Using Poetry for Economic Analysis

Using Poetry for Economic Analysis:

Economics Meets Literature

By

Ky-Hyang Yuhn

Cambridge Scholars Publishing

Using Poetry for Economic Analysis: Economics Meets Literature

By Ky-Hyang Yuhn

This book first published 2023

Cambridge Scholars Publishing

Lady Stephenson Library, Newcastle upon Tyne, NE6 2PA, UK

British Library Cataloguing in Publication Data
A catalogue record for this book is available from the British Library

ISBN (10): 1-5275-1968-6
ISBN (13): 978-1-5275-1968-8

CONTENTS

Part 1. The Economics of Crisis and the Crisis of Economics

1 2
Snow Falling in the Village of Chagall: The Aftermath of the COVID-19 Recession
<Painting> *Moi et Le Village* (Marc Chagall)
<Poem> Snow Falling in the Village of Chagall (Kim Choon-soo)

2 12
The New Millennium and Irrational Exuberance

3 16
The Global Economic Crisis and the Dark Clouds of Greed

4 22
The Roaring Twenties and the Great Depression

5 27
The Tragedies of the Great Depression: Splendor in the Grass
<Poem> Splendor in the Grass (William Wordsworth)

6 29
The Two Oil Shocks of the 1970s and Stagflation

7 35
The 1997 Asian Financial Crisis: They Popped Up the Champagne Bottle Too Early
<Poem> The Wind Is Blowing (Lee So-ra)

8 40
Japan's "Lost Two Decades"

9 45
Abenomics and the Three Arrows
<Poem> The Arrow and the Song (Henry Longfellow)

10 54
The Uneasy Alliance of the Eurozone
<Painting> Europa and the Bull on a Greek Vase

11 61
The U.S.-China Confrontation and the Thucydides Trap
<Poem> The Waste Land (T.S. Eliot)

12 67
Will American-Style Market Capitalism Decline? The Micawber Principle

13 72
Can the Owl of Minerva Predict an Economic Crisis?
<Painting> Athena Holding a Helmet and a Spear with an Owl
<Poem> The Clock of Life (Robert Smith)

14 77
The Crisis of Economics?

Part 2. The Market and Capitalism

1 82
Two Different Views on the Economy

2 88
Is the Chinese Economy a Socialist Economic System
or a Capitalist Economic System?

3 92
The Market and the 'Invisible Hand'

4 97
Market Failures, the Tragedy of the Commons and the Coase Theorem

5 102
Game Rules of Market Participants

6 108
Opportunity Cost: Bygones Are Bygones
<Poem> Yesterday (The Beatles)

**Part 3. An Overview of Macroeconomics:
Classical and Keynesian Perspectives**

Chapter 1. A Self-Adjusting Economy: Classical Economics

1 114
Adam Smith and the Birth of Classical Economics

2 116
The Water-Diamond Paradox and Da Vinci's *Salvator Mundi*
<Painting> *Salvator Mundi* (Leonardo Da Vinci)

3 121
The Market Has Self-Correcting Forces

4 125
How Are Output and Employment Determined in the Classical System? Supply Determines

5 130
Money as a Veil: Money Has No Effect on Output and Employment

6 134
The Economy through the Lens of the Classical Economist: Charlie Chaplin's Quip

7 137
The Role of the Government in the Classical System

8 139
The Sirens' Melliferous Songs and Rules for Monetary Policy
<Photo> Ulysses and the Sirens (Leon Belly)

9 141
Supply-Side Economics

Chapter 2. A Government-Connected Economy: Keynesian Economics

1 146
The Legend of Autumn
<Poem> Autumn Day (Rainer Maria Rilke)

2 148
The Collapse of the Classical Doctrine and the Birth of Keynesian Economics

3 151
The Economy through the Lens of the Keynesian: *Carpe Diem* and *Memento Mori*
<Poem> O Me! O Life! (Walt Whitman)
<Movie> Dead Poets Society

4 154
Aggregate Demand (AD) Matters in the Determination of Output

5 157
Consumption Is the Largest Component of Aggregate Demand (AD)

6 162
Investment, Government Purchases, and Net Exports; The Rest of the Chariot Wheels

7 166
How Are Output and Employment Determined in the Keynesian System: Demand Determines

8 171
The Magic of the Economy: The Multiplier Effect

9 176
There Is No 'Free Lunch'

10 179
Effects of Fiscal Policy in the Keynesian System

11 182
Effects of Monetary Policy in the Keynesian System

12 185
Rules versus Discretion: The Mississippi River Parable

Chapter 3. Neoliberalism

1 190
The Reflux of Keynesianism and the Rise of Neoliberalism

2 193
Reaganomics and Trickle-Down Economics

3 195
Thatcherism
<Poem> Little Gidding (T.S. Eliot)

4 197
<Four Quartets> and <A Late Quartet>
<Poem> Burnt Norton (T.S. Eliot)
<Movie> A Late Quartet

5 200
"Occupy the Wall Street": The America Fall

Part 4. Measurement of Macroeconomic Performance: Seeing the Trees for the Forest

1 204
Measuring the Size of an Economy: GDP, GNP, and GNI

2 206
Measurement of GDP: You Cannot Add Apples and Oranges

3 209
The Underground Economy and GDP

4 212
Nominal GDP versus Real GDP

5 215
A Simple Comparison of Income between 2020 and 1961
Is like Ignoring Perspective

6 219
Which Movie Has Grossed the Highest Box Office Earnings?

7 222
Nominal GDP versus Purchasing Power Parity (PPP) GDP

8 226
GDP Increases as the Rent Increases but GDP Does Not
Increase as the House Price Rises

9 229
GDP as Value Added and Value-Added Tax (VAT)

10 232
Production and Expenditure Are Two Sides of a Coin

11 235
Production and Income Are Two Sides of a Coin

12 238
From Gross Income (GDI or GNI) to Personal Income

13 241
GDP Does Not Measure Happiness: The Easterlin Paradox
<Poem> Duino Elegies (Rainer Maria Rilke)

14 245
In Search of Shangri-La
<Novel> Lost Horizon (James Hilton)

Part 5. Income Inequality and Welfare: The Sphinx's Conundrum

1 250
The Sphinx's Conundrum and Welfare Issues
<Painting> *Oedipe Explique L'enigme du Sphinx*
(Jean-Auguste-Dominique Ingres)

2 253
What Is Economic Justice?
<Poem> The People, Oh Yes (Carl Sandburg)

3 257
Piketty's *Capital in the Twenty-First Century* and the Kuznets Curve

4 264
The Lorenz Curve and the Gini Coefficient

5 270
The World's Billionaires: "Everyone Wants More"

6 274
Which Comes First, Growth or Welfare?
<Poem> A True Travel (Nazim Hikmet)

7 277
Do More Welfares Require More Taxes? The Eureka of Archimedes

Part 6. ..Savings and Investment: The Building Blocks of the Economy

1 282
Savings and the Psalm of Life
<Poem> A Psalm of Life (Henry Longfellow)
<Poem> Savings (Toyo Shibata)

2 286
Why Are Statistics on Savings Seesawed?

3 288
Savings Are the Source of Domestic and Foreign Investment

4 293
The Paradox of Thrift

5 297
Chimerica (China-America): China Earns Dollars from the United States, and the United States Borrows Dollars from China
<Poem> The Flower (Kim Choon-soo)

6 302
Volatility of Investment

Part 7. Inflation and Unemployment: Two Macroeconomic Diseases

1 306
Inflation Is the Thermometer of the Health of an Economy

2 310
The Measurement of Inflation

3 313
The Official Inflation Rate Tends to Overestimate True Inflation

4 316
The Causes and Types of Inflation

5 320
Hyperinflation

6 323
Fear of Deflation?

7 327
Is Zero Inflation Feasible and Desirable?

8 329
Consequences of Inflation

9 332
Inflation and Interest Rates: The Fisher Equation

10 335
Measurement of Unemployment

11 339
The Causes and Types of Unemployment

12 341
The Full-Employment Rate of Unemployment and the Natural Unemployment Rate

13 344
Is Zero Unemployment Feasible and Desirable?

14 346
Economic and Social Costs of Unemployment and the Misery Index

Part 8. Low Inflation and Low Unemployment: Catching Two Hares at Once?

1 350
The Great Debate between Keynesians and Monetarists and Okun's Law

2 355
The Phillips Curve: Tradeoff between Inflation and Unemployment

3 358
Stagflation: The Disappearance of the Phillips Curve

4 361
Friedman's 'Misperception Theory' and the Natural Rate Hypothesis
<Painting> Sisyphus (Tiziano Vecelli)

5 368
NAIRU

6 370
The Birth of Monetarism

7 374
Lucas' Rational Expectations Revolution and New Classical Economics

8 379
The Policy Ineffectiveness Theorem and 'Fooling Theory'

9 381
The Keynesian Attack on the Policy Ineffectiveness Theorem:
New Keynesian Economics

Part 9. Money: The Artery of the Economy

1 386
What Is Money? "Too Much Money or Too Little Money, That Is the Question""

2 390
Stone Money on the Island of Yap

3 393
Money Is "What Money Does"

4 396
Evolution of the Monetary System

5 400
Functions of Money

6 402
Measurement of Money

7 407
Can Bitcoin and Other Cryptocurrencies Be Money?

8 411
The Economics of Gold: Gold and the U.S. Dollar

9 414
Can We Predict the Future Price of Gold?

Part 10. Short-Run Economic Fluctuations: The Four Seasons of the Economy

1 418
The Curse of Skyscrapers
<Poem> Dead Leaves (Jacques Prevert)
<Poem> Autumn Leaves (Edith Piaf)

2 423
The Characteristics of a Business Cycle

3 426
The Pattern of the Business Cycle Has Been Changing

4 429
The Inflationary Gap and the Recessionary Gap

5 433
Why Does the Economy Have a Cycle? The Multiplier-Accelerator Model

Part 11. Long-Run Economic Growth: A Dance Marathon

1 440
Economic Growth and Living Standards: Australia Was the Richest Country 150 Years Ago

2 443
Ascension of the Asian Dragons

3 446
Technological Progress Is the Source of Long-term Economic Growth
<Poem> A Song of the Japanese Knife (Ouyang Xiu)

4 450
Solow's Growth Accounting Equation

5 454
Economic Growth and Living Standards

6 457
How Could Singapore Catch Up the United States?
The Convergence of Living Standards

7 462
Economic Growth and Population: Malthus, Solow, and Kremer

8 466
Will the Growth of the Four Asian Tigers Stagnate?
From Mount Olympus to the Thessaly Plains?

Part 12. Monetary Policy and Economic Stabilization

1 470
What Does Economic Policy Aim For?

2 475
The Magic of Money Creation: Tools of the Magic

3 479
The Magic of Money Creation: Preliminaries

4 483
The Magic of Money Creation: The Complete Model

5 488
The Causes of the Great Depression

6 490
Monetary Policy Tools: Open Market Operations

7 493
Monetary Policy Tools: Discount Policy

8 496
Monetary Policy Tools: Reserve Requirements

9 500
New Monetary Policy Tools: Quantitative Easing (QE)
<Poem> The Road Not Taken (Robert Frost)

10 504
How Does the Central Bank Set the Benchmark Interest Rate (Federal Funds Rate)?

11 510
The Goldilocks Economy and the Neutral Interest Rate: The Taylor Rule

Part 13. Fiscal Policy and Economic Coordination

1 518
How Fiscal Policy Differs from Monetary Policy

2 523
Equitable Taxation: "Pulling the Most Feathers with the Least Screams"
<Painting> Wife Godiva (John Collier)
<Painting> The Scream (Edvard Munch)

3 529
Is a Balanced Budget Necessary and Desirable?

4 532
Is the National Debt Explosive?

5 537
Fiscal Deficits and Ricardian Equivalence: "The Buck Stops Here"

6 541
The Crowding-out Effect versus the Crowding-in Effect

7 544
Fiscal Deficits and Seigniorage: Windfall Gains to the Government?

8 547
The Laffer Curve: Do Lower Tax Rates Increase Tax Revenues?

**Part 14. International Trade and Finance:
Sailing Before the Tradewinds**

1 552
International Trade and Income

2 557
The Balance of Payments (BOP)

3 562
The Current Account versus the Capital Account: *Quid Pro Quo*

4 565
How Is the Exchange Rate Measured?

5 571
The Effective Exchange Rate and the U.S. Dollar Index (USDX)

6 574
Exchange Rates and Economic Activities

7 578
The Rise and Fall of the Gold Standard

8 582
The Wizard of Oz

9 584
From the Fixed Exchange Rate System to the Floating Exchange Rate System

10 587
Determination of Exchange Rates in the Long Run: Purchasing Power Parity (PPP)

11 591
Purchasing Power Parity and the Big Mac Price Index

12 598
Determination of Exchange Rates in the Medium Run: Business Cycles

13 601
Determination of Exchange Rates in the Short Run: Interest Rate Parity (IRP)

14 606
The Marshall-Lerner Condition and the J-Curve

15 611
The Triffin Paradox and the Confidence Problem

16 613
High Inflation, High Interest Rates, and High Exchange Rates: An Economic Tripledemic?

Bibliography 617

PART 1

THE ECONOMICS OF CRISIS AND THE CRISIS OF ECONOMICS

1

Snow Falling in the Village of Chagall: The Aftermath of the COVID-19 Recession

A dark age swooped down on the Earth in 2020 when the coronavirus invaded the planet. Since the first coronavirus case was reported on December 31, 2019 in Wuhan, China, the world has been seized with fear and panic. No human being on the planet could escape from the sphere of influence of the COVID-19 crisis. It is not an exaggeration to say that the COVID-19 pandemic has divided the human history into BC (before the coronavirus pandemic) and AC (after the coronavirus pandemic). As the world was filled with darkness, human activities also froze, and economic activities stopped beginning March 2020: Production slowed down, and consumption cooled down. As the economy stepped back, unemployment rose, and income fell. The economy was faced with a cold wave as if it snowed in the village of Chagall in March.

The poem, <Snow Falling in the Village of Chagall> was published by Choon-soo Kim, a famous Korean poet, in 1969. In that poem, he sings the vitality of spring as follows:

It snows in March in the village of Chagall.
On the temples of a man who stood hoping for spring
New veins tremble.
To the temples of the man who trembles
Rubbing the new veins,
Snow with tens of thousands of wings
Falling from the sky,
Cover the roofs and chimneys in the village of Chagall.
When it snows in March
The color of the winter fruits of the size of a pellet in the village of Chagall
Turns into olive again.
At night,
The women kindle the most beautiful fire of the year in the fireplace.

<Snow Falling in the Village of Chagall> is evaluated as a 'poem of meaninglessness' in that it attempted to convey the vitality of spring as an image rather than as a meaning. In fact, it is known that Kim Choon-soo drew the inspiration for the poem from the painting *<Moi et Le Village>* (I and the Village) (1911) by Marc Chagall, an expressionist painter. As is well known, Chagall was a surrealist painter. He was born in Russia and went to Paris to study art at the age of 23. In the painting *<Moi et Le Village>*, you can see the view of the village in the distance, where the head of a large horse, a human face, and a large tree of life painted in red, green, blue, and yellow dominate the canvas. It looks like a fairy tale village landscape that is surreal. Kim Choon-soo may have experimented with a meaningless poem from Chagall's surreal painting that emphasizes images.

<Painting> *Moi et Le Village* (Marc Chagall)

However, it is not right to say that his poem contains only images. Many people may accept snow falling in the spring as a cold snap in the flowering season. But snow falling in the spring may be welcomed by farmers as auspicious snow. When it snows in March, winter plants will bear appetizing fruits that will be colored in olive, and women will light a burning fire to warm the cold night air. We have often been told that when it snows a lot in winter, the land becomes fertile, and farmers produce a good harvest in that year. Freezing cold weather with snow in March does not necessarily bring only coldness and depression. Kim Choon-soo's poem symbolizes the positive image of snow falling in the spring and sings hope.

Shocks such as typhoons and hurricanes can sometimes bring a virtuous cycle to the ecosystem. Some studies have shown that if a typhoon blows hard and stirs the seawater from the bottom, the ecosystem of the sea becomes healthier. This virtuous circle can work not only in natural ecosystems, but also in economic ecosystems. Economic metabolism takes place. When an economic crisis hits, in the short run, it can scratch the economy like a typhoon scratching nature, but in the long run, it can make the economy stronger by strengthening the structure and functioning of the economic system. It is in a similar vein to the saying that "every cloud has a silver lining". At the time of the Great Depression in the 1930s, there were some worries that the market economy capitalist system would end, and that the communist revolution would take place in the United States, but the American-style market economy became even stronger after the Great Depression.

The COVID-19 economic crisis is quite different from the previous economic crises in many respects. What has made the COVID-19 recession distinct is that the world has been growingly integrating into a global village, and the coronavirus pandemic made the whole world stand still in one moment. During the COVID-19 crisis, we were on a path we had never taken before, and the world economy suffered a chain reaction it had never experienced. The world economy is now a structure that prevents any country from escaping this kind of crisis. When the Great Depression broke out in the 1930s, many Asian countries remained quite tranquil. The COVID-19 recession is particularly serious in that the shock wave on the demand side has been intertwined across countries, and the global supply chain has collapsed. Until now, there have been few crises in which both the supply-side and demand-side shocks have hit the economy at the same time. The Great Depression of the 1930s, the Great Recession of 2008, and the Asian financial crisis of 1997 were economic recessions caused mainly by shocks on the demand side of the economy, and the recessions caused by the oil shocks in the 1970s were economic downturns caused by shocks on the supply side of the economy.

<Figure 1.1> University of Michigan Consumer Sentiment Index, 2006~21

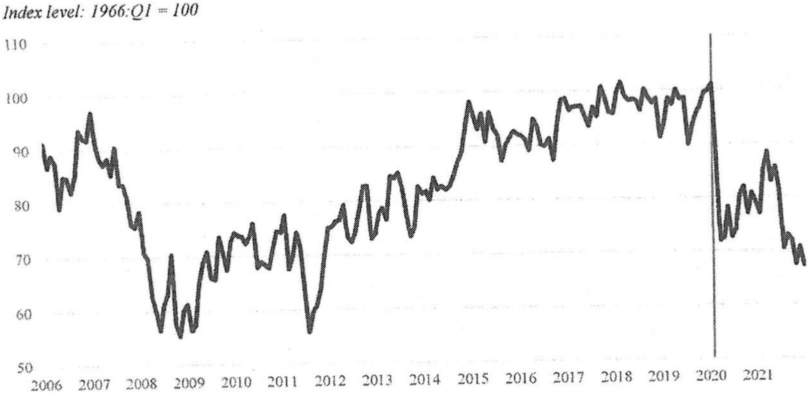

Sources: Haver Analytics; CEA calculations.
Note: The red line denotes start of the pandemic.

As the COVID-19 crisis deepened, the world economy rapidly cooled off. The Consumer Sentiment Index surveyed by the University of Michigan began to nosedive. It dropped from 103 in January 2020 to almost 70 in March 2020. The world economy grew at the annual rate of 3.3% from 2013 to 2019 prior to the COVID-19 crisis, but it contracted by 3.4% in 2020. The U.S. economy was no exception. U.S. GDP decreased by 5.1% in the first quarter of 2020 and by 31.2% in the second quarter. As a matter of fact, U.S. GDP decreased only for two months in March and April 2020, but the decline in GDP in March and April was so large that the quarterly GDP growth rate was -5.1% in the first quarter and -31.2% in the second quarter of 2020. The U.S. unemployment rate soared from 4.4% in March 2020 to 14.7% in April 2020, which was the second highest after the Great Depression. The stock price (Dow Jones Industrial Average) plunged by 37% from its pre-pandemic peak of 29,551 (February 12, 2020) to 18,592 (March 23, 2020). The comparison of U.S. quarterly GDP growth rate between the prior- and post-COVID 19 crisis speaks volumes for the severity of the crisis:

<Table 1.1> U.S. Quarterly Growth Rate During the COVID-19 Crisis

	Q1	Q2	Q3	Q4
2019	2.4%	3.2%	2.8%	1.9%
2020	−5.1%	−31.2%	33.8%	4.5%.
2021	6.3%	6.7%	2.3%	7.0%

Other major economies, except for China, also experienced negative growth in 2020. The euro-zone countries witnessed a decline in their GDP by 6.5% in 2020, which was a sharp decline from the annual growth rate of 1.9% from 2013 to 2019. Japanese GDP increased at the annual rate of 0.6% from 2013 to 2019 but shrank by 4.6% in 2020. The COVID-19 crisis had the most devastating effect on the U.K. economy. The British economy grew at the annual rate of 1.5% from 2013 to 2019, but its GDP decreased by 9.7% in 2020. The Indian economy was also hit hard by the COVID-19 crisis. The Indian economy grew at the annual rate of 6.8% from 2013 to 2019, but its GDP retracted by 7.3% in 2020. In contrast, the Chinese economy grew at the rate of 2.3% in 2020, although its growth rate in 2020 was much lower than the annual growth rate of 4.3% during the 2013-2019 period.

<Table 1.2> Economic Growth Rates and Forecasts for Major Economies

Country[1]	2013~2019	2019		2020		2021	2022 (Forecast: OECD)
	Growth rate (%): Average	GDP (in Billions)	Growth rate (%)	GDP (in billions)	Growth rate (%)[2]	Growth rate (%)	Growth rate (%):
World	3.3%	$87,265	2.8%	$84,298	-3.4	5.6%	4.5%
United States	2.4%	$21,439	2.3%	$20,937	-3.4	5.7%	3.7%
Euro Area	1.9%	$18,705	1.3%	$17,508	-6.5	5.2%	4.3%
China	4.3%	$14,140	6.1%	$14,723	2.3	8.1%	5.1%
Japan	0.6%	$5,154	0.7%	$4,975	-4.6	1.6%	3.4%
United Kingdom	1.5%	$2,879	1.7%	$2,757	-9.3	7.4%	9.5%
India	6.8%	$2,936	4.2%	$2,623	-7.3	8.9%	8.1%
South Korea	2.9%	$1,647	2.2%	$1,631	-0.9	4.0%	3.0%

Data: IMF

Interestingly, the world economy, including the U.S. economy, began to revive rapidly in the third quarter of 2020. The world economy could be out of the woods thanks to the act of pair trawling by the government and the central bank in major countries. The U.S. economy began to turn around in the third quarter of 2020, achieving the astonishing growth rate of 33.8% in the third quarter. As a result, the growth rate of the U.S. economy increased from −3.4% in 2020 to 5.7% in 2021. The U.S. unemployment rate also steadily fell, reaching its pre-pandemic level of 4.2% by November 2021. The stock market also regained its pre-pandemic record on September 2, 2021. Most major economies also exhibited a V-shaped recovery. The growth rate of the Chinese economy increased from 2.3% in 2020 to 8.1% in 2021. In particular, the recovery of the Indian economy is very impressive. The Indian economy grew at the rate of 9.4% in 2021, which was a quantum leap from deep negative growth (−7.3%) in 2020. Overall, the world economy grew at the rate of 5.6% in 2021, which was a significant improvement from negative growth (−3.4%) in 2020.

<Figure 1.2> Real GDP by Country

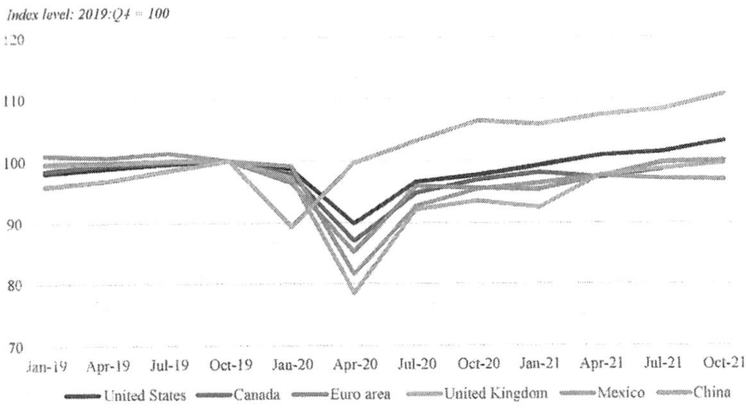

Sources: National data organizations.
Note: Data are seasonally adjusted.

The most important contributor to the rapid recovery of the world economy from the COVID-19 recession was massive spending programs initiated by the governments and central banks in almost all countries. In the United States, the Biden Administration embarked on its major spending program (Infrastructure Bill) on November 15, 2021, which requires the spending of $1 trillion. Of course, the Trump Administration also spent a lot of money to cope with the COVID-19 crisis.

On the other hand, the Federal Reserve System (for short, the Fed), the central bank of the United States, continued to lower its benchmark interest rate (federal funds rate) from 1.50% to 1.00% by 0.50% point on March 4, 2020 as the COVID-19 pandemic was looming. The Fed lowered the federal funds rate again from 1.00% to 0% by 1% point on March 15, 2020 as the dark cloud of the crisis was on the horizon. The Fed also implemented its Phase 4 quantitative easing (Q4) on March 15, 2020 and purchased $700 billion worth of long-term government bonds and mortgage-backed securities. The Fed's bond purchase programs poured $2 trillion into the U.S. economy by the summer of 2020. This is the Fed's fourth quantitative easing policy. The Fed previously implemented the three phases of bond-purchase programs (Q1, Q2, and Q3) during the global economic crisis in 2008. Other countries also poured huge amounts of money into the economy through quantitative easing and government spending programs. This kind of policy mix (combination of monetary and fiscal policies) has proved to be effective in extinguishing the impending fire. However, such a spending spree has boomeranged to the U.S. economy and the world economy in the form of inflation.

There have been four major economic crises in modern times since the Great Depression. These include the Great Depression, the oil recessions in the 1970s and early 1980s associated with the two oil crises in the 1970s, the global economic crisis (also called the Great Recession) during the 2008 ~ 2009 period and the COVID-19 recession in 2020. There is no question that the Great Depression during the 1930s was the worst economic crisis in U.S. history. During the Great Depression, the unemployment rate soared to 24.9% in 1933. In 1929, just before the Great Depression, the unemployment rate was 4.0%. The Great Depression lasted for more than 10 years, leaving a deep scar in American life. Which of the crises was the second worst economic crisis after the Great Depression? In the early stage of the COVID-19 crisis, people were worried that the economic crisis would develop into a major economic crisis that was comparable to the Great Depression.

The COVID-19 crisis was the most severe in terms of the strength of the shock, but the shortest in terms of the duration of the shock. Four months after the occurrence of the COVID-19 crisis, the U.S. unemployment rate rose from 3.5% in February to 14.7% in April 2020, the highest level since March 1933 (24.9%). The unemployment rate during the oil recessions hit 10.8% in November and December of 1982, the third highest unemployment rate in U.S. history. The unemployment rate during the Great Recession climbed to 10.0% in October 2009. Thus, in terms of the level of unemployment, the COVID-19 recession was the second worst recession in the United States.

<Table 1.3> Stock Prices Before and After the Crisis

Recession	Highest before the Crisis	Lowest during the Crisis	Rebound to the Prior Highest
Great Depression	381 (9/3/1929)	40 (8/8/1932)	380 (11/20/1954)
Great Recession	14,066 (10/5/2007)	7,170 (3/12/2009)	14.010 (2/1/2013)
COVID Recession	29,551 (2/12/2020)	18,592 (3/23/2020)	29,101 (9/2/2020)

<Table 1.4> Comparison of Major Recessions in the U.S.

Economic Crisis	Starting & Ending Dates	Recession Duration (Months)	Unemployment Rate (Highest)	Inflation (Highest/Lowest)
Great Depression	8/1929 ~ 3/1933 5/1937 ~ 6/1938	3 years & 7 months 1 year & 1 month	25% (3/1933)	-10.7% (10/1932) -4.1% (10/1938)
Oil Recessions	11/1973 ~ 3/1975 1/1980 ~ 7/1980 7/1981 ~ 11/1982	1 year & 4 months 6 months 1 year & 4 months	9.0% (5/1975) 7.8% (7/1980) 10.8% (11,12/1982)	12.3% (12/1974) 14.8% (3/1980) 11.8% (1/1981)
Great Recession	12/2007 ~ 6/2009	1 year & 6 months	10.0% (10/2009)	-2.1% (7/2009)
COVID 19 Recession	2/2020 ~ 4/2020	2 months	14.7% (4/2020)	7.4% (1/2022)

However, the COVID-19 recession lasted only for two months, whereas the Great Depression lasted for more than 10 years. The oil recession lasted for 38 months (11/1973 ~ 3/1975: 16 months; 1/1980 ~ 7/1980: 6 months; 7/1981 ~ 11/1982: 16 months), and the Great Recession lasted for 18 months. Thus, as far as the duration of recession is concerned, the COVID-19 recession was the shortest. The U.S. stock market also behaved differently during each crisis. It took more than 25 years for the Dow Jones

Industrial Average (DJIA) to recover its previous level during the Great Depression. It took almost six years for the Dow Jones to regain its previous level during the Great Recession. However, it took only seven months for the Dow Jones to reach its previous level during the COVID-19 recession. Thus, the COVID-19 recession could be characterized as a mini-recession. The COVID-19 recession ended up in anticlimax.

The U.S. government and the Fed succeeded in resuscitating the economy from the COVID-19 crisis, but the success met with mixed blessings. As the COVID-19 virus subsided, inflation began to go viral. The U.S. annual inflation rate had never exceeded 2.5% except for 2011 (3.2%) since 2009 until the COVID-19 crisis. The Fed has made every effort to maintain its target inflation rate of 2.0% over the past several decades. However, the annual inflation rate in 2021 soared to 4.7%, and the consumer price index (CPI) rose by 7.5% in January 2022 and by 8.5% in March 2022 compared with a year ago. The March 2022 inflation rate has been the highest in 40 years since 1982. At last, the Fed began to reverse its monetary policy position by raising its policy interest rate from 0% to 0.25% on March 15, 2022. The federal funds rate was raised for the first time in 3 years and 3 months. The last interest rate hike was made on December 20, 2018 when the Fed raised the federal funds rate from 2.00% to 2.25%. The Fed continued its battle against inflation by raising its benchmark interest rate from 0~0.25% (March 15, 2022) to 4.25~4.5% (December 15, 2022) seven times in 2022 alone, and the federal funds rate reached its highest level in 15 years.

<Figure 1.3> Consumer Price Index (CPI) Inflation, 2007 ~ 21

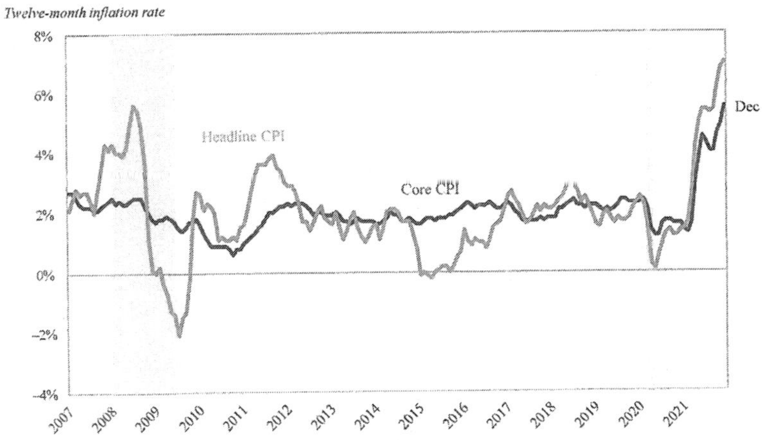

Sources: Bureau of Labor Statistics; National Bureau of Economic Research.

2

THE NEW MILLENNIUM AND IRRATIONAL EXUBERANCE

January 1, 2000 is a point in the eternal flow of time. However, people were excited to give a special meaning to the first day of the year 2000, which breaks once every millennium. When people celebrated the first day of the year 2000, they would dream of good fortune as the bells of the year-end night sounded. On January 1, 2000, they were bustling, waiting for the bright sun to rise from the horizon. However, they did not see dark clouds coming from the other side of the dazzling sun.

The Information Technology Revolution, which began around the mid-1990s, heightened expectations for the new millennium. The IT Revolution advanced to the realm of the real economy, ringing a fanfare for a new economy. Productivity began to increase noticeably. Workers worked the same hours and produced more output. Companies hired more workers because they were more productive, and the unemployment rate continued to decrease. Inflation fell while wages rose. Workers earned higher wages because they were able to fully compensate for their wage increases with high productivity. Thanks to this virtuous cycle of productivity, the U.S. unemployment rate fell to 3.8% in April 2000. This was the lowest level since the unemployment rate reached 3.5% in December 1969, the last golden era of the U.S. economy.

Now, the U.S. economy saw hope for the future that had never been experienced, such as the coexistence of low unemployment and low inflation. The U.S. economy couldn't have been better. The coexistence of low unemployment and low inflation was called the New Economy. The U.S. economy grew at the full-employment level of output with no inflation during the second half of the 1990s (1996 – 2000). The U.S. full-employment rate of unemployment was estimated to be 5.0% during this period. Here are some statistics:

<Table 1.5> U.S. Economic Performance During the IT Revolution

Year	Economic Growth Rate (%)	Unemployment Rate (%)	Inflation Rate (%)
1996	3.8	5.4	2.9
1997	4.4	4.9	2.3
1998	4.5	4.5	1.6
1999	4.8	4.2	2.2
2000	4.1	4.0	3.4

Reflecting the expectations of the IT Revolution, the stock price continued its high streak. Let's look at the Nasdaq Composite index which contains a lot of technology stocks. It surpassed 1,000 highs in July 1995, then exceeded 2,000 in October 1998, and 3,000 in November 1999, and a month later it climbed to 4,000 in December 1999. In March 2000, it jumped to the long-awaited 5,000 plateau and peaked at 5,049 on March 10, 2000. This was the 'world of wonder' that the Nasdaq had never reached before.

In less than five years, from July 1995 to March 2000, the Nasdaq stock index jumped more than five times. Anyone who invested $1,000 in Nasdaq stocks in 1995 would have earned more than $5,000 in March 2000, just before the bubble collapsed. This speculative frenzy was commonly dubbed as a dot-com bubble; Alan Greenspan who was the Chairman of the U.S. Federal Reserve System at that time called the frenzy as "irrational exuberance".

However, expectations for the new millennium could not keep on going to infinity. The vertical rise of the stock prices was suddenly halted. When the excitement for the new millennium was rising to the fullest, the Nasdaq Composite began to nosedive. On April 14, 2000, a month after the Nasdaq peaked, the Nasdaq stock index plunged 34% to 3,321. After the continuous free fall of the Nasdaq Composite index until October 9, 2002, it plunged to 1,114. This was less than a quarter of the peak of 5,049.

A person who invested $1,000 in the Nasdaq stocks in 1995 would have earned $5,049 if he held the stocks for about 5 years until March 2000, and if he had retained the stocks for another 2 years until October 2002, he would only have $1,114 in his pocket. During this period, investors would have experienced heaven and hell, and hot and cold. The situation was similar for the Dow Jones Industrial Average (DJIA). The DJIA index, which soared to 11,723 on January 14, 2000, fell to 7,286 by October 9, 2002, which was almost half of the peak.

Although the dot-com bubble rocked the U.S. stock market, it had trifling effects on the real economy. During the dot-com bubble crisis, the annual growth rate fluctuated from 4.1% (2000) to 1.0% (2001) and 1.7% (2002). Thus the U.S. economy did not exhibit negative growth and slip into a recession. The U.S. unemployment rate also remained at a relatively stable level between 3.8% (April 2000) and 6.0% (December 2002). The U.S. inflation rate also remained quite low: 3.4% (2000) 2.8% (2001) 1.6% (2002). Thus, we could say that the dot-com bubble was a storm in a teacup. Here is a reality check on what happened to the economy during the crisis:

<Table 1.6> U.S. Economic Performance after the IT Revolution

Year	Economic Growth Rate (%)	Unemployment Rate (%)	Inflation Rate (%)
1999	4.8	4.0	2.2
2000	4.1	3.9	3.4
2001	1.0	5.7	2.8
2002	1.7	6.0	1.6
2003	2.8	5.7	2.3

What caused the dot-com bubble in the stock market and what were the consequences of the crisis? The dot-com bubble seems to be different in nature and pattern from the previous bubbles that occurred in the United States. Over the past 100 years or so, there were several major eruptions and subsequent collapses of seeming bubbles: 1929~1940 (Great Depression), 2000 (IT Revolution), and 2007~2008 (Great Recession). There is a close resemblance between the Great Depression and the Great Recession in the nature of the bubble, but the dot-com bubble had distinguishing features from the bubble during the Great Depression and the Great Recession.

The stock market crash during the Great Depression and the stock market collapse during the Great Recession occurred concomitantly with the boom and the subsequent bust of the real estate market. It is worth noting that the 1929 stock market crash during the Great Depression and the 2008 stock market collapse during the Great Recession had something to do with unsustainable real estate bubbles. The stock market crash that triggered the Great Depression occurred amid the construction boom and bust in 1929, and the stock market crash that brought about the global economic crisis was the concomitance of the boom and collapse of the housing market. However, the boom of the stock market during the dot-com bubble, starting in the middle of the 1990s and lasting until August 2000, reflected buoyant productivity growth nurtured by the IT Revolution in the latter half of the 1990s. One distinguishing feature of stock price movements during the 1929 Great Depression and the 2008 Great Recession was that the stock price curve was synchronized with the housing price curve, but the dot-com bubble during the millennium year was driven by optimistic market moods. In this regard, the dot-com bubble was more likely to be an extraneous bubble that was not directly related to real estate bubbles and thus was less likely to have a ripple effect on the real economy.

3

The Global Economic Crisis and the Dark Clouds of Greed

Greed blurs reason and judgment. Even if you are a rational economic person, you may not be able to escape from irrational decisions. Some people easily indulge in speculation, believing that the collapse of the bubble will not come to them. If people are blind to greed, their speculative behavior could be uncontrollable. People tend to have a short memory once they succumb to greed. Short memory refers to the propensity of people to easily forget past wrong doings. Less than five years after the collapse of the dot-com bubble economy in 2000, some signs of anomalies began to appear in the housing market. The chickens came home to roost.

Homes were not considered targets for speculation in the United States except for a few hot regions until the 2007 subprime mortgage crisis hit the U.S. economy. However, in the middle of the 2000s, house prices began to rise sharply around the Sun Belt region, which refers to the southern part of the United States. From January 2000 to July 2006, mainly in Sun Belt cities like Miami (178%), Los Angeles (174%), San Diego (149%), Tampa (138%), Las Vegas (134%), Phoenix (127%) and San Francisco (115%), house prices more than doubled. Such speculation then spread to other regions. Even in the Washington D.C. area, the house prices rose by 150%. At that time, subprime loans were popular. Banks lent up to nearly 100% of house prices to those with lower credit scores or lower incomes than those eligible for the loans. To make matters worse, the 'head-first' attitude by greedy home buyers played a role, too. Low interest rates also fueled soaring house prices.

Fortune is always met with some mishap. When the information technology bubble fizzled out in early 2000, the U.S. economy began to slow down rapidly, and the stock price plummeted. The embarrassed Fed shifted gears toward expansionary phase and lowered the federal funds rate in a row. The federal funds rate is gauged as an important policy interest rate because the Fed mainly manipulates the federal funds rate to influence market interest rates and consequently economic activity. The federal funds rate rose to 6.5% on May 16, 2000 before the collapse of the dot-com bubble, but the federal funds rate fell to 1% by June 25, 2003 as the Fed cut the rate 11 times from to stimulate the economy. Market interest rates such as mortgage interest rates also began to fall. As the market interest rates fell, both house prices and stock prices continued to rise. On October 9, 2007, the Dow Jones Index recovered to a record high of 14,165, and the Nasdaq index rose to 2,862 on October 31, 2007. The dark clouds of the IT bubble seemed to have lifted.

Alan Greenspan, once called a maestro in the conduct of monetary policy, not only initiated interest rate cuts to stimulate the economy after the collapse of the IT bubble economy, but also led home buyers to confuse the central bank's policy intention. He even encouraged homeowners to refinance mortgage loans and recommended homeowners to switch from fixed-rate mortgages to variable-rate mortgages to reduce interest costs. His attitude prompted financial institutions to provide reckless mortgage loans to people with low income or low credit scores. For this reason, Greenspan was criticized for fanning the overheating of the housing market that had continued until 2007. It is for this reason that the2007 housing market boom was also called the 'Greenspan Bubble'.

The financial crisis that started with the U.S. subprime mortgage problem quickly devastated the financial markets around the world as if the *tsunami* swept. It was like a war without bombardment. War clouds began to smash Bear Sterns with its 85-year history in the wake of the subprime mortgage crisis in early 2007. Bear Stearns was America's fifth-largest investment bank with assets of $350 billion as of November 2006. In March 2008, the Federal Reserve Bank of New York gave a rescue loan to the bank, but it was not enough to save Bear Stearns. Finally, Bear Stearns was sold to JP Morgan Chase in May of that year for $10 per share. (Bear Stearns' stock price was $133.20 before the crisis.)

After Wall Street's fifth-largest investment bank collapsed, the clouds of war spread to Lehman Brothers, the fourth-largest investment bank in the United States with a 161-year tradition. Lehman Brothers was twice as big and twice as old as Bear Sterns. Just before bankruptcy in September 2007, Lehman Brothers' assets totaled $691 billion. When Lehman Brothers collapsed on September 15th, 2008, the stragglers who dressed up poured out to the street, and they joined the "Occupy the Wall Street" demonstration. Unfortunately, the war front began to expand to Europe and Asia.

Earlier, Merrill Lynch, the third largest investment bank, was sold to the Bank of America (BOA) in September 2008. Now, among the investment banks that swayed the world's financial community, only survivors were Morgan Stanley (2nd) and Goldman Saks (1st). In the midst of the crisis,

Goldman Sachs and Morgan Stanley also transformed from investment banks to commercial banks to survive, which implies that they would surrender to the oversight and regulation of financial regulators. Their transformation was no different than a white flag.

The flames started to move from investment banks to insurance companies, mortgage companies and commercial banks. In September 2008, there was an unprecedent market intervention in the United States. The U.S. government took over two major U.S. housing mortgage firms, Fannie Mae and Freddie Mac with the price tag of $200 billion. Subsequently, as the American International Group (AIG), the largest American insurance company, faced an insolvency crisis, the Fed urgently transfused $85 billion to the company in September 2008. Founded in 1812, Citibank, the largest commercial bank in the United States, was also in bankruptcy crisis due to a decline in asset value. The U.S. government provided $50 billion in bailouts to Citibank in November 2008.

The crisis spread from Wall Street to the main street. Sufferings shifted from the financial sector to the real sector, and the war front line expanded globally from the United States to Europe and Asia. In particular, the most vulnerable automakers in the U.S. industry were hit hard by the global economic crisis. In November 2008, three major U.S. automakers (GM, Ford, and Chrysler) asked the U.S. government to provide $50 billion to avoid bankruptcy. (Ford filed the rescue money but did not actually receive the bailout money.) Over the next five years, the total amount of bailouts the U.S. government provided to the automobile industry amounted to $80 billion, resulting in securing 340,000 jobs.

GM agreed to provide common stock and preferred stock (60% of the total) to the government as collateral in exchange for receiving a bailout and agreed to repay the loans by 2012. In the U.S. economy, something previously unthinkable happened. The U.S. government became a shareholder of a private company for a while. This kind of government intervention in the private economy during the global economic crisis led people to wonder: "Is the U.S. economy a capitalist market economy?" The government's active intervention in the market economy took place to the extent of the borderline between capitalism and socialism. Some criticism was raised that the U.S. economy reached the level of a socialist-controlled economy. There was an increasing sentiment that the global economic crisis in 2007 was a prelude to ending the American-style market capitalism and the U.S.-led financial order.

The U.S. economy entered a recession phase in December 2007. In 2008 alone (until November) 2 million jobs were lost. The U.S. unemployment rate jumped to 10.0% in October 2009, up from 3.8% in April 2000, just before the last flash of the IT frenzy was quenched. The unemployment rate of 10% during the global economic crisis was the highest level since the unemployment rate reached 10.8% in December 1982 during the oil crises. During and after the global economic crisis of 2008, 485 U.S. banks went under. The global economic crisis began to be called the Great Recession.

<Table 1.7> U.S. Economic Performance During the Great Recession

Year	Economic Growth Rate (%)	Unemployment Rate (%)	Inflation Rate (%)
2007	2.0	5.0	2.9
2008	0.1	7.3	3.8
2009	−2.6	9.9	−0.4
2010	2.7	9.3	1.6
2011	1.5	8.5	3.2

The amount of money that the Bush and Obama administrations spent to rescue the economy was astronomical. The Bush administration and Congress took drastic steps to supply $700 billion in bailouts to financial institutions, and the Obama administration that inherited the crisis also poured in $780 billion as economic stimulus packages. The Fed lowered the federal funds rate, the benchmark interest rate to almost 0% to cope with the global economic crisis and maintained the zero-interest rate for years. It also used a new financial policy tool, quantitative easing (QE) that had never been used in the Fed's 100-year history. In extreme situations, extreme measures were needed. Traditional monetary policy until then was to buy short-term Treasury securities from banks to increase the amount of money in the economy, and the central bank supplied new money to banks in exchange for the short-term securities. However, the Fed was no longer able to use the traditional monetary policy tools because the short-term interest rates (federal funds rate) reached 0%. This phenomenon is known to be the zero-lower-bound problem. Quantitative easing is a new tool for monetary policy in which the Fed buys long-term Treasury securities and mortgage-backed securities (MBS) to provide long-term funds to the market (especially mortgage market) and to stabilize the housing market. Quantitative easing policy has become a game changer in the operation of monetary policy.

Criticism has been raised at home and abroad regarding quantitative easing. In the United States, concerns have been raised that such QE policy would increase inflationary expectations in the long run. Criticism has also been heightened outside the United States, stating that quantitative easing would have a negative impact on the exchange rates of other countries by declining the value of the U.S. dollar. Thus, such quantitative easing would make other countries' currencies stronger, which would adversely affect their competitiveness in the world market and their exports. Confronted with such criticisms, then Fed Chairman Ben Bernanke said he was confident that the U.S. economy would be able to absorb the shock of quantitative easing without fear of inflation, given that the U.S. economic growth rate was well below the potential growth rate.

The global economic crisis in 2008 had been the most painful economic ordeal since the Great Depression in the 1930s. Many people were worried that the Great Recession would spread far and wide to the extent of an economic disaster comparable to the Great Depression. In some ways, the Great Recession in 2008 was not as severe as the Great Depression in depth, but in terms of scope, it could be much more global than the Great Depression. So many people suffered so much. The Great Depression was confined to the United States and European countries, but almost all countries on the planet (except a few closed countries) fell within the influence of the global economic crisis.

Many economists and political and religious leaders agree that greed was at the root of the global economic crisis. The Dalai Lama, the spiritual leader of Tibetan Buddhism, who rarely mentions economic issues, maintained that greed was the cause of the global economic crisis. Pope Francis also criticized the greed of capitalism by quoting the words of Saint Basil the Great (or Basil of Caesarea), who said that "The greed for money is the 'dung of the evil'" (Source: https://www.cnn.com/2015/07/07/world/pope-mass-ecuador-quito/index.html). There is no denying that the global economic crisis was caused by the excessive love of money rather than the lack of money. When people saw the value of the house rising more than twice, they would be tempted to buy houses without doubting the risk involved in such investment. It was the easiest way to make money with no sweat and labor. All they cared about was that even if they bought a house for a ridiculous price, they would expect to sell it at an even higher price. People forgot what a house was for. However, history has taught us that wealth beyond rational profit pursuit eventually disappears. (Yuhn et al., 2015)

In addition, deregulation played a part in the global economic crisis. In 1999, the U.S. Congress abolished the Glass-Steagall Act of 1933 that was enacted during the Great Depression. The law aimed at separating banking, insurance, and investment to prohibit banks from engaging in risky investment projects. As a result of the abolition of the Glass-Steagall Act, securities and insurance companies were able to buy banks, and banks were also able to engage in insurance and investment businesses. As financial regulations were abolished, Dinosaurian financial institutions that synthesized banks, insurance and investment firms were born, and financial institutions entered an era of fierce and endless competition. Banks were still strongly regulated for the protection of depositors, but investment banks were almost out of regulation because investors were investing at their own risk. Thus, we can't dispute the argument that deregulation was a remote cause of the financial crisis.

The Obama administration's aggressive market intervention and the Fed's unprecedented quantitative easing policy restored people's trust in the economy. The Great Recession finally ended in December 2010. Although the U.S. unemployment rate remained at 9.3% in December 2010, it steadily declined to 5.3% by June 2015 (the lowest level since April 2008), and to 3.5% in February 2020 just before the outbreak of the coronavirus pandemic. As the economy was recovering, the U.S. stock market also began to rebound. The Dow Jones Industrial Average returned to its pre-recession level (14,066 on October 10, 2007), reaching the 14,000 mark on February 1, 2013. It took almost six years for the DJIA to regain its prior-crisis level. Also, the Nasdaq Composite index which slowly recover like a slug finally topped the 3,000 mark (March 13, 2012) for the first time since 1998. It took more than 12 years for the Nasdaq to reach the milestone of the 3,000 level.

Since the U.S. economy recovered from one of the worst recessions in 2011, the U.S. economy has emerged as a stronger and more productive economy. The U.S. stock market has squared away like sailing with a tailwind, entering the longest expansion phase in U.S. history. The Dow Jones index has kept on rising to the record level of 36,799.65 (January 4, 2022), except for a brief drop to 18,591.93 (March 23, 2020) during the corona pandemic crisis. The Nasdaq index has also been running along smoothly. The Nasdaq index surpassed the 9,000 mark (9,022.39) on December 26, 2019, just before the arrival of the coronavirus pandemic. The Nasdaq index, after briefly dipping to the level of 6,860.67 on March 23, 2020, climbed to 16,057.44 on November 18, 2021, the highest level so far. Both the Dow-Jones and Nasdaq indexes broke the previous peaks that had never been reached ever. The Great Recession that had been the most serious recession after the Great Depression ended with a great fanfare, making the U.S. economy more resilient.

4

THE ROARING TWENTIES AND THE GREAT DEPRESSION

The 1920s was a heyday for the U.S. economy. The 1920s was commonly called the 'Roaring Twenties'. Just as there is a saying that "There is no success without fear", American people in the 1920s indulged in portfolio investment without fear for the accumulation of their wealth. The U.S. economy in 1929 was like a balloon inflated with full air. On a typical day in October 1929, the sun rose again, but all of a sudden fear swept over American people. The stock market collapsed like a falling dam. The Great Depression began on October 29, 1929 when the U.S. stock market lost 25% of its value in one week (Black Tuesday).

From the Black Tuesday of 1929 to the bank holidays of 1933, U.S. gross domestic product (GDP) decreased by as much as 30%, and the unemployment rate rose from 3.2% to 25%. Prices fell 25% during this period, and the money supply fell 35%. More than 9,000 banks out of 25,000 banks disappeared by 1933. After three years of the most tumultuous convulsion in U.S. history, the U.S. economy began to recover from its worst trough in 1933. However, this recovery was transient, and a second wave recession struck again in 1937. Even though the second phase of the Depression officially ended in June 1938, the U.S. economy remained fragile. At last, the U.S. economy was able to get out of the long tunnel of the Great Depression around the end of 1941 when the United States participated in World War II. Here is are some data on what happened during the crisis:

<Table 1.8> U.S. Economic Performance During the Great Depression

Year	Economic Growth Rate (%)	Unemployment Rate (%)	Inflation Rate (%)
1929	N.A.	3.2%	0.0%
1930	−8.5%	8.7%	−2.7%
1931	−6.4%	15.9%	−8.9%

1932	−12.9%	23.6%	−10.3%
1933	−1.2%	24.9%	−5.2%
1934	10.8%	21.7%	3.5%

The Great Depression fundamentally changed the landscape of the U.S. economy. Most notably, more than 9,000 banks went bankrupt for about three years after the crisis. One reason for the bank failures was that there were severe bank runs during the first phase of the Great Depression from 1929 to 1933. Initially a few people would suddenly fear that they wouldn't be able to get their money from their bank. They would run down to their bank to get their money. Other people would see them getting their money out of their bank and follow suit. This is referred to as a bank run. As a result, their bank would have to close because of the drain of funds. If a bank closed, people would worry about other banks closing, and they would run to their banks. This phenomenon is referred to as a financial panic. The financial panic spread uncontrollably during the early stage of the Great Depression.

Another reason why a huge number of banks failed during the Great Depression is that banks engaged in too-risky businesses. They heavily pursued more profitable investment activities such as project financing (loans to finance construction projects). This kind of excessive speculation by banks made situations worse. In addition to the traditional business activities in which banks received deposits and made loans with the deposit funds, they expanded their operations to project financing, securities, and insurance. As a result of these risky investments, 9,000 banks were closed in just three years during the Great Depression. In 1933, when the Great Depression reached its bottom, U.S. Congress passed the Glass-Steagall Act to separate the financial institutions into three areas: banking, insurance, and investment (securities). The law aimed at effectively preventing financial institutions from invading each other.

The deposit withdrawals (bank runs) also subsided when President Franklin Roosevelt took extreme measures to stabilize the financial panics. He suspended the operations of all banks for one month in March 1933. This drastic measure was known as the bank holidays. The bank holidays together with President Roosevelt's 'New Deal' policy designed to pour large-scale public spending finally helped the U.S. economy escape from the Great Depression. President Roosevelt, in his 1933 inaugural address, declared that "The only thing we have to fear is fear itself." The economic crisis had begun to slow down to some extent. But again in 1937, the specter of the Depression began to wander, and it was only after the United States began to enter World War II in 1941 that the U.S. economy was completely out of the dark cloud of the Great Depression. The U.S. economy exhibited a W-shaped recession during the Great Depression.

Now let's look back to the 1920s just before the Great Depression broke out. Long before the Great Depression, speculations on real estate and stocks went wild. The U.S. stock market in 1929 enjoyed the last of the "Roar of 1920s," and the year was the festival for making money for many people. In 1929, about 10 million people flocked to the stock market. They couldn't foresee the serious economic catastrophe that was on the horizon. Their eyes only focused on the stock quotations. They enjoyed seeing the money invested in stocks growing as if they saw trees bear tasteful fruits. Just as the passengers of the sinking Titanic had been unable to foresee the coming disaster a few hours later and were intoxicated by the dance of joy, American people soaked themselves in the money-making game without realizing the coming disaster in a few months. Reporter Edward Lefevre described the fever of stock investment at that time as follows:

> "A janitor who was cleaning the windows of a stockbroker's office is taking a break to look into the stock market through the window. He was about to invest the money he had earned from cleaning into Simons' stock. A stockbroker's assistant earned nearly $250,000 in stock investments, and a nurse earned $300,000 following a patient's recommendation. Also, a farmer herding cattle in a remote village in Wyoming, 30 miles away from the nearest railway station, bought 1,000 shares a day."

Obviously, these investment crazes contained a lot of bubbles, but the risk of such investment was overshadowed by the irrational exuberance. If a person invested $1,000 in the U.S. stock market in 1921, the value of the investment would have increased to $20,000 by 1929. Who could fathom out the risk of investing in assets where investment values increased exponentially? The three-month rise in stock prices from June to August 1929 significantly outpaced the one-year increase in stock prices in the previous year. At that time, almost everyone was concerned with investing in stocks to become rich and had little interest in anything else other than borrowing and saving money to buy stocks.

The bubble in the U.S. stock market burst without any warning sign, as if an air balloon popped up. The stock market collapsed in an instant as selling orders surged like an avalanche. Buying orders were missing and only selling orders were flooded over the counter. On the day of October 29th alone, the amount of the market value in the U.S. stock market that was equivalent to the increase over the previous year evaporated like smoke in the air. Investment bank Goldman Sachs lost half of its market value in just one day on October 29th. When the stock market boom crumbled, the situation was like a huge dam collapsed.

Until the Great Depression occurred, classical economics, which believed in the self-correcting forces of the economy, prevailed. Classical economists had the belief that the economy would take care of itself if economic agents pursued their own best interests, and the free market worked in full competition. The Great Depression, however, devastated the classical economists' belief in the self-correcting economy. The economy failed to restore stability and drifted out of equilibrium for more than 10 years. The Great Depression ruined the doctrine of the classical school.

Around that time, white knight John Maynard Keynes turned up. The appearance of Keynes signaled the birth of a new paradigm advocating government intervention in the economy. Keynes visited the United States three times during the Great Depression and met with President Roosevelt for economic advice. Although President Roosevelt was known to confess that he was not much impressed with Keynes' advice, Keynes certainly had some influence on President Roosevelt's New Deal policy, which served as a gateway to escaping from the Great Depression. Had the Keynesian Revolution not happened, some scholars argued that totalism could have emerged on the U.S. territory. It would be fair to say that thanks to the Keynesian Revolution, the Great Depression had the consequence of not destroying but strengthening U.S. capitalism.

There are many explanations for the cause of the Great Depression, but the exact cause of the Great Depression is still not known. Economists like Friedman argue that the sharp decline in the money supply was the main culprit of the Great Depression. In fact, the central bank of the United States, the Federal Reserve System, was founded in 1913, and the Great Depression broke out 16 years later. The Fed encountered a severe panic such as the Great Depression for the first time and showed immaturity in dealing with the crisis. The money supply declined by 35% during the first three years of the Great Depression, and Friedman blamed the economic crisis on the drastic decline in the supply of money.

On the other hand, Keynes maintained that insufficient aggregate demand had caused the Great Depression. Consumers spent less for consumption, and businesses spent less for investment because they were precarious about the future of the economy for some reasons. As a consequence, business firms could not sell their products, and inventories accumulated. Business firms would have to lay off workers.

Even though no one has a definitive answer as to what caused the collapse of the U.S. stock market, one thing is clear: The investment frenzy before the Great Depression was the result of greed far beyond the behavior of rational profit seeking. There are some similarities between the 2008

Great Recession and the Great Depression of the 1930s. What they have in common is that “the market was driven by fear, not by fact,” and greed was at the root of the two economic crises.

5

THE TRAGEDIES OF THE GREAT DEPRESSION: SPLENDOR IN THE GRASS

There has been a proliferation of novels and movies that dealt with the tragedies of the Great Depression. Among them, <Splendor in the Grass> and <The Grapes of Wrath> have been shining. As the Great Depression deepened, millions of investors who had mistaken an increase in paper assets (stocks) for the accumulation of wealth went stone-broke overnight. Suicides took place here and there, and the number of people who took their lives continued to increase. <Splendor in the Grass> was not a movie about the Great Depression but was shot against the backdrop of tragedies inflicted by the Great Depression. .

The title of the movie, <Splendor in the Grass>, was taken from a verse of <Ode, Intimations of Immortality from Reflections of Early Childhood> written by British romantic poet, William Wordsworth.

> What though the radiance which was once so bright
> Be now for ever taken from my sight,
> Though nothing can bring back the hour
> Of splendor in the grass, of glory in the flower,
> We will grieve not, rather find
> Strength in what remains behind.

The time was the early 1930s, and the scene was a rural village in Kansas, United States. The film depicts the tragic ending that the Great Depression brought about. The movie traces a journey toward which the protagonists of the movie, Wilma 'Deanie' Loomis (Nathalie Wood) and Arthur 'Bud' Stamper (Warren Beatty) were gradually adapting to a new environment in the aftermath of the Great Depression. The movie ends with a sense of sadness that the radiant brilliance of the past glory disappears from sight, but people embrace the reality of being unable to escape from the tragedy of the Great Depression. The Great Depression left them in a dangerous limbo, but they could not have the luxury of just grieving.

'Deanie' Loomis and 'Bud' Stamper were high-school sweethearts. Deanie's parents had a very pious attitude toward indulgence. Her mother strongly advised Deanie not to play with her boyfriend until she got married. Deanie's parents were from poor families. All the property they owned was the shares of the Stamper Oil Company owned by Bud's father.

Bud's father, Mr. Stamper, made a lot of money from the development of oil fields. Bud's father also did not want Bud to be too close to Deanie for other reasons. His father wanted Bud to attend Yale University to study for four years and to take over his business. The two youngsters agonize over their parents' incomprehensible demands and become conflicted and rebellious. After this wandering, Deanie suffers from severe depression and is admitted to a psychotherapy ward. In the meanwhile, Bud goes to Yale University.

Deanie's parents visited their daughter six months after she was hospitalized. They listened to the radio in the hospital. It was the news that the New York Stock Exchange (NYSE) had its worst drop since its opening and that the asset value of $14 million had been lost in one day. Deanie's parents, who owned some of the Stamper Oil Company stocks, became very despondent at the news. Around that time, Mr. Stamper was also on a visit to his son at Yale University, and he also heard the news. When he learned that his company's stock price plunged, he was shocked and jumped out of the hotel window that night to commit suicide. The next morning, Bud discovered the body of his father, who was piled up on a blanket. The tragedy of the Stamper family illustrates how the Great Depression inflicted devastating pains to American families.

6

THE TWO OIL SHOCKS OF THE 1970S AND STAGFLATION

The first oil shock occurred in October 1973 through March 1974 when OPEC (Organization of the Petroleum Exporting Countries) nearly quadrupled crude oil prices. OPEC's dramatic increases in crude oil prices were not based on economic principles of demand and supply but were made from the geopolitical dynamics of the Middle East. In the six-day war between Israel and nine Arab nations in 1967, Israel won a great victory in the war with the Arab nations. The war was like a thunderbolt operation. Israel occupied the Sinai Peninsula and Golan Heights. On October 6, 1973, on the day of Yom Kippur, the Day of Atonement of Judaism, Syria and Egypt attacked Israel with assistance from other Arab countries to restore their territories. This was the Yom Kippur War.

When the war broke out, the United States decided to provide Israel with weapons and war supplies. In opposition to the U.S. aid to Israel, OPEC increased its crude oil price from $3 to $5.11 per barrel by 70%. The United States again urgently provided $2.2 billion to prevent the collapse of Israel. In response, almost all OPEC countries took petroleum embargoes against the United States, and the embargoes extended to Western European countries and Japan. As a result, crude oil prices jumped nearly four times to $12 a barrel by 1974. Oil became a new weapon.

The second oil crisis (1979 ~ 1980) was triggered by the collapse of the Mohammad Reza Pahlavi regime, the pro-American regime in Iran. The Shah of Iran fled Iran in 1979, and Ayatollah Ruhollah Khomeini seized the power. The new government of Iran took hostages of the U.S. embassy personnel and declared a confrontation with the United States. Over the next 12 months after the new state ruled by Khomeini was established, the price of crude oil increased to $39.50 per barrel. The price of West Texas Intermediate (WTI) crude oil also increased by 205% from 1978 to 1980. The two oil crises put the global economy into shock and chaos. They affected many short-term and long-term economic and political impacts on the world economy.

The first oil crisis that occurred in 1973 and the second oil crisis that occurred in 1979 led the U.S. economy to experience a series of recessions from 1973 to 1982. The first oil recession occurred in November 1973 and lasted for 16 months until March 1975. The second oil recession that occurred in January 1980 was short-lived, ending in July 1980. The third oil recession that may be called the Volker recession occurred in July 1981 and lasted 16 months until November 1982. Here is a reality check on what happened to the U.S. economy during the oil recessions:

<Table 1.9> U.S. Economic Performance During the Oil Crises

Year	Economic Growth Rate (%)	Unemployment Rate (%)	Inflation Rate (%)
1973	5.6	4.9	6.2
1974	−0.5	7.2	11.1
1975	−0.2	8.2	9.1
1976	5.4	7.8	5.7
1979	3.2	6.0	11.3
1980	−0.3	7.2	13.6
1981	2.5	8.5	10.3
1982	−1.8	10.8	6.1
1983	4.6	8.3	3.2

In the United States, prices and interest rates started to rise precipitously. Gasoline prices rose from 38.5 cents per gallon in May 1973 to 55.1 cents in June 1974. As oil accounted for a large proportion of production costs, companies shifted higher production costs to their product prices. In addition, in the United States, where the proportion of gasoline in personal consumption was large, the real income of households was reduced so much that it was necessary for households to reduce consumption in other items. Companies began to cut production and laid off employees. It was the beginning of a long journey that made the 1970s gloomy.

In the United States, gasoline quotas were implemented on a weekly basis, and the even-odd day refueling system was introduced. For American consumers who accustomed to using gasoline like water, such a restriction was a painful experience. U.S. consumers prior to the oil shocks preferred gas guzzlers but after the oil crises, they had to turn to small cars. Thus, the oil shocks changed the U.S. automobile industry significantly, forcing the American automakers to face the Japanese raid on the car market.

The second oil crisis once again put the world economy on the spiral of rising inflation. Inflation in the United States developed to almost uncontrollable phases with conventional economic policy. The annual inflation rate rose to nearly 15%, and the 30-year mortgage rate also jumped to over 18% in 1980. People could not afford to make mortgage payments. They protested the exorbitant interest rates in front of the White House. An extraordinary prescription for extraordinary situations was needed.

President Carter at last implemented a direct price control policy that puts an upper limit on the prices of some items to ease inflationary expectations. This kind of policy is called income policy. It was the first and the last time the United States implemented the income policy. Carter further appointed Paul Volker, known as the 'Inflation Czar' as the Chairman of the Fed. Volcker took drastic measures to calm down the inflationary spiral. He implemented a very restrictive monetary policy to allow interest rates to soar. Volker's Fed raised the federal funds rate to 20.0% on March 18, 1980, the highest level in U.S. history. The third oil recession ensued.

The federal funds rate is extremely important because it is a benchmark interest rate on which market interest rates are based. The federal funds rate is the cheapest money available to banks. Banks borrow funds from other banks in the federal funds market and make consumer loans, business loans, and mortgage loans with the borrowed funds. Thanks to Volker's drastic measures, American people began to have confidence in the government's determination to end the inflationary spiral, and the 'diehard' inflation gradually began to lose steam in the middle of the 1980s. The U.S. inflation that was 13.6% in 1980 fell to 3.2% in 1983. The inflation rate of 13.6% was the highest level ever recorded in the Unites States.

In addition to the United States, the global economy was confronted with a new phenomenon called stagflation, the coexistence of high unemployment (stagnation) and high inflation. Before the oil crises, it was common for prices to fall along with the stagnation of economic activity. However, the oil shocks rocked this pattern. The development of stagflation was a counterpunch on the mainstream Keynesian economics that had dominated Western economic thoughts for the past several decades after the Great Depression. Keynesian economics could neither explain stagflation nor give proper remedies for it.

The economic recessions brought by the oil crises had several distinct features from previous economic crises. First, the oil crises in the 1970s affected the economies of almost all countries that depended on oil imports, regardless of whether they were developed or less developed. Not only the United States and Japan, but also India and South Korea did not escape from the influence of the crises. Second, the previous crises were mainly associated with the demand side of the economy caused by human greed, but the economic recessions in the 1970s and early 1980s were primarily ascribed to the supply side of the economy caused by skyrocketing oil prices. A supply shock to the economy is worse than a demand shock because a supply shock such as an oil crisis leads to higher inflation and higher unemployment. Finally, previous crises were touched off by economic factors, but the economic crises of the 1970s and early 1980s were triggered mainly by political conflicts.

As an Inflation-inflicted economy became the norm of the global economy after the oil crises, economic policy in most major countries was shifted toward placing on combating inflation. Since then, the specter of double-digit inflation has not again rambled about in the U.S. economy and in other advanced economies. Nonetheless policymakers have been on the alert to put inflation under control until the end of the 20th century. In many countries, policymakers set the goal of inflation at a certain level and made every effort to achieve the target inflation rate. This kind of policy is called inflation targeting. Inflation targeting has become the highest priority in monetary policy in many advanced economies. For example, the Fed's target inflation rate has been set at 2% per year. The Bank of Japan pursued even a stricter inflation targeting policy by setting the target inflation rate at 1%. The Bank of Korea also set the target inflation rate between 2.5% and 3.5%.

Thus, the oil crises in the 1970s and early 1980s led central bankers in major countries to turn into a hawkish position on inflation. The hawk is a position that places more importance on the suppression of inflation than on the promotion of growth, and the hawks prevailed at least until the global economic crisis in 2008. The dove became the minority in the initiative of monetary policy. But things come full circle, and the influence of the hawk has been diminishing since the global economic crisis in 2008. For instance, Japan has been trying hard to stimulate the inflation rate to 2% since Abe became the new prime minister.

Will another oil crisis come? Historically, oil prices have been much more volatile than the prices of assets such as equities and bonds. After the oil crises in the 1970s, oil prices trended downwardly. The West Texas Intermediate (WTI) crude oil prices (nominal) once fell to $12.07 per barrel in 1998 (average), but rose to $127.77 per barrel in July 2008, just before the deepening of the global economic crisis. However, downward trends in oil prices accelerated since October 2014 when shale oil and shale gas got down to the market. Oil prices fell to $16.74 in March 2020 again when the coronavirus pandemic began to spread rapidly. The coronavirus pandemic crisis was another external shock that dampened the demand for oil on a global scale. Daily oil prices fluctuated between $11 to $80 per barrel during the coronavirus pandemic period (January 2020 ~ December 2021), and the WTI crude oil futures once traded at negative prices on April 20, 2020. However, as geopolitical tensions in the Middle East were heightened, the WTI oil price rose again to $88 (January 18, 2022), the highest level since October 2014 when the oil price began to fall. As Russia invaded Ukraine in February 2022, the WTI price further jumped to $123.70 per barrel (March 8, 2022). Although the oil price is expected to go up and down beyond the level of $100 per barrel, the price of $100 per barrel seems to be the upper limit to the future oil price.

Oil prices have been volatile because they have been affected by more than the laws of demand and supply. Above all, many experts have blamed wide fluctuations in oil prices on international speculations in crude oil and geopolitical tensions. Oil prices are also heavily affected in the short run by oil futures contracts on the commodities markets. However, many economic and geopolitical factors indicate that the likelihood of a major oil crisis is slim. Recent efforts by advanced countries to reduce the use of fossil fuels such as petroleum makes the next oil crisis on a global scale less likely. Fossil fuels have been blamed to be the main culprit of the global warming of the earth. A host of countries have made commitments to significantly reduce their carbon emissions. Their goal is to achieve 'net zero' by the year 2050. Net zero means that each nation which has joined the Paris Climate Agreement is not adding new emissions to the earth. The Paris Agreement aims to maintain the global temperature within the 2^oC above the pre-industrial era level. There is a promising report that the U.K. economic growth rate has increased in proportion to decreases in carbon emission.

Furthermore, shifts to renewable energy have been accelerated, and there have been new technologies in the development of alternative energy sources. These alternative energy sources include bioenergy, solar, wind, and hydrogen. However, no single energy source or technology advancement is sufficient to achieve a 2^oC pathway. Also, gasoline cars will be speedily replaced by electrical cars or hybrid cars in the near future. Thus, the supply of renewable energy is expected to continue to increase while the demand for fossil fuels is expected to continue to decrease, which will eventually reduce the upward pressure on the prices of oil. Most importantly, the full-dress production of shale oil and shale gas in the United States has significantly changed the landscape for the global supply of oil.

<Figure 1.5> Changes in U.K. Greenhouse Gas Emissions and Real GDP since 1990

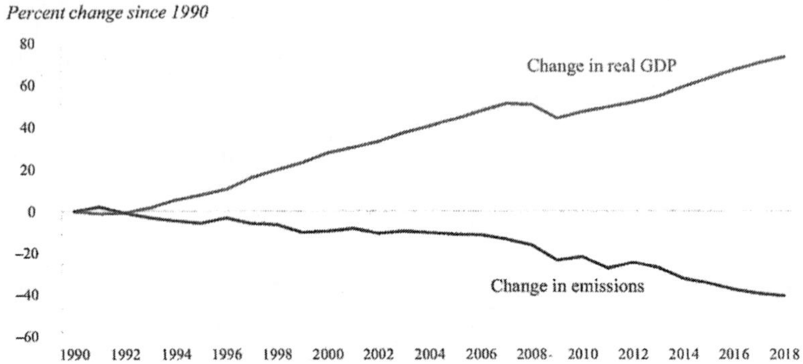

Sources: Climate Watch; U.K. Office for National Statistics; CEA calculations.
Note: Real GDP is reported in chained 2019 pounds. Greenhouse gases are reported in megatons and use production-based accounting

7

THE 1997 ASIAN FINANCIAL CRISIS: THEY POPPED UP THE CHAMPAGNE BOTTLE TOO EARLY

The Asian economic crisis of 1997 was a pain that left scars on the lives of many Asian people. Many people lost their jobs and homes. Many people took their lives. The scars have not been completely erased from their lives. Suddenly in the summer of 1997, a cold wind shook the streets in many Asian cities, and the streets were filled with outcast unemployed people. The dark shadow of the crisis devoured people and their neighbors as if the rain came in torrents, and everything was wiped out. It was a lonely scenery that reminded us of a poem entitled *The Wind Blows* by Korean poet, Lee So-ra (2004).

> The wind blows.
> A dreary scenery blows into a sad heart.
> On my way home with my hair cut
> I shed tears that formed in my eyes.
> The sky is wet.
> Cold raindrops fall on the bleak street.
> The rain that follows me in a multitude.
> It's far from me.
> It seems to have already stopped.
> The world is like yesterday
> Time is passing.

The 1997 Asian economic crisis might have many causes, but human greed and speculation on foreign currencies appear to have been the major causes of the crisis. The economic crisis that struck Asia in 1997 was initially set off by speculators' attack on some Asian currencies. As the Great Depression came without any sign of crisis, the attack on the Thai baht came suddenly in July 1997. On July 2, 1997, the day after Hong Kong's sovereignty was transferred from the United Kingdom to China, speculators' attack on the Thai baht started. On the surface, the plunge of the value of the Thai baht happened abruptly, but, in fact, the crisis was brewing long before. Speculators began to sell the baht in anticipation that the baht would drop further. The attacks of these speculators spread rapidly into the Korean won, Philippine pesos, and Indonesian rupees by October of that year.

Some Asian countries indulged in the euphoria of affluence in the 1990s. They enjoyed rapid economic growth and wealth accumulation achieved at a dizzying pace in the 1990s, but ironically, this fortune sowed the seeds of misfortune. People in these countries went on a shopping spree to buy luxurious foreign goods and to travel to foreign countries. Their foreign reserve assets decreased drastically as their imports of foreign goods and services increased, and their foreign currency reserves were quickly emptying. As someone put it adequately, they popped up the champagne too early.

A common feature that characterized these countries was that they were soaked in the mood to show off their newly created wealth. These nations began to open their domestic markets with a sense of confidence. Consumers were beginning to turn their appetite to foreign products, and they were eager to travel to foreign countries. Companies also began to turn their attention to foreign investment in the wake of liberalization. Excessive consumption and over-investment were the dominant trend in the 1990s in these countries. Excessive consumption and excessive investment inevitably accompanied excessive borrowing.

Although people in these countries saw their income increasing like the fruits hanging on trees ripening, the soil on which the trees were growing began to dry out. In most of these countries, the annual economic growth rate was cut in half beginning in the middle of the 1990s. For example, South Korea's economic growth rate reached close to 8% from 1980 to 1995, but the growth rate fell to half during the 1996-2010 period. In many Asian countries, the growth engine already began to cool down from the middle of the 1990s.

Furthermore, most of the Asian capital markets were not fully open when the Asian financial crisis occurred, although their domestic markets for goods and services were considerably opened. Thus, their financial sectors lacked market forces that could adjust their exchange rates in response to such an external shock. Their currencies became the targets of international speculators who expected the values of the local currencies to fall in value. Speculators began to sell the local currencies in exchange for U.S. dollars, and international investors moved their funds invested in these countries to safe places because they expected the local currencies to fall further. Consequently, the values of the currencies in these countries nosedived, and the exchange rates between their currencies and the U.S. dollar began to soar. The value of the Asian currencies during the 1997 financial crisis plummeted vertically from July 1997 to July 1998.

Thailand baht:	24.5 baht: $1 ⇒ 41.0 baht: $1 (↓ 40.2%)
Malaysian ringgit:	2.48 ringgit: $1 ⇒ 4.88 ringgit: $1 (↓ 45.0%)
Korean won:	850 won: $1 ⇒ 1,290 won: $1 (↓ 34.1%)
Indonesian rupee:	2,380 rupee: $1 ⇒ 14,150 rupee: $1 (↓ 83.2%)
Philippine peso:	26.3 peso: $1 ⇒ 42. 0 peso: $1 (↓ 37.4%)

Let's take a closer look at the crisis experienced by South Korea. The Korean won fell in value by 34.1% for one year from July 1997 to July 1998. The exchange rate between the Korean won and the U.S. dollar was 850 won per dollar just before the financial crisis but rose almost as high as 1,900 won per dollar by the end of 1997. There was an intensive attack on the Korean won by speculators during this period. Just before the 1997 financial crisis, Korea's foreign exchange reserves almost ran out. This was the result of over-consumption by Korean consumers and over-investment by Korean businesses. When a country's foreign exchange reserves almost emptied out, speculators found that the country would not be able to defend the value of its currency at an appropriate level. This currency becomes good prey for international speculators.

South Korea first decided not to reach out to the IMF for help and to endure to the end, but as its economy was approaching the cliff, it finally decided to ask for a bailout from the IMF. On December 3, 1997, the memorandum for the bailout money was signed. The bailouts included $19.5 billion from the IMF and $7 billion from the World Bank (IBRD) and $3.7 billion from the Asian Development Bank (ADB), respectively. These bailouts helped South Korea bring the crisis under control. The exchange rate began to drop gradually, and the foreign exchange market finally began to stabilize. At that time, the voluntary movement for "gold donations" by Korean people attracted the attention of the world, but many Korean firms including Daewoo faced an avalanche of bankruptcy.

Under the current international financial system where the U.S. dollar is overwhelmingly used in international transactions of goods and capital and is a dominant form of official reserve assets, a country's currency can always be the target of international speculation, if its dollar reserves are not sufficient. Although the current international financial system is not a dollar standard system under which the exchange rate is fixed to the U.S. dollar, the influence of the dollar in international transactions is still dominant. In this sense, almost all countries except for the United States are exposed to some degree of foreign exchange crisis. Moreover, the more open the economy is, the greater is the exposure to exchange risk.

One characteristic phenomenon in the Asian financial crisis was that the shock wave of the crisis rapidly transmitted to other countries. This is a phenomenon known as the contagion effect. Of course, a similar phenomenon had been observed before. For example, in the 1990s, South American countries fell into a series of currency devaluations, like dominoes. In the current state of rapid globalization and liberalization, almost all economic crises tend to spread to other countries. However, before the Asian financial crisis, the epicenters of a crisis mainly originated in large, developed countries such as the United States, and the ripple effect spread to small open economies.

However, the Asian financial crisis showed different characteristics from the previous ones in that like a pandemic, the crisis that occurred in a small economy quickly spread to other large economies. The term 'contagion effect' was used for the first time during the Asian foreign exchange crisis. It took less than two months for the Thai crisis to spread to South Korea, the Philippines, Malaysia, and Hong Kong. Later it spread to Russia and Brazil. It is interesting, however, to find that the Asian financial crisis did not spread to the Japanese yen, Chinese yuan and the Indian rupee by contagion. How could these economies escape from the Asian financial crisis? One possible explanation is that these countries were immune from the crisis because they had enough dollar reserves to counterattack the attacks of speculators on their currencies. This issue deserves further investigation.

Another phenomenon similar to the contagion effect is the butterfly effect. The butterfly effect is the idea that the tiny wing of a butterfly can drive a typhoon later. The butterfly effect originates from quantum physics and chaos theory, which means that a small change in one place can lead to a large change in another place later. The term 'butterfly effect' was first coined by Edward Lorenz. He explained the butterfly effect in the parable: "When a butterfly flies with a flap of its wings in Brazil, a hurricane comes to Texas." In 1961, Lorenz conducted a computer experiment. He used computer simulations to predict the butterfly effect and made weather forecasts. He tried to predict the weather by entering 0.506 rounded to the value of the initial condition without using the original number, 0.506127, but the results of the weather forecast were very different. The difference was only 0.000127, but the result was a sizable and significant difference.

Can the butterfly effect occur in economic events? The butterfly effect can be quite common in fiction, but in the real world, it is not easy to identify the causal relationship between a small change in the initial condition and a large-scale result. Especially in the real economy, the butterfly effect is limited. However, in the asset market, where self-fulfilling expectations prevail, the butterfly effect can occur. For example, the stock price collapse in 1988 known as the 'Black Monday,' was usually difficult to explain by theory. One plausible explanation for the Black Monday was that President Reagan's wife, Nancy Reagan, was known to come down with the flu, and her illness caused such a selloff. Some people argue that the Black Monday was difficult to explain without the aid of the butterfly effect. The outbreak of World War I was also prompted by a tiny event. The event that fired the fuse of WWI was the assassination of Archduke Prince Franz Ferdinand of Austria and his wife Sophie by Bosnian Serb nationalist Gavrilo Princip. This small event sparked one of the two most tragic wars in human history.

8

JAPAN'S 'LOST TWO DECADES'

The Japanese economy was burning like the red sun rising above the horizon until 1990, but it suddenly began to lose its aura in the early 1990s as if it had met a total solar eclipse. What stopped Japan's unstoppable sprint? The downturn of the Japanese economy, which began in the early 1990s, is often referred to as Japan's 'Lost Decade'. The size of the Japanese economy (real GDP) grew at the average rate of 4.3% per year for 20 years from 1970 until 1990, but during the Lost Decade period (1992~2002), the real GDP growth rate fell to 1.3% per year. The level of per capita income was 86% of that of the United States in 1991 but fell to 70% in 2002. The unemployment rate rose from 2.1% in 1991 to 5.4% in 2002. The Japanese economic downturn did not stop there but lasted almost 20 years more until Prime Minister Abe took office in 2012. People began to talk about Japan's 'Lost Two Decades'.

The stock market index (The Nikkei Stock Average or Nikkei 225 Index) which symbolizes Japan's economic power deviated abnormally from the path predicted by the asset pricing model such as the present value(PV) model. In fact, the Nikkei Average grew at an exponential rate for almost 40 years from 1950 to 1990. The Japanese stock index grew sixfold during the decade of the 1980s. Then the Nikkei Average reached its all-time high on December 29, 1989 when it hit an intra-day high of 38,957.44, before it closed at 38,915.87. This stock market performance was at the blossom of the Japanese asset price bubble. At the zenith of the Japanese economy, it began to falter, and the Nikkei Average also began its downturn. By March 10, 2009 near the end of the 'Lost Two Decades,' it fell to 7,054.98, losing nearly all of its previous gains in the 1980s. The Japanese stock price was 81.9% below its peak nearly 20 years earlier. This was at the nadir of the Japanese economy. When the bubble burst, the impact on the Japanese economy, society and politics was nothing short but devastating. A speculative bubble was incubated by an unfettered pursuit of greed. The crisis that began in the financial market sent shock waves throughout the entire economy.

Does history repeat itself? In the 1940s, Japan attacked Pearl Harbor in Hawaii, and the war eventually ended with Japan's defeat. From the 1970s until the early 1990s, Japan invaded the United States economically with the vigor of overwhelming the U.S. economy, the world's largest economy. Japanese firms bought landmark buildings in major U.S. cities such as Honolulu, Los Angeles, and New York and swallowed the MGM film company and the Pebble Beach golf courses which were American emblems and prides. Japan's carpet bombing of the U.S. economic territory in the 1970s and 1980s was likened to the Kamikaze attack on the Pearl Harbor in the 1940s. Japanese management techniques such as the Toyota method were accepted as textbook management models for American companies to learn. Suddenly, from the early 1990s, the Japanese economy began to lose its aura.

What brought about Japan's Lost Decades? Japan's Lost Decades might not be as severe as the Great Depression of the United States in the 1930s, but the duration of the Lost Decades was much longer than that of the Great Depression. The two economic disasters were similar in some respects. First, both economic crises began with a collapse in stock and real estate markets. Japan's share price in 2002 (8,578) at the end of the 'Lost Decade' was less than one fourth of its peak in 1989 (38,916). Japan's land price, which had soared since 1980 also plummeted. When the real estate bubble in Japan was in full swing, there was a joke that "if you sell the land of Tokyo, you can buy the entire land of the United States, and if you sell the land of the Emperor's Palace, you can buy the entire land of California."

As stock and real estate prices fell, Japanese consumers experienced their wealth slipping out of the ground day after day, and they began to tighten their belts by reducing consumption. This was also very similar to the situation before the Great Depression in the United States. The surge in stock prices and real estate prices in Japan in the 1970s and 1980s was due to the speculation fever that investors expected the stock and real estate prices to rise without a ceiling, because the stock and land prices rose exponentially during the high growth period.

Second, the Japanese financial system was not so efficient. Japanese banks that had been overprotected began to crumble in the wake of falling stock and real estate prices. In the United States, more than 9,000 banks were closed during the Great Depression (October 1929 ~ March 1933). In the 1980s, Japanese banks heavily engaged in project financing (PF) with holding stocks or land as collaterals. As the collateral values declined, borrowers fell into insolvency, and the insolvency of borrowers significantly undermined banks' ability to make profits. This credit crunch made it more difficult for companies to borrow funds for their investment projects from banks and consequently significantly reduced corporate investment.

Third, the dollar exchange rate of the yen began to fall sharply from the early 1990s. This means that the value of the yen increased rapidly. The strong yen was the result of the Plaza Agreement. Representatives from five advanced countries, the United States, Japan, the United Kingdom, West Germany, and France, gathered at the Plaza Hotel in New York in 1985 and agreed to cut the exchange rate of the yen to the dollar in half, thus making the value of the yen twice as strong as before. Until the early 1990s before the beginning of the 'Lost Decade,' the yen's exchange rate to the dollar was almost 250 yen per dollar. The yen was weak, which made Japanese products in the international marketplace highly competitive. This advantage suddenly disappeared.

In fact, the 'Low Yen' was the driving force behind the explosive growth of Japanese exports. A weaker currency is an essential condition for an export-led growth strategy. Japanese automobiles and electronic products dominated the U.S. market, cornering the American industries in the 1970s and 1980s. It is in this background that the United States, Japan, and other three nations entered into the Plaza Agreement to keep the exchange rate of the yen to the dollar low and the value of the yen strong. Japan's export competitiveness began to decline abruptly. We have already discussed that the two major components of private aggregate demand, consumption and investment suffered a significant decline in the first "Lost Decade". Now, the third component of aggregate demand, exports also began to decline.

Fourth, the Japanese economic disaster has solidified deflation to the Japanese economy. The government initially kept the policy interest rate (commonly called the call rate in Japan, which is equivalent to the U.S. federal funds rate) at very low levels to stimulate the economy. To make matters worse, as the economy slowed down, market interest rates fell further, and the economy was trapped in low interest rates. In Japan, short-term interest rates had fallen below 1% since 1995, and remained at 0.1% from 2001 to 2005. The United States experienced a similar situation during the Great Depression. The U.S. short-term interest rate had fallen below 1% since 1931 and dropped to 0.05% from 1938 to 1940. The Japanese economy was caught in a liquidity trap during the Lost Decades, and the U.S. economy suffered a liquidity trap during the Great Depression. When deflation sets in, consumers tend to delay purchasing products, expecting product prices to fall further in the future. Firms would not be able to make profits and have to cut production and employment further.

Fifth, the choice of policy by the Japanese government was not proper. It would be more accurate to say that Japan's policymakers mismanaged fiscal and monetary policy in a passive and shortsighted manner. The Bank of Japan, the central bank of Japan, judged that there was not much they could do because Japan's interest rates remained near zero. The Japanese government also thought that there was not much they could do in the situation where the public debt exceeded 100% of GDP. Japanese policymakers worried that if they cut taxes or increased government expenditures to stimulate the economy, the public debt would uncontrollably increase. Japan was in a policy dilemma.

When the exit seems to be blocked, a Copernican change of thought is necessary. If the Bank of Japan had issued new money and lent it to the Japanese government, this policy mix could have been a good idea for rescuing Japan from the policy dilemma. The mechanism by which the Bank of Japan lends money to the Japanese government is simple. The Japanese government issues government bonds, and the Bank of Japan buys them by printing new money. This is a policy mix of monetary expansion and financial expansion without incurring further debt from the public. However, Japanese policymakers were occupied with the belief that such a bond purchase program could be a sure road to high inflation, even though the Japanese economy suffered long-sustained deflation.

Financing tax cuts or fiscal expenditures through an increase in the money supply can have the effect of killing three birds with one stone. First, the newly created money can be used by the government as a resource to finance tax cuts or spending increases. Furthermore, if the government uses such money newly issued by the central bank, the money will go around the economy. In other words, the economy can escape from the swamp of stagnation. Third, since the Japanese government does not have to borrow from the public, it will not be a burden on the fiscal deficit and public debt. (Japan increased its fiscal spending mainly through borrowing from the domestic private sector.) Lastly, the newly issued currency can bring new vitality to the economy by boosting inflation. Incidentally, Japan could escape from the low interest rate trap. Thus, it is even possible to kill four birds with one stone.

The policy option of financing the fiscal deficit through the creation of new money by the central bank is called the 'monetization of the deficit'. This practice has been a taboo in developed countries because this kind of policy inevitably leads to an increase in the money supply and to inflation. However, as far as deflation rather than inflation is a worry, financing the government deficit through the creation of new money is no longer a policy option to be tabooed. The United States took a large-scale fiscal expansion policy through military expenditures between 1940 and 1941 and was finally able to escape from the Great Depression.

Unfortunately, Japan did not take this road. Even though many economists advised that large-scale tax cuts were necessary to overcome the

Lost Decades, the Japanese government did not take appropriate actions. The Japanese government was passive in reducing taxes because of concerns about the explosive increase in the national debt. Instead, the Japanese government increased the consumption tax twice during the Lost Two Decades. When Japan needed aggressive expansionary policy actions, Japan took restrictive policy measures.

In addition, the Bank of Japan was reluctant to increase the money supply because it aimed at 1% inflation targeting for a long period. However, if the central bankers had been willing to embrace the idea that the annual inflation rate of 2% is acceptable and the perception that the central bank can issue new money and lend it to the government, Japan could have been out of the tunnel earlier. Until Prime Minister Abe emerged as a rescuer and put three arrows in the barrel, the Japanese policymakers lost the opportunity to win the battle against the 'Lost Decades'.

9

ABENOMICS AND THE THREE ARROWS

Japan that was once an envy of industrialized nations in the world turned into a laggard student who failed in almost every subject during the 'Lost Two Decades'. Abe Shinzo was elected as Japan's new Prime Minister in December 2012 in the midst of the quagmire of the Japanese economy. Like a warrior, Abe's heart was filled with the determination to reclaim the glory of Japan that had been lost for 20 years.

Slowing growth (high unemployment) and falling prices (deflation) are typical of a recession, but an economic downturn lasting nearly 20 years is a rare experience in advanced economies. The United States also experienced slow growth and falling prices during the Great Depression, but the depression combined with deflation lasted about a decade. The U.S. economy suffered the longest falling prices in the 1870s that lasted 20 years. Since then, the United States has never experienced such a long-lasting combination of stagnation and deflation.

When Abe took office, he pulled out three arrows. He set the top priority of economic policy at breaking the vicious cycle of falling prices. His economic policy is often referred to as 'Abenomics,' which is based on three economic reforms: unlimited monetary expansion (= quantitative easing), active fiscal spending, and structural reform. Abe expressed his willingness to shoot these three arrows at a time, arguing that if these three policy measures were implemented separately, they would be ineffective. The first breakthrough he tried was to increase the annual inflation rate to 2%. This means that a fundamental shift was made in the conduct of monetary policy of the Bank of Japan that targeted maintaining annual inflation below 1%. To this end, he shot the first arrow in April 2013, pursuing unlimited quantitative easing. In June 2013, the third arrow, the structural reform plan, was shot.

In order to promote inflation, the central bank normally uses its monetary policy as a main tool. Monetary policy is a policy that affects the economy by controlling the amount of money and interest rates. Until recently, policymakers in many advanced economies focused on policy aimed at lowering inflation, which was generally accepted as a common-sense principle. Why was Prime Minister Abe so obsessed with raising inflation? As we discussed, the Bank of Japan regarded an inflation rate of 1% per year as a golden rule.

In economic activity, continuous increases in prices (inflation) are a serious problem, but continuous decreases in prices (deflation) are just as serious as inflation. In a sense, deflation may have more harmful effects on the economy than inflation. First, if deflation continues, consumers tend to postpone consumption, expecting prices to fall further in the future. Goods and services are not selling well in the market. Also, in a situation where prices continue to fall, companies cannot raise product prices and as a result, their profits decrease. Decreasing profits inevitably lead to a decrease in corporate investment. Third, when deflation occurs, borrowers' real debt increases. If you borrow \$100, and prices are falling at the rate of 10%, your real debt burden will increase to \$110 one year later, although your nominal debt remains the same at \$100. The government and firms could be borrowers, but consumers as borrowers are at the most serious disadvantage. Consumers are forced to reduce consumption as the real burden of debt increases.

Finally, deflation increases the currency value of a country in the long run. Inflation is the process by which a country's currency value falls. Deflation is the opposite of inflation and increases currency value. An increase in the currency value of a country (i.e., yen) relative to the dollar means that the yen becomes relatively more expensive than the dollar. Consequently, Japanese goods become more expensive in the international marketplace, which has an adverse effect on Japanese exports. The strong yen was the main cause that the Japanese economy could not get out of the woods for more than two decades. Thus, ending deflation was the most urgent and important task Abe faced.

The market reacted enthusiastically as Abe pushed his Abenomics forward. The yen's value continued to decline, the unemployment rate continued to fall, and the share price turned to a bull market from the bear market. In the first six months following Prime Minister Abe's implementation of Abenomics, the value of the yen against the dollar fell 30%, and the Nikkei Stock Average rose 80%. His midterm (2012 ~ 2015) score card was even better: At the time of the start of the Abe regime, the exchange rate was around 80 yen per dollar, but it rose to 126 yen by June 5, 2015. This was the highest level since May 20, 2002. The unemployment rate was 4.5% in 2011 but fell to 3.4% in 2015. The annual growth rate of GDP was −0.12 % in 2011 but rose to1.22% in 2015. The seeds sown by Abenomics were starting to bear fruit.

A more dramatic upsurge occurred in the stock market. At the time of his inauguration on December 26, 2012, the Nikkei Stock Average was

10,230, but the Nikkei 225 index began to bounce back, regaining the 20,000 level by 2015. It climbed to 20,134 (April 22, 2015), breaking through the 20,000 mark in two years and making it one of the fastest growing stock market indexes in the world. It was the first time in 15 years since April 14, 2000 (20,435) for the Nikkei 225 index to surpass the 20,000 level. That level was almost doubled compared with 10,230 at the time when Prime Minister Abe took office.

Abenomics was shining in the splendid revival of the Japanese economy. Since Abe began the longest uninterrupted run as Japanese leader, he had successfully managed Japan's recovery from the devastating economy, earthquake, *tsunami,* and nuclear disaster and restored the country to the semblance of its old glory. Now let's look at his final report card. Although Prime Minister Abe left office on September 16, 2020, his legacy is still ongoing. Here, we compare the performance of the Japanese economy between the Lost Two Decades (1992 ~ 2012) and the decade of Abenomics (2013 ~ 2021). (The numbers represent the annual average.)

<Table 1.10> Japan's 'Lost Two Decades'

Period	Economic Growth Rate (%)	Unemployment Rate (%)	Inflation Rate (%)
Lost Decades (1992~2012)	0.83	4.14	0.10
Abenomics Era (2013~2021)	0.45 (1.08)[1]	3.06	0.62

1) The number in the parenthesis is the average annual growth rate that excludes the 2020 growth rate. The Japanese economic growth rate fell to −4.59% in 2020 due to the COVID-19 crisis, which was an outlier.

<Figure 1.6> Japanese Economic Performance During the 'Lost Decades'

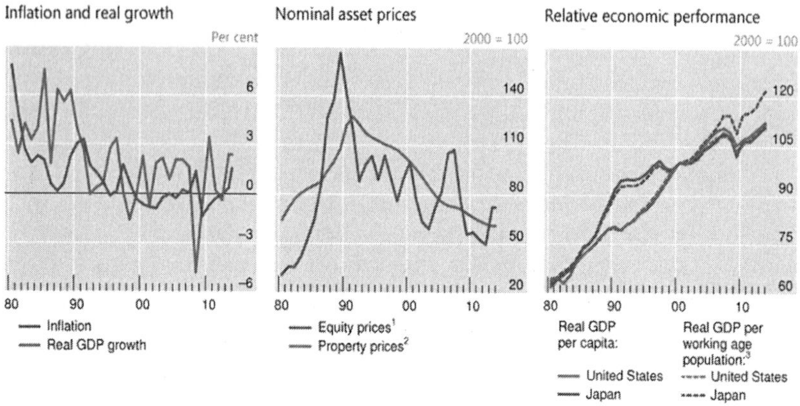

Overall, Abenomics was a driving force behind higher economic growth, higher employment (or lower unemployment), higher stock prices, and higher exchange rates (or lower yen). These indicators point to the exit of the Japanese economy out of the long tunnel of the Lost Two Decades. The average annual growth rate of the Japanese economy (GDP) during the Abenomics era was 1.08% once we exclude the negative economic growth rate (−4.59%) of 2020, which was an anomalous decline due to the COVID-19 pandemic. The Japanese annual growth rate during the Lost Two Decades was 0.83%. Second, the Japanese unemployment rate (annual average) also dropped from 4.14% during the Lost Two Decades to 3.06% during the Abenomics era. Thus, as far as economic growth and employment are concerned, Abenomics seems to have succeeded.

<Figure 1.6> Japan's Unemployment Rate During the 'Lost Decades'

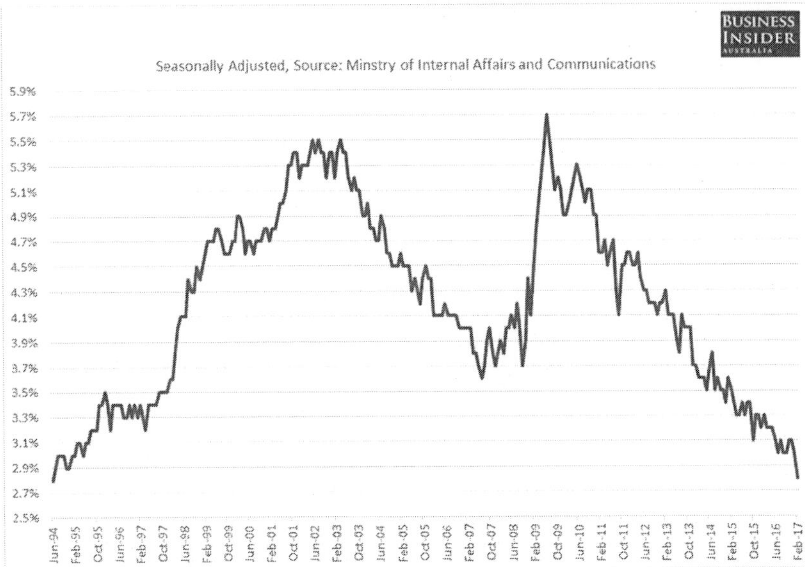

Next we'll look at the performance of the stock price (Nikkei Average) and the exchange rate. Since Prime Minister Abe took office, the Japanese stock price has continued to be on the rise. The Nikkei index was 10,230 when Abe took office on December 26, 2012, and it jumped to 23,476 when he left the office on September 16, 2020. The Japanese stock price rose nearly 2.3-fold during his tenure. The Japanese stock market continued to march toward the 30,000 plateau even after Abe left office. It finally surpassed the 30,000 mark on February 15, 2021 (30,084). It took more than 30 years for the Nikkei Average to regain 30,000. However, this level is still 77% of its all-time high of 38,915 that the Nikkei Index achieved on December 29, 1989.

<Figure 1.7> Japan's Stock Prices During the 'Lost Decades'

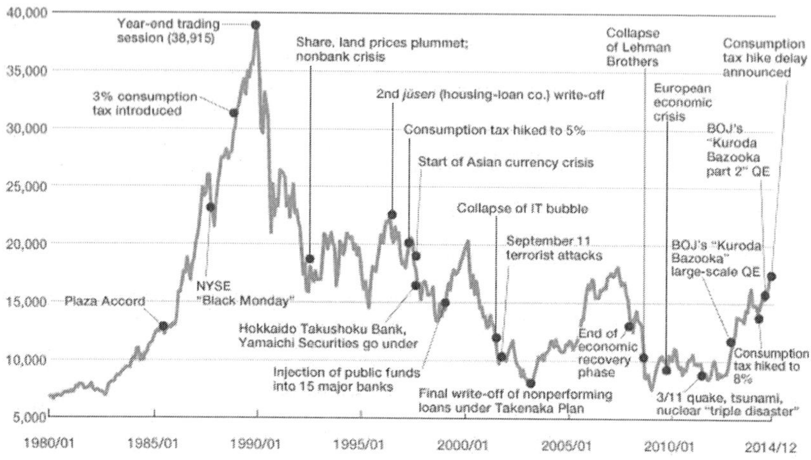

Source: Compiled using data from the Tokyo Stock Exchange.

The exchange rate of the yen to the dollar had remained quite high until 1985 when the Plaza Agreement was signed. From 1971 to 1985, the exchange rate (annual average) moved between ¥210: $1 (1978) and ¥303: $1 (1972). This means that Japan took full advantage of a super low yen during the amazing era of explosive growth. But for the first time, the exchange rate fell below ¥200: $1 in 1986 (¥168: $1), which was a sharp decline from the long-run trend of the low yen. However, the exchange rate did not fall as low as ¥100: $1 until 2009 (except for 1995) when the exchange rate fell to ¥94: $1 and further to ¥79: $1 in 2012. The exchange rate of 79 yen per dollar was the exchange rate Abe inherited when he became the Prime Minister in 2012. This indicates that the yen became a super strong currency, and this strong yen was the remote cause of the 'Lost Two Decades'. After Abe took office, the exchange rate began to gradually rise from ¥79: $1 (2012) to ¥98: $1 (2013). Since the exchange rate rose to ¥106: $1 in 2014, it has never fallen below ¥100: $1 as of 2021. (On April 13, 2022, the exchange rate rose as high as ¥126: $1.) (The exchange rate rose as high as ¥131: $1 at the end of 2022.) A comparison of the exchange rate between the pre-Abenomics and post-Abenomics years reveals the crystal-clear turnaround in the exchange rate movement after Abe became the Prime Minister.

Pre-Abenomics: ¥94: $1 (2009); ¥88: $1 (2010); ¥80: $1 (2011); ¥80: $1 (2012)

Post-Abenomics: ¥98: $1 (2013); ¥106: $1 ((2014); ¥121: $1 (2015); ¥109: $1 (2016); ¥112: $1 (2017); ¥98: $110: $1 (2018); ¥109: $1 (2019); ¥107: $1 (2020); ¥110: $1 (2021) –

However, Abenomics failed in achieving higher inflation and lower public debt. We are particularly interested in whether Japan's unlimited quantitative easing policy has succeeded in boosting inflation. The Japanese experience with unlimited quantitative easing was an adventure like walking on a new road that had never been taken before. The Fed also took quantitative easing policy during the global economic crisis in 2008, and the COVID-19 crisis in 2020 but did not pursue unlimited monetary easing. In contrast, Japan's quantitative easing policy was the strongest form of its kind in that the Bank of Japan promised to supply unlimited money to financial institutions until inflation reaches 2%. Abenomics made some contributions to stimulating inflation. The annual inflation rate rose from 0.10% during the Lost Two Decades to 0.62% during the Abenomics era. It is thus evident that despite Abe's immense effort, Abenomics has not been quite successful in achieving the 2% inflation rate target.

Abenomics has also failed in reducing the public debt. The biggest challenge faced by the Japanese government is how to stimulate the economy while managing the government debt at a reasonable level. In 2020, the ratio of the Japanese government's debt to GDP (254.1%) was the highest in the major economies, dwarfing Greece (211.2%) whose national financial system failed. (The ratio of national debt to GDP is as follows: U.S.A.: 133.4%, U.K.: 104.5%, South Korea: 47.8%.) In order to reduce the public debt, the Japanese government consecutively raised the consumption tax which is an indirect tax, while lowering the corporate tax which is a direct tax. In general, an indirect tax has less tax resistance from taxpayers. In 2014, Japan's corporate tax rate was 34.62%, which was higher than any other major countries except for the United States (Germany: 29.59%, China: 25%, Singapore: 17%) The U.S. corporate income tax rates ranged from 15% to 39% depending on taxable income brackets, but the U.S. tax rate was lowered to 21% for all taxable income brackets in 2018. The Japanese government lowered the corporate tax rate to 29.74% from 34.62% in 2018. On the other hand, in order to increase tax revenues, the Japanese government consecutively raised the consumption tax from 5% to 8% in 2014 and raised again from 8% to 10%, while lowering the corporate tax. The biggest challenge to the Japanese economy is the achievement of fiscal soundness. The Japanese government aims to reach a fiscal surplus by 2027, but its feasibility is doubtful. To achieve the fiscal surplus, the nominal growth rate of GDP must reach 3.1 to 3.5% over the period 2020~2027. However, this is the level that Japan has never reached since the bubble collapsed in the early 1990s.

<Figure 1.8> Japan's Fiscal Deficits During the 'Lost Decades'

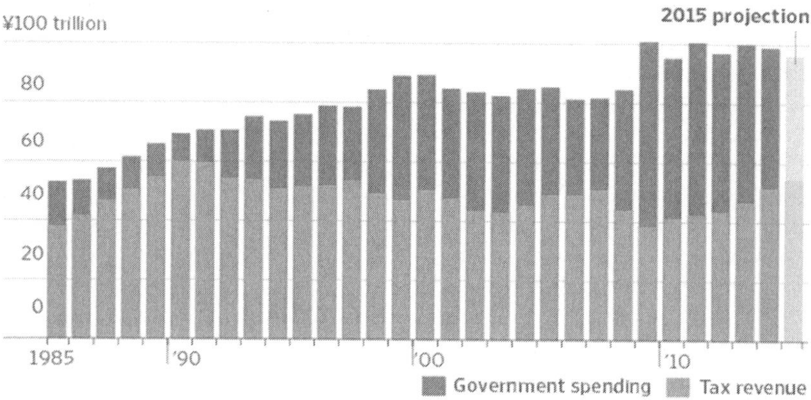

Source: Japan Finance Ministry

Abenomics has some undesirable effects on the market by promoting extremely low interest rates and high exchange rates (low yen). One by-product of Abenomics is the 'Yen Carry,' which is a money game that exploits Japan's low interest rates and high exchange rates. The 'Yen Carry' refers to a transaction in which investors borrow yen-denominated funds at a low interest rate (for example, 1%) in the Japan and lend them to foreign fund management companies at higher interest rates (for example, 4%). Recently, even domestic housewives (Watanabe women), who were disappointed at low interest rates in Japan, are known to be actively engaged in the Yen Carry investment. (This phenomenon is called Mrs. Watanabe syndrome.)

In sum, Abenomics did a good job in boosting economic growth, employment and stock prices and lowering the value of the Japanese yen but did a poor job in stimulating inflation and reducing the government debt. The Japanese experience suggests that there is a limit to the policy of inducing inflation by simply pumping more money into the economy. This is because inflation boosted by quantitative easing may be a burden if it is not supported by wage increases. Ultimately, the rise in wages will increase consumer purchasing power and increase demand for goods, which will boost inflation more effectively. In fact, Japan's average real wages had declined since 1997 until 2014. Thus, it remains unclear whether Abenomics will hit the inflation target of 2% in the long run.

Abenomics has run on an unexpected rock. The Japanese warrior succumbed to terrorism committed by a lonely wolf named *Yamagami Detsya* in July 2022. In Japan, many youngsters have become *hikikomori* (lonely wolves) since the early 1990s when the 'Lost Two Decades' began. They are not eager to seek a job and have often committed crimes. Ironically, Abe Shinzo who was so eager to end the Lost Two Decades became a victim of a *hikikomori* who was nurtured by the long-standing stagnation. The fate of Abenomics has also been fogged. Although Abe was gone, his legacy is not gone.

Abe's three arrows reminds us of Longfellow's <The Arrow and the Song>. His unlimited quantitative easing policy came as fast as a flying arrow. We can't keep an eye on it. We don't know if Abe's three arrows will hit the target in the long run, just like Longfellow found an arrow in an oak after a long time.

> I shot an arrow into the air;
> It fell to earth, I knew not where;
> For, so swiftly it flew, the sight
> Could not follow it in its flight.
> I breathed a song into the air;
> It fell to earth, I knew not where;
> For who has sight so keen and strong
> That it can follow the flight of song?
> Long, long afterward, in an oak
> I found the arrow, still unbroken,
> And the song, from beginning to end,
> I found again in the heart of a friend.

10

The Uneasy Alliance of the Eurozone

Since World War II, European countries have pursued economic integration as an effective way to prevent further wars and tensions among European countries. The first form of economic integration in Europe was a customs union signed in 1948 by three countries: Belgium, the Netherlands and Luxembourg (Benelux). This economic union was aimed at the elimination of all customs and non-tariff barriers among these countries and the imposition of the same trade barriers to non-participating countries.

Then in 1951 Belgium, France, Italy, Luxembourg, West Germany, and the Netherlands formed the European Coal & Steel Community, and in 1957 these countries signed the Treaty of Rome, which led to the creation of the European Economic Community (ECC). In 1973, Britain, Ireland, and Denmark joined the EEC, and the EEC continued to expand its boundary by accepting Greece (1981), Spain, and Portugal (1987) as members. The EEC membership increased to a total of 12 countries by 1987.

In 1993 the European Economic Community (EEC) was expanded and reorganized into the European Union (EU) by the Maastricht Treaty. In 1995 Austria, Finland, and Sweden joined the EU, and the European Union grew to a total of 15 countries. After the collapse of the former Soviet Union, ten central and eastern European countries participated in the EU in 2004. Most lately, Bulgaria and Romania joined the club in 2007. Thus, the total EU members increased to 28 countries. (Then the United Kingdom exited from the EU membership on January 1, 2020, and the EU is currently comprised of 27 members.)

The EU (made up of 28 countries) emerged as the largest economic bloc on the planet when the euro was launched, and the EU took the lead over the United States in terms of the size of the economy (GDP) and population until 2017. In 2012, the Nobel Peace Prize was awarded to the EU, which was quite controversial. However, in 2018 the United States ($21.4 trillion) regained the title of the world's largest economy, followed by EU ($18.7 trillion) and China ($14.1 trillion), Japan ($5.2 trillion), Germany ($3.9 trillion), and India ($2.9 trillion).

As the United Kingdom withdrew its membership from the EU on January 31, 2020, the influence of the EU could not have been the same as before. The population and GDP of the EU were shrunken to 447.3 million and $15.2 trillion, respectively as of the end of 2020. On the other hand, the population and GDP of the United States were increased to 332.6 million and $20.9 trillion as of the end of 2020, widening the gap between the two economic blocs. The population and GDP of the United Kingdom were 67.1 million and $2.7 trillion in 2020.

The three East Asian countries (China, Japan, and South Korea), although they have not formed an economic bloc, could emerge as a rival to the United States and the EU in terms of population and GDP if they were integrated into a single economic entity. The combined GDP of these three countries sums to $21.4 trillion in 2020 (= $14.8 trillion (China) + $5 trillion (Japan) + $1.6 trillion (Korea)), which is slightly larger than that of the United States ($20.9 trillion) and considerably bigger than that of the EU ($15.2 trillion). In 2020, the world's total GDP amounts to $84.7 trillion. (It increased to $93.9 trillion in 2021.) The combined population of the three countries totals 1.590 million (China: 1,413 million, Japan: 126 million, Korea: 51 million), which is by far the largest (U.S.: 330 million; EU: 450 million. In 2020, the world population reached 7.8 billion.) On the trade side, the three East Asian countries are far ahead of the United States and the EU. In 2013, the world trade volume reached $37 trillion, of which the three East Asian countries accounted for $6.7 trillion, the EU for $4.5 trillion, and the United States for $4.6 trillion.

Of these three economic blocs, the United States is the single federal state, and the EU's Eurozone countries use a single currency, making the Eurozone countries highly cohesive. Although the three East Asian countries are economically interdependent, they have been politically and historically in conflicts and tensions. Thus, they have high mutual economic dependence, but weak cohesion. Whether the three East Asian countries could achieve economic integration using a single currency like the Eurozone remains challengeable, but highly unlikely in the foreseeable future. Such an integration is a Herculean challenge for the three nations because of their intertwined historical, cultural, and geopolitical interests.

The EU achieved a common market in 1972. Thus, the member nations agreed not to impose tariffs on intra-regional transactions, but the leaders of the EU wanted a stronger form of economic integration, which was essential for establishing a monetary union with a single central bank and a single currency. The Maastricht Treaty signed by 15 EU member countries in 1991 declared the realization of the monetary alliance and set the goal of creating a single common currency by January 1, 2002. The Maastricht Treaty established the so-called convergence criteria. The convergence criteria require that in order to join the monetary union, potential member nations must satisfy some conditions that ensure similar economic performance with other countries.

- Price stability: The inflation rate in each prospective member country should not exceed 1.5 percentage points above the average inflation rate of the three countries with the lowest inflation rates.
- Interest rate stability: Long-term interest rates in each prospective member country should not exceed 2.0 percentage points higher than the average interest rates of the three countries with the lowest interest rates.
- Exchange rate stability: The exchange rate in each prospective member country should have been kept within the target bands of the European Monetary Union with no devaluations for at least two years prior to joining the monetary union.
- Sound public finance: The budget deficit in a prospective member country should not exceed 3% of the country's GDP, and government debt should not exceed 60% of the country's GDP.

When the Maastricht Treaty was first signed in 1991, the EU consisted of 15 countries. These 15 countries include Austria, Belgium, Denmark, Finland, France, West Germany, Greece, Ireland, Italy, Luxembourg, the Netherlands, Portugal, Spain, Sweden, and the United Kingdom. Britain and Denmark refused to join the monetary union, and Greece and Sweden did not fulfill the economic tests as mandated by the Maastricht Treaty. Thus, only 11 of these member countries became the founding members of the European Monetary Union (EMU).

Finally, on January 1, 1999, the euro, the single currency of these 11 EMU member countries, was born. Although the euro became the legal currency of the 11 Eurozone countries, the physical currency began to be used in real transactions on January 1, 2002. Thus, in 2002, the full-fledged European Monetary Union with a single currency and a single central bank was born. The EMU that was comprised of 11 nations in 1999 was later joined by Greece (2001), Slovenia (2007), Cyprus and Malta (2008), and Slovakia (2009). Most recently, the three Baltic countries, Estonia (2011), Latvia (2014), and Lithuania (2015) joined the monetary union. Thus, as of December 2022, 19 out of a total of 27 member countries of the European Union (after the exit of the United Kingdom from the EU) joined the Eurozone, adopting the euro as their legal currency.

The name of the Eurozone's common currency unit, euro, was derived from Europe, and Europe originated in the Greek mythology, Europe or Europa. Europa was the daughter of Agenor, king of the Phoenicians. Zeus, who ruled as king of the gods of Mount Olympus was mesmerized into her beauty and approached Europa. Zeus disguised himself as a white bull when she was playing on the beach. Zeus who became a bull accosted her. Europa stroked the bull and climbed to the top of the bull. Zeus did not miss this opportunity. He picked her up, went to the sea and swam to Crete. Europe became the region where Europa roamed. She had three sons with Zeus: Minos, Rhadamanthus, and Sarpedon. Minos later became the king of Crete.

Zeus' abduction of Europa became the subject of numerous arts and sculptures. Among them 'Europa and the Bull' painted on a vase made around 480 BC and 'The Rape of Europa' by Italian painter, Titian are particularly famous. Zeus gives her the bronze Talos (or Talon), a bronze human who protects her from pirates and invaders, the hunting dog Laelaps (or Lailaps) that never misses a prey when it finds it, and a javelin that never misses the target. Laelaps was later given to King Minos, Cephalus (or Kephalos).

<Painting> Europa and the Bull on a Greek Vase

Cephalus decided to use the hunting dog to hunt the Teumessian fox. The Teumessian fox was a fox that is never caught. This was clearly a contradiction. The Laelaps dog that never missed any target, and the Teumessian fox that was never caught were antinomic. Perhaps this antinomy suggests the fate of the Eurozone today. The Eurozone was created in order to create unity in Europe, but the Eurozone might be in jeopardy if it is not divided, because there seems to be some incongruence between the northern states such as France and Germany and southern states such as Greece and Italy. This irony resembles the contradiction of the Laelaps hound and the Teumessian fox.

Since the introduction of the euro in 1999, the euro has greatly increased its prominence, soon surpassing the Japanese yen and the British pound in international transactions and foreign exchange reserves. In 1999, the share of the dollar, the euro, and the yen among reserve assets in the world was 70.9%, 17.9%, and 6.4%, respectively. But in 2008, the share of the dollar and the yen shrank to 64.0% and 3.3%, respectively, but the share of the euro increased to 26.5%. The share of the euro peaked at 28.0% in 2009. Since 2010 the debt crisis in some Eurozone countries (especially, in PIGS (Portugal, Ireland, Greece, and Spain) has intensified and the role of the euro has begun to show a downward trend. At the end of 2020, the share of the euro fell to 20.1%, while the share of the dollar and the yen remained at 62.7% and 5.7%, respectively. Some believe that the euro and the dollar will have a hegemony battle in the future for the world's key currency, but it is premature to see the power of the dollar decline soon, given the recent trend of the dollar's strength.

What are the benefits of the euro as a single currency? The Eurozone's single currency makes it easy and clear to compare prices among Eurozone countries, with prices of all goods and services displayed in a single currency unit and all transactions made in a single currency unit. Thus, the use of a single currency has the effect of lowering prices in countries that use the single currency. In addition, the use of a single currency eliminates the exchange of currencies between countries, which greatly simplifies transactions and eliminates exchange rate risks caused by exchange rate fluctuations. Furthermore, financial assets such as stocks and bonds are all quoted in a single currency, making asset trading within the single currency bloc more active.

Despite these microeconomic advantages, there are also many problems in macroeconomic aspects. All independent countries have their own central banks and attempt to influence economic conditions through their own monetary policy. However, the Eurozone countries have transferred their monetary sovereignty (such as the right to issue money) to the European

Central Bank (ECB), a transnational organization. Accordingly, monetary policy and foreign exchange policy are also carried out by the European Central Bank. Therefore, each member country cannot independently conduct its own monetary or foreign exchange policy. Some researchers believe that the macroeconomic costs (abandonment of monetary and exchange rate policies) outweigh the microeconomic benefits (efficiency of economic transactions). Greater macroeconomic disadvantages over microeconomic advantages might be the reason why the United Kingdom had initially refused to join the Eurozone even before it exited from the EU membership. Of course, in some small economies, microeconomic merits may be greater than macroeconomic costs.

To achieve internal and external stability when a country is in an economic crisis, policymakers use three economic policy instruments: fiscal policy, monetary policy, and exchange rate policy. Among the three policy tools, the Eurozone countries have abandoned monetary and exchange rate policy tools. If an economic crisis does not hit the entire Eurozone and is limited only to individual countries, each individual country must overcome the crisis by using only fiscal policy such as increasing government spending or reducing taxes. However, it is well established that the use of a mixture of fiscal policy and monetary policy, or a mixture of monetary policy and exchange rate policy is far more effective than using only one policy measure. Such a policy mix could achieve the maximum effect.

In the aftermath of the 2008 global economic crisis, fiscal deficits and government debt increased dramatically in some Eurozone countries, causing them to deviate significantly from the original convergence criteria. In general, the economic performance of the northern Eurozone countries was in a good shape, while the economic performance and fiscal situations of the southern Eurozone countries deteriorated significantly after the global economic crisis. In particular, the economic situations of countries known as PIGS (Portugal, Italy, Greece, Spain) became shaky, making it difficult for the Eurozone to maintain a harmony in the conduct of economic policy. The unemployment of the 'Four Pigs' in 2015 reveals how troublesome the economies of the southern Eurozone countries were: Greece: 26.0%, Spain: 23.7%, Portugal: 13.5%, Italy: 12.6%. (The average unemployment rate of the EU was 9.8%.) Ireland's economy was also in trouble, which led people to coin the term, PIIGS adding Ireland to PIGS.

The uncertainty in the Eurozone is largely due to the fact that some countries in the Eurozone deviated significantly from the original convergence criteria, and that these countries cannot use their own monetary and exchange rate policies. The Eurozone, which is composed of 19 countries, is currently like playing an insecure running game of 19 players with their legs tied up with a string. They do not sometimes rhyme with other players, faltering in the running race. If the Eurozone collapses, the world financial order is likely to fall into a great vortex once again, and its shock wave will not be comparable to that of the 2008 global economic crisis.

11

THE U.S.-CHINA CONFRONTATION AND THE THUCYDIDES TRAP

The Thucydides trap is a phenomenon in which an extreme structural tension arises when a newly emerging force threatens to take the place of the dominant force. In his book *Destined for War* (2017), political scientist Graham Allison, former head of the Belper Center for Science and International Affairs at Harvard University argues that such a tension could head toward a war. According to Allison, the Peloponnesian War (431~ 404 B.C.) described by Greek historian Thucydides was the result of a structural tension between the newly emerging Athens and the existing power, Sparta that tried to contain the rising power. Allison called it the 'Thucydides trap'. Allison maintains that in the past 500 years, there were 16 Thucydides traps, and 12 of them developed into a full-fledged war.

The current confrontation existing between the United States and China is reminiscent of the Thucydides trap. China that took the place of the United States economically (in terms of PPP GDP) in 2014 has imposed a threat to the United States, whereas the United States has a long way to give up its hegemony. China's President Xi Jinping who has initiated 'OBOR' (One Belt and One Road) and then-U.S. President Donald Trump, who shouted 'MAGA' (Make America Great Again) have been destined to clash out. Allison's grim diagnosis is that there is the possibility of an all-out war between the United States and China. Unless China tones down its ambition to be the first place or the United States is not ready to give up its 'number one' position and to back down to be satisfied with the 'number two' position in the back seat, the two nations might be caught in a Thucydides trap. There are many on-going issues surrounding the two nations. Especially, trade disputes, cyber-attacks, Taiwan-related issues, and confrontations at Indochina Sea are close call situations that can lead the G2 nations to a war. The two nations have been pulling some strings through the OBOR initiative and its antithesis.

China was the most powerful nation in the Middle Ages or Medieval Times (AD 500~1500). This period corresponded to European history ranging from the collapse of the Roman empire in the 5th century to the rise of the Ottoman Empire. The Chinese heyday era also encompassed the Renaissance period of the 13th~15th centuries. China especially flourished during the Tang Dynasty (AD 618~907) and the Song Dynasty (AD 960~1279). In contrast, Europe was devastated by the Black Plague (AD 1346~1353), but China was less affected by the pandemic. After the pest pandemic subsided, the world economy was slowly resuscitated with the increase of population and trade. The Silk Road was a conduit for trading between Europe and China. Xi Jinping's OROR is the modern-day revival of the glory of the Silk Road.

However, China began to go downhill beginning the late 19th century. It was the first time that China's population growth rate turned negative since the beginning of the Qing Dynasty. The population of China dropped from a peak of 440 million in 1852 to the low of 358 million in 1870. Around that time, China turned over Hong Kong to England as a result of the defeat to England in the Opium War (1840~1842), and China was derided as a paper tiger for a long while. The eagle (United States), on the other hand, began to spread its wings. The United States took over China in terms of the size of the economy (nominal GDP) around 1880 and surpassed the British Empire after WWI. The United States emerged as the world's largest economy and has dominated the world economy as an economic superpower since then.

History repeats itself. China's ascension to the economic powerhouse is astonishing. In 2010, Chinese GDP ($5.8 trillion) surpassed Japanese GDP ($5.5 trillion) for the first time, making China the world's second-largest economy. In 2021, China ($17.7 trillion) overtook the EU in GDP. China's GDP is forecasted to surpass that of the United States by 2030. China already surpassed the United States in terms of purchasing power parity (PPP) GDP in 2014. According to IMF statistics, China's purchasing power parity (PPP) GDP in 2014 was $$17.6 trillion (16.5% of the world's PPP GDP), and U.S. PPP GDP in 2014 was $17.4 trillion (16.3% of the world's PPP GDP). The PPP GDP of a country refers to a calculated GDP that reflects the country's price level. If the country's price level is lower, its PPP GDP becomes larger than its nominal GDP and vice versa.

Until China stepped up to the G2 status, rivalling the United States, an old saying told us that when the United States sneezed, the world caught a cold. However, the axis of the world economy has been shifting. China's sneeze has also become stronger. The health of the Chinese economy has become essential for the growth and stability of the world economy. China is now replacing the United States as an important growth engine for the global economy. China's contribution to global economic growth became more than tripled from 10% in the 1990s to 34% in 2014. Instead, the U.S. contribution fell from 32% to 17% over the same period. Europe's position is even poorer. Europe's contribution has shrunk from 23% to 8%.

The war for the economic hegemony between the United States and China is looming up in the fog. Although China was defeated by the Western forces in the Opium War, it is interesting to see who will win the 21st century Red Cliff War. In the Red Cliff War described in the *Romance of the Three Kingdoms* written by *Luo Guanzhong*, the allied forces of *Liu Bei* and *Sun Quan* defeated the *Cao Cao* forces. The allied forces of the United States and Europe still dominate the world in terms of firepower, tactics, and strategies, but China is powerful in terms of numbers and morale like the *Cao Cao* army. The momentum of China is so strong, and the southeastern wind may blow. The allied *Liu Bei* and *Sun Quan* forces were able to defeat the *Cao Cao* fleet by taking advantage of the southeastern wind.

China pursued the strategy of *Taoguangyanghui* under the leadership of *Deng Xiao Ping*. The Chinese word, *Taoguangyanghui* implies that the dragon (China) hides its claws until it becomes sufficiently strong. The *Taoguangyanghui* strategy was a red herring tactic for hiding China's ambition. China finally did the finishing touch under the leadership of *Xi Jinping* by drawing the eyes of the dragon on the painting of the dragon (*Hualongdianjing*), which means that the dragon finally began to ascend to the sky. About 142 years after the global economic leadership passed from Europe (UK) to the United States in 1872, the hegemony of the global economy is again shifting from the United States to China. China is no longer a paper tiger. Now the West has begun to watch how the Chinese wind blows. There has been some criticism that Europe, the home of capitalism, has shown a handful of fears in front of Chinese money. The Eurozone, which was formed in order to become One Europe and to become a more powerful Europe, has been lackluster in economic growth for many years. Europe needs Chinese money. Even the United States, where capitalism has blossomed is standing in front of fiscal cliffs that cannot be sustained without borrowing money from China. Now the West has begun to watch how the Chinese wind blows. We realize that the reorganization of the world economic order is under way. Will Europe be a setting sun, and China a rising sun?

T.S. Eliot already lamented the decline of Europe in his poem <The Waste Land> (1922). Eliot contemplated the European civilization which became increasingly divided and devastated after the First World War. He depicted the crisis and uncertainty embedded in European civilization in an eloquent language from the perspective of apocalyptic eschatology. Eliot was a representative English poet who added dark religious colors to his poems. April is the month of the resurrection (Easter). In the British Shakespearean era, Romantic poet Chaucer (1342~1400) who wrote *The Canterbury Tale* in 1380 depicted April as 'Hopeful April'. In a sense, Eliot's poem is the negation of Hopeful April. His expression of April as the cruelest month can be seen as a manifestation of his deep skepticism about European civilization. Such a sense of crisis is imbuing the continent of Europe again.

April is the cruelest month, breeding
Lilacs out of the dead land, mixing
Memory and desire, stirring
Dull roots with spring rain.
Winter kept us warm, covering
Earth in forgetful snow, feeding
A little life with dried tubers.
Summer surprised us, coming over the Starnberger see
With a shower of rain, we stopped in the colonnade,
And went on in sunlight, into Hofgarten,
And drank coffee and talked for an hour.
Bin gar keine Russin, stamm' aus Litauen echt Deutsch.
And when we were children, stay at the archduke's,
My cousin's, he took we out on a sled,
And I was frightened. He said, Marie,
Marie, hold on tight. And down we went.
In the mountains, there you feel free.
I read, much of the night, and go south in the winter.
What are the roots that clutch, what branches grow
Out of this stony rubbish? Son of man,
You cannot say, or guess, for you know only
A heap of broken images, where the sun beats,
And the dead tree gives no shelter, the cricket no relief,
And the dry stone no sound of water. Only
There is shadow under this red rock,
(Come in under the shadow of this red rock),
And I will show you something different from either
Your shadow at morning striding behind you
Or your shadow at evening rising to meet you;
I will show you fear in a handful of dust.

China's climbing to the world's second-largest economy may create a threat to the United States and Europe. But some critique of the Chinese economy from the Western point of view denies such a possibility. China's growth has been largely due to the rapid increase in labor and capital, just as the Four Tigers in Asia have done so far. Economic growth without technological progress will eventually reach a limit. Technological progress takes place through innovation, and innovation is an essence of capitalism that cannot be separated from competition. Innovation grows under the forces and incentives of the market mechanism. In other words, innovation blossoms in an environment where the market functions properly. Any innovation may be hard to flourish in China unless the Chinese economy is transformed into complete market capitalism. Also, the transition to true market capitalism would not be possible without a change in the political system. Chinese leaders still do not fully appreciate the market dynamics. If people's demand for democracy becomes stronger, the resulting economic burden and costs may be a serious challenge to the Chinese leadership. This is the dilemma China will face in the future.

The argument on 'China's likelihood of overtaking the United States' is also a rosy picture. It is true that in terms of PPP GDP, the Chinese economy surpassed the U.S. economy, but this is because the Chinese price level is relatively low compared with the U.S. price level. As China's price level rises, China's GDP on the basis of purchasing power parity will also fall. In the future, as China's income increases, it can be foreseen that the Chinese price level will gradually accelerate, and that will bring China's purchasing power-based GDP closer to its actual nominal GDP.

In 2020, U.S. GDP was $20.9 trillion, and China's GDP was $14.7 trillion. Assuming that the U.S. economy is growing at an average annual rate of 3.3% and the Chinese economy is growing at 7% in the future, China's GDP will become equal to that of the United States about 10 years from 2020. This means that by 2030, China's nominal GDP will catch up the United States. However, there is no question that China's economic growth rate will gradually decrease in the future, too. It is only a matter of time. The United States is expected to maintain its current 3.3% growth rate, but China's growth rate may even fall to 4 ~ 5%. Even a sharp drop in the growth rate (hard landing) could happen in China. From this point of view, the timing of China's taking over the United States could be delayed.

Consider a scenario that is a bit more pessimistic for China, but it is not unlikely. If China's economic growth rate falls to the same level as the U.S. average annual growth rate of 3.3% by 2030, when China's nominal GDP is expected to catch up that of the United States, China's ambition to surpass the U.S. economy will remain as a wishful thinking. At that point, the two nations may run parallel with each other, without taking overwhelmingly over the hegemony of the global economy. In the 1950s, some predicted that the Soviet Union would exceed the United States in GDP by 1970. However, the result was the collapse of the Soviet Union system, ending the cold-war era. Of course, the competition between the United States and China is different from the competition between the United States and the Soviet Union, and thus the Soviet experience cannot be applied by analogy to China.

Just as physical fitness is an important factor in the final victory in a marathon race, the economic constitution is an important issue in a race for economic hegemony. The economic constitution is largely determined by political stability (establishment of law and order) and economic efficiency (establishment of free competition). From this point of view, the goddess of victory, Nike, might rather beckon the United States. The logo of the sporting goods company Nike is simple, yet reminiscent of an upward flying. It is difficult to predict for now which country will fly higher and will be in the bosom of Nike, the goddess of victory.

12

WILL AMERICAN-STYLE MARKET CAPITALISM DECLINE? THE MICAWBER PRINCIPLE

The global economic crisis that was originated in the U.S. subprime problem in the summer of 2007 remodeled the U.S. financial system and reshaped the market economy. Financial giants such as Bear Sterns, Lehman Brothers, Merrill Lynch, AIG, Fannie Mae, Freddie Mac, and Citigroup either disappeared or were rescued through large government bailouts. Goldman Sachs and Morgan Stanley were converted to bank holding companies, marking the end of an era for investment banking in the United States. Many people agree that the 2007-2008 global economic crisis, also called the Great Recession, was the worst economic contraction after the Great Depression that occurred in 1929. The Great Depression in the 1930s brought a fundamental shift in people's thinking about the market economy and capitalism.

Will the economic crises brought about by the subprime problems change the principles and ideas of capitalism that have been enshrined for many years? The U.S. government's partial nationalization of banks and massive intervention in the private sector during the global economic crisis were unimaginable merely before the crisis. In fact, there was a suspicion that the United States was heading for abandoning the basic tenets of capitalist orthodoxy that brought prosperity to the United States over the past several decades. Some ideological leaders in Europe and Asia have argued that the global economic crisis marked the beginning of the end of the superiority of the U.S. economic model and free-market capitalism. They further claim that it is inevitable to establish a new international financial and monetary system that is not dominated by the United States. Such a sentiment has been echoed in the form of China's intiative for OBOR (One Belt, One Road) and establishment of AIIB (Asian Infrastructure Investment Bank).

Each country has a different ability and direction to deal with an economic crisis. The main difference is the flexibility of the economic system and policy. In every crisis, some countries tend to rely on a 'cold head' (efficiency), and some other countries tend to rely on a 'warm heart' (equity). Economic flexibility cannot be achieved only with a warm heart or a cold head. Since the Great Depression, the United States has taken measures to use both regulations and deregulations on economic activities. U.S. policymakers sometimes strengthen regulations to protect consumers, depositors, and workers and to prevent monopoly power and in other times promote deregulation to induce competition. Put it differently, in the United States, the government (equity) and the market (efficiency) have come together in tandem when it encounters an economic crisis.

The U.S. model has made the U.S. economy more competitive and accommodative than any other industrialized economies, and as a consequence, the U.S. economy became more resilient and flexible after an economic crisis. As President Reagan took office in 1980, he began to pursue a market-oriented policy. He boldly lowered taxes, retouched the 'from the cradle to the grave' welfare system in favor of flexible benefits, and put a strong grip on illegal union activities. Owing to such market solutions, the U.S. labor market became more flexible. The median wage was reported to have fallen by about 23% during the global economic crisis period, which was helpful in restoring the jobs. This attests to the flexibility of the U.S. labor market and the strength of the U.S. economy.

However, the United States also is not shy of 'warm heart' remedies. During the global economic crisis and the coronavirus pandemic crisis, millions of jobs disappeared, and the unemployment rate soared. The U.S. government poured astronomical amounts of money into the economy to take care of the poor and needy. Thanks to the government interventions, most of the lost jobs were quickly recovered as the crises calmed down. Reflecting the resiliency of the U.S. economy, the U.S. stock market enjoyed the longest bull market after the global economic crisis until the corona pandemic crisis. Amazingly, the U.S. stock prices reached the highest plateau after the corona pandemic crisis. The Dow Jones Industrial Average reached 36,799.65 on January 4, 2022, an all-time high, and the Nasdaq Index climbed to 4,796.56 on January 3, 2022, the highest level ever reached. Subsequent decreases in the stock prices after the corona pandemic crisis reflected some worries about inflation.

On the other hand, many European countries have failed to increase the flexibility of the labor market. In many European countries, the unemployment rate, which was only 1 to 3% even in the early 1970s, jumped to almost double digits in the 1980s as they went through the long recession tunnel of the 1970s. The persistent high unemployment rate and the long-lasting economic recession in many countries in Europe have been often termed as 'Euro-sclerosis' (European sclerosis). Although there are many factors that led to the Euro-sclerosis, experts point to strong unions and almost perfect social welfare systems as important factors. These institutional guarantees have weakened unemployed people's willingness to actively seek jobs, and as a result, the unemployment rate has not dropped and remained at a high level even after the crisis was gone. The labor market in Europe is likened to the hardening of the arteries.

Anatole Kaletsky, an economist and a regular contributor to *The Economist* published *Capitalism 4.0: The Birth of a New Economy in the Aftermath of Crisis* (2010). In his book, he divided capitalism into four stages.

- Capitalism 1 (1776 - 1930): Classical capitalism or laissez-faire capitalism
- Capitalism 2 (1931 - 1979): Keynesian capitalism or social capitalism
- Capitalism 3 (1980 - 2007): Fundamental capitalism or Neoliberal capitalism
- Capitalism 4 (2008 -): Future form of capitalism

Capitalism 1 refers to the original capitalist system built on the vision of Adam Smith in 1776 and maintained until the Great Depression of the 1930s. Classical capitalism is an economic system that is close to laissez-faire ideals. Classical capitalism is a capitalist system in which economic agents pursue their own best interest in a perfectly competitive market without government interventions and regulations. Capitalism 2 refers to the capitalist system newly designed by Keynes after the Great Depression. When classical capitalism was facing the Great Depression in the 1930s, Keynes believed that only reformed capitalism through government intervention and regulation could save capitalism not only from the crisis, but also from totalism. Capitalism 3 refers to capitalism that was restored after the emergence of neoliberalism in the late 1970s and early 1980s. However, unlike the original classical capitalism, neoliberal capitalism aims for a small government, but requires a strong government to maintain the order of the free market.

Kaletsky predicted that the market economy and capitalism would continue to evolve further into the form of 'capitalism 4.0'. Capitalism 4 is a type of capitalism that will be reborn in a more efficient form by adapting to the new environment that has changed since the global economic crisis in 2008. Capitalism 4 is a form of capitalism, where the market and the government, and growth and welfare go together. Capitalism 4 has several characteristics. First, businesses and governments work closer together than ever before. The second characteristic is that the size of the government will be reduced. However, government influence or responsibility will increase. Third, there will be a clearer distinction between the twin goals of taxation (expenditure and well-being), and the marketization and privatization of industries will be promoted more actively.

The 2008 global economic crisis was the fourth economic crisis in which capitalism was forced to change. As the driving force for capitalism to survive these challenges, Kaletsky cites the Micawber principle. Wilkins Micawber is the protagonist in *David Copperfield* written by Charles Dickens. In this novel, Micawber is depicted as a utopian optimist. Micawber says that “if you make an annual income of 20 pounds, and spend 19.975 pounds, you are happy. However, if you make an annual income of 20 pounds and spend 20.025 pounds, you are miserable" (Dickens, 1850). Micawber has become synonymous with someone who lives in hopeful expectations. Kaletsky interprets the Micawber principle in a little bit different way. The Micawber principle refers to a vague belief that “things will get better in the future without any clear ground" or a faith that “something will turn up”.

According to Kaletsky, the Micawber principle has the following implication. If people don’t recognize a problem as a problem for a long time and leave it alone, the problem is no longer a problem. Kaletsky’s interpretation is that the global economic crisis did not lead to the collapse of capitalism because people believed that American-style market capitalism was problematic, but that it would continue to work. The Micawber principle is consistent with the ‘invisible hand’ notion of Smith saying that “the whole economy is in harmony when individuals pursue their own best interest.” Even if people don’t recognize the harmony of the whole economy, it works.

Two thoughts have always been in conflict in the historical evolution of capitalism. One is the claim that the market is always right, and the government is almost always wrong (classicism), and the other is that the government is always right, and the market is almost always wrong (Keynesianism). According to Kaletsky, future capitalism, represented by capitalism 4, is based on the perception that the government and the market alone may not be right, and sometimes their errors can be fatal. This perception emphasizes that the government and the market must go together, and not function separately.

This means that in the era of capitalism 4, it is necessary to solve economic problems with a ‘cold head’ and a ‘warm heart’. In that case, it is possible to reduce errors that can be made by the government or the market alone. He sees this as an opportunity for creativity, experimental curiosity, and talent. Kaletsky's conclusion is that the global economic crisis in 2008 was just a trigger to bring about new changes to the economic system. Kaletsky concludes that if the West makes good use of opportunities for change – evolution, new experimentation, and innovation, American-style free-market capitalism will continue to be the best economic model in the future. However, he warns that if the West fails to adapt to these new challenges, the world's economic system will be designed and dominated by China.

China has already begun taking the first steps toward restructuring the world financial order. The AIIB (Asian Infrastructure Investment Bank), the first international financial institution established by China, was established in June 2015. AIIB has emerged as a renowned international financial institution with a total of 57 member countries including China, Germany, France, the United Kingdom, and Italy, as well as South Korea, Australia, and Singapore. As the number of participating countries increased, the amount of capital increased from the originally targeted $50 billion to $100 billion. Currently, only the United States and Japan as major developed countries refused to participate in AIIB.

13

CAN THE OWL OF MINERVA PREDICT AN ECONOMIC CRISIS?

Robert H. Smith's poem <The Clock of Life> sings that no one has the ability to predict the future.

The clock of life is wound but once,
And no man has the power
To tell just when the hands will stop
At late or early hour.
To lose one's wealth is sad indeed,
To lose one's health is more,
To lose one's soul is such a loss
That no man can restore.
The present only is our own,
So Live, Love, toil with a will
Place no faith in "Tomorrow"
For the clock may then be still.

In the 19th-century, German philosopher Georg Friedrich Hegel (1820) left the famous dictum: "The Owl of Minerva takes its flight only when the shades of night are gathering," or "The Owl of Minerva spreads its wings only with the falling of the dusk".

Minerva is the Roman name of Athena in Greek mythology. Athena was the virgin goddess of wisdom, and a little owl always accompanied her. Because of the accompaniment of the owl to Minerva, the 'Owl of Athena' or the 'Owl of Minerva' has been used as a synonym for knowledge, wisdom, and erudition.

Why was Minerva associated with the owl? There are several explanations. Martin Nilsson (1950) and David Kinsley (1989) suggest that she might descend from a Minoa palace goddess associated with birds. On the other hand, Cynthia Berger (2005) notes the ability of owls to see in the dark, and this ability can be interpreted as the symbol of wisdom. In short, Hegel's reference to the Owl of Minerva is that as the Owl of Minerva (i.e.

wisdom or philosophy) spreads its wings in the day and at night, philosophy does not predict the future, but only after the historical conditions have already passed.

<Painting> Athena Holding a Helmet and a Spear with an Owl

Once a cyber writer named as Minerva became famous in South Korea because he was known to predict the bankruptcy of Lehman Brothers and to predict a sharp decline in the value of the Korean won against the dollar during the global economic crisis.There was a syndrome in South Korea that people believed in Minerva's predictions, even if they didn't believe what economists said, and his popularity made the Korean economists bewildered. The Korean government was also embarrassed because he led many people to distrust the government's policy. He was once touted as the 'Internet Economic President'. The Korean Minerva pushed Korean society into a controversial furnace during the global economic crisis.

Was the Korean Minerva a prophet with magical powers? Did he indeed have occult arts to save the economy? If he predicted that Lehman Brothers would be in a very difficult situation, then his predictions would have a logical basis. However, if he predicted Lehman Brothers' bankruptcy like a tweezer, his prediction would be less magical. It is a coincidence, and it is no different than divination. In fact, the fall of Lehman Brothers was like a coin toss. Lehman Brothers was the card that could have been kept or been abandoned by three players: U.S. Treasury Secretary Henry Paulson, Fed Chairman Ben Bernanke, and Timothy Geithner, an appointee for the next Treasury Secretary by President Obama. The likelihood of Lehman Brothers' bankruptcy was half-and-half; the Korean Minerva bet on the back of the coin, and it happened to hit by chance.

Like the Owl of Minerva, the purpose of economics is not to predict the future, but to analyze what happened in the past. Economics aims to diagnose economic problems and to present solutions. However, people expect economists to have the ability to predict future economic developments. Can economists predict the future of the economy or the next economic crisis? In the natural world, it is not difficult to predict future happenings. We can predict exactly the sunset time and sunrise time even over a long period of time. However, even in the natural world, there are many areas in which human beings cannot predict the future. For example, it is almost impossible to predict the next coming of a hurricane, unless it is close to the area. Even weather forecasts looking forward to a day or two days are often wrong. There is a famous episode in this regard. The British Meteorological Agency issued the following weather forecast on October 14, 1987: "Tomorrow will have some showers, moderate weather, and some wind." But the next day, one of the worst cyclones known as the 'Great Storm of 1987' hit the United Kingdom (Source: chatGPT: U.K. 1987 Storm).

A disciple of Confucius asked his teacher: "How well does fortunetelling fit?" Confucius said: "70% of it is right" (Source: The Analects of Confucius). Confucius believed that fortunetelling is correct seven times out of ten. However, the conclusion of statistics theory is that the probability that fortunetelling is correct is about five out of ten. Of course, the odds of getting some specific numbers right will be much less. Russian writer Tolstoy (1884) said that "God does not allow humans to predict the future". Harvard economist John Galbraith (who was an eminent theorist of economic development and served as a U.S. ambassador to India in the Kennedy Administration once said that "The only function of economic forecasting is to make astrology look respectable" (Casiorek, 2021).

In the Middle Ages, predicting the future through crystal balls was popular. People believed that future things were projected onto the crystal ball, and people could see into the future through it. Indeed, Dr. John Dee (1527~1608), a British mathematician, astronomer, geographer, and advisor to Queen Elizabeth I of England, was known to have used the crystal ball in his research. However, it is almost impossible to accurately predict the future economic phenomena, no matter how crystal-clear the crystal ball is.

Economic forecasting is different from predicting the lead-lag relationship. It is said that when the halo occurs, the wind blows, and when the cornerstone becomes wet, it rains. This relationship established from the rule of empirics can be viewed as a lead-lag relationship rather than a prediction. This sequential relationship is sometimes referred to as 'post hoc ergo propter hoc' (after this, therefore because of this), which means that "since event B followed event A, event B must have been caused by event A". The ergo propter hoc' assumption is a wrong reasoning because it does not establish any causal relationship. Economic forecasting is designed to predict a causal relationship that will happen in an uncertain future.

Economists try to predict the future economy using complex economic models. However, the result may be different depending on what information is used in such a model. The term GIGO (Garbage In, Garbage Out) is used in computer terminology. "If you put in garbage-like information, you get a garbage-like result." Even a sophisticated economic model cannot be free from this kind of error.

All economic forecasts are based on current economic trends. Economic forecasts are made based on the 'ceteris paribus' assumption, the assumption that all other things remain the same. No one knows how the current situation will change in the future. It might be reasonable to assume that the current trend will not change much for a short period of time, say six to 12 months, and the economic forecast may hit the target in this time span. However, predicting the economy after two, ten, or twenty years is not much different from fortunetelling. Milton Friedman (1968) who won the Nobel prize in economics once said, "I do not make forecasts longer than six months". Friedman believes that the ceteris paribus assumptions will hold valid roughly over a period of about six months.

Many economic experts were not able to predict the Great Depression of the 1930s, the most serious economic crisis in U.S, history. Even after the stock market crash in 1929, the prelude to the Great Depression, many economists expected the economy to recover soon. Even in the midst of the deepening economic downturn in 1931, Professor Irving Fisher of Yale University, the most prominent economist of the time, predicted that the U.S. economy would recover soon. But contrary to his predictions, the Great Depression lasted more than a decade.

Founded in 1969 by Lawrence Klein, a professor of economics at the University of Pennsylvania who won the Nobel prize in economics, the Wharton Econometric Forecasting Associates (WEFA) is world-renowned as an economic forecasting institution. The WEFA designs economic forecasting models using hundreds of equations and makes economic forecasts every quarter using high-performance computer programs. However, the fact that such forecasts are also updated every quarter show that it is very difficult to accurately make economic forecasts over the long horizon. We learn from the IMF's forecasts how it is difficult to predict future events even within a short period of time. The IMF forecast the world's economic growth rates for 2020 and 2021 that would be under the influence of the COVID recession. The IMF predicted in June 2020 that the 2020 U.S. economic growth rate would be -8.0%, but four months later, it revised the 2020 U.S. economic growth rate to -4.3%. The forecast difference for the U.S. economic growth rate was almost 3.7% points just in four months.

Harvard economist Mankiw analyzed how well economic forecasting models predicted the unemployment rate in the 1982 recession. The median unemployment rate predicted by 20 professional economic forecasting agencies was compared with the actual unemployment rate. Predicting the next 5 quarters (1 year and 3 months later) at 6 time points (1981:Q2, 1981:Q4, 1982:Q2, 1982:Q4, 1983:Q2, 1983:Q4) was relatively correct in the first quarter, but overall, it missed the prediction significantly after the second quarter (6 months ahead). His study shows that it is not easy to predict even six months ahead.

Long-term predictions are just imaginations of the future. We should not place much confidence in any economic forecast that is beyond six months. If you accept a long-term prediction as a 'Believe It or Not' game, it will be for the fun of it, but if you take it seriously, you might be fooled in five cases out of 10. One thing is clear: serious economists rarely make long-term economic predictions.

14

The Crisis of Economics?

Some people say that modern economics is in crisis. Their main criticism is that economics that is not able to predict the forthcoming of an economic crisis in advance is of little use. People also argue that although thousands of economists with advanced degrees in economics are produced, and celebrated Nobel prize laureates are awarded every year, there are still many economic problems that remain unresolved.

However, most economists would disagree with the claim that economics is in crisis because economics is not able to forecast an economic crisis in advance. As a matter of fact, predicting the future is not the primary purpose of economics. Of course, in practice, there is a field of economics that focuses on predicting what will happen in the economy, but such a discipline is primarily based on the needs of business or policymaking and is not a mainstream field of economics. In addition, it is not uncommon for such predictions to become useless. Ben Bernanke, who headed the U.S. monetary policy as the chairman of the U.S. Federal Reserve System (2006~2014) during the 2008 global economic crisis, once said that "Economics is the best discipline to find out where the past policy went wrong, but it is not good at predicting the future."

Second, it is not reasonable to say that economics is in crisis because there are still many unresolved economic problems. As long as there is a problem of relative scarcity, economic problems always exist. The problem of relative scarcity is the fundamental problem that does not disappear forever as long as mankind lives in the limited space of the earth. Resources are relatively limited, but human wants or desires are unlimited. The imbalance existing between limited resources and unlimited human desires creates relative scarcity. Water that appears to exist indefinitely is also relatively scarce in this context. It is the realm and purpose of economics to analyze the problems arising from relative scarcity and to seek the best choice for limited resources.

Economics is sometimes called dismal science. The *alias* attached to economics is misleading because it can give the impression that economics is a boring or dull discipline. This term was first used in the mid-19th century by historian Thomas Carlyle. At that time, the study of mastering the skills necessary for poetry was called gay science, *alias dictus* (= otherwise called) poem, where 'gay' means 'bright'. Carlyle referred to economics as 'dismal science' with the purpose of using the term symmetric to gay science.

In the background of Carlyle's use of the term was the grim prediction of Pastor Thomas Malthus, who was famous for his demographics. In *An Essay on the Principle of Population* (1798), he argued that "a society's population increases exponentially, whereas its food supply increases arithmetically." According to Malthus, this trend would inevitably lead to massive starvation. Malthus believed that through preventive checks such as war, famine, disease, and moral abstinence, the population would be controlled to balance between the food supply and the population growth. Carlyle, in his *Occasional Discourse on the Negro Question* (1849), insisted on the existence and preservation of slavery as a solution to Malthus' gloomy prediction. He further argued that the emancipation of slavery would exacerbate the food shortage problem. Thus, Carlyle preferred to maintain slavery rather than to rely on the market forces of supply and demand to solve the food shortage problem. It is known that economists who opposed Carlyle's proposition characterized economics as 'dismal science'.

Sociologist Peter Berger is the author of *Adventures of an Accidental Sociologist*. In his book, he introduced an interesting parable on a cancer patient. A cancer patient heard the shocking news from her doctor that she would live only for one year. She pondered for a long while and asked the doctor what to do. Her doctor responded to her:

> "Marry a sociologist and go to North Dakota."
> "Then, would I be cured?"
> "No, you'll feel that one year is like a very long time."

North Dakota is a state located in the northwestern part of the United States, with only a large plain and no good things to enjoy. Is North Dakota really a place where you do not have much fun, and you feel that one year is like ten years? On the contrary, there are some places you would like to visit in North Dakota. These attractions are the ghost towns where old houses of the pioneers lived in the West frontier years, and the barren lands called 'Bad Lands'. Bad Lands attracts many tourists with the mysterious appearance of yellow-pink sedimentary rocks. The situation is now completely changing, however. In North Dakota, shale oil and shale gas have been discovered in large quantities. North Dakota is now leading the second oil boom in the United States and is emerging as America's hope.

Paul Samuelson was the first American Nobel Laureate in economics. In his famous book, *Economics,* Samuelson says that "Economics is the queen of social science which is the newest as a science and the oldest as an art." If the starting point of modern economics can go back to Adam Smith's *Wealth of Nations* published in 1776, then the history of economics as a science exceeds a bit 200 years. In this context, economics can be viewed as the newest science. However, the economic decision-making problem started with the advent of human beings. Economic decisions are processes in which optimal solutions are sought under the given economic conditions. The decision-making process that attempts to derive the best results can be claimed to be the most basic of a human being's artistic activity. In this sense, economics is the oldest art.

Let's go to London, one of the most vital cities in the world, and study economics there. 10 years may feel like a year.

PART 2

THE MARKET AND CAPITALISM

1

TWO DIFFERENT VIEWS ON THE ECONOMY

A common analogy of half a bottle of wine is often cited to contrast two different views. When people look at a bottle of wine with half of it filled, some people think that the wine is still half full, while others see that the wine is already half empty. People look at the same thing differently depending on their views. The fact is that half of the wine bottle is filled. Looking at the same thing and showing different views reflect different values formed by the person's different background, growth environment, family gene, education, and the like. People can also be born with a tendency (DNA) to look at the world more optimistically or more pessimistically. The truth is that either the view that "wine is still half full" or the view that "wine is already half empty" is not wrong. It is in a similar vein that beauty is in the eye of the beholder.

Historically, there have been two largely different views on the working of the economy, too. Some argue that the economy has the capability to self-cure itself, and therefore the government should let the economy itself flow. This position is called classical economics. Some other economists maintain that the self-correcting forces of the economy may be weak or sometimes ineffective, and therefore the government should actively intervene in the economy to solve economic problems. This position is called Keynesian economics. It should be obvious that a dichotomous judgment about the correctness of the two different schools is not correct. We cannot say that one theory is right, and the other theory is wrong, just as in the analogy of half a bottle of wine.

Of course, there are various spectrums of economic thought. The view that half a bottle of wine is filled can be characterized as the middle-of-the-road position. If we move from the middle to the right, we first encounter classical orthodoxy. Orthodox classical economics was constructed based on faith in the role of the market and the distrust in the government's interference in the economy. Adam Smith, who published a monumental work, *The Wealth of Nations,* in 1776 set forth the economic doctrine which was termed as classical economics later by John Keynes. In his book, Smith argued that if people pursued their own best interest, and there were free markets, then the economy would take care of itself. His theory laid the foundations for market capitalism.

Classical orthodoxy was refined into neo-classical economics by marginalists such as William Jevons, Carl Menger, von Bohm-Bawerk, and Alfred Marshall. Marginalists developed important economic concepts such as marginal utility, marginal product, marginal costs, and marginal revenues that were the essential analytical tools in modern economics. Classical economists were not able to resolve the so-called water-diamond paradox. The paradox shows that water that is essential for the subsistence of human life has almost no price, whereas diamond that is not essential for human life has very high price. Neoclassical economists were able to resolve the water-diamond paradox with the aid of marginal analysis. Water exists in almost unlimited amounts, and the marginal utility of water is almost zero, whereas diamonds exist in the limited amount, and the marginal utility of diamonds is extremely high. Neoclassical economists believed the value (or price) of a product had something to do with its marginal utility.

Classical economics was further developed into the modern-day offspring such as monetarism, new-classical economics (rational expectations school), and supply-side economics. Milton Friedman who established monetarism maintains that money is the dominant influence on the level of economic activity, and therefore policymakers should be cautious about using money as a tool for stabilizing the economy. His theme is that if the central bank controls the money supply at discretion to stabilize the economy, such a discretionary policy would rather destabilize the economy. Thus, the central bank should control the money supply according to rules, not discretion.

Robert Lucas who was the main architect of the rational expectations school of economics has proposed that people form their expectations of economic variables such as inflation rationally using all the information available to them. Because they do not make systematic errors in forming their expectations of economic variables, they can nullify anticipated government policy actions. Thus, any anticipated government policy has no effect on real economic activity. In short, monetarism and rational expectations theory stress that when incorporating people's expectations into economic behavior, private economic agents have the ability to neutralize the anticipated policies of the government and the central bank. Thus, according to rational expectations theorists, any active government role in economic activity will do harm to the economy.

If we move to the right further, we meet a more conservative position than the orthodox classical school, libertarianism, which places importance on individual freedom, limited government, private property, and free competition. Friedrich Hayek of the Austrian school of economics argues that personal liberty is the most important element of economic activity, and social goals such as public interest are next. His position can be seen as being closer to classical liberalism (laissez-faire) in terms of ideology. The theoretical framework established by Friedman and Hayek led to the advent of neoliberalism in the 1970s and 1980s. Neoliberalism promotes deregulation, liberalism, and free trade and favors a small government, but a strong government to maintain the function of the free market, which differentiates itself from classical liberalism.

More radical libertarians place more emphasis on individual liberty and consider the government as a system that hinders individual liberty. The school of radical economics opposes any government interference in private property or individual activities. It also favors the legalization of drugs and opposes taxation on earned income from forced labor. In addition, it supports abolishing the monopoly of the monetary system by the government. This position can be seen as radical liberalism. At the far right of the spectrum is anarchism, which puts individual freedom at its highest value and rejects all oppressive institutions or social practices. In the East, the idea of *Taoism* is close to anarchism.

The main Keynesian school is located a little to the left of the middle. It values private property and market functions, but advocates government intervention in economic activity because it sees the market as imperfect. Keynesianism, as opposed to free market capitalism built by Smith, is sometimes referred to as revisionist (or modified) capitalism. The original Keynesian economics is also called 'depression economics'. It was born during the Great Depression, and it was mainly concerned with rescuing the economy from depression. When the economy is in deep stagnation, wages, prices, and interest rates tend to fall, or at least to remain unchanged. In such a situation, the market system does not function properly, and consequently the government should intervene in the market to correct market failures. Thus, the starting point for original Keynesian economics is the assumption that prices, wages, and interest rates are fixed at least in the short run. For this reason, original Keynesian economics is sometimes called 'fixed-price model'. The orthodox Keynesian economics places much emphasis on the role of fiscal policy such as government spending and taxation.

The orthodox Keynesian doctrine has developed into neo-Keynesian economics, post-Keynesian economics, and new-Keynesian economics. Because original Keynesian economics was constructed based on the premise of constant prices, wages, and interest rates, these prices were supposed to be given, which means that the effects of changes in prices, wages and interest rates on economic activity were ignored. Early Keynesians including Keynes himself doubted the effectiveness of monetary policy as a tool for revitalizing the economy, because the role of flexible prices, wages and interest rates in the economy was put aside.

In contrast to the original Keynesian orthodoxy that doubted the effectiveness of monetary policy as a stabilization tool, neo-Keynesian economics emphasizes the role of money and interest rates in the stabilization of the economy. In this context, neo-Keynesian economics is sometimes called Keynesian-classical synthesis, because it introduces some elements of classical economics such as variable interest rates into the economic model. Classical economists maintain that the interest rate is freely determined by the supply of and demand for money in the market, and the interest rate is an important determinant of investment and savings. Paul Samuelson, John Hicks, and Franco Modigliani who were all Nobel prize winners in economics were the representative neo-Keynesians.

New Keynesian economics emerged in the 1970s amid the oil shocks. New-Keynesian economics grafted people's expectations into economic behavior in response to new-classical economists' criticisms that Keynesian economics lacks the foundations of the microeconomic decision-making process. New Keynesian economics aims to demonstrate that the government's intervention is still effective in stabilizing the economy even when people form their expectations rationally in their decision making, although the government intervention might not be as powerful as the traditional Keynesian model. In contrast to new Keynesian economics, the original Keynesian model is sometimes called old-Keynesian economics.

Moving a little further to the left is post-Keynesian economics, where the progressive tints are strongly built in. Post-Keynesian economists view market failures as a serious problem and advocate active and extensive interventions in the economy by the government. They insist on the regulation of major national industries and the control of prices, wages, and profits, and support the introduction of a wide range of incentives and punishments through government subsidies and taxes. They also favor the strengthening of the government's economic planning function. One of the leading economists who led the post-Keynesian school is Joan Robinson.

If we continue to move to the left, we meet institutional economics. Institutional economists believe that the laws and institutions that are the basis of the function of the market are more important for economic activity than the market itself. Behavioral economics can also be included in the category of institutional economics. Institutionalists have greatly contributed to the establishment of welfare state policies such as the U.S. Social Security system during the Great Depression.

There are anti-market economists who see the market as a strange institution that destroys the traditional function of human society. A representative scholar is Karl Polanyi. He argues that the market has been in confrontation of human and natural traits and exhibited culturally destructive impacts on humanity and dignity since the massive transformation of the Industrial Revolution occurred. The central theme of his theory is that capitalism inevitably implies instability by commercializing labor, money, and nature (land). Polanyi called the transition from classical liberalism to the Keynesian welfare state the 'Great Transformation.'

Radical economists who stand at the far left of the spectrum do not believe in the market's self-regulating forces. They support the nationalization of production resources. One of the main figures is Paul Sweezy. Samuelson praised him as "the best student ever produced by Harvard and one of the most promising economists of his time". According to Sweezy, the capitalist system goes through the three phases of evolution: monopoly, stagnation, and financial meltdown. At the end of our journey to the left is Marxian economics, where the state determines the production and distribution of resources without recognizing private property rights. Marxian economists rely on Marx's theory of class struggle as their theoretical framework.

We have looked at various spectrums of economic thoughts and ideologies from the right to the left. Here we need to distinguish between liberalism and libertarianism. Both liberalism and libertarianism could be presumably influenced by the theory of liberty advanced by John Locke. Locke was commonly known as the 'Father of Liberalism'. His idea of liberty had great influences on enlightenment thinkers and American revolutionaries and was reflected in the U.S. Declaration of Independence. Locke's theory of liberty focused on the freedom of religion, freedom of speech, fair elections, civil rights, free trade, and private property rights. The original liberalism based on Locke's ideas was a political ideology with liberty and equality as key elements. Of the two axes of liberalism, conservatism emphasizes freedom, while progressivism stresses equality.

In the 20th century, Locke's liberalism evolved into two directions: libertarianism (laissez-faire) that has emphasized liberty and liberalism that has valued equality. The former has been linked to classical liberalism and neoliberalism. Neoliberalism was theoretically refined by Hayek and Friedman, and politically implemented by British Prime Minister Thatcher and U.S. President Reagan. On the other hand, the latter has been associated with welfarism, a new paradigm that emerged in the midst of the Great Depression. Welfarism was theoretically advanced by Keynes, and politically implemented by President Roosevelt's 'New Deal' in the 1930s and by President Johnson's 'Great Society' in the 1960s.

2

Is the Chinese Economy a Socialist Economic System or a Capitalist Economic System?

On September 20, 2014, a Chinese firm was in the limelight when it debuted at the New York Stock Exchange (NYSE), the heart of capitalism. It was the day when Chinese e-commerce company Alibaba listed its stock, the flower of capitalism, and raised the largest IPO (initial public offering) in the history of the U.S. stock market. This event symbolized China's climbing to the status of G2, which means that China could compete with the United States shoulder-to-shoulder, thanks to the unprecedented economic growth over the past three decades or so.

Alibaba's total public offering amounted to $21.7 billion, which renewed the previous IPO recorded in the information technology and communications industry achieved by Facebook ($16 billion) as well as Visa Card's IPO ($19.7 billion) that was the largest IPO before the arrival of Alibaba in the NYSE. Based on the IPO at the time of listing, Alibaba's market capitalization was $167.6 billion, and it ranked third among Internet companies after Google ($398.6 billion) and Facebook ($200.2 billion). Alibaba's stock price had continued to rise since its IPO, but met a bump on a road in February 2016, hitting an all-time low at 60.89. Since then, it had burned up the road again toward its high plateau, and finally reached $317.14, an all-time high on October 27, 2020. Alibaba's market capitalization also increased to $$835 billion. Alibaba's market value more than quadrupled over the past six years from 2014 to 2020.

Ma Yun (or Jack Ma, his English name) who was the founder and then-executive chairman of the Alibaba Group entered the gate of the NYSE with two thumbs up like a triumphant general and pushed the NYSE opening bell. It was as if the New York Stock Exchange's door opened when Ma Yun said, "Open sesame!" As Alibaba's share price rose sharply since the company went public in September 2014, his wealth also increased conspicuously. His net assets increased to $25 billion by December of that year. This quickly led him to the rank of the richest man in China. Before he became the richest man in China, Li Ka-shing, the Chairman of the Cheung Kong Group in Hong Kong, was the richest person in the Greater China. However, by December 2014, Jack Ma's assets amounted to $28.6 billion. Not only he became the wealthiest person in the Greater China at the time, but also no individual in the Greater China had enjoyed the grandiosity of Jack Ma's wealth in Chinese history.

This was the success story of China until 2020 when the Chinese economy as well as the world economy was hit hard by the corona pandemic crisis, and the relationship between the United States and China began to be twisted. Since Alibaba's stock reached its peak in October 2020, it has continued to skid, plunging to $63.22 on October 25, 2022, and its market value shrank to $167.4 billion. This market value is less than one quarter of its previous peak. Alibaba's stock price and market capitalization have taken a rollercoaster since its debut at the NYSE. Alibaba's ups and downs may epitomize the rocky relationship between China and the United States.

Looking at the remarkable achievement of the Chinese economy over the past several decades, many people wonder whether the Chinese economy is a communist or socialist economy. Capitalism refers to an economic system in which private property rights are guaranteed, and production and resource allocations are determined in the market by individual economic agents. Any society or nation faces the three fundamental economic problems: (1) what to produce; (2) how to produce, and (3) for whom to produce. In free market capitalism, decisions on the three fundamental economic problems are made by individual economic agents through the invisible hands (price mechanism) in the market.

Socialism and communism tend to be used often interchangeably. Both socialism and communism aim to achieve an equal society by removing class privilege and to fix the problems created by market capitalism. The communist economy and the socialist economy can be grouped into a command economy. In the command economy, the government intervenes in the determination of 'what to produce', 'how to produce' and 'for whom to produce' problems, although there are various levels of intervention. The socialist economy is a system in which resources are allocated by the government, and at the same time private ownership and private enterprises within a limited range are allowed. Government intervention in the economy is seen as inevitable to meet the basic needs of its members. It is justified to collect high taxes from private business activities to meet the basic needs of the members of society.

In principle, the communist economy is an economic system in which private property rights to resources are not allowed, and the allocation of resources is evenly made by the government. The communist economic system can be viewed as a hard-core form of the socialist economic system. In the extreme case, under a communist utopia, the government has no reason to exist anymore. If such a utopia comes true, the role of government is no longer necessary because members of society receive their share of product corresponding to their work. It is evident that the Chinese economy no longer operates under a communist economic system.

Is China a capitalist economy or a socialist economy? As China's top leader Deng Xiaoping initiated a policy to open the Chinese economy to foreign markets in 1978, China allowed private firms to make profits. However, public enterprises owned by local governments still dominate the financial, transportation, telecommunications, and energy sectors, although their shares in the Chinese economy are gradually shrinking. Currently, state-owned enterprises (SOEs) account for about 30% of the total Chinese economy (GDP), and private enterprises account for nearly 70%. This statistic indicates that the government determines about 30% of the problems of 'what to produce,' 'how to produce,' and 'for whom to produce,' but 70% of the fundamental problems are resolved in the market. From this standpoint, it seems clear that China is no longer a communist economic system even though it is politically a communist country. In China, however, the government has been implementing the five-year plan for economic developments since its inception, allocating resources at its command. Many prices and costs are determined and controlled by government intervention, not the market's invisible hands. In addition, private ownership of land is limited.

Then, what is the standing of China's economic system? Ronald Coase (2012), who won the Nobel prize in economics collaborated on the Chinese economy with Ning Wang. In their co-authored book titled *How China Became Capitalist?* they characterized the Chinese economy as a capitalist system. However, the Chinese economy has yet to reach the level of a capitalist market economy. China's economy can be claimed to be 'centralized capitalism' or a 'socialist market economy,' a kind of hybrid capitalism. In fact, when Deng Xiaoping initiated his South-bound trip in 1992, he outlined the goal of his reform under the slogan of a 'socialist market economy.'

However, from a legal point of view, China was scheduled to be given the status of a market economy in 2016. China joined the World Trade Organization (WTO) in 2001, and it expressed its intention to accept the norms of the market economy by becoming a member of the global economic system. At the same time, China opened the financial, capital, insurance and telecommunications markets. When China joined the WTO in 2001, its major trading partners promised to give China a 'market-economy treatment' beginning December 2016, 15 years later. The market economy status has become an important issue, because if China were granted the market economy status, it could be difficult for foreign companies to impose high retaliatory tariffs on Chinese companies selling products at a lower price than domestic production costs (dumping) in the world market.

Under the WTO system, if a product is sold in an overseas market at a price lower than the domestic production cost, the affected country is allowed to impose high retaliatory tariffs on it. However, in the case of the socialist economic system, the domestic price is maintained at an artificially low level with the support of government subsidies, and thus production cost cannot be estimated based on the domestic price. Instead, China's production cost should be estimated based on the price of a similar foreign product, which could increase the estimate of the Chinese production cost, and many Chinese products could not be freed from the suspicion of dumping. However, if China acquires the status of a market economy, the production cost can be calculated based on the domestic price in China, and in many cases, Chinese companies will be free from dumping charges. It is for this reason that China has been obsessed with its status as a market economy.

As some experts predicted, in 2016, the United States and the EU formally notified the WTO that they would oppose granting China a market economy status, which would allow the United States and the EU to maintain high anti-dumping duties on Chinese products. The United States and the EU have argued that China's pervasive intervention in the private economy, including subsidies, would cause China's domestic prices to deviate from market-determined prices and to severely distort resource allocations. As of December 2020, China was not yet granted a market economy status from the United States, the EU and Japan. Only South Korea among China's major trading partners took a favorable step in 2005 to give China a market economy status. That's why Chinese firms could be subject to high tariffs when they sell their products at a dumping rate in the U.S. and EU markets. The Trump administration was able to wield exorbitant tariffs on some Chinese products by using the non-market economy status of China as a weapon.

3

THE MARKET AND THE 'INVISIBLE HAND'

Markets and capitalism are inseparably linked. Naturally enough, we are concerned with what a market is and what capitalism is. Can macroeconomic problems such as growth, inflation, unemployment, business cycles, foreign trade, and asset market stability be solved by the market forces of the economy, or should the government actively intervene to solve these problems? To answer the question, we need to first look at the role of the market in the economy.

When economists use the term 'market,' it sometimes has a general and abstract meaning such as the mechanism through which prices are determined by the interaction of demand and supply forces in the economy. Of course, the market originated from a specific place where sellers and buyers gathered in one place to buy and sell products. The market pointing to this specific place remains in the form of a 5-day market or a farmer's market, and in the form of more modernized markets such as groceries, supermarkets, department stores, shopping malls, convenience stores, etc., or highly sophisticated markets such as stock exchanges, futures markets, auctions, etc. The market also exists in electronic forms such as television shopping channels and online shopping websites such as Amazon, eBay, Alibaba's *Taobao*.

Thus, the market in the economic sense is not confined to a physical place where the seller and the buyer meet and trade, but rather refers to a mechanism through which an equilibrium price is determined through the interaction between the seller and the buyer. This interaction can be done verbally through meeting in a physical location like the traditional market, or through other forms of mediation such as letters, telephones, fax machines, emails, and Internet messages. More fundamentally, any form of mediation itself is not important.

The capitalist economic system is based on private properties and market functions. The function of the market in the capitalist economic system is that the equilibrium price is determined by the interaction of the opposing forces of supply and demand in the market, and that the equilibrium price determined in the market provides information for decision making to economic agents participating in economic activities. Thus, there are two elements of the market: demand and supply. In economic analysis, demand refers to the amount of goods or services that a consumer (or buyer) is willing and able to buy for a certain period of time, and supply refers to the amount of goods or services that a producer (or seller) is willing and able to sell for a certain period of time. Thus, demand and supply contain two elements: willingness to buy (or sell) and ability to buy (or sell). If you want to buy an expensive car (such as the Lamborghini, for example), but if you cannot afford to buy it, you only want or desire the car, and do not demand the car.

The quantity demanded of a product is negatively related to the price of the product if other conditions are equal. This inverse relationship between price and quantity demanded is called the law of demand. It is important to make the assumption that other things are equal or constant. The assumption of other-things-being equal is sometimes referred to as the *ceteris paribus* assumption. Thus, the law of demand means that when the price of a product rises (falls), the quantity demanded of the product decreases (increases) if other things such as income, interest rates, family size, education, gender, age, and tastes and preferences are held constant or the same.

We often observe that although car prices keep on rising, people buy more cars. Thus, on the surface, there seems to be a positive association between the quantity demanded of a car and its price, refuting the law of demand. However, this observation is made without holding other conditions such as income, interest rates, tastes, preferences constant. More consumers buy cars despite higher car prices because their income might have increased, or interest rates on car loans might have fallen. Of course, in the real world, we cannot keep other things constant. Nevertheless, if we analyze the relationship between the price of cars and the quantity demanded of cars using some statistical techniques, we usually find that there is an inverse relationship between price and quantity demanded. This analytic technique works as if we held the consumer's income, interest rates, age, education, and family size constant.

There are two anomalies to the law of demand. The first anomaly is a Giffen good. A Giffen good refers to a good that is so inferior that a fall in its price leads to a decrease in the quantity demanded of the good. Thus, the demand curve for a Giffen good has an upward slope. The Giffen good is named after Sir Robert Giffen, a British economist. Historically potatoes, wheat, and rice appeared as Giffen goods.

The second anomaly is a Veblen good. While the Giffen good is associated with non-luxury and inferior products, a Veblen good is a type of a luxury good for which the quantity demanded of the good increases as its price rises. Thus, the Veblen good has an upward-sloping demand curve, which seems to be a contradiction of the law of demand. The Veblen good is named after Thorstein Veblen, an American economist. Veblen (1899) observed an anomalous consumption behavior as consumers purchased more luxury goods as their prices increased. This kind of behavior has been explained as a mode of status-seeking behavior, which is attributable to the 'keeping up with the Joneses' effect (or the snob effect).

<Figure 2.1> The Demand and Supply Curves

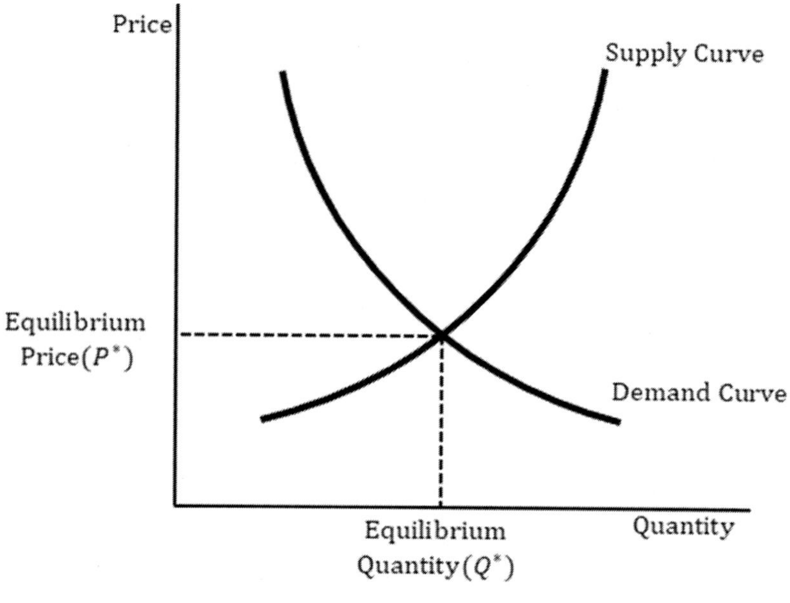

On the other hand, the quantity supplied of a product is positively related to the price of the product if other conditions are held constant. This positive relationship is called the law of supply. When the price of a product rises, the producer is willing to increase the supply of the product because the producer can make more profits at higher prices. On the contrary, when the price of a product falls, the producer's profit decreases, and the producer is willing to decrease the quantity supplied of the product. It is also important to note that the law of supply holds true under the *ceteris paribus* assumption. The *ceteris paribus* factors include the prices of factor inputs such as labor (wages) and capital (interest rates), the prices of raw materials, the prices of energy and electricity, and productivity. Sometimes, we observe that producers produce more of their goods even if the market prices of the products do not rise or even fall. This happens because some favorable *ceteris paribus* factors are in motion. For example, if wages or interest rates go down, or electricity and oil prices fall or workers' productivity increases, producers can make profits even at lower prices. This observation does not contradict the law of supply.

In this way, supply and demand forces move in opposite directions through prices in the market. When these two opposing forces working in opposite directions become equal, the market is in equilibrium. In other words, the market achieves a balance by matching supply and demand. The price determined at the equilibrium point is called the equilibrium price, and the volume of transactions determined at the equilibrium price is called the equilibrium quantity transacted.

There are many different types of markets. There are goods markets where goods and services are traded, labor markets where labor services are traded, and asset markets or financial markets where assets are traded. In the goods market, the equilibrium price of goods and services is determined; in the labor market, the equilibrium wage is determined; and in the financial market, the equilibrium asset price and the equilibrium interest rate are determined. The issues of how freely equilibrium prices are determined in these markets, how quickly the information contained in the equilibrium prices is disseminated among market participants, and how much restriction is imposed on the determination of the equilibrium prices are the dividing lines that distinguish between classical economics and Keynesian economics, between liberalism (laissez-faire) and market interventionism, between a capitalist economy and a socialist economy, and between a market economy and a command economy.

The main characteristic of the market economy is that the equilibrium price freely fluctuates in response to market disturbances. If the current market price is higher than the equilibrium price for some reason, producers can expect to earn more profit at the price, and they want to supply more of the product than the equilibrium quantity of transaction. However, because this price is too high for consumers, consumers try to cut down on their purchases. Therefore, at the market price, the supply exceeds the demand. Thus, at a price level higher than the equilibrium price, an excess supply or a surplus occurs. In such a case, the market is out of equilibrium because the two opposing forces are not equal. This imbalance will not last long, however, if market prices move freely. In a disequilibrium state, some of the product produced will not be sold because the supply of the product is more than the demand for the product, and producers are forced to lower the price to reduce the increased inventory. As such, the current market price will decrease until the disequilibrium disappears, and ultimately the equilibrium price will be restored.

Conversely, if the current market price is lower than the equilibrium price for some reason, less competitive producers will not make profits at this price and will eventually leave the market. Only highly competitive producers will remain in the market. Thus, the quantity of the product supplied will decrease. On the other hand, since this low price is sufficient to stimulate the consumer's desire to purchase, consumers are willing and able to purchase more of the product. Thus, at a price level lower than the equilibrium price, the demand for the product exceeds the supply of the product. This is called excess demand, and there is a shortage of products in the market. Some consumers who cannot purchase the product will bid up a higher price to get the product, and the market price will continue to rise until the equilibrium price is restored.

Of course, how quickly and how perfectly these market adjustments and corrections are made is constrained by social and historical backgrounds and political and institutional practices. American economist Arthur Okun describes the social and historical background as the 'invisible handshake,' and American economist Stephen Magee describes the political and legal system as the 'invisible foot'. Even under the market economy, there are many differences in the degree to which an invisible hand can function depending on the society's invisible handshake (social and historical background) and invisible foot (political and legal system).

As discussed, economists' views on the market's ability to adjust in response to disturbances are also divided. Economic theory is largely divided into classical economics and Keynesian economics. Classical economists have faith in the market function as the solution of macroeconomic problems, and Keynesian economists support the government role as the solution of macroeconomic problems. Classical economists believe that prices, wages, and interest rates move quickly and flexibly when the economy is in a disequilibrium, while Keynesian economists maintain that prices, wages, and interest rates do not move as quickly as classical economists believe.

4

MARKET FAILURE, THE TRAGEDY OF THE COMMONS, AND THE COASE THEOREM

Market failure means a situation in which the market is unable to allocate resources efficiently. This means that society has not reached Pareto efficiency because the market failure leads to the inefficient allocation of resources. Pareto efficiency is an important criterion for evaluating economic efficiency. Pareto efficiency is closely related to Pareto improvement. A Pareto improvement refers to a situation in which at least one person of society is made better off without making at least one other person worse off. The state in which such a Pareto improvement is no longer possible is called Pareto efficiency or Pareto optimum. Thus, when society reaches Pareto efficiency, it is not possible to make at least one person better off without making others worse off. If there is a market failure, it is possible to increase the welfare of an individual without harming the welfare of others.

Many economists, particularly Keynesian economists, argue that the government should intervene in the market to correct market failure because they result in the inefficient allocation of resources. They argue that the government should redress market failure by using tax or subsidy policies, or by using wage and price controls or regulations. The question is whether the government can correct the market failure. Classical economists maintain that the measures the government use to correct market failure can introduce another type of inefficiency in the allocation of resources. This is sometimes referred to as a government failure. They object to the government's intervention in the allocation of resources because the government failure incurs greater social costs than market failure. Here, we will look at market failure from a microeconomic point of view, not the Keynesian position advocating government intervention.

Market failure in the capitalist system is an inevitable phenomenon. If there is no market failure, production is determined in such a way that social marginal benefits equal social marginal costs. If a market failure exists, however, this condition is not met. In other words, society as a whole produces more or less than the most socially desirable level of output. Suppose that from the perspective of society, the most desirable level of production is 100 units. If there is a market failure, society may produce less than 100 units (say, 90 units) or more than 100 units (say, 110 units).

Why does a market failure occur in an economy? First, we can consider the case in which the market is dominated by one firm (monopoly) or several firms (oligopoly). When the market takes the form of monopoly, the price and output determined in the market are no longer Pareto optimal. The problem with a monopoly firm is that it does not produce at a level at which the social marginal cost of producing one more unit of goods equals the social marginal benefit of having one more unit of goods. The monopolist seeks to raise the market price to a level that is higher than the price determined in a competitive market. A monopoly firm is a price setter and has the power to influence the market price of its products. As a result, a monopoly firm can make higher profits than firms in a fully competitive market. It is for this reason that monopolies are heavily regulated in many countries. When the market is dominated by oligopolistic firms, the problem may be less severe than the case of monopoly, but still the social marginal cost is greater than the social marginal benefit under oligopoly.

The second type of market failure occurs when a society produces public goods or common goods. Public goods are goods that society members can consume or use without paying for them. Defense, police, firefighting, roads and parks are examples of typical public goods. Public goods have non-excludability and non-rivalry properties. Non-exclusivity refers to the property that a person who has not purchased the public goods cannot be excluded from the consumption or use of them by the producer of the public goods. Non-rivalry refers to the characteristic that one person's consumption does not reduce the consumption of another person.

In the case of private goods, if one person consumes them, the consumption or use of the goods by others is reduced by that amount, and thus, people compete for the consumption of the goods. However, in the case of public goods, the consumption of public goods by one person does not decrease the chances of other people consuming them. For example, the fact that one person receives defense benefits does not diminish the defense benefits received by others. By the same token, defense providers cannot exclude some people from defense benefits. Because of this non-excludability and non-rivalry, private firms are not willing to participate in the production of public goods. In the case of private goods, output is determined at the level where social marginal benefits and social marginal costs are equal, whereas in the case of public goods, it is common that the level of output is determined at a lower level than the socially desirable level.

Even if public goods are produced by private firms seeking profits, investment and production are made at a level lower than the level of Pareto efficiency, because private firms cannot prevent public goods from being used for free. Or private firms may stop producing public goods or leave the market altogether. Therefore, in many countries, the production of public goods is made by governments or public firms, not private firms. Or the government may ensure that private firms make profits from producing public goods such as roads and bridges. It is for this reason that some countries entrust private firms with the construction and operation of roads and bridges and allow them to collect usage fees.

Examples of public goods are not limited to defense, police, firefighting, parks, roads, etc. For example, when a new technology is developed, it can be freely disseminated to other individuals or businesses unless the technology is protected by patents or laws. Even in this case, non-excludability and non-rivalry properties exist. Anyone can use such technology, and the availability of one person does not limit the availability of others.

The third case where market failure occurs is when externalities exist. Externalities can be divided into positive externalities and negative externalities. Positive externalities are sometimes referred to as external economies. When people benefit from the outside in the process of production or distribution, we have positive externalities. For example, if one family runs a flower garden, and the other engages in beekeeping in a village, the two families will enjoy a positive externality effect. First, the flower grower benefits the beekeeper because bees can extract the nectar from the neighbor's flower gardens. Second, the beekeeper benefits the flower grower because bees propagate cauliflower, which can bring the garden into beautiful flowers.

We also have negative externalities. Negative externalities are sometimes referred to as external diseconomies, which causes external damage to production or distribution in the neighborhood. Suppose a fabric manufacturer operates a factory on the riverside of a village and engages in the production of fabric and dyeing material. In this case, the textile company will emit pollutants to the river, which would greatly reduce the number of fish in the river. As a result, fishermen who earn their income by catching fish in the river suffer some damage. This is an example of a negative externality.

If the fabric company is not forced to pay these social costs, then the costs are borne by society, not by the company. Therefore, the market price for textiles does not reflect these social costs, and the production cost of the textile company is lower than the social cost. As a result, the textile company produces more textiles than the quantity dictated by Pareto efficiency. In this case, the social marginal cost is greater than the social marginal benefit because the social marginal cost must include negative externalities.

Lastly, information asymmetry is another factor causing market failure. Information asymmetry refers to a case in which the amount of information existing between the parties involved in transactions is not the same. There are two types of information asymmetry: adverse selection and moral hazard. Adverse selection is the asymmetry of information that exists before a transaction occurs, and moral hazard is the asymmetry of information that exists after a transaction occurs. An important feature of information asymmetry is that when information asymmetry prevails, a party with a small amount of information does not trust the other party, and the transaction may not be made at all. Even if a transaction is made, the quantity or price of a product is determined at a level that is not socially desirable in the market. Transactions can be made at a level that does not satisfy Pareto efficiency.

If market failure exists, should the government intervene in the market to correct the market failure? One study shows that a solution by market coordination can lead to the most efficient allocation of resources, albeit less equitable. In this regard, there is an interesting paper concerning the tragedy of the commons. The tragedy of the commons is the title of a paper (1968) published by ecological economist Garrett Hardin (1968) in the *Science Journal*. The notion of the 'tragedy of the commons' is similar to that of public goods.

Suppose a village has a public pasture. Many people in the village are engaged in cattle breeding. Initially, a villager grazes his cattle on a common pasture. In this case, the marginal cost of raising cattle is almost zero. This is clearly a rational behavior to maximize profits. Other residents who have seen him grazing cattle on the pasture bring their cattle to the pasture to graze, too. The number of cattle on the pasture gradually increases. The grass will eventually run out, and the grassland will be devastated. The cattle will leave the pasture one by one, and finally all the cattle will be gone. This phenomenon has been termed the tragedy of the commons by Hardin. The tragedy of the commons shows that individuals' behavior of maximizing their own interest can result in social inefficiency. Although we have taken pastures as an example, the depletion of fishery resources and the devastation of forests are all the phenomenon of the tragedy of the commons.

To deal with the tragedy of the commons, the government can think of ways to limit the number of cattle each individual can graze, limit the number of days they can graze, or limit the area of the commons. However, these methods are not a fundamental solution. Fundamentally, the tragedy of the commons occurs due to the fact that the ownership of pastures is not established. The commons are like public goods, and there is no market mechanism through which market prices are determined. If the government grants ownership to individuals and allows each to manage the commons, then the tragedy of the commons can be resolved. In this case, a person who has the ownership of a portion of the grassland will take steps such as collecting fees to prevent other people's cattle from entering the land. However, simply establishing ownership by law or the government is not the best solution that maximizes efficiency. The Coase Theorem demonstrates that a more efficient solution than legal or government regulations is to negotiate deals between parties through the market.

Ronald Coase (1960) proposed a surprising theorem showing that a negotiation-based agreement rather than law or regulations could lead to a more efficient solution for the allocation of resources. Coase was awarded the Nobel prize in economics for his contribution to this work. His theory shows that the allocation of resources by voluntary coordination of the market can be more efficient than the legal solution or government intervention in establishing ownership. The gist of the Coase theorem is that economic solutions by the market are superior to economic solutions by the government, although the market solutions are less equitable.

5

GAME RULES OF MARKET PARTICIPANTS

The market is a place where information needed by market participants is produced and disseminated. Equilibrium prices determined in the market convey information on demand and supply to economic agents. Market participants take this information as a signal and act to maximize their own best interest: Consumers act to maximize their utility, and firms act to maximize their profits. Workers act to maximize their earnings, and investors act to maximize their returns. In order for market participants to make decisions that maximize their best interest, they must follow some basic principles for decision making. The basic principles that are kind of hors d'oeuvres for decision making can be summarized as follows.

◈ Economic decisions are made based on real value, not nominal value.
◈ Economic decisions are made based on relative prices, not absolute prices.
◈ Economic decisions are made based on the comparison of marginal costs and marginal benefits.
◈ Economic cost is measured as opportunity cost, not accounting cost.

Here we raise the fundamental question of whether market participants have the knowledge of the basic principles and behave according to the rules of decision making. Of course, most market participants might not be aware of these rules. Even if they know the rules, they might not make decisions by following them strictly. However, many studies show that if market participants act rationally, in most cases these rules are satisfied. This is true even if they act without knowing the rules of decision making.

Let's look at the first rule. We intuitively know that when prices rise, the money and income we possess become less valuable. This indicates that we are more concerned with the real value of money. The nominal value is the value measured at the current market price, and the real value is the value measured using the price level that prevailed in a given base year. In simple terms, the real value is the value obtained after adjusting for inflation. What we observe is the nominal value such as nominal income, nominal wages, nominal interest rates, and nominal exchange rates, but variables affecting economic decisions are real income, real wages, real interest rates, and real exchange rates. It is the real wage that matters in decisions on whether to work or not. It is the real interest rate that matters in decisions on borrowing and lending. It is the real exchange rate that matters in international transactions. On the surface, our decisions seem to be made based on nominal values, but a careful examination reveals that our decisions are consistent with real values.

When the labor union negotiates wages with the management, union representatives usually insist that the rate of increase in (nominal) wages this year should be at least 4%, as the inflation rate is expected to rise by 4% this year. The union leaders insist on a 4% wage increase or higher, because they are aware that at this wage increase workers will not lose in real terms. Thus, the union representatives recognize that real wages, not nominal wages, are the key to the wage negotiation process. Nominal variables such as nominal income, nominal interest rates, and nominal wages tend to increase proportionally with price increases. Because a nominal variable includes the inflation effect, any decisions made based on the nominal variable may not result in the best interest of economic agents.

When you are lending $1000 to a borrower, you will figure out in advance what the expected rate of inflation will be. For example, if inflation is expected to rise by 4% this year, you will never lend money at an interest rate lower than 4%. If you lend money at 3%, for example, you will lose money in real terms from lending the money. You earn 3% interest from your lending, but you lose 4% of the loan value from inflation. Thus, you end up with a loss of 1% when the inflation rate reaches 4%. In other words, the interest you earn in real terms is −1%. Thus, the real interest rate should be a guide to your economic decisions.

The principle can also be applied to macroeconomic variables. Almost all economic variables that we encounter as measures of macroeconomic performance such as consumption, savings, investment, imports and exports, and government spending, as well as national income are measured and published in nominal terms. Nominal income (or GDP) is the value of gross domestic product measured at the current market price (say, the price level in 2020), and real GDP is the value of gross domestic product measured at the base-year price (say, the price level in 2015). Nominal GDP is not suitable as an indicator of economic performance because nominal GDP includes both the increase of real output and the increase of inflation. Nominal GDP could increase as the price level rises even if there is no increase in the real quantity of output.

Thus, when evaluating economic performance based on nominal GDP, we arrive at the unreasonable conclusion that as prices rise higher, the amount of nominal GDP becomes larger. This shows that we should use real GDP when calculating the economic growth rate. This approach is especially true when we want to compare economic performance over time, because prices tend to rise over time. By the same logic, a comparison of income per capita over time should also be based on real income, so that the true comparison of living standards between different time points is possible. However, nominal GDP and nominal income per person are usually used for comparison across countries during the same period, because in this case we are concerned with comparing economic performance on the same footing across countries (not over time).

We do not observe real variables. Thus, in order to obtain real variables, we have to calculate them from their corresponding nominal variables. In general, the real variable is obtained by dividing the nominal variable by the price index. When the nominal variable represents the amount (income, consumption, savings, investment, wages, etc.), the real variable is calculated by dividing the nominal variable by the price index such as the consumer price index. (CPI) Thus, we obtain real GDP by dividing nominal GDP by the CPI.

$$\text{Real GDP} = \frac{Nominal\ GDP}{Price\ level}$$

When the nominal variable is expressed as a percentage or rate (%) (interest rate, wage rate, etc.), the real variable is obtained by subtracting the expected inflation rate from the nominal variable. Thus, we obtain the real interest rate by subtracting the inflation rate from the nominal interest rate. Similarly, we can obtain the real wage rate by subtracting the inflation rate from the nominal wage rate.

$$\text{Real interest rate} = \text{Nominal interest rate} - \text{Inflation rate}$$

We'll next talk about Rule 2. In economic decision making, the distinction between absolute prices and relative prices is as important as the distinction between real and nominal variables. Let's take the following example. When we go to a restaurant and order meals, we look at the price tag and compare the prices. For example, when a pan of pizza is \$10, it is not possible to know whether this price is high or cheap. This price can be regarded as an absolute price, but the absolute price itself does not contain much information for economic decision making. You can tell whether a meal is expensive or not by comparing it with the prices of other meals.

Now, if one hamburger meal at a fast-food restaurant is $5, and one serving of beefsteak is $20, it is possible to compare the price of pizzas with the prices of hamburgers and beefsteaks. The pan pizza is relatively expensive compared with the hamburger, but it is relatively cheap compared with the beefsteak. Based on this comparison, we can easily make decisions. In this case, we can say that the relative price of the pan pizza to the hamburger is $10/$5 = 2, and the relative price of the pan pizza to the beefsteak is $10/$20 = 0.5.

Microeconomic theory of consumer choice is constructed based on the premise that consumers and producers make decisions by looking at relative prices, not absolute prices. It is relative prices, not absolute prices, that contain market information. This is because the relative price represents the opportunity cost of a product. The relative price of the pizza to the hamburger (= 2) means the cost of giving up the consumption of the hamburger in order to buy the pizza. In other words, the consumer must give up two hamburgers to consume one pan pizza. This indicates that the opportunity cost of one pan pizza is two hamburgers. (We'll discuss the opportunity cost in more detail in the next chapter.)

To see why absolute prices are not important for economic decision making, suppose that absolute prices have doubled. So, the price of one pan pizza rose to $20, the price of one hamburger to $10, and the price of one beefsteak to $40. Given that all other conditions are constant (*ceteris paribus*), this change in absolute prices will have no effect on your choice of meals, because there is no change in the relative price. However, if only the price of pizzas rose to $15 per pan, and the prices of hamburgers and beefsteaks remained unchanged, then pizzas become relatively expensive compared with hamburgers or beef steaks. A rational consumer will try to change the choice of lunch menu from pizzas to either hamburgers or beefsteaks

Now we will take the case of producers as an example. Producers produce goods using labor and capital. Producers examine the relative price of labor to capital to determine how to combine labor and capital. For example, if the price of one unit of labor is $1,000 per month, and the price of one unit of machinery is $2,000, the relative price of labor to capital is $1,000/$2,000 = 0.5. If the price of one unit of labor has risen to $2,000 and the price of one unit of capital has risen to $3,000, the relative price of labor is now $2,000/$3,000 = 0.67, making labor relatively expensive compared with capital. Producers will adopt a production method that uses more capital and less labor. However, if price of labor increases to $2,000, and the price of capital to $4,000, then there will be no change in the relative price of labor to capital, and this change will not affect the producer's decision to employ labor and capital.

Finally, Rule 3 implies that all economic decisions that maximize self-interest are made at the margin. A marginal value in the economic sense means the additional value or extra value of a variable. For example, the marginal utility of a product refers to the amount of utility that you obtain when your consumption of the product increases by one additional unit. In this manner, the marginal product of labor refers to the amount of output that increases when labor is increased by one additional unit, and the marginal product of capital refers to the amount of output that increases when capital is increased by one additional unit. Similarly, the marginal cost of a product refers to the increase in production cost when output is increased by one additional unit, and the marginal revenue of a product is the increase in total revenue that increases when output is increased by one additional unit.

When the tax rate on wage income goes down, people have an incentive to work harder. It is the marginal income tax rate, not the average income tax rate that induces people to work more. The marginal income tax rate is the increase in the amount of taxes when income increases by one additional unit ($1). Income tax rates vary for each income segment. Suppose that the income tax is 5% for individuals who earn up to $20,000 per year; 15% for individuals who earn from $20,001 to $50,000; 25% for individuals who earn $50,001 to $100,000; and 35% for individuals who earn $100,000 or more per year. Then, these tax rates are the marginal income tax rates. On the other hand, the average income tax rate is the ratio of total taxes divided by total income. This average income tax rate does not affect people's decision to work.

If we make decisions based on average numbers, the results could be nonsensical. When 100 people with an average height of 170 centimeters jump into a 160-centimeter-deep pond, we can conclude on the basis of the average height that no one would drown. However, there may be some people who do not reach 160cm in height and would drown.

How much of income people spend and how much of it people save have a significant impact on the household's budget and play an important role in the determination of national income. Again, what is important is the marginal propensity to consume and the marginal propensity to save. The marginal propensity to consume (MPC) is a ratio that shows how much consumption increases when income increases by $1. If consumption increases by $0.9 when income increases by $1, the MPC is

0.9. Similarly, the marginal propensity to save (MPS) is a ratio that shows how much savings increase when income increases by \$1. If savings increase by 10 cents when income increases by \$1, the MPS 0.1. On the other hand, we obtain the average propensity to consume (APC) by dividing total consumption by total income, and the average propensity to save (APS) by dividing total savings by total income. Although the APC and the APS may be useful as an indicator for statistical comparison, they are not variables that affect the national economy.

Here are some examples of how the decision-making principles can be applied. First, consumers purchase goods or services in such a way that they maximize their utility. Assuming that the consumer buys only two products, clothing (C) and food (F), consumers maximize their utility when the marginal utility of clothing they obtain by spending \$1 for clothing is equal to the marginal utility of food they obtain by spending \$1 for food. This happens when the marginal utility (MU^F) of food divided by the price of the food (P^F) is equal to the marginal utility (MU^C) of clothing divided by the price of the clothing (P^C)

$$MU^F/P^F = MU^C/P^C$$

This means that the consumer's utility is maximized when products are purchased until the marginal utility of each product per dollar is the same.

Next, producers employ labor and capital in such a way that they maximize their profits. First, in order to maximize profit, the producer hires labor until the marginal product of labor (MP^L) equals the real wage (w).

$$MP^L = w$$

This tells us that if workers are hired until the amount of output that the additional worker produces (MP^L) is equal to the real wage paid to the worker, the producer will make the most profit. Also, in order to maximize profit, the producer produces a product until the marginal cost (MC) of the product equals the marginal revenue (MR) of the product.

$$MR = MC$$

In this context, all rational economic decisions are made at the margin.

Most economic agents act without knowing the concepts or principles of economic decision-making. However, many studies show that if they behave rationally to maximize their own best interest, their optimizing behavior is consistent with the decision-making rules.

6

OPPORTUNITY COST: BYGONES ARE BYGONES

Opportunity cost is one of the important rules for economic decision making (Rule 4). Economic rationality tells us that "bygones are bygones". It also teaches us that "you should forget the past expenses that you incurred from your past decisions". However, human emotion cannot forget the beautiful memories of the past. The Beatles' <Yesterday> is known to be one of the most beloved pop songs in the world and is the most covered song in history with over 2,000 versions having been recorded. In those days when the Beatles' popularity was sky-high, <Yesterday> shook the emotions of many people with its sweet melody. The lyric says that "I long for yesterday". Let's go back to the memories of the past by listening to the Beatles' <Yesterday>.

> Yesterday
> All my troubles seemed so far away,
> Now it looks as though they're here to stay.
> Oh, I believe in yesterday.
> Suddenly,
> I'm not half the man I used to be,
> There is a shadow hanging over me,
> Oh, yesterday came suddenly.
> Why she had to go,
> I don't know, she wouldn't say.
> I said something wrong.
> Now I long for yesterday.
> Yesterday,
> Love was such an easy game to play,
> Now I need a place to hide away,
> Oh, I believe in yesterday.

Although the Beatles believe in yesterday, the science of economics believes in today. Economic theory teaches us that if we believe in the past in assessing the cost of any activity, we might sink into a wrong decision.

If we make an economic decision based on the cost of something we incurred in the past, our decision cannot produce the optimal outcome in the economic sense. People make economic decisions by comparing costs and benefits, but the cost spent in the past does not correctly measure the economic cost of decisions. The cost in the economic sense is used in a very different way than the accounting cost we normally use.

The cost in economics is defined as the cost of a decision. When we make a decision, we must give up other valuable alternatives. If you decide to watch a football game on the weekend, you should give up other valuable activities, such as part-time work at a convenience store, going to a movie, or meeting a friend. In this case, watching a football game is costly in the sense that it sacrifices other alternative activities. This is the concept of cost in economics, and this cost is called opportunity cost. Thus, the opportunity cost of something is defined as the value of the next best alternative that must be sacrificed.

In the previous example, it is assumed that you spend all the Saturday afternoon (four hours) watching a college football game. Possible alternatives to watching the football game include (1) part-time work at a convenience store, (2) going to a movie, (3) playing tennis, and (4) preparing for exams. Let's assume that the next best alternative you would choose is a part-time job that pays $20 per hour. Then, the opportunity cost of watching the football game is $80. If you chose to work at the convenience store instead of watching the football game, you would have an opportunity to earn $80, but you gave up this opportunity. This forgone value of the next best alternative ($80) is the opportunity cost of watching the football game, and this cost is sometimes called an implicit cost, because you did not explicitly incur this cost.

You also incur some explicit costs such as the ticket price, automobile fuel and parking fees. This cost is called an explicit cost. Thus, economic costs include both implicit and explicit costs. The explicit cost can also be viewed as an opportunity cost. Suppose that the ticket price, gasoline cost, and parking fees amount to $100. Then you could use this $100 for other purposes such as purchasing a pair of jeans, but you have forgone the opportunity to buy a pair of jeans. Because the price of a pair of jeans is $100, the explicit cost paid for the football game ($100) can also be considered as an opportunity cost.

Even if you get a free admission ticket from a friend, and your friend gives you a ride to the football stadium, the cost in the economic sense is not zero. By watching the football game, you give up an opportunity to earn $80 from your part-time job. Thus, the economic cost of watching the football game is still $80. As the saying goes, "Time is money". This opportunity cost is not a special kind of cost, but any cost of economic activity is measured as an opportunity cost. From jeans to cars, costs must be calculated as opportunity costs.

The concept that should be distinguished from the opportunity cost is the sunk cost. This is not the cost associated with the current decision, but the cost that already occurred in the past. Because the cost that occurred in the past is an expense that was already spent in the past, the sunk cost has nothing to do with the current decision, nor can it be recovered by the current decision. When we make a decision based on costs that have already been incurred in the past, that decision can have economically irrational outcomes. There is a proverb that says, "Bygones are bygones," which is a good analogy to explain the sunk cost. There is a Korean song that sings, "Don't ask the past," which is in sync with the notion of an opportunity cost.

As a good example of the sunk cost, suppose you have already waited an hour to buy a ticket for a concert by a famous opera singer, and then see the signpost showing that "It takes two hours from where you stand to get the ticket". If you think leaving without watching the concert after already having waited for an hour (time which you deem as being worth quite a lot) is wasteful, and decide to wait for two more hours, then your decision is based on the sunk cost. However, if you think that although you have waited an hour so far, waiting for another two hours to attend the concert is of no value, your decision is based on the opportunity cost. The cost of waiting two hours from now should be the basis for your current decision making. If the cost is bigger than the benefits you obtain from attending the concert, you should not wait. In Shakespeare's (1606) *Macbeth,* King Macbeth of Scotland confessed that "Things without all remedy should be without regard: what's done is done". That confession captures the essence of opportunity cost.

PART 3

AN OVERVIEW OF MACROECONOMICS: CLASSICAL AND KEYNESIAN PERSPECTIVES

Chapter 1

A Self-Adjusting Economy: Classical Economics

1

ADAM SMITH AND THE BIRTH OF CLASSICAL ECONOMICS

1776 was a year that made an epoch in world history both politically and economically. In political history, the United States (13 Eastern states) declared the independence from the United Kingdom in 1776, which marked the birth of a new country in the New World. From an economic perspective, Adam Smith published *The Wealth of Nations* in 1776, which heralded the birth of a new discipline of economics, the classical school of economics. His masterpiece laid the foundations of modern economics and paved the way for free-market capitalism. Smith's theory dominated Western economic thought for more than 160 years until the Great Depression devastated the classical doctrine in the 1930s and opened the door to the Keynesian Revolution.

Of course, Smith never called his theory the classical theory of economics. The term 'classical economics' was coined by Keynes who published *The General Theory of Employment, Interest and Money* in 1936. He used the term classical economics in order to differentiate his new theory from any economic doctrine that existed before his work. According to Keynes, the term was first used by Karl Marx to describe the economic thoughts of David Ricardo and earlier economists. Keynes systematically reconstructed the basic doctrines of classical economists in *The General Theory* (Chapter 2) in accordance with his own interpretation.

Prior to the publication of *The General Theory* by Keynes, economics was mainly concerned with how the prices of goods and resources were determined in an individual market, how resources were allocated efficiently, and how the welfare of individuals was maximized in a free and competitive market under an economic system where private properties were established. Thus, the analysis of economic problems faced by individual economic agents such as consumers, producers, and workers became the dominant subject of classical economics. In this way, classical economists were mainly concerned with microeconomic issues.

It would have been no coincidence that the year when Smith's *The Wealth of Nations* was published (1776) happened to be the year when the American Independence was declared. The sentiment of political freedom from the European monarchy could be easily combined with the aspiration for a market economy that was economically free from government intervention and be also well matched with the dream for a laissez-faire system that entrusted the self-functioning of the economy. The idea of a self-correcting economy became a key element of classical economics.

Classical economists maintained that if the economy had problems such as unemployment or inflation, prices, wages, and interest rates determined in the market would respond quickly to such disequilibrium, resulting in flexible adjustment of the economy. Thus, by claiming that prices, wages, and interest rates move flexibly to solve any economic problems, classical economists believe in the economy's self-correcting forces. It was a belief that if a free market existed and people acted for their own best interest, then the whole economy would take care of itself. Classical economists maintained that the self-adjusting mechanism would lead the economy to harmony, not to chaos. Expressing this harmony economically means that "the economy always tends to return to the state of full employment equilibrium".

The notion that "The economy takes care of itself" was first introduced by Smith under the name of the invisible hand. The idea of the 'invisible hand' means that the decisions of economic agents that are guided by unobservable prices, wages, and interest rates always lead the economy to a harmonious state of equilibrium The classical school of economics thus reflects a more optimistic view on the working of the economy.

The theory of the classical school and the theory of the Keynesian school are not the relics of the past displayed in the museum of history but are alive today and affect every aspect of our lives. In the United States, politically, most Republicans support classical prescriptions, and most Democrats favor Keynesian conclusions. When the 2008 global economic crisis broke out, President Obama and the central bank of the United States, went on to "saving private businesses" under Keynesian prescriptions. However, many Republicans opposed such spending programs, criticizing that increased spending associated with economic stimulus packages would only lead to inflation in the future. There was a replica of the debate surrounding spending programs between Democrats and Republicans during the COVID-19 crisis.

Now we will explore how these two contrasting economic theories and ideologies were formed, what their main features are, and how they are positioned in today's economic policy.

2

THE WATER-DIAMOND PARADOX AND DA VINCI'S *SALVATOR MUNDI*

In a free market economy, the equilibrium price of a product is determined in the market by supply and demand forces. However, prices determined in the market sometimes make people tilt their heads. <The Card Players> drawn by Paul Cezanne in 1893 was sold for an eye-opening price of $250 million in 2011, which set the highest price ever paid for a work of art up to that time. However, this seemingly exorbitant price was a temporary record to be broken. There is a saying that "a record-breaking event exists only to be broken." The price of Cezanne's work was soon broken by an oil painting by French impressionist Paul Gauguin, <When Will You Marry?> (*Quand te maries-tu*?) (1892), which was sold for $300 million. However, this insane price was also not that surprising after all. There was indeed a jaw dropper.

The painting that amazed many people was <*Salvator Mundi*> (Latin for 'Savior of the World') drawn by Leonardo Da Vinci (1452-1519), a genius artist in Italy in the 16th century. The painting was sold at a whopping price of $450.30 million at the Christie Auction in New York on November 15, 2017, the highest price ever paid in the history of art auction. Many people stood aghast at the price of the painting. Abu Dhabi's Ministry of Culture and Tourism was known to purchase the painting. The painting was expected to be open to the public at the Abu Dhabi Louvre Museum, which opened in early December 2017, but the release has not been made yet. It is difficult for our cognitive ability to understand the mechanism through which the price of a priceless painting is determined in the market. Classical economists had a similar confusion regarding how the price of a commodity was determined.

Early classical economists were faithful to laissez-faire (or hands-off) liberalism and paid much attention to subjects such as value theory. However, classical economists did not distinguish between total utility and marginal utility, and their value theory led many classicists into the labyrinth. As discussed previously, utility refers to the satisfaction obtained from consuming a product. Total utility measures the aggregate satisfaction an individual receives from consuming a certain quantity of a product, and marginal utility is the increase in satisfaction an individual receives from consuming one additional unit of a product. An important principle of economics is that as consumers increase the consumption of a product, the marginal utility that consumers derive from the consumption of the product decreases. This phenomenon is called the law of diminishing marginal utility.

<Figure 3.1> *Salvator Mundi* (Leonardo da Vinci)

A buffet restaurant is a business method that operates based on the law of diminishing marginal utility. If the law of diminishing marginal utility does not work, all buffet restaurants are bound to go broke. Suppose that the utility a consumer obtains from eating the first lobster is \$30 in monetary value. (This indicates that the consumer is willing to pay as much as \$30 for the consumption of the first lobster.) Then the marginal utility the consumer receives from consuming the second lobster would be less than \$30, say, \$20. If the marginal utility from the consumption of the third lobster is \$10 and the marginal utility from the consumption of the fourth lobster is 0, then the consumer will not eat the lobster anymore after eating up to the fourth. At the time when the consumer eats the fourth lobster, the marginal utility he gets is 0, but the total utility he has derived from consumption of the lobsters was \$60 (\$30 + \$20 + \$10 + \$0). Thus, marginal utility and total utility are two different concepts.

Classical economists, including Adam Smith, understood the price of a commodity being determined by the value it had, and they thought that the value of a commodity was closely related to the total utility that the commodity awarded. However, their value theory did not solve the so-called water-diamond paradox. Water is an indispensable commodity for humans, that is, it is a very valuable commodity, while diamond is not so essential for human life. However, water has almost little price, whereas diamond is priceless. According to their value theory, the price of water should be high, whereas the price of diamonds should be low. Thus, classical economists were not able to solve the paradox of why the price of water is almost nil, and the price of diamonds is sky-high.

With the advent of marginalism, this problem could have been solved. After all, water exists in almost unlimited amounts, but the reserves of diamonds are limited. Although the total utility of water is much greater than the total utility of diamonds, the marginal utility of water is near zero since water exists almost indefinitely, and the marginal utility of diamonds is very high by the law of diminishing marginal utility. Since the price is determined by the marginal utility rather than the total utility, marginalists could maintain that the price of water is almost zero and the price of diamonds is very high. It is interesting to note that the phrase, 'a diamond of the first water' means the best quality diamond or a first-rate figure.

But Marx, in his *Das Kapital* (1867) developed the 'labor theory of value,' where he proposed that the value of a commodity was determined by the labor time socially necessary to make the commodity. He further claimed that capitalists did not pay workers the full value of the commodity workers produce, but only paid enough to provide workers with the means they needed to survive, and that capitalists exploited the rest of the value of the commodity. Marx's labor theory of value was a fundamental departure from the classical theory of value.

<Figure 3.2> The Water-Diamond Paradox

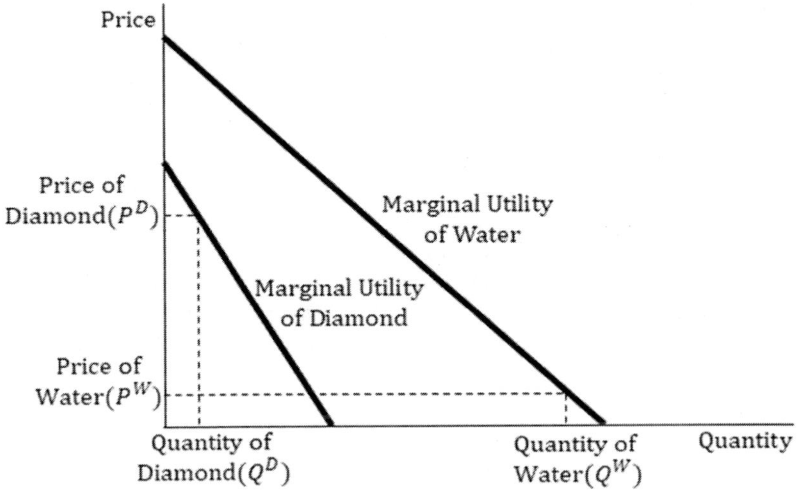

Price theory was further advanced by neoclassical economists such as Alfred Marshall. The theory of pricing that was systematically developed by Marshall was a significant step forward in the development of modern economics as a science. Marshall's theory was recognized as synonymous with neoclassical economics. Keynes and Arthur Pigou, who had a great influence on modern economics, were also Marshall's students. The demand-supply model we use today to analyze the determination of the equilibrium price in the market was the analytical tool developed by Marshall.

The most important contribution of Marshall was to combine the value theory of the classical school and the utility theory of the marginalist school to develop the demand-supply model. Smith and other classical economists argued that the value of a good or service was largely determined by the cost of production, and marginalists maintained that the value of a good was principally determined by the marginal utility of the good. Marshall viewed that the cost of production determined the supply of the good, and the utility of a good determined the demand for the good. Then the equilibrium price of a good is determined by the interaction between the supply side, which represents the cost of production, and the demand side, which represents the marginal utility. Marshall's combination of the value theory and the utility theory into the supply-demand model was a restoration, reinterpretation, and extension of the vision drawn by Smith. Marshall successfully overcame the pessimism of 'dismal science' that Malthus and Ricardo depicted and restored the harmony and optimism that Smith envisioned in his *The Wealth of Nations*.

Using the demand-supply model, we can recast the water-diamond paradox and explain why the masterpieces drawn by Da Vinci, Gauguin, and Cezanne commanded seemingly nonsensical prices. Since water exists in almost unlimited amount, the water supply curve is almost horizontal. Even if demand changes, prices of water rarely change. (The case of bottled water may be different.) On the other hand, since the supply of diamonds is very scarce, the supply curve of diamonds is almost vertical. Even if the demand for diamonds changes slightly, prices can jump significantly. The supply curve for Da Vinci's *Salvator Mundi* is virtually undefined. This is because there is only one supply. It can be drawn as a point, and that point lies on the demand curve, so the price of the person who called the highest price is the market price.

3

THE MARKET HAS SELF-CORRECTING FORCES

The basic assumption on the behavior of economic agents maintained in classical economics was that people pursued their self-interest. The pursuit of self-interest has been recognized as human nature and not regarded as a selfish act. Smith transformed the selfishness of human behavior into the rationality of economic decisions. In Smith's view, the pursuit of an individual's own best interest in the exchange economy was seen as a means of ensuring social harmony.

Furthermore, it is assumed that in conducting economic activities, the individual does not intend to pursue public interest, or even does not know that he is doing so. In *The Wealth of Nations,* Smith (1776) wrote as follows: "It is not from the benevolence of the butcher, the brewer, or the baker that we expect our dinner, but from their regard to their own interest." The pursuit of self-interest is materialized in the form of the maximization of utility by consumers and the maximization of profits by business firms. Consumers purchase goods and services using limited income to maximize their utility. Generally, people prefer more to less, but they cannot pursue the goal of 'the more, the better' because their income is limited. Thus, consumers are concerned with the maximization of utility given the level of income.

Business firms produce goods and services using limited production resources to maximize profits. Making optimal decisions for profit maximization by the representative firm is constrained by limited resources. Again, the representative firm cannot pursue the goal of 'the more, the better,' because their production resources are limited. Thus, firms are concerned with the maximization of output given the level of production costs or the minimization of production costs given the level of output.

In order to build an edifice of classical theory, classical economists further assumed that when external disturbances occurred in the economy, market prices such as prices, wages, and interest rates would move quickly to eliminate such disturbances. The upward and downward flexibility of prices, wages and interest rates is the essential tenet of classical economics. This classical assumption is in sharp contrast with Keynesian economics that is built on the downward rigidity of wages and prices. The flexible movement of prices, wages and interest rates presupposes the existence of a free, competitive market.

We'll see how flexible prices eliminate disturbances such as inflation and unemployment. Inflation develops when the economy is in a booming cycle. When the economy is booming, the prices of goods and services tend to rise. As inflation rises, wages and interests also tend to rise. Higher prices and interest rates discourage people from buying goods and services, which in turn leads prices to go down. Thus, inflation will begin to cool down. On the other hand, unemployment occurs when the economy is in a recession cycle. When the economy slows down, the prices of goods and services tend to fall, and consequently wages and interest rates also tend to fall. Wages and interest payments constitute a significant portion of production costs. Lower wages and interest rates encourage business firms to expand production and to hire more workers, which in turn leads unemployment to decrease. Classical economists argue that this kind of adjustment of prices, wages, and interest rates occurs quickly without help from the government.

Thus, classical economists argue that when external shocks such as the COVID-19 crisis create excess demand or excess supply, the price mechanism works to eliminate such disequilibrium in the market. The invisible price system guides every sector of the economy (commodity market, labor market, asset market, housing market etc.) to reach a harmonious state of the economy, just as the invisible immune system guides every branch of the body (organs and viscera) to reach a healthy state of the body. At this point, if the government attempts to intervene in the private economy to eliminate excess demand or excess supply and the resulting inflation or unemployment, it may temporarily solve the problem, but in the long run, the side effects are greater.

The invisible hand envisioned by classical economists, especially Smith, works nicely when there are perfectly competitive markets, and prices, wages, and interest rates are freely determined in such markets. Classical economists' passion for laissez-faire liberalism naturally incorporated anti-feudal, anti-mercantilist, anti-monopoly, and anti-government elements into their theoretical threads. The classical position was a decentralized economic system and a fully competitive market economy. In fact, 18th-century England, where Smith worked on his theory, was not much different from his envisioned model of business. At that time, the British economy had tens of thousands of small factories and stores competing with each other.

However, from the turn of the 19th century, some institutional factors that imposed hindrance on the working of the competitive market were looming. In particular, large corporations began to emerge thanks to corporate mergers that heated up in the United States and Europe in the late 19th century. With the emergence of large corporations, the form of monopoly or incomplete competition began to appear in the market, and the prototype of perfectly competitive markets plotted by Smith gradually faded. As a result, there were attempts to modify the classical position regarding perfect competition. That was an orbital modification that embraced the market form of monopolistic competition. This modification foreshadowed the emergence of a new branch (neoclassical economics) within the classical school. Many neoclassical economists noted that the real world was not characterized by a monotonous form of perfect competition, but by diverse forms of market. The new theory of competition among neoclassical economists meant a significant departure from Smith's principle of laissez-faire liberalism. However, their efforts as a reform within the system were not enough to defend the classical doctrine and the capitalist system in the face of the forthcoming Great Depression.

In practice, there was a movement to regulate the tyranny of big companies through the establishment of antitrust laws in advance of the Great Depression. The U.S. antitrust laws aimed to protect consumers and promote competition by regulating the formation of corporate cartels. The U.S. antitrust law consists of three main statutes. They include the Sherman Act of 1890, the Clayton Act of 1914, and the Federal Trade Commission Act of 1914. The Sherman Act prohibits price fixing and the operation of cartels and collusion. The Clayton Act restricts the mergers and acquisitions (M&A) of firms that may substantially reduce competition or create a monopoly. Thus, the antitrust laws were mainly designed to prohibit the formation of monopolies and the abuse of monopoly power. However, the U.S. government was not quite successful in anti-monopoly cases.

The landmark anti-monopoly case achieved by the U.S. government happened in 1911. The Justice Department claimed that American petroleum conglomerate Standard Oil had violated the Sherman Act, and the Supreme Court ruled that Standard Oil's high market share was proof of its monopoly power and ordered it to break itself up into 34 separate companies. Another anti-monopoly victory was the breakup of AT&T Corporation into seven 'baby bells' in 1984. The 'baby bells' include NYNEX, Pacific Telesis, Ameritech, Bell Atlantic, Southwestern Bell Corporation (SBC), BellSouth, and U.S. West. AT&T relinquished control of the Bell Operating Companies, which had provided local telephone service in the United States but continued to be a provider of long-distance service. AT&T Corporation, the original parent company, was later acquired by SBC in 2005, which renamed itself AT&T. It is a case of the tail wagging the dog. The new company acquired BellSouth in 2007.

Classical economics that was built based on the premise of a self-regulating economy hung by a thread in the front of the big waves of the Great Depression.

4

How Are Output and Employment Determined in the Classical System? Supply Determines

Say's law is one of the cornerstones of classical economics. Say's law is attributed to Jean Baptiste Say, a French classical economist who first discussed the law. The law states that "supply creates its own demand". More specifically, the supply of a product creates a corresponding demand for the product. When a certain amount of goods or services is supplied, there is no overproduction of goods and services because the corresponding demand for the goods and services is always created. If Say's law is valid, the possibility that the supply of goods exceeds the demand for goods (excess or surplus) or the supply of goods falls short of the demand for goods (excess demand or shortage) is ruled out. Thus, the economy always tends to move toward the state of equilibrium.

Does Say's law hold true in the real world? We'll first consider the supply of homes. Say's law means that if a home builder builds and supplies 10 new homes, the demand for the 10 homes will be created, and all the homes will be sold. Let's look at the Chinese experience. In China, the housing sector accounts for about 30% of GDP. (In the United States, the housing sector accounts for less than 5%.) When the housing boom went viral before the global economic crisis in China, Say's law seemed to hold true. However, when the Chinese economy slid into a stagnation after the global economic crisis, many Chinese construction companies could not sell condominiums supplied, thus building up a lot of inventories. Many condominiums remained unsold for an extended period deemed to be much longer than the classical economist presumes. Many empty condominiums with lights turned off made towns look like ghost towns.

It appears that Say's law did not work in China because condominium prices were downwardly inflexible when the economy was in stagnation. Say's law was based on the downward and upward flexibility of prices, wages, and interest rates. In the classical system, such an oversupply does not occur in principle. Even if it occurs, it is assumed that the prices of homes will drop quickly, and eventually supply will be matched by demand. In other words, the departure from Say's law is a temporary phenomenon in the classical system. The main reason for Say's law not to work in China may be the fact that prices, wages, and interest rates are not flexible enough to eliminate such excess supply of homes quickly. There are at least two factors that make home prices inflexible in China. First, home prices are in general insensitive to demand changes and are heavily affected by supply-side factors. Second, many prices in China are controlled by the central and local governments.

In general, there are many factors that keep Say's law from holding true in the real world. First, when there are some institutional factors that keep prices, wages, and interest rates from moving freely, Say's law may not work smoothly. Consider the minimum wage law. In the United States, the national minimum wage was established in 1938 under the Fair Labor Standards Act. When the federal minimum wage was created, the minimum hourly wage of workers was $0.25 (October 24, 1938). Since then, the federal minimum wage has continued to be raised. Most recently, the federal minimum wage was increased to $7.25 on July 24, 2009. Of course, each state can set its own minimum wage, which should not be lower than the federal minimum wage.

Also, individual firms can pay their own minimum wages, which should not be lower than the federal minimum wage and their state minimum wages. Sometimes, the minimum wage could be higher than the equilibrium wage determined in the market by demand and supply forces. In such a case, the employer has two options: Hiring workers at the minimum wage that is higher than the market wage or giving up hiring workers at the minimum wage. Thus, if the minimum wage law is enforced, and the minimum wage is higher than the market-determined wage, the wage will not fall below the equilibrium wage. Say's law will not work, and unemployment will persist.

Second, if a labor union is strong, and the wage supported by the union is higher than the equilibrium wage, the wage will not fall below the equilibrium wage, thus making the wage inflexible. If there are no restrictions on the labor market, such as minimum wages or strong unions, wages will converge to an equilibrium wage that equilibrates supply and demand. Classical economics is a theory that makes sense under free markets and perfect competition. Thus, Say's law holds in an economy where prices and wages move flexibly, and there are no institutional restrictions and barriers that hinder prices and wages from adjusting in response to external shocks. Thus, excess supply or excess demand is quickly eliminated.

Flexible prices and free markets (without restrictions and constraints) are the two pillars of classical economics. Classical economists such as Say could claim that "supply creates its own demand," because the business environments of the time were similar to the classical assumptions. Any imbalance between supply and demand would be adjusted instantaneously if there were free markets and prices moved freely without interruptions. Thus, any departure from Say's law was considered to be temporary during the adjustment period. They further argued that in the long run, supply would almost surely be matched with demand. Classical economics is concerned with the long-term adjustment of the economy.

However, the real world is different from the classical prototype. Say's law is not squarely applied in many economies, because there are varying levels of restrictions and constraints on the market. The closer an economy is to the prototype of the classical model, the higher is the likelihood of Say's law to hold. Put differently, the fewer the constraints on the market and the greater the flexibility of prices, the faster will the market adjustment be. The U.S. economy together with the Singaporean economy may be most close to the classical model. The problem is a short-run solution. As Keynes mentioned, if the adjustment period is too long, the prescription of the classical school will be empty for those who need a solution right now.

Say's law suggests that "supply creates its own demand", and this is reflected in the classical aggregate supply curve. Since Say's law indicates that the supply of labor by workers is equal to the demand for labor by firms, anyone who wants to work can find a job. This situation is nothing but a state of full employment. Thus, the employment of labor by firms is always determined at the full employment level. In order to derive the classical aggregate supply (AS) curve, suppose that the initial full employment level of labor is 100 workers with the nominal wage of $10 per hour, and that the price level (CPI) is 1.0. The amount of real output that a hypothetical economy produces is $100 million.

Now assume that the price level increases to 1.1 by 10%. Then the real wage will decrease to $9 by 10%. The worker will not be happy with the decrease in the real wage and demand a 10% increase in the nominal wage. Thus, the nominal wage increases to $11 in response to the price increase. This adjustment will occur quickly because wages are flexible enough. The real wage that was temporarily decreased to $9 as a result of the higher price level will return to its original level $10 ($11/1.1). Since workers make a decision on the supply of labor based on the real wage, and the real wage is the same as before, the level of employment is still determined at the level of 100 workers. As a consequence, there is no change in real output at $100 million, because output is determined by the quantity of labor (in the short run).

We can consider another level of prices, say, 1.2. It can be shown that the real wage will again return to the original level ($10) at this higher level of price, and real output will remain at $100 million. The aggregate supply curve is the locus of the combinations of real output at various price levels. When we connect all these combinations, we obtain a vertical aggregate supply curve. Thus, in the classical system, the aggregate supply curve is represented by a vertical line at the full-employment level of output. The vertical aggregate supply curve is the consequence of the classical assumption that prices, wages, and interest rates are flexible.

<Figure 3.3> The Classical Aggregate Supply Curve and Full-employment Output

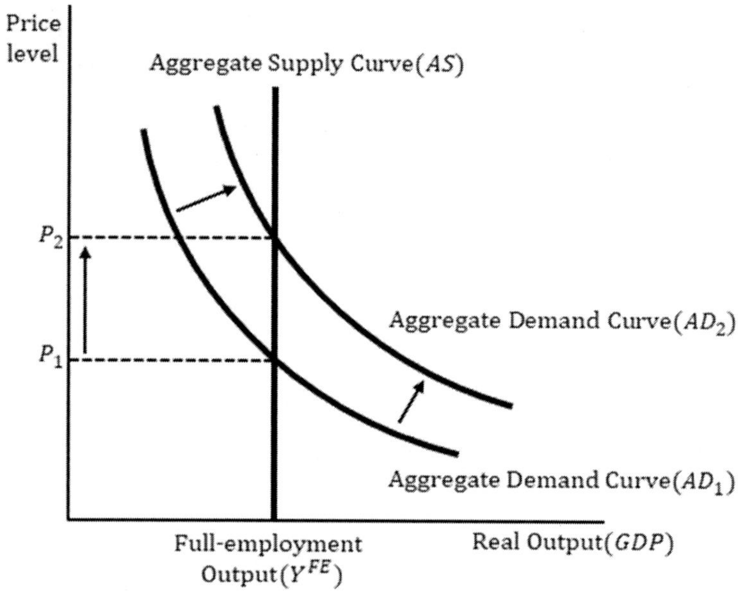

When the aggregate supply curve is given vertically, the demand side of the economy has no effect on output and employment. An increase in aggregate demand will only lead to a rise in prices (from P_1 to P_2) with no effect on real output and employment. In this regard, classical economics is a supply-side theory in the sense that the supply side of the economy determines total output and employment. Aggregate demand is generated by fiscal expansion or monetary expansion. Thus, when the government increases expenditures or reduces taxes, the aggregate demand curve shifts upwardly, resulting in a higher price level. Similarly, when the central bank increases the money supply or lowers interest rates, the aggregate demand curve shifts upwardly, leading to a higher price level. It is natural for classical economists to be skeptical of the effectiveness of such aggregate demand management policies. Under the classical system, the government has little to do when it comes to economic problems such as stagnation and unemployment. Thus, classical economists argue that the government does not need to be involved in the economy.

5

MONEY AS A VEIL: MONEY HAS NO EFFECT ON OUTPUT AND EMPLOYMENT

We have seen that in the classical system, employment is determined at the level of full employment, and real GDP (total output) is determined at the full-employment level of output. How is it possible for an economy to produce goods and services at the full-employment level of output? The classicist's answer to the question lies in the flexibility of prices, wages, and interest rates in a free market. Classical economists have also held that the full-employment level of output is determined by physical factor inputs such as labor and capital, and technological progress in the real sector and is not affected by the amount of money. Then, what role does money play in the determination of employment and output?

In the classical system, money plays only the role of a lubricant that facilitates transactions of goods and services produced in the economy. People want to hold money to use it as a medium for transactions. The role of money is simply a medium of exchange. Classical economists have understood that people do not want to hold money for the purpose of portfolio choice, but rather as a means to buy and sell goods and services and to pay financial obligations. In the classical system, real variables such as real GDP and employment are determined by labor, capital, and technology in the real sector of the economy, and thus money has no effect on real variables. Classical economists view money as a veil that covers the real sector of the economy. We must take off the veil of money to see what is happening in the real sector of the economy.

The view that money is a veil was theoretically established as the quantity theory of money mainly by Alfred Marshall at Cambridge University in the United Kingdom and Irving Fisher at Yale University in the United States around the turn of the 20th century. First, Fisher figured out how the quantity of a country's money is related to its nominal GDP. Nominal GDP is the current market value of all goods and services produced in an economy during a specified period of time. For example, suppose that the U.S. economy produced \$22 trillion worth of goods and services (= nominal GDP) in 2020, and the daily outstanding balance (average) of money in 2020 was \$5.5 trillion. Here we ask the following question: How many times did American people use money in 2020 to buy the goods and services produced in the United States in 2020? People would have used one unit of money about 5.5 times in 2020 to purchase goods and services produced in 2020, This number is obtained by dividing nominal GDP by the amount of money (\$22trillion/\$5 trillion = 5.5). This number is called the velocity of circulation or the income velocity of money (V). Thus, we have the following relation:

$$V = \frac{Nominal\ GDP}{Money} = \frac{PY}{M}$$

where P is the price level, Y is real GDP, and M is the stock of money. Nominal GDP (PY) is equal to real GDP (Y) multiplied by the price level (P).

From the definition of the velocity of money, we can derive the following relation:

$$MV = PY$$

The above equation shows that the stock of money (M) multiplied by the velocity (V) equals nominal GDP. This relation is called Fisher's equation of exchange, named after Irving Fisher who first discussed the relation. Since the equation of exchange is derived from the definition of the velocity of money, it is only an identity. In other words, it is not a monetary theory that shows a relationship between the quantity of money and nominal income. In order for the equation of exchange to be established as a theory of money, a certain functional relationship between the amount of money and nominal income must be established.

If the velocity of money is variable, the equation of exchange is not very helpful in understanding the relationship between money and economic activity. However, if V is constant (at least stable), we can derive a meaningful relationship between the quantity of money and nominal GDP. In fact, classical economists argued that the income velocity of money was determined mainly by institutional factors such as the organizational efficiency and stability of banks and financial institutions, and therefore they thought that the income velocity of money was constant in the short term.

Under the assumption that V is constant, we can derive a functional relationship between the money supply and nominal GDP from the equation of exchange. If the quantity of money increases by 10%, then the left-hand side of the equation (MV) increases by 10% because V is constant.

Accordingly, the right-hand side of the equation (PY) will also increase by 10%. Thus, the equation of exchange predicts that nominal GDP (PY) will increase by 10%. Going one step further, real GDP (Y) in the classical system is determined at the level of full employment by labor, capital, and technology in the real sector of the economy, and thus real GDP is not affected by money. This means that if the quantity of money increases by 10%, only the price level (P) rises by 10%, and real output or employment is not affected by the increase in the quantity of money. This proposal is called the neutrality of money. Money is neutral with respect to output and employment.

This conclusion has important implications for monetary policy. As the U.S. economy plunged into a deep slump in 2008 during the global economic crisis, the Fed, the central bank of the United States, supplied $85 billion of money each month to the banking system, which was known as quantitative easing. (The Fed gradually decreased the size of quantitative easing and ended it in October 2014.) In the United States, most Republicans who adhered to the classical doctrine were opposed to the Fed's quantitative easing policy, arguing that such a policy was more likely to increase inflation in the long run. By the same logic, Republicans were also opposed to President Biden's $1.9 trillion economic stimulus packages. The equation of exchange shows why Republicans were opposed to such increases in the amount of money. They believed that monetary expansions would lead to higher inflation later.

Japan also pursued unlimited quantitative easing (Abenomics) as Abe took office as new Prime Minister. However, the two nations pursued quantitative easing policy with different goals and motivations. In the United States, some people have been opposed to quantitative easing because of the fear of inflation. In Japan, policymakers have favored quantitative easing with the purpose of stimulating inflation. Japan's goal was to boost inflation through quantitative easing. Japan suffered the 'Lost Two Decades' because of severe deflation.

We have seen that classical economists maintain that a 10% increase in the quantity of money only leads to a 10% increase in inflation with no effect on real output. However, there is not a clear one-to-one relationship between the quantity of money and inflation, as the equation of exchange suggests. One of the main reasons is that the velocity of money is not constant. The classical quantity theory of money is valid under the assumption that the income velocity of money is constant. However, many empirical studies show that the assumption may not be tenable. If the velocity of money is variable, inflation is affected not only by the quantity of money, but also by the speed of the velocity.

Even when the supply of money is constant, inflation could increase as the velocity of money increases, other things being equal (= ceteris paribus). This means that as people use money more frequently, the velocity of money increases, which ultimately leads to higher inflation. Conversely, if the velocity of money falls, inflation tends to fall, ceteris paribus. From this point of view, even if the Japanese central banker tries to increase inflation to 2% with unlimited quantitative easing, it is unclear whether the policy could hit the inflation target of 2%. If Japanese people do not spend money, the goal of boosting inflation to 2% could not be an easy task.

We can analyze the relationship between the velocity of money and economic activity from different angles. When the economy is in recession, people are cautious about spending money because of uncertainty about the future. Some people such as Paul Krugman (2011) refer to this phenomenon as sclerosis. Thus, during the economic downturn, the velocity of money tends to decrease. In order to stimulate economic activity, it is thus necessary to provide an incentive for people to spend money more frequently. On the other hand, when the economy is booming, people tend to spend more money. This means that the velocity of money tends to increase during the economic boom. However, it is not a pushover for policymakers to influence the velocity of money by stimulating people to use more money or less money.

6

THE ECONOMY THROUGH THE LENS OF THE CLASSICAL ECONOMIST: CHARLIE CHAPLIN'S QUIP

Charlie Chaplin, who dominated an era as a comic actor, once said: "Life is a tragedy when seen in close-up, but a comedy in long-shot" (Source: www.charliechaplin.com).The economy seen through the lens of the classical economist is similar to Chaplin's quip. We can rephrase the conclusion of classical economics from Chaplin's standpoint: "The economy is a chaos in the short run, but a harmony in the long run". In the short run, the economy may experience some ups and downs such as unemployment or inflation, but in the long run, it has the power to cure these problems on its own, and it moves toward the level of full employment.

Since the economy approaches a full-employment equilibrium in the long run, classical economists oppose any attempt by the government to use money or government spending to solve economic problems such as unemployment or inflation. They insist that the economy should be left as it flows. This policy proposal is called *laissez-faire* policy or hands-off policy. The word, '*laissez faire*' comes from a French phrase, *laissez faire et laissez passer*, meaning that "let it alone and let it flow". Thus, classical economics is primarily interested in a harmonious state of long-term phenomena and full employment equilibrium. As a natural consequence, classical economists favored the notion of 'small government' rather than a 'big government' and were more concerned with the problem of inflation rather than unemployment.

One important aspect that distinguishes between classical economics and Keynesian economics is the distinction between the short run and the long run. Classical economists are more concerned with long-term economic problems, whereas Keynesian economists pay more attention to short-term economic problems. Here it is important to distinguish between the short run and the long run. The effect of economic policy varies greatly with the passage of time. The division between the short run and the long run is not based on the number of years or months on the calendar but is based on the nature of economic behaviors and economic relations.

Of course, the distinction between the short run and the long run is sometimes defined according to the calendar years. For example, short-term securities (or short-term loans) refer to securities (or loans) whose maturity (or loan period) is less than one year; mid-term securities are securities whose maturity is from 1 year to 10 years; and long-term securities are securities whose maturity is over 10 years. However, the distinction between the short and long runs used in economics focuses mainly on the period of adjustment of economic behavior. There is no difference in the purpose of distinguishing them between microeconomics and macroeconomics, but there is a difference between microeconomics and macroeconomics in the criterion of measuring them.

In microeconomics, the short term is defined as the period during which at least one of the factors of production (usually fixed inputs such as capital) is fixed and the other factors of production (usually variable inputs such as labor) can be changed at any time. Microeconomics views the period of changing the fixed input (capital) as a long term. We cannot tell exactly how many years or months it takes to build a new factory and to install machinery, but it is obvious that building a new factory cannot be completed in a short period of time such as a few weeks or a few months. It is a bit vague, but it takes a long time to build a factory or to install machines. In this way, the long run is defined as a period during which all factors of production, including capital, can be altered. In other words, in the long run, all factors of production are variable. In the long run, capital is not a fixed input, but a variable input, because capital can also increase or decrease in the long run.

The short term in macroeconomics can be viewed as the state in which economic agents (consumers, producers, and workers) do not have enough time to recognize a change in economic conditions and to adapt to the change. Suppose, for example, that the central bank has increased the money supply. If a lot of money is supplied into the economy, prices will rise. However, it takes some time for workers to realize that prices have risen and to demand wage increases. The short run is a period during which the full adjustment of the economic agent to changes in economic conditions is not completed.

Over time, the government agencies survey various prices in the market, collect and process data on prices and publish statistics on inflation (the consumer price index). At this stage, the economic agent will be able to realize that prices have risen. Accordingly, consumers and workers adjust their economic behavior according to changes in prices. Consumers will change their consumption or workers will demand wage increases. This period is a long term. In other words, the long term in macroeconomics is a period during which economic agents are fully aware of changes in economic conditions (especially inflation) and can fully reflect such changes in their economic activities.

The practical merit of distinguishing between the short run and the long run should be obvious: Not only the behavior of economic agents varies, but also the effect of economic policy can vary greatly between the short and long runs. It is generally understood that when more money is supplied into the economy, interest rates fall. However, this conclusion is true only in the short term. In the long run, an increase in the amount of money may lead to an increase in the nominal interest rate. The reason is that an increase in the supply of money is likely to cause inflation in the long run, and an increase in inflation rate will lead interest rates to rise. The relationship between inflation and interest rates is called the Fisher equation.

7

The Role of the Government in the Classical System

The main role of the government in the classical system is to protect individual freedom and private property rights and to remove factors that hinder the functioning of the market, such as competition. Classical economists have one thing in common: they maintain that the government should be least involved in economic activity. The government should limit its engagement in economic activity to the extent that it maintains a balanced budget, eliminates or loosens regulations on economic activities, and promotes free competition.

Classical economists see the private sector as much better than the government sector in the efficient allocation of resources. The private sector allocates resources more efficiently because economic agents in the private sector act in such a way that maximizes their own best interest. The government sector is less efficient than the private sector in resource allocation because politicians are more concerned with winning elections. If a policy action is helpful for increasing the chances of winning elections, then politicians adopt even a policy that leads to the inefficient allocation of resources.

The government uses fiscal policy to influence the economy, and the central bank uses monetary policy to influence the economy. Fiscal policy and monetary policy are collectively referred to as aggregate demand policy. Classical economists believe that aggregate demand policy has little effect on real economic activity, such as employment or real output (real GDP). Rather, classical economists argue that the government or the central bank should be very cautious about using aggregate demand policy because it can do harm to the economy rather than do good to it. Classical economists further believe that monetary policy is more harmful than fiscal policy in stabilizing the economy.

First, fiscal policy is an economic policy in which the government affects economic activities through government purchases, government subsidies (transfer payments), and taxes. Classical economists had a very different philosophy in terms of fiscal policy than the post-Keynesian economists. Under the atmosphere of the Victorian Age (1837~1901) in the 19th century, classical economists supported sound finances, that is, a balanced budget with annual revenues being matched with annual expenditures. In the United States, the budget remained almost balanced until the Keynesian Revolution occurred in 1936. The philosophical background of the balanced budget was driven by the perception that it was morally incorrect for the government to spend more than taxes collected from the people.

In the classical system, fiscal policy affects the economy by changing aggregate demand in the economy. This mechanism is similar to monetary policy that affects the economy through changes in aggregate demand. However, fiscal policy is different from monetary policy in two important ways. First, fiscal policy does not indiscriminately affect the economy. Second, fiscal policy uses the money that already exists in the economy unless the government borrows money from the central bank to finance government spending.

The two types of aggregate demand policy are also different in terms of their effectiveness. First, monetary expansion tends to lower the nominal interest rate, while fiscal expansion tends to increase the interest rate, *ceteris paribus*. If the government experiences a fiscal deficit due to an increase in fiscal expenditure, it will usually borrow money from the private capital market to make up the deficit. The government will enter the private capital market as a new borrower, and now the government will compete with private firms and households for limited amounts of funds available in the economy. The existing funds were previously used primarily by businesses for investment and by households for consumption, but now the government wants to get some of funds to finance budget deficits. As a result, the interest rate will rise.

When interest rates rise, investment by business firms will decrease. Thus, government spending tends to crowd out private investment. This phenomenon is called the crowding-out effect. Classical economists argue that the net effect of fiscal expenditure on real GDP is almost zero, as the decrease in investment is almost the same as the increase in fiscal expenditure by the government. The classical position on fiscal policy is in sharp contrast with the Keynesian position on fiscal policy. Keynesians view fiscal policy to be the most powerful economic policy, especially when the economy is in a deep stagnation. Keynesians believe in the multiplier effect of fiscal policy, whereas classical economists emphasize the crowding-out effect of fiscal policy.

8

THE SIRENS' MELLIFEROUS SONGS AND RULES FOR MONETARY POLICY

When we hear about the word 'siren', we are reminded of a loud noise. However, in the Greek-Roman mythology, the Siren is a sea fairy who seduces sailors by singing in a beautiful voice that no one could dare to imitate. Finn Kydland and Edward Prescott intensively studied the question of whether to use monetary policy at discretion as Keynesians favor, or mechanically according to the rule as monetarists (modern-day classical economists) support. They won the Nobel prize in economics for their contribution to their work on the subject. They advocated the superiority of the classical rule over the Keynesian discretion by citing the Greek poet Homer's epic <Odyssey>.

<Figure 3.4> Ulysses and the Sirens (Leon Belly, 1867)

<Odyssey> is the sequel to Homer's series <Iliad>, which dealt with the Trojan War. <Odyssey> described the journey back to Odysseus' hometown 10 years after the Trojan War was over. Odysseus is sometimes called Ulysses, which is the Latin name for Odysseus. Odysseus was the legendary Greek king of Ithaka. The Sirens were sisters, sea fairies with half a woman and half a bird. They lived outside the inaccessible coral reefs and sang very sweet songs, seducing sailors passing by. When nearby sailors tried to get close to the Sirens, being enchanted with the beautiful sound of the songs, they were shipwrecked off the coast of the island, and died. Only two groups of people escaped this fatal attraction. They were Odysseus and his soldiers and captain Jason of the Argo ship and his sailors. The English word, 'siren song' (or siren call)' is used to mean something that is mesmerizing or deceiving. The word sometimes means "something that is very appealing and makes a person want to do something but that may have bad results" (Source: Merriam-Webster).

After winning the Trojan War, Odysseus was sailing to his hometown of Ithaca. Odysseus had beeswax sealed in the ears of his soldiers, so that they could not hear the Sirens' songs, and he tied himself to the mast. In this manner he could see off the challenge of the Sirens' temptation. Captain Jason and his sailors were also able to escape the danger with the help of Orpheus, who outperformed the Sirens' singing. Orpheus was a legendary musician, poet, and prophet in Greek mythology, and even stones were touched by the sound of his song.

The classical economist's monetary policy rule is to tie the growth rate of the money supply to some predetermined rule, as if Odysseus was tied up to the mast, so that he could do nothing and safely flow along the river. When the economy is in a recession or a boom, policymakers are easily tempted to take some discretionary policy actions. But classical economists warn of the danger of such discretionary policy. The message of the warning is that just because the economy is in a swamp of stagnation, the central bank should not take actions to lower interest rates by increasing the amount of money. By the same token, just because the economy is in a state of booming, the central bank should not take measures to raise interest rates by reducing the amount of money. Classical economists argue that regardless of whether the economy is in a recession or a boom, keeping the growth of the money supply constant at the rate of potential growth is the key to stabilizing the economy. This proposition is called the constant growth rate rule (CGRR). The constant growth rate rule contrasts with Keynesian discretionary monetary policy, which is a counter-cyclical policy rule. If the economy is in a recession, the central bank should expand the money supply; conversely if the economy is booming, the central bank should contract the money supply. The debate concerning classical 'rule' versus Keynesian discretion will be revisited later.

9

SUPPLY-SIDE ECONOMICS

Supply-side economics, rooted in classical economics (especially Say's law), emerged as a solution to stagflation in the late 1970s, and began to draw an increasing attention with the start of the Reagan government in the United States. Supply-side economics is often criticized as 'trickle-down economics' by opponents, but it is called free-market economics by supporters. The English word, 'trickle down' means dripping water from the top to the bottom. The name of trickle-down economics is given in the sense that if taxes, especially taxes on interest and dividend income earned by wealthy people were lowered, then they would spend a lot of money, and the effect of such spending would flow downwardly from the rich to the poor and stimulate the entire economy.

Trickle-down economics sharply contrasts with Keynesian economics and President Obama's 'bottom-up economics'. 'Bottom-up' means rising up from the bottom to the top. It is the opposite of trickle-down, indicating the countercurrent of water. Just as the warm air gradually spreads to the ceiling, thus making the entire room warm when one makes a fire in the stove on the floor, the entire economy will be stimulated as more subsidies are provided to the poor.

Recently, interest in supply-side economics has been growing among the media and some conservative politicians. Prominent economists, such as Nobel prize-winning economists, Gary Becker of the University of Chicago and Robert Mundell of the University of Columbia, also agree with the proposals of supply-side economics. Politicians who are in favor of supply-side economics include Bob Dole and Jack Kemp, former Republican presidential candidates. Steve Forbes, the publisher of economics magazine, *Forbes* is also in sympathy with supply-side economics.

Economists who have been working on supply-side economics include Arthur Laffer, Jude Waniski, and George Guilder. Particularly, Laffer is famous for developing the Laffer curve. Some supply-side economists such as McNamee even argue that supply-side economics has risen to the status of mainstream economics that has replaced Keynesian economics. Supply-side economics is an economic discipline that emphasizes the importance of the supply side of the economy, that is, labor productivity, savings, and investment. The rationale for supply-side economics is that by increasing the economy's total supply capacity, it can control inflation and promote economic growth in the long run, thus strengthening the economy's self-regulating capabilities.

According to supply-side economists, the most effective way to deal with inflation and unemployment simultaneously is to increase the supply side of the economy. As the economy's total supply capacity increases, inflation will drop and employment will increase, and naturally the economy will reach its goal of low inflation and low unemployment. The most important and effective policy to promote economic growth without inflation is to give workers an incentive to work more, capitalists an incentive to save more, and entrepreneurs an incentive to invest more. As the natural consequence, they pay much attention to the factors that shift the economy's aggregate supply curve to the right. They propose lowering the marginal income tax rate on labor income earned by workers, lowering the marginal income tax rate on capital income such as interest and dividend income earned by capitalists, and lowering the marginal income tax rate on profits earned by entrepreneurs.

Supply-side economists argue that lowering the marginal tax rate on labor income and capital income such as interest and dividends not only induces more labor, more savings, and more investment, but also more tax revenues through the revitalization of the economy. Supply-siders argue that if people work harder and more, output will increase, and accordingly tax revenues will increase. Since the government's tax revenues are given by taxable income multiplied by the tax rate (tax revenue = taxable income x tax rates), the taxable income must increase more proportionally than the tax reduction in order for the tax revenues to increase. Supply-side economists argue that it is possible for a lower tax rate to bring greater tax revenues.

This proposition is implied in a simple illustration of the relationship between tax rates and tax revenues, known as the Laffer curve. The Laffer curve will be discussed in detail later, but simply speaking, there is an optimal income tax rate that maximizes tax revenues. The Laffer curve indicates that if the current tax rate is higher than the optimal tax rate, the government can increase tax revenues by lowering the tax rate. However, if the current income tax rate is lower than the optimal income tax rate, the tax rate reduction will simply result in a decrease in tax revenues. According to one study, the optimal income tax rate that maximizes tax revenue in the United States is about 79%, which is more than three times higher than the current average income tax rate. The results of this study indicate that the current income tax rate in the United States is much lower than the optimal tax rate on the Laffer curve. Thus, contrary to the argument of supply-siders, if the income tax rate is lowered further from the current level, U.S. tax revenues may decrease.

We cannot say that the conclusion of supply-side economics is wrong because the current income tax rate in the United States is lower than the optimal tax rate on the Laffer curve. Even if the current tax rate is lower than the optimal tax rate on the Laffer curve, the reduction of the marginal income tax rate could promote savings and investment. There is no question that increases in savings and investment are conducive to economic growth.

CHAPTER 2

A GOVERNMENT-CONNECTED ECONOMY: KEYNESIAN ECONOMICS

1

THE LEGEND OF AUTUMN

The two most painful economic disasters over the past 100 years took place in the autumn. The Great Depression that was triggered by a sudden crash of the U.S. stock market occurred in October 1929, and the Great Recession in 2008 that was sparked by the fall of Lehman Brothers occurred in September 2008. In addition, the Black Monday crash that slashed the Dow Jones Industrial Average by 22% in a single day also took place in October 1988. Mark Twain (1876), who wrote <The Adventures of Tom Sawyer>, once said that “October is one of the particularly dangerous months in the equity investment”. Twain’s quip hints that economic disasters might be related to emptiness and anxiety cherished in people’s minds in a season of falling leaves.

In the autumn of 2011 when the shadow of the global economic crisis was hanging down, many highly educated unemployed people began protesting on Wall Street, the heart of the world’s capital markets, shouting the slogan “Occupy Wall Street”. The demonstrations were touched off in the autumn of falling leaves on the streets. In the background of these protests of anger, there was a perception that the main culprit behind the global economic crisis was the financial capitalists’ greed. Subsequently, protests began to spread on a national scale, and the throng of demonstrators was getting bigger. Some people called the protests the 'America Fall,’ likening it to the 'Arab Spring’.

Is there any causal relationship between autumn and an economic disaster? Autumn is the season of melancholy following the summer which was shining and lustrous. As Rainer Maria Rilke sang in the <Autumn Day>, people may feel empty and fall into solitude when autumn colors become yellowish brown, and leaves are falling. People who have no homes may no longer want to build their homes, and people who are alone may be left with hollowness and wish to remain alone for so long.

Lord, it’s time. The summer was immense.
Lay your shadow on the sundials
and let loose the wind in the fields.

Bid the last fruits to be full.
give them another two more southerly days.
Press them to ripeness, and chase
the last sweetness into the heavy wine.
Whoever has no house now will not build one anymore.
Whoever is alone now will remain so for a long time,
will stay up, read, write long letters
and wander the avenues, up and down,
restlessly, while the leaves are blowing.

Even if there is no direct link between autumn and an economic crisis, there is high likelihood that economic disasters occur more often in autumn, if people's expectations play an important role in economic behavior. As you can see from self-fulfilling expectations, when people expect something to happen in the future and many act according to such expectations, it can actually happen. Autumn is the transit to winter. People may have a feeling of loss in their heart and experience loneliness. Sometimes people feel let down. When uncertainty about the future increases, fear can prevail, and it can have a major impact on people's economic activities. During the Great Depression, President Roosevelt (1933) said that "The only thing we have to fear is fear itself". Bank runs and financial panics in most cases occur as a result of people's fear.

In fact, modern economic theory shows that people's psychological expectations have an undeniable effect on individual decision making, and that they are directly related to economic fluctuations. Behavioral economics explores how people's psychological and behavioral motives affect economic phenomena. In mainstream economics, expectations have long been incorporated into economic decisions. Most notably, the theories of adaptive expectations and rational expectations emerged in the 1960s and 1970s as major rivals to Keynesian economics. It would be interesting to further study whether the occurrence of more economic disasters in autumn is simply a coincidence or a causal consequence of psychological expectations and to delve into the relationship between an economic depression and psychological depression. Keynesian economics was born to deal with economic depressions.

2

THE COLLAPSE OF THE CLASSICAL DOCTRINE AND THE BIRTH OF KEYNESIAN ECONOMICS

The rosy picture of the economy painted by classical economists was torn apart in the midst of the Great Depression that ruined the U.S. and European economies in the 1930s. In 1933, when the Great Depression reached its nadir, the U.S. unemployment rate soared to 25%. The Great Depression was not only the worst economic disaster that made many people miserable, but it also brought about the fall of the classical doctrine that dominated Western economic thought for 160 years. The Great Depression lasted for more than 10 years without showing any sign that the economy would move toward full-employment equilibrium. This means that the classical self-correcting model did not work, and the failure of the classical doctrine heralded the birth of a new breed of economics. The Keynesian Revolution occurred in 1936 and shook the economic paradigm.

When the Great Depression devastated the U.S. and European economies, Keynes proposed new prescriptions that were totally different from those of the classical school. It was a transition from the microeconomic approach of the classical school, which focused on the behavior of individual economic agents and the efficient allocation of resources by market forces, to the macroeconomic approach which focused on the management of aggregate demand and the government's active role in the allocation of resources.

The imminent threat brought about by the Great Depression was a possible revolt against the capitalist system, and Keynes thought that a Copernican shift of thinking was needed to avoid any emergence of totalitarianism such as communism or fascism. Keynes published a monumental work titled *The General Theory of Employment, Interest, and Money* (commonly known as *The General Theory*) in 1936 when the Great Depression was in full swing. He challenged the classical foundations in the introduction of *The General Theory*.

"I have named the title of the book *The General Theory of Employment, Interest and Money*, putting emphasis on the prefix 'General'. The purpose of such a title is to contrast the characteristics of my arguments and conclusions with those of classical theory. I would argue in this book that the propositions of classical theory can only be applied in special cases and not in general cases. Moreover, the characteristics of the special case assumed by classical theorists may not be consistent with the economic reality in which we actually live, and the conclusion of classical theory is that if we try to apply it to the facts of experience, it will lead to misleading and absurd results" (Source, Keynes, 1936).

Keynes disagreed with classical economists' claim that the economy always tends to gravitate toward a state of full employment equilibrium. He emphasizes that prices and wages do not move flexibly, as classical theorists thought. He saw the power of monopolistic firms that had control over the prices of their products and the existence of strong labor unions that made wages downwardly inflexible even under severe recession. According to Keynes, unemployment is not a temporary phenomenon that exists only in the period during which wages are adjusted to equilibrium wages but is a more general phenomenon. The existence of strong labor unions makes not only wages sticky, but also the laying off and displacement of workers difficult.

Then how did Keynes and his followers (Keynesian economists) diagnose the cause of unemployment? When consumers are not willing to consume, and firms are not willing to invest due to uncertainty about the future state of the economy, some of products and services produced by firms remain unsold and are stocked up as inventory. As this happens, firms have no choice but to lay off workers and reduce production. Thus, unemployment is caused by a decrease in aggregate demand by consumers and business firms in the private sector. In short, insufficient effective aggregate demand is the main cause of unemployment. Therefore, the government must increase its spending or lower taxes to supplement the insufficient aggregate demand in the private sector.

Keynes was more concerned with the unemployment problem, and the inflation issue was not his main concern. For this reason, Keynesian economics is sometimes called depression economics. Keynesian economics was constructed based on the assumption that prices, wages, and interest rates were fixed. When the economy is in depression, prices, wages, and interest rates tend to remain unchanged. That's why Keynesian economics is also called the fixed-price model. The rigidity of prices and wages in the market is the major source of market failure. A market failure is a situation in which the market cannot achieve optimal allocation of resources. As we discussed previously, there are many factors for market failure: market failure occurs frequently when the market takes the form of monopoly or oligopoly; when there is an external economy; when public goods are produced; and when information asymmetry and transaction costs exist. In such cases, the optimal allocation of resources is not achieved by the market.

Thus, Keynesian economists advocate for the government's active role in the management of aggregate demand in the economy. They argue that the government can and should manage the economy appropriately by the use of aggregate demand policy such as fiscal and monetary policy. Keynesian economics is an economic discipline emphasizing the government-led management of aggregate demand, whereas classical economics is an economic discipline emphasizing the working of self-curing forces of the economy.

3

THE ECONOMY THROUGH THE LENS OF THE KEYNESIAN ECONOMIST: *CARPE DIEM* AND *MEMENTO MORI*

There are famous Latin sayings that best describe life and death. They are two maxims, *carpe diem* and *memento mori*. *Carpe diem* is known to have originated from a Latin poem (*carpe diem. quam minimum credula postero*) by Roman poet Horatius. *Carpe diem* means "Seize the day". The message can be phrased as meaning "Do your best to live today" or "Enjoy this moment".

This phrase became famous because of the movie <Dead Poets Society>. Keating, a high school teacher who was the protagonist of the movie, introduced the word, '*carpe diem*' to students. Keating told the students: "We don't read and write poetry because it's cute. We read and write poetry because we are members of the human race. And humans are filled with passion. Medicine, law, business, engineering, these are noble pursuits and necessary to sustain life. But poetry, beauty, romance, love, these are what we stay alive for." And he said to them: "*Carpe diem*. Enjoy the present" (Source: www.wikipedia.org/Dead Poets Society).

His remark that medicine, law, economics, and technology are important means to sustain life, but-poems, beauty, romance, and love are the purpose of life may sound romantic, but no one would deny that materialistic happiness does not necessarily bring about true happiness, and spiritual enjoyment such as beauty, romance, and love may be more important for true happiness. Keating's word of "Enjoying the present" is in parallel with the purpose of life symbolized by poems, beauty, romance, and love. The movie got even more attention because actor Robin Williams who starred as Keating killed himself in September 2014. He lived as a famous actor and a top-class comedian who amused many people, but ended his life without overcoming anguish. He became a dead poet, like the movie title. Before Keating finished his lecture, he cited Walt Whitman's poem entitled "O Me, O Life!"

O me! O life! of the questions of these recurring,
Of the endless trains of the faithless, of cities fill'd with the foolish,
Of myself forever reproaching myself,
(for who more foolish than I and who more faithless?)
Of eyes that vainly crave the light, of the objects mean, of the struggle ever
renew'd,
Of the poor results of all, of the plodding and sordid crowds I see around me,
Of the empty and useless years of the rest, with the rest me intertwined,
The question, O me! so sad, recurring--what good amid these,
O me, O life!
Answer:
That you are here—that life exists and identity,
That the powerful play goes on, and you may contribute a verse.

Another maxim that is more closely related to the Keynesian position is '*memento mori*'. This Latin epigram means that "Remember that you shall die" or "Remember death". The message that this proverb delivers is that "Don't be proud and intoxicated as if you would live forever". You must remember that you will surely die. *Carpe diem* and *memento mori* are like the two sides of the same coin. We all should remember that one day we must die and realize that my life given today is a gift, and we should enjoy the pleasure of the moment without concern for the future.

Keynes might also have *carpe diem* and *memento mori* in his mind when he wrote *The General Theory.* Keynes witnessed the tragedy of the Great Depression and said: "In the long run, we all die". When looking at people who were on the streets looking for food, he might think that we would have to do something today. Paul Samuelson who won the Nobel prize in economics described the atmosphere of the Depression era from the Keynesian perspective in his famous economics textbook, *Economics*:

"After the Great Depression, critics had regarded the classical doctrine as outdated theory. They looked at people waiting in line to get bread and people selling apples at the corner of the street and raised the question of "Why talk about scarcity? Or efficiency? Or growth? Or equity? Throw away the tools of supply and demand that describe the function of market prices. We are now living in a new era where everything has changed. Saving is now a harm to the economy rather than a virtue. Typhoons and wars are blessings in that they increase jobs and provide food for hungry unemployed people" (Source: Samuelson, 1948).

As long as the economy runs smoothly, the classical proposition that the economy moves toward equilibrium in the long run may sound great. It is natural, however, that the classical doctrine is no longer convincing when the economy is in a state of deep stagnation for a long period. For those who don't have a job and worry about meals right away, the short run is meaningful, and the rosy promise for the long run is meaningless.

Keynes' message was that "Let's forget the long run and focus on short run problems". Instead of clinging to the question of whether the economy could ultimately reach an equilibrium state, he asked what short-term factors caused the Great Depression and what society could do to cure it. When Keynes said "we all die in the long run", he didn't mean that long-term economic problems weren't important at all. What he tried to emphasize was that if the government took a 'wait and see' attitude, for practical purposes there would be no way out of the Great Depression.

Keynes sensed a very desperate political and social atmosphere in which people could not wait until the market cured the Depression and brought full employment to the economy. Keynes feared that citizens might choose some form of totalism that swept Germany and Italy or even communism that took place in Russia if immediate measures to alleviate unemployment were not taken in the short run. He argued that all of the classical choices were of no use in front of such threats. He voiced his worry, saying that the government should take policies to reduce unemployment right now and not wait for a long-run equilibrium to prevent such a political upheaval. In conclusion, Keynesian economics focuses on government intervention and on short-term policy measures tailored to underemployment equilibrium.

4

AGGREGATE DEMAND (AD) MATTERS IN THE DETERMINATION OF OUTPUT

Keynes challenged Say's law, which states that "Supply creates its own demand". Keynes reversed this theme, arguing that "Demand creates supply". Keynes said that the economic downturn, like the Great Depression, occurs as the result of a lack of effective aggregate demand in the private sector. Therefore, the government needs to replenish insufficient private demand by using government spending, subsidies and taxes to stimulate the economy and lower unemployment.

A country's macroeconomy consists of four sectors: households, firms, governments, and foreign sectors. First, households purchase goods and services produced by firms with the income they earn from selling their production resources. The purchase of goods and services by households is called consumption (C). Firms produce goods and services using capital and labor. The purchase of capital goods (factories, machines, tools, etc.) by firms is called investment (I). The governments (federal, state, and local) collect taxes and use a portion of the collected taxes to purchase goods and services, which is called government purchases (G). The government also uses part of the taxes to finance subsidies for the poor and the needy, which is called transfer payments (TP). Lastly, firms sell goods and services produced to households, firms, governments, and foreigners. Selling goods and services to foreigners is called exports (EX) and buying goods and services from foreigners is called imports (IM). The difference between exports and imports is called net exports (NX = exports - imports). Net exports are sometimes called trade balances in trade theory.

What is aggregate demand (AD) and how is it determined? Aggregate demand is the amount of goods and services that economic agents (households, firms, governments, and foreigners) are willing and able to purchase. In other words, aggregate demand is the demand for aggregate output (GDP). GDP is equal to the total market value of all final goods and services produced in an economy during a specified period. The final goods and service produced in the economy are purchased by households (consumption), business firms (investment), federal, state, and local governments (government purchases) and foreigners (exports).

GDP = Consumption + Investment + Government purchases
+ Exports – Imports

Imports are the purchases of foreign goods by domestic buyers. We subtract imports from GDP because imported goods are produced in foreign countries. Aggregate demand (AD) is then defined as the sum of desired or planned consumption by households, planned investment by firms, planned purchases of goods and services by the governments, and planned purchases of goods and services by foreigners minus planned purchases of foreign goods and services by domestic buyers.

AD = Planned consumption + Planned investment
+ Planned government purchases +Planned net exports

Here we note that the components of GDP are *ex post* (realized or actual) consumption, investment, government purchases, and net exports, and the components of AD are *ex ante* (planned or desired) consumption, investment, government purchases, and net exports. When the economy is in a normal situation, households usually realize their desired consumption plan, so that there is no significant difference between planned and realized consumption. Similarly, governments set up their budgets and execute their planned programs (or purchases) according to their budgets, so that there is no significant difference between planned and realized government purchases. However, business investment is different. It is quite common that there is a big difference between planned and realized investment. Firms often change their planned investment projects as the prospects for the economy change, which makes investment highly volatile. There is also quite a big difference between planned and realized net exports, because net exports are heavily affected by foreign business cycles.

In the Keynesian system, AD is a key variable in the determination of national income (GDP). The Keynesian theory of income determination is a significant departure from the classical theory of income determination. As represented by Say's law, in the classical system, GDP is determined at the full-employment level by supply side factors such as physical quantities of labor and capital, and technological progress, and aggregate demand has no effect on the determination of output. However, in the Keynesian system, aggregate demand is a pivotal variable in the determination of output. When aggregate demand is not sufficient, then output is determined at the level below the full-employment output, and unemployment occurs.

5

CONSUMPTION IS THE LARGEST COMPONENT OF AGGREGATE DEMAND (AD)

Consumption is the buttress of the economy. This is true for both developed and underdeveloped countries. However, the importance of consumption in the determination of GDP is different across countries. For example, consumption constitutes about 70% of GDP in the United States, but the proportion of consumption to GDP is much lower in Japan (60%), South Korea (50%) and China (35%). As an economy becomes more advanced and richer, the share of consumption in GDP tends to rise, and it plays a more crucial role in stabilizing the economy.

Let's look in more detail at how consumption is determined. Consumption decisions are made by households. Consumption by households has a major impact on the short- and long-term performance of the economy. Consumption is the most stable component of GDP and functions as a buffer for the economy. When household income falls, people reduce consumption, but do not decrease consumption in proportion to the decline in income, thus mitigating the effect of the decline in income on the economy. Likewise, when income increases, people increase consumption, but do not increase in proportion to the increase in income, thus smoothing out economic fluctuations. Modern consumption theory finds that consumers try to keep consumption stable and even. This is because people have the propensity to keep their standard of living stable. This characteristic of consumption makes consumption the most stable component of GDP.

Since consumption demand is the largest component of aggregate demand, even a small change in consumption demand can significantly affect GDP. Thus, consumption demand is a macroeconomic variable that has a direct and strong impact on short-term economic fluctuations. In addition, households' current consumption decisions are closely related to savings. Since consumption affects household savings that is a key to sustainable economic growth, consumption demand also plays an important role in long-term economic growth. If households consume more, they save less, and vice versa. The United States has the highest share of consumption in GDP in the world, but the American savings rate is among the lowest.

Consumption is defined as the purchase of final goods and services by households. Consumption can be divided into the purchase of durable goods, the purchase of nondurable goods, and the consumption of services (consumer services). Durable consumer goods are consumer goods that can be used over a year or more, such as automobiles, furniture, TVs, and refrigerators. Non-durable consumer goods are consumer goods that are consumed within a year, such as food, beverages, gasoline, cigarettes, clothing, and shoes. Consumer services include intangible goods (services), such as education, travel, insurance, health care and medical treatments.

There are some subtle categories of consumption. First, the purchase of houses and buildings by households is not considered as consumption and is classified as investment. This is an exception to the measure of consumption which is defined as the purchase of final goods and services by consumers. Second, the purchase of stocks, bonds, and cryptocurrencies such as bitcoins is not considered as consumption, because stocks, bonds, and bitcoins are financial assets rather than goods, and thus the purchase of financial assets has no effect on GDP. As an illustration, we'll consider the purchase of various kinds of gold. If a consumer buys gold mines, such a purchase is not the behavior of consumption, but the behavior of investment because the consumer buys a title to gold mines. However, the purchase of gold jewelry by a consumer is classified as consumption. Finally, the purchase of intermediary goods by a consumer is not included in consumption because intermediary goods are not final goods for consumption. In this sense, if a consumer buys gold bars, such a purchase is not counted as consumption. The purchase of gold bars by consumers is treated as a portfolio investment.

In general, consumption of nondurable goods such as foods and consumer services such as medical treatments show a stable movement. However, the purchase of durable goods such as cars exhibit a very sensitive response to economic fluctuations. When the economy is in good condition, people buy more luxury cars and expensive furniture, but when the economy is not good, they first reduce spending on durable goods. Although overall consumption is the most stable component of GDP, consumption demand on durable goods could have an impact on short-term economic fluctuations.

However, the amount of durable goods that consumers purchase each year accounts for a very small portion of the total amount of existing durable goods that consumers already hold, and thus spending on new durable consumption goods in each year is small. (In the United States, spending on durable goods accounts for about only 9% of total consumption.) Therefore, even if spending on durable goods fluctuates significantly each year, the impact on the overall economy is negligible. Thus, we can conclude that consumption moves with income, but is more stable than income fluctuations. The stability of consumption seems to be related to people's tendency to keep the standard of living stable. Annual income fluctuates quite sharply, but people try to maintain the distribution of consumption quite smoothly.

Several theories have been proposed to explain consumption smoothing. Keynes' theory of consumption is the basic consumption framework. Keynes in *The General Theory* maintained that current consumption depends on current disposable income, which is known as the absolute income hypothesis (AIH). Disposable income is income that people have after they pay various taxes to the government and receive various subsidies (transfer payments) from the government. Keynes proposed the following linear relationship between disposable income (DY) and consumption (C):

$$C = a + b\,DY$$

where a is the intercept, and b is the slope. The intercept term (a) indicates how much people consume when income is zero. Even if income is zero, we could not stop consumption.

How do people consume without having income? First, you could get help from your family members, relatives, or friends. Or you might withdraw money from your bank accounts or sell stocks or bonds or even real estate. In the worst case, you may use credit cards or borrow money to support your consumption. The portion of consumption represented by the intercept measures consumption supported by these non-income factors. This kind of consumption is called autonomous consumption. In macroeconomics, any expenditure that is not induced by income is called autonomous expenditure. The slope (b) indicates how much consumption increases when disposable income increases by $1. For example, if the slope is 0.8, it means that when income increases by $100, people increase their consumption by $80. In macroeconomics, this ratio is called marginal propensity to consume (MPC).

Keynes assumes that the MPC is greater than 0 but less than 1. This is because the consumer does not spend all of the increased disposable income for consumption and saves part of it. Individuals' MPC could be greater than 1, but in the economy as a whole the MPC is less than 1. Before the global economic crisis in 2008, a very unusual phenomenon occurred in the United States. The U.S. MPC was greater than 1 for a while (about two quarters). It tells us that American consumers consumed more than their disposable income during this period. This overconsumption partly contributed to the 2008 economic crisis.

Keynes also assumes the MPC to be highly stable. The stability of the MPC has very important policy implications. This is because policymakers can predict the effect of fiscal policy or monetary policy on the economy based on the stable MPC. The assumption that the MPC is stable is in a similar vein to the classical assumption that the income velocity of money is constant or at least stable. The stability of the MPC is the underpinning of the Keynesian income-determination model, and the stability of the income velocity of money forms the core of the classical quantity theory of money. Looking at it from a different aspect, the stability of the MPC means that the goods market is stable in the Keynesian world, and the stability of the income velocity of money means that the money market is stable in the classical world.

In contrast to Keynes' view that current income is an important variable in consumption decisions, Friedman proposed the permanent income hypothesis (PIH), which states that current consumption is influenced by the expected future income that is the discounted present value of a future income stream. According to Friedman, people's income undergoes fluctuations due to unexpected factors, but nonetheless, consumption is relatively stable because consumption depends on permanent income, not current income. Permanent income is the average income people expect to earn over the long term and is therefore stable.

MIT Professor Franco Modigliani who won the Nobel prize in economics developed the life cycle hypothesis (LCH). The life cycle hypothesis demonstrates that current consumption is determined by the earnings consumers expect to make during their life cycle. Modigliani argues that the total earnings including labor income and capital income that an individual is expected to make throughout his life has the most significant impact on consumption.

The most important variable affecting life cycle income is retirement. Many people plan to retire at the age of about 60~70, and their income drops sharply when they retire. However, consumers do not want their living standards to drop sharply, too. In other words, they generally want to maintain the same standard of living they enjoyed before retirement. Therefore, in order to maintain the same level of consumption as before retirement, they must save more and consume less when they earn more during the peak of their life cycle. Modigliani's life cycle hypothesis provides a very appealing framework for consumption theory, as the population is rapidly aging, and the 100-year-old life cycle is not a distant future. The sharp decline in earned income after retirement and the need for an even distribution of consumption tells us that it is important to balance life-time consumption and life-time savings.

We have overviewed the three representative theories of consumption: Keynes' absolute income hypothesis (AIH), Friedman's permanent income hypothesis (PIH), and Modigliani's life cycle hypothesis (LCH). They all attempt to explain consumption smoothening. Each theory has some merits and weaknesses, but Modigliani's LCH has received most empirical support.

6

INVESTMENT, GOVERNMENT PURCHASES AND NET EXPORTS: THE REST OF THE CHARIOT WHEELS

We have seen that aggregate demand in an open economy is equal to the sum of planned (or desired) expenditures on consumption, investment, government purchases, and net exports. Although the sum of investment, government purchases, and net exports constitutes only 30% of GDP in the United States, the small sum does not mean a small role in the determination of GDP. It is as if any of the four wheels of a chariot did not function well, the chariot could not roll forward smoothly.

In the Keynesian system, investment accounts for only a small portion of GDP, but it is the most volatile component of GDP, and the volatility of investment is the main culprit of business cycles. In the United States, the proportion of investment in GDP has varied from 2.9% to 20% over the past 100 years or so. At the same time, business investment is also the main source of technological progress. Thus, every country is vital in promoting investment.

Where does the variability of investment come from? First, one explanation for the volatility of investment is that income (GDP) is not an important determinant of investment demand. Keynes argues that investment does not depend on income. This kind of investment is called autonomous investment. Autonomous expenditure in the Keynesian system refers to any expenditure category that does not depend on the level of income. Instead, investment is heavily affected by interest rates in the Keynesian system. The volatility of investment primarily comes from the sensitivity of investment to interest rates. Second, although interest rates are the most important determinant of investment when the economy is in a normal state, interest rates have little effect on investment when the economy is in deep stagnation. When the economy is in recession, investment is overwhelmingly affected by expectations of the future state of the economy.

Expectations of the future state of the economy are precarious. If business firms are optimistic about their future profitability, they invest more. If they are pessimistic about their profitability, they invest less. When the economy is expected to slow down, firms will not be able to sell their products and they are not willing to invest, even though interest rates are low. When Japan experienced the 'Lost Two Decades', Japan vigorously pursued low interest rate policy, but could not revive investment sentiment. During the global economic crisis in 2008, the United States also maintained an interest rate of almost zero, but U.S. investment fell sharply on the contrary. Thus, even if policymakers try to promote investment by lowering interest rates, such a policy has little effect when the economy is in a deep stagnation. These lessons tell us that it is important to stimulate investment sentiment rather than to lower interest rates when the economy is in recession.

Because of the vital importance of investment, many countries often attempt to promote private investment using a carrot and stick strategy. In the capitalist system, the government cannot force firms to increase their investment. The government usually uses investment incentives and tax policy. Can policymakers stimulate investment by lowering taxes on investment? What is a prime for investment is a challenging issue to many economists. Classical economists maintain that it is most important to lower the marginal tax rate on capital gains and corporate profits. However, Keynesian economists argue that it is important to restore confidence in the future of the economy through drastic fiscal spending. Existing studies have reported conflicting results on the effectiveness of tax incentives in stimulating business investment. Yuhn and Bennett (2016) have investigated the effects of the Bush tax cuts enacted in 2001 and 2003 in the United States and found little impact of the tax cuts on marginal investment incentives. This conclusion seems to support the Keynesian position. After all, business firms determine their investment decisions mainly based on the future profitability of their investment projects. Where there is profit, there is investment

The third component item of aggregate demand is government purchases (G). Government purchases consist of government consumption and government investment. First, government consumption includes purchasing consumer goods such as gasoline, cars, computer hardware and software, etc. It also includes paying salaries and wages for government officials and military personnel. Government investment includes space exploration, defense system build-ups, and infrastructure construction such as highways, roads, bridges, airports, fire stations, police stations, However, government purchases do not include any social welfare expenditures such as social security benefits, unemployment compensations, childcare money, Medicare and Medicaid because these transfer payments are kind of gifts from the government and not part of GDP. The share of government purchases in GDP varies from country to country. If a country engages in the private economy and social programs more heavily, the proportion of government purchases in GDP tends to be larger. Some research shows that countries with a high proportion of government spending in GDP have lower income inequality, but such a finding is still controversial.

In the Keynesian system, it is assumed that government purchases are given exogenously and are not determined within the model. In other words, government purchases are determined by the government as part of its fiscal policy, and not influenced by income (real GDP). Thus, government purchases are treated as an exogenous variable or an autonomous expenditure in the Keynesian system.

The last component of aggregate demand is net exports. Net exports are given by the difference between exports (EX) and imports (IM). Exports are sales of domestically produced goods and services to foreigners, which represents the inflow of foreign income into the domestic economy. On the other hand, imports are the purchases of foreign goods and services by domestic buyers, which represents the leakage of domestic income out of the domestic economy. A country's exports depend on foreign income, which is beyond the control of the domestic economy. Thus, exports are treated as 'given' or an exogenous variable. On the other hand, a country's imports are heavily dependent on domestic income. Thus, U.S. imports are induced by U.S. income, and therefore imports are treated as an induced expenditure. If we assume that imports increase linearly with income, the relationship between imports (IM) and income (Y) is given by

$$IM = c + m\,Y$$

where the intercept term (c) represents autonomous imports that do not depend on income and the slope (m) represents the marginal propensity to import (MPI). The MPI shows how much imports increase when domestic income increases by \$1. If the MPI is 0.3, this means that if domestic income increases by \$1, imports increase by \$0.3. The U.S. MPI is close to 0.3, which is the largest among advanced countries.

We have discussed four components of aggregate demand (AD). They include consumption (C), investment (I), government purchases (G), and net exports (EX–IM). Out of the components of AD, consumption and imports depend on the level of domestic income, and thus, they are induced expenditures. On the other hand, investment, government purchases, and exports do not depend on the level of domestic income, and thus, they are treated as autonomous expenditures. The distinction between autonomous expenditures and induced expenditures is important in the Keynesian system, because only autonomous expenditures exert a multiplier effect, which will be discussed later.

7

How Are Output and Employment Determined in the Keynesian System? Demand Determines

When the Great Depression occurred in 1929, many people including Irving Fisher who were in the tradition of classical theory thought that the depression would end soon through the working of market forces. Against the backdrop of the optimistic atmosphere, Keynes provided a totally new paradigm of economics to reduce unemployment and revitalize the economy. He argued in *The General Theory* that an economic downturn, like the Great Depression, was due to a lack of effective aggregate demand in the private sector, and the depression of this nature could not be resolved by the market. He further argued that unemployment was not a transitory phenomenon, but rather a general phenomenon. In such a situation, the government should not leave the economy alone and instead should use its policy tools such as spending and taxes to make up the shortage of aggregate demand in the private sector. The Keynesian influence was not a storm in a teacup, but his idea was revolutionary at the time. Because the influence of the Keynesian doctrine was so great and strong that the Keynesian theory has been called the 'Keynesian revolution'.

Keynes was mainly concerned with how unemployment occurred and why national income (GDP) fluctuated in the short run. The main theme of his work was to demonstrate that government policy such as fiscal and monetary policy could be effectively used to cope with the depression. The Keynesian model was constructed based on the assumption that prices, wages, and interest rates were fixed. This assumption was made because his analysis mainly focused on depression and unemployment issues. For this reason, Keynesian theory is sometimes called 'depression economics'. When unemployment is widespread, it is not unreasonable to assume that prices, wages, and interest rates are fixed, and this assumption is not far from reality.

We previously defined aggregate demand (AD) as the sum of planned expenditures on consumption by households, investment by firms, government purchases by federal, state, and local governments, and net exports by foreigners. In the Keynesian system, the equilibrium level of aggregate output (real GDP) is determined when real GDP produced in the economy is matched by aggregate demand for the output.

Keynes' equilibrium condition: Real GDP = Aggregate demand (AD)

Since real GDP produced by a country represents the country's aggregate supply, Keynes' equilibrium condition means that the equilibrium level of output is determined at the point where aggregate supply is equal to aggregate demand. There is no fundamental difference between the Keynesian model and the classical model in that at the equilibrium level of output, aggregate demand is equal to aggregate supply. However, the implications of the equilibrium condition are quite different. The difference between the two schools is that the Keynesian aggregate supply curve is almost horizontal at some predetermined price level, whereas the classical aggregate supply curve is almost vertical at the full-employment level of output. Thus, in the Keynesian model, equilibrium output is determined by aggregate demand, whereas in the classical model, equilibrium output is determined by aggregate supply.

In short, classical equilibrium output is determined at the full-employment level of output, whereas Keynesian equilibrium output can be determined at the level lower than full-employment output. This equilibrium output is called underemployment level of output.

Since the aggregate supply curve shows the amount of output at various price levels, and the price level is fixed, the Keynesian aggregate supply (AS) curve is almost horizontal at the predetermined price level. Therefore, the Keynesian model does not rule out the possibility that the aggregate demand curve intersects the aggregate supply curve at the horizontal portion of the aggregate supply curve. Thus, aggregate output (GDP) could be determined at a level lower than full-employment output. In fact, Keynes thought that the underemployment level of output was a norm, not an exception. Since equilibrium output could be lower than full-employment output, unlike the classical model, aggregate output can be increased or decreased by the appropriate management of aggregate demand in the Keynesian system, As can be seen from the diagram, policymakers can increase equilibrium output to the level of full-employment output by shifting the aggregate demand curve to the right.

The idea that aggregate output was not determined at the full-employment equilibrium level and could be increased or decreased by government policies was a fresh shock. In particular, Keynes' theory came as a blessing for many suffering people inflicted by the Great Depression. People began to be fascinated by the new theory.

If the economy suffers external shocks, households and businesses will reduce consumption and investment due to uncertainty about the future of the economy. If the external impact on the economy is not serious, households and businesses will gradually reduce consumption or investment, and the economy will be able to restore resilience again. However, when external shocks come suddenly or with a force that is difficult to handle, households and businesses sharply reduce consumption and investment. As a consequence, aggregate demand in the private sector will decrease significantly.

If the decline in aggregate demand is large, however, the economy will not be able to recover by itself. The resilience of the economy can be likened to that of a ship. If the ship is tilted about 30 degrees, the hull may recover its resilience, but if the hull is tilted more than 45 degrees, it is difficult to return to its original position. Similarly, if the economy is on a severe downturn, the economy is no longer able to recover from the downturn. In such a case, Keynes' prescription would be that the government should use a crane or other tools to restore the tilted hull. In this way, if aggregate demand is revitalized again, the economy will come into action again. The economy recovers its equilibrium with the aid of government intervention, and the two intertwining forces of supply and demand are equalized.

We'll illustrate using the example of the U.S. economy how equilibrium output is determined in the Keynesian system. The U.S. economy produced about $21 trillion worth of goods and services in 2020. This amount is the equilibrium level of aggregate output. We can say that the U.S. economy produced $21 trillion worth of goods and services, and consumers, businesses, governments, and foreign buyers also wanted to buy $21 trillion worth of goods and services in 2020. In this sense, equilibrium aggregate output (real GDP) is determined at the level where real GDP is equal to aggregate demand.

Aggregate demand (AD) = Real GDP = $21 trillion

If the U.S. economy produced $22 trillion worth of goods and services (aggregate supply), but households, businesses, governments, and overseas buyers wanted to buy only $21 trillion worth of goods and services (aggregate demand), some products and services would not be sold. There would be an excess supply or a surplus of goods and services by $1 trillion in the economy. Firms would try to reduce production because of the build-up of inventory, which in turn leads to a reduction in real GDP (aggregate supply) to the level of $21 trillion.

AS (= $22 billion) > AD (= $21 billion): Excess supply

<Figure 3.5> The Keynesian Aggregate Supply Curve (AS)

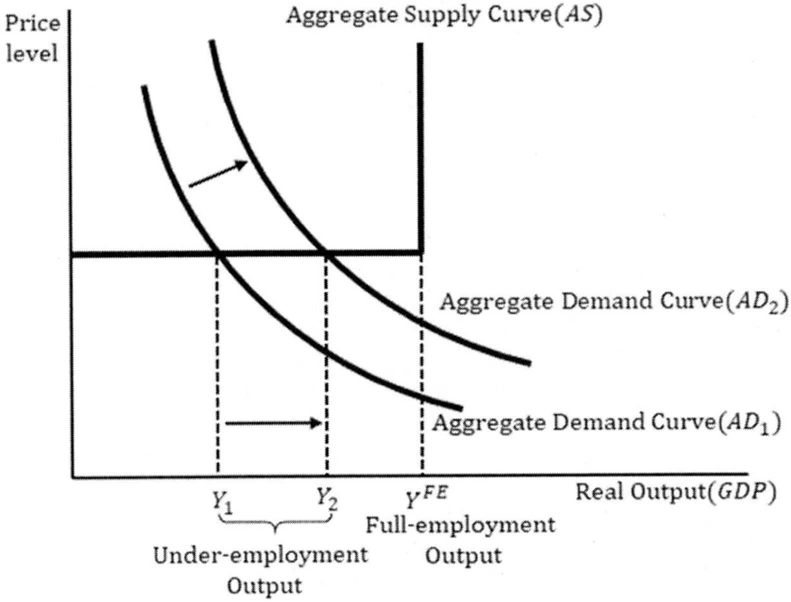

Conversely, if the U.S. economy produced 20 trillion worth of goods and services (aggregate supply), and households, businesses, governments, and overseas buyers wanted to purchase $21 trillion worth of goods and services (aggregate, demand), the economy would have an excess demand or a shortage of goods and services by $1 trillion in the economy. Firms will try to increase production to make additional profits. Firms will increase production to the level of $21 trillion until real GDP (aggregate supply) equals aggregate demand.

AS (= $20 billion) < AD (= $21 billion): Excess demand

Thus, the equilibrium level of real GDP will be determined at the level of $21 trillion, because at the level of output, there will be neither a surplus nor a shortage of goods and services in the economy. That's why real GDP of $21 trillion is called the equilibrium level of output. Unlike the classical model, however, the equilibrium level of output determined in the Keynesian model does not always coincide with the full-employment level of output. Rather, it is a common phenomenon that the equilibrium level of output is below the full-employment level of output. The underemployment level of equilibrium output is an important feature that distinguishes the Keynesian model from the classical model.

As an illustration, suppose that the U.S. economy could produce $22 trillion worth of goods and services without promoting inflation. The maximum level of aggregate output that the U.S. economy could produce without promoting inflation is called the full-employment level of output or potential output. Put differently, potential output refers to the maximum level of output that the economy could produce when its resources such as labor and capital are fully utilized. If U.S. potential GDP is $22 trillion, but the United States actually produces only $21 trillion, then actual GDP falls short of potential GDP by $1 trillion. The U.S. economy is in a recessionary phase, and the U.S. unemployment rate is below the full-employment level of unemployment. In such a situation, the Keynesian model for income determination recommends that the government should use its policy to boost aggregate demand to the level of $22 trillion. The U.S. government can increase aggregate demand by increasing fiscal spending or by reducing taxes. The Keynesian model suggests that the government should continue to increase aggregate demand until actual GDP ($21 trillion) increases to potential GDP ($22 trillion). The Keynesian model concludes that as aggregate demand increases, so does aggregate output (GDP), which in turn leads the unemployment rate to fall to the full-employment level.

AS (= $22 billion) = AD (= $22 billion): Full-employment output

Are there any side effects of the Keynesian prescriptions? The most serious side effect is that inflation can rise. Another side effect is that an increase in government spending inevitably increases government deficits, which in turn leads to an increase in national debt. Because of these side effects, classical economists do not favor Keynesian policy prescriptions.

8

THE MAGIC OF THE ECONOMY: THE MULTIPLIER EFFECT

Classical economists (especially Adam Smith) argue that the invisible hand leads the economy to a state of equilibrium as if the economy is guided by the invisible hand. However, Keynesians show another magic that works in the economy. The Keynesian magic is the working of the multiplier. Keynesian economists see a virtuous cycle in the economy as aggregate demand comes into play. First, consider the case where investment increases in a closed economy with no trade and no income taxes in which there are only three sectors: households, businesses, and governments. Thus, we assume away the foreign sector. For convenience of discussion, we assume that all taxes consist of autonomous taxes that do not depend on income. In other words, there are no personal income taxes and corporate income taxes, and all taxes consist of sales taxes (or value-added taxes), property taxes, and inheritance taxes that do not depend on income. The sum of these autonomous taxes may be called lump-sum taxes.

When the prospect for the future economy looks good, firms plan to increase their investment. Suppose a firm decided to build a factory by investing $10 million. In order to build a factory, the company will first hire an architecture firm and construction workers needed to build the factory. The firm will also purchase construction materials such as iron beams and timbers. To simplify our discussion, we assume that the initial investment of $10 million is used to pay both the labor costs of architects and construction workers and the purchase of construction materials and equipment. Thus, incomes earned by architects and construction workers and the producers of construction materials and equipment will increase by $10 million. They are all consumers too, so they will use their increased income for consumption.

Let's say architects buy computers, construction workers buy clothes, and construction equipment producers buy trucks. If their marginal propensity to consume (MPC) is 0.8, they will use 80% of their increased income ($10 million x 0.8 = $8 million) to purchase these products. Now computer makers, apparel makers, and truck makers will earn \$8 million as the result of the initial investment. Since they are also consumers, they will use their increased income (\$8 million) for consumption.

Now computer makers buy furniture, clothing makers buy fabrics, and truck makers buy refrigerators. If their marginal propensity to consume (MPC) is also 0.8, they will spend 80% of their increased income (\$8 million x 0.8 = \$6.4 million) to buy the products. The economy is like a living organism. This income generation process does not end here. It goes on endlessly until additional income reaches zero. How will total income be generated in this country after going through such infinite progression? In a simple model in which a country's economy has no income taxes and no foreign trade, total income generated by the initial increase in investment (\$10 million) is given by:

$$\text{Increase in total income} = \left[\frac{1}{1-MPC}\right] \text{ x Increase in initial investment}$$

Plugging the numbers into this formula, we get:

$$\text{Increase in total income} = \left[\frac{1}{1-0.8}\right] \text{ x \$10 million}$$

$$= 5 \text{ x \$10 million} = \text{\$50 million}$$

In this simple model, if private investment increases by \$10 million, total income (GDP) will increase by \$50 million. There is a five-fold increase in GDP. The number 5 here is called the investment multiplier. This shows that some magical forces are working in the economy. No individual would make a killing in investment, but the economy as a whole would bring about a surprising result.

This multiplier effect is not confined only to an increase in investment. All autonomous expenditures have a multiplier effect. Thus, government expenditure and autonomous consumption also have a multiplier effect. The government expenditure multiplier is an important tool which Keynesian economists particularly emphasize. They maintain that the government should stimulate the economy by increasing fiscal expenditure when the economy is in recession because the increase in government expenditure has a strong multiplier effect. Thus, we have the following formulas:

$$\text{Increase in total income} = \left[\frac{1}{1-MPC}\right] \text{ x Increase in government expenditure}$$

$$\text{Increase in total income} = \left[\frac{1}{1-MPC}\right] \text{ x Increase in autonomous consumption}$$

It is worth noting that all the expenditure multipliers such as the investment multiplier, the government expenditure multiplier, and the autonomous-consumption multiplier have the same magnitude. They are all given by 1/(1-MPC). In our example, the government expenditure multiplier is 5, and the autonomous- consumption multiplier is also 5. This is because the multiplier works through the consumption of goods and services by households.

Is the multiplier effect so great in the real world? The answer is 'no'. The simple multiplier effect we havc so far discussed is greatly exaggerated for several reasons. First, we assumed that taxes all consisted of lump-sum taxes that did not depend on income. However, in the real world, personal income taxes and corporate income taxes depend on the level of income. If we introduce the income taxes into our income determination model, the story will be quite different. Some of the income we earn is taxed, and there is a leakage of income out of the circular flow of income. The inclusion of personal and corporate income taxes into the model makes the size of the expenditure multiplier much smaller. When we introduce income taxes into the model, the multiplier effect is given by

$$\text{Increase in total income} = \left[\frac{1}{1-MPC\ (1-Income\ tax\ rate)}\right] \text{ x Increase in government expenditure}$$

If the average income tax rate is 25% (0.25), the size of the expenditure multiplier is reduced to 2.5. If the government increases its spending by \$10 million to stimulate the economy, the multiplier effect becomes:

$$\text{Increase in total income} = \left[\frac{1}{1-0.8\ (1-0.25)}\right] \text{ x \$10 million}$$
$$= (2.5) \text{ x \$10 million} = \text{\$25 million}$$

Second, we looked at a closed economy that did not trade with foreign countries. Now, if we deal with an open economy that trades with foreign countries, the size of the expenditure multiplier becomes further smaller. In an open economy some of the domestic income we earn leaks out of the country, because a portion of our income goes abroad to purchase foreign goods and services. If the marginal propensity to import (MPI) is 0.3, this indicates that people spend 30 cents to buy foreign goods and services for every \$1 increase in domestic income. If the marginal propensity to import is included in the income determination model, the multiplier becomes even smaller.

$$\text{Increase in total income} = \left[\frac{1}{1-MPC\ (1-Tax\ rate)+MPI}\right] \text{ x}$$
$$\text{Increase in government expenditure}$$

In our example, the expenditure multiplier shrinks to 1.4.

$$\text{Increase in total income} = \left[\frac{1}{1-0.8\ (1-0.25\ )+\ 0.3}\right] \text{ x \$10 million}$$
$$= (1.4) \text{ x \$10 million} = \text{\$14 million}$$

So how big is the real-world multiplier? The size of the multiplier depends largely on the size of the income tax rate, the marginal propensity to consume (CPI) and the marginal propensity to import (MPI). Generally speaking, the higher the MPC, and the smaller the income tax rate and the smaller the MPI, the greater is the multiplier, and vice versa. Here we note that the size of the expenditure multiplier moves positively with the MPC but negatively with the income tax rate and the MPI. The reason is that domestic consumption stimulates the flows of goods and services, but income taxes and imports work as leakages of income out of the circular flow of income. Therefore, the size of the multiplier is different in each country. In the case of the United States, the marginal propensity to consume is greater than in any other country, but the marginal propensity to import is also greater than in any other country. Thus, it cannot be said that the multiplier of the United States is greater than that of other countries, because a larger MPC and a larger MPI could cancel out each other in the multiplier effect.

In addition, the Keynesian income-determination model is constructed under the assumption that prices, wages, and interest rates are fixed, so that the multiplier could become further smaller in an economy where prices, wages, and interest rates move more flexibly. Keynes himself conjectured in *The General Theory* that the actual multiplier would be less than 3 and fairly stable in the neighborhood of 2.5. However, classical economists are very skeptical of this multiplier effect. Economists such as Robert Barro criticize the multiplier effect as something of a voodoo myth. He called the Keynesian multiplier a voodoo multiplier.

Large-scale econometric models used by professional research institutes or universities for economic forecasting use hundreds of structural equations covering all sectors of the economy (monetary sector, tax, prices, wages, interest rates, and foreign sector). The actual size (average) of the expenditure multiplier estimated by the large-scale econometric models is slightly larger than 1. A recent study (Bryant, Holthau and Hooper, 1988) calculated the average of government expenditure multipliers estimated by eight large econometric models. According to their study, the multiplier reached about 1.4 in the first year of government expenditure, but after two years, the multiplier effect gradually began to diminish as the influence of the overseas sector exerted, and the multiplier effect of government expenditure almost disappeared in the fifth year.

Year	1	2	3	4	5
Multiplier	1.4	1.3	1.2	1.1	1.0

Is there such a thing as a multiplier effect in life? Sir William Golding, who was a British novelist, playwright, and poet says that there is a mystery in our lives as well, which resembles the working of the multiplier in the economy. Sir Golding is best known for his debut novel, *Lord of Flies* (1954). He was awarded the Booker Prize for *Rites of Passage* in 1980 and the Nobel Prize in Literature in 1983. *Time* magazine ranked him third on its list of "The 50 Greatest British Writers since 1945". He was known to write the following epigram titled <The Truth>.

> I think women are foolish to pretend they are equal to men,
> they are far superior and always have been.
> Whatever you give a woman, she will make greater.
> If you give her sperm, she'll give you a baby.
> If you give her a house, she'll give you a home.
> If you give her groceries, she'll give you a meal.
> If you give her a smile, she'll give you her heart.
> She multiplies and enlarges what is given to her.
> So if you give her any crap, be ready to receive a ton of shit.

<The Truth> is like applying the Keynesian multiplier effect to life. Amazingly, the multiplier effect of life feels more mysterious than the Keynesian multiplier effect.

9

THERE IS NO 'FREE LUNCH'

The expenditure multiplier seems to work like a will-o'-the wisp in the Keynesian system. If the magnitude of the multiplier is greater than 1, as the Keynesian model claims, this has very important policy implications. If that's the case, then the government can indeed enjoy a 'free lunch'. If the government pours \$1 trillion into the economy to boost the economy, national income (GDP) would increase by even more than \$1 trillion. Thus, policymakers will be tempted to boost the economy by expanding fiscal expenditure.

Moreover, Keynesian economists argue that the expenditure multiplier of the balanced budget is 1 in the simple model. This is called the balanced-budget multiplier theorem. A balanced budget is a policy in which the government collects, say, \$1 trillion in taxes to finance its spending of \$1 trillion. If the balanced-budget multiplier works, then the government would indeed have a magical policy tool. More specifically, the government collects \$1 trillion more in taxes and uses the tax revenues for its spending programs. In this way, the government can increase GDP by \$1 trillion without incurring any budget deficit. Let's look at the tax multiplier to learn more about the balanced-budget multiplier.

In the Keynesian system, not only government spending, but all other autonomous expenditures have a multiplier effect. Taxes can be divided into income taxes that depend on the level of income and autonomous taxes that do not. We have seen that government spending, business investment and autonomous consumption that do not depend on income all have the same multiplier, but the multiplier for autonomous taxes and transfer payments is different from the autonomous expenditure multiplier. The autonomous tax has the following multiplier effect in the simple model in which there are no income taxes and no foreign trade.

$$\text{Increase in total income} = \left[\frac{-MPC}{1-MPC}\right] \text{x Increase in autonomous taxes}$$

If the MPC is 0.8, the autonomous-tax multiplier becomes $-0.8/(1-0.8) =-4$.

We have the negative sign (−) in the tax multiplier because as taxes increase, national income decreases, *ceteris paribus*. Also, we have the MPC in the numerator of the tax multiplier. The reason is that taxes do not directly affect aggregate demand. Taxes first affect consumption, which in turn affects aggregate demand. On the other hand, transfer payments such as subsidies for low-income families and the stimulus checks during the coronavirus pandemic crisis have also a multiplier effect. The transfer payment multiplier is similar to the autonomous tax multiplier, but it has a positive effect on income.

$$\text{Increase in total income} = \left[\frac{MPC}{1-MPC}\right] \text{ x Increase in transfer payments}$$

Like taxes, transfer payments do not directly affect aggregate demand, but first affect consumption, and then consumption affects aggregate demand. Unlike taxes, however, transfer payments have a positive effect on income. As transfer payments increase, national income (GDP) increases, *ceteris paribus*. We have seen that in the real-world economy, the expenditure multiplier is about 1.4 to 1.0, but the size of the autonomous-tax multiplier and transfer payment multipliers will be smaller than the expenditure multiplier, because the tax and transfer payment multipliers affect indirectly GDP through their effects on consumption. This is one reason why Keynesians argue that spending increases are more effective and powerful than tax cuts in stimulating the economy.

Now we are ready to calculate the balance budget multiplier. If the government expenditure is financed by the same amount of tax increases (balanced budget), the net effect of these two fiscal policy actions on the economy is given by the sum of the government expenditure multiplier and the tax multiplier.

$$\text{Net increase in total income} = \left[\frac{1}{1-MPC}\right] \text{ x Increase in government spending}$$
$$+\left[\frac{-MPC}{1-MPC}\right] \text{ x Increase in taxes (= government spending)}$$

$$= \left[\frac{1-MPC}{1-MPC}\right] \text{ x Increase in government spending}$$
$$= [1] \text{ x Increase in government spending}$$

The balanced budget multiplier is equal to 1. The balanced-budget multiplier formula shows that national income increases as much as government spending increases. If the government increases its spending by $1 trillion financed by an equal amount of new taxes, GDP will increase by

$1 trillion. What is more surprising is that the government would not have to worry about budget deficits because the government maintains its balanced budget. This means that the government can indeed enjoy a free lunch.

In the Keynesian system, the size of all expenditure multipliers such as the investment, consumption and government purchase multipliers is greater than 1, except for the balanced-budget multiplier. The size of the balanced-budget multiplier is the smallest in the Keynesian system. However, most monetarists argue that the expenditure multiplier is actually smaller than one. In particular, Harvard economist Robert Barro and Stanford economist Robert Hall argue that government expenditure multiplier is around 0.8 under a war time economy and statistically equal to zero in the peace-time economy.

A government spending multiplier of zero means that there is no multiplier effect. It also tells us that there is no free lunch. Barro sarcastically says that "if an increase in government spending brings about an equal increase in national income (GDP), then there should be no reason why the government does not increase GDP by increasing its spending continuously and why unemployment occurs". Classical economists maintain that when the government increases its spending to stimulate the economy, spending in the private sector, especially investment spending, decreases almost by the same amount, so that government spending has little impact on the economy. It is argued by classical economists that spending in the government sector crowds out spending in the private sector such as investment, consumption, and net exports. This phenomenon is called the crowding-out effect. Put differently, any increase in government spending has the side effect of reducing private investment, consumption, and exports.

10

EFFECTS OF FISCAL POLICY IN THE KEYNESIAN SYSTEM

There are two types of aggregate demand policy. Both fiscal policy and monetary policy affect the economy through their effects on aggregate demand. However, the way in which fiscal policy and monetary policy affect aggregate demand is quite different. Fiscal policy is implemented by the government and Congress through changes in government expenditures, taxes, and transfer payments. Monetary policy is implemented by the central bank (the Fed in the United States and the Bank of England in the United Kingdom) through changes in the money supply and monetary conditions such as interest rates.

Professor Paul Krugman at New York University, a Nobel prize winner in economics and a preacher of Keynesian economics, has been crusading to prove the superiority of Keynesian economics in the real world. He has regularly contributed to the *New York Times* and received both accolades and criticisms from a large audience. The essence of Keynesian demand policy elaborated by Krugman can be summarized as follows.

- "Something is better than nothing." It is better for the government to roll up the sleeves and do something than to have the arms folded, leaving the economy alone. The reason is that when the economy is in deep stagnation, the market is not functioning properly.
- "Fiscal policy is better than monetary policy when the economy is in a crisis." When the economy is in a normal state, monetary policy through the adjustment of the money supply and interest rates may be more effective in stabilizing the economy than fiscal policy. However, when the economy is in a stagnation, fiscal policy is more effective as a policy tool to boost the economy than monetary policy. Monetary policy mainly affects the economy through the working of interest rates. When the economy is in a recession, it is difficult to expect the economy to be revitalized through lower interest rates. When the economy is cooling off, it is important to stimulate the

sentiment for consumption and investment. Adjusting interest rates may not be sufficient to kindle the economy and to revive it from deep stagnation.

- In this context, one can say that fiscal policy is better in dealing with unemployment, whereas monetary policy may be better in coping with inflation. The government could reduce government spending or increase taxes to solve the inflation problem, but such fiscal actions may be indirect and not be effective in curbing inflationary expectations. The central bank can easily cool off inflationary expectations by raising interest rates. On the other hand, monetary policy affects the economy across the board, but fiscal policy can target economically inflicted areas or people like a surgical operation. Inflation has an adverse effect on everyone, and no one can escape from inflation, but unemployment afflicts only people who are unemployed and their family members. Thus, monetary policy may not be proper for targeting only unemployed people, but fiscal policy can specifically focus on unemployed people.
- "Spending increases are better than tax cuts." Among fiscal policy tools, an expansion of expenditures is more effective than a reduction of taxes. The expansion of fiscal expenditure has a direct impact on certain sectors of the economy, while tax cuts have an indirect effect. Increased fiscal spending leads to increased consumption, but tax cuts are mainly used as savings by households. Furthermore, the government spending multiplier is greater than the tax cut multiplier, which indicates that an increase in government spending has a greater effect on income than a tax cut of the same size.
- "Fiscal spending in a gutty scale is better than fiscal spending in dribs and drabs." President Obama increased fiscal spending by $870 billion to revitalize the economy when the 2008 global economic crisis broke out. Krugman supported Obama's economic stimulus package but argued that the economic stimulus spending should have increased by about three times more than the stimulus package in order to quickly get the economy out of the woods. On the other hand, interest rate adjustments should be made by a small step (say, 0.25 percentage point adjustment at a time) in order for monetary policy to be more accurate and less shocking. When inflation is serious, the Fed sometimes adopts a big step (0.5 percentage point increase) or a giant step (0.75 percentage point increase).

The main theme of Keynesian economics is that aggregate demand plays a key role in determining national income and in managing economic fluctuations. In the capitalist economy, aggregate demand in the private sector (consumption, investment and exports) can sometimes be insufficient to buttress the ailing economy. In such a case the government can and should stimulate the economy by supplementing insufficient aggregate demand in the private sector through fiscal expansion. It is not a surprise that early Keynesian economists believed in the omnipotence of fiscal policy. It is also true that such Keynesian policy prescriptions generally worked well until the end of the 1960s after the Great Depression.

Of course, the side effects of Keynesian policy prescriptions were also serious. For example, prior to the Great Depression, developed countries such as the United States and the United Kingdom generally maintained a balanced budget, but the major developed countries have experienced budget deficits almost every year since the Great Depression, which might be blamed on Keynesian economics. Many nations have tended to resort to massive government spending whenever they have encountered a major recession. For instance, after the global economic crisis in 2008, the Obama administration made a massive increase in fiscal spending to rescue the economy from the crisis, and the fiscal deficit was snowballing, exceeding $1 trillion per year. When the coronavirus pandemic swept the globe, similar situations occurred. Many nations have attempted to overcome the crisis by pouring astronomical money into the economy.

In the Keynesian system, expansion of fiscal spending is considered the most effective policy tool to reduce unemployment, especially when the economy is in a severe recession. A serious adverse effect associated with lowering unemployment is that it could accompany inflation as a byproduct. Until the Great Depression, many countries including the United States were crippled by falling prices, deflation, except for hyperinflation in some European countries during World War I, but inflation has emerged as a major economic disease since the end of WWII. The latter half of the 21st century could be characterized as an anti-inflation period, and Keynesian economics was a contributor to the die-hard inflation in the latter half of the 21st century.

In sum, obsessed with the Keynesian model, the government may be easily tempted to raise GDP to the full-employment level through spending increases or tax cuts. However, in many countries these policy prescriptions are not easily adopted, nor do they have the effect that the government wants to achieve This is because an increase in government spending or a reduction in taxes has the side effects of raising inflation and market interest rates and increasing budget deficits and national debt.

11

EFFECTS OF MONETARY POLICY IN THE KEYNESIAN SYSTEM

Keynesian economists are a bit skeptical about the effectiveness of monetary policy in stimulating the economy, and this skepticism was even more pronounced among early Keynesians including Keynes himself. Unlike fiscal policy that has a direct effect on aggregate demand, monetary policy goes through several channels to affect aggregate demand. If the central bank pursues expansionary monetary policy by increasing the supply of money, interest rates first tend to fall. The interest rate is one of the key factors that determines the demand for investment in the Keynesian model. Firms mainly finance their investment by borrowing from banks. Thus, if the interest rate rises, the cost of investment increases, and accordingly firms reduce their investment. Conversely, if interest rates fall, firms expand their investment. In the second channel, lower interest rates lead to an increase in business investment. Investment is a component of aggregate demand. If investment demand increases, so does aggregate demand. We have already seen that an increase in aggregate demand leads to an increase in real GDP. Thus, we have the following channels of monetary policy.

$$\text{Money} \uparrow \Rightarrow \text{Interest rates} \downarrow \Rightarrow \text{Investment} \uparrow \Rightarrow \text{Aggregate demand} \uparrow \Rightarrow \text{GDP (Income)} \uparrow$$

This channel of monetary policy is called the Keynesian transmission mechanism of monetary policy.

On the surface, monetary policy in the Keynesian system also seems to be very effective in increasing employment and output. However, the effectiveness of monetary policy is guaranteed only when all channels in the Keynesian transmission mechanism work well. In this regard, Keynes himself and early Keynesians believed that monetary policy was not very effective. The ineffectiveness of monetary policy is mainly due to the following two reasons.

The first reason is that when the economy is in a recession, an increase in the amount of money does not lead to a drop in interest rates. Suppose that the central bank increases the money supply to stimulate economic activity. However, when the economy is in deep stagnation, the economy tends to fall into a liquidity trap. The liquidity trap is a phenomenon in which interest rates remain so low that any increase in the money supply does not lead to a further reduction in interest rates. During the global economic crisis and the corona pandemic crisis, the Fed implemented a new monetary policy tool known as quantitative easing (QE), because the short-term interest rate was so low that the Fed's traditional monetary policy tool such as open market operations did not work.

When the economy is caught in a liquidity trap, people don't want to deposit money because they receive interest close to 0%. In such a situation, bonds or stocks are not a good alternative to bank deposits, either. The yield on bonds or the return on stocks is also extremely low. People have no choice but to simply hold their increased money. Thus, if the economy is caught in a liquidity trap, interest rates will not move much, because money will not be circulated even if the monetary authorities increase the money supply. Thus, when the economy slips into a swamp of stagnation, the first channel does not work. The United States fell into the liquidity trap during the Great Depression in the 1930s and the Great Recession in 2008. Japan also experienced a liquidity trap during the period of the 'Lost Two Decades' in the 1990s and 2000s.

The second factor that makes monetary policy ineffective is that investment is not very sensitive to changes in interest rates. Keynes argues that when the economy is in a normal condition, business investment is highly sensitive to interest rates. However, when the economy is in deep stagnation, the effect of interest rates on investment goes haywire. If the prospects for the future economy are uncertain and pessimistic, firms will be cautious about investment, no matter how low the interest rate is. As a result, investment will not be able to absorb domestic savings. The supply of funds (savings) exceeds the demand for funds (investment), and this excess supply will not be eliminated, because interest rates will not fall further. This means that there is a problem with the second channel in the Keynesian transmission mechanism.

For these reasons, early Keynesians claimed that money does not matter. This position was related to the fact that Keynesian economics was more concerned with the unemployment problem and that monetary policy was not quite effective in resolving the unemployment problem. However, Keynesians gradually began to recognize the importance of monetary policy, and there were shifts in their attitude toward the importance of monetary policy. Their position has changed to "Money matters a little" to "Money matters" to "Money matters much".

In conclusion, in the Keynesian system, the government can use fiscal or monetary policy at its discretion to adjust aggregate demand and to manage the economy. Keynesian discretionary policy is termed under many different names such as aggregate demand management policy, economic stabilization policy, activist policy, fine-tuning policy, or counter-cyclical policy. They all emphasize that the government could manage the economy by intervening in the economy.

12

Rules versus Discretion: The Mississippi River Parable

When the monetary authorities conduct monetary policy, the question remains as to how to operate it. The question is related to whether to operate monetary policy passively according to predetermined rules or to use it actively at discretion that is deemed most desirable considering changes in economic conditions. There has been heated debate concerning the choice of rules versus discretion between modern classical economists (monetarists) and Keynesians. The debate is still on-going without a clear winner. We have seen earlier that classical economists use the Sirens analogy to emphasize the superiority of the rules.

Classical economists contend that monetary policy only affects inflation in the long run and has no real effect on the economy, while Keynesian economists maintain that monetary policy affects employment and real output to some extent even in the long run. Most economists today agree that monetary policy should be used as a tool to maintain low and stable inflation in the long run. However, there is a sharp debate between Keynesian economists and monetarists as to whether monetary policy should be used to alleviate economic fluctuations and business cycles.

The problem is that managing the economy is fundamentally different from managing natural phenomena or machines. One reason why it is difficult to manage the economy is that economic activity is greatly affected by people's expectations and psychologies that are uncontrollable. Unlike machines, people know that they are influenced by economic policy and have the ability to learn from past economic actions used by policymakers. As a result, economic representatives respond to such policy actions and behave in the best way to protect their interests. The focus of the debate is whether economic policies based on fixed rules minimize economic uncertainty in response to people's reactions, or whether policies based on discretionary management minimize uncertainty.

People (mainly Keynesian economists) who prefer discretion to rules would argue that the central bank should use policy tools that are deemed to be appropriate to achieve the ultimate goals of monetary policy: price stability, economic growth, high employment, etc. Supporters of discretionary policy further argue that it is silly for policymakers not to make the most of the new arrival of information for policy implementation. By tying itself up to a set of rules, the central bank gives up an advantageous position to use new information. They argue that it was too passive in dealing with the Sirens' temptation for Odysseus to tie himself to the mat of the ship to distance himself from the Sirens.

Meanwhile, economists (mainly monetarists) who support the rules have a philosophy that monetary policy should be autonomous in nature, and the central bank should implement monetary policy in accordance with a set of simple, pre-defined and announced rules to maintain the consistency and transparency of monetary policy. By doing so, policymakers could minimize the uncertainty of the economy arising from fluctuations in the supply of money.

Economists who advocate the rules argue that for a number of reasons the discretionary management of monetary policy is not only ineffective, but also even dangerous. First, the extent to which changes in the money supply or fiscal expenditure affect the real economy is variable in length and depth. Especially, it is not clear how long it will take for changes in the money supply or fiscal expenditure to take effect. This is called the time inconsistency problem of policy effect.

Generally, the effect of monetary policy on target variables appears differently until it has its final effect on the target variables. For example, it is known that the effect of a change in the amount of money on unemployment, inflation, or business investment takes about 6 to 18 months. On the other hand, the time path of the effect of monetary policy on prices and wages appears to be shorter, and the time path of the effect of monetary policy on asset prices such as interest rates, stock prices and bond prices is even shorter. The advocates of the fixed rules point out that due to the time lag, discretionary monetary policy could destabilize the economy by influencing the target variable only after the target variable was already stabilized.

They also argue that even if monetary policy plays a role in alleviating economic fluctuations to some extent, it is not advisable to use discretionary monetary policy because the central bank may be politically lenient to government pressures (especially during the election season). In particular, Friedman argues that in order to stabilize the economy, the central bank should increase the money supply at a constant rate that is consistent with the growth rate of potential GDP regardless of economic conditions. If the growth rate of potential GDP is 4 percent, then the money supply should grow at the rate of 4 percent or at a little bit higher rate each year. This proposition is known as the ‘constant growth rate rule‘ (CGRR). Friedman’s constant growth rate rule is in sharp contrast with the Keynesian discretion, which suggests the central bank to increase the money supply when the economy is in a recession and to decrease the money supply when the economy is overheated.

Keynesian economist Modigliani (1977) criticizes the proposal of the fixed rule in the following analogy: “The fixed rule is like telling a person who travels from St. Paul (the capital city of Minnesota which is close to the beginning of the Mississippi River) to New Orleans (a port city in southern Louisiana, where the Mississippi River ends) on an important business that it is silly to drive a car and instead to take a boat and to drift down the Mississippi River. This way, he can be sure that the Mississippi River’s water stream will take him to his destination safely. On the other hand, if he drives a car, he may change directions incorrectly, and even before he realizes that he has taken the wrong direction, he may soon be getting farther away from the final destination and may soon arrive in Alaska. There he is almost certain that he will come down with pneumonia, so that he may never get to New Orleans.” The Keynesian analogy of the Mississippi River is comparable to the classical analogy of the Sirens.

CHAPTER 3

NEOLIBERALISM

1

THE REFLUX OF KEYNESIANISM AND THE RISE OF NEOLIBERALISM

Classical economics had dominated Western economic thought for almost 160 years until the Great Depression. The Great Depression which ravaged the U.S. and European economies in the 1930s also shipwrecked the classical school of economics, the orthodox economics of the time. The influence of classical economics rapidly diminished in 1936 when Keynes published his monumental work, *The General Theory*. In academia, economics textbooks only dealt with Keynesian economics until the late 1960s, and classical economics was almost extinct in economics textbooks. Until the 1960s, most economists acknowledged themselves to be Keynesians. This kind of confession came from an unexpected person: Republican President Nixon was known to say, "We are now all Keynesians" (Source: *Time,* 1965)

However, classical economists centered around the University of Chicago in the United States, under the leadership of Milton Friedman, tried to rebuild the collapsed classical edifice in the late 1960s. Particularly, two oil crises that occurred in 1973 and 1978 struck a blow on Keynesian economics. In the aftermath of the two oil crises, the world economy faced the coexistence of high inflation and high unemployment. This phenomenon is known as stagflation, the combination of stagnation and inflation. Stagflation was a new phenomenon to Keynesians because they ruled out the possibility of the coexistence of high inflation and high unemployment. Keynesians believed that the government could achieve one goal (say, low unemployment) by sacrificing another goal (say, low inflation) using aggregate demand policy, although it is not possible to catch the two hares of low inflation and low unemployment at the same time.

It is said that history repeats itself. Just as the Great Depression of the 1930s uprooted the theoretical foundations of classical economics, the oil crises of the 1970s rocked the theoretical foundations of Keynesian economics. Keynesian economics could neither explain the coexistence of high unemployment and high inflation nor provide any solutions to stagflation. This new development confirmed that the Keynesian model no longer worked like a panacea.

Friedman, who was devoted to the reconstruction of the classical school since the 1960s, had already predicted the demise of the Keynesian model long before the occurrence of the oil shocks. As the stagflation problem became more stubborn, Friedman doubled down on his effort to reconstruct classical economics almost single-handed. He accepted John Locke's liberal ideology which values the free activity of human beings. From the perspective of economic thought, he raised the torch of neoliberalism that has purposed the restoration of Smith's liberalism. Friedman advocated individual freedom and private ownership, the government's nonintervention and deregulation, corporate privatization, incentive-based welfare, labor market flexibility and productivity-linked wages, free trade and liberalization, and rule-based monetary policy.

Neoliberalism was an attempt to revive the ideology of free market capitalism envisioned by Smith after it collapsed following the Great Depression. In this context, neoliberalism is an economic thought that was born against the backdrop of Keynesian orientation toward welfare state. Neoliberalism emphasizes that when the government intervenes in the free market, the economy's ability to self-regulate decreases, and the efficiency of the economy decreases. In addition, the economy becomes more government-dependent, and the government's burden of costs rises.

However, there is no universally accepted definition of neoliberalism. This is because neoliberalism has been interpreted differently in different times and in different circumstances. Neoliberalism is a political and economic ideology that is rooted in liberalism, and the fact that liberalism itself is used in various contexts makes the definition of neoliberalism more difficult. Thus, it is not strange at all to expect the advocates of neoliberalism such as Hayek, Friedman, David Harvey, and Noam Chomsky to have different thoughts on neoliberalism.

Originally neoliberalism was an economic philosophy advocated by European liberal scholars who were looking for a 'Third Way' or 'Middle Way' between the conflicting ideologies of classical liberalism and collective central planning (socialist system) in the 1930s. The Third Way tended to oppose the libertarian doctrine reflecting the hindsight of the failure of classical laissez-fare in the 1930s. Instead, the Third Way promoted a market economy, called the 'social market economy' that operated under strong governmental guidance and rules. As a result, the usage of the term 'neoliberalism' greatly dwindled in the 1960s.

There were two developments in terms of theoretical constructs and practical fields. The theoretical foundations for neoliberalism burgeoned with the works of Hayek and Friedman in the 1960s. Then, in the 1980s, the term neoliberalism was splendidly revived with the advent of the conservative regimes in both the United Kingdom (Prime Minister Margaret Thatcher) and the United States (President Ronald Reagan), and the term was also reborn with the tint of individual freedom and free market capitalism as opposed to a modest form of liberalism.

There were two great works that had a significant influence on the development of neoliberalism: Hayek's *The Constitution of Liberty* (1960) and Friedman's *Capitalism and Freedom* (1962). Hayek's book was published in 1960, and Friedman's book was published two years later. Interestingly, Friedman won the Nobel prize in economics two years later than Hayek did. It has been more than 60 years since these two pieces of *magnum opus* were published, but they still have profound impacts on many intellectual explorers and policymakers in many countries around the world.

Another notable fact is that Keynes and Hayek, who were polar opposites, tried to find a happy medium point between revisionist capitalism supporting the government's intervention and neoliberalism advocating the government's 'hands-off'. Their effort has been confirmed in many correspondences between Keynes and Hayek, which shows that the two intellectuals tried to intercede for the common thread between Keynesianism (or revisionist capitalism) and neoliberalism (or free-market capitalism).

2

REAGANOMICS AND TRICKLE-DOWN ECONOMICS

Margaret Thatcher, who was praised as a conservative Amazonian (female warrior), was elected as British Prime Minister in 1979, and conservative actor Ronald Reagan in cowboy attire was elected as the President of the United States in 1980. As the flag of conservatism flapped in the two continents, the influence of neoliberalism began to gather momentum.

Reagan pursued major policies to return to free enterprise principles and free market capitalism that prevailed prior to the Great Depression and Roosevelt's New Deal policy. He further declared a turn from Keynes' demand-driven economics to supply-side economics. The Laffer curve showing that the excessive tax rate could rather lead to a decrease in tax revenues became his theoretical weapon for his economic policy, which is commonly called Reaganomics. However, in 1984 George Bush who competed with Reagan for the Republican presidential nomination criticized Reaganomics as Voodoo economics.

Reagan began to implement a series of economic policies based on neoliberalism. Since the emergence of Reaganomics, names that imitate it have been sprouting: Clintonomics, Abenomics, etc. Clintonomics is epitomized by the slogan that "It's the economy. Stupid!" and Abenomics refer to the economic policy of Japanese Prime Minister Shinzo Abe. Whether these names are appropriate is controversial because the original Reaganomics meant economic policies based on the principles of neoliberalism. President Reagan's economic policy consisted of four pillars: (1) reducing the growth of government spending, (2) lowering the federal income tax and capital gains tax rates, (3) eliminating government regulations and (4) curbing inflation. These policies meant a great shift from the economic policies of his predecessors.

He also took a scalpel to reform the welfare system Before President Reagan, some people were reluctant to work because they were entitled to more child-care compensations if they gave birth to more children. Thus, they chose to receive welfare money rather than to work to support their children. President Reagan mended this practice. He lowered taxes on the high-income class more proportionally relative to the lower income class, eliminated many tax credits, and significantly lowered the highest marginal income tax rate from 70% to 39%.

The prescription of supply-side economics on which Reaganomics was based would be a very ideal economic solution if its intended goal were realized in the real economy as anticipated. However, questions have been raised as to whether the rosy supply-side economic policy could achieve the desired goal in the real economy. During the period between 1981 and 1982 when President Reagan implemented tax cuts, federal tax revenues fell by more than 6%, and annual tax revenues from 1983 to 1984 were lower than those of 1981. In 1980, when Reagan's predecessor was President Carter, the federal budget deficit was 2.7% of GDP, but increased to 4.2% when Reagan was in office.

The transcript for Reaganomics was mixed. The annual growth rate of real government spending decreased from 4% (President Carter) to 2.5% (President Reagan), while the average worker's income increased only 0.8% during President Carter's presidency but increased by 1.8% when President Reagan was in office. The increase in labor productivity was even more impressive. During the Carter administration, it did not increase, but during the Reagan administration, it increased at the rate of 1.4% per year.

However, it might be inappropriate to simply compare President Carter's economic performance with President Reagan's. Because in 1979 when President Carter was in office, the second oil crisis broke out, and the world economy, including the United States, was in shatters. Some economists criticize that under the Reagan regime, the significant reductions in tax rates and the resulting decreases in tax revenues were responsible for the ballooning deficit in the subsequent years. The budget deficit problem was one of the biggest problems faced by the U.S. economy in the 1980s and thereafter. On the other hand, the New Economy, the coexistence of low inflation and low unemployment enjoyed by the U.S. economy in the late 1990s, is also viewed as the result of the seeds sown by Reaganomics.

Thus, Reaganomics that can be seen as the economic experiment of neoliberalism has received both applauses and criticisms. Supporters of Reaganomics argue that its merits outweigh its problems, whereas critics of Reaganomics maintain that its costs outweigh its benefits.

3

THATCHERISM

British Prime Minister Margaret Thatcher was another fighter for neoliberalism. Now it is time to look at the performance of Prime Minister Thatcher who led the movements of neoliberalism together with President Reagan in the 1980s. Thatcher's politics and economic policy left a big footprint in history, which was confirmed by words such as Thatcherism and Thatcherites. Most of all, she left her mark in history as a liberal warrior who ended the cold war era together with President Reagan in the 1980s. Thatcher served as the leader of the British Conservative Party from 1975 to 1990 and served as the British Prime Minister from May 1979 to October 1990.

The essence of Thatcherism is characterized by the enhancement of free market capitalism, realization of small government, and maintenance of low inflation through the control of the money supply. There are also other achievements such as deregulation, privatization of major state-owned enterprises, reforms of the labor market, performance-based principles in the labor market, and transfer of central government policy decisions to local governments. From this point of view, Thatcherism contains the elements of neoliberalism that was closer to classical liberalism. It is well known that Thatcher maintained a close friendship with Hayek and Friedman who were the pioneers of neoliberalism. Hayek's masterpiece, *The Road to Serfdom,* became the theoretical reference for Thatcherism. Friedman once said that "one thing that people do not know about her is that she claimed to be a 19th-century liberal rather than to be evaluated as having the beliefs of the Conservative Party." (Source: www.wikipedia.org/Thatcherism)

In terms of economic policy, Thatcherism is based on monetarism. Monetarism is a school of economic thought established by Friedman, which has its roots in classical theory. The purpose of monetarism is to show that money is the dominant influence on economic activity such as inflation. Monetarism puts more emphasis on controlling inflation over unemployment. Thatcherism placed emphasis on strict regulations of the money supply, as low inflation is one of its core policies. In addition, reducing government spending and lowering taxes are prerequisites for realizing a small government and cores of Thatcherism.

Thatcher was known to have loved to recite T.S. Eliot's <Four Quartets>, especially <Little Gidding>. The last verse of <Little Gidding> decorated the first page of Prime Minister Thatcher's funeral service (April 18, 2013) program. Eliot's <Little Gidding> is a poem full of religious color, which gives us a glimpse of Thatcher's religious piety. <Little Gidding> is the last quartet of a series of Eliot's poems, <Four Quartets>. <Four Quartets> consist of' <Burnt Norton>, <East Coker>, <The Dry Salvages>, and <Little Gidding>. Little Gidding is the name of a small city in England that was the home of the British Anglican faith community founded by Nicholas Ferrar in 1626. Eliot was known to have visited the town in 1936 and wrote the poem.

<Little Gidding> focuses on the past, present, and future and says that a people without history is not redeemed from time, for history is a pattern of timeless moments. It is important to understand the continuity of the past, present and future for salvation. Critics classify <Little Gidding> as a poem of purification and the fire of Pentecost (holy spirit). The poem listed here is the last part of <Little Gidding>, a favorite verse of former Prime Minister Thatcher.

What we call the beginning is often the end
And to make an end is to make a beginning.
The end is where we start from.
We die with the dying:
See, they depart, and we go with them.
We are born with the dead:
See, they return, and bring us with them.
The moment of the rose and the moment of the yew-tree
Are of equal duration. A people without history
Is not redeemed from time, for history is a pattern
Of timeless moments. So while the light fails
On a winter's afternoon, in a secluded chapel
History is now and England.
With the drawing of this Love and the voice of this Calling
We shall not cease from exploration
And the end of all our exploring
Will be to arrive where we started
And know the place for the first time.

4

<FOUR QUARTETS> AND <A LATE QUARTET>

The economy could be out of equilibrium and be driven into the state of disharmony. However, the economy has the resilience of returning to its equilibrium state. Classicists and Keyncsians do not have disagreements in this regard. The differences between the two schools center around the length of the period of the adjustment toward equilibrium and the method of reaching the equilibrium state. Classicists hold the position that the adjustment of the economy toward the equilibrium state occurs in the short run through self-correcting forces of the market, whereas Keynesians maintain the position that it would take a long while for the economy to adjust toward the equilibrium state without government intervention. We get some clue to these issues through T.S. Eliot's poem that Thatcher loved during her life, <Burnt Norton>. *The poem* begins with the following famous verse:

> Time present and time past
> Are both perhaps present in time future.
> And time future contained in time past.
> If all time is eternally present
> All time is unredeemable.
> ....
> Time past and time future
> What might have been and what has been,
> Point to one end, which is always present.

We could divide the time into the past, the present, and the future, and divide into 'what might have been' and 'what has been'. But all time points to one end, which is always present. Eliot's view of the time is reminiscent of St. Augustine's time. In his *Time and Eternity*, St. Augustine argued that it was not right to divide the time simply into the past, the present, and the future: There is the present that belongs to the past; there is the present that belongs to the present; and there is the present that belongs to the future. In this way, what we call the beginning is often the end, and there is the eternality of time. Thus, Eliot's view of time is in sync with the Christian perception of time.

<Burnt Norton> that is the first quartet of <Four Quartets> is introduced in the prologue of the movie <A Late Quartet>. It is known that T.S. Eliot's <Four Quartets> was inspired by Beethoven's late quartets. A quartet refers to a musical ensemble having four instruments or voices or a group of four performers. However, a string quartet typically consists of two violinists, a violist, and a cellist. The protagonist of the movie is cellist Peter Mitchell who developed Parkinson's disease around the 25th anniversary of the founding of the Fugue String Quartet. His health condition gives the quartet members some time to look at the relationships that they have maintained for so long. After Peter was diagnosed with Parkinson's disease, he announces his decision to have the last concert before he retires. Meanwhile, on this occasion, Robert, the second violinist reveals his intention to take on the role of the first violinist Daniel has played for a long time. Robert is married to Juliet, the viola player of the group.

After Robert knew that his wife Juliet did not support his plan, he engaged in a 'one-night stand,' and Juliet asked him to leave the house. What makes the matter more twisting is that their daughter, Alexandra, began to have a relationship with Daniel, whom her mother once adored. Their relationship went haywire. These extreme dissonances led the relationship among the quartet members to be almost crushed, but just before their relationship went to the brink of collapsing, they were able to restore their long-maintained relationship once again for the last farewell concert in honor of Peter. They played Beethoven's String Quartet No. 14

The String Quartet No. 14 was composed after Beethoven lost his hearing completely. It is known that Beethoven wrote the String Quartet No. 14 in the hope that it would be played with continuity from start to finish. The movie <A Late Quartet> cited Eliot's poem, <Four Quartets> to compare it to the eternity of the time. Peter cited the first verse of <Burnt Norton> to students to explain Beethoven's String Quartet No. 14.

> "If you continue playing for a long time like this, the pitch of each instrument will not match.
> Since instruments cannot be tuned in the middle, dissonance occurs in the notes.
> So, what will you do? Will you stop playing?
> If not, shouldn't everyone try to fit each other to suit others somehow
> even if they are discordant?"

Life is like performing a quartet. As in the case of the performance of the Fugue String Quartet, there could be some disharmony in relationships.

It is life that has little time for tuning up, while resting for a while. However, such discord could be patched up through love and caring or someone's help, and harmony would come back again. Love and caring work like self-curing forces or someone's help will work as a shot in the arm. Peter emphasizes that the future life is an extension of the past life in the eternity of time, citing that "Time future contained in time past" (Source: <Burnt Norton>)

The economy is also like performing a quartet. The behavior of individuals is so erratic that there could be disturbances in the economy. However, such disequilibrium could be adjusted toward the state of equilibrium through market forces or government intervention. The coordination that encompasses the vagaries of individual economic agents is a healing process of the economy toward the equilibrium of the whole economy. This state was a picture of the economy drawn by classical economists, especially Adam Smith. In the world of Smith, when individual economic agents act in pursuit of their own interest, there could be conflicts and discord among them, but the behavior of individuals is guided into an equilibrium state by the invisible hand. Keynesian economists also argue that the economy will eventually be adjusted toward an equilibrium state, but the adjustment process could be lengthy and costlier without the government's help.

The preachers of neoliberalism such as Prime Minister Thatcher and President Reagan envisioned the harmony of the whole through individual freedom and liberalism. However, individual freedom and liberalism sometimes clash with social justice and collective consensus and could provoke anger such as the "Occupy Wall Street" protests.

5

"OCCUPY WALL STREET": THE AMERICA FALL

Thatcherism shone in the 1990s when the Soviet Union and its blocs collapsed, and people chanted individual freedom. Thatcher's hope was that the value of neoliberalism she had treasured would continue in the future, as in the phrase in *Burnt Norton*:

> Time past and time future
> What might have been and what has been
> Point to one end, which is always present.

Can the value of human society based on individual freedom keep on moving forward on the continuity of time? Human value has historically progressed through the dialectical process of thesis-antithesis-synthesis. Neoliberalism is also the product of such a dialectical process: Classical liberalism was dominated by Keynesian interventionism, which was challenged by neoliberalism. However, amid the global economic crisis of 2008, neoliberalism was once again attacked and became subject to controversy. The controversy has centered on the fundamental choice between liberalism and interventionism, between efficiency and equity, and between regulation and deregulation. Since the global economic crisis in 2008, the term neoliberalism has been ironically used as a rather derogatory term, meaning liberalization, deregulation, and greed, which could worsen income inequality.

The global economic crisis in 2008 has shown that when deregulation, one of the core values of neoliberalism, was combined with human greed, individual freedom could lead to collective anger, rather than collective harmony. When regulations on banks and big corporations are removed, these capitalists could seek to maximize their profits with no limit and could not be content with proper profit. Even Pope Francisco criticizes the global economic system as a system of "profit ahead of people". It is known that all animals on the planet, except for racehorses, eat only until they feel full according to their natural appetite and no longer predate. However, human beings and racehorses are known to be not satisfied with the proper amount of fullness and are gluttonous.

People who were critical of neoliberalism argue that when regulations were abolished, banks and corporations were occupied with octopus-style management to get even bigger. Also, big banks and corporations sought monopolistic market dominance through collusion and unfair transactions. Monopolistic firms distort the function of the market because they charge prices higher than those in a perfectly competitive market. Big banks also try to maximize profits by making predatory loans. Workers could be easily laid off and driven into the streets by the predatory behavior of firms and banks that seek only profit maximization. The social safety net for the economically disadvantaged people should be prepared, but neoliberalism has been criticized to be indifferent to such social welfare issues. The advocates of liberalism have tried to resolve the problem only with the power of the market. Neoliberalism anchored in liberalization, deregulation, and privatization could sow the apple of discord.

As the global economic crisis in 2008 deepened in the United States, many unemployed white-collar workers who lost their jobs came out on the streets and shouted the slogan "Occupy Wall Street". Protests to occupy the heart of the world financial system began in September 2011. Many highly educated unemployed people were driven out of the workplace and wandered the streets. At the root of the protests, there was the increasing sentiment that Wall Street's greed was the main driver of the global economic crisis. Demonstrators settled in Zuccotti Park in Manhattan as a base camp and continued their protests for several months. The "Occupy Wall Street" movement was a peculiar social phenomenon in the United States.

At first, only a few dozen people participated, but the number of sympathizers gradually increased, and later the number of protesters increased to thousands. The protests also began to spread to San Francisco, Boston, Chicago, Los Angeles, and Seattle across the country. Protesters shouted the slogans: "We represent 99% of American people and resist the 1% richest in the United States"; "The top 1% richest people in the United States occupy the 50% of American wealth" (Source: www.wikipedia.org/Occupy Wall Street). Coincidentally, a study was published around that time, showing that 1% of the world's wealthiest people would occupy more than 50% of the world's wealth by 2016. Some people called the "Occupy the Wall Street" movement as the 'America Fall', comparing it to the 'Arab Spring'. The Arab Spring was a song of hope with new buds for individual freedom sprouting up on the ground (although it was an unfinished song), but the America Fall was the expression of anger against the greedy capitalists. The scene in the

Zuccotti Park with leaves falling onto the ground symbolized the bleakness of the 'America Fall'. The "Occupy Wall Street" movement was a grassroots reaction to economic inequality, corporate greed, and political apathy.

Those who took part in the "Occupy Wall Street" protests did not directly express a sense of hostility toward neoliberalism. However, the movement reflected their belief that deregulation and liberalization which were the core value of neoliberalism fanned the global economic crisis. The perception that the greed brought by deregulation lay at the bottom of the "Occupy Wall Street" movement. Protesters believed that they were victims of such deregulation and greed. In September 2011, when the protests began, the U.S. unemployment rate was 9.0%, which was far higher than the U.S. potential unemployment rate. The "Occupy Wall Street" movement symbolizes the dark side of neoliberalism. In order to overcome the global economic crisis and to placate angry people, the Obama government borrowed the astronomical amount of money and poured the money into the economy. The U.S. national debt began to exceed more than 100% of its GDP at the end of the global economic crisis. This might be a turnaround from neoliberalism, but the U.S. government faced the fiscal cliff. Although the "Occupy Wall Street" protests were over, the debate surrounding the choice between liberalism and interventionism and between efficiency and equity is not over.

PART 4

MEASUREMENT OF MACROECONOMIC PERFORMANCE: SEEING THE TREES FOR THE FOREST

1

Measuring the Size of the Economy: GDP, GNP, and GNI

The most commonly used measure of the size of an economy is gross domestic product (GDP). GDP is defined as the sum of the total market value of all final goods and services produced domestically during a specified period. For example, British GDP includes all the goods and services which are produced in the geographical domain of the United Kingdom regardless of who produces the goods and services. There is another measure of the size of an economy. Gross national product (GNP) measures the total market value of all final goods and services produced by the nationals (businesses and self-employed) of a country. Thus, British GNP includes all the goods and services which are produced by British nationals regardless of where they produce the goods and services. The value of automobiles produced by Toyota in the United Kingdom is included in British GDP, but not in British GNP. It is included in Japan's GNP. Similarly, Jaguar cars are produced in the United Kingdom, but the company is owned by Tata Motors, an Indian automaker. Thus, the value of automobiles produced by Jaguar in the United Kingdom is included in British GDP, but not in British GNP. However, the value of petroleum produced by BP (British Petroleum) in Saudi Arabia is included in British GNP, but not in British GDP.

GNP was used in almost all countries until 1992, but the United States changed from GNP to GDP in 1992 to measure the size of the economy and other countries followed suit. The main reason is that as many countries move toward openness and globalization, GDP becomes more suitable for the purpose of measuring the size of the economy. For the United States, there is little difference between these two measures. This is because the overseas earnings of U.S. firms are about the same as the earnings of foreign firms in the United States. The difference between GDP and GNP is large for a country like Canada where there is much more foreign investment in Canada than there is Canadian investment abroad (GDP > GNP) or the Philippines where a large number of Filipinos work overseas (GNP > GDP).

There is a close relationship between GDP and GNP. Let's see how we get GNP from GDP. First, British GDP includes goods and services produced by foreigners in the United Kingdom. In order to obtain the total value of goods and services produced by British nationals during a certain year, the value of goods and services produced by foreigners in the United Kingdom must be subtracted from British GDP. Next, British GDP does not include goods and services produced by British nationals abroad. Therefore, the value of goods and services produced by British nationals abroad must be added to GDP to obtain the total value of goods and services produced by the British people.

GNP = GDP – Value of goods and service produced by foreigners in the U.K.+ Value of goods and services produced by the British overseas

If the value of goods and services produced by the British (corporations and self-employees) from foreign production activities is greater than the value of goods and services produced by foreigners (corporations and self-employees) in the United Kingdom, British GNP is greater than British GDP.

Sometimes, we are concerned with comparing the income of consumers across countries. For this purpose, either GDP or GNP may not be appropriate. It is more common to use GNI (gross national income) for the purpose of international comparison of the earnings of consumers across countries. GNI is the total income (including taxes) earned by a country's nationals domestically and abroad, and GNP is the total market value of goods and services produced by a country's nationals, domestically and abroad. In the national income accounting, the total market value of final products should be the same as the amount of total income, and thus GNP and GNI should be identical. Just as we distinguish between GDP and GNP, we can also distinguish between GDI (gross domestic income) and GNI (gross national income). We have the following relationship (we'll discuss the distinction between GDP and GDI (and between GNP and GNI) in more detail later):

GNI = GDI − Income earned by foreigners (corporations and self-employees) in the U.K.+ Income earned by the British (corporations and self-employees) overseas

2

MEASUREMENT OF GDP: YOU CANNOT ADD APPLES AND ORANGES

There are basically three different approaches to measuring GDP. First, we can measure GDP by adding the market values of all final goods and services produced in the economy during a given period. This approach is called the product approach. Second, we can measure GDP by summing all expenditures on final goods and services spent by different economic agents—households, business firms, governments, and foreigners. This approach is called the expenditure approach. Finally, we can measure GDP by summing all incomes earned by factor owners who participate in the production of final goods and services. This approach is called the income approach. Since these different approaches look at the same thing from different aspects, we should obtain the same number no matter what approach we use. This principle is known as the national income accounting identity.

GDP measured by the product approach
= GDP measured by the expenditure approach
= GDP measured by the income approach.

We'll first discuss the measurement of GDP by the product approach. According to this approach, GDP is equal to the sum of market values of all final goods and services produced in a country (say, United States) during a given period. First, GDP is a *market value* concept. U.S. GDP is measured in dollar values. On a typical day, firms produce millions of loaves of bread, thousands of suits of clothes, hundreds of units of houses, and so on. These are different products, and each is measured in its own unit such as loaves, suits, and units. As an old saying tells us, we can't add apples and oranges. In order to obtain the total value of goods and services produced in an economy, we must combine all of them into a single number (i.e., GDP) using a common unit. Suppose there are 10 apples and 20 oranges. We cannot add these two numbers to obtain the total of the produces, because apples and oranges are different products. Similar problems arise when we calculate GDP. The product approach is to add up the market value of every good or service—the number of dollars each product is sold for in the market. In this way, "we can add apples and oranges".

Some economic activity that cannot be measured at market price is excluded from GDP. For example, homemakers' work, do-it-yourself activities, underground transactions are usually excluded from GDP. Homemakers' housework is a valuable production activity and greatly contributes to the wellbeing of a nation, but such housework is not included in GDP because it is difficult to evaluate the market price of such housework. Under the same logic, underground economic transactions such as drug trafficking and prostitution, are also economic activities, but are excluded from GDP because there are no legal market prices. (However, several attempts have recently been made to include them in GDP in some countries.)

Second, GDP measures the value of *final goods and services*. Final goods and services refer to those goods and services acquired for final use, not for resale or further processing. Goods that are used in the process of producing other goods are called intermediate goods and are excluded from GDP. Raw materials such as crude oil and iron ores and semi-finished goods such as steel are not for final consumption, and thus they are intermediate goods. If intermediate goods are included in the measure of GDP, then they will be double counted in the measure of GDP. However, automobiles made of steel and gasoline made of crude oil are final consumer goods, and they are included in GDP. For the same reason, gold bars are intermediate goods, but accessories made of gold bars are final goods and included in GDP.

Third, GDP refers only to the value of the goods and services that are *produced* during the current period. Hence, goods and services that were produced in a previous period but are now transacted are excluded from current GDP. For example, the sales of used cars produced in previous years are not included in this period's GDP. From this line of reasoning, the sales of existing homes, buildings, condominiums, factories that were built in previous years are also excluded from current GDP. The value of land is also excluded from GDP, because land exists in its natural state and is not produced. By the same token, the value of assets such as stocks, bonds, derivatives, foreign currencies, and cryptocurrencies are not included in GDP, because assets are not goods or services and are thus not produced.

Fourth, only the value of goods and services produced in the *geographical domain of a nation* (say, United States) is included in the nation's GDP (U.S. GDP). This is the natural consequence of the definition of GDP. GDP includes only the value of domestically produced goods and services whereas GNP includes the value of goods and services produced by the nationals of a country.

Finally, GDP refers to the production that takes place *during a certain period* (usually a quarter or a year). In this context, GDP is a flow variable. Economic variables are divided into flows and stocks. A flow variable such as GDP measures the value of the variable that occurs during some time interval. Thus, we are talking about GDP during the period of 2020 (yearly GDP) or the fourth quarter of 2020 (quarterly GDP). On the other hand, a stock variable such as the money supply measures the value of the variable at a specific point in time. Thus, we are talking about the amount of money at the end of December 2020.

To understand the measurement of GDP, we'll consider a simple economy in which the economy produces 10,000 loaves of bread, 1,000 suits of clothes, and 100 units of houses. We cannot simply sum them up to get GDP. For example, the country's GDP is not 10,000 + 1,000 + 100 = 11,100. As we discussed, we cannot simply add apples and oranges. Now, if the price (average) of bread is $10 per loaf, the price (average) of clothes is $500 per suit, and the price (average) of a house is $300,000, the market value of the produced bread is $100,000, the market value of the produced clothes is $500,000, and the market value of the produced houses is $30,000,000. Now the value of each product is measured in a common unit, the dollar value, and we can add up these market values: $100,000 + $500,000 + $30,000,000 = $30,600,000 = $30.6 million. From this, we can say that the amount of GDP produced in this economy is equal to $30.6 million.

3

THE UNDERGROUND ECONOMY AND GDP

The underground economy refers to economic activities that are illegally conducted, such as drug trafficking or prostitution. The underground economy is not limited to such illegal transactions, however. The scope of the underground economy is quite wide. Underground-economic activities also include the transactions of counterfeit goods or fake medicines, illegal copying of software, illegal copying of books, and illegal gambling. However, not all underground economic activities are illegal. Broadly speaking, the case of not reporting or abbreviating the transaction details for the purpose of evading taxes is also considered as underground-economic activities. In addition, unreported transactions of assets and antiques fall into the category of the underground economy. Economic activities that do not violate the law and whose transaction details are not reported are sometimes referred to as a shadow economy or a black market.

Thus, most underground-economic activities are not reported and are traded only in cash. Due to this nature of the underground economy, most underground-economic activities do not have market prices, and it is not easy to measure the size of the underground economy. Since underground-economic activities are difficult for the government authorities to detect, the government could not impose taxes on such economic activities, and tax revenues would be reduced. GDP is also reduced by the size of the underground economy.

The actual price of a product or service transacted in the underground economy may be lower or higher than the market price of the same kind of product or service in the market. When the transaction of a product or service is illegal, then the price of a product prevailed in underground-economic transactions is usually set to be lower than the market price of the same product. Counterfeit goods, fake medicines, and piracy are examples of such transactions. In some underground-economic activities, transactions are made at a price higher than the market price, because it is not easy to produce such products or services, and a risk premium is added to the price. This happens in the underground transactions of drugs such as marijuana. This is one reason why some economists have been supporting the legalization of drugs. They argue that legalizing drugs can lower the price of drugs, reduce the trafficking of drugs, and increase tax revenues.

Because there is no way of calculating the size of the underground economy directly, national income accountants in many countries make every effort to estimate the size of the underground economy. Since transactions in the underground economy are mostly conducted in cash, it is possible to approximate the size of the underground economy by looking at the trend in the usage of cash issued by the central bank. The most comprehensive and authoritative research on the size of the underground economy in each country was conducted by Professors Friedrich Schneider and Andreas Buehn of Johannes Kepler University in Austria.

Schneider and Buehn (2012) calculated the size of the underground economy (as a percentage of GDP) of 39 OECD countries. They have calculated and averaged this percentage annually from 1999 to 2010. According to this study, Bulgaria (34.6%) has the highest rate, and Switzerland (8.3%) the lowest rate. The average estimates for the major countries during the 1999-2010 period are as follows:

> (1) Switzerland: 8.3%; (2) United States: 8.7%; (3) Austria: 9.8%; (4) Luxembourg: 9.6%; (5) Japan: 11.0%; (6) New Zealand: 12.2%; (7) United Kingdom: 12.5%; (8) Netherlands: 13.2%; (9) Australia: 13.8%; (10) Canada: 15.6%; (11) Germany: 15.7%; (12) Denmark: 17.3%; (13) Finland: 17.4%; (14) Norway: 18.6%; (14) Sweden: 18.6%; (16) Belgium: 21.5%; (17) Portugal: 22.7%; (18) Spain: 22.8%; (19) South Korea: 26.3%; (20) Italy: 26.9%; (21) Mexico: 30.0%; (22) Turkey: 30.6%; (23) Bulgaria: 34.6%.

These numbers may be viewed as an indirect indicator of the average honesty of a country. Advanced countries that have a ratio of 20% or higher include Italy (26.9%), South Korea (26.3%), Spain (22.8%), Portugal (22.7%) and Belgium (21.5%). This record might leave a bitter aftertaste to the nations. In contrast, advanced countries that have a relatively low ratio include Switzerland (8.3%), United States (8.7%), Austria (9.8%) and Luxemburg (9.6%). Japan (11.0%), New Zealand, and the United Kingdom (12.5%). Russia and China are not included in the study because they are not OECD member countries. Russia has traditionally been considered as one of countries with the highest share of the underground economy.

In 2020, U.S. GDP was about $20.9 trillion, Italy's GDP was $1.9 trillion, and South Korea's GDP was $1.6 trillion. Based on the Schneider-Buehn study, we can estimate the size of the underground economy in these countries: U.S.: $1,822 billion, Italy: $507 billion, and South Korea: $429 billion. When converting South Korea's underground economy into Korean won, it is about 350 trillion won. If the government authorities were able to detect the underground economic transactions, they could increase not only the government's tax revenues, but also the nation's GDP.

In fact, there was a country that attempted to increase GDP by surfacing the underground economy. Former South Korean President Park Geun-hye promised to detect the underground economy as one of her campaign pledges during the Presidential election in 2014. (Park's estimate of the size of the South Korean underground economy in 2014 was 370 trillion won, which was close to the size of the Korean underground economy estimated by the Schneider-Buehn model.) Her pledge was to uncover about 6% (22 trillion won) of the underground economy, which would increase more than 1.6 trillion won in taxes annually and use it to cover the cost of the welfare budget. However, as discussed above, it is not easy to uncover underground-economic transactions, and after all, President Park's ambitious plan ended in failure.

4

NOMINAL GDP VERSUS REAL GDP

We have seen that in order to estimate GDP, we must assess the value of goods and services produced in a country at market prices. Depending on how the market value is measured, we can consider two different measures of GDP: nominal GDP and real GDP. Nominal GDP (or current-value GDP) is calculated by evaluating the quantity of goods and services produced in a year using the market prices of the year. For example, we obtain nominal GDP for 2020 by multiplying the quantity of each product or service produced in 2020 by the 2020 price of the good or service.

On the other hand, real GDP is calculated using the price that prevailed in a base year chosen for the purpose of calculating real GDP. Suppose that the base year chosen is 2015. Then we measure the market value of each good or service produced in 2020 using the price of the good and service that prevailed in 2015. The national income accountants usually change the base year every several years.

There is good reason for the government to publish two different measures of GDP. The most fundamental reason is that the value of $1 in the past (say, 2015) is different from the value of $1 today. Nominal GDP increases as market prices rise. As such, even if output does not increase, nominal GDP could increase if prices rise. The more the price rises, the greater is the amount of nominal GDP of the year. Thus, nominal GDP is not a good indicator for measuring real economic activity. Because nominal GDP contains the effect of price increases on GDP, we need another measure of output, real GDP to eliminate the effect of inflation on GDP.

The superiority of real GDP over nominal GDP as a measure of economic growth should be obvious. Since real GDP measures the value of goods and services produced in any given year (say, 1960, 2000, 2010, 2020) using the same base-year (2015) prices, any increase in GDP due to price changes from year to year is eliminated in real GDP. Thus, real GDP enables us to compare the growth of real output over time. For instance, since real GDP in 2020 and real GDP in 1960 are measured at the same base-year (2015) prices, real GDP enables us to compare the size of the economy at different time periods (1960 and 2020). However, nominal GDP includes an increase in the value of goods and services associated with increases in prices over time. Thus, it does not make sense to directly compare 1960 nominal GDP with 2020 nominal GDP, because 2020 nominal GDP is inflated by price increases from 1960 to 2020. The real value of $1 in 1960 is not the same as the real value of $1 in 2020.

In the base year, real GDP is the same as nominal GDP, because both measures of GDP use the same-base year prices. Thus, nominal GDP in 2015 is the same as real GDP in 2015. However, nominal GDP in 2020 is different from real GDP in 2020. If the prices of goods and services rose from the base year (2015) to the given year (2020), nominal GDP in 2020 would be larger than real GDP in 2020. If the prices of goods and services fell from the base year to the given year, then nominal GDP in 2020 would be smaller than real GDP in 2020.

We'll compare nominal GDP (NGDP) with real GDP (RGDP) in the United States. The base year is 2012, and the unit is in billions of dollars.

<Table 4.1> U.S. Nominal and Real GDP

Year	NGDP	RGDP	Difference (NGDP – RGDP)
2010	15,049.0	15,649.0	−600.0
2011	15,599.7	15,891.5	−291.8
2012	16,254.0	16,254.0	0
2013	16,843.2	16,553.3	289.9
2014	17,550.7	16,932.1	618.6
2015	18,206.0	17,390.3	815.7
2016	18,695.1	17,680.3	1,014.8
2017	19,479.6	18,079.1	1,400.5
2018	20,257.2	18,606.8	1,650.4
2019	21,372.6	19,032.7	2,339.9
2020	20,893.7	18,384.7	2,509.0
2021^{P}	22,997.5	19,428.4	3,569.1

1) The figures for 2021 are preliminary values.
2) Source: *The Economic Report of the President 2022.*

U.S. nominal GDP in 2020 (measured at 2020 prices) was $20,893.7 billion, whereas U.S. real GDP in 2020 (measured at 2012 prices) was $18,384.7. The difference between the nominal GDP and real GDP in 2020 was $2,509.0, which was due to price increases (inflation) between 2012 (base year) and 2020. This increase in nominal GDP due to inflation has nothing to do with the growth of the quantity of output. For this reason, a country's economic growth rate should be calculated based on real GDP, not nominal GDP. If we use nominal GDP to calculate the economic growth rate, the growth rate balloons by the magnitude of inflation.

We also need to distinguish between nominal and real values for interest rates, wages, and exchange rates, as we do between nominal GDP and real GDP. As discussed earlier, our economic decision-making can be misleading if we do not differentiate between nominal interest rates and real interest rates, between nominal wages and real wages, and between nominal exchange rates and real exchange rates. The real interest rate is the interest rate adjusted for inflation, and the real wage is the wage adjusted for inflation. This distinction is important because rational economic agents (consumers, workers, producers, etc.) make their economic decisions based on real variables, not nominal variables to pursue their best interest.

5

A SIMPLE COMPARISON OF INCOME BETWEEN 2020 AND 1961 IS LIKE IGNORING PERSPECTIVE

In order to compare the records of runners in a running race, it is important for runners to start at the same starting line on the same track. Similarly, when we compare the size of the economy (GDP) or income over time, it is necessary to measure GDP or income at the same starting line to make meaningful comparisons over time. Evaluating the size of the economy by the same standards means that the size of the economy should be measured on an equal footing, that is, based on the same base year. Measuring GDP and income per capita at the same base-year price means that we use real GDP or real income per capita, not nominal GDP or nominal income per capita.

Some confusion concerning the distinction between nominal and real variables often occurs when we make comparisons of living standards over time or across countries. The indicator that is widely used as a measure of living standards in each country is GDP per capita or GNI per capita. GDP per capita is obtained by dividing a country's nominal GDP by the total population, and GNI per capita is calculated by dividing a country's nominal GNI (gross national income) by the total population. In the United States, there is no significant difference between these two indicators because GDP and GNI are not much different. International institutions such as the IMF, IBRD, UN, etc. usually use GDP per capita for cross-country comparisons of per capita income. In order to compare and evaluate living standards in each country, it is convenient to measure per capita GDP of each country using a common denominator. It is common to compare income per capita measured in the U.S. dollar.

Since GDP and income per capita in each country are converted into U.S. dollars using exchange rates for international comparison, GDP and income per capita are sensitive to changes in exchange rates. They change if each country's dollar exchange rate fluctuates, even though there is no change in GDP and income per capita in local currency. As an extreme example, if the exchange rate of the Japanese yen to the dollar suddenly fell from 140 yen per dollar to 70 yen per dollar, income per capita denoted in the yen remains the same, but Japanese income per capita in the U.S. dollar increases twice. In this case, the value of the Japanese yen has increased relative to the U.S. dollar, which makes Japanese income per capita greater. This is, of course, an extreme case, but it is not unlikely. When the exchange rate between the yen and the dollar fell to ¥70: $1 in the 1980s, Japanese income per capita exceeded that of the United States. However, when the exchange rate rose to ¥150: $1 in 2022, Japanese income per capita is forecasted to be exceeded by Taiwanese GDP per capita. Thus, it is true that a nation's GDP and income per capita in dollar terms could increase or decrease at any time, as the result of exchange rate fluctuations.

Now consider the comparison of income per capita over time. In this case, a meaningful year-by-year comparison is possible only when real GDP is used. Many South Korean people are proud to say that South Korea's GDP per capita was only $80 in 1961, but it increased to $30,000 by 2020. They would like to boast that income per capita increased by nearly 375 times over the past 60 years. Simply speaking, this claim is not correct.

Volt and Zanden (2013) reported GDP per capita in several countries over time at the 1990-dollar value. According to their study, South Korea's GDP per capita was $485 in 1913, $854 in 1950, $2,824 in 1973. Then South Korea's GDP per capita continued to increase to $15,481 in 2001 and to $21,701 in 2010. (Bolt and van Zanden, *The First Update of the Maddison Project*, Maddison Project Working Paper 4, 2013.) Their research shows that in 1961, South Korea's GDP per capita had already reached around $1,500 at the 1990-dollar value. South Korea's official income per capita was $80 in 1961, but Volt and Zanden's estimate was $1,500 in 1961. South Korea's income per capita in 1961 was $80 if it was measured at the 1961 price (= nominal income per capita), but was $1,500 if it was measured at the 1990 price (real income). In other words, these two income measures are not measured on an equal basis. $80 in 1961 is equivalent to $1,500 at the 1990 market price.

Thus, it is misleading to compare nominal GDP per capita in 1961 ($80) with nominal GDP per capita in 2020 ($30,000), because the market prices (inflation) have increased by hundreds of times from 1961 to 2020 in South Korea. Put simply, ignoring inflation over time, and making a simple comparison on the basis of nominal income is no different from drawing a picture ignoring the principle of perspective.$1 in the distant past could not be the same as $1 today in value.

Since income per capita is expressed in U.S. dollars, we could figure out how much the value of the U.S. dollar has fallen over time from 1961 to

2020. The U.S. consumer price index (CPI) jumped 8.6 times from 29.9 in 1961 to 255.7 in 2020, which means that $1 in 1961 would be the same as $8.6 in 2020 in real value. If we convert $80 in 1961 to the 2020-dollar value, income per capita in 1961 ($80) is equivalent to $688. Thus, it would be more accurate to say that South Korea's income per capita increased 44 times from $688 in 1961 to $30,000 in 2020, not 375 times from $80 to $30,000. Equivalently, we can say that $30,000 in 2020 is equivalent to $3,488 at the 1961 price. Then we can also say that income per capita increased from $80 in 1961 to $3,488 in 2020 at the 1961 market value. In this case, income per capita also increased 44 times from 1961 to 2020.

The principle of perspective also applies even when we compare economic performance across countries. The principle is that we should make comparisons of economic performance across countries using the same base year. For instance, South Korea's nominal GDP per capita reached $10,000 in 1995 and exceeded the long-awaited $20,000 mark in 2007, but then stepped back during the global economic crisis and then again exceeded $20,000 in 2010. However, when we compare the year of reaching the $10,000 nominal income level across countries, we should be cautious about the timing of reaching the $10,000 level. The United States reached the landmark level of $10,000 in 1978, Canada in 1980, and Japan in 1984. The fact that South Korea achieved the $10,000 level in 1995, and Japan achieved the level in 1984 does not mean that South Korea was just 11 years behind Japan in reaching the $10,000 level, because the income figures are nominal values. Japan's income of $10,000 in 1984 is not the same as South Korea's income of $10,000 in 1995.

In fact, Japan had achieved the $10,000 level much earlier than 1984 at the 1995 market prices, and South Korea was more than 11 years behind Japan when we used the same criteria, that is, the 1995 prices. When we estimate each country's year of reaching the $10,000 level using the 1995 market value, we have a quite different story. It has been figured out that the United States achieved $10,000 in the 1940s, Canada in 1952, and Japan in 1972. Thus, South Korea was 23 years (not 11 years) behind Japan in achieving the income level of $10,000 in real terms.

<Figure 4.1> U.S. Real GDP per Person, 1870 ~ 2021

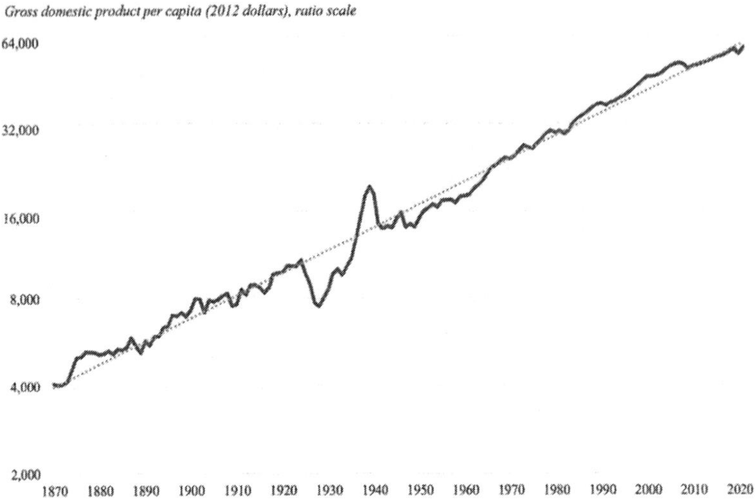

Source: Updated and reproduced from Fernald and Jones (2014). Data for 1870 to 1929 are from Madison (2008). Data for 1929 to 2021 are from the Bureau of Economic Analysis.
Note: Orange dots represent the fitted line.

In conclusion, in order to make a meaningful comparison of economic performance such as GDP or income per capita over time, we should evaluate economic performance using real or constant-price GDP, not nominal or current-price GDP.

6

WHICH MOVIE HAS GROSSED THE HIGHEST BOX OFFICE EARNINGS?

Box Office Mojo, which provides information on earnings of movies, has published 50 films that have earned the highest box office revenues as of 2021. Box office earnings come from various sources including theatrical exhibitions, home video and DVD sales and rentals, television broadcasting rights and merchandising. However, all earnings listed on the table include only the revenues of box office sales. This ranking is based on the revenues expressed in U.S. dollars at their nominal value at the time the movie was released.

<Table 4.2> Highest-Grossing Films at Current Prices (in millions of $)

Rank	Movie Title	Performance Year	World-wide Revenues (Nominal)
1	Avatar	2009	$2,847.2
2	Avengers: Endgame	2019	$2,797.5
3	Titanic	1997	$2,187.4
4	Star Wars: The Force Awakens	2015	$2.068.2
5	Avengers: Infinity War	2018	$2,048.4
6	Jurassic World	2015	$1,671.7
7	The Lion King	2019	$1,656.9
8	The Avengers	2012	$1,518.8
9	Furious 7	2015	$1,516.0
10	Frozen II	2019	$1,450.0

Which movie has earned the highest box office revenues? According to the revenues (nominal value) grossed by movies at the time when they played, the film that earned the highest revenues was Avatar that was released in 2009 and earned $2.8 trillion in box office sales worldwide. The second highest grossing film was Avengers: Endgame (2019) that earned $2.8 trillion, and Titanic (1997) that earned $2.2 trillion (2009) ranks in the third place. The ranking is based on the nominal revenues that were measured at the prices that prevailed when the movies were in theaters. The ranking based on nominal values, however, involves some flaws of containing inflation. In fact, some monumental movies such as Gone with the Wind, The Sound of Music, ET, The Ten Commandments, and Doctor Zhivago which were smashing hits around the world were not included even in the top-ten list of highest-grossing films. Most of these blockbuster movies were released many years ago, and the ticket prices were very low when the movies were in theaters.

For a meaningful comparison of the ticket sales over time, we need to compare them on the basis of real revenues that are measured at the constant price that prevailed in a certain base year. <Table 4.3> presents the highest-grossing films at the 2020 price adjusted for inflation are as follows:

<Table 4.3> Highest-Earning Films Adjusted for Inflation (in millions of $)

Rank	Movie Title	Performance Year	World-wide Revenues (Real Value)
1	Gone With the Wind	1939	$3,739.0
2	Avatar	2009	$3,286.0
3	Titanic	1997	$3,108.0
4	Star Wars	1977	$3,071.0
5	Avengers: Endgame	2019	$2,823.0
6	The Sound of Music	1965	$2,572.0
7	IT: the Extra-Terrestrial	1982	$2,511.0
8	The Ten Commandments	1956	$2,377.0
9	Doctor Zhivago	1965	$2,253.0
10	Star Wars: The Force Awakens	2015	$2,221.0

The ranking of highest-grossing films at the 2020 constant dollar means that the comparison is made based on the 2000 purchasing power. The top ten movies that earned the highest box office revenues in real terms According to the Box Office Mojo's data, Gone with the Wind, that was staged in 1939, has earned the highest box office revenues so far. At the time of the show, the film earned $198.7 million in box office sales, which is translated into $3,739 million at the 2020 price. No film has broken this record yet and is the highest-grossing film of all time. The second highest-earning movie is Avatar. The film earned $2,847.2 in 2009 when it played in theaters, which was equivalent to $3,286 million at the 2020 price. The real earnings of Avatar look dwarfish compared with those of Gone with the Wind. Thus, no film will compete with Gone with the Wind for the title of the all-time high grossing film for many years to come.

The third highest earning movie in real terms was Titanic ($3.1 trillion, 1997) followed by Star Wars ($3.1 trillion, 1977). Avengers: Endgame ($2.8 trillion, 2019) which earned the second highest box office revenues in nominal terms ranks in the 5th place in real terms. Some old blockbusters form an array of high rankings at the 2020 price. The memorable movies of old days include The Sound of Music (1965, $2.6 trillion, 6th place), ET: The Extra-Terrestrial (1982, $2.5 trillion, 7th place), The Ten Commandments (1956, $2.4 trillion, 8th place), and Doctor Zhivago (1965, $2.3 trillion, 9th place) in real terms.

7

Nominal GDP versus Purchasing Power Parity (PPP) GDP

Some readers might get confused between nominal GDP and purchasing power parity (PPP) GDP, because China's GDP in PPP terms already surpassed that of the United States in 2014, but China's nominal GDP is expected to overtake that of the United States around 2030. We have seen earlier that nominal GDP is frequently used to compare the size of the economy (GDP) or income per capita across countries. Official nominal GDP, however, has some problems in comparing living standards across countries, because it does not reflect price level differences among countries. Thus, we might need another measure of nominal GDP that takes different price levels among countries into account. The measure of GDP designed to meet this need is purchasing power parity (PPP) GDP.

To compare GDP and living standards across countries, we need to measure each nation's GDP using a common denominator and commonly use the dollar exchange rate to convert each nation's GDP (denominated in local currency) into the dollar amount. The exchange rate applied to obtain the dollar-denominated GDP is the official exchange rate determined in the foreign exchange market. Some examples of dollar-denominated GDP for major countries in 2021 are as follows: U.S.: $22.7 trillion, China: $16.6 trillion, Japan: $5.4 trillion, U.K.: $3.1 trillion, India: $3.1 trillion, and South Korea: $1.8 trillion. This dollar-denominated GDP is no problem if the market exchange rate accurately reflects price level differences across countries. However, there has been some criticism that the market exchange rate does not reflect differences in price levels across countries.

Although the market exchange rate moves toward reflecting the price level of each country in the long run, it is not necessarily true in the short run. A country's market exchange rate may overestimate or underestimate its price level in the short run. Especially when we convert GDP of a developing country into dollar-denominated GDP using the market exchange rate, the GDP figure may underestimate the living standard of the country. The reason is that the prices of goods and services (especially in the service sector) in developing countries are considerably lower than those in developed countries, and market exchange rates do not properly reflect these purchasing power differences.

For example, consider the case of a haircut. In the United States most haircuts are made at barber shops or beauty salons. Thus, haircuts have a market price, and the market value of haircuts is included in U.S. GDP. Suppose that the average market price of a haircut is $20 in the United States, and there are 300 million haircuts every two weeks. Then the market value of haircuts in the United States is ($20) x (300 million) x (26) = $156 billion per year, and the service of haircuts will add $156 billion to U.S. GDP every year.

However, in developing countries such as Bhutan, the picture is quite different. First, many haircuts are made at home in developing countries. Like many do-it-yourself activities, haircuts have no market prices, which means that the value of many haircuts is not included in GDP in developing countries. Even if haircuts are done at barber shops, the market price of a haircut in developing countries is much lower than the market price in developed countries. It may be true that a haircut costs $20 in the United States, but it costs only $1 in Bhutan. Thus, if the United States produces one haircut service, its GDP will increase by $20, but if Bhutan produces one haircut service, Bhutan's GDP will increase only by $1. This is not fair in comparing living standards across countries. The two countries produce almost identical services (haircuts), but Bhutan's GDP would increase only by one twentieth of U.S. GDP. Thus, GDP figures in developing countries tend to underestimate the true wealth of nations. PPP GDP corrects these deficiencies by reflecting price differences across countries in calculating GDP.

For the purpose of calculating GDP adjusted for price differences across countries, economists apply the PPP exchange rate to convert a nation's GDP into dollar-denominated GDP. Thus, PPP GDP is different from official dollar-denominated GDP in that the latter uses the market-determined exchange rate (under floating exchange rates) or the official exchange rate (under fixed exchange rates), whereas PPP GDP uses the calculated PPP exchange rate. The PPP exchange rate is not an actual exchange rate, but it is an estimated exchange rate. Suppose that the United States and Japan produce only one product, the Big Mac hamburger. If the price of the Big Mac hamburger in the United States is $4, and an identical Big Mac hamburger in Japan sells for 400 yen, then the PPP exchange rate is calculated as ¥400/$4 or ¥100 per dollar. If the market exchange rate is ¥130 per dollar, Japan's official dollar-denominated GDP is calculated based on 130 yen per dollar, whereas Japan's PPP GDP is calculated based on 100 yen per dollar.

<Table 4.4> Nominal GDP versus PPP GDP (2021, in billions of $)

Ranking	Country	Nominal GDP	Country	PPP GDP
1	United States	22,675.3	China	26,656.8
2	China	16,642.3	United States	22,675.3
3	Japan	5,378.1	India	10,207.3
4	Germany	4,319.3	Japan	5,585.8
5	United Kingdom	3,124.7	Germany	4,743.7
6	India	3,049.7	Russia	4,328.1
7	France	2,938.3	Indonesia	3,507.2
8	Italy	2,106.3	Brazil	3,328.5
9	Canada	1,883.5	France	3,231.9
10	South Korea	1,806.7	United Kingdom	3,174.9
11	Russia	1,710.7	Turkey	2,749.6
12	Brazil	1,491.8	Mexico	2,613.8

Let's take the example of China and India to see how much these two measures of GDP make difference. In 2021, China's nominal GDP was $16.6 trillion, but China's PPP GDP in 2021 jumped to $26.7 trillion, which dwarfs U.S. PPP GDP (= $22.7 trillion). China is the second largest economy in the world by nominal GDP, but the largest economy by PPP GDP. India's case is more dramatic. In 2021, India's nominal GDP was $3.1 trillion, ranking 6th in the world, but its PPP GDP reached $10.2 trillion, becoming the world's third largest economy. India's PPP GDP is three times larger than its nominal GDP.

An increase in PPP GDP per capita in China and India is eye-popping. According to IMF, China's nominal GDP per capita in 2022 (estimate) was $14,096, but its PPP GDP per capita in 2022 was $21,364. India's nominal GDP per capita in 2022 was $2,515, but its PPP GDP per capita jumps to $8,358. The vertical jump of PPP GDP in both China and India is attributed partly to the rapid growth of their economies and partly to the lower prices in these countries. Between 1990 and 2018, China's economy grew by over 1,000% whilst India's economy grew by nearly 500%.

In the United States, nominal GDP (= 22.7 trillion) is the same as PPP GDP (= $22.7 trillion). This is because the U.S. price level is used as a reference point for calculating each country's PPP GDP. The United

Kingdom and Japan are one of a few countries where PPP GDP is almost the same as or smaller than its nominal GDP.

We have examined nominal GDP, real GDP, and PPP GDP. Nominal GDP evaluates the market value of final goods and services using current-year prices. Real GDP evaluates the market value of final goods and services using past base-year prices. Thus, real GDP is GDP adjusted for different price levels over time. In other words, real GDP is inflation-eliminated GDP. PPP GDP is nominal GDP adjusted for different price levels across countries.

The difference between official nominal GDP and PPP GDP provides useful information on a country's price level relative to that of the United States. If a country's price level is lower than the United States, the PPP GDP of the country is greater than its official GDP, because official GDP tends to underestimate the true market value of goods and services. Conversely, if a country's price level is higher than that of the United States, the country's PPP GDP is smaller than its official GDP, because official GDP overestimates the true market value of goods and services. Put it differently, if a country's PPP GDP is greater than its official GDP, we can infer that the country's price level is generally lower than that of the United States; if a country's PPP GDP is smaller than its official GDP, we infer that the country's price level is generally higher than that of the United States.

In the table above, China, India, Russia, Brazil, Mexico, and Indonesia are countries whose PPP GDP is much greater than their official GDP. It can be thus inferred that the prices of these countries are generally lower than those of the United States. By contrast, Japan, Germany, the United Kingdom, France, Italy, and Canada are countries whose PPP GDP is not much different from official GDP. The prices of these countries are not much different from those of the United States.

Should we use official GDP or PPP GDP to compare the size of the economy (GDP) or income per capita across countries? PPP GDP can provide useful information on living costs and living standards to people who travel to foreign countries or do business abroad. A fly in the ointment in the measurement of PPP GDP is that the PPP exchange rate is not an actual, but calculated exchange rate, and therefore is less accurate. Thus, for the international comparison of the size of the economy, nominal GDP should be a better measure.

8

GDP Increases as the Rent Increases, but GDP Does Not Increase When the House Price Rises

The distinction between consumption and investment is often ambiguous and confusing. A good example is housing. In macroeconomics, consumption is defined as the purchases of final goods and services by consumers (or households). There is one exception to this accounting principle. The exception is the purchase of houses by households, which is considered as investment, not consumption. When a construction company builds 100 units of houses and sells each unit for $500,000 to consumers, then the sales revenues of $50 million are included in the investment component of GDP. However, if an automobile company manufactures 100 units of trucks and sells each truck for $20,000 to consumers, then the sales revenues of $2 million are included in the consumption component of GDP.

Suppose that you bought a newly built house for $500,000. As we discussed, your purchase of the house is not regarded as consumption but is included in the investment category of GDP. However, if you bought a 10-year-old vacation house for $500,000, your purchase of the house is not included in either the consumption or investment category of GDP. Your purchase of the existing vacation home falls into portfolio investment and has nothing to with GDP. Now suppose that you rent a house (either the newly built house or 10-year-old vacation house) for $30,000 per year. Then your rental fee will be included in the measure of GDP (consumption). There is no problem with including the rental fees of a house in GDP because renting a house from someone belongs to the category of consumer services. However, there is a delicate case in calculating GDP. If, instead of renting a house in the market, you live in your own house, is there any rental income that will affect GDP?

In order to delve into this question further, suppose that Tom and Jerry own almost identical houses whose market prices are $500,000 each. Tom's house is close to an elementary school, and Jerry's house is close to a hospital. Jerry has a 10-year-old child, and Tom works at the hospital. They agree to rent their houses to each other. Tom agrees to pay $30,000 as a rental fee to Jerry, and Jerry agrees to pay $30,000 to Tom. This transaction was made in the market and will increase GDP by $60,000 per year. Now consider the case of owner-occupancy. Tom and Jerry decide to reside in their own houses. If Tom and Jerry are both owner-occupiers, there are no explicit transactions of rents, even though the same economic relationship as the case of tenant-occupancy exists: There are still two owners and two occupiers, but the transactions between them no longer go through the market. Is there any rental income in the case of owner-occupancy?

The owner of a house can be viewed as having two entities: One (right hand) is a business firm that buys and owns a house, and the other (left hand) is a consumer who consumes the services the house provides. My right hand owns the house, and my left hand rents the house from my right hand and pays the rent. In the national income accounting, the virtual rent that does not have explicit monetary payments is called an imputed rent.

The rationale for the imputed rent can be found in the concept of opportunity cost. If you own a house and rent your house to a third party in the market, you'll receive $30,000 as a rental fee from the tenant. The rental fee becomes your disposable income, which will increase GDP by that amount. If you instead live in the house you own, you do not have to pay the rent. However, this rental fee can be considered as your opportunity cost of living in your own house. If you rented your house to someone else, you would earn $30,000 per year, but you gave up this opportunity to earn $30,000. Thus, in the spirit of national income accounting, this imputed rent should also be included in GDP. However, many countries are divergent about this issue.

Since there is no market price for the imputed rent, the national income accountants should estimate it. As we discussed, the annual rent for a similar house on the market will be an estimate for the imputed rent. This is the only exception to the national income accounting principle that "GDP is measured by market price". (If prostitution and drug transactions were included in GDP, this would also be an exception to this principle.) Theoretically imputed rent should be included in the amount of GDP just as explicit rent is included in GDP. However, many nations are reluctant to include imputed rents in the category of GDP, because there could be some taxation implications. Some countries such as the United Kingdom Belgium, Iceland, Luxembourg, the Netherlands, Slovenia, Spain, and Switzerland have attempted to tax the imputed rent.

Assuming that the imputed rent is included in GDP, we calculate GDP in our example. Your friend bought a newly built house for $500,000 and rented it to a third party for the annual rent of $30,000. You buy a 10-year-old vacation house for $500,000 and live in the house. Your neighbor rents a house similar to your house for $25,000. The transactions would increase GDP as follows:

Your friend's purchase of the house (investment):	$500,000
Your purchase of the 10-year-old house:	0
Your friend's rental income (consumer service):	$30,000
Your imputed rent (consumer service):	$25,000

The amount of GDP as the result of the transactions will increase by $555,000 (= $500,000 + $30,000 + $25,000). If the imputed rent is excluded from GDP, then GDP will increase by $530,000 (= $500,000 + $30,000) In conclusion, no matter how much the price of an existing house built in the past rises, it does not affect national income (and thus income per capita). However, if a higher house price raises rental fees. GDP will increase to the extent that the rental fees increase.

9

GDP AS VALUE ADDED AND VALUE-ADDED TAX (VAT)

GDP is defined as the market value of all final goods and services produced in a country, but the calculation is not as simple as it might seem. Above all, it is possible to double count or triple count the value of products. We have seen that GDP measured on the product side does not include intermediate goods such as raw materials (iron ores) and semifinished goods (iron). The exclusion of intermediate goods from GDP is to avoid double counting. To this end, the national income accountants calculate GDP by adding only the value added at each stage of production of goods and services. According to the value-added approach, GDP is equal to the sum of values added at each stage of production and distribution of goods and services.

Value added refers to the difference between the selling price of a good or service and the cost of the production factors used to make the good or service. Many countries except for several countries such as the United States adopt value-added taxes (VAT), which impose taxes on the value added at each stage of production.

To understand the concept of value added, we will consider a simplified economy that produces only coffee products. First, let's say that a coffee bean grower produces coffee beans in the state of Karnataka in India. Luckily, coffee trees grew naturally in the garden of his home. He picks up coffee beans by hand using simple homemade tools (ladders and baskets). There will be some production costs for making the tools, but we ignore these costs, because they are one-time costs (fixed costs) and small. The coffee farmer harvests $10,000 worth of coffee beans per month. He sold the coffee beans for $10,000 to a coffee roasting (processing beans) company. In the first production stage, the value added by the coffee bean grower is $10,000.

The roasting company processed beans and sold them for $15,000 to a coffee cafe. In the second stage of transaction, the value added by the roasting company is $5,000 ($15,000 – $10,000). The cafe owner used roasted coffee beans to make 500 cups of coffee, and he sold them for $5 per cup. The total sales of the coffee drinks he sold were $25,000. The café owner newly added $10,000 worth of value in the production of coffee drinks ($25,000 – $15,000) by providing his service to final consumers. Adding up the value added at each stage of production and distribution, we get $10, 000 (value added by the coffee bean farmer) + $5,000 (bean roaster) + $10,000 (cafe owner) = $25,000. The total sum of values added at all stages of production and distribution of coffees is exactly the same as the market value of coffee drinks, the final consumer product.

	Coffee farmer	Roasting firm	Cafe owner	Final price
Sale price	$10,000	$15,000	$25,000	$25,000
Value added	$10,000	$5,000	$10,000	

However, if we sum up the market values of all goods and services produced at each stage of production and distribution, we obtain $50,000 (= $10,000 + $15,000 + $25,000). The sum of the market value of all goods and services is double- or triple- counted, which greatly exaggerates the amount of GDP. Here we note that the value of roasted coffee beans ($15,000) includes the value of raw coffee beans ($10,000), which is already counted in the calculation of GDP. Thus, $10,000 is double counted at this stage. Similarly, the market value of $25,000 earned by the café owner also includes the value of raw coffee beans ($10,000) and roasting services ($5,000). Raw coffee beans or roasted coffee beans are intermediate goods, and their market value should not be included in GDP. In fact, summing up value added at each stage of production and distribution is consistent with the market value of final goods and services. It should be clear that the value-added approach to measuring GDP has the advantage of avoiding the double counting of GDP.

Value added taxes (VAT) adopted by many countries in the world, including the United Kingdom, EU countries, India, Japan, South Korea, and many other countries, is a tax levied on newly added value at each stage of transaction. VAT is a form of consumption tax and an indirect tax that is passed from the business owner (who has the obligation to pay the tax) to the final consumer. Since the price of the product or service includes value added taxes, when the final consumer purchases the product (coffee drinks), the business owner pays the VAT included in the final product to the tax collector. The value added tax is distinguished from the sales tax adopted in the United States and other countries. The sales tax is levied on the sales of goods or services, while the value added tax is imposed on the value added to the goods or services at each stage of production and distribution.

France was the first country to adopt a value added tax. France introduced the new tax system in 1955 to replace the tax system imposed on manufacturing processes with the value added tax. Since then, many countries have adopted value added taxes. The background of the introduction of the VAT was to modernize the indirect tax system and to implement their economic development plans more efficiently by simplifying taxable items and tax rates.

The Organization for Economic Cooperation and Development (OECD) has published the annual VAT rates of member nations since 1975. According to the database, VAT rates in member countries (33 countries) range from 5% to 27%. The average standard VAT rate in 2015 was 19.2%, which is higher than the average standard VAT rate of 17.8% in 2000 and the average standard VAT rate of 15.6% in 1975. Thus, VAT rates in OECD countries have been on the rise. These average rates exclude reduced rates or zero-rated goods and services, as they are difficult to compare across countries. It is interesting to note that the average value added tax rate of 33 OECD member nations is higher than the average sales tax rate of the United States. Do higher tax rates lead to more welfares for people? (We'll discuss this issue later.)

10

Production and Expenditure Are Two Sides of a Coin

We have discussed the product approach to measuring GDP, which states that GDP is measured as the sum of the market value of all final goods and services produced in an economy during a certain period. There is another approach to measuring GDP commonly known as the expenditure approach. There is an important principle in national income accounting: The total value of products produced by firms is identical to the total amount of expenditures on the products spent by economic agents. This national income accounting principle follows from the presumption that all goods and services *produced* during a certain year are normally all *purchased* in that year. Put differently, the total value of products and the total amount of expenditure on the products are eventually the same. Thus, we can measure GDP either by summing the market values of all goods and services *produced* by firms or by summing *expenditures* on all goods and services spent by economic agents. We have seen that there are four main economic agents in the economy who purchase final goods and services: consumers, firms, governments, and foreigners.

Thus, aggregate expenditure on final goods and services can be divided into four categories. First, households (or consumers) purchase consumption goods produced in a country. Consumption goods are goods produced for final consumption such as coffee drinks and automobiles. Coffee beans and steel are not consumption goods, because they are intermediate goods that are used to produce final goods. Consumption goods include durable goods such as automobiles, nondurable goods such as food, and consumer services such as medical treatments, education, and travel. In any country, consumption is the largest component of GDP. In general, as the living standards of a country rises, the country moves toward a mass consumption economy, and the proportion of consumption becomes greater. Currently, in the United States, the share of consumption in GDP is almost 70%, the highest level in the world, and the share of consumption in China's GDP remains at less than 40% of GDP.

The second component of aggregate expenditure is investment by business firms. Investment in macroeconomics refers to the purchases of capital goods such as tools, machinery, equipment, and plants by firms. Put simply, investment is an increase in capital. Firms include corporations, limited liability companies, unlimited liability companies, and self-employed enterprises. Thus, if a homemaker buys a sewing machine to make sweaters with the purpose of selling them in the market, the purchase of the sewing machine falls into investment. However, if a homemaker buys a sewing machine to make clothes for her children, the purchase of the sewing machine is treated as consumption.

Business investment can be divided into three categories: First, business fixed investment (= construction investment) occurs when firms buy investment goods to increase the production of goods and services. Business fixed investment refers to expenditures on production facilities such as tools, machines, plants and intellectual property products. The second category of investment is residential fixed investment. Residential fixed investment refers to expenditures on residential buildings such as single-family homes, condominiums, townhouses, and other residential facilities. We have defined consumption as spending on goods and services by households, but residential construction investment is an exception to the definition of consumption. Residential construction investment is a household expenditure on housing, but it is viewed as an investment rather than as the consumption of durable goods. The last component of investment is inventory investment. Inventories held by a firm are treated as if the firm purchased its own products for future sales. With this accounting principle, a country's total production and expenditure become equal.

The government also purchases goods or services produced in a country. Government purchases are divided into government consumption and government investment. Government consumption refers to expenditures on consumption goods such as cars and gasoline, computer hardware and software, and office supplies. Government consumption also includes salaries and wages for government officials and military personnel. Government investment refers to expenditures on the construction of highways, railroads, ports, fire stations, police stations, courts, etc. The state and local governments also buy goods and services. Government purchases (G) include the purchase of final goods and services by the federal, state, and local governments. Government purchases are part of the government's fiscal policy. However, transfer payments such as social security payments, unemployment benefits, and interest payments are not included in government purchases. The proportion of government purchases in GDP is very stable compared with investment. The proportion of government purchases in GDP is a measure of the size of the government. There has been heated debate concerning 'big government' versus 'small government'. If a government involves more in the private economy, the ratio tends to be high. Conversely, if a government involves less in the economy, the ratio tends to be low. In the United States, the ratio remains quite stable around 20% of GDP.

Finally, net exports are also an important expenditure item. First, exports are the sales of domestic goods and services to foreigners. Therefore, exports should be included in the country's GDP. On the other hand, imports are the purchases of foreign goods and services by domestic consumers, firms, and governments and therefore should not be included in the country's GDP because they are produced in foreign countries. However, in reality, domestic consumption by households includes many imported goods and services. Chinese clothes, German cars, French wines, etc. are purchased by American consumers. In addition, firms also buy many foreign-made investment goods such as cranes, trucks, and machines. The government also buys foreign-made products such as computers. We need to subtract the imports of foreign goods and services to get the total amount of goods and services produced domestically. The difference between exports (EX) and imports (IM) is called net exports (NX), and the net exports constitute part of GDP.

Thus, GDP measured by the expenditure side is equal to the sum of expenditures on consumption (C) by consumers, investment (I) by firms, government purchases (G) by federal, state, and local governments, and net exports (NX) by foreigners.

$$\text{GDP} = \text{Consumption (C)} + \text{Investment (I)}$$
$$+ \text{Government purchases (G)} + \text{Net exports (NX)}$$

The national income accounting identity shows that the total amount of expenditures spent on final goods and services by economic agents (GDP measured in terms of expenditure) is equal to the total market value of all final goods and services produced domestically (GDP measured in terms of production).

11

Production and Income Are Two Sides of a Coin

We have shown that GDP measured by the expenditure approach is identical to GDP measured by the product approach. We can now show that the market value of all final goods and services is equal to the sum of income earned by the owners of production factors. In order to produce goods and services, firms use production factors such as labor, capital, land, and entrepreneurship. Firms use sales revenues from selling their products to pay for labor, capital, land, and entrepreneurship. Therefore, the sum of income earned by the owners of production factors is in principle equal to the sales revenues (or market value) of final goods and services produced by firms.

First, workers provide labor to firms and receive wages. Second, capital owners provide funds to firms and earn interest. Third, landowners provide land to firms and earn rents. Finally, anything left after firms pay wages, interest, and rents out of their sales revenues constitutes profits that go to entrepreneurs who provide entrepreneurial skills to firms. When we sum wages, interest, rents, and profits that factor owners earn, we obtain factor income. If factor owners earn factor income domestically (say, in the United Kingdom) regardless of their nationality, we obtain domestic income. On the other hand, when we sum wages, interest, rents and profits that British factor owners earn regardless of where they earn, we obtain British national income. The distinction between domestic income and national income corresponds to the distinction between GDP (gross domestic product) and GNP (gross national product).

Domestic income = Wages earned by workers in the U.K. + Interest earned by capitalists in the U.K. + Rents earned landowners in U.K. + Profits earned by entrepreneurs in the U.K.

National income = Wages earned by British workers + Interest earned by British capitalists +Rents earned by British landowners. + Profits earned by British entrepreneurs

Domestic income (or national income) defined above does not exactly match GDP (or GNP). If GDP is solely used for payment of wages, interest, rents, and profits, domestic income and GDP will be the same. However, some of the sales revenues (GDP) received by firms from selling their goods and services are used to replace worn-out capital. Capital goods used by firms tend to wear out in the process of production. The amount required for the replacement of worn-out capital is depreciation. It should be noted that the depreciation of capital goods is not a payment to production factors but represents production cost. Firms must replace the worn-out parts of factories and machines every year to maintain a certain quantity and quality of capital goods. Since depreciation does not represent a payment to the owners of production factors, it is not included in domestic income (or national income) but is included in GDP (or GNP) because it is part of the sales revenues received by firms from selling final goods and services.

The second adjustment is the indirect business tax. An indirect tax is a tax that is imposed on goods and services, not individual payers. The indirect tax is paid by sellers or producers, and then shifts to final consumers. There are two types of indirect taxes. The sales tax or value-added tax is levied as a certain percentage of the sales of goods and services, and the excise tax is imposed on any particular product such as cigarettes, alcohol or gasoline as a certain amount. On the other hand, a direct tax refers to the tax that the person who is obligated to pay a tax and the person who pays the tax are the same. The indirect tax is the tax that these two identities are different, and the tax burden is passed on to another payer. The consumer is ultimately responsible for paying the indirect tax that is included in the price of the goods or services purchased.

Let's take the example of VAT (10%) that is levied on goods and services. If you buy a $100 garment at the Harrods department store, the price includes the VAT of, say, $10. The department store pays the VAT to the tax collector first and receives the tax from the final consumer later. In this way, firms use a portion of GDP as payments to factor owners and the rest of it for depreciation and indirect tax payments. If we add depreciation and indirect business taxes to domestic income, we obtain GDP, which is commonly called GDI (gross domestic income):

$$\begin{aligned}\text{GDI} &= \text{Domestic income} + \text{Depreciation} + \text{Indirect business taxes}\\ &= \text{Wages} + \text{Interest} + \text{Rents} + \text{Profits} + \text{Depreciation}\\ &\quad + \text{Indirect business taxes}\end{aligned}$$

Similarly, when we add depreciation and indirect business taxes to national income, we obtain GNI (gross national income):

GNI = National income + Depreciation + Indirect business taxes

As we discussed, GDI is identical to GDP, and GNI is identical to GNP. GDP and GDI are two sides of the same coin, and GNP and GNI are two sides of the same coin. Thus, we have the following identities:

GDP = GDI
GNP = GNI

Finally, the relationship between GNI and GDI (for the U.K. economy) is derived as follows:

GNI = GDI – Income earned by foreigners (corporations and self-employees) in the U.K.+ Income earned by the British nationals (corporations and self-employees) overseas

12

From Gross Income (GDI or GNI) to Personal Income

It is important to know the gross income (GDI or GNI) of a country, but it is also important to understand how much individuals earn. There is a saying that one does not see the forest for the trees. Also, the opposite might hold true. One does not see the trees for the forest. It is important to see both the forest and the trees.

Factor income (domestic income or national income) is the sum of income earned by the owners of production factors who participate in the production of goods and services. However, some people receive a certain amount of income as gifts from the government, even though they don't participate in the production of goods and services. This type of income is called transfer payments. The transfer payments include food stamps, unemployment compensations, Social Security benefits, civil service pensions, and subsidies for the elderly with low income. Transfer payments are an important source of income for individuals to use, and we need a measure of income that individuals can use for consumption. In order to find out how much an individual actually earns, income from transfer payments must be added to factor income that the owners of production factors (labor, capital, land, and entrepreneurship) earn from participating in the production of goods and services.

Second, corporate income taxes and corporate retained earnings should be subtracted from factor income because corporate income taxes and retained earnings by firms do not actually go to the income of factor owners. Corporate retained earnings are corporate profits that are retained after some portion of profits is allocated to shareholders as dividends. The following defines personal income (PI) that goes to individuals.

Personal income (PI) = Factor income + Transfer income –
(Corporate income taxes + Corporate retained earnings)

This personal income is the total amount of income that individuals receive, but individuals cannot use all of personal income to purchase final goods and services. This is because part of personal income is used to pay personal income taxes. Thus, the amount of income we obtain after subtracting personal income taxes from personal income becomes the income that individuals can dispose of for the purchase of final goods and services. This final income is called disposable income and defined as follows:

Disposable Income (DI) = Personal income −Personal income taxes

In sum, disposable income is obtained by adding transfer payments to GDP and subtracting various taxes (indirect business taxes, corporate income taxes, and personal income taxes) from GDP. Disposable income is the key determinant of consumption in the Keynesian model.

Individuals use disposable income mainly for consumption and save any remaining income after they spend it.

Disposable income = Consumption (C) + Savings (S)

From this relationship, savings are defined as the remaining portion of disposable income consumed.

Savings = Disposable income − Consumption

Alternatively, we can obtain disposable income by adding transfer income to GDI (gross domestic income) and subtracting various taxes from GDI.

Disposable Income = GDI + Transfer Income – Various taxes
= GDI − Net taxes (NT)

where net taxes (NT) = taxes – transfer income, and include indirect business taxes, corporate income taxes, personal income taxes, corporate retained earnings, and depreciation. Thus, GDI is given as follows:

GDI (or GDP) = Disposable income + Net taxes
= Consumption + Savings + Net taxes

This measurement of GDP may be called the disposition approach to measuring GDP. This relation shows how GDI is disposed of in the economy. First, GDP is used for consumption. Some of GDP is used for paying net taxes (taxes – transfer payments). The remaining GDP is used for savings.

So far, we have seen that GDP can be measured in three different ways: They include the product approach, expenditure approach, and income approach. There is another way of measuring GDP, that is, the disposition approach. No matter what approach we use, we arrive at the same GDP figure, because we are looking at the same thing from different aspects. This principle is known as the national income accounting identity.

GDP measured by the product approach
= GDP measured by the expenditure approach
= GDP measured by the income approach
= GDP measured by the disposition approach

13

GDP DOES NOT MEASURE HAPPINESS: THE EASTERLIN PARADOX

There has been some criticism that GDP measuring the size of an economy is inaccurate as an indicator of people's welfare or happiness. A country's standard of living is usually measured on the basis of GDP (or GNI) per capita, and GDP per capita is obtained by dividing the country's GDP by the number of its people. However, GDP per capita may measure only people's material satisfaction.

One of the criticisms is that GDP includes the value of 'bads' as well as the value of 'goods'. A country's GDP tends to increase with war. Obviously, war kills many people, destroys factories, houses, buildings, roads, and even the splendid cultural heritage that humanity has achieved in its long history. Nonetheless, war increases GDP without reference to the tragic destruction of human achievements. When war breaks out, government spending tends to increase to support the war, and the utilization of the country's production facilities tends to increase to produce arms and other military supplies. Furthermore, after war, large-scale investment is made to rebuild production facilities, homes, roads, bridges destroyed by war. As a result, the country's GDP tends to increase. The United States was able to escape from the Great Depression after the United States entered World War II. The U.S. economy boomed during the periods of the Korean War, Vietnam War, and Gulf War. Japan was also able to rise from the ashes after WWII when it benefitted from the Korean war. Natural disasters such as earthquakes, hurricanes, tornados, floodings, fires devastate human lives and human achievements, but they all tend to increase GDP due to reconstruction projects.

Even a car accident also tends to increase GDP. Car accidents certainly harm the welfare of people, and there would be no benefit from any car accident. However, a car accident could significantly increase GDP. First, if an auto repair shop spends $5,000 to repair the damaged car, GDP will increase by that amount. Second, the treatment of the injured by a doctor is an act of consumer service. If the treatment costs $10,000, GDP will increase by that amount. If the injured file a lawsuit against the injurer for the compensation of any physical injury, GDP also increases because a lawyer service is a consumer service. If the legal expenses are $3,000, this amount is added to GDP. As a result of the car accident, nothing is better from the standpoint of the wellbeing of the person who suffered from the accident, but the nation's GDP will increase by $18,000 in our example. It is obviously preposterous that a car accident which does not contribute to the well-being of the people at all increases national income.

Another critique of GDP is that it excludes economic activities that are difficult to measure at market prices, because GDP only includes economic activities that have market prices. Thus, any economic activities done by homemakers or do-it-yourselfers are excluded from GDP. However, there is no question that such valuable economic activities provided by homemakers and do-it-yourselfers make a significant contribution to the welfare of the country. Some studies show that the monetary value of homemakers' housework could be greater than the income they earn at work. While such a claim may be true, nonetheless, housework and do-it-yourself activities are not included in GDP. If a homemaker makes a meal at home for a party, such expenses are not included in GDP, but if she orders the same meal by catering, such expenses are included in GDP. Do-it-yourself work has a greater share in economic activity in underdeveloped countries than in developed countries.

In addition, GDP does not include the value of leisure activities. This is because it is not easy to measure leisure activities at market price. It goes without saying that leisure activities increase workers' productivity and promote workers' health, which in turn enhances the public welfare.

Finally, GDP per capita used as a measure of national welfare is the average of total national income, and it does not take income inequality into account. The average numbers sometimes belie the truth. For simplicity, consider two countries (Atlantis and Shangri-La) with two people each. In Atlantis, one person earns $40,000 and the other person earns $10,000. The country's income distribution is biased towards the rich person. On the other hand, in Shangri-La one person earns $26,000, and the other person earns $24,000. In both countries, GDP per capita is $25,000. But half of the people living in Atlantis will live under poverty and not be happy. The average level of happiness felt by people living in Shangri-La will be much higher than the average level of happiness felt by people living in Atlantis.

GDP measures material civilization. However, material abundance does not necessarily ensure spiritual happiness. There is an interesting study concerning the relationship between income and happiness. Richard Easterlin (1974) who investigated the relationship has found that individual happiness increases with income within a nation, and average happiness increases among nations at a point in time, but happiness does not increase as income continues to increase over time. He has further found that there is little correlation between income and happiness when the annual income exceeds $75,000 (The threshold income would be much higher at current prices). This phenomenon is known as the Easterlin paradox. Put it simply, the Easterlin paradox indicates that happiness has not changed over time despite sharp increases in GDP per capita. One plausible explanation for the Easterlin paradox is that income may be evaluated relative to others (social comparison or social relation) or to oneself in the past (habituation). However, spiritual comforts may also be an important element of happiness.

King Solomon, who is known to have possessed the greatest amount of wealth, lamented at the end, “Vanity of vanities. All is vanity” (Source: The Bible, Ecclesiastes 1:2). It is said that when Native Americans ride a horse for a long time, they stand for a while and look back at the road they ran. It’s not for them to take a break, and it’s not for giving the horse a break, either. It is a stop to see whether there is a soul that could not catch up with the running, because the horse ran too fast. Homo sapiens (modern people), who have been running fast toward mammonism, may need this kind of stop. Bhutan is one of the few countries in the world that does not yet have a Starbucks cafe. It may be the business policy of the Starbucks headquarters, but it may be that the Bhutanese government has taken some measures because it is concerned about the spread of material civilization and the retreat of its spiritual culture. Starbucks is a symbol of modern materialism.

Over the past several thousand years, religion and philosophy have struggled over the subject of "what happiness is,” but have not yet reached a satisfactory answer. We are curious about how a poet sees happiness. Rainer Maria Rilke’s definition of happiness is very philosophical. He composed 10 series of <Duino Elegies> (<*Duineser Elegien*> in German) in 1912 at the castle of Duino on the beach of the Adrian Sea. The name Duino Elegies comes from the name of the place (Duino) where he wrote the poem. Rilke tried to seek after the truth of what a human being is. Life, death, love, happiness are the main themes of his poem. According to him, true happiness comes not from religion or Marxism, or politics, or materials, but from a state of unity encompassing ‘life and death’ and ‘time and space’ together. Particularly, Rilke saw happiness in his Ninth Elegy as “a hurried gain in front of an impending loss”. Does it mean that happiness is a drifting cloud after all? The following is part of the Ninth Elegy of <Duino Elegies>.

Why, if it could begin as laurel, and be spent so,
This space of Being, a little darker than all
the surrounding green, with little waves at the edge
of every leaf (like a breeze's smile)—why then
have to be human—and shunning destiny
long for destiny?
Oh, not because happiness exists,
that over-hasty profit from imminent loss,
not out of curiosity, or to practice the heart,
which could exist in the laurel…
But because being here is much, and because all
That's here seems to need us, the ephemeral, that
strangely concerns us. We: the most ephemeral. Once,
for each thing, only once. Once, and no more. And we too,
once. Never again. But this
once, to have been, though only once,
to have been an earthly thing—seems irrevocable.
……..
Earth, is it not this that you want: to rise
invisibly in us? —Is that not your dream,
to be invisible, one day? —Earth! Invisible!
What is your urgent command if not transformation?
Earth, beloved, I will. O, believe me, you need
no more Spring-times to win me: only one,
ah, one, is already more than my blood can stand.
Namelessly, I have been truly yours, from the first.
You were always right, and your most sacred inspiration
is that familiar Death.
See I live. On what? Neither childhood nor future
grows less…Excess of being
wells up in my heart.

14

IN SEARCH OF SHANGRI-LA

Criticism that GDP has a limitation as a measure of wellbeing and happiness has long been raised. Efforts to replace or improve GDP have been made steadily. One of such efforts is to develop broader national welfare measures that include not only material satisfaction but also spiritual happiness. These indicators differ from the traditional GDP measure in that they attempt to include the value of economic activity that cannot be assessed based on market prices.

A representative example is the Human Development Index (HDI), which is released annually by the UNDP (UN Development Program). The Human Development Index was originally developed in 1990 by Nobel prize-winning Indian economist Amartya Sen and Pakistani economist Mahbub ul Haq. In addition to the income index, the HDI is calculated by obtaining the life expectancy index and education index for each country and then geometrically averaging them. The UNDP began to publish the income inequality-adjusted human development index (IHDI) in 2014. Either HDI or IHDI is not a quantified indicator because it is expressed as an index. However, the IHDI is considered to be a step closer to the development of an indicator that measures people's happiness. According to the United Nations' 2014 IHDI, the order of happy countries is as follows.

> (1) Norway (0.891); (2) Australia (0.860); (3) Netherlands (0.854); (4) Switzerland (0.847); (5) Germany (0.846); (6) Iceland (0.843); (7) Sweden (0.840); (8) Denmark (0.833); (8) Canada (0.833); (10) Ireland (0.832); (16) United Kingdom (0.812), (18) France (0.804); (19) Japan (0.799); (23) Italy (0.755); (28) United States (0.755); (33) South Korea (0.736).

One interesting feature in this statistic is that the United States ranks fifth in HDI without the adjustment of income inequality, and South Korea ranks 16th which is better than Japan, but the United States ranks 28th and South Korea 33rd in IHDI, when income inequality is adjusted. This indirectly indicates that income inequality in the United States and South Korea is much worse than in Japan.

Another alternative indicator to GDP is the Measure of Economic Welfare (MEW) developed by William Nordhaus of Yale University together with James Tobin who won the Nobel prize in economics in 1972. Based on the Measure of Economic Welfare, Herman Daly and John Cobb developed the Index of Sustainable Economic Welfare (ISEW) in 1987. The ISEW index is quantified as follows.

$$\text{ISEW} = \text{Personal consumption} + \text{Public expenditure (excluding defense expenses)} + \text{Private safety costs} + \text{Capital formation} + \text{Domestic labor service} - \text{Environmental deterioration cost} - \text{Natural capital depreciation}$$

In addition to these indexes, there are several attempts to develop an alternative to GDP such as the Genuine Progress Index (GPI), but no satisfactory indicators to replace GDP have been developed yet. The biggest weakness of these alternative indicators is that it is not easy to quantify spiritual happiness and create an objective indicator that everyone can agree on.

There has been a remarkable effort toward developing an index that can be used for actual policy evaluations by quantifying spiritual happiness. The Bhutanese government has developed the Gross National Happiness (GNH) index and used the index officially to evaluate the feasibility of its economic projects. The index is a combination of seven items used to determine the national gross well-being: (1) economic health; (2) environmental health; (3) physical health; (4) mental health; (5) job satisfaction; (6) social health; (7) political soundness. The Bhutan government uses the GNH index to evaluate how well the country's development of resources can help people's happiness. Joseph Stiglitz, who won the Nobel prize in economics, is also sympathetic to Bhutan's GNH index.

Bhutan may be Shangri-La that is the major scene of *Lost Horizon*, a novel by James Hilton published in 1933. *Lost Horizon* is a novel depicting a truth-seeking life experienced by Hugh Conway, a veteran of the First World War in Shangri-La, a Utopian land that is believed to exist in a valley in the Himalayas. In May 1931, 80 white people living in a village in India escaped to a place called Pashawar because of the riot that erupted in the region. Some of passengers in the plane included British Consul Conway, a British vice-consul, an American, and a British missionary. However, the plane was kidnapped during flight and turned to Tibet, where it was forced to land. In the process of the hijacking, the pilot died. Before he died, he told passengers to flee to nearby Shangri-La. The four of them journeyed to find Shangri-La.

Conway meets High Lama in the village. Conway became aware that when people entered the valley, they aged slowly, but once they left the village, people quickly aged and died soon. He was told that the Lama Temple was founded in the early 18th century by Perrault, a Catholic priest in Luxembourg. After meeting the High Lama, Conway sensed that the high priest might be Ferrol. His guess was correct. The high priest was 300 years old. Ferrol had a feeling that his final day was numbered when he became 300 years old and asked Conway to lead the Lama Temple after him.

In 2020, GDP per capita was $3,122 in Bhutan (153rd), $63,414 in the United States (12th), and $31,632 in South Korea (38th) (Data: World Bank). Based on this comparison, we cannot conclude that American people are happier about 20 times more than Bhutanese people, and South Korean people are happier about 10 times more than Bhutanese people. We have noted that in underdeveloped countries, many economic activities such as food, clothing, haircuts, etc. become self-sufficient. Most of these economic activities are not included in GDP because they don't have market prices. Even if the economic activities are measured at market value, the prices of goods and services in underdeveloped countries are much lower than those of developed countries.

Although Bhutan's GDP per capita ranked 153rd in the world, Bhutan is often ranked among the top 10 nations in the world in the survey of happiness. In 2010, it ranked first in the National Happiness Index ranking published by the European New Economic Foundation (NEF): 97 out of 100 people in Bhutan responded that they were happy. South Korea's GDP per capita ranked 38th, but in the survey of happiness, South Korea was placed in the 67th. These survey results once again remind us that material abundance is not an absolute criterion for happiness, and that GDP is not enough as an indicator of well-being and happiness. We might not find a utopia such as Shangri-La, forever in the real world. However, we should not give up our effort to move one step closer to an economic Shangri-La, through continuously improving economic welfare and income inequality. That is a mission and a privilege given to people who are interested in economics.

PART 5

INCOME INEQUALITY AND WELFARE: THE SPHINX'S CONUNDRUM

1

THE SPHINX'S CONUNDRUM AND WELFARE ISSUES

In ancient Egypt, the Sphinx was depicted as a monster with a human face and the body of a lion. At the same time the Sphinx which stood in front of the entrance to the pyramids or temples was usually recognized as a guardian of people. However, in Greek mythology, the Sphinx is depicted as a wicked being with a woman's face and chest, an eagle's wings, and a snake's tail.

The most widely known story about the Sphinx was the work written by Sophocles around 450 B.C. Sophocles wrote several plays, of which seven plays have been passed down completely until today. The most famous one is the trilogy of Thebes (*Oedipus the King*, *Oedipus at Colonus*, and *Antigone*). In his play *Oedipus the King*, Oedipus received a prophecy that stated that he would kill his father and marry his mother. Oedipus was the son of Laius, the king of Thebes and Jocasta.

After unknowingly killing his father, he meets the Sphinx on his way to his hometown of Thebes. The Sphinx throws a riddle to a passing traveler and kills him if he doesn't get it right. The conundrum the Sphinx gives to Oedipus is: "Which animal walks on all four legs in the morning, on two legs during the daytime, and on three legs in the evening?" The question the Sphinx asked was about human life. The riddle hints a human being who crawls as a child, walks vigorously with two legs in adolescence and eventually relies on a walking stick in old age. The Sphinx's riddle hints at two essentials. First, it is inevitable for the old to need a certain type of support, whether the support is physical or financial. Second, it is not an easy task to get an answer to the challenging issue of getting old. Jean-Auguste-Dominique Ingres created a famous painting (1808) called <Oedipus Who Explains the Riddle of the Sphinx>.

Oedipus not only saved his life because he satisfactorily answered the riddle, but he was also destined to become the King of Thebes and to marry his mother. The sexual compassion that a son has unconsciously about his mother was called the Oedipus complex by psychoanalyst Sigmund Freud.

<Figure 5.1> Oedipus Who Explains the Riddle of the Sphinx

On the other hand, psychologist Carl Gustav Jung used the term Electra complex to describe the tendency of a daughter to have sexual compassion for her father while hating her mother. Electra is the daughter of Agamemnon in Greek mythology. Agamemnon, king of Mycenae, returned to his homeland after the 10-year Trojan War. The king was killed by his wife Clytemnestra and her lover, Aegisthus, on the night of his return home. Electra joins forces with her brother, Orestes, to kill her mother and her paramour and pay back their father's enemies. Eugene O'Neill published a novel, *Mourning Becomes Electra* in 1931, which was based on the Electra complex. The novel was considered as a representative work that dealt with love-hate affairs and conflicts in a family such as murder, adultery, incest, affection, and revenge from the perspective of the Electra complex.

Let's go back to the Sphinx's conundrum. Isn't it that the Sphinx asks such a riddle because the Sphinx knows that the greatest problem faced by the human being is the fate of man who is destined to walk on three legs in the age? And isn't it that the problem of the old is recognized as a conundrum that could not be solved easily? In fact, the issue of welfare is a problem that cannot be easily resolved, but it is also a problem that makes many people suffer and leads them to die if they do not find an answer, just like the Sphinx's conundrum.

Keynes also discussed the urgency of the welfare problem, maintaining that if we did not solve the welfare problem quickly, we would be in big trouble later. He says that "In the long run we are all dead". He argued that during the Great Depression, we saw people waiting in line to get bread and other people selling apples at the corner of the street, and people would die if we waited until the economy solved its problem for itself. He believed that the government's immediate intervention in the economy through spending increases, tax cuts, transfer payments could create jobs, provide food and save the lives of many unemployed people.

Keynes presented a new paradigm to deal with the Great Depression and was mainly concerned with resolving the unemployment problem. According to Keynes, it is a dereliction of duty for the government to take a hands-off attitude toward the unemployment problem. Amid rising unemployment during the Great Depression, many welfare programs were introduced and implemented.

2

WHAT IS ECONOMIC JUSTICE?

Economic justice is a field of welfare economics, and the subject is a major concern of normative economics. Normative economics is a field of economics that deals with the issues of 'what should be'. In contrast, positive economics is a field of economics that deals with the issues of 'what is'. Economic justice refers to a set of economic principles that create equal opportunities, just processes and fair outcomes. In the practical context, economic justice requires the redistribution of income and wealth, so that the fruits of economic growth can spread squarely to people who are economically and socially at a disadvantage.

The term 'economic justice' is sometimes used in parallel with 'economic equity' or 'economic equality' or 'economic democracy'. Economic justice may be a new concept in developing countries, but it is not new in advanced countries including the United States and European countries. Particularly, economic justice was considered as a vital issue during the Great Depression in the United States and European countries, and through trial and error, it has been polished to completion. On the other hand, in communist and socialist economies, the issue of economic justice has been the core of governance and policy.

The natural question is: how we achieve the goal of economic justice and on what basis income will be redistributed? This is an issue that has annoyed many economists, politicians, and philosophers for centuries. Different opinions on this question have been presented, and diverse ideas and solutions have been proposed. Various thoughts have existed from libertarians to radicals, from classical economists to Keynesian economists and to Marxian economists. In the diverse spectrum of thoughts, orthodox Keynesian economics is in the middle. Thus, orthodox Keynesian economics can be used as a reference point. Keynes made clear that a new paradigm is needed to defend the free-market economy and to prevent the emergence of collectivism and totalitarianism. Originally, Keynesianism was a belief that the government should actively intervene in the economy for those who need support right away because they have no jobs or the ability to work.

Many different ideas and philosophies concerning economic justice have been discussed as early as the Aristotelian era. They have ranged from egalitarianism to the principle of 'survival of the fittest'. The most radical claim about income inequality is of course the unjust endowment of income. Those who believe in the original injustice argue that income inequality did not happen by accident, but in an unjust way from the beginning. According to them, all human beings were born equal, with all the capabilities and skills to do almost anything. Anyone can do farm work, become a company manager, or teach classics. But why did income inequality occur? It is because the unequal distribution of property has resulted in the unequal distribution of income. Then why did the unequal distribution of property occur? The extreme egalitarians attribute it to the 'result of stealing'. American poet and three-time Pulitzer Prize winner Carl Sandburg expresses this idea in his poem entitled *The People, Oh, Yes*:

> "Get off this estate."
> "What for?"
> "Because it's mine."
> "Where did you get it?"
> "From my father."
> "Where did he get it?"
> "From his father."
> "And where did he get it?"
> "He fought for it."
> "Well, I'll fight you for it."

Sandburg's poem can be seen as the basic philosophy underlying extreme equalitarianism. According to Sandberg, the solution to correcting income inequality is clear: As income inequality comes from the unjust distribution of property made in an unfair way, the unjust distribution of property, which is the root cause, must be corrected.

Egalitarianism advocates the idea that income should be equally distributed among all members of the society. If there are 10 members of a society and the endowed wealth includes 50 pieces of clothing and 100 bags of flour, each should have 5 pieces of clothing and 10 bags of flour. Marxism is based on class conflicts and argues that capitalists exploit surplus value created by workers. Thus, in order to give the surplus value back to workers, the government should own production resources. Marxism does not demand universal equality, but it aims to distribute income according to each person's needs.

Jeremy Bentham's utilitarianism has had significant influence not only on income distribution, but also on politics and philosophy such as 'one person, one vote'. Utilitarianism is the ideology of pursuing the 'greatest happiness of the greatest number'. Utilitarianism dreams of a society where the maximum number of members of a society can enjoy as much happiness as possible, which is known as the greatest happiness principle. The goal of the utilitarianist is to achieve the welfare system for as many people as possible.

Darwinism takes a position on welfare opposite to the previous three philosophies. It takes the position that the distribution of income should be determined in the market according to the 'survival of the fittest' and rejects any government involvement in redistributing income. It was not a coincidence for many economists to advocate the laissez-faire distribution of income in the 19th century when Darwinism was in full swing in European intellectual society. It is believed that the welfare system that neoliberalism has supported in modern times was influenced by Darwinism.

Lastly, the American political philosopher John Rawls emphasizes economic justice from the perspective of fairness in the liberal tradition. Rawl's theory of social justice is in the middle between egalitarianism and Darwinism. He argues that the redistribution of income should be done to maximize the utility of the least advantaged members of society in any case where economic inequality is an issue. In his *A Theory of Justice* (1971), Rawls argues that "a society in which the most fortunate help the least fortunate is not only a moral society but a logical one". Rawls admits that a more egalitarian redistribution can undermine the work desires of the most productive members of society. He took the position that more productive members of society should be given the corresponding incentives. His justice as fairness' means that the more productive class should be rewarded with a higher income to the extent that it does not reduce the income of the poorest in society. According to him, the goal of a society should be aimed at maximizing the well-being of the 'least fortunate' (or 'the least cared', or 'the worst-off' members of society).

Here we consider a society of 100 people to see how Rawlsianism differs from utilitarianism in the pursuit of economic justice. The members of this society have the same income of $50,000 a year, except for two people (Tom and Jerry). Tom has an annual income of $100,000, and Jerry has an income of $10,000. Suppose now that a law has been enacted to charge Tom $50,000 in tax. It is further assumed that $40,000 of subsidies out of Tom's tax is given to Jerry and the remaining tax of $10,000 is thrown into the Atlantic Ocean.

All members of society now have an equal income of $50,000. This redistribution of income will certainly reduce utilitarian social welfare. That is because Tom's loss of utility from the tax of $50,000 is much greater than

Jerry's gain of utility from the welfare of $10,000. However, Rawls' social justice increases, because Jerry is the least advantaged member of society, and his utility has increased. We see that overall economic justice increases in the Rawlsian sense. There is a Chinese axiom saying that "People are not angry at poorness but are angry at unevenness" (不患貧, 患不均). This is taken from the Analects of Confucius: "People are not worried about insufficiency but are worried about unevenness; people are not worried about poorness but areworried about unfairness" (不患寡而 患不均 不患貧而 患不安) (Source: Confucius). The Confucian teaching indicates that it is relative inequality that makes people unhappy.

It can be said that Rawlsianism aimed at maximum benefit to the least fortunate is a happy medium point between egalitarianism and Darwinism. In this sense, Rawls' emphasis on equal basic liberties, the equality of opportunity, and the promotion of the maximum benefit to the least fortunate can be characterized as a middle-of-the-road position on economic justice. In this regard, Rawlsianism is in line with the principle of *Zhongyong* meaning a happy medium point or a 'golden mean'. *Zhongyong* is a key element of Confucian thought. The core content of *Zhongyong* is that "Too much is as bad as too little".

On the surface, egalitarianism and liberalism seem to be mutually exclusive concepts. Emphasizing egalitarianism can shrink liberalism and emphasizing liberalism can undermine egalitarianism. If the distribution of income is completely entrusted to the free competition of the market, it becomes the '*bellum omnium contra omnes*' (the war of all against all) expounded by Thomas Hobbes. The gap between the rich and the poor is widened, and the inequality of opportunity is intensified. Rawls argues that such a society cannot be viewed as a just society.

Therefore, in order to achieve social justice, the government should actively intervene in the redistribution of income to the benefit of the least fortunate members of society, but not decrease the work incentives of the most productive members. The government should prepare a safety net for social welfare and social security to increase the welfare of the least fortunate in society. This position poses a dilemma of how to resolve the conflict between liberalism that values individual freedom, and egalitarianism that emphasizes universal equality. Rawls attempts to resolve this conflict through the concept of' 'justice as fairness'.

3

PIKETTY'S *CAPITAL IN THE TWENTY-FIRST CENTURY* AND THE KUZNETS CURVE

The most acclaimed economics book that was published in 2014 may be *Capital in the Twenty-First Century* written by French economist Thomas Piketty. We take note of this book because much of the book has been devoted to diagnosing the causes of income inequality and giving explanations for the issue of welfare. He used a wide range of long-term statistical data ranging from 1770 to 2010. (Some parts trace to the first century.)

The central theme of *Capital in the Twenty-First Century* is that when the rate of return on capital is higher than the rate of economic growth, income inequality progresses in favor of the capitalist, and a small difference between the return on capital and the economic growth rate leads to a large income inequality in the long run. In order to delve into the subject, we need to understand the meaning and measurement of the economic growth rate and the rate of return on capital.

The economic growth rate is a measure of how much real GDP has increased in a given year compared with a previous year. If the annual economic growth rate is 4%, it means that the total amount of goods and services (real GDP) produced this year increased by 4% compared with the previous year. On the other hand, it is not straightforward to measure the rate of return on capital. In economics, capital refers to all human-made means of production used to produce goods and services. It includes all devices of production such as factories, machines, and tools. Thus, a capitalist is not a person who has a lot of money, but rather a person who owns capital as a means of production.

It is important to distinguish between capital income and labor income to understand the essence of Piketty's work. After all, the issue of income inequality is related to the division of income between capital income and labor income. Simply speaking, if labor income increases faster than capital income, income inequality improves in favor of workers, and *vice versa*. In economics, capital income is usually defined as returns on capital earned by capital owners, and labor income as wages, salaries, and benefits earned by workers. This definition is closely related to national income accounting. In national income accounting, gross income (domestic or national income) includes wages earned by workers, interest (or returns) earned by capital owners, rents earned by landowners, and profits earned by entrepreneurs.

Gross income (Domestic or national income)
= Wages earned by workers + Returns on capital earned
by capital owners + Rents earned by landowners + Profits

However, Piketty uses the term capital income in a broader sense. Piketty's measure of capital income includes returns on capital, rents on land, and profits. In this context, capitalists refer to the group of capital owners, landowners, and entrepreneurs.

Capital income = Returns earned by capital owners
+ Rents earned by landowners + Profits earned by entrepreneurs

Labor income = Wages, salaries and benefits earned by workers

The calculation of capital income is not straightforward. Returns on capital cannot be measured directly. The total amount of interest paid on funds spent on the purchases of capital goods can be viewed as returns on capital. First, we can consider a case in which capital owners use their own funds to buy capital goods. Then the amount of interest they would earn if they deposited the funds in their bank accounts instead of buying capital goods is the return on capital. (This kind of interest may be called implicit interest.) In most cases, however, capital owners purchase capital goods by borrowing from banks or by issuing bonds and/or stocks. In such cases, returns on capital can be viewed as the sum of interest paid on borrowings from banks (= explicit interest payment), interest paid to bond holders and dividends paid to shareholders.

Returns on capital = Implicit interest on own funds
+ Explicit interest paid on bank borrowings
+ Interest paid on bonds + Dividends paid on shares.

Capital income in the Piketty sense
= Returns on capital + Rents on land + Profits

Thus, the rate of return on capital in the Piketty sense can be obtained by dividing the sum of returns on capital, rents on land, and profits in national income accounting by the total amount of money spent on capital goods.

The key theme of Piketty's argument in his *Capital in the Twenty-First Century* is that if the rate of return on capital (capital yield) earned by capitalists is higher than the rate of economic growth, the distribution of income is favorable to the capitalist and against the worker. Piketty has argued that in this regard, income inequality has aggravated since 1700. According to Piketty, from 1700 to the early 20th century (1913, before the start of World War I), the rate of return on capital continued to surpass the rate of economic growth, but the gap gradually narrowed in the 20th century. However, he expects the gap to widen again in the 21st century.

First, the fact that the rate of return on capital exceeded the rate of economic growth before the outbreak of WWI means that income inequality worsened against workers during this period. However, the narrowing of the gap between the rate of return on capital and the rate of economic growth after WWI in the 20th century indicates that income inequality continued to improve. During the period from 1914 to 1945, income inequality improved in almost all rich countries. This was mainly due to wars such as World War II, economic shocks such as the Great Depression and oil crises and was not attributed to the ability of the economy to self-correct income inequality.

He points out that if the rate of return on capital exceeds the rate of economic growth, the inherited wealth from parents will be much greater than the wealth accumulated through labor by workers, and as a result, income inequality will worsen further. In order to corroborate his claim, Piketty has used the following two simple equations. Although these two equations are simple, they are very useful in explaining the cause of income inequality.

The First Fundamental Law of Capitalism is given as

Share of capital income in total income = Rate of return on capital x Ratio of total capital to gross income (GDP or GNP)

The Second Fundamental Law of Capitalism is given as

Ratio of total capital to gross income = Savings rate/Economic growth rate

He called the first relation the First Fundamental Law of Capitalism and the second relation the Second Fundamental Law of Capitalism. To understand the First Fundamental Law of Capitalism, we need to find out what the share of capital income in gross income means. (Here gross income means either GDP or GNP.) Dividing capital income by GDP gives us the share of capital income in gross income. The share of gross income going to workers and capitalists varies from country to country. In the United States, the share of gross income that goes to workers is about 0.7, and the share of gross income that goes to capitalists is around 0.3. The United States is one of the countries with the highest share of income going to workers. In South Korea, the share of income going to workers is much lower than in the United States. In 2013, the share of income going to workers was about 44%, and the share of income going to capitalists was 56%. The share of labor income is even smaller in China.

On the other hand, the ratio of total capital to gross income is obtained by dividing the amount (dollar value) of capital goods used to produce goods and services by GDP. The amount of capital used to produce goods and services is usually several times larger than GDP. This ratio of total capital to gross income (total capital/GDP) is around 2.5 in the United States.

When we combine the First Law of Capitalism with the Second Law of Capitalism, we get the following relationship. This equation is the essence of Piketty's theme in his *Capital in the Twenty-First Century*.

Share of capital income in gross income
= [Rate of return on capital/Economic growth rate] x Savings rate

If the share of capital income in gross income increases, the distribution of income progresses in favor of capitalists. From the above equation, we can easily see that if the savings rate is constant, and the rate of return on capital (numerator) is greater than the rate of economic growth (denominator), then the share of capital income in gross income increases. In other words, the pie of the income earned by capitalists in GDP becomes larger, and the pie of the income earned by workers becomes smaller. Thus, income inequality will deteriorate. Piketty concludes that the share of income going to the capitalist will not decrease by itself, even if technological progress takes place in a favorable direction for labor.

Piketty emphasizes that capital ownership has always had inegalitarian outcomes far greater than labor in human history. This trend was reversed only during economic disasters such as wars and only when the government used public policy to mitigate it, but the effect was temporary. Piketty further warns that it is a misjudgment that simply by looking at the temporary trend in income inequality, one concludes that capitalism is moving towards a more universal egalitarian society.

According to Piketty's estimates, the world's annual economic growth rate never exceeded 0.1 to 0.2% from the first century to the 17th century. However, it was estimated that the rate of return on capital (mainly from land) reached 4 to 5% per year. In particular, the rate of return on capital began to exceed 5% in the 20th century. The economic growth rate also had begun to increase to more than 1% since the Industrial Revolution, and in the 20th century, it reached an average of 3%. Nevertheless, the rate of return on capital was always higher than the rate of economic growth. He maintains that the rate of return on capital in human history was at least 10 to 20 times higher than the rate of economic growth (p. 353).

The gist of Piketty's argument is that market forces in the capitalist system have led to a worsening of income inequality. However, Piketty's conclusion that income distribution has been worsening with the progress of capitalism has been at variance with the conclusion of the Kuznets curve. The Kuznets curve is a hypothesis proposed by Simon Kuznets, an American economist who won the Nobel prize in economics in 1971. Kuznets discovered in the 1950s and 1960s that as the economy developed, market forces would first deteriorate income distribution and then improve economic inequality. Thus, the Kuznets curve is described as a reverse U-shaped curve on a graph with income inequality being measured on the vertical axis and income per capita being measured on the horizontal axis. Contrary to Kuznets' proposal, however, economic inequality has deteriorated in most developed countries since the 1960s.

<Figure 5.2> The Kuznets Curve

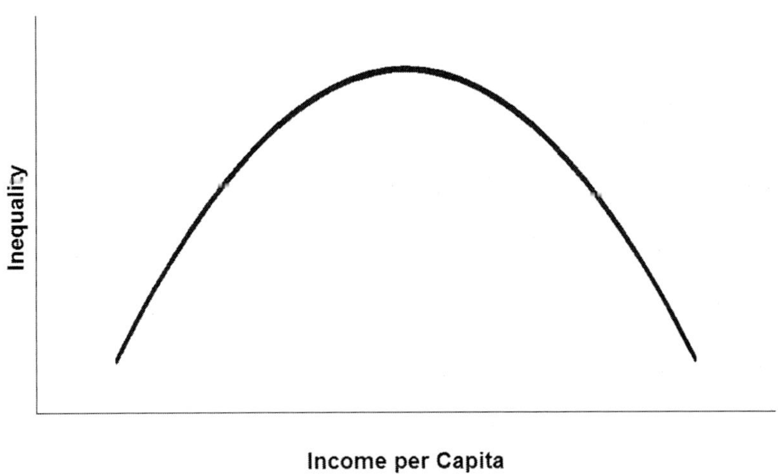

Piketty goes further by saying that the ‘rich-get-richer-and-the-poor-get-poorer’ phenomenon is a characteristic of capitalism. If the average return on capital is 4% per year, the return on capital to the 'super rich' is about 6 to 7%, and the return to those who are less rich is about 2 to 3%. From 1987 to 2013, the wealth of the super-rich, 1 in 100 million people (about 70 people worldwide) increased at the average rate of 6.8% per year, and the wealth of semi-super rich, 1 in 20 million people (about 350 in the world) increased at the average rate of 6.4% per year, but the world’s wealth increased at the average rate of 2.1% per year. According to one study, in 2016, the top 1% of the world's richest people owned more than 50% of the world’s wealth.

Piketty proposes to implement a progressive global tax on capital worldwide to reduce income inequality, as capitalism does not function to reduce income inequality by itself. He said that imposing an 80% tax on capital incomes of $500,000 to $1 million a year would not deter economic growth in the United States but would deter economically meaningless (sometimes even harmful) luxuriant consumption behavior. He further argues that such a wealth tax would make the fruit of growth distributed more widely. In addition, it would not be impossible to implement a global wealth tax if the transparency of international financial transactions were guaranteed. He also maintains that his global wealth tax plan is not intended to establish a socialist state but aims to promote economic democracy by effectively regulating capitalism. By doing so, he concluded that we could avoid a new crisis by breaking the ever-intensifying income inequality and imposing effective regulations on financial markets.

Piketty is inspired by the works of French writer Honore de Balzac and British novelist Jane Austin, among others. Piketty frequently quoted many contents from <*Le Pere Goriot*> (<Old Goriot> or <Father Goriot> in English). One reason why Piketty cited Balzac’s work frequently is that the circumstance surrounding the characters of the novel fit well into his theme. First, in the early 19th century when Balzac wrote <Old Goriot>, wealth existed mainly in the form of rent on land or interest on government bonds. However, the lower classes were frustrated and unable to escape poverty because they did not own either land or bonds. At that time, about three-quarters of Parisians did not earn the lowest cost of living. Balzac himself, too, engaged in the printing business but failed, and he was left behind a debt of 50,000 francs. He had to write a novel to pay off his debt. While suffering economic hardships, he realized the power of money in a capitalist society, and it became a valuable subject of his novel.

In the novel, Vautrin, a fugitive who lives in a boarding house with Rastignac, an ambitious law school student, teaches him a more realistic and somewhat cynical approach to success. Vautrin says, "If you think social success can be achieved by studying, talent, and hard work, that's an illusion." He further tells Rastignac that "There are many other possible career paths that could earn him much more income. Even if you climbed to the top of your professional career in law or medicine, your income would not be great." And Vautrin encouraged him to fold his hopes of becoming rich through hard work.

What Piketty tried to convey in <Old Goriot> was that in the French society in the 19th and 20th centuries, labor income (income earned from work) was too low to enjoy a standard of living that could be enjoyed with capital income. The story of <Old Goriot> may not be unique to France in the early 19th century. It is a scene that could happen everywhere in the 21st century. Piketty believes that the rate of growth in capital income is still higher than the rate of growth in labor income. Bolzac's <Old Goriot> tells us that in a society where capital income (the rate of return on capital) is greater than labor income (the wage rate), people easily pursue the 'get-rich-quick attitude', plunging into the flame of desires for success and fortunes.

4

THE LORENZ CURVE AND THE GINI COEFFICIENT

The Gini coefficient developed by Italian statistician and sociologist Corrado Gini in 1912 is the most widely used measure of income inequality. The Gini coefficient is sometimes called the Gini index or Gini ratio. The Gini coefficient is measured based on the Lorenz curve, which was developed by Max Lorenz in 1905 to represent the inequality of income distribution. The Lorenz curve displays the *cumulative share (in %) of population* from the lowest to highest income groups on the horizontal axis and the *cumulative share (in %) of income* from the lowest to highest income groups on the vertical axis. Suppose that the entire population is lined up from the lowest to highest income groups. Here we first take 10% of the population from the bottom, then 20% of the population from the bottom, and so on until we finally take 100% of the population up to the top. This is the cumulative share (in %) of the population.

In the next step, we obtain the cumulative share (in %) of income earned by the cumulative 10% of the population from the bottom. Let this cumulative share of income be 5%. Then this indicates that the cumulative 10% of the population have 5% of total income. Thus, we can find a combination of (10%, 5%). Next, we obtain the cumulative share (in %) of income earned by the cumulative 20% of the population from the bottom. Let this cumulative share of income be 15%. Then this indicates that the cumulative 20% of the population have 15% of total income. Thus, we can find another combination of (20%, 15%). We continue this procedure until we find the cumulative share (in %) of income earned by the cumulative 100% of the population. Of course, the cumulative 100% of the population will have the cumulative 100% of income. Thus, we can find the combination of (100%, 100%). Connecting all these points gives us the Lorenz curve. In deriving the Lorenz curve, we take the cumulative 10%, 20%, 30% … 100% of the population for analytical convenience, but we can take any other cumulative percentages of population.

<Figure 5.3> The Lorenz Curve

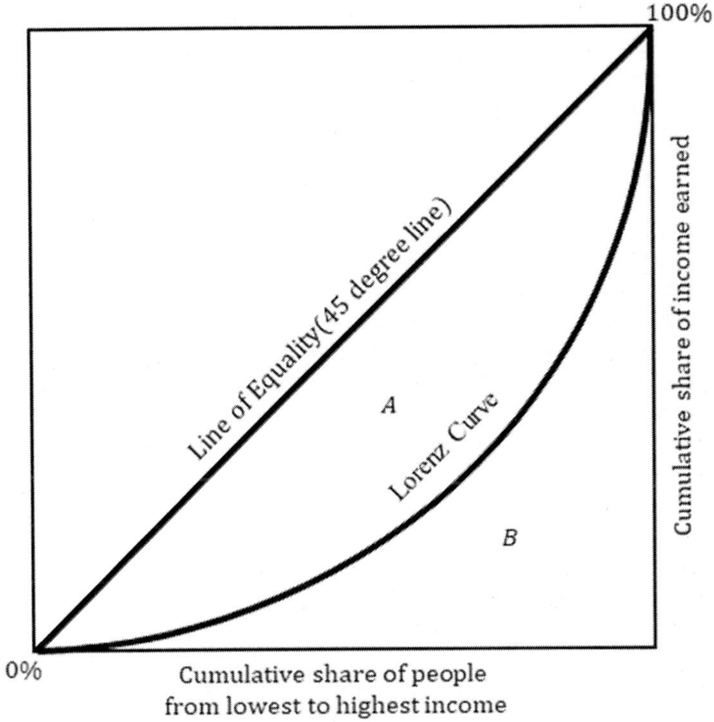

If the cumulative 10% of the population earns 10% of total incomes, the cumulative 20% of the population earns 20% of total incomes, and the cumulative 90% of the population earns 90% of total incomes, income is perfectly evenly distributed, and the Lorenz curve will be represented by a diagonal line (a 45-degree straight line). Thus, a diagonal Lorenz curve (line) represents the perfectly even income distribution line. The Lorenz curve usually has a convex curve below the diagonal. We find the half-moon shaped area (A) formed by the diagonal line and the Lorenz curve and the area (B) surrounded by the Lorenz curve and the horizontal and vertical axes. The Gini coefficient is then given as the ratio of these two areas.

Gini coefficient = Half-moon shaped area/Triangle formed by the diagonal line and the horizontal and vertical axes = A/(A + B)

The Gini coefficient ranges theoretically between 0 to 1 (100%) if there is no negative wealth (i.e., debts). Consider two extreme cases: (1) In Atlantis, all income is concentrated on one person. Then the Lorentz curve will be the line equal to the horizontal axis and the vertical axis, and the half-moon area is equal to the triangle are (A+B). In this case, the ratio of the two areas (Gini coefficient) is 1. In Shangri-La where income distribution is completely equal, the Lorenz curve coincides with the 45-degree diagonal line, and the half-moon area equals 0. In this case, the ratio of the two areas (Gini coefficient) is zero. Thus, the closer the value of the Gini coefficient to 0, the lower is the degree of income inequality. Conversely, the closer the value of the Gini coefficient to 1, the higher is the level of income inequality. Visually speaking, as the half-moon-shaped area becomes larger, income inequality becomes worse and vice versa. In general, if the Gini coefficient in a society is greater than 0.4 (40%), income inequality is severe.

The World Bank's Gini coefficients for representative countries are as follows.

Gini Coefficient	Countries
Gini <0.3	Slovak Republic: 0.23 (2019); Slovenia: 0.24 (2019); Belarus: 0.24 (2020); Czech Republic: 0.25 (2019); Ukraine: 0.26 (2020); Moldova: 0.26 (2019); Iceland: 0.26 (2017); Belgium: 0.27 (2019); Azerbaijan: 0.27 (2005); Norway: 0.28 (2019); Denmark: 0.28 (2019); Finland: 0.28 (2019); Kazakhstan: 0.28 (2018); Kosovo: 0.29 (2017); Croatia: 0.29 (2019); Netherlands: 0.29 (2019); Sweden: 0.29 (2019).
0.3 ≤Gini< 0.4	Austria: 0.30 (2019); Ireland: 0.31 (2018); S. Korea: 0.31 (2016); Bangladesh: 0.32 (2016); Germany: 0.32 (2018); France: 0.32 (2018); Switzerland: 0.33 (2018); Japan: 0.33 (2013); Canada: 0.33 (2017); Spain: 0.34 (2019); Australia: 034 (2018); U.K.: 0.35 (2017); Italy: 0.35 (2018); India: 0.36 (2011); Russia: 0.36 (2020); Bhutan: 0.37 (2017); Indonesia: 0.37 (2021); China: 0.38 (2019); Israel: 0.39 (2018).
0.4 ≤Gini< 0.5	Uruguay: 0.40 (2020); Bulgaria: 0.40 (2019); U.S.A.: 0.42 (2019); Philippines: 0.42 (2018); Togo: 0.42 (2018); Argentina: 0.42 (2020); Paraguay: 0.44 (2020); Peru: 0.44 (2018); Chile: 0.45 (2020); Cameron: 0.47 (2014); Mexico: 0.45 (2020); Nicaragua: 0.46 (2014); Ecuador: 0.47 (2020); Guatemala: 0.48 (2014); Honduras: 0.48 (2019); Brazil: 0.49 (2020); Costa Rica: 0.49 (2020); Panama: 0.498 (2019).

0.5 ≤Gini	Zimbabwe: 0.50 (2019); Angola: 0.51 (2018); Botswana: 0.53 (2015); Columbia: 00.54 (2020); Central African Republic: 0.56 (2008); Zambia: 0.57 (2015); Namibia: 0.59 (2015); South Africa: 0.63 (2014).

In terms of the Gini coefficient, Slovak Republic (0.23), Slovenia (0.24), and Belarus (0.24) are the countries with the most equally distributed income on the planet. The countries with the most uneven distribution of income are South Africa (0.63), Namibia (0.59), Zambia (0.57), and Botswana (0.53).

Interestingly, the Gini coefficient in Namibia and Botswana have decreased impressively over the past two decades or so. Namibia's Gini coefficient decreased from 0.74 in 1993 to 0.59 in 2015, and Botswana's Gini coefficient decreased from 0.61 in 1994 to 0.53 in 2015. This lesson shows that a country could improve its income inequality by appropriate policy for a relatively short period of time.

In many African countries, the Gini coefficient is greater than 0.5, and in most of South and Latin American countries, the Gini coefficient is higher than 0.4. On the other hand, in many European countries, the Gini coefficient is less than 0.3. The United States, a symbol of the free-market economy, has a relatively high Gini coefficient of 0.42 (2019), while China (0.38 in 2019), a symbol of the planned economy, has a Gini coefficient lower than that of the United States. Among the Four Tigers in Asia, South Korea (0.31) and Japan (0.33) have a relatively low Gini coefficient, which is followed by Singapore (0.42) and Hong Kong (0.43). However, South Korea's relatively low Gini coefficient may be perceived as a somewhat surprise because the *chaebol* (Korean conglomerates) dominates the Korean economy.

The Gini coefficient provides not only useful information to compare the degree of income inequality across countries, but also valuable information to understand how the degree of income inequality in a country has changed over time. The Gini coefficient itself is important, but the trend movement of the Gini coefficient is equally important. Looking at the trends in the Gini coefficient in the United States, the income inequality in the United States continued to improve from 1929 (Great Depression) until 1970, but it has been steadily on the rise again since 1970.

Year	U.S. Gini Coefficient
1929	0.45 (estimated) (The Great Depression occurred)
1947	0.38 (estimated)
1968	0.38 (lowest in official statistics) (The Great Society began in 1964 and 1965.)
1970	0.39
1980	0.40 (The stagflation hit the U.S. economy)
1990	0.43
2000	0.46
2006	0.472 (highest in official statistics) (The global economic crisis was looming.)
2009	0.468
2016	0.414

The trend in the U.S. Gini coefficient is informative on income inequality. The trend suggests that income inequality could be improved by the government's social policy programs, which seem to be in line with Piketty's argument. Until the outbreak of the Great Depression in 1929, the U.S. economy was under the influence of the classical doctrine that emphasized hands-off policy. The classical position was that economic problems including income inequality would be resolved by the market forces. It is not a surprise to see that the U.S. Gini coefficient was very high just before the start of the Great Depression.

After the Great Depression, the U.S. governments pursued ambitious economic programs aimed at increasing the welfare of the socially disadvantaged people, and concomitantly the Gini coefficient also steadily decreased until 1980. In particular, the Gini coefficient reached the lowest level in 1968, which seemed to be partly attributed to President Johnson's Great Society. The Great Society was an ambitious set of social policy programs initiated by President Johnson during the 1964-1965 period, mainly aiming at eliminating economic injustice and ending poverty in the United States. The Gini coefficient again turned into a worsening after 1980. The 1980s was the period characterized by deregulation, liberalization, and globalization under the banner of neoliberalism. Economic policy based on neoliberalism prompted the "Occupy Wall Street" movements.

Along with the Gini coefficient, the quintile of income is often used as an indicator of the degree of income inequality. This is a multiplier that indicates how many times the average income at the top 20% (5th quintile) of the income bracket is the average income at the bottom 20% (1st quintile). For example, if the income quintile ratio is 10, it means that the average income of the top 20% is ten times larger than the average income of the bottom 20%. While the Gini coefficient is for all income groups, the income quintile ratio measures income inequality across different income groups.

5

THE WORLD'S BILLIONAIRES: "EVERYONE WANTS MORE"

"In 2016, the wealth of the richest 1% of the world's population will exceed the wealth of the rest of the 99%." This prediction was made by OXFAM before the annual World Economic Forum (WEF) meeting in Davos, Switzerland in January 2016. OXFAM (Oxford Committee for Famine Relief) is a poverty relief organization founded in Britain in 1942. The Davos report prepared by Hardoon (2015) was released under the title of 'Wealth: Having It All and Wanting More'. OXFAM's prediction means that in 2016, 1% of the world population would own more than half of the world's wealth. The prediction became a reality. For the first time in human history, 1% of the world's richest people owned more than 50% of the world's wealth in 2016.

In 2009, the ratio of the wealth owned by the 1% richest people to the world's wealth was only 44%, but in 2014 it quickly rose to 48%, and it exceeded 50% in 2016. According to the report, the average per capita wealth of the world's 80 richest people (0.000001% of the world's population) was $23.7 billion, while the bottom 50% of the world's population (3.5 billion people) had an average per capita wealth of $540. This statistic shows that income inequality is getting worse as income increases worldwide.

Many people expect that as the economy grows and income increases, income inequality will improve. This expectation is congruous with the Kuznets curve. However, in reality the income distribution has progressed in the opposite direction. The worsening of income inequality is also confirmed in the statistics on the quintile income distribution. In order to obtain the quintile income distribution, we first arrange the total income earned by people from the low-income group to the high-income group; next we divide the total income arrangement into 5 quintiles: the income of people in the lowest 20%, the income of people in the next lowest 20%, the income of people in the median 20%, the income of people in the next highest 20%, and the income of people in the highest 20%. Finally, we obtain the quintile income distribution by dividing income in each group by total income.

<Table 5.2> Household Quintile Income Distribution in the U.S. (%)

Income Group	1970	1980	1990	2000	2010	2020
Lowest quintile	4.1	4.2	3.8	3.6	3.3	3.0
Second quintile	10.8	10.2	9.6	8.9	8.5	8.1
Third quintile	17.4	16.8	15.9	14.8	14.6	14.0
Fourth quintile	24.5	24.6	24.0	23.0	23.4	22.6
Highest quintile	43.3	44.2	46.6	49.8	50.3	52.2

Source: Statista Research Department

As the above statistics clearly show, in the United States only the share of income in the highest 20% quintile group increased over the past 50 years. Their income accounted for only 43.3% of the total income in 1970, but in 2020 the ratio increased to 52.2%. For the rest of the income groups, the percentage declined over the past 50 years. Clearly, these statistics are frustrating for many policymakers. This trend supports Piketty's argument that income inequality tends to worsen as income increases. He argues in his book that capitalism has the characteristic that income inequality tends to worsen if we leave it to the market.

We'll look at the quintile distribution of income in other countries. The following is a comparison of the distribution of quintile income between the United States and other OECD member countries (average). In OECD countries, the concentration of income at the highest level is not as severe as that of the United States.

The worsening of income inequality can also be confirmed in the number of the world's billionaires. Although the number of the world's billionaires declined temporarily during the corona pandemic crisis, the number of billionaires over the past several decades had persistently increased until the corona pandemic crisis, which suggests that income inequality has been widening worldwide. When we compare the number of 'the super-rich' in 2020 with that of 2015, the numbers are more revealing. The number of billionaires was 1,826 in 2015, and their total net wealth was \$7.5 trillion. Over the past six years from 2015 to 2021, the number of the super-rich increased by 929 from 1,826 to 2,755. This is more than 50% increase in the number of billionaires during the 2015 ~ 2021 period. The number of billionaires increased almost 10% every year.

<Table 5.3> Comparison of Income Distribution across Countries (%)

Income Quintile	U.S.	OECD Average	South Korea (1998)
Lowest 20%	3.0	7.7	7.9
Second lowest 20%	8.1	12.7	13.6
Median 20%	14.0	16.8	18.0
Second highest 20%	22.6	22.3	23.1
Highest 20%	52.2	40.5	37.5

The corona pandemic crisis changed the landscape for the distribution of wealth worldwide. The world's billionaires could not dodge the crisis. According to the annual Forbes list of the 2022 World's Billionaires, the number of the world's billionaires in 2021 was 2,755 with a total net wealth of $13.1 trillion, but in 2022 the number of billionaires on the Forbes' list decreased to 2,668, 87 fewer than 2021 (Source: *Forbes,* 2022). Their net wealth also decreased to $12.7 trillion, $400 billion less than in the previous year.

The United States still tops in the list of the richest persons in 2022. The United States has 735 billionaires who owned the collective worth of $4.7 trillion. China (including Hong Kong and Macau) remains number two, with 607 billionaires with the collective worth of $2.3 trillion. China had 87 fewer billionaires in 2022 than in 2021 presumably due to the corona pandemic crisis and the Chinese government's crackdown on information and technology companies. However, China's ascension to the wealth pyramid was amazing. In 2014, there were only 213 Chinese people on the billionaire list. The most dramatic change occurred in Russia. Russia had 34 fewer billionaires in 2022 than in the previous year following Putin's invasion of Ukraine.

The wealthiest person in the world according to the Forbes 2022 list was Elon Musk (founder of Tesla and Space X, U.S.) who possessed a net wealth of $219 billion, and the second richest person was Jeff Bezos (owner of Amazon, U.S.) with a net wealth of $177. Their rankings, however, went topsy-turvy in 2022. In 2021, the world's wealthiest person was Jeff Bezos with a net wealth of $177 billon, and the second richest person was Elon Musk with a net wealth of $151 billion. There was another turnaround in the ranking of the wealthiest at the end of 2022. Elon Musk was dethroned from the wealthiest person due to a decline in the price of the Tesla stock.

<Table 5.4> Distribution of World Billionaires
(2014, Source: *Forbes*, March 23, 2015)

Ranking	Country	# of Billionaires	Total Assets
1	U.S.A.	735 (2022)	$4.7 trillion (2022)
2.	China	607 (2022)	$2.3 trillion (2022)
3	Germany	103	$435.0 billion
4	India	90	$294.3 billion
5	Russia	88	$336.5 billion
6	Hong Kong	55	$246.1 billion
7	Brazil	54	$181.1 billion
8	U.K.	53	$171.2 billion
9	France	47	$253.4 billion
10	Taiwan	33	$82.1 billion
	South Korea	30	$77.5 billion
	Japan	24	$97.8 billion
	Singapore	19	$53.8 billion
	Total	1,826	$53.6 trillion

6

WHICH COMES FIRST, GROWTH OR WELFARE?

Since the Great Depression, many countries have pursued two goals of economic policy: growth and welfare. In advanced countries such as the United States and European countries, welfare programs were beefed up during the Great Depression. On the surface, these two goals are conflicting. If too much emphasis is given to economic growth, then efficiency becomes the priority of economic policy. If too much emphasis is given to welfare, then equity becomes the priority of economic policy. Efficiency is at odds with equity.

The debate of whether we should pursue growth first or welfare first is a perennial issue in many countries. The demand for more welfare by the disadvantaged people in many countries has driven people into a whirl of debate over which goal should come first, growth or welfare. In general, the debate surfaces as a hotter issue in a country whose income per capita exceeds $10,000. China just joined the $10,000 income club in 2019 and is facing an increasing demand for welfare. The Asian Four Tigers (South Korea, Taiwan, Singapore, and Hong Kong) reached the $10,000 income level in the 1990s and already started a true travel toward a welfare state, but their most glorious journey has not been finished yet. As Nazim Hikmet sang in <A True Travel>, their magnificent poem for welfare hasn't been written yet, and their most beautiful song hasn't been sung yet.

> The most magnificent poem hasn't been written yet.
> The most beautiful song hasn't been sung yet.
> The most glorious day hasn't been lived yet.
> The most immense sea hasn't been pioneered yet.
> The most prolonged travel hasn't been done yet.
> The immortal dance hasn't been performed yet.
> The most shine star hasn't been discovered yet.
> When we don't know any more what we are supposed to do,
> it's the time when we can do true something.
> When we don't know any more where we are supposed to go,
> it's the start when the true travel has just begun.

Although in many countries, the debate of whether to choose 'growth first or welfare first' is a recurrent issue, economists and policymakers are still divisive about what to choose first. Hikmet sings that our true journey begins at the time when we no longer know which way to go. Unlike Western welfare nations that have been embracing high burden-high welfare, latecomers such as the Four Tigers have pursued low burden-low welfare. The question of "growth first or welfare first" may be a Sphinx conundrum that could not be answered easily. The debate is similar to the debate of 'Which came first, the chicken or the egg?' However, the seemingly unresolved puzzle of "the chicken first or the egg first" seems to have been solved at last with the aid of two different research methods. One is evidence based on biological science, and the other is evidence based on statistical methods.

First, from the biological point of view, a study reached a conclusion that the chicken came first. Sri Lanka's *Daily Mirror* (April 19, 2012) reported that a group of researchers ended up obtaining the answer to the conundrum. It is observed that in the area of Welimada in Sri Lanka, a chicken was not born from breaking the eggshell but from the mother chicken's body. The chick was in the mother chicken's womb for 21 days and hatched. There was no abnormality in health, and the physical condition was like a normal chick. A local veterinarian dissecting the mother chicken said, "The test revealed that the fertilized egg was found in the mother chicken's genitals." Thus, the evidence seems to indicate that the chicken came first.

However, research based on statistical methodology has arrived at the opposite. A paper jointly published by Walter Thurman and Mark Fisher (1988) has obtained the result that 'Eggs precede chickens'. They used a sophisticated research method known as Granger's causality tests developed by Cline Granger (1969), a Nobel prize winner in economics to test whether the chicken is the cause of the egg, or the egg is the cause of the chicken. Using data on the number of spawned chickens per year and the number of eggs produced annually, they concluded that 'Eggs precede chickens'. Two studies using different methodologies have arrived at contradictory results. Thus, the question of "the chicken first or the egg first" seems to have been solved, but rather results have driven us into a bigger labyrinth.

As seen in the egg-chicken debate, the question of whether 'growth comes first, or welfare comes first' has no definitive answer or basis for determining it clearly. However, if we had to choose one of the positions, the choice between Reaganomics and Obamanomics would be informative. President Reagan's economic policy is based on trickle-down economics emphasizing the flow of benefits of economic growth from the top to the bottom. The proponents of trickle-down economics believe that economic growth leads to the spreading of welfare to the lower end of the income spectrum. On the other hand, President Obama's economic policy focuses on the 'bottom-up effect,' stressing that the strengthening of the economic welfare of low-income people eventually promotes economic growth. Reaganomics is rooted in the belief that when the economy is strong at the upper spectrum, the benefits of such economic growth flow from the top to the bottom, as water flows from the high to the low. They argue that as the economy grows, tax revenues will increase, and as a result, financial resources for welfare programs can be secured. This is the stance that growth precedes welfare.

On the other hand, Obamanomics starts from the perception that when the bottom is warmed up, then warm air puffs up from the floor to the ceiling. This is the stance that welfare precedes growth. In his 2015 State of the Union address, President Obama declares: "Should we choose an economy that is good for only a small number of the wealthy or an economy that expands everyone's income and opportunity? The answer is self-evident. It's an economy for the middle-class" (Obama, 2015). If the economy is strengthened from the bottom, the constitution of the economy also becomes strong, and economic growth is followed. It is known that President Kennedy said that "A rising tide lifts all boats". The choice pertains to the question of which of the two approaches, economic policy based on trickle-down economics or economic policy based on bottom-up economics works better for lifting all boats.

However, what might be more important than the debate is the feasibility of welfare programs, that is, how to secure resources for welfare programs. Policymakers should focus on how to finance welfare programs rather than the consumable debate on the 'growth first or welfare first'. And how to set the scope of welfare should also be the core content of welfare policy. People who are unable to work should benefit from welfare. People who have the ability to work but are not able to work because they are behind the competition should be provided with the motivation to work.

7

Do More Welfares Require More Taxes? The Eureka of Archimedes

People are divisive about whether welfare benefits should be universal or selective. In many countries, policymakers aim for 'welfare for working', not for 'welfare for living'. The message is that welfare recipients should not count on the government to provide welfare for a 'life from the cradle to the grave' and that they should know that the work will always pay. This is the same spirit as the Jewish proverb, "Teach your children how to catch fish instead of giving them fish" (Source: *Talmud)*

There is an interesting case study in this regard. There are many fishing spots along the coast of Monterey, California in the United States. Anglers caught fish there and threw leftovers after filleting fish to pelicans rushing for the fish offal. Pelicans flocked to the fishing area one by one, and the number of pelicans in the area increased over time. Pelicans enjoyed eating fish leftovers thrown by anglers instead of going into the water themselves and catching fish. When too many pelicans flocked into the area, Monterey city officials had a headache over the increasing number of pelicans. The city banned anglers from giving fish leftovers to pelicans. After the action, dead pelicans were found here and there along the beach. Pelicans died because they starved. Researchers were curious about the death of pelicans and found that pelicans forgot how to catch fish in the sea. Researchers brought pelicans from the southern coast of California that were not addicted to the habit of eating thrown fish offal. Dead pelicans were no longer found on the Monterey coast (LA Times, 1988).

An increase in social welfare inevitably entails an increase in government spending. As government spending increases, the government's budget deficit also increases unless the budget maintains a surplus. The government must secure resources necessary for welfare. There are limits to government resources to support welfare spending. Thus, the amount of money required to finance welfare programs must come from somewhere else. We may need the wisdom of Eureka, a shout made by Greek philosopher Archimedes.

Archimedes was ordered by the king to find out the purity of gold in the gold crown newly made. Archimedes, who was in agony, went into a public bath, and dipped himself into the tub fully filled with water. He saw the overflowing water, and got a hint and shouted, 'Eureka'. Eureka means "I got it," or "I have found it". He observed the water coming out of the bathtub was exactly the same as the volume of the body dipped in the tub. He got an inspiration from this observation and discovered the answer. He was so excited that he stepped out of the bath and ran naked on the streets of his hometown, Syracuse. Financing welfare is similar to the 'Eureka' case. An increase in welfare spending requires a cut in other government spending by the same amount or an increase in tax revenues by the same amount.

We can consider four possibilities for financing welfare. The first is to adjust the government's spending programs to secure financial resources for welfare. Because government revenues are limited, it might be necessary to re-prioritize government spending. For example, the government might want to reduce spending on defense or education to increase spending on welfare. The second option is to increase taxes. However, politicians are reluctant to raise taxes, because raising taxes risks their political career. Either of these two options is challenging. Raising taxes is a political torpedo in any country. For politicians, it's like stepping on a minefield.

The third option is to have the central bank print more money and borrow money from the central bank to secure welfare money. However, this is also as difficult as raising taxes in developed countries. Central banks in developed countries are politically independent from the government. Thus, even if the government asks the central bank to print more money, the central bank is not easily inclined to accept such a pressure.

Finally, the government borrows money from the public. When the government borrows money, it issues government bonds (Treasury securities in the United States) with various maturities and sells them to investors (including foreign governments and central banks) in the capital market. The government's borrowing results in an increase in the amount of government debt. Government debt is not necessarily bad but becomes a serious problem if the size of government debt is too big to be out of control. As government debt increases, interest payments on the debt increase, which must be added to budget payment items in the following year.

The U.S. government is in a relatively better position than any other countries in borrowing money. The United States is a reserve currency country, and there is a strong demand for U.S. government securities such as Treasury bills, Treasury notes, and Treasury bonds issued in the U.S. dollar. Thus, there is virtually no limit to the borrowing by the U.S. government (but there is a limit set by U.S. Congress). However, other countries do not enjoy this kind of privilege. Nonetheless, increasing government debt is a big burden on the U.S. economy. The amount of debt in the United States has increased sharply due to the war in Iraq and Afghanistan and the stimulus packages following the 2008 financial crisis and 2020 corona pandemic crisis. In 2007, before the global economic crisis broke out, the ratio of U.S. government debt to GDP was 36.8%, but it increased to 97% in 2010 and exceeded 100% in 2011. The ratio snowballed to 134% in 2020. Even though there is a ceiling on the amount of debt that the U.S. government can borrow, such an effort is not quite effective.

Does an increase in government debt have the effect of reducing income inequality? Not all government debt is used to improve welfare and to reduce income inequality. However, the results of simple regression analysis based on the data provided in the table below show that the Gini coefficient decreases as government debt increases. More specifically, as government debt increases by 1%, the Gini coefficient decreases by 0.015%. This means that as government debt increases, the degree of income inequality tends to decrease. Thus, we can argue that increases in government spending and government debt have the effect of alleviating income inequality.

The following table shows government debt as a percentage of GDP in 2020 in major countries. The size of government debt or public debt (or sovereign debt) is the total amount of the debt borne by the government, which does not include the debts of public enterprises and various pensions (national pensions and government employee pensions, etc.) that must be covered by national taxes. China and South Korea have high debts of public enterprises. If the debts of public enterprises are included in the category of government debt, the share will be much higher in these countries.

<Table 5.5> Government Debt (% of GDP) in 2020

country	Total debt		Gini coefficient
	2020	2012	
Venezuela	304.1	30.1	0.47 (2006)
Japan	259.0	237.9	0.31 (2016)
Greece	211.9	158.5	0.34 (2017)
Italy	155.3	127.0	0.35 (2018)
Singapore	152.0	111.0	0.42 (1998)
Portugal	135.2	123.0	0.38
Spain	120.0	84.1	0.34 (2019)

U.S.A.	134.2	106.5	0.42 (2019)
U.K.	102.6	90.3	0.35 (2017)
France	115.2	90.3	0.32 (2018)
Brazil	98.7	68.5	0.54 (2018)
Germany	68.7	82.0	0.32 (2018)
China	68.1	22.8	0.38 (2019)
Ireland	58.4	117.1	0.26 (2017)
South Korea	48.9	33.7	0.31 (2016)
Hong Kong	1.0	32.4	0.43 (1996)

Source: IMF and World Economic Outlook Database (OECD)

However, even if the government's fiscal deficit and an increase in government debt have the effect of reducing income inequality, the government cannot make a welfare feast by increasing its debt indefinitely. Financing welfare programs through borrowing is a patch-up solution. From this point of view, the most responsible choice among the four possible options (reducing government spending, borrowing from the central bank, borrowing from private sectors including foreign investors, and increasing taxes) will be a tax increase. However, the financing of welfare costs through taxation should be considered as a 'last resort'. This is because tax increases have a negative effect on the economy. To minimize the negative effects of higher taxes, a tax increase should be designed in such a way that they have the least impact on the economy.

PART 6

SAVINGS AND INVESTMENT: THE BUILDING BLOCKS OF THE ECONOMY

1

SAVINGS AND THE PSALM OF LIFE

The most important factors in the determination of economic growth in a country are investment and technological progress. In a sense the relationship between investment and economic growth is similar to the relationship between nutrients and the power of muscle. Investment refers to an increase in capital such as factories, machines, and tools. Investment further nourishes technological progress. Funding for investment is provided by a country's savings. The role of investment and savings in economic growth is like the two wheels of a chariot.

In fact, equilibrium in the private sector of the economy (households and businesses) is achieved when private savings and private investment are equal. This condition means that if domestic savings are just enough to finance domestic investment, there is no shortage of funds or a surplus of funds for investment, and the economy reaches equilibrium Savings represent the supply of funds by households, and investment represents the demand for funds by business firms.

What will happen to the economy if savings are not equal to investment? First, if savings are greater than investment, there is a surplus of funds in the economy. This excess supply of funds leads to lower interest rates, and investment will eventually increase, thus restoring the equality of savings and investment. On the other hand, if savings are smaller than investment, there is a shortage of funds. This excess demand for funds leads to higher interest rates, and investment will eventually decrease, thus restoring the equality of savings and investment. The adjustment of savings and investment toward equilibrium through interest rates is mainly supported by classical economists. Keynesians have a little different view. Keynesians argue that savings are primarily determined by income, and the adjustment of savings and investment toward equality is made slowly.

Savings are not only the foundation of investment and economic growth, but also a source of personal wealth. Savings are the amount of money left after an individual spends his disposable income for consumption.

$$\text{Savings} = \text{Disposable income} - \text{Consumption}$$

As can be seen from this relationship, if an individual consumes more, his income for saving decreases. Conversely if an individual consumes less, his ability to save increases. Thus, savings are closely related to disposable income. If you sell a house or stocks and deposits capital gains from the sale of the house or stocks in your bank account, your deposits do not represent an increase in savings, but an increase in wealth, because capital gains do not come from increases in disposable income. A few months before the 2008 global economic crisis broke out, personal savings in the United States fell to a negative range for about two quarters. This means that American people spent more than they earned. People could spend more than their income by selling their assets or borrowing money from their relatives or banks.

In the 1960s and 1970s, when Japan and the Four Tigers were eagerly pursuing economic development, people in these countries tightened their belt under the slogan that "Saving is a virtue". The Korean government selected the 'King of Savings' every year and encouraged people to save more. However, this kind of celebration became a thing of the past. Most of these countries went on a spending spree as they enjoyed fruits of high growth in the 1970s and 1980s, embracing the high consumption era. As a consequence, personal savings in these countries began to decrease rapidly.

The saving behavior of Japanese people is more dramatic in recent years. When we talk about Japan, the first thing that comes to our mind is that they save a lot. The Japanese savings rate was among the highest in the world and was the driving force behind Japan's rapid economic growth in the 1960s and 1970s. The Japanese personal (or household) savings rate ranged between 15% and 25% during the 1979~1985 period, which was more than double the U.S. savings rate, but it fell to −1.3% in 2014. This means that if the individual's disposable income is 100 yen, the Japanese spent 101.3 yen for consumption. The Japanese mythology surrounding their saving behavior has been gone. During the corona pandemic crisis, however, the Japanese savings rate again rose to 11.8% (2020).

Savings are a very important source of personal wealth. In the United States and other developed economies with well-developed social safety networks for retirement, savings from wages and salaries, interest and dividend income, and transfer income are the main source of post-retirement income. However, in many countries where social security networks are not well developed, personal savings are not an important means of retirement funds. For instance, in South Korea, wealth earned from real estate investments rather than savings have been the primary source of income after retirement. However, capital income from real estate investments makes the flow of retirement income precarious and unstable, which makes retired people more miserable. This structure of retirement income makes the rich richer and the poor poorer, thus intensifying income inequality. South Korea was the 10th largest economy, and income per GDP was $34,994 (IMF estimate) in 2022. Nonetheless South Korea's poverty rate of the old people is the highest, and its suicide rate of the old people is the highest among the OECD member countries. Since the accumulation of assets through savings is relatively stable and has a more predictable flow of retirement income, the proportion of savings in the portfolio of retirement income should be high for stable consumption after retirement. This conclusion is consistent with Modigliani's life cycle hypothesis (LCH).

We have seen that savings are given by the difference between disposable income and consumption. People often confuse savings with assets. Suppose you made a capital gain of $200,000 from selling your house, and you deposited the money in your savings account. In this case, savings did not increase by $200,000 in the economic sense. Assets increased by $200,000. Savings include only disposable income left after consumption. When we calculate the savings rate, we divide total savings by total income. Thus, it is important to clearly distinguish between savings and assets. Otherwise, we might measure the savings rate incorrectly. Of course, savings are an important component of assets.

Saving can be viewed as an act of not spending today and waiting for future consumption. In order for us to sing a psalm of life after we retire, it is important to work hard and save more in preparation for retirement. Longfellow sings that "Tell me not in mournful numbers, "Life is but an empty". He further says, "Life is real! Life is earnest! Act in the living present. Learn to labor and to wait." His poem sounds like a song that encourages savings.

> Tell me not, in mournful numbers,
> "Life is but an empty dream!"
> For the soul is dead that slumbers
> And things are not what they seem.
> Life is real! Life is earnest!
> And the grave is not its goal.
> "Dust thou art, to dust returnest."
> Was not spoken of the soul.
> Not enjoyment, and not sorrow
> Is our destined end or way.
> But to act, that each tomorrow
> Find us farther than today.
> Art is long, and time is fleeting:
> And our hearts, though strong and brave,
> Still, like muffled drums, are beating

Funeral marches to the grave.
In the world's broad field of battle,
In the bivouac of life,
Be not like dumb, driven cattle…
Be a hero in the strife!
Trust no future, howe'er pleasant;
Let the dead past bury its dead.
Act,… act in the living present,
Heart within, and God o'erhead!
Lives of great men all remind us.
We can make our lives sublime.
And, departing, leave behind us
Footprints on the sands of time.
Footprints, that perhaps another,
Sailing o'er life's solemn main
A forlorn and shipwrecked brother
Seeing, shall take heart again.
Let us, then, be up and doing.
With a heart for any fate;
Still achieving, still pursuing.
Learn to labor and to wait.

There is a poem that might touch the heart of people more than Long Fellow's <A Psalm of Life>. That is <Saving> written by Japanese poet, Toyo Shibata. Shibata was a 100-year-old lady in 2015 when she published her first poetry title< Don't Be Weak>. Shibata had savings of 1 million yen in her bank account for her funeral expenses, but she used the savings to publish her poetry. The poetry aroused a sensational response, and more than 1 million copies of her poetry were sold.

I mean,
If people offer kindness
I save it in my mind.
When I'm lonely
I take it out and
Become energetic.
Why don't you save it from now on.
It's better than a pension.

2

WHY ARE STATISTICS ON SAVINGS SEESAWED?

Savings, investment, and trade form a triangle of a country's economic health. There have been misunderstandings and confusions about savings. We often get confused when we come across mass media reports or data on the savings rate. For example, South Korea's savings rate in 2013 was 30.1% in some data sources and 3.1% in other data sources. No matter how inaccurate statistical numbers are, you may be bewildered by this magnitude of disparity between the two statistics. However, the above statistics are correct numbers. The difference comes from how we define the savings rate.

To avoid this confusion, we need to understand the exact meaning of savings. As discussed, savings are defined as the remaining disposable income that is not consumed. These savings are called household savings. Business firms also save. They retain some profits after they pay production costs (such as wages) and corporate income taxes. These savings are called corporate savings. The sum of household savings and business savings defines private savings. Finally, the government can also save. If the government spends less than its tax revenues, the government has a budget surplus. The budget surplus is called government savings. When we add government savings to private savings, we obtain total savings or national savings.

Private savings = Household savings + Corporate savings

National savings = Private savings + Government savings
= Household savings + Corporate savings + Budget surpluses

The savings rate is then expressed as a percentage (%) of savings divided by GDP. Thus, we have the following savings rates:

Household savings rate = Household savings/GDP

Private savings rate = Private savings/GDP

National savings rate = National savings/GDP

Now we can resolve the mystery surrounding the numbers on the savings rate. South Korea's household savings rate was 3.1% in 2013. However, the national savings rate was 30.1%. The difference means that households saved only 3.1% of their disposable income and spent the rest of income on consumption. However, the fact that the national savings rate reached 30.1% means that business firms held substantial profits as retained earnings, and the South Korean government also maintained a large amount of a budget surplus in 2013. In the United States, the national savings rate in 2013 was 13.%, but the household savings rate was low at 4.0%. In the United States, the government had a large budget deficit. Thus, government savings were negative, but there were large corporate savings, and thanks to corporate savings, the national savings rate was far greater than the household savings rate. However, in China, the national savings rate was 49.7% and the household savings rate was also 38.0%, which was very high compared with other countries. Thus, in China, much of national savings comes from household savings.

3

SAVINGS ARE THE SOURCE OF DOMESTIC AND FOREIGN INVESTMENT

We have seen that savings are income not spent on consumption. It follows from the national income accounting identity that private savings can be expressed as

$$\text{Private savings} + [(\text{Government Purchases} + \text{Transfer payments}) - \text{Taxes}] = \text{Investment} + [\text{Exports} - \text{Imports}]$$

Savings on the left-hand side (LHS) indicate private savings. Private savings include household savings made by individuals and corporate savings held by firms. The sum of government purchases and transfer payments on the LHS is the government's total expenditures, and taxes are the total revenues that the government collects from individuals and firms. If tax revenues are greater than the government's expenditures, the government has a fiscal (or budget) surplus; if the government's expenditures are greater than tax revenues, the government has a fiscal (or budget) deficit. The fiscal surplus is often called government savings. The sum of private savings and government savings is total savings or national savings and represents the total supply of funds available in a country.

Among the items on the right-hand side (RHS), investment is total private investment by business firms. Thus, government investment is not included in the category of investment and instead included in the category of government purchases. Private investment includes not only the installation of new plants, machinery, and tools by firms (investment for structures, equipment, and intellectual property products), but also the construction of new residences by builders (residential investment). The second item on the RHS, the difference between exports and imports, is called net exports and represents the trade balance. If a country's exports are greater than its imports, the country has a trade surplus; if a country's imports are greater than its exports, the country has a trade deficit.

It is very informative to look at trade surpluses and deficits in terms of the flow of funds. Any trade of goods and services between two countries entails the flows of funds between the two countries. Let's look at a trade between the United Kingdom and the United States. We'll show that a country's trade surplus represents a loan to a foreign country and a trade deficit a borrowing from a foreign country. This is the key to solving the puzzle of why the United States borrows from China, and China lends money to the United States for an extended period.

To understand this relation, suppose there are only two countries on the planet: the United States and the United Kingdom. Suppose that the United Kingdom exports $56 billion worth of goods and services to the United States and imports $61 billion worth of goods and services from the United States. The United Kingdom has a deficit of $5 billion in trade with the United States, and the United States records a surplus of $5 billion in trade with the United Kingdom. In other words, the United Kingdom spends $5 billion more than it earns from its exports to the United States. In this case, the trade between the two countries would not be possible if the United Kingdom did not borrow $5 billion from the United States. Thus, the United Kingdom, a trade deficit country, will borrow $5 billion dollars from the United States, and the United States, a trade surplus country, will lend $5 billion to the United Kingdom.

U.K. trade deficit with U.S. ⇒ U.K. borrowings from U.S.
⇒ U.S. investment in U.K.

If the United Kingdom exhibits a trade surplus with United States, we have the following relationship:

U.K. trade surplus with U.S.⇒ U.K. loans to U.S.
⇒ U.K. investment in U.S.

Of course, there are more than 200 countries in the world, not just two. However, even if the relationship does not exactly hold between any two countries via-a-vis in a multiple-country model, the relationship still holds between a country and all other trading countries. In this regard, a country's trade surplus (exports > imports) represents a loan to other countries or foreign investment, and a country's trade deficit (imports > exports) represents a borrowing from other countries.

The national income accounting identity can be rearranged as follows.

Savings = Investment + [(Government purchases
+ Transfer payments) − Taxes] + [Exports −Imports]

The national income accounting identity shows that private savings can be used for three purposes. First, private savings can be used to finance business investment. Second, private savings can also be used to finance the government's budget deficit (government purchases + transfer payments – tax revenues). Lastly, private savings can be used to make loans to foreign countries that experience trade deficits. In this way, savings function like the artery of the economy.

The national income accounting identity can also be rearranged as

$$\text{Savings} + [\text{Taxes} - (\text{Government purchases} + \text{Transfer payments})]$$
$$= \text{Investment} + [\text{Exports} - \text{Imports}]$$

This relation can be rearranged as

$$\text{Private savings} + \text{Government savings}$$
$$= \text{Domestic investment} + \text{Loans to foreign countries}$$

Since a trade surplus represents investment in foreign countries in terms of the flow of funds, investment and trade surpluses on the RHS can be seen as the sum of domestic and foreign investments, which is the total investment of a country. On the other hand, the sum of private savings and government savings defines total savings or national savings. The above equation shows that a country's total savings are equal to its total investment.

$$\text{Total Savings } (= \text{National savings})$$
$$= \text{Total Investment } (= \text{Domestic and Overseas Investment})$$

Since total savings are the total supply of funds in a country, and total investment is the total demand for funds, the relation implies that total savings equal total investment, which is the general equilibrium condition for an open economy. This equilibrium condition seems to hold almost exactly for the world economy. In 2013, the total savings rate of the world was 24.4% of the world's GDP, and the total investment rate of the world was 24.2% of the world's GDP.

This relationship provides an important perspective on the working of an open economy. Many countries around the globe have become increasingly open and closely connected to each other through trade and financial transactions. The world is truly merging into a global village. Previously, many countries had a closed-economy structure. In the closed economy system, the equilibrium of the domestic economy was achieved at the point where private savings (S) are equal to private investment (I).

In a closed-economy model, when private savings are smaller than private investment, domestic investment will have to be reduced, and the economy is likely to find a new equilibrium position at the levels of lower savings and lower investment, which results in lower GDP. However, this kind of prediction did not happen in the United States. The U.S. private savings rate remained at a very low level until the 2008 global economic crisis. In some periods, it reached almost 0%. On the other hand, the U.S. demand for investment was very strong. In such a situation, according to the closed-economy model, the demand for investment in the United States should have been reduced, and the model would predict that the U.S. economy would slip into a recession. However, this scenario did not happen. The main reason is that the United States was able to make up the lack of domestic savings by borrowing from foreign countries. Thus, U.S. investment was not reduced despite the shortage of domestic savings. The insufficient domestic savings were made up through foreign borrowings (or trade deficits). Under an open-economy model, the economy reaches an equilibrium in the direction that national savings are equal to total investment (domestic investment + foreign investment).

We can now use the open-economy national income accounting identity to solve the mystery of why the United States has been borrowing from China, Japan, and South Korea, whereas China, Japan and South Korea have been lending money to the United States.

National and Household Savings Rates in Major Countries (2013)

Country	National savings rate (% of GDP)	Investment rate (% of GDP)	Annual growth rate (2013-2021)
Kuwait	59.2	18.4	−0.96
China	49.7 (38.0)	47.1	6.56
Singapore	44.6	27.7	3.13
India	30.2 (34.7)	35.1	5.49
South Korea	30.1 (3.1)	27.4	3.06
Taiwan	30.1	19.7	3.29
Hong Kong	27.3	26.1	1.70
Germany	23.5 (10.6)	26.1	1.12
Japan	22.4 (1.9)	21.2	0.47
France	17.9 (15.8)	19.2	1.03
Italy	17.9 (4.5)	17.6	−0.25
U.S.A.	13.8 (4.0)	16.8	2.03
U.K.	10.7 (5.4)	15.1	1.49
World	24.4	24.2	

1) The numbers in parentheses represent household savings rates.
Source: National Saving Rate and Investment Rate: IMF; Household Saving Rate: OECD

It is interesting to find that in East Asian countries including China, Japan, and the Four Tigers (South Korea, Taiwan, Singapore, and Hong Kong), the national savings rate is higher than the investment rate, which indicates that in these countries, domestic savings are more than sufficient to finance private investment. For example, in China, national savings were 49.7% of GDP, while private investment was 47.1% of GDP in 2013. In Japan, total savings were 22.4% of GDP, while private investment was 21.2% of GDP. The Four Tigers all have a similar pattern. The savings rate (as the percentage of GDP) is higher than the investment rate (as the percentage of GDP) in all four countries.

In contrast, in the United States and Western European countries including the United Kingdom, Germany, France, the total savings rate is smaller than the investment rate. For example, in the United States, total savings (national savings) were 13.8% of GDP, while private investment was 16.8% of GDP in 2013. In the United Kingdom, total savings were 10.7% of GDP, but private investment was 15.1% of GDP. These statistics show that the United States and Western European countries are unable to fully support domestic investment demand without borrowing from foreign countries. Otherwise, these countries would have to curtail their investment projects.

4

THE PARADOX OF THRIFT

There is a proverb that "From saving comes having". Early about 2000 years ago, Chinese historian *Sima Qian* said that "Thrift and saving are the only way to become rich" (Sima Qian, B.C. 145 ~ B.C. 86). The slogan that "Saving is a virtue" has been ubiquitous in many developing countries. As a matter of fact, thrift and saving are the norm of living in any society and at any time. It goes without saying that savings are essential to maintaining a decent living standard after retirement.

However, savings are like a double-edged sword. First, we need to understand the fallacy of composition to see why this is the case. The fallacy of composition is a wrong reasoning, which states that 'what is true for a part is also true for the whole'. Some phenomena may be partially true, but they are not necessarily true entirely. If a country issues new money of $10 million and gives $100,000 to 100 people as a gift, these 100 people will be happy and become rich. However, this phenomenon is only partially true for some individuals. If a country prints more money and gives $100,000 to every member of society as a gift, the real value of income or wealth owned by each member of society will not increase, and they will not be better off after all. Thus, the argument that giving money to all people in the nation will make them better off is not true. The reason is that more money without any production of goods will only lead to higher inflation, thus making real income and wealth almost unchanged.

The fallacy of composition can be applied to savings. Savings have a double-faced role in the economy. Savings are a key to promoting economic growth by supporting investment in the long run, but in the short run, savings can be a hurdle that leads to economic fluctuations. Personally, as you save more, you'll have more, and you'll be better off. But if everyone saves more, the country as a whole will not become better off. More savings could pour cold water over the recovery of the economy. To examine the dual properties of savings, let's look at the effects of savings on short-term economic fluctuations and long-term economic growth.

In order to maintain long-term economic growth, continual investment must be made. Building new factories, installing machinery and equipment, and developing new technologies are crucial for long-term economic growth. The resources needed for business investment are mainly provided by household savings deposited in financial institutions or retained earnings held by firms. Government savings (budget surpluses) are also an indirect source of investment. Therefore, as people save more, more funds are available for business investment, and investment is made at a lower cost. Of course, business firms can also issue bonds or stocks to finance their investment, but in many countries, borrowings from financial institutions account for the largest portion of financing business investment.

We find some interesting patterns between the East Asian countries (China, Japan, South Korea, Taiwan, Singapore, and Hong Kong) and the United States and the West European countries (United Kingdom, Germany, France, Italy) in the behavior of saving. Here we classify the East Asian countries as high-savings countries (with the national savings rate being higher than 20%), and the United States and the West European countries as low-savings countries (with the national savings rate being lower than 20%), according to the data presented in the previous table.

◈ The savings (total savings) rate as the percentage of GDP in the high-savings countries is more than double the low-savings countries. The average savings rate of the high-savings countries is 34.0% whereas the average savings rate of the low-savings countries is 16.5%

◈ The investment rate as the percentage of GDP in the high-savings countries is also relatively high compared with the low-savings countries. The average investment rate of the high-savings countries is 29.0% whereas the average investment rate of the low-savings countries is 19.3%

◈ The savings rate (34.0%) is higher than the investment rate (29.0%) in the high-savings countries, but the investment rate (19.3%) is higher than the savings rate (16.5%) in the low-savings countries. This means that in the high-savings countries, their domestic total savings are sufficient to finance their investment, and thus they don't need to borrow funds for investment from foreign countries. However, in the low-savings countries, domestic total savings are not sufficient enough to support investment, and thus, they would have to borrow funds for investment from foreign countries. Otherwise, they would have to cut their investment projects.

◈ The countries with high savings have trade surpluses, whereas the countries with low savings have trade deficits. Thus, the high savings countries can afford to lend money to other countries, but the low savings countries would have to borrow money to support their trade deficits.

◈ The countries with high savings own the large portion of U.S. Treasury securities. In 2014, China (1st), Japan (2nd), Taiwan (7th) and Hong Kong (10th) were among the top 10 countries that owned most U.S.

Treasury securities, which indicates that these countries lend money to the United States.

◈ The countries with high savings have a higher economic growth rate than the countries with lower savings. The average annual economic growth rate of the high savings countries from 2013 to 2021 was 3.1%, whereas the average annual economic growth rate of the low savings countries was 1.1%.

◈ Interestingly, the world's savings rate is 24.4% and the world's investment rate is 24.2%. Thus, on a global scale, savings are almost the same as investment. In other words, the supply of funds (= savings) and the demand for funds (= investment) are almost equal for the world as a whole, and the world economy is approximately in equilibrium.

It is clear from our discussion that high savings lead to high economic growth, *ceteris paribus*. However, as long as the impact of savings on short-term economic fluctuations is concerned, we have a different picture. When people save more, they sacrifice their current consumption for future consumption. When people save more to prepare for the future, they say that they tighten their belt, which indicates that they consume less. When people save more instead of consuming, goods and services produced by firms are not sold and remain as inventories. Firms are forced to reduce the production of goods and services and to lay off workers. The economy slows down, and unemployment increases. Thus, policymakers have a dilemma: if people save too much, the economy is likely to slip into a recession in the short run; if people save too little, the economy is likely to grow slowly in the long run. This dilemma is called the paradox of thrift. Particularly, in a high-consumption society like the United States, where consumption accounts for almost two-thirds of GDP, consumption plays a critical role in stabilizing the economy, and the impact of consumption on short-term economic fluctuations carries weight.

Then, is it better to save more or less? There is no such thing as an optimal savings rate or desired savings rate. We cannot say that the savings rate should be a certain level of GDP. In order for the economy to maintain its potential growth rate in the long term, continuous investment must be made. From this perspective, theoretically, it can be said that the desired level of total savings should be the one that can support domestic investment without relying on foreign borrowing. However, this criterion is not absolute. Some countries have more investment opportunities than others, and these countries usually have higher investment demand than domestic savings. In such countries, increasing investment by increasing foreign borrowing can bring more benefits to the economy. Ultimately, in a free market economy, real interest rates will move in the direction of equalizing savings (supply of funds) and investment (demand for funds). When savings are higher than investment, the real interest rate tends to fall, and *vice versa*. We have noted that the speed of the adjustment of the real interest rate in response to the surplus or shortage of savings differs depending on whether the market is more competitive or less competitive.

5

CHIMERICA (CHINA-AMERICA): CHINA EARNS DOLLARS FROM THE UNITED STATES AND THE UNITED STATES BORROWS DOLLARS FROM CHINA

There have been tensions and conflicts surrounding trade and currency disputes between the United States and China over the past several years. Tensions between the two nations were especially heightened to a plosive during the Trump presidency. It was not long ago that the two nations led the world economy in tandem after the two nations had established a diplomatic relation in 1978, and China had pursued an open-economy policy.

The United States trades with more than 200 countries (223 countries as of 2022) in the world and has recorded perennial trade deficits with the rest of the world over the past several decades. Particularly, U.S. trade deficits with China have been snowballing every year until the recent tension between the two nations. The total value of U.S. exports to 223 countries amounted to approximately $2,500 billion, and the total value of U.S. imports amounted to $3,400 billion in 2021. Thus, the United States had a trade deficit of $900 billion with the rest of the world. In this case, the United States must borrow $900 billion in the form of selling its assets to domestic and foreign investors including foreign governments and central banks.

In addition to these trade deficits, the United States has been recording fiscal deficits annually over the past five decades or so, except for only several years. The U.S. government mainly relies on borrowings from domestic and foreign investors, particularly from China and East Asian countries. The U.S. government issues various types of government securities (mainly Treasury securities) with maturities of 1 month to 30 years and sells them to borrow money. Particularly, the U.S. national debt increased explosively during the coronavirus pandemic crisis. The U.S. government's gross debt (= national debt) increased to $27.7 trillion at the end of 2020 in the midst of the coronavirus pandemic crisis and to $29.6 trillion by the end of 2021. The U.S. national debt currently reaches $30.6 trillion as of July 31, 2022.

<Table 6.1> U.S. Debt-GDP Ratio During the COVID-19 Crisis

Year	National Debt (in trillions of $)	Percent of GDP	Remarks
2018	$21.5	105%	
2019	$22.7	107%	
2020	$27.7	129%	COVID-19 crisis
2021	$29.6	124%	COVID -19 crisis

About 48% of the national debt in 2021 is owned by government agencies such as the Fed (U.S. central bank) and the intragovernmental agencies (for example, Social Security Trust Fund) and 28% of the debt is owned by foreign investors (including foreign governments and central banks) and international agencies such as the United Nation and IMF. The rest is owned by mutual funds, banks, insurance companies, pension funds, and private investors.

The breakdown of the U.S. national debt owned by foreigners is revealing. Foreigners owned $7 trillion, approximately 25% of the total debt of $27.7 trillion as of December 2020, Of the $7 trillion foreign debt, $4.1 trillion (59%) was held by foreign governments including foreign central banks, and $2.8 trillion (41%) was owned by foreign investors. The top three holders of the U.S. debt were Japan ($1.2 trillion or 17.7% of foreign holdings of the U.S. debt), China ($1.21 trillion or 15.2%), and the United Kingdom ($0.4 trillion or 6.2%). China was the largest holder of the U.S. debt until 2011 when China's holding of the U.S. debt reached $1.3 trillion. However, China gradually diversified its holdings of foreign currencies and reduced the holding of U.S. dollars (U.S. Treasury securities) and increased the holding of the euro.

The U.S. national debt was the result of U.S. trade deficits and budget deficits over the past several decades. The coexistence of trade deficits and budget deficits is called the 'twin deficits'. The only country that can sustain the twin deficits for an extended period of time is the United States. The reason for this privilege is that the U.S. dollar is the *de facto* key currency or reserve currency in the world, and that the United States is the only country that can print the dollar endlessly. Why does a twin deficit problem occur? To answer this question, we revisit the national income accounting identity which is given by

Private savings + [Taxes − (Government Purchases + Transfer payments)]
= Investment + [Exports − Imports]

Assuming that the private sector is in equilibrium, so that savings are equal to investment, we can derive the following relationship from the national income accounting identity:

Taxes − (Government purchase + Transfer payments)
= Exports −Imports

⟹ Budget surplus = Trade surplus

This relation shows that a country which has a budget surplus tends to have a trade surplus. This is the case of the twin surplus. By multiplying both sides by (−1), we also have

(Government purchase + Transfer payments) − Taxes
= Imports - Exports

⟹ Budget deficit = Trade deficit

This relation is the opposite of the twin surplus. This relation shows that a country which has a budget deficit tends to have a trade deficit. This is the case of the twin deficit. It is interesting to see that a budget surplus tends to go together with a trade surplus, and that a budget deficit tends to go hand in hand with a trade deficit. China, Japan and the four Asian Tigers have long enjoyed the twin surplus, whereas the United States has long suffered the twin deficit. The twin deficit problem is one of the most pressing issues faced by the United States, although the United States could manage the twin deficit problem as a key currency country. Here we need to note that the twin deficit occurs only under the assumption that savings are equal to investment in the private sector.

Despite the twin deficit problem, central banks in many countries and many private investors are willing to buy U.S. Treasury securities. The market for U.S. Treasury securities is not only huge, but also well developed. Any individuals and institutions who invest in U.S. Treasury securities can easily buy and sell them in the financial market at any time. Thus, U.S. Treasury securities are highly liquid. Because U.S. Treasury securities are issued by the U.S. government, they are the most secure of all securities. Everyone knows that the U.S. government cannot default on its debt. Although Standard & Poor's downgraded the U.S. credit rating from AAA to AAA- in 2013, U.S. Treasury securities are still welcomed as the safest and most attractive investment for international investors. Thus, the U.S. government seems to have no problem with borrowing funds by selling its securities in international financial markets.

Some politicians in China once argued that the Chinese government should use its holdings of U.S. Treasury securities as a weapon against the United States. Selling the U.S. Treasury securities that they hold would cause U.S. interest rates to rise and thus drive the U.S. economy to a great turmoil. However, using U.S. Treasury securities held by foreign countries as a weapon could be more difficult than launching a missile. CNBC said that "China's card of selling U.S. Treasury securities is a self-destructive nuclear option, and the likelihood of using that option is very low." (Cox, 2019). If they dump U.S. Treasury securities in the market, the value of the U.S. dollar will nosedive, and U.S. interest rates will skyrocket. However, at the same time the price of Treasury securities will plummet, and the ones who suffer the most are the investors who hold U.S. Treasury securities.

Thus dumping U.S. government securities is not a plausible scenario, but some countries including China have recently begun to reduce the holdings of U.S. Treasury securities. Some believe that China intended to sell U.S. Treasury securities as a non-tariff trade retaliation card. China's holdings of U.S. Treasury securities have been the lowest level since June 2006. China's holdings of U.S. Treasury bonds amount to $1.21 trillion as of the end of December 2020. This is still the second largest holder of U.S. Treasury bonds in the world next to Japan.

East Asian countries including China, Japan, and South Korea earn U.S. dollars by selling goods to the United States, thus recording trade surpluses with the United States. The United States needs the outflown dollars to import foreign goods. The United States borrows dollars from these countries to make up trade and budget deficits. Thus, U.S. dollars are flown into the East Asian countries and then recycled back into the United States. There seem to be some mutual dependence between the United States and the East Asian countries.

These mutual benefits are economically called 'interdependence' and are poetically called 'flowers' in Kim Chun-so's poem. Kim Choon-soo composed the poem titled <Flowers> in 1952 when he was fascinated with the poems of Rainer Maria Rilke. In the poem, Kim Choon-soo sings that I wish you were an unforgettable wink to me, and I were an unforgettable wink to you. Like "you and I exchange winks each other" in the poem, the United States and China exchanged the benefits of trade until the two nations exchanged tirades. The United States became a flower to China in the form of trade surpluses, and China became a flower to the United States in the form of capital inflows.

Before I called his name
He was just a gesture.
When I called his name
He came to me
And became a flower.
Like I called his name
I want someone to call my name
Suitable for my color and scent.
I go to him and
I want to be his flower.
We all want to be something.
I wish you were an unforgettable wink to me,
And I were an unforgettable wink to you.

6

VOLATILITY OF INVESTMENT

Investment is a catalyst for long-term economic growth, but it is also a source of short-term economic fluctuations because investment is the most volatile component of GDP. Although investment constitutes a small portion of GDP, it plays a crucial role in the stabilization of the economy. In the United States, the proportion of investment in GDP has ranged from 3% to 20% over the past 100 years, whereas consumption has accounted for about 70% of GDP. We frequently hear that firms have cut and adjusted their investment projects, because the prospects for the future economy do not look promising. This is a good example of how investment variability has a major impact on economic fluctuations. Among the four components of aggregate demand (AD), consumption and government purchases are the most stable and predictable components. They perform as economic stabilizers. Net exports are somewhat unstable and unpredictable because exports are heavily affected by foreign business cycles. Business investment is the most volatile and precarious aggregate demand component and is the main culprit of destabilizing the economy. Where do the volatility and instability of investment come from?

The volatility of investment is attributable to three sources. First, investment is affected by financial conditions. The majority of investment by business firms is financed through their borrowing of external funds from financial institutions. Therefore, the demand for investment can be greatly influenced by changes in financial conditions, especially interest rates. In the market economy, interest rates are not only determined by supply and demand forces in the asset market but are also influenced by monetary policy. Thus, market interest rates can fluctuate widely, and therefore investment is highly unstable. Especially when the economy is in a normal state, investment is sensitive to fluctuations in interest rates. This view is mainly maintained by classical economists. Classical economists emphasize the sensitivity of investment to changes in interest rates. In this regard, there is a big divergence between classical economists and Keynesian economists because Keynesians are doubtful of the sensitivity of investment to changes in interest rates.

Second, investment can also be influenced by changes in real GDP (gross output). This view is primarily held by Keynesians. Keynesians argue that when the economy is in recession, the relationship between investment and interest rates becomes insignificant. The relationship between investment and GDP is often explained by the accelerator principle. The accelerator principle shows the amplifying effect of GDP on investment. Some studies have found that in the United States, real GDP fluctuations and investment movements have shown incredibly similar patterns. When real GDP increases, investment also increases, but with some time lag and wider amplitudes. When the accelerator principle is combined with the multiplier effect, the economy exhibits an oscillating pattern of fluctuations. The multiplier effect indicates that an increase in investment leads to a larger increase in GDP, and the accelerator principle indicates that an increase in GDP results in a greater increase in investment.

However, the relationship between investment and GDP is not confirmed uniformly in all countries. For example, the accelerator effect in Japan and South Korea is not as strong as in the U.S. economy. Many studies show that fluctuations in investment in the Japanese economy are not sensitively linked to fluctuations in GDP. In the South Korean economy, as in the case of the Japanese economy, the investment behavior of firms is not well explained by the accelerator principle. Since the 1990s, investment and GDP have been moving in the same direction in South Korea, but in the 1980s, investment continued to increase despite the ups and downs of economic activity.

Lastly, a firm's investment plan (= investment demand) can be greatly influenced by expectations about the future state of the economy. If the future state of the economy looks bright, firms plan to increase their investment projects. Conversely, when the future of the economy is uncertain, firms plan to curtail their investment projects. The future state of the economy can fluctuate at any time due to unpredictable shocks and disturbances inherent in the economy. As such, investment based on precarious prospects is bound to be unstable.

According to the expectations hypothesis, the volatility of investment is mainly attributable to the investor sentiment of business firms. Thus, it may be more important to stimulate the depressed investor sentiment of entrepreneurs than to lower interest rates. Many policymakers try to lower interest rates or to increase fiscal expenditure to reinvigorate investment when the economy slows down. Lowering interest rates is typical of classical prescriptions and increasing government spending is representative of Keynesian recipes. Such policies may not be futile but may be ineffective when the economy is in deep stagnation.

These policy prescriptions also have some side effects on the economy. An increase in the money supply aimed at lowering interest rates could lead to higher inflation, and an increase in government spending could bring about higher interest rates and larger budget deficits. In fact, the government cannot do much to stimulate private investment. At most, the government can give firms a shot in the arm by providing tax incentives such as lower corporate taxes or lower taxes on capital gains. However, the effect of such tax incentives on business investment is also dubious. Yuhn and Bennet (2016) presented evidence showing that the Bush tax cuts had no effect on stimulating U.S. business investment. In conclusion, the most dominant factor that affects investment is expectations on profitability, and profitability is mainly determined by the market mechanism.

PART 7

INFLATION AND UNEMPLOYMENT: TWO MACROECONOMIC DISEASES

1

INFLATION IS THE THERMOMETER OF THE HEALTH OF THE ECONOMY

We have seen that when we calculate GDP, we cannot directly add apples and oranges. A country produces millions of goods and services during a certain period, and they are measured in different units. One common method to calculate GDP is to add the *market values* of all goods and services produced in an economy. The market values of goods and services are measured by market prices. The logic of obtaining the general price level is like calculating GDP. A country produces a myriad of goods and services, and the prices of goods and services produced are a million and one. We cannot simply sum all the prices of goods and services and divide them by the number of goods and services transacted. The general price level is the weighted average of the prices of goods and services with the quantity of each good or service being used as a weight. In this way, we can obtain a single index number for all prices of goods and services.

The most commonly used measures of the general price level are the GDP price deflator, the consumer price index (CPI), and the producer price index (PPI). First, we need to know the meaning of an index. An index is a number showing how much the price of goods in a specific year changes compared with the base-year price which is set equal to 100. Thus, the price index does not represent actual prices expressed in monetary units. The three price indices have different base years, and the number and composition of products included in the indices are also different.

The price level works like a thermometer that measures the health of the economy. Our body maintains the temperature of 97.5 degrees when our body is in an optimal condition. If the body temperature rises above or falls below the optimal temperature, the abnormal temperature is a signal that we have some health problems. A higher temperature than the normal temperature is problematic, but a lower temperature than the normal temperature is also troublesome. Likewise, if the price level rises (inflation) or falls (deflation) significantly, the abnormal price change is a sign that the economy has some problems. In order to find out whether the price level is rising or falling, we need a price index.

The GDP price deflator is calculated by dividing nominal GDP by real GDP. We have seen that nominal GDP measures the market value of goods and services using current prices. Thus, nominal GDP increases or decreases as prices are rising or falling, even if there is no change in the quantity of goods and services produced. On the other hand, real GDP measures the market value of goods and services using the prices that prevailed in the base year chosen for the purpose of calculating real GDP. Real GDP excludes any price changes from nominal GDP. Thus, the ratio of nominal GDP to real GDP is an indicator of how much the overall prices in a given year have risen compared with the base year.

$$GDP\ price\ deflator = \frac{Nominal\ GDP}{Reall\ GDP}\ x\ 100$$

The GDP deflator is sometimes called an implicit price deflator because government agencies do not actually survey the prices of all goods and services, but they first obtain nominal and real GDP and then divide nominal GDP by real GDP. We multiply this ratio by 100 to obtain an index. Because the GDP deflator includes the prices of all goods and services produced in a country, it can be viewed as the broadest measure of the general price level.

<Table 7.1> U.S. GDP Deflator

Year	Nominal GDP	Real GDP	GDP Deflator
2012 (Base year)	16,254.0	16,254.0	100.0
2019	21,372.6	19,032.7	112.3
2020	20,893.7	18,384.7	113.6
2021	22,997.5	19,681.7	116.8

Source: *The Economic Report of the President*, 2022

The consumer price index (CPI) or cost-of-living index is a composite price index calculated as the weighted average of the retail prices of 211 consumption items in 38 geographical areas in the United States. The items of goods and services included in the CPI are called a 'market basket'. The CPI compares the cost of purchasing market basket items in the base year (for example, 1982) measured at the price of the base year (1982) and the cost of purchasing the same items measured at the given-year (2020) price. Thus, the CPI index in 2020 measures how much the cost of purchasing the items in the market basket has increased from the base year (1982) to the given year (2020). Since the CPI is a weighted average of retail prices, the composition of the weight is important. Currently the weight of the U.S. CPI is as follows: food: 13.4%, energy: 8.7%. commodities: 21.3%, housing: 32.3%, health care: 6.8%, transportation: 5.9%, other items: 11.6%.

It is worth noting that the rentals of houses (i.e., housing) are included in the CPI, but the prices of houses and condominiums are not included in the category of the CPI. The rentals of houses and condominiums are included in the category of consumption as consumer services, but the purchases of houses and condominiums built in the given year are considered as business investment, not as household consumption, and consequently the purchase prices of houses and condominiums are not included in the CPI. However, the prices of newly built houses and condominiums are included in the calculation of the GDP deflator because the GDP deflator includes the prices of all final goods and services produced.

The government agency (the Bureau of Labor Statistics in the United States or the Office for National Statistics in the United Kingdoms) chooses the base year for computing the consumer price index. Currently the base year for the U.S. CPI is 1982-84. The Bureau of Labor Statistics (BLS), instead of changing the base year, updated the expenditure weights and the geographic areas and survey samples every 10 years until 2002 from 1940. The U.S. Government Accountability Office (GAO) recommended in 1998 that the BLS should update the CPI's market basket more frequently than every 10 years to make it timelier in its representation of consumer expenditures and consumer tastes. The BLS has begun to update the expenditure weights every 2 years since January 2002.

<Table 7. 2> U.S. Consumer Price Index

Year	CPI
1920	20.0
1930	16.7
1940	14.0
1950	24.1
1960	29.6
1970	38.8
1980	82.4
1980~82	100.0
1990	130.7
2000	172.2
2010	219.2
2019	255.7
2020	258.8
2021	271.0

The consumer price index differs from the GDP deflator in many respects. First, the consumer price index is an explicit price index in that the staff of the government statistical agency visit retail centers and survey the prices of the items in the market basket. Second, the items included in the market basket are fixed until the composition of the items are updated by the government, but the number of goods and services included in the GDP deflator is variable, depending on how many goods and services are produced each year. Thus, the items included in the GDP deflator vary every year. Third, the consumer price index includes the prices of goods and services imported from abroad, but the GDP deflator includes only the prices of goods and services produced domestically. Thus, if the prices of imported goods rise due to fluctuations in exchange rates and other factors, the CPI rises, but it does not affect the GDP deflator. For this reason, inflation based on the consumer price index could be higher or lower than inflation based on the GDP deflator.

2

THE MEASUREMENT OF INFLATION

The inflation rate is measured based on some price indexes such as the consumer price index (CPI) and the GDP deflator. The general price index is a weighted average of prices with the weight being equal to the quantity of a good purchased by consumers in a specific year. The index means that the weighted average price in a specific year (base year) is set equal to 100, and the weighted average price index of a given year is compared with the weighted average price index of the base year. Then, the annual inflation rate in year t based on the GDP deflator is measured as

$$GDP\ deflator\ inflation\ rate_t = \frac{GDP\ deflator_t - GDP\ deflator_{t-1}}{GDP\ deflator_{t-1}}.$$

The inflation rate shows how much the GDP deflator rises from year t-1 (previous year) to year t (current year). In order to obtain the percentage change of the price level, we multiply the inflation rate by 100.

On the other hand, the annual inflation rate in year t based on the CPI is measured as

$$CPI\ inflation\ rate_t = \frac{CPI_t - CPI_{t-1}}{CPI_{t-1}}.$$

The inflation rate shows how much the CPI rises from year t-1 (previous year) to year t (current year). The CPI inflation rate is not the same as the GDP deflator inflation rate, because the two inflation measures have different market baskets and different calculation methods. The GDP deflator includes the prices of all final goods and services produced in an economy, whereas the CPI includes the prices of certain goods and services purchased by urban households. Thus, the GDP deflator inflation rate does not include the prices of imported goods and services whereas the CPI inflation rate includes the prices of imported goods and services.

More fundamentally, it is important to understand the methods of calculating the GDP deflator inflation rate and the CPI inflation rate. There are two different approaches to measuring the price index. The Paasche price index compares the cost of purchasing the *current-year (2020) quantities of goods and services* at the current-year price with the cost of purchasing the *same quantities* at the base-year (1982) price. This method uses the *current-year quantities* as a weight to measure the price change between the two periods. Suppose there are n goods and services that consumers buy in 2020. Then the Paasche price index in 2020 (P^P_{2020}) is given by

$$P^P_{2020} = \frac{p^1_{2020}\, q^1_{2020} + p^2_{2020}\, q^2_{2020} + \cdots + p^n_{2020}\, q^n_{2020}}{p^1_{1982} q^1_{2020} + p^2_{1982}\, q^2_{2020} + \cdots + p^n_{1982}\, q^n_{2020}}$$

The GDP deflator is a Paasche index, Thus, the GDP deflator inflation rate measures how much the cost of purchasing currently produced goods and services at current prices has risen compared with the cost of purchasing the same quantities of goods and services at base-year prices.

On the other hand, the Laspeyres price index compares the cost of purchasing the base-year (1982) *quantities of goods and services* at the current-year price with the cost of purchasing the *same quantities* at the base-year (1982) price. This method uses the base-year *quantities* as a weight to measure the price change between the two periods.

$$P^L_{2020} = \frac{p^1_{2020}\, q^1_{1982} + p^2_{2020}\, q^2_{1982} + \cdots + p^n_{2020}\, q^n_{1982}}{p^1_{1982} q^1_{1982} + p^2_{1982}\, q^2_{1982} + \cdots + p^n_{1982}\, q^n_{1982}}$$

The consumer price index is a Laspeyres index. Thus, the CPI inflation rate measures how much the cost of purchasing goods and services produced in the base year at current prices has risen compared with the cost of purchasing the same quantities of goods and services at base-year prices.

The Paasche price index (GDP deflator) tends to underestimate the true price increase, whereas the Laspeyres price index (CPI) tends to overestimate the true price increase. In this context, the CPI represents the upper limit of inflation, and the GDP deflator represents the lower limit of inflation, and the true inflation rate is likely to be in between the two indexes. The price index developed by Irving Fisher can be claimed to be 'ideal' (ideal Fisher index) in that the Fischer index is a geometrically averaged index of the Paasche index and the Laspeyres index, which seems to be the most accurate measure of true inflation.

The consumer price index is often referred to as the cost-of-living index. This is because many wages are linked to the CPI, meaning that they are adjusted as the CPI changes. In addition, pensions and other government subsidies are usually linked to the CPI. This adjustment is often called a cost-of-living adjustment (COLA). In this regard, it is important to accurately measure the CPI inflation rate, because fluctuations in the CPI can significantly affect the government's budget management. In the United States, the size of government subsidies including Social Security benefits is very large, and even if the inflation rate rises slightly, the cost-of-living adjustments could be very large.

For this reason, the problem of over-estimation of inflation based on the CPI has become a political issue. The U.S. Congress formed an advisory committee consisting of five economists (chairperson: Professor Boskin at Stanford University) and commissioned the issue to be reviewed. The Boskin Advisory Council concluded that the inflation rate based on the CPI overestimates the actual inflation rate by about 0.2 to 0.8 percentage points and estimated that the adjustment of the over-estimation of inflation could save the U.S. budget by $633 billion over the next 10 years. Greenspan, chairman of the Fed at that time, also testified that the inflation rate based on the CPI was overestimated by about 0.5% to 1.5%.

3

THE OFFICIAL INFLATION RATE TENDS TO OVERESTIMATE TRUE INFLATION

The consumer price index (CPI) is based on the Laspeyres index. A price index based on the Laspeyres method has several problems. Most of all, the Laspeyres index has been criticized for not properly reflecting changes in consumption patterns, product quality improvements, and price changes caused by new product developments.

The composition of goods and services included in the CPI is fixed for a certain period, and the market basket's weights were updated every 10 years in the past in many countries. In other words, the items included in the market basket have been used for the measurement of the CPI without any adjustment for a considerable time. However, consumer preferences, new product developments, and quality improvements steadily change. There is a criticism that the CPI is not able to adjust quickly such changes in the behavior of consumers.

The first issue is concerned with changes in consumption patterns. Consumers' tastes and preferences for products change frequently, and people have a tendency to change their buying behavior toward cheaper products. For example, renting a videotape at Blockbuster, a rental chain of videotapes, was cheaper than going to a movie theater, and people liked to borrow more videotapes than to go to the movies. But even these consumption patterns became a bygone. Blockbusters once dominated the market from 1992 until its 9,094 stores were closed in 2014. Since then, videotape rentals have disappeared from the market, and watching movies through streaming via Netflix on the Internet has become a common consumer preference.

Although videotape rentals accounted for a large portion of the household budget during the period of the middle of the 1990s to the middle of the 2010s, videotape rentals were not included in the market basket of the CPI until the market basket was readjusted. After videotape rentals almost disappeared in 2014, the share of videotape rentals in the household budget was almost nil. Nonetheless, if the expenditure weights of the CPI were to be updated every 10 years, videotape rentals would continue to account for a large part in the CPI until the readjustment of the expenditure weights is made. Thus, if the updates of the market weights in consumption expenditures took place only after a long period of time, the CPI could not properly reflect changes in consumption patterns.

The second issue is related to the development of new products. When a new product is first introduced onto the market, its price is very high due to development costs, but it is not uncommon for the price to drop significantly over time. However, the consumer price index does not reflect such a drop in price until such a new product is included in the market basket. For example, in South Korea, CD records, camcorders, electronic calculators, video tapes, mobile phones, international airfare, etc. have been included in the market basket since 1997, and thus the price fluctuations of these items began to be reflected in the CPI after 1997. The CPI prior to 1997 did not reflect any changes in the price of these items, although some of the items were already purchased by consumers. In the United States, microwave ovens included in the market basket in 1978, and VCRs and personal computers were not included until 1987. Personal computers began to be widely used by consumers from the late 1970s, and until 1987, their prices began to drop significantly. Until 1987, the CPI did not reflect the price drop of personal computers at all.

The third issue is related to quality improvements. As technological progress occurs, product quality also improves, but the CPI does not reflect quality improvements. A new washing machine can handle more laundry using less energy than an old washing machine. For example, if an old GE washing machine was $1,000 in 2010 and a new power-saving GE washing machine in 2020 was $1,200, then it may not be appropriate to treat the price increase as the result of inflation in the computation of the 2020 CPI. If there is a proper method of reflecting any quality improvement in the computation of the CPI, it is true that the price of the new washing machine might have fallen during this period.

Lastly, the CPI is based on the tagged price of a product and not the discount price transacted. Also, the price of a product sold in a department store and the price of the same product sold in a discount store or a convenience store can be different. Thus, the CPI can be different depending on different sample retail centers. Because of the problems with the CPI, economists conclude that the CPI overestimates true inflation. In the United States, the market weights of the consumer price index are updated every two years, but the updates alone do not completely resolve the problems inherent in the method of computing the CPI. For a more fundamental solution, we must find a way to reflect the quality improvement of products measurement of the consumer price index. in the measurement of the consumer price index. By updating the expenditure weights in the market basket more frequently, the problem has been on the mend, although the improvement is not perfect.

Faced with the criticism that the CPI is biased toward overestimating inflation, U.S. Congress formed a Congressional Advisory Commission in 1996. The Commission that was led by Michael Boskin at Stanford University concluded that the CPI overstated inflation by 1.1% points a year. Thus, if the CPI reports that the inflation rate is 3.1% a year, the true inflation rate is most likely to be 2% per year. This proposition stirred a considerable amount political controversy. Many government programs such as Social Security benefits and wages are indexed to the CPI, implying that they have provisions for automatic increases geared to increases in the CPI. This adjustment is called the COLA (cost-of-living adjustment). If the conclusion reached by the Boskin Commission were true, and the government accepted such a proposal, the government could save billions of dollars per year.

In contrast, there is another kind of criticism that there is a big difference between the official prices published by the government and shopping cart prices. The criticism is that the official inflation rate tends to underestimate actual inflation. This claim may be legitimate in a sense. The proportion of products purchased by a particular family in the household budget may not be the same as that of the market basket of the CPI. For example, spending on apparel, dining out, and going to the movies may account for a very large portion of the budget for a particular family while the expenditure weights of these items in the CPI could be small. Particularly, daily necessities such as vegetables, salt, instant food, etc. may constitute a small portion in the market basket, although expenditures on such daily necessities are big items in a family's budget. Meanwhile, the weight of gasoline and electricity is large in the market basket of the CPI.

Thus, even if the prices of the items that some households purchase intensively rise a lot, the price increases may have a minor impact on the CPI. Accordingly, if the prices of daily necessities rise steeply, but the prices of gasoline and electricity do not change or fall, then the overall CPI could rise slightly or even fall. In such a case consumers could feel differently. In this way, there may be a difference between the inflation rate based on the official CPI and the inflation rate consumers perceive while shopping in the market. Consumers feel the details, but macroeconomic statistics deal with the average. Just like "the devil is in the details", the average number often beguiles people.

4

THE CAUSES AND TYPES OF INFLATION

The specter of inflation is roaming again as the aftermath of the coronavirus pandemic crisis has been lingering. Inflation was considered as the relic of the past over the past four decades or so. However, the coronavirus pandemic crisis awakened the danger of inflation again. The U.S. inflation rate rose to 9.1% (annual) in June 2022, the highest level in 40 years since 1981 and is estimated to reach 8.7% in 2022. Many other countries have been experiencing a similar upsurge of inflation.

Inflation is a phenomenon in which the overall prices of the economy measured by the general price level rise continuously and significantly. Therefore, if the overall prices rise temporarily or mildly, such a rise is not considered to be inflation. Basically, inflation is caused by a shortage of the supply of goods and services or a surplus of the demand for goods and services or both. Thus, inflation is an imbalance that occurs as the result of an increase in aggregate demand or a decrease in the aggregate supply or both.

First, let's see how an increase in aggregate demand causes inflation. If the amount of goods and services people want to purchase (= aggregate demand) is greater than the amount of goods and services produced in the economy (= aggregate supply), producers try to raise prices to make more profits in response to the excess demand for goods and services. The overall prices rise, and inflation occurs. This inflation is called demand-side inflation or demand-pull inflation.

An increase in aggregate demand is primarily induced by expansionary aggregate demand policy such as fiscal expansion and monetary expansion. Expansionary fiscal policy aimed at increasing aggregate demand includes an increase in government purchases and transfer payments and a reduction in taxes. Expansionary monetary policy targeting increasing aggregate demand includes an increase in the money supply and a reduction in interest rates. Here we are interested in the question of whether the expansion of government spending itself could be the cause of inflation. Put it differently, we are concerned with whether inflation can be caused by an increase in government spending (or a tax cut) that is not accompanied by an increase in the supply of money. The conclusion of modern economic theory is that a one-time increase in fiscal expenditure (or a tax cut) induces only one-time inflation without inducing sustained inflation, and inflation ceases at a higher price level when there is no further increase in government spending. The reason is that a government spending increase has a limit. Government spending in excess of its tax revenues cannot be continuously increased. Thus, an increase in government spending itself cannot be inflationary. Today, most economists, regardless of whether they are monetarists or Keynesians, agree with Milton Friedman's assertion that "inflation is always and everywhere a monetary phenomenon" (Friedman and Schwartz, 1963).

Thus, unless the government continues to borrow money from the central bank to finance its budget deficits, spending increases cannot induce a continual increase in inflation. Borrowing money from the central bank seems to be an easy choice but borrowing from the central bank is not a popular option and is not easily adopted in developed countries, because borrowing from the central bank is certainly a sure road to inflation. However, in many developing countries, a dictatorial or authoritarian regime can easily pressure its central bank to print more money and to borrow money. This practice is called the monetization of the deficit. The monetization of the deficit has been the main cause of hyperinflation in many South and Central American countries and African countries.

Another important source of increasing aggregate demand is an increase in the supply of money. The mechanism through which an increase in the money supply causes inflation is similar to an increase in fiscal spending. An important difference is that there is some limit to the continual increase of fiscal spending, but the supply of money can be increased without limit. If the central bank decides to do so, it can print as much money as it can and supply money to financial institutions. Thus, there are no bounds in increasing the money supply.

In modern times many countries experienced demand-pull inflation except for the inflation associated with the oil crises in the late 1970s, and early 1980s Thus, many countries were concerned with managing aggregate demand to curb demand-pull inflation. The top priority of central banks was to achieve price stability. Many advanced countries set the 2% inflation rate as a target and made every effort to achieve the goal. Many countries including the United States succeeded in maintaining the inflation rate within the target range of 2% per year. Thus, the inflation issue was forgotten for many years until the coronavirus pandemic issued an alert to the world economy in 2020.

On the other hand, the Japanese government and the Bank of Japan took a different path to achieve the 2% inflation goal. Japan suffered from the long-sustained stagnation for almost two decades from the early 1990s. Japan experienced severe deflation caused by Japanese people's unwilling to spend and the resulting insufficient aggregate demand. The Japanese government and the Bank of Japan poured money into the economy to increase aggregate demand which was aimed at boosting the annual inflation rate to 2%. Japan was not successful in boosting the inflation rate until recently.

So far, we have discussed demand-pull inflation, but inflation can also be caused by supply-side factors. Inflation that is caused by supply-side factors is called supply-side inflation or cost-push inflation, because supply-side bottlenecks usually lead to higher production costs, and higher production costs are passed to the prices of products. Factors that increase production costs include higher wages, higher energy prices, higher raw material prices, lower labor productivity, and supply chain bottlenecks. The aggregate supply of goods and services is also negatively affected by natural disasters such as droughts, flooding, hurricanes, and earthquakes, and external shocks such as war and diseases. The supply-side inflation that is particularly caused by the shortage of production factors is sometimes called bottleneck inflation. In order to contrast supply-side inflation with the traditional Keynesian demand-side inflation, supply-side inflation is sometimes called 'new inflation'.

A rise in the price level caused by a supply shock results in only one-time inflation and does not develop into sustained inflation unless continuous supply shocks occur. Once such a supply shock disappears, overall prices stop rising. Just like fiscal expenditures cannot be the source of persistent inflation, a one-time supply shock itself is not the source of continual inflation. Nonetheless, the economy suffers persistent inflation when a supply shock such as the COVID-19 crisis hit the economy. because policymakers are pursuing an accommodating policy by continuously increasing the money supply to mitigate the adverse effects of supply shocks. In this context, we can say that inflation is a monetary phenomenon.

One characteristic of cost-push inflation is that it accompanies lower output and higher unemployment. In contrast, demand-pull inflation results in higher output and lower unemployment. In this sense, supply-side inflation is worse than demand-pull inflation. The coexistence of stagnation and inflation is called stagflation, and the phenomenon of stagflation appeared for the first time during the two oil crises in the 1970s. Then the unwelcome guest of stagflation again revisited the world economy in 2022 during the coronavirus pandemic crisis. The inflation that we experienced after the COVID-19 crisis is in fact a mix of demand-pull inflation and cost-push inflation. It was triggered by supply-chain bottlenecks and exacerbated by a surge in aggregate demand. During the COVID-19 crisis some supply chains collapsed, and at the same time, astronomical amounts of government spending and money were poured into the economy in many countries, which fueled both demand-pull and cost-push inflation.

One merit of distinguishing between demand-pull inflation and cost-push inflation is that restrictive aggregate demand policy such as an increase in interest rates or a decrease in government expenditures is not effective in curing supply-side inflation, although it may be effective in controlling inflation expectations. Thus, when supply-side inflation or stagflation hits the economy, policymakers encounter a policy dilemma. The first dilemma is whether policymakers should put a break on the economy to control inflation or to step on the accelerator to stimulate the economy and lower unemployment. In order to control inflation, policymakers should use contractionary monetary or fiscal policy. Thus, policymakers should raise interest rates or decrease fiscal expenditures. On the other hand, in order to reduce unemployment, policymakers should use expansionary monetary or fiscal policy. Thus, policymakers should lower interest rates or increase fiscal expenditures.

The second dilemma is that if policymakers choose to fight inflation and use contractionary monetary policy instead of stimulating the economy, such a policy option could drag the recovery of the economy. During the oil shocks and the COVID-19 crisis, policymakers (the Fed) chose to control inflation, raising the federal funds rate several times.

Lastly, inflation is not only caused by demand-pull and cost-push factors, but also by inflationary expectations. Especially, inflationary expectations play a critical role in the spiral of inflation. We'll discuss the role of inflationary expectations later in more detail.

5

HYPERINFLATION

We have discussed Friedman's statement that "Inflation is always and everywhere a monetary phenomenon" (Friedman and Schwartz, 1963). There is a category of inflation that corroborates Friedman's statement. Historically severe price increases showed up sporadically in a number of countries in a number of periods and devastated the economy. Hyperinflation has been the most notorious human-made calamity in economic history. Hyperinflation is to a hurricane what inflation is to a wind. In many developing countries (especially countries in South America and Africa), the governments have engaged in excessive borrowing from their central banks to finance budget deficits. Such a practice led to uncontrollably berserk inflation.

Most of hyperinflation is the result of the monetization of the deficit. There is no official definition of hyperinflation. Most economists follow Phillip Cagan's definition of hyperinflation. According to his definition, hyperinflation refers to a situation in which the period from the month when the monthly inflation rate rose above 50% to the month when the monthly inflation rate fell below 50% lasts more than a year. In other words, hyperinflation occurs when the monthly rate of inflation is 50% or higher at least for one year. This monthly rate is equivalent to the annual inflation rate of 12,874%.

There have been many episodes that tell us how painful and stressful hyperinflation was. For instance, people came to a shopping store with a truck filled with money and left the store with goods put in a small shopping bag. People rushed to a store immediately after they received a salary to buy groceries, because they worried that grocery prices would rise the next morning. In Germany during the hyperinflation period, it was less expensive to burn the paper currency than to buy firewood to warm the house. Historically, hyperinflation has occurred in many countries on and off. The most notorious ones took place in Germany after World War I, in Hungary after World War II, and most recently in Zimbabwe in 2008 and in Venezuela in 2018.

In 1923, during the ruling of the Weimar Republic of Germany, the Reichsbank issued a 2 trillion Deutsche mark-denominated note, and the government issued a stamp with a face value of 50 billion Deutsche marks. The highest value issued by the Reichsbank was a 100 trillion Deutsche mark bill. At that time, one U.S. dollar was exchanged for 4 trillion marks. The Mint Bureau that printed the mark billed the Reichsbank for a 3.28 $x10^{19}$ marks for the expense of printing the Deutsche mark. The pengo was the basic monetary unit of Hungary from 1927 until 1946. The highest face value bill issued by the Hungarian National Bank that was circulated in 1946 was 10^{20} pengos, which is equivalent to 100,000,000,000,000,000,000 pengos. At that time, Hungary's inflation rate was 41,900,000,000,000,000% (4.19 x 10^{16}%) per month.

The most recent hyperinflation is the inflation experienced by Zimbabwe in Africa in 2008 and by Venezuela in 2018. The Zimbabwean central bank, the Reserve Bank of Zimbabwe (RBZ) increased the money supply at an annual rate of 7,500% beginning 2004 as the country's economic situation became worsened. The result was an increase in the inflation rate from an already high rate of 130% to more than 231,000,000 percent by 2008. The exchange rate between the Zimbabwean dollar and the U.S. dollar was 1,000 Zimbabwean dollars per U.S. dollar in 2004 but rose to 10,000,000,000,000,000 Zimbabwean dollars per U.S. dollar by the end of 2009.

A businessman of Zimbabwe at the time said: "you'd have to pay for your coffee before you drank it because if you waited, the cost would rise within minutes." (Nurse, 2016). Zimbabwe issued a 100 trillion Zimbabwe dollar bill, but when it was no longer possible to issue such high face-value Zimbabwean dollar bills, it abandoned issuing its own currency in March 2009 and took steps to use the U.S. dollar as its national currency. Through the dollarization of its currency, Zimbabwe was finally able to escape from its notorious hyperinflation.

In modern times, in addition to Zimbabwe, many Latin American countries such as Argentina, Bolivia, Brazil, Nicaragua, and Peru experienced hyperinflation or pseudo-hyperinflation in the 1980s and 1990s. However, the hyperinflation Venezuela experienced in the 2010s went sky-high. In 2014, Venezuela's annual inflation rate reached 69%, the highest level in the world in the year. In 2015, the inflation rate rose to 181%, again the highest in the world in the same year and the highest in Venezuela's history. Since then, the inflation rate accelerated out of control. The inflation rate reached 274% in 2016, 863% in 2017, 130,060% in 2018, and 9,586% in 2019. The Central Bank of Venezuela (BCV) officially estimated that the inflation rate increased to 53,798,500% between 2016 and August 2019. In

April 2019, the IMF estimated that inflation would reach 10,000,000% by the end of 2019. In December 2021, the Central Bank of Venezuela announced that Venezuela would reach the monthly inflation rate below 50% in the first quarter of 2022 after more than four years of a hyperinflation cycle, which would indicate Venezuela's exit from hyperinflation.

Many studies have shown that almost all types of hyperinflation that occurred in different countries and at different times have all been caused by a dramatic increase in the quantity of money and that there was no exception to this pattern. Thus, hyperinflation is genuinely a monetary phenomenon. Today, countries that suffer hyperinflation are few and far between. Some economists have declared that mankind finally won the war against inflation. Some developed countries were even concerned about deflation. However, that was then before the outbreak of the coronavirus. There is a saying that "Now he laughs, then he weeps." (Source: The Bible, Luke 6:25)

6

FEAR OF DEFLATION?

Long before the rekindling of inflation triggered by the coronavirus pandemic crisis, people screamed out for the 'fear of D' in which 'D' stands for deflation. Deflation is the opposite of inflation. Deflation indicates a significant and sustained fall in the general price level measured by price indexes such as the consumer price index (CPI) and the GDP deflator. Deflation is a phenomenon in which the inflation rate becomes negative. A phenomenon that should be distinguished from deflation is disinflation. Disinflation refers to a slowdown in inflation. Disinflation is a phenomenon in which the inflation rate becomes smaller. Many South American countries experienced sky-high inflation in the 1980s and 1990s, with annual inflation rates ranging from a few hundred percent to a few thousand percent. Particularly, the IMF reported that the inflation rate in Venezuela reached 929,790% in 2018. However, Latin American countries have been successful in curbing such ferocious inflation, and now most Latin American countries except for Venezuela have shown a single-digit inflation rate.

Many countries did not experience deflation after WWII until the global economic crisis in 2008, except for Japan. Thus, many people did not feel the severity of deflation. However, in the United States, overall prices generally declined until the end of the 19th century. The periods of 1818~1821, 1837~1843, and 1875~1896 were characterized as the periods of falling prices. In particular, the U.S. prices continued to fall for more than 20 years from 1875 to 1896, which was called the "Great Deflation". During the Great Depression in the 1930s, prices fell sharply, and again during the Great Recession in 2008, overall prices fell intermittently.

Japan has been known as one of the countries with the highest price levels in the world, but Japan suffered die-hard deflation beginning in the early 1990s as the Japanese economy turned into a severe recession commonly known as the 'Lost Two Decades'. During this period, Japan's price level almost ceased to rise or fell continually. The deflation Japan experienced for more than 20 years was the first phenomenon in world history since the United States had experienced the Great Deflation in the late 19th century.

Until the global economic crisis in 2008, the top priority of economic policy in major developed countries was to curb inflation. Developed countries as well as developing countries had suffered from inflation until the 2008 Great Recession since WWII, and pronouncedly since the oil crisis in the 1970s. This long lasting and cumbersome inflation worldwide led many economists as well as policymakers to believe that inflation is bad, and deflation is corrigible. This can be confirmed by the fact that central banks in many countries place the top-priority goal of monetary policy in controlling inflation. Japan's annual inflation rate target was 1%. The United States and major European countries had an inflation rate target of 2%. South Korea's inflation target was 2.5% to 3.5% per year.

However, since the middle of the 2000s, inflation in many developed countries has no longer been on the list of economic headaches. The China effect played a part. Since China's cheap products began to flood into the U.S. market, the U.S. price level has not risen above 3% per year for an extended period. In addition, as labor productivity continued to increase due to the influence of the IT (information technology) revolution, firms could significantly reduce production costs, and the price level began to rise at a snail's pace. Furthermore, as the global economic crisis in 2008 hit the world economy, inflation almost stopped at least in major developed economies.

As the general price level continued to slow down, many countries began to worry about deflation. It is the so-called 'fear of D'. This situation is as if the economic constitution in many countries changed from hyperthermia to hypothermia, and many countries were on the alert to prepare for falling prices. In Japan, the Abe regime implemented an unlimited quantitative easing policy to raise the inflation rate to 2%. The 'fear of D' was also looming in the United States as well as in the eurozone countries.

These efforts reveal that policymakers have begun to realize that deflation may be more harmful to the economy than inflation. Why are people afraid of deflation? Usually, inflation accelerates concurrently with rising GDP and falling unemployment. This is an indication that at least one of the two economic diseases is healthy. The problem is deflation. Deflation usually comes in tandem with falling GDP and rising unemployment. The two economic diseases take place simultaneously.

First, if deflation proceeds, prices are generally falling. Naturally consumers expect the prices to fall further in the future and delay their purchasing of products (especially expensive ones). Thus, when deflation deepens, consumption also tends to decrease. From firms' perspective, deflation is not good at all. With prices falling overall, firms cannot raise prices for their products. To make matters worse, the products are not selling well because consumption is reduced and delayed. Corporate profits will fall. Companies are hesitant to invest when profits fall, and sales prospects are murky. Thus, deflation leads private consumption and private investment to contract.

Private exports are also negatively affected by deflation. Inflation is the process by which a country's real currency value falls. Deflation, the opposite of inflation, can be seen as the process by which a country's real currency value rises. An increase in the value of a country's currency also means that the value of the currency against other currencies becomes stronger. If the value of the British pound becomes stronger against the U.S. dollar, British exports will be adversely affected, because British products become more expensive in the international marketplace. For example, if the exchange rate between the British pound and the U.S. dollar rises from $1.2 per pound to $1.4 per pound, British products become relatively expensive abroad, and now people need $1.4 to buy a £1 British product in the world market. Before the exchange rate changes, people needed only $1.2 to buy the same product.

Thus, deflation has a negative impact on the three private components of GDP (consumption, investment, and exports). Deflation is not a trivial economic disease, and it can lead the economy to stagnation. The primary reason that Japan was not able to escape from the 'Lost Two Decades' is that it did not break the vicious circle of deflation.

Deflation can also disarrange an individual's life. Falling prices could increase households' real income and increase purchasing power, but these benefits apply only to people who have a lot of money or have loans. Deflation can be a nightmare for those who are in debt. Deflation can increase the real value of debt, making debt payments more burdensome. If the price level falls by 2% per year, households with a debt of $100,000 will be burdened with additional debts of $2,000 in real terms each year. Thus, for those who struggle with debt, deflation will make their struggle harder.

Not long ago, many people thought that deflation was not a big deal. Few countries have suffered serious deflation except for Japan since the Great Depression. Furthermore, there was a widespread perception that central bankers could easily overcome deflation by pouring money into the economy. Even economists thought that controlling inflation is a difficult job, but controlling deflation is a 'pushover'. However, as seen in the case of Japan, deflation does not easily lend itself to the central bank's policy such as 'unlimited quantitative easing' pursued by the Bank of Japan.

Recently, people have begun to realize that deflation has some structural inertia as well as psychological elements and that simply pouring money into the economy could not defeat deflation. Until the outbreak of coronavirus pandemic, the 'fear of D' (deflation) was greater than the fear of inflation, but deflation gave in to both demand shock-therapy (quantitative easing) and the collapse of supply chains. People have also changed their perception, believing that inflation could be recurrent at any time.

7

Is Zero Inflation Feasible and Desirable?

We have learned that neither inflation nor deflation is desirable. Then is zero inflation desirable and feasible? The answer to this question is 'No'. As discussed previously, persistent demand-side inflation is primarily caused by an increase in the quantity of money. We have also seen that supply-side inflation is mainly caused by supply shocks or rising production costs such as nominal wages and energy prices If so, then can inflation be zero provided that the supply of money increases at the same rate as the potential economic growth rate and that there is no external supply shock, and the nominal wage increases only by the increase of labor productivity?

However, we need to distinguish between the question of whether zero inflation is possible or not and the question of whether zero inflation is desirable or not. Zero inflation is theoretically feasible and possible. Inflation could reach zero if the growth rate of the money supply equals the growth rate of potential output, and the rate of increase in wages equals the rate of increase in labor productivity. A nation's potential output is determined by technological progress and the quantity of factor inputs such as labor and capital. The growth rate of potential output is about 3.5% in the United States. Therefore, it would be possible for the U.S. economy to achieve zero inflation if its economy (real GDP) grew at the rate of 3.5%, and the money supply increased at the rate of about 4%. Also, if labor productivity increases about by 2% per year (that is, if workers produce 2% more each year), it will be possible to achieve zero inflation even if the nominal wage increases by 2% annually.

However, a country's inflation rate of 0% means that overall prices of goods and services do not rise. If the prices of goods and services do not rise, it is difficult for firms to make profits. This leads to a decrease in corporate investment. Under zero inflation, firms should cut production costs to make a profit, but it is not easy to reduce production costs every year. There is no choice but to reduce employment or cut wages, and these extreme measures will lead to a decrease in production and income through the multiplier effect. This pushes the economy into a vicious cycle of shrinking investment-recession-low income. Japan's 'Lost Two Decades' was typical of such a shrinking economy.

Rather, it is a more desirable policy option to give investment incentives to firms by allowing inflation within a limited range and ensuring corporate profits. In this way, the economy will be on a virtuous cycle. Although zero inflation is feasible, it is not necessarily desirable for the whole economy.

The idea of limited inflation was first proposed in the 1950s by Harvard economist Sumner Slichter who maintained that inflation to some extent is vital to the economy. The proponents of the limited inflation idea are often called 'limited inflationists'. The term 'limited inflationist' was first used by Time magazine to refer to a group of economists who shared the idea. When many countries experienced low inflation or deflation in the 2000s, and the economy lost vitality, a sentiment began to emerge among Keynesian economists that a certain amount of inflation was needed to stimulate the economy. The inflation rate favored by limited inflationists is about 2 to 2.5% per year. Former Japanese Prime Minister Abe who aspired to raise Japan's annual inflation rate to 2% would be certainly classified as a limited inflationist.

8

CONSEQUENCES OF INFLATION

The most obvious consequence of inflation is the decline of the real value of money, although the nominal value of money remains the same. For instance, if the annual inflation rate is 10%, then the real value of a $100 bill will decrease to approximately $90 at the end of the year, although the nominal value of the $100 bill remains unchanged. However, the effects of inflation on the national economy and the lives of individuals are multi-faceted. Some quizzes are here.

- Is inflation or deflation good for people who are borrowers?
- Is inflation or deflation good for people who are lenders?
- Is inflation or deflation good for people who own real estate such as land and houses?
- Is inflation or deflation good for people who own financial assets such as stocks, bonds, and foreign currencies?
- Is inflation or deflation good for people who live on fixed income and pensions?

In general, if inflation occurs, financial asset owners, lenders, and fixed-income earners such as wage earners and pensioners will lose, and real estate owners and borrowers will gain. If deflation occurs, the opposite occurs. However, the redistribution of income and wealth is largely dependent on how accurately economic agents (consumers, lenders, borrowers, workers, companies, etc.) can predict inflation before making economic transactions. If economic agents can predict inflation accurately before the transaction occurs, they try to minimize the adverse effects of inflation by fully reflecting the expected inflation in their wage contracts, loan contracts, and leasing contracts. Generally speaking, expected inflation has much less damage to people than unexpected inflation. (Here we'll focus on the effects of inflation, not deflation.)

First, we'll examine the effect of expected inflation on economic activity. As we discussed, the obvious effect of expected inflation is a decline in the real value of money. Next, as the cost of expected inflation, we can consider shoe leather costs and menu costs. Because inflation reduces the real value of money, people try to reduce the holdings of cash and to convert cash into stocks, bonds, gold, or savings deposits that pay interest when they expect inflation. Consequently, when you need money to pay rent or hospital bills, you will have to go to the bank to get cash or go to the financial market to sell stocks or bonds. Thus, if inflation is expected to rise, people incur some economic costs in terms of time and effort to reduce cash holdings. These costs are called 'shoe leather costs'. As inflation rises, shoe leather costs increase as well. The shoe leather costs seem to be trifling, but according to a study by Stanley Fischer, the shoe leather costs associated with an expected 10% inflation rate are estimated to be about 0.3% of GDP. (Since U.S. GDP is $21 trillion in 2021, the annual shoe leather costs are estimated to be about $63 billion.) The theory of shoe leather costs was proposed by Harvard economist N. Gregory Mankiw. However, the significance of shoe leather costs seems to be considerably diminishing, because many banking transactions are now carried out through online banking.

Another cost of expected inflation is the menu cost. If inflation is expected, department stores, groceries, or restaurants will have to change their menu prices, and thus they'll have to print new catalogs or menus. As inflation becomes more severe, these changes will occur more frequently, and the menu costs will also increase. The menu costs may not be great in the overall economy, but according to Mankiw, the effect of such costs on the economy is not trivial. Again, the significance of the menu cost is considerably diminishing in the age of Internet shopping.

If inflation is not expected, the costs of inflation are much larger and more serious than the costs of expected inflation. If economic agents do not accurately anticipate inflation, economic losses due to inflation will not be avoided, and the allocation of resources will be made in an arbitrary way, not by market forces. Unexpected inflation results in the redistribution of income and wealth among economic agents. The redistribution of wealth depends on how accurately inflation is predicted.

If inflation is accurately predicted and actual inflation equals expected inflation, then, the redistribution of income and wealth between lenders and borrowers does not occur in principle. If the inflation rate is expected to reach 5%, then lenders will charge at least 5% of nominal interest on their loans. Therefore, if the actual inflation rate reaches 5%, neither the lender nor the borrower will lose.

However, if the actual inflation rate (7%) is higher than the expected inflation rate (5%), lenders will lose, and borrowers will gain. If a lender expects the annual inflation rate to be 5% during the life of the loan, the lender will demand at least 5% interest. The lender asks for at least a 5%

interest on the loan, because the lender predicts the real value of his loan to drop by 5% due to inflation. In order to compensate for the decline in the real value of the loan, the interest rate will be set equal to 5% in the loan contract. However, if inflation actually rises by 7%, the real value of the loan will be reduced by 7%. The 5% nominal interest rate is not sufficient to compensate for the decrease in the real value of the loan by 7%. Thus, the lender will lose, and the borrower will benefit.

However, if the actual inflation rate (3%) is lower than the expected inflation rate (5%), the opposite occurs between the lender and the borrower. The lender will gain, and the borrower will lose. In such a case, the lender expects the real value of the loan to decline by 5%, but the real value of the loan actually decreases only by 3%. The 2% interest is an unexpected gain for the lender. We can summarize our discussion as follows: (We assume that the market expects the inflation rate in year t to be 5%.)

- If the actual inflation rate (= 5%) is the same as the expected inflation rate (= 5%), neither the lender nor the borrower will gain.
- If the actual inflation rate (=7%) is greater than the expected inflation rate (= 5%), the lender will lose, and the borrower will gain.
- If the actual inflation rate (=3%) is less than the expected inflation rate (= 5%), the lender will gain, and the borrower will lose.

Households are the major borrowers in the economy, but governments and corporations are also borrowers. Will the governments and business firms also benefit from unexpected inflation? Inflation will certainly help reduce the burden of the debt borne by the governments and business firms, but the inflation rate should be higher than the expected inflation rate at the time when the governments or firms repay their debts.

9

INFLATION AND INTEREST RATES: THE FISHER EQUATION

We have seen that when people anticipate inflation, they try to minimize the damage from inflation by reflecting the anticipated inflation in their wage contracts, loan contracts, or lease contracts. Taking the loan contract as an example, the lender usually sets the interest rate on the loan by adding the anticipated inflation to the cost of the loan. The cost of a loan should be measured by the real interest rate. We have the following relationship:

Nominal interest rate = Real interest rate + Expected inflation rate

The relationship between the nominal interest rate and the expected inflation rate is often called the Fisher equation named after Irving Fisher who first discussed it. The real interest rate can be viewed as compensation for the sacrifice that a lender embraces by giving up current consumption. Suppose you lend \$1,000 to your friend for one year. Then you cannot use this money for current consumption for one year. Thus, you'll require some compensation for the sacrifice of current consumption. This compensation is the real interest rate. Thus, the real interest rate is the time value of money for not using your money today. If the lender lends a certain amount of money when the real interest rate is 2%, the lender will require 2% interest on the loan in exchange for sacrificing current consumption.

Fisher further presumed that the real interest rate was quite constant. It was assumed that the real interest rate was not affected by aggregate demand policy such as the money supply or fiscal spending. This suggests that if the money supply increases, it almost surely leads to an increase in inflation, which in turn increases the nominal interest rate without affecting the real interest rate. This proposition is known as the Fisher hypothesis.

The Fisher equation shows that the nominal interest rate consists of two parts: (1) the real interest rate or the compensation for the sacrifice of current consumption and (2) the expected inflation rate. The real interest rate is not directly observable and may be different among individuals, because individuals have a different time preference for money. Nonetheless, we can calculate the average real interest rate from the Fisher equation as follows:

Real interest rate = Nominal interest rate – Expected inflation rate

The *ex-ante* real interest rate cannot be negative in principle because it is a reward for the sacrifice of current consumption. When the lender makes a loan, the lender figures out the real interest rate *ex-ante* before the loan contract is made. Thus, the *ex-ante* real interest rate cannot go below 0%.

However, if the real interest rate is calculated *ex post* at the end of the year after the loan contract was made, the real interest rate may drop below 0%. For example, if the real interest rate is figured out to be 2% and the inflation rate is expected to be 3% before the loan contract is made, the nominal interest rate will be set equal to 5% in the loan contract. However, if the inflation rate turns out to be 7% *ex-post* after the loan contract is made, the real interest rate becomes negative 2%.

Ex-post real interest rate = Nominal interest rate – Actual inflation rate

⇒ *Ex-post* real interest rate = 5% – 7% = –2%

On the other hand, the real interest rate that was calculated before the loan contract was made is the *ex-ante* real interest rate.

Ex-ante real interest rate = Nominal interest rate – Expected inflation rate

⇒ *Ex-ante* real interest rate = 5% – 3% = 2%

Since it is difficult to measure accurately the expected inflation rate, researchers like to use the *ex post* real interest rate as an approximation to the *ex-ante* real interest rate.

We have seen that the real interest rate matters in making decisions on lending and borrowing. Can policymakers make the *ex-post* real interest rate negative? Policymakers could make the real interest rate negative by promoting inflation. The most effective way to promote inflation is to increase the quantity of money available in the economy. Negative real interest rates have important implications for business investment. Just as lenders or borrowers make a loan contract based on the real interest rate, firms also make a decision on their investment on the basis of the real interest rate. When the real interest rate goes down, firms invest more, and vice versa.

In this way, when corporate investment is dull, policymakers could promote inflation and lower the real interest rate below 0% to promote investment. Such a policy has some side effects but could be effective. Some economists argue that lowering interest rates is not sufficient to stimulate business investment. According to this view, policymakers should induce negative real interest rates to stimulate investment. Larry Summers who served as the U.S. Treasury Secretary and the President of Harvard University is in sympathy with this view. However, such a policy scheme works only when the inflation rate is higher than the nominal interest rate. Policymakers cannot make the *ex post* real interest rate negative for an extended period because the nominal interest rate will soon catch up with the inflation rate.

10

THE MEASUREMENT OF UNEMPLOYMENT

Unemployment and inflation are described as two macroeconomic diseases or two macroeconomic evils. Naturally, the goal of a country's economic policy is to prevent or cure these two diseases. Unemployment is a situation in which a person who has the ability and willingness to work cannot find a job. The unemployment rate varies across countries, and changes over time. To understand why unemployment occurs, we need to know how unemployment is defined and measured.

To compute the unemployment rate, the Bureau of Labor Statistics first divides the total population into the working-age population (civilian non-institutional population) and the non-working-age population. People in the non-working-age population include those who are too young to work or cannot work because they live in some types of institutions such as the military, prisons, and mental hospitals. In the United States, people under the age of 16 years are considered to be too young to work. The working age varies among countries. In South Korea, people under the age of 15 years are not allowed to work. Thus, people who belong to the working-age population are those who are 'able to work', and people who fall into the category of non-working-age population are those who are 'unable to work'.

The working-age population is divided into two groups: People who are in the labor force and people who are not in the labor force. People who are in the labor force are those who are 'willing to work', and people who are classified as 'not in the labor force' are those who are not willing to work, although they are able to work. Homemakers, full-time students, and people who are retired fall into this group. The Bureau of Labor Statistics finally divides the labor force into two categories: The employed who are currently working and the unemployed who are not currently working, but actively looking for work.

The Bureau of Labor Statistics randomly selects about 60,000 households each month and surveys a questionnaire that contains a number of questions about the job market situations of household members. Based on the surveyed data, the Bureau of Labor Statistics estimates the unemployment rate as follows:

$$Unemployment\ rate = \frac{Number\ of\ people\ unemployed}{Labor\ force}\ x\ 100(\%)$$

In addition to the unemployment rate, we have two useful measures of job market situations:

$$Labor\ force\ participation\ rate = \frac{Labor\ force}{Working-age\ population}\ x\ 100(\%)$$

$$Employment\text{-}to\text{-}population\ ratio = \frac{Employed\ people}{Working-age\ population}\ x\ 100(\%)$$

The labor force participation rate measures how many people who are able to work are currently in the job market, that is, how many people are willing to work. The employment-to-population ratio measures how many people who are able to work currently have jobs.

<Table 7.3> U.S. Unemployment Rate (in thousands)

	2019	2020	2021
Population	330,151	329,484	332,915
Working-age Population	259,175	260,329	261,445
Labor force	163,539	160,742	161,204
Not in labor force	95,636	99,587	100,241
Employed	157,538	147,795	152,581
Unemployed	6,001	12,947	8,623
Unemployment Rate	3.7%	8.1%	5.3%

Source: *The Economic Report of the President*, 2022.

In order for a person to be included in the category of the 'unemployed', the person must have searched for a job at least once in the preceding four weeks. Anyone who has been actively looking for work in the preceding four weeks but has not yet found a job is considered unemployed. However, if a person who has been out of work for the past four weeks or more and has given up looking for work because of poor job prospects, she is not considered unemployed, because she is treated as a person who has left the labor market. The person is instead treated as being 'not in the labor force', because she is not willing to work. We can show the statistics for the unemployment rate in 2021 as follows (unit: thousands):

- ◈ Population (332,915) = Civilian noninstitutional people (261,445) + Others (71,470)
- ◈ Civilian noninstitutional people (261,445) = In labor force (161,204) + Not in labor force (100,241)
- ◈ Labor force (161,204) = Employed (152,581) + Unemployed (8,623)

The U.S. unemployment in 2021 was 5.3%.

$$U.S. unemployment\ rate = \frac{8,602}{161,204}\ x\ 100 = 5.3(\%)$$

The estimated unemployment rate is the official unemployment rate published by the government each month. In the United States, the unemployment rate is one of the most frequently used economic variables for policy making. Even if the unemployment rate rises slightly, the stock and bond markets react sensitively, and U.S. monetary and fiscal policy is adjusted accordingly. However, the official unemployment rate has many loopholes. The official unemployment rate is criticized for underestimating actual unemployment. It is mainly due to the presence of discouraged workers.

The definition of unemployed people seems to be straightforward at first glance. However, in practice, the distinction between the unemployed and the employed is sometimes ambiguous. This confusion is mainly due to two types of unemployment: discouraged workers and involuntary part-time workers.

Discouraged workers are people who have tried to find a job but eventually given up their job search because they have been unable to find a job. The discouraged unemployed are not included in the labor force because they have left the job market and are therefore not classified as unemployed. If an unemployed person is looking for a job without losing hope, she is unemployed, but if she gives up hope and no longer seeks a job, she is not treated as unemployed. She is neither employed nor unemployed. Under the current method of estimating unemployment, the unemployment rate falls when the unemployed give up hope.

Next, the Bureau of Labor Statistics does not differentiate between full-time workers and part-time workers when calculating the unemployment rate. If a worker chooses to work only a few hours per week voluntarily, she is counted as 'employed' in the unemployment statistics. Even if a worker works only one hour per week, there will be no problem with treating her as an ‘employed’ person as long as the worker wants to work only one hour per week, and the employer offers such a job.

Involuntary part-time workers are another factor that leads the official unemployment rate to underestimate true unemployment. For example, if an employer reduces the number of working days or shortens working hours instead of laying off workers when the economy is in a bad shape, this is involuntary part-time employment. In such a case, the job market situation has been worsening, but the unemployment rate remains unaffected. Let’s take the example of golf caddies. They usually work six days per week and eight hours per day. However, if the management of a golf club shortens the working days from six days to three days per week or working hours from eight hours to four hours per day, caddies would become involuntary part-time workers.

Discouraged workers are not classified as unemployed because they left the job market, and therefore are not included in the labor force. Involuntary part-time workers are not counted as unemployed, because they are treated as ‘employed’. Discouraged unemployment and involuntary part-time employment are sometimes referred to as disguised unemployment. The official unemployment rate tends to underestimate the actual unemployment situation because of the existence of disguised unemployment.

11

THE CAUSES AND TYPES OF UNEMPLOYMENT

There are many different types of unemployment. First, frictional unemployment is unemployment caused by temporary factors such as moving and turnovers. When people move to a better place or are relocated, they'll quit their old jobs. People also quit their previous jobs to get a better job, or their previous jobs are closed. Frictional unemployment is sometimes called turnover unemployment. In a democratic society where people are free to move and free to choose jobs, the existence of frictional unemployment is inevitable and of considerable size.

Structural unemployment is unemployment caused by changes in industrial structure and technological change, whereas frictional unemployment is caused by temporary factors. Structural unemployment occurs because the qualifications required by jobs do not match the skills of workers. A structurally unemployed person is the case of 'a round peg in a square hole' or 'a square peg in a round hole'. For example, in the 1980s, a number of typewriters who had a small office were scattered all over the place, but as typewriters were replaced by word processors, all the typewriting jobs disappeared. Also, until personal computers were popularized, the demand for key punchers typing computer languages was very high. But such jobs were eliminated due to technological advances in computers. For this reason, structural unemployment is sometimes called mismatch unemployment. Structural unemployment can be seen as an essential trait of capitalism.

As office and factory automations accelerate, structural unemployment is expected to become a serious issue in the future. Many traditional jobs are rapidly being replaced by robots and AI (artificial intelligence) machines. The age of 'jobless growth' is approaching light-footedly. Structural unemployment imposes more serious problems than frictional unemployment, because workers are not voluntarily quitting their jobs to find a better job or a better place but because their previous jobs were gone due to the reorientation of the economy and the restructuring of the industry brought by technological progress.

Seasonal unemployment is unemployment that occurs due to seasonal fluctuations in job opportunities. Employment opportunities in some industries are subject to seasonal changes. Workers in the construction industry usually do not get jobs in winter, which is an example of seasonal unemployment. People in the tourist industry in U.S. northern states have difficulty in finding jobs in the winter. Seasonal unemployment is common in agriculture, construction, and tourism industries. This type of unemployment exists in any society or under any economic system (even under a command economy).

Finally, there is cyclical unemployment. The three types of unemployment discussed above always exist regardless of the business cycle of the economy. These types of unemployment do not go away just because the economy is booming. However, cyclical unemployment is unemployment associated with a business cycle. In other words, cyclical unemployment increases as the economy stagnates and decreases as the economy booms. Firms lay off workers when the economy contracts and hire more workers when the economy expands.

Let's take the U.S. economy as an example to see how total unemployment is decomposed into the four types of unemployment. When the U.S. unemployment rate was 6.8%, the unemployment rate was broken down into the following categories:

- ◈ Friction unemployment rate: 2.8%
- ◈ Structural unemployment rate: 2.5%
- ◈ Seasonal unemployment rate: 0.2%
- ◈ Cyclical unemployment rate: 1.3%
- ◈ Total unemployment rate: 6.8%

In most advanced economies, frictional unemployment and structural unemployment account for a large portion of the total unemployment rate. The fact that frictional unemployment and structural unemployment are very high in the United States indicates that the U.S. labor market is highly flexible. As the labor market is more flexible, workers have much freedom to move to better jobs or better places, and firms have much leeway to lay off workers in response to changing economic conditions.

12

THE FULL-EMPLOYMENT RATE OF UNEMPLOYMENT AND THE NATURAL UNEMPLOYMENT RATE

If everyone who wants to work can get a job, such a job market situation is characterized as full employment. However, even when the economy reaches full employment, the unemployment rate cannot be zero. We have seen that there are always some types of unemployment in any society. Frictional, structural, and seasonal unemployment always exist regardless of the state of the economy. Even if the economy is in an expansion phase, such unemployment does not go away. At best, the government can eliminate cyclical unemployment by using an expansionary aggregate demand policy. In other words, even if the economy is in full-employment equilibrium, the unemployment rate cannot fall to zero. Thus, the full-employment level of unemployment can be defined as the sum of the frictional, structural, and seasonal unemployment rates with the cyclical unemployment rate being equal to zero.

The term 'full-employment rate of unemployment' is a term favored by Keynesian economists. The term reflects Keynesians' confidence in achieving the full-employment level of unemployment by the appropriate use of aggregate demand policy such as fiscal and monetary policy. There are several other terms that refer to the full-employment rate of unemployment. Monetarists, modern-day classical economists, prefer to use the term, 'natural unemployment rate'. Some economists like to use the term, 'potential unemployment rate'. These terms are used almost interchangeably, but there is a subtle difference among them.

The natural rate of unemployment was first used by Friedman and Edmund Phelps. The natural unemployment rate is the unemployment rate toward which the economy gravitates in the long run. The economy reaches the natural unemployment rate in the long run when economic agents fully incorporate all the available information on expected inflation into their economic behavior, and they do not make any systematic errors in predicting the inflation rate. On the other hand, the potential unemployment rate is the unemployment rate that the economy achieves when the economy produces potential output. Potential output (or potential GDP) is the maximum level of output that the economy can produce when production resources such as labor and capital are fully utilized without promoting inflation. Put simply, the potential unemployment rate is a long-run trend in the unemployment rate.

Whatever term is used, one clear fact is that the natural or potential unemployment rate is outside the influence of monetary or fiscal policy. Potential output is determined by a nation's quantities of labor and capital together with technological progress and is not affected by fiscal or monetary policy. Thus, it will be futile for policymakers to attempt to lower the potential unemployment rate further using aggregate demand policy. One merit of discussing the potential unemployment rate is that potential unemployment in a country can be lowered only by increasing productivity through education, training or technological advancement.

One important practical advantage of discussing the natural unemployment rate is that when the economy reaches the natural unemployment rate, inflation is neither accelerating nor decelerating. Thus, the natural unemployment rate is also defined as the unemployment rate that does not accelerate inflation. This level of unemployment is called NAIRU (non-accelerating inflation rate of unemployment).

The full-employment rate of unemployment in the United States was estimated to be 4% in the 1960s, when the U.S. economy was enjoying a golden era. This means that even when the economy reaches full employment, 4% of people in the job market remain unemployed. These unemployed people are comprised of frictionally unemployed people, structurally unemployed people, and seasonally unemployed people.

Then, in the 1970s, the economic environment rapidly changed as the effects of two oil crises changed the structure of the economy into an inflation-oriented constitution, and accordingly, the full-employment rate of unemployment also changed upwardly. This upward trend in the full-employment rate of unemployment was made mainly due to major changes in the composition of the working population. During this period, the influx of adolescents and female workers into the labor market had a significant impact on the potential rate of unemployment. It is known that those adolescent and female workers have relatively low levels of skills and often have higher levels of frictional and structural unemployment compared with the existing male workforce and often leave the labor market for other alternative activities such as education and homemaking.

As a result of the change in the composition of the working population, the full-employment rate of unemployment rose to 6.5% from the mid-

1970s through the 1980s. As the full employment rate of unemployment rose in the 1980s to 6.5 percent, some economists began to use the term, 'high-employment rate of unemployment', instead of the term 'full-employment rate of unemployment'. The most recent estimate of the full-employment rate of unemployment has been about 5.5% of the civilian labor force during the 2000s. However, it is presumed that the COVID-19 pandemic crisis would have certainly changed the full-employment rate of unemployment in many countries. Lastly, the downsizing and restructuring of industries in the midst of the advancement of information technology such as AI (artificial intelligence) and robots have also fueled the upward trend in the full-employment rate of unemployment.

13

Is Zero Unemployment Feasible and Desirable?

In a free society, frictional unemployment is inevitable. Structural unemployment is also an essential characteristic of the capitalist system. Seasonal unemployment always exists in any society as long as there are seasonal changes. Thus, frictional, structural, and seasonal unemployment cannot be avoided. These three types of unemployment can be characterized as noncyclical unemployment and cannot be changed or reduced by fiscal or monetary policy. Even if the government increases spending, and the central bank increases the money supply, noncyclical unemployment does not go away easily.

This kind of unemployment has, of course, some economic and social costs, but sometimes it can be a vital force for the economy. Frictional unemployment, for example, performs the function of placing 'the right man in the right place'. If a worker finds that his current job does not fit into his aptitudes, but there is no way out for better opportunities, he cannot perform his capabilities in full force, and hence his productivity will not be fully enhanced. However, if he is free to move from job to job and from place to place, he can find a new job or a new place that suits better his aptitudes, or to achieve his talents and capabilities more efficiently. Thus, frictional unemployment performs the function of putting 'a round peg in a round hole' or 'a square peg in a square peg'. In such a case, any economic and social losses from temporary unemployment will not be an issue.

Since frictional unemployment acts as a lubricant that keeps the economy running well, it can increase the flexibility of the labor market and the efficiency of the economy. The more flexible the labor market, the higher is the level of frictional unemployment. Under the communist system, where the freedom to choose jobs and to move to other places is restricted, such frictional unemployment cannot exist in principle. Thus, people under the totalitarian system are deprived of the opportunities to choose a job and to maximize their productivity and talents. In a free society, frictional unemployment cannot be either zero or desirable.

Structural unemployment and seasonal unemployment are also outside the scope of fiscal or monetary policy. Structural unemployment is the byproduct of industrialization and technological progress. If there were no advancement in industrialization or technological progress, we could avoid structural unemployment. However, such a situation would be unimaginable in a capitalist economy. Thus, the government cannot eliminate frictional, structural, and seasonal unemployment by the use of its aggregate demand policy. The government can, at best, eliminate cyclical unemployment by using monetary and fiscal policies. Thus, even when the economy achieves full employment, the unemployment rate cannot be zero. Just as zero inflation is neither feasible nor desirable, zero unemployment is neither feasible nor desirable in a free-market capitalist economy. In short, frictional and structural unemployment can be a shot in the arm for the flexibility of the labor market and the efficiency of the economy.

14

Economic and Social Costs of Unemployment and the Misery Index

Unemployment means that an economy does not fully utilize human resources. As a result, the economy loses some of the goods and services it could produce if there were no unemployment. This lost output is the economic cost of unemployment. How can we measure the economic cost of unemployment? We can first estimate potential output. Potential output is the maximum level of output that the economy can produce when its production resources are fully employed. When unemployment exists in the economy, the total amount of goods and services that the economy produces does not reach its potential output. The difference between potential GDP and actual GDP is the measure of the economic cost of unemployment.

In measuring the cost of unemployment, we also need to think about the human suffering from unemployment as well as trillions of dollars of lost output. Inflation affects almost everyone's life in an indiscriminatory way , and the impact of inflation is indirect. However, the unemployment of a family head not only has a direct effect on the family, but it can also drive the family into tragedy.

Bluestone and Harrison (1982) have found that for every 1 percentage point increase in the unemployment rate in the United States, 920 people committed suicide, 650 people committed murder, and 500 people died from heart attacks and illnesses related to unemployment. It is also reported that 4,000 people are admitted to mental hospitals and 3,300 people are going to jail.

These statistics eloquently indicate that as unemployment rises and is widespread, the number of people who suffer also increases. When the suffering of unemployment is combined with the pressure of inflation, people feel miserable. There is an index that quantifies the hardships inflicted by unemployment and inflation. The misery index is the sum of the unemployment rate and the inflation rate. Adding an unemployment rate and an inflation rate doesn't make sense economically, but the misery index is often used as a popular measure of economic performance. In particular, the misery index attracts a considerable amount of attention during election years because it can be seen as a report card for the government's economic performance. The higher the misery index, the greater the economic pain people feel and the deeper are the wrinkles in the economic lives of people.

There seems to be a strong correlation between the misery index and the outcomes of the presidential and parliamentary elections. The results of the past U.S. presidential elections demonstrate that the lower the misery index, the more likely the incumbent president or ruling party wins the election. Let's look at the relationship between the U.S. misery index and the election outcomes. The U.S. misery index began to rise significantly in the mid-1970s after the first oil crisis in 1973. The rising misery index was a huge burden for President Gerald Ford (Republican), and American voters elected Jimmy Carter (Democrat) in 1976 who promised new hopes. However, as the inflation rate soared to double-digit numbers during the second oil crisis in the late 1970s, the misery index jumped to the all-time high during the Carter presidency. The misery index reached 19.6 in 1980, and the high misery index derailed Carter's challenge for reelection.

After President Ronald Reagan took office, the misery index continued to fall, reaching 11.4 at the end of his first term (1984). Thanks to his economic achievements, President Reagan defeated Walter Mondale, a Democratic candidate with a landslide margin and became the second-term president in nearly 20 years. In 1988, when President Reagan's second term was nearing the end, the misery index fell to a single digit number (9.6), and George H.W. Bush (Republican) who served as Vice President in the Reagan administration easily won the election.

Until 1992, there seemed to be no obstacle to President Bush's reelection avenue. However, President Bush had to embrace the painful misery index. The misery index again rose to a two-digit number (10.4) in 1992, which cost Bush's presidency. Bush was a hero in the Gulf War, but he lost in the battle against the misery index. In 1992, when President Bill Clinton finished his first term, he was embroiled in a sex scandal with Monica Lewinski who worked as an intern at the White House. His chances of being reelected dimmed. However, the IT revolution, which started in the middle of the 1990s, was in full blossom during his presidency, and the U.S. economy experienced a new phenomenon known as the 'New Economy'. The New Economy was characterized as the coexistence of low inflation and low unemployment, and the misery index fell to 8.7 in 1996, the lowest level since 1970. He was reelected as President, overcoming all political obstacles. Clinton's catchphrase in the 1996 election was "It's the economy. Stupid!" In the 2020 Presidential election, the misery index (9.5) was quite high, because the unemployment rate rose from 3.7% in 2019 to 8.1% in

2020 due to the impacts of the COVID-19 pandemic on the economy. President Trump lost to Joe Biden by a big margin.

<Table 7.4> U.S. Misery Index

Election Year	Inflation Rate	Unemployment Rate	Misery Index	President Elected
1976	4.9%	7.7%	12.6	Jimmy Carter (D)
1980	12.5%	7.1%	19.6	Ronald Reagan (R)
1984	3.9%	7.5%	11.4	Ronald Reagan (R)
1988	4.4%	5.5%	9.6	George H.W. Bush (R)
1992	2.9%	7.5%	10.4	Bill Clinton (D)
1996	3.3%	5.4%	8.7	Bill Clinton (D)
2000	3.4%	4.0%	7.4	George W. Bush (R)
2004	3.3%	5.5%	8.8	George W. Bush (R)
2008	0.1%	5.8%	5.9	Barack Obama (D)
2012	1.7%	8.1%	9.8	Barack Obama (D)
2016	2.1%	4.9%	7.0	Donald Trump (R)
2020	1.4%	8.1%	9.5	Joe Biden (D)

Source: *The Economic Report of the President*, 2022

PART 8

LOW INFLATION AND LOW UNEMPLOYMENT: IN SEARCH OF TWO HARES

1

The Great Debate between Keynesians and Monetarists and Okun's Law

We have examined the two macroeconomic evils: inflation and unemployment. Although they are unwelcome, they are not easily chased away either. Thus, achieving low inflation and low unemployment is not an easy task for policymakers. For this reason, achieving low inflation and low unemployment is the top priority of economic policy in almost all countries. Is it possible to catch two hares, low inflation and low unemployment at once or to kill two birds with one stone? This question is a long-standing issue that has driven the economics profession into the furnace of debate for decades.

The generally accepted conclusion so far is that it is not possible to achieve both goals of low inflation and low unemployment using monetary or fiscal policy. In other words, many economists, especially Keynesians agree that 'two hares could not be caught all at once'. They believe in the proverb that anyone who runs after two hares will catch neither. Of course, some non-mainstream economists such as supply-side economists maintain that policymakers can achieve both low inflation and low unemployment by shifting a country's aggregate supply curve to the right. As we have already seen, supply-side economists favor lowering the income tax rate primarily to shift the aggregate supply curve to the right. This position is fundamentally different from that of mainstream economics such as Keynesian economics and classical economics.

Then, if we give up one hare, can we catch the other hare? There are two different views. Keynesian economists argue that it is not possible to achieve these two goals at the same time, but it is possible to achieve one goal by sacrificing the other goal. On the other hand, monetarists (modern-day classical economists) claim that it is not even possible to achieve one goal by sacrificing another goal by the use of fiscal policy or monetary policy.

The conflict between the two schools about the relationship between inflation and unemployment was commonly called the Great Debate, which has lasted more than half a century. At the heart of the debate is the Phillips curve. Since Philips discovered the Phillips curve in the late 1950s, there has been heated debate surrounding the relevance of the Phillips curve between Keynesian economists and monetarists. The debate has been extended to a new debate between new Keynesian economists and new classical economists since the 1980s. The Phillips curve is a useful tool that allows us to assess the performance of the economy in terms of inflation and unemployment. To understand the Phillips curve, we first need to know Okun's law, which represents the relationship between output (GDP) and unemployment.

In general, gross output and inflation move together in the same period. During the same period, output and inflation have a *positive* correlation. However, over time, inflation has a negative effect on output, because inflation distorts the allocation of resources. Meanwhile, there is a negative correlation between output (GDP) and unemployment in the same period. When the economy slows down, and output decreases, unemployment increases. Okun's law is concerned with a contemporaneous correlation between output and unemployment. When we combine these two correlations, we obtain the Phillips curve.

Thus, in order to understand the Phillips curve, we first need to know Okun's law. Okun derived the empirical relationship between unemployment and output by introducing the concept of potential unemployment. As we discussed, the potential unemployment rate is the unemployment rate that exists when the economy produces at the level of potential output. Okun's law can be expressed as

$$\text{Real GDP growth rate (\%)} = \text{Potential growth rate (\%)} \\ - 2[\text{Actual unemployment rate} - \text{Potential unemployment rate}]$$

The above relationship can be rewritten as

$$\text{Real GDP growth rate (\%)} - \text{Potential growth rate (\%)} = \\ - 2[\text{Actual unemployment rate} - \text{Potential unemployment rate}]$$

Okun's law shows how much the growth rate of real GDP will drop if the actual unemployment rate rises above the potential unemployment rate. First, if the actual unemployment rate equals the potential unemployment rate (= full employment rate of unemployment), the real GDP growth rate equals the potential growth rate. This is obviously a predictable result. When the economy achieves its potential unemployment rate, it will produce at the level of potential output. Next, Okun's law shows that if the actual unemployment rate rises by 1 percentage point above the potential unemployment rate, the growth rate of real GDP falls by 2 percentage points from the potential growth rate. For example, if the potential unemployment rate is 5.0% and the actual unemployment rate rises to 6.0%, the real GDP growth rate will drop by 2 percentage points from the potential growth rate. Here, the number 2 is called Okun's coefficient.

Okun's law is the result of empirical analysis obtained from the U.S. economy. Therefore, Okun's law not only varies considerably from country to country, but also varies over time even in the same country. The differences in the Okun coefficient largely reflect differences in the practice of hiring and firing workers in different countries, and the relationship between firms and workers. Thus, Okun's coefficient can be seen as an indirect indicator of how flexible the labor market is in a country. MIT economist Olivier Blanchard estimated the reciprocal of Okun's coefficient by readjusting Okun's law as

$$\text{Actual unemployment rate} - \text{Potential unemployment rate}$$
$$= a - b\,[\text{Real GDP growth rate} - \text{Potential growth rate}]$$

where b is the inverse of Okun's coefficient (b = 1/Okun's coefficient). We call b the Blanchard coefficient. The Blanchard coefficient represents how much the actual unemployment rate fluctuates when real GDP changes from its potential GDP, and thus measures the flexibility of the labor market. The more flexible the labor market in a country, the larger is the Blanchard coefficient, because the actual unemployment rate will move more flexibly. In the extreme case, if the actual unemployment rate does not respond to economic fluctuations at all, the value of the Blanchard coefficient will be zero. If the value of the Blanchard coefficient is 1, as GDP falls 1 percentage point from the potential growth rate, the actual unemployment rate rises 1 percentage point from the potential unemployment rate. The estimated value of the Blanchard coefficient (b) in major countries is as follows:

U.S.:	1960 ~ 1980: 0.40, 1981 ~ 1994: 0.47
Japan:	1960 ~ 1980: 0.15, 1981 ~ 1994: 0.23
Germany:	1960 ~ 1980: 0.27, 1981 ~ 1994: 0.42
U.K.:	1960 ~ 1980: 0.17, 1981 ~ 1994: 0.49

We note that the Blanchard coefficient (b) or the coefficient of labor market flexibility is high in the United States, but it is quite low in Japan. This difference seems to be due to differences in the business culture between the two countries. Japanese firms have provided their workers with a 'lifetime job' security (at least until the early 1980s). Even if the economy was not good, the tradition of the Japanese labor management was that they treated their employees like family members. Therefore, it is natural that fluctuations in output in Japan have had little impact on Japanese employment and consequently the unemployment rate. In the United States, however, there is a corporate culture in which firms can lay off workers at any time if the economy is sluggish. Two European countries (Germany and the United Kingdom) seem to be in between these two extreme labor-management practices. We see that their Okun's coefficients are also between the United States and Japan.

However, in the turbulent era of 1980s~1990s, the situation changed greatly. First of all, the value of the Blanchard coefficient showed an upward trend in all countries. This shows that the practice of laying off marginal workers at any time when the economy is not good became more prevalent in these countries. This management practice might be inevitable for business firms to survive in the environment of immense competition in the international marketplace after the oil crises of the 1970s. In particular, the rise in the value of the Blanchard coefficient in Japan in the 1980s demonstrates that the tradition of permanent employment in Japan, which had been the subject of interest in the United States and European countries has been gradually collapsing. Under the rapidly changing environment, layoffs in response to economic fluctuations have been more easily made.

Japan and other Asian countries including the Four Tigers have long been under the influence of the Confucian work ethos, which is in contrast with the Protestant work ethics that has dominated the United States and European countries. Confucius' morality has been recently challenged. It is no wonder that employment in Japan has now become sensitive to economic fluctuations, and the value of the Blanchard coefficient has also become larger.

The second link between unemployment and inflation is that as the gap between actual output and potential output (actual output − potential output) becomes larger, prices rise higher because the economy is overheated. Thus, an increase in actual output will accompany higher prices or an increase in inflation (positive correlation).

$$\text{Output} \uparrow \Longrightarrow \text{Unemployment} \downarrow \text{ (Okun's law)}$$

Or

$$\text{Output} \uparrow \Longrightarrow \text{Inflation} \uparrow \text{ (Price adjustment)}$$

By linking these two relations together, one can conclude that a decrease in unemployment leads to an increase in inflation, or an increase in unemployment leads to a decrease in inflation. The Phillips curve is an empirical representation of this relationship.

$$\text{Unemployment} \downarrow \Rightarrow \text{Inflation} \uparrow$$

Or

$$\text{Unemployment} \uparrow \Rightarrow \text{Inflation} \downarrow$$

In fact, until Philips discovered a tradeoff between unemployment and inflation, the Keynesian school was criticized for not having a proper theory of inflation. As discussed, the original Keynesian economics was mainly concerned with the unemployment issue. As Phillips discovered a stable, negative relation between inflation and unemployment, Keynesians were able to predict the inflation rate given the level of unemployment. The Phillips curve was a blessing that enabled Keynesians to find a missing link between output and unemployment.

2

THE PHILLIPS CURVE: TRADEOFF BETWEEN INFLATION AND UNEMPLOYMENT

In 1958, British economist A.W. Phillips conducted an empirical analysis of the relationship between the rate of change of nominal wages (sometimes called wage inflation) and the unemployment rate in the United Kingdom. Philips began to study how the unemployment rate as a measure of supply and demand conditions of the labor market is related to the nominal wages employers are willing to pay in the labor market. He analyzed long-term data spanning almost a century (1861 to 1957) and found that there was a stable, non-linear negative correlation or tradeoff between the rate of change of money wages and the unemployment rate.

<Figure 8.1> The Original Phillips Curve

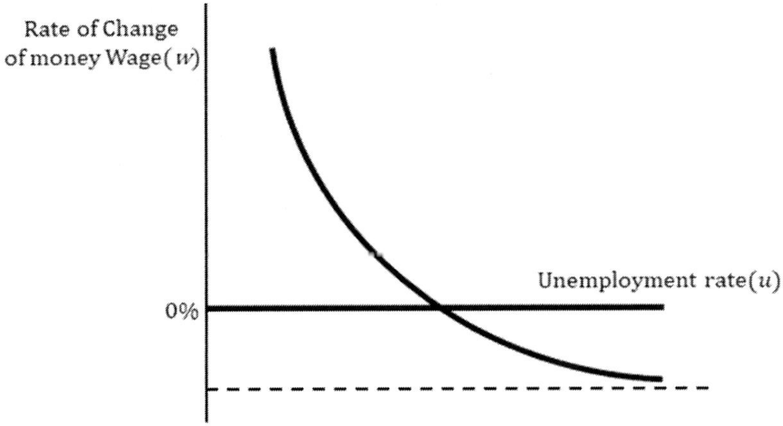

The Phillips curve was a significant development in that it proved empirically the theoretical tradeoff between inflation and unemployment we established earlier. In the original Phillips curve, the rate of change of money wages was specified as a nonlinear function of the deviation of the actual unemployment rate from the potential unemployment rate. In 1958, when Philips published his paper, it was a time before the advent of computers, and computer statistical programs capable of estimating nonlinear functional relationships were not even in the offing. Estimating a complicated nonlinear function with a simple calculator would have been a Herculean task. He was able to overcome these difficulties and to estimate the nonlinear Phillips curve equation. His academic background in engineering would have been of great help.

When Philips published his work, many economists (mainly Keynesians) welcomed his findings, expecting the Phillips curve to be the basis for macroeconomic theory of inflation. The Phillips curve related the unemployment rate, the key variable in Keynesian economics, to money wages. Keynesian economists thought the Phillips curve was consistent with the Keynesian rationale for the downward rigidity of money wages. British economist Lipsey immediately derived a linear equation as an approximation to the nonlinear Phillips curve and applied it to the British economy. He also confirmed that the Phillips curve explained the relationship between U.K. unemployment and inflation remarkably well.

In the United States, MIT economists, Paul Samuelson and Robert Solow, applied the Phillips curve to the U.S. economy to provide a rationale for anti-inflationary policy in the United States. Unlike the original Philips and Lipsey models, Samuelson and Solow used the inflation rate instead of the rate of change of nominal wages. When we talk about the Phillips curve today, it usually means the inverse relationship between the inflation rate and the unemployment rate. Thus, the Phillips curve now means that as inflation goes up, unemployment goes down, and vice versa. Samuelson and Solow confirmed that there was a stable negative correlation between the inflation rate and the unemployment rate in the U.S. economy.

As influential studies provided mounting evidence in support of the Phillips curve, the theoretical foundation of the Philips curve was strengthened, and the practical influence of the Phillips curve was further cemented. The Phillips curve has now become a powerful analytical tool that provides the 'menu of choices' to policymakers. If policymakers set low unemployment as a priority of economic policy, the Phillips curve suggests that they could achieve this goal by tolerating some degree of inflation. Conversely, if policy makers set low inflation as a policy goal, they could achieve this goal by allowing for a slightly higher unemployment rate.

The policy implications of the Phillips curve should be obvious. Policymakers could manage or fine-tune the economy by appropriately using aggregate demand policy such as fiscal policy or monetary policy. Thus, the Phillips curve clearly shows that policymakers could achieve one goal (say, low inflation) by sacrificing another goal (say, low unemployment). As an auxiliary proposition, the Phillips curve also implies that it is not possible for policymakers to achieve both goals, low inflation, and low unemployment. The simultaneous pursuit of low inflation and low unemployment is not on the policy menu of the Phillips curve. By the same logic, the choice of high unemployment and high inflation is also not on the menu of the Phillips curve. Of course, there will be no insane policymakers trying to pursue both high inflation and high unemployment.

Keynesian economists maintain that policymakers could choose any combination of unemployment and inflation on the Phillips curve. Liberal policymakers such as Democrats would like to choose lower unemployment combined with relatively high inflation. In contrast, conservative policymakers such as Republicans would like to choose lower inflation combined with relatively high unemployment. In fact, in the United States, the economic policy options implemented by the Kennedy-Johnson administration during the 1960s and the economic policy mixes pursued by the Obama administration and the Fed during the global economic crisis in 2008, can be viewed as laboratory tests for the Phillips curve.

3

STAGFLATION: THE DISAPPEARANCE OF THE PHILLIPS CURVE

The Phillips curve, which represents the quantitative tradeoff between unemployment and inflation, was relatively well consonant with the real economy until the early 1970s. In particular, the inverse correlation between unemployment and inflation was very impressively observed in the U.S. and U.K. economies. If we plot the inflation rate on the vertical axis and the unemployment rate on the horizontal axis over the 1948~1969 period, we obtain a downwardly sloped curve. This is manifest evidence that there was a stable trade-off between unemployment and inflation in the U.S. economy until 1970.

But if we plot the observations of inflation and unemployment from 1970 to 1994 on the same plane, the inverse relationship between inflation and unemployment is not found, and we obtain the scatters of the pairs of inflation and unemployment. The tradeoff between unemployment and inflation implied by the Phillips curve seems to have disappeared during this period. In almost all years during this period, the inflation rate was much higher than the inflation rate predicted by the Phillips curve. Thus, from the early 1970s throughout 1990s, the U.S. economy was characterized as the coexistence of high inflation and high unemployment. This is a new pattern that the U.S. economy has never experienced before.

The new phenomenon of the coexistence of unemployment and inflation was an anomaly that Keynesian economics cannot explain. This new development has come to be known as stagflation, which is the combination of *stag*nation (indicating unemployment) and in*flation*. Stagflation was a phenomenon that plagued almost all countries in the late 1970s and the early 1980s. No economy could escape from the fallout of stagflation, although its severity was different among countries. For example, stagflation was more severe in the United Kingdom than in the United States. Here is a comparison of stagflation between the United States and the United Kingdom.

<Figure 8.2> The U.S. Phillips Curve

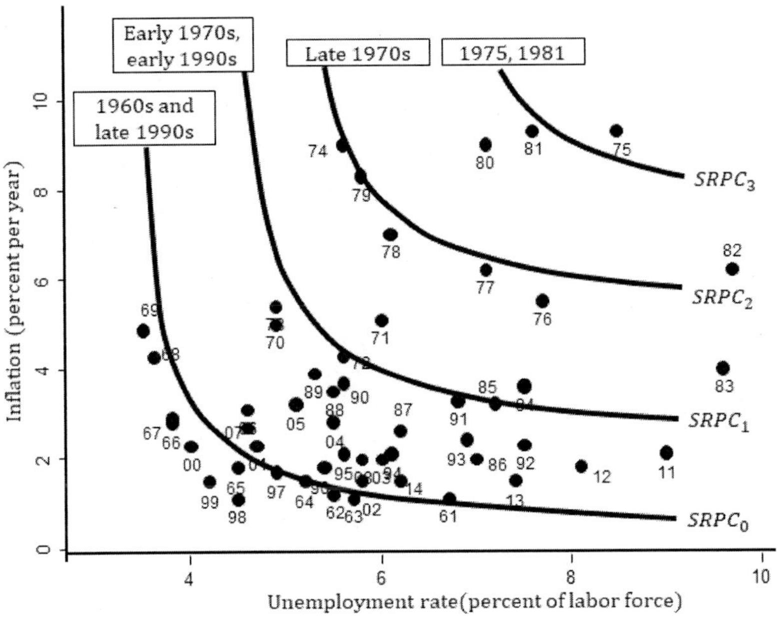

The main cause of stagflation was, of course, the two oil crises that hit the world economy in the 1970s. The first oil crisis in 1973 raised the world's crude oil prices more than four times, and the second oil crisis in 1978 further fueled the flames of inflation in most countries. Most importantly, due to the ripple effect of higher oil prices on all industries, the oil crises brought about supply-side inflation, which accompanied stagnation. One serious problem with stagflation is that traditional aggregate demand policy such as monetary or fiscal policy does not work well in dealing with it.

Stagflation was considered to be the 'public enemy number one'. Paul Volker, who served as the Chair of the Federal Reserve System from 1979 to 1987 was in the forefront of this war. Volker, who was preferably called the 'inflation czar', took drastic measures to fight against stagflation. Volker's Fed raised the federal funds rate to a peak of 20% in June 1981, the highest level in U.S. history. The federal funds rate had averaged 11.2% in 1979. Stagflation began to retreat as major central banks waged an all-out war against it. Stagflation was forgotten by people as a thing of the past until it revisited many countries during the COVID-19 pandemic in 2020.

The world economy has been on the alert again for combating stagflation for the first time in almost 40 years.

<Table 8.1> Comparison of Stagflation between the U.S. and the U.K.

	United States			United Kingdom		
Year	Inflation Rate (%)	Unemploy-ment Rate	Misery Index	Inflation Rate	Unemploy-ment Rate	Misery Inde
1973	6.2	4.9	11.1	9.2	3.7	12.9
1974	11.0	5.6	16.6	16.0	3.6	19.6
1975	9.2	8.5	17.7	24.2	4.4	28.6
1976	5.8	7.7	13.5	16.6	5.4	22.0
1977	6.5	7.1	13.6	15.8	5.6	21.4
1978	7.6	6.1	13.7	8.3	5.5	13.8
1979	11.2	5.8	17.0	13.4	5.4	18.8
1980	13.6	7.1	20.7	18.0	6.6	24.6
1981	10.4	7.6	18.0	11.9	9.5	21.4
1982	6.2	9.7	15.9	8.6	10.7	19.3

Source: U.S. data: *The Economic Report of the President*
U.K. data: Office for National Statistics

Just as the Great Depression in the 1930s devasted classical economics, stagflation in the 1970s ruined Keynesian economics and paved the way for the triumphant comeback of the classical doctrine in the names of monetarism and new classical economics.

4

FRIEDMAN'S 'MISPERCEPTION THEORY' AND THE NATURAL RAYE HYPOTHESIS (NRH)

Friedman attempted to reconstruct the collapsed edifice of the classical school almost single-handed in the 1960s when most mainstream economists joined the Keynesian camp. He devoted himself to demonstrating the validity of classical theory using more sophisticated econometric techniques and the vast set of data. His new theory is called monetarism.

First, he raised the banner of the counter-Keynesian revolution by attacking the Phillips curve, which was welcomed by Keynesian economists as a blessing for Keynesian economics. Friedman argued that the Phillips curve, which represents a trade-off between unemployment and inflation, exists only during which the economic agent makes an error in predicting the expected inflation. He further argues that this perception error occurs only in the short run. With the passage of time, the economic agent will gradually gather information about the inflation and have the correct perception of the expected inflation. When the economic agent readjusts his behavior according to the correctly perceived expected inflation, then there is no disparity between actual inflation and expected inflation. Therefore, the downward-sloping Phillips curve also ceases to exist and disappears. When this situation happens, Keynesian aggregate demand management policy to lower unemployment in exchange for inflation is not successful and promotes only inflation in the long run. This proposition is the contrary of the conclusion of Keynesian theory.

The gist of Friedman's 'misperception theory' is that when the economic agent correctly perceives the expected inflation and makes economic decisions according to the correctly perceived information, he will not make any errors. When this situation happens, the unemployment rate tends to gravitate toward a long-term equilibrium level, which is known as the natural unemployment rate. This proposition is called the natural rate hypothesis (NRH). Friedman's theory is sometimes referred to as the misperception theory because the downward-sloping Phillips curve exists only while there is a discrepancy between the actual inflation rate and the expected inflation rate.

Friedman's misperception theory has important policy implications. When economic agents have correct information on the future expected inflation, the unemployment rate remains at the natural unemployment rate. Thus, if policymakers want to lower the unemployment rate further, they must fool economic agents, so that they will not correctly perceive the future expected inflation. This unconventional, but pathbreaking policy proposal is more exquisitely developed by Lucas' rational expectations hypothesis later.

In order to understand Friedman's natural rate hypothesis, we assume that the economy initially operates at a high unemployment rate (5%) and a relatively low inflation rate (3%). In such a situation, the priority of economic policy faced by policymakers is to lower the unemployment rate. Policymakers (the government or the central bank) will pursue an expansionary policy to increase aggregate demand and to lower the unemployment rate below 5%. As we have seen earlier, the expansion of aggregate demand exerts an upward pressure on inflation. Now we assume that the inflation rate has risen from 3% to 6% as the result of the expansionary aggregate demand policy. When the inflation rate rises, the real wage (nominal wage/inflation rate) will fall. This follows from the presumption that nominal wages do not change in the short term.

At this point, producers will immediately recognize that inflation has risen to 6% because the prices of their products have risen. Thus, they will soon realize that real wages have also fallen. Since the real wages that firms pay fall, and the prices of the products they sell rise, firms' profits will increase. Thus, firms will increase production and hire more workers. Consequently, unemployment will fall as firms employ more workers. Now let's say that the unemployment rate has fallen from 5% to 4% thanks to the expansionary aggregate demand policy. We arrive at the traditional Philips curve conclusion that low unemployment comes at the expense of high inflation.

Monetarists, however, argue that this decline in unemployment is only a short-term phenomenon. In the short run, workers are unaware that inflation rose from 3% to 6%. In other words, they expect the current inflation rate to still remain at 3%. Thus, they make an error in forming the expectation of the inflation rate.

$$\text{Actual inflation rate (6\%)} \neq \text{Expected inflation rate (3\%)}$$

There can be many reasons why economic agents make this kind of error. First, in order to publish the CPI (consumer price index), the Bureau of Labor Statistics (BLS) surveys the prices of individual products sold in retail stores. Then, based on these surveyed prices, the BLS computes the general price level and publishes the CPI. It takes a while for the BLS to survey and process individual product prices and publish the CPI. It also takes some time for consumers and workers to obtain the CPI statistics. Until they obtain the complete set of data on the CPI, it is common for economic agents to make mistakes about expected inflation, and there is a discrepancy between actual and expected inflation in the short run.

However, over time, economic agents will collect and analyze information on the movements in the general price level. Initially, economic agents will not get complete information about the general price level. They will gather only a fraction of it and revise their expected inflation based on the piece of new information. For example, based on the initial information, they may recognize that the inflation rate rose from 3% to 4%. In other words, they realize that there was an error in their initial perception of inflation and revise their expected inflation from 3% to 4%.

$$\text{Actual inflation rate (6\%)} \neq \text{Expected inflation rate (4\%)}$$

However, as more information arrives, they are aware that their expected inflation rate of 4% is wrong, and they will revise their expected inflation rate again from 4% to, say, 5%.

$$\text{Actual inflation rate (6\%)} \neq \text{Expected inflation rate (5\%)}$$

This revision of expected inflation will continue as more information arrives on the market. Finally, when they get the full information on the price movements, they finally realize that the inflation rate has risen to 6%, and they will revise their expected inflation to 6%. At this stage, their adjustment of expectations will be completed. Thus, in the long run, the discrepancy between the actual inflation rate and the expected inflation rate disappears, and economic agents no longer make systematic errors in predicting the inflation rate.

$$\text{Actual inflation rate (6\%)} = \text{Expected inflation rate (6\%)}$$

When the inflation rate is completely and correctly anticipated, workers will realize that their real wages have been eroded by higher inflation, and they will demand higher nominal wages to compensate for the drop in real wages. If the employer raises the nominal wage by 6% in response to a 6% increase in the price level, the real wage, which has fallen as the result of the higher inflation, will start rising again. The nominal wage will continue to increase until the real wage reaches the initial real wage level. In this way, the adjustment of the economic agent in response to changes in the price level is completed in the long term.

Now that real wages have risen again, firms will begin to lay off less productive workers, and consequently, the unemployment rate which has been lowered to 3% (from 5%) will begin to rise again. There will be a gradual rise in unemployment from 3% to 4% and finally to 5%. As such, the net effect of the expansion of aggregate demand in the long run is a high inflation rate (6%) with no real effect on unemployment (5%). There is a temporary decrease in the unemployment rate in the short run when economic agents make an error in predicting expected inflation, but the unemployment rate goes back to the original level. There is no permanent decrease in the unemployment rate as suggested by the Phillips curve.

As the unemployment rate has returned to its original level (5%), policymakers discover that the unemployment problem remains unresolved, and may be tempted again to lower the unemployment rate by using expansionary aggregate demand policy. However, another increase in aggregate demand reduces the unemployment rate only temporarily while economic agents make errors in predicting expected inflation. The unemployment rate again returns to its initial level as they revise their expected inflation rate in accordance with the arrival of more information on the price level and demand an increase in nominal wages.

Thus, when the discrepancy between the expected inflation rate and the actual inflation rate disappears, the tradeoff between unemployment and inflation disappears, and the unemployment rate returns to the long-term equilibrium level that monetarists call the natural rate of unemployment. Based on the natural unemployment rate hypothesis, monetarists argue that the Phillips curve tends to slope downward in the short run, but in the long run it becomes a vertical line at the level of the natural unemployment rate. The fact that the Philips curve is vertical is equivalent to denying the existence of the Philips curve itself. The vertical long-term Phillips curve is closely related to the neutrality of money we discussed earlier. Classical economists argue that increases in the money supply have no effect on real variables including unemployment in the long run. The natural rate hypothesis and the neutrality of money are fundamental elements of monetarism.

The implication of the natural rate hypothesis is that once the economy reaches the natural unemployment rate, monetary or fiscal policy has no role in changing the natural unemployment rate. Any attempt to lower the unemployment rate below the natural unemployment rate will not succeed because the unemployment rate will return to the natural unemployment rate in the long run. Lowering the unemployment rate below the natural unemployment rate does not belong to the territory of monetary or fiscal policy. Policymakers should look at the structure of the labor market and technological breakthroughs. For example, we can think of reforms such as improving the level of education and strengthening job training programs to increase labor productivity, or to abolish or alleviate regulations detrimental to technological progress to lower the natural rate of unemployment.

<Figure 8.3> The Monetarist Phillips Curve

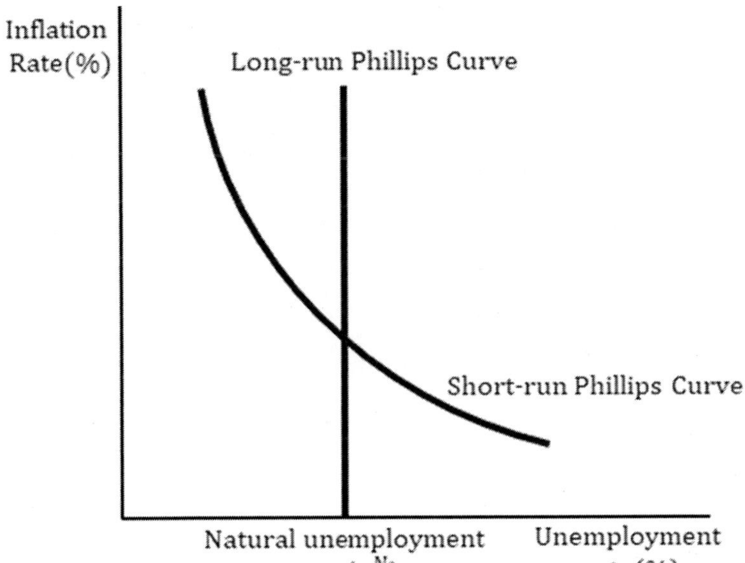

The essence of Friedman's misperception theory is that any attempts to lower the unemployment rate below the natural rate of unemployment will not succeed. Policymakers could lower the unemployment rate by fooling economic agents, but the unemployment rate would return to the natural unemployment rate once economic agents get disillusioned from the misperception. Thus, any attempt to lower the unemployment rate below the natural unemployment rate is like reinventing the wheel. In this respect, Friedman's misperception theory reminds us of the story of Sisyphus. In

Greek mythology, Sisyphus did a lot of bad things during his reign. After he died, he was punished with the task of rolling a large rock to the top of a mountain. When he lifted the stone to the top of the mountain, the stone rolled back down into the ground. Such a task was forever recurring.

<Figure 8.4> Sisyphus (Tiziano Vecelli)

Sisyphus was also a king who had the ability to skillfully cheat people. Even Autolycus, who learned the skill of stealing from his father, Hermes, without being detected, could not cheat Sisyphus. Autolycus stole Sisyphus' cow and changed the color and shape of the cow, so that the cow could not be detected. However, Sisyphus was able to find the stolen cow because he had marked on the hoof of the cow in advance.

The Sisyphus mythology is often cited as a metaphor for a futile effort and an endless frustration. The monetarist characterizes Keynesian aggregate demand management policy as a futile effort and an unsuccessful frustration. Friedman's misperception theory and Lucas fooling theory suggest that economic policy becomes more effective and powerful if policymakers fool economic agents more cleverly.

5

NAIRU

What are the practical merits of discussing the natural rate of unemployment? When the actual unemployment rate reaches the natural unemployment rate or the full employment rate of unemployment, cyclical unemployment approaches zero. The natural unemployment rate is the level of unemployment at which everyone who wants to work can find jobs, except those who are currently frictionally, structurally, and seasonally unemployed.

First, when a country's unemployment rate equals its natural rate of unemployment, the amount of goods and services that it produces equals its potential output (or potential GDP). Potential output is the maximum amount of goods and services that a country can produce without promoting inflation. Another implication of the natural unemployment rate is that when the actual unemployment rate equals the natural unemployment rate, inflation does not accelerate or decelerate but tends to stay stable. If inflation remains constant or at least stable, people expect tomorrow's inflation rate (= expected inflation rate) to be equal to today's inflation rate. Thus, we have the following relationship.

Expected inflation rate = Today's (or actual) inflation rate

If inflation does not rise and remains constant, economic agents make decisions, expecting future inflation to be the same as current inflation, which has a major impact on economic agents' behavior. If the inflation rate in the future is expected to be the same as the current inflation rate, economic agents no longer take expected inflation into their decision making. In other words, workers will not demand higher nominal wages, and therefore, wage increases can be stable and predictable.

In this regard, George Akerlof, William Dickens, and George Perry (2000) have found that economic agents have a tendency to ignore past inflation when the annual inflation rate stays between 0% and 4%, and they do not incorporate expected inflation into their wage negotiations. This study shows that the inflation rate as low as two to three percent per year is not a hurdle to the operation of the economy.

The unemployment rate that does not accelerate inflation is sometimes called the non-accelerating inflation rate of unemployment, or shortly, NAIRU. Thus, NAIRU is a synonym for the natural unemployment rate. One important lesson we learn from the natural rate hypothesis is that inflation accelerates when policymakers try to lower the unemployment rate below the natural unemployment rate, but if policymakers maintain the unemployment rate at the natural unemployment rate, they could prevent the inflation rate from accelerating. As a corollary, the natural rate hypothesis has an implication that if the unemployment rate is higher than the natural unemployment rate, policy makers could lower the unemployment rate to the level of the natural unemployment rate by the use of aggregate demand policy. Thus, the natural unemployment rate is a reference point for monetary policy.

Our discussion suggests that the gap between the actual unemployment rate and the natural unemployment rate can be used as a predictor of future inflation. If the actual unemployment rate falls below the natural rate of unemployment, this can be viewed as a sign of future inflation. As a matter of fact, in the U.S. economy, the predictability of inflation based on the gap holds almost exactly true. The U.S. economy experienced four serious inflation periods from 1959 to 1995. In all of these cases, the rise in inflation occurred when the actual unemployment rate fell below the natural rate of unemployment. The prediction of inflation based on the gap between the actual unemployment rate and the natural unemployment rate has never missed the mark. Three inflation cases out of the four inflation episodes showed up shortly after the actual unemployment rate fell below the natural unemployment rate, and inflation from 1987 to 1991 appeared almost simultaneously when the actual unemployment rate fell below the natural unemployment rate.

Finally, the natural rate of unemployment is more than a theoretical argument. It serves as a practical guideline for the implementation of monetary or fiscal policy. On October 31, 2014, the United States ended quantitative easing policy taken during the global economic crisis in 2008. The Fed made it clear that it would maintain the quantitative easing policy until the U.S. unemployment rate falls to the level of the natural unemployment rate. The U.S. unemployment rate fell to 5.7% in October 2014, which was close to the U.S. natural unemployment rate. The U.S. natural unemployment rate is estimated to be around 5.5%. (The Fed's estimate of the U.S. natural unemployment rate is 5.2% to 5.9%.) The Fed's decision to end quantitative easing was made because the U.S. unemployment rate almost reached its natural unemployment level.

6

THE BIRTH OF MONETARISM

Monetarism is a revival of classical economics rebuilt by Milton Friedman of the University of Chicago in the 1950s and 1960s when Keynesian economics swept the economics profession. Almost all economists at that time were under the influence of Keynesian economics that favored the government's active role in the economy. Keynesians had a belief that the government could fine-tune the economy through aggregate demand management policy, especially fiscal policy. Because monetarism was incubated at the University of Chicago, monetarism is often identified as a synonym for the Chicago school. The economic philosophy and policy pursued by Prime Minister Thatcher of the United Kingdom and President Reagan of the United States was rooted in monetarism.

Monetarism can be viewed as the modern-day version of classical economics. This is because the foundations of monetarism are based on classical doctrine. This does not, however, mean that monetarists follow all the assumptions of the classical school. Monetarism is a new evolution of classical theory equipped with empirical analysis and ample data. Let's look at some of the characteristics of monetarism that differ from the original classical school. First, monetarists maintain the position that fluctuations in the supply of money affect not only prices, but also gross output and employment in the short run. However, in the long run, the increase in the quantity of money only leads to higher prices with no real effect on output and employment, which is the same as the conclusion of classical theory. Second, the income velocity of money is not considered to be fixed as classical economists presumed, but it is very stable and therefore predictable.

The period from World War II to the end of the 1960s was the heyday for Keynesian economics. At that time, some sentiment prevailed among economists that monetary policy was not important in managing aggregate demand. Many economists were very skeptical of the notion that policymakers could affect the economy using monetary policy given the fact that there are many financial assets that can be substitutes for money. The statement that "Controlling inflation by limiting the supply of money is like controlling drinking by limiting the supply of whiskey" represents Keynesians' skepticism about the effectiveness of monetary policy. Limiting the supply of whiskey would not be able to keep people from getting drunk, because people would easily switch to gin or vodka.

As we have seen before, stagflation which ravaged the world economy in the 1970s was an epochal event that changed the pendulum of the thoughts of economics. The coexistence of unemployment and inflation was at odds with Keynesian theory. Keynesian economics was neither able to explain stagflation nor to offer any solutions to the malaise. On the other hand, monetarists successfully explained the coexistence of unemployment and inflation with the aid of misperception theory. Thus, the development of stagflation strengthened the influence of monetarism and stepped up the decline of the Keynesian school. Monetarists emphasize the importance of money in the stabilization of the economy from a different perspective: Money can be a holy grail in the management of the economy, but it could be a poisonous grail if it is mismanaged.

Although there are many different layers in monetarism, their views are largely in line with the proposition that "money is the most important influence on economic activity". Keynesian economists argue that it is ineffective to regulate money because there are many substitute assets for money, but monetarists disagree to the view that money is not important. According to the monetarist, money is still important because the substitutability between money and other financial assets is not as high as that of commodities.

Monetarists' emphasis on the importance of money can be analyzed from the perspective of both money demand and money supply. First, the monetarist theory of money demand focuses on reaffirming the stability of the money demand function denied by Keynesians. Monetarists, particularly Friedman, aimed at rebuilding the classical quantity theory of money to counter the Keynesian view that "money is not important". Friedman's quantity theory of money was reborn as a more sophisticated version of the classical quantity theory of money. The monetarist's quantity theory of money stresses that the income velocity of money is highly stable and therefore predictable and uses sophisticated statistical methods and vast data to prove the stability of the income velocity of money. The stability of the income velocity of money means that there is a clear and predictable relationship between the quantity of money and nominal GDP.

Second, the monetarist theory of money supply can be summarized by the argument that "money is important, and therefore monetary policy should not be used recklessly". This position of the monetarist is also reflected in the natural rate hypothesis we have discussed. It is the monetarist conclusion that a discretionary increase in the amount of money does more harm than it does good to the economy. The natural rate hypothesis clearly demonstrates that such an increase in the money supply only leads to inflation in the long run.

From the equation of exchange (MV = PY), we can obtain the following money growth equation under the premise that the income velocity of money (V) is stable:

Money growth rate = Inflation rate + Potential economic growth rate

We can derive several important implications of monetarism from the money growth equation:

- The money growth equation shows that the effect of an increase in the supply of money on economic activity is divided between inflation and economic growth in the short run. This division of the effect of monetary policy is merely another expression of the natural rate hypothesis. In the short run, if the economic agent makes a mistake in predicting inflation, an increase in the money supply temporarily results in an increase in inflation and a decrease in the unemployment rate. The money growth equation is simply a re-statement of the short-term Phillips curve from the monetarist point of view.
- There is a considerable amount of controversy as to whether an increase in the amount of money affects inflation first or output first, and how the effect is divided between the two variables. Although the answer to these questions should be obtained from the results of empirical analysis, Friedman's natural rate hypothesis shows that the increase in the supply of money affects inflation first, and then output.
- However, with the passage of time, the effect of an increase in money on real output tapers off, and the effect on inflation gathers strength gradually. Thus, the net effect of an increase in the money supply is only higher inflation in the long run.
- The direction of causality between money and inflation is that a change in money causes a change in inflation, that is, the causality runs from the money supply to inflation and does not run from inflation to the money supply.
- Finally Friedman proposes increasing the money supply at a constant rate that is consistent with the growth rate of potential output. This proposition is known as the constant growth rate rule (CGRR).

In sum, monetarists maintain that policymakers should be cautious about using monetary policy, because any discretionary use of monetary policy is more likely to destabilize the economy. Monetarists conclude that even if the economy runs into a temporary disequilibrium state, it will return to equilibrium in the long run, because the economy has the forces to fix problems for itself through the price mechanism. Therefore, the best monetary policy is to increase the money supply in a stable and predictable way.

Then, what is the optimal rate of money growth? Monetarists insist that the rate of money growth should be roughly equal to the growth rate of potential output in order to prevent inflation from accelerating. This conclusion is derived from the money growth equation. When inflation is zero, the money growth equation becomes:

$$\text{Money growth rate} = \text{Potential economic growth rate}$$

In the United States, the potential GDP growth rate has remained around 3.5% until the COVID-19 pandemic. Monetarists would argue that in order for the U.S. economy to operate stably, the supply of money should increase at the rate of about 3 to 5% per year. Let's take Friedman's word:

> "I myself have largely supported the rate of increase in the money supply that would help stabilize the price level of final goods and services. I have estimated such a rate to be on average 3% to 5% per year in the case of M2 (= currency + all bank deposits) and to be slightly lower than that in the case of M1 (currency + bank demand deposits" (Friedman, 1968a)

But will inflation go away in our economy if the growth rate of money equals the growth rate of potential GDP? The money growth formula is based on the simple equation of exchange that ignores the supply side of the economy. Thus, monetarists' money growth rate rule does not necessarily hold true. In other words, inflation can occur at any time in the event of a supply shock, even if the growth rate of the money supply remains fixed around 3% to 5%, which is roughly the same as the potential growth rate.

Furthermore, many economists accept the view that some inflation is necessary for the economy to roll along. In particular, 'limited inflationists' are sympathetic to the argument that some inflation is vital to the economy. Currently, the annual inflation rate that limited inflationists generally accept is around 2% to 2.5%. If we consider the positions of monetarists and limited inflationists, the desirable money growth rate would be around the potential growth rate plus the inflation rate of 2% to 2.5%.

7

THE RATIONAL EXPECTATIONS REVOLUTION AND NEW CLASSICAL ECONOMICS

In the 1970s, the world economy went through a major transition. The oil war initiated by OPEC in 1973 was powerful enough to fundamentally shake up the landscape of the world economy. The economy of each nation was like a candle in the wind in front of tumultuous inflation. To make matters worse, the shades of stagnation overlaid the flame of inflation. It became increasingly difficult to continue sailing through the rough waves with the conventional navigation, i.e., Keynesian prescriptions.

Many countries pursued a tightening aggregate demand policy to curb ferocious inflation in accordance with the Keynesian recipes, but the contractionary aggregate demand policy led to the exacerbation of chronic unemployment. In many countries including the United States and European countries, income policy was implemented that aimed at controlling prices and wages directly, but it did not work well. In many European countries, a phenomenon of persistent, high unemployment known as Euro-sclerosis appeared.

Against the backdrop of the dark clouds of stagflation, new economic thought rooted in the principles of classical economics emerged in the early 1970s. This new paradigm of economics led by Robert Lucas at the University of Chicago, often called the rational expectations theory, spearheaded the attack against Keynesian economics. By claiming that the Keynesian aggregate demand policy had no effect on output and employment if economic agents form their expectations rationally, Lucas was in the forefront of counter-revolution against the Keynesian revolution that overthrew the classical system in the 1930s.

In fact, since the influence of rational expectations theory on economic thought could be compared to that of Keynesian economics, this new theory is sometimes called the rational expectations revolution or Lucas revolution. The rational expectations school was led by a group of young economists, especially Robert Lucas, Thomas Sargent, Robert Barro, Edward Prescott, and Finn Kydland, among others. All but Barro won the Nobel prizes in economics.

The theory of rational expectations has something in common with monetarism in many areas such as the natural rate of unemployment, but it is more skeptical than monetarism about the effectiveness of active economic stabilization policy through aggregate demand management. Both monetarism and rational expectations theory have their roots in classical economics, but rational expectations theory is closer to the ideology of the classical doctrine. That's why rational expectations theory is sometimes called new classical economics. The debate that developed between Keynesian economists and monetarists until the mid-1970s tended to be merged into the debate between new Keynesian economists and new classical economists after the emergence of the rational expectations school. The essence of rational expectations theory can be summarized as follows:

- ◈ Full information: People use all the information available to them when they form expectations for economic variables.
- ◈ Flexible prices: Prices, wages, and interest rates move instantaneously in response to changes in economic conditions.
- ◈ Market clearing: The market always clears. In other words, if there is any excess demand or excess supply in the market, this disequilibrium is immediately eliminated. At the equilibrium point, there is no unemployment (excess supply of labor) or the shortage of labor (excess demand for labor) because demand and supply are always equalized.

In order to understand Lucas' theory, it is important to first distinguish between a change in relative prices and a change in the general price level, which can be viewed as the inflation rate. For the purpose of illustrating the difference between a change in relative prices and a change in the general price level, let's assume that the economy produces only three goods: hamburgers, pizzas, and beefsteaks and that a hamburger sells for $5, a pan pizza for $10, and a beefsteak for $20. If the hamburger price rose to $10, the pizza price rose to $20, and the beefsteak price rose to $40 in the market, all prices are doubled, and relative prices remain the same, but there is a change in the general price level caused by inflation. However, in the market, if the price of the hamburger rose from $5 to $10 while the prices of the pizza and beefsteak remain unchanged, this change means that the price of the hamburger is now relatively high compared with the prices of the pizza and the beefsteak. In other words, relative prices have changed.

Lucas' theory is constructed based on the difference between a change in relative prices and a change in the general price level:

- ◈ Economic agents (consumers, workers, firms, etc.) respond to a change in relative prices, and do not respond to a change in the general price level, that is, inflation.
- ◈ If economic agents perceive mistakenly a change in the general price level as a change in relative prices, they react to such a change in the general price level.
- ◈ Changes in real variables such as real GDP and employment depend on the extent to which the economic agent misperceives a change in the general price level as a change in relative prices.

Now suppose that individual economic agents form expectations about the general price level (CPI) and the prices of the products they produce (relative prices). Economic agents can directly observe the prices of the goods they produce, but the general price level can only be observed after some time. This is because the general price level is not known to the public until the government agencies first survey the prices of individual goods and services included in the market basket, process the raw data, and computes the weighted average of the individual prices. When the government publishes the weighted average of prices, the general price level is finally available to the public. Thus, when the producer of a certain product such as hamburgers observes a change in the price of the product in the market, he must determine whether such a change in the price of his product reflects a change in the relative price, or a change in the general price level.

If the relative price of the hamburger rises, it means that the hamburger is sold at a higher price relative to the pizza and the beefsteak. Therefore, producers who produce hamburgers will increase the production of hamburgers and hire more workers. However, if the rise in the price of the hamburger the producer observes is only a result of an increase in the general price level (i.e., inflation), the producer has no incentive to increase the production of hamburgers. This is because the prices of other products will also rise by the same proportion, and production costs will rise accordingly. In this case, the increase in the hamburger price does not benefit only the hamburger producer in his favor. Thus, there is no incentive for the producers of hamburgers to increase the production of hamburgers and to hire more workers. However, if economic agents mistakenly perceive a change in the general price level as a change in relative prices, we have a different story.

If economic agents form their expectations of inflation rationally, they are very unlikely to confuse a change in the general price level with a change in relative prices because they use all the available information. That is, the possibility that the economic agent makes a systematic error in predicting the general price level is very small even in the short run. Thus, as long as rational expectations prevail, producers will not respond to any change in the general price level, that is, inflation. This indicates that a higher inflation rate does not lead to an increase in output and a fall in unemployment, which means that there is no tradeoff between inflation and unemployment. Thus, there is no downward-sloping Philips curve even in the short run.

There is an exceptional case in which economic agents make an error in predicting the inflation rate even if they use all available information. If there is an unexpected increase in the general price level, the producer is likely to confuse the increase in the general price level with an increase in relative prices in his favor and to respond by increasing the production of products (say, hamburgers) and hiring more workers. Simply speaking, he is fooled into thinking that the observed increase in the hamburger price is due to a rise in relative prices although the increase in the hamburger price is due to an increase in inflation. Especially, this kind of error can occur more frequently in countries where prices are stable. In a stable-price country like the United States, people have been long accustomed to low and stable inflation. Thus, when they observe a rise in the price of products, they normally perceive this price increase as a rise in relative prices. In other words, they would not consider the price increase as the result of an increase in the general price level, and they respond to such an unexpected change in the general price level. Here we have the following propositions:

Proposition 1: Economic agents (consumers, producers, and workers) respond to only a change in relative prices.

Proposition 2: Economic agents sometimes respond to a change in the general price level when they wrongly perceive the change in the general price level as a change in relative prices.

These propositions are the core of the new classical model of Lucas. Suppose that the CPI inflation rate has remained at the average rate of 3% per year for a long period. Then the inflation rate, which is significantly lower or higher than 3%, could be perceived as an unexpected inflation rate. Thus, if the inflation rate suddenly rises unexpectedly to a level above 3% (say, 6%), the producer will be fooled into thinking that this rise is a rise in relative prices in his favor and accordingly increase production and employment, which leads to lower unemployment. Conversely, if the inflation rate suddenly falls to a much lower level than 3%, the producer will perceive it as a drop in the relative price to the disadvantage of him. The producer will reduce production and employment, which leads to higher unemployment. If we show this relationship on a graph with the inflation rate on the vertical axis and the unemployment rate on the horizontal axis, we have a downward-sloping curve. This is the traditional Philips curve. We have the traditional Phillips curve under a circumstance in which economic agents are fooled.

Thus, the economic agent sometimes makes an error which is beyond his control. No matter how rational the economic agent is, he can sometimes make a mistake which is due to factors that cannot be attributed to his error. For example, even if all available information is used, the economic agent is not able to recognize the shocks or events that are outside his information set. Thus, if policymakers subtly or intentionally hide or mislead the contents of their policy or the timing of enforcement, even rational people are not able to realize the effects of such policy in advance and may make errors in predicting future inflation. This happens even if they act according to rational expectations. This kind of error is called a random or stochastic error. Only when economic agents make random errors do we have a traditional Philips curve. In other words, there is an inverse relationship between unemployment and inflation.

In this context, Lucas' rational expectations hypothesis is more skeptical than Friedman's natural rate hypothesis as to the effectiveness of aggregate demand policy. In Friedman's natural rate hypothesis, there is a trade-off between inflation and unemployment in the short run because people don't have enough information in the short run, so that they are confused between a change in the general price level and a change in relative prices. This is a systematic error, not a random error. As long as they make a systematic error, there is a trade-off between inflation and unemployment. To sum up, in Friedman's model, the economic agent commits a systematic error in predicting the general price level in the short run, but in the Lucas model, the economic agent does not commit such a systematic error even in the short term. Thus, in the Friedman model, there is a downward-sloping Phillips curve in the short run, but in the Lucas model, there is no downward-sloping Phillips curve even in the short run.

8

THE POLICY INEFFECTIVENESS THEOREM AND 'FOOLING THEORY'

We can summarize the policy implications of the rational expectations hypothesis as follows. First, the anticipated aggregate demand policy (monetary and fiscal policy) has no effect on real variables such as output (GDP) and employment. Because economic agents do not make systematic errors in forming expectations for future inflation, they understand the content and implication of any anticipated aggregate demand policy and correctly predict its effects on prices and output. Therefore, they respond immediately to the anticipated policy and can nullify the effects of such policy.

For example, if expansionary monetary policy is implemented and anticipated, people predict accurately how much the general price level will rise and realize that their real wages will be eroded accordingly. They demand an increase in nominal wages, at least as much as inflation, to cover the decrease in real wages. Thus, the real wage, which has been temporarily reduced due to the rise in the price level, will immediately return to the original level, and therefore firms have no incentive to increase employment and production. The expected aggregate demand policy has no effect on aggregate output. This is because economic agents are fully equipped with information that can neutralize the effects of anticipated policy if they form their expectations rationally. This proposal is called policy ineffectiveness theorem.

The conclusion of the rational expectation hypothesis contrasts with that of the monetarist natural rate hypothesis. According to the natural rate hypothesis, economic agents temporarily (or in the short term) make mistakes in predicting the price level. In other words, they can't correctly predict a rise in inflation in the short run because they gradually adapt their expectations to changes in inflation and in the process of these adjustments, they make systematic errors. This misperception of economic agents about expected inflation leads to a drop in real wages, which in turn leads to increased employment and output. Therefore, in the short run, there is a trade-off between unemployment and inflation.

However, according to the rational expectation hypothesis, economic agents do not make such an error even in the short term because they use all the information available to them. Thus, they seek appropriate and prompt countermeasures against the anticipated policy to protect their best interest. The rational expectations hypothesis has revolutionary implications in relation to macroeconomic policy. Any anticipated aggregate demand policy aimed to stimulate or fine-tune the economy will not succeed.

Second, as an auxiliary theorem to the policy ineffectiveness theorem, rational expectations theorists argue that only unanticipated aggregate demand policy affects output and employment. An example of an unanticipated aggregate demand policy is a policy shock. The proponents of the rational expectations hypothesis do not argue that economic agents accurately predict a change in the general price level caused by unanticipated policy shocks. In this case, economic agents do not predict such an unexpected rise in the price level and will not demand an increase in nominal wages. Thus, they do not respond immediately and appropriately to government policy actions. As real wages fall due to higher inflation, firms increase employment and expand production. Thus, the advocates of the rational expectations hypothesis maintain that only unanticipated aggregate demand policy has an impact on output and employment.

If we put the rational expectations theory in the extreme, we'll come to a conclusion that the government can affect employment and output only by fooling economic agents, because any anticipated policy cannot increase output and reduce unemployment. For this reason, the rational expectations hypothesis is sometimes called fooling theory. However, cheating policy is not always tenable. As Abraham Lincoln, the 16th President of the United States said, the government can fool all the people some of the time, and some of the people all the time, but the government can't fool all the people all the time (Shapiro, 2006). Even if Lucas' theory of rational expectations is theoretically elegant, there is a limit to its practical applications.

9

THE KEYNESIAN ATTACK ON THE POLICY INEFFECTIVENESS THEOREM: NEW KEYNESIAN ECONOMICS

Keynesian economics was born during the Great Depression in the 1930s. Keynes published his book titled *The General Theory* in 1936, which heralded the birth of a new economic paradigm known as Keynesian economics. Keynesian economics dominated Western economic thought until the late 1960s. Then the oil crises in the 1970s hit the world economy and brought a new phenomenon known as stagflation to the world economy.

We have seen that stagflation in the 1970s and early 1980s was a catastrophe for Keynesian economics and at the same time was a catalyst for reviving the classical doctrine in the form of monetarism and rational expectations theory. Keynes emphasized in *The General Theory* that unemployment was not a temporary phenomenon, but rather a general phenomenon of the economy. He further argued that unemployment could last for a long time due to the rigidity of nominal wages. Here is the point of division between the classical and Keynesian schools. In such a situation, classical economists believe that market (nominal) wages fall quickly, thus lowering real wages. Again, firms will increase production and employment, and eventually full employment will be achieved. On the other hand, Keynesian economists maintain that due to the rigidity of nominal wages, nominal wages do not fall as quickly as classical economists thought. The inflexibility of nominal wages is attributed to the influence of labor unions and some institutional factors such as minimum wage laws.

In the 1980s, as the influence of monetarism and neoclassical economics increased, and the wave of neo-liberalism in the political arena began to rise, the influence of Keynesian economics was significantly shrunk. New classical economics was in the forefront of criticizing Keynesian economics for the lack of microeconomic foundations. In fact, macroeconomic relations are a result of the aggregation of the decisions of individual economic agents, but Keynesian economics has been criticized for not paying much attention to the behavior of individual economic agents. In addition, there is some criticism that Keynesian economics does not pay much attention to the process of how economic agents form their expectations for inflation.

In response to such criticism of Keynesian economics by new classical economists, new Keynesian economics emerged. New Keynesian economics, of course, has distinct features from neo-Keynesian economics that emphasizes the importance of money, and, on the other hand, post-Keynesian economics that is more Keynesian than Keynes. Although new Keynesian economics shows diversity in the contents and colors of its positions, new Keynesian economists accept the critiques of new classical economics and incorporate the notion of rational expectations into their theoretical framework. One thing in common among the diverse spectrums of new Keynesian economics is that they still maintain the Keynesian premise that wages and prices are inflexible. The goal of new Keynesian economics is to show that even if individual economic agents form their expectations rationally, aggregate demand management policy can still be a useful tool for stimulating the economy and promoting price stability.

The underpinning of new classical theory is that all markets function like an auction market. In the auction market, the market is immediately cleared by demand and supply forces in the market, and the equilibrium price determined in the market provides market participants with information for the maximization of their best interest. In the auction market, institutional arrangements do not help improve the results obtained from the information produced in the market. Let's consider a house that is put up at auction. The successful bid price is the equilibrium price at which the supply and demand for the house are equal. Other institutional arrangements such as wage contracts or labor unions are not a constraint on reaching the equilibrium price.

However, an economic system such as an auction market is far from being a reality, and a real economy does not operate like an auction market. In the labor market, for instance, market rigidity by contracts dominates, and market clearance by auction does not occur. In the auction market, any slight disequilibrium is removed instantaneously. However, in the labor market, even if there is an excess demand for labor or an excess supply of labor, workers and employers refrain from competitive behavior to correct disequilibrium situations in the labor market because of the cost and time associated with eliminating such disequilibrium. Instead, they agree to a contract that binds their behavior for a certain period.

Workers and employers agree to long-term labor contracts and enter long-term wage contracts (1 to 3 years), although they know that the conditions of the labor market will be constantly changing. Thus, the contract brings rigidity to the labor market, which prevents the equilibrium wage from being established at all times. Thus, there are restraints on competitive behaviors such as layoffs or hirings and wage increases or wage cuts. The advocates of new Keynesian economics argue that the existence of such long-term contracts must be incorporated into the macroeconomic framework.

In a situation where wage rigidity bound by contracts dominates, individual economic agents cannot nullify the effect of anticipated stabilization policy, even if they form their expectations of inflation rationally. Because contracts introduce the rigidity of wages, workers could not demand higher wages in response to higher inflation triggered by expansionary aggregate demand policy during the contract period, even though they correctly anticipate higher inflation using all the available information. As a result, real wages fall, which leads firms to increase production and employment. Thus, workers could not respond to the government's stabilization policy to maximize their own interest. This conclusion is known as the theory of overlapping contracts proposed by Stanley Fischer (1977)

In conclusion, if the labor market is governed by a contract, economic agents could not completely nullify or neutralize the effect of government policy, even if they act according to rational expectations. New Keynesian economists maintain that aggregate demand policy such as fiscal and monetary policy still work as important policy tools for stabilizing the economy. Prominent economists who lead new Keynesian economics include Olivier Blanchard, Ben Bernanke, Stanley Fisher, Robert Gordon, N. Gregory Mankiw, and Larry Summers.

Part 9

Money: The Artery of the Economy

1

WHAT IS MONEY? "TOO MUCH MONEY OR TOO LITTLE MONEY, THAT IS THE QUESTION"

A transaction of goods and services produced is necessarily accompanied by an exchange of money. Just as a car cannot run without gasoline, the real economy cannot go around without money. Money functions like an artery of the economy. It is thus important to know how much money we have in the economy. As a first step, we should know what money is and how money is measured.

We first need to recognize that money is not the same as what you think it is. When people talk about money, they usually think of cash such as dollar bills and coins. However, money used in economics is much broader than cash. Anything that can be used as a means of payment in the transactions of goods, services and assets can be included in the measure of money even if it is not a dollar bill or a coin. Demand deposits we have in bank accounts can also be included in the measure of money because they can be used as a means of payment.

Second, you might think that money is only issued and supplied by the central bank such as the Federal Reserve System in the United States, the Bank of England in the United Kingdom, and the European Central Bank (ECB) in the euro-zone countries. However, if the measure of money includes demand and some savings deposits as well as dollar bills and coins, it is easy to see that not only central banks but also depositors and financial institutions also play an important role in the creation of money. If you know that you also take part in creating or destroying money in our economy, you will feel proud as an economic agent.

Third, many people think that money itself has some intrinsic value. Before money emerged as a medium of exchange, people exchanged one product for another. This practice is called a barter system. The barter system developed into a system under which some commodities such as shells, salt, cows, and tobaccos were used as a medium of exchange. These goods were used as commodity money. Under the commodity money system, commodity money had some intrinsic value. However, it is not necessary for money to have some value itself. People on the Island of Yap used donut-shaped stones as money for many years. The commodity money system evolved into a system in which precious metals such as silver and gold were used as a medium of exchange. These precious metals had intrinsic value that was on a par with the nominal denomination of the medium. However, under the current paper money system, money has no intrinsic value. The value of paper money is based on people's faith in the usefulness of money as a medium of exchange.

Today, paper currency and coins are simply legal tender. A legal tender functions as money not because it has its own intrinsic value, but because the government declares that it is money by law. On the face of a dollar bill, the phrase, "This note is legal tender for all debts, public and private" is printed. This kind of money is sometimes referred to as fiat money. It is not accepted by people as a medium of exchange because it is valuable, but because the government requires that it be accepted as a means of payment. If a nation loses sovereignty through war, fiat money becomes just a piece of paper or a piece of metal. More fundamentally, the intrinsic value of money is not important and necessary as long as people have confidence in its usefulness as a medium of exchange.

The face value (or par value) of paper money we use is usually far above the value of the material made of it. This kind of money is called token money. A good example of token money is stone money, which was used for more than 1500 years by the residents of Yap Island. In this sense, today's paper currency and coins are no different from stone money. However, if the value of money falls sharply due to inflation, sometimes the face value of a coin falls below its material value.

Many people talk about money almost every day, and many people want to have more money. Is it good for the economy as a whole to have more money? "To be or not to be, that is the question" is the most famous quote in the writings of Shakespeare. A policymaker who is truly concerned with the wellbeing of people would also wonder, "Too much money or too little money, that is the question." If an economy has too much money, that is a problem. If an economy has too little money, that is also a problem. Historically, too much money rather than too little money has caused serious economic disruptions. The world economy was out on a limb for a while after the COVID-19 pandemic crisis. Many countries suffered serious inflation because too much money was poured into the economy during the crisis. Over the past 100 years or so, economists have been endeavoring to get a solution to the question of what the 'just right amount of money' is for the economy, but they have not reached any consensus yet. Finding the right amount of money, 'not too much, not too little, but just right' might be a mirage, but economists have not given up their efforts to find an answer to such a question.

George Bernard Shaw, who was a British playwriter and philosopher and impressed people with witty epigrams, once said: "The lack of money is the source of all kinds of evil." He was also famous for leaving an epitaph, which says that "I knew if I stayed long enough, something like this would happen" (Source: https://www.goodreads.com/author/quotes/5217_George_Bernard_Shaw). But the Bible sees money from different angles. "The love of money is a root of all kinds of evil" (Source: 1 Timothy 6:10). Cyndi Lauper, a famous singer who recently wrote and composed a Broadway hit musical <Kinky Boots> sang a song titled "Money changes everything" (Source: YouTube, CyndiLauperVEVO, February 21, 2014). The poet Hilaire Belloc (1870-1957) said: "I am tired of love, more tired of poems, but money always pleases me" (Source: https://www.brainyquote.com/quotes/bilaire-belloc).There is also a quip saying that "Yesterday is a cancelled check; tomorrow is a promissory note; today is cash and enjoy it" (Source: https://www.goodreads.com/quotes/197755-yesterday-is-a-cancelled-check).

There are also many interesting aphorisms about money.

- ◈ Money isn't everything (Cyndi Lauper).
- ◈ Money will do almost everything for people, and people will do almost everything for money.
- ◈ People who love money are never satisfied.

Human history over the past thousands of years has been a history of human greed to get more money. Midas' story in Greek mythology dating back to the ancient time teaches us that too much money (gold) does not necessarily make people happy. King Midas begged the god Dionysus to turn everything he touched into gold. Dionysus is the god of the grape-harvest, fertility, and alcohol, and in Roman mythology Dionysus is known as Bacchus, Roman god of wine. Dionysus granted Midas his wish. The phrase 'Midas touch' has been used to mean the ability to make money out of anything one undertakes.

Midas touched a pebble as a test, and the pebble turned into gold. Now, when he picked an apple from the apple tree and rubbed it, the apple soon became a golden apple. He has been intoxicated with happiness and joy as if the world belonged to him. If he had been reborn today, Bill Gates would have been dwarfed in front of Midas. He ordered his servants to invite the people of the village he ruled over and to prepare a feast for them. Surprisingly, however, when he touched bread to eat it, the bread quickly turned into gold. When he drank wine in a glass, the wine flowed into the neck like melted gold.

The Midas touch now became his shackles. Midas, surrounded entirely by gold, was waiting for a starving day because there was nothing to eat. So, he begged Dionysus again to release himself from this magic bondage. Dionysus promised Midas that "If you go to Pactolus River and wash your sins, I will release you from the magic" (Source: www.wikipedia.org/Midas). It was the sin of greed. After Midas was freed from the magic, he went down to the countryside, leaving his secular fortune behind him and lived in worship of the god of the wild.

There is a saying that "money begets money", which suggests that money should go around. It is also said that coins are made round because money should go around like a merry-go-round. No one denies that the economy will become brisk if money circulates well. In fact, there is an interesting story about people who used round, donut-shaped stones as money for almost 1500 years.

2

STONE MONEY ON THE ISLAND OF YAP

Before the money we currently use emerged, various forms of commodities were used as a means of payment. The most famous one that human beings used as money was round, donut-shaped stone money that was used by residents of Yap, an island located in the Micronesian archipelago of the South Pacific. Yap Island is one of the three federal states of Micronesia in the Pacific Ocean. Residents of Yap Island had used large donut-shaped stones, also known as Rai or Fei as money for nearly 1500 years. Some were more than 3 meters in diameter and weighed hundreds of kilograms.

Residents of Yap carried these stones on rafts pulled by canoes from Palau Island about 400 kilometers from the island. The Island of Iwo Jima is located on the south side of Palau where a fierce battle (Battle of Iwo Jima) took place between the U.S. marines and the Imperial Army of Japan in early 1945.

<Figure 9.1> Stone Money on the Yap Island>

On the Island of Yap, the value of each stone as money was determined by the characteristics and shape of the stone. The larger the stone, the more perfect its shape, and the greater the effort to bring it to Yap Island, the higher the value of the stone as money. Stones carried to the island could be placed around the island, or erected on the side of the road, or placed in front of a house.

The ownership of stone money, of course, belongs to the person who carried it to the island. Since the ownership of stone money was transferred by an oral contract, there was no need to move the physical stone to pay the transaction. Each stone had unique characteristics, and thus the islanders were able to know who the original owner had been and who the current owner was. Some stones had very high monetary value. Some stones had a monetary value of $10,000. There is a record showing that Hilrary Tacheliol, the island's vice-governor, was quoted as saying that "I recently bought a house for $12,000 and paid $2,000 in cash, and the rest of $10,000 in stone money" (Angell, 1929, Boyes and Melvin, 1991).

Stone money on Yap Island shows how important people's faith is in determining the value of money. In *The Story of Money* (1929), Norman Angell, introduces a story about a Yapese family who owns very precious stone money. None of the Yapese had ever seen the stone money. Nevertheless, the owner and value of the stone money were recognized by everyone on the island. The story of the family's stone money is as follows:

> "The stone was known to lie deep in the sea for generations. A long time ago, when an ancestor carried the stone from Palau Island, he met a ferocious storm. He was forced to break the raft that was carrying it. When he arrived at Yap Island, people who sailed on the same boat testified to how large and how perfect the lost stone was. After hearing the story, the islanders recognized the value of the stone and the ownership of the original owner, even though they had never seen the stone. Over the years, the ownership of the stone lying deep in the sea was transferred from person to person by verbal contract, and the lost stone performed the function of the means of payment" (Angell, 1929, Boyes and Melvin, 1991).

Any form of money is acceptable if people believe that it has value. It is not necessary for money to possess physically any value or to be backed by any promise of redemption in gold or other precious metals. As long as people have faith in something as money, it functions as money. Stone money on Yap Island is a good example showing that if people believe something has value as a means of payment, it can be used as money.

Are the dollar bills we use today fundamentally different from the stone money that the citizens of Yap used? Of course, the nature of the dollar bill is different from that of stone money in that the dollar bill is a legal tender.

A legal tender means that the law stipulates that the dollar bill must be accepted as a means of payment. However, the 100-dollar bill itself has no intrinsic value. It is worth $100 because people believe that it is worth $100. In this regard, the dollar bill is no different from the stone money used by the Yapese.

However, a certain kind of money has intrinsic value as a commodity rather than as money. Sometimes it is more profitable to use money as a commodity than actual money. Old and rare coins are often traded at much higher prices than their par values. Recently, a penny issued in 1793 was sold for $2 million. Gold and silver coins also contain some intrinsic value on a par with their nominal denominations.

3

MONEY IS "WHAT MONEY DOES"

We have seen that on the Island of Yap, people used donut-shaped stones as money for many years. The fact that stones could be used as money suggests that drawing the border line between moneyness and non-moneyness based on the composition of money is ambiguous. Some economists such as University of Chicago economist, Jacob Viner (1937) say that "money is what money does". Although this definition of money might sound like tautology, it captures the essential features of money. Here are several episodes (in addition to the story of stone money) which do justice to the definition of money.

Under the barter system, it will be possible to exchange violin lessons and barber services. Under the monetary system, no one would imagine a deal in which one takes a violin lesson and provides a haircut service in return. But a similar situation actually happened. British economist William Stanley Jevons (1875) conveyed a story on the uncomfortable bargain of the barter he witnessed when he traveled to the South Pacific in the 19th century (Also, see Fayzmanesh, 2006).

At that time, the well-known French singer Mademoiselle Zelie was performing on Society Islands near Taiti Island as part of her world tour. She signed a contract to perform in exchange for a third of the ticket sales. At the end of the show, her performance fees consisted of three pigs, 23 turkeys, 44 chickens, 5,000 coconuts, and a fair number of bananas, lemons, and oranges. These items were the products received from the sales of tickets under the barter system that took place on the island.

Jevons calculated the value of these items based on the prices of the same products traded in Paris at the time. The market value of the items Zelie received as a performance fee was about 4,000 francs. It was a very good reward for the performance. The problem is that no one on Society Islands had any currency to buy and sell these products. Zelie did not have adequate transportations to bring the goods she received to France, but she also had no time to eat the pigs, turkeys, chickens, and fruits while staying on the South Pacific Island. She had no choice but to leave the products on the island. She fed the fruits to pigs, turkeys, and chickens before she left the island.

Jevons also conveyed a story about the experience of Wallace who traveled to the Islands of Malay. The islanders there did not use any currency. It was no wonder that Wallace had to barter some items for his dinner every night. Unfortunately, people with food on the island sometimes didn't want Wallace's barter items. 'The double coincidence of wants between Wallace and the islanders did not happen. He was sometimes starving. So, he had to go somewhere else to get the food he wanted and had to travel with a big bag full of knives, clothes, and liquor that the locals would like to have. His suitcase became heavier, but this heavy bag was inevitable for bartering with people at his destinations.

During World War II, a unique commodity money was circulated in the prison camps operated under the Nazis regime. The International Red Cross provided various kinds of goods to prisoners held in the Nazi concentration camps. These items included cheese, chocolates, clothes, cigarettes and so on. The International Red Cross distributed a certain amount of these items to the prisoners of war (POW) without asking them for their preferences or choices (Radford, 1945). It soon became apparent that this quota system was inefficient. For example, one prisoner liked chocolates, the other prisoner preferred cheese, while another prisoner wanted shirts. Prisoner A who wanted chocolate but received cheese and shirts began to barter cheese for chocolate with Prisoner B who received chocolate but wanted cheese, and to barter shirts for chocolates with Prisoner C who received chocolates but wanted shirts. Barters occurred among prisoners.

The barters in the concentration camps presented the problem of the 'double coincidence of wants,' which will be discussed in the next chapter. This is because such a transaction could be achieved only when the wants of prisoners matched with each other. Prisoner A had to find Prisoner B to barter cheese for chocolates and Prisoner C to barter shirts for chocolates. This barter system made their transactions very inefficient and inconvenient. Under the scheme of the double coincidence of wants, prisoners might not be able to get the items they liked the most. This is an example which shows that even a transaction within a limited area of concentration camps needed some form of a medium of exchange.

In response to such needs, cigarettes eventually emerged as a medium of exchange. All the values of rationed products in the prison camps were determined by the number of cigarettes. Thus, transactions were made based on the number of cigarettes. For example, one shirt was exchanged for 80 cigarettes, and a pack of chocolates was priced as having five cigarettes. Even the price of services was set by the number of cigarettes. Some prisoners received two cigarettes and washed a suit of clothes for other prisoners. Prisoners who did not smoke also used cigarettes as a medium of exchange because they could use them to purchase the goods they would need in the future. In this way, cigarettes in the prison camps were used as a medium of exchange, as a unit of account and as a store of value. Cigarettes fully functioned as money.

Tobacco or cigarettes were not only used as money in the prison camps under the Nazis regime. In British colonies, Maryland and Virginia used tobacco as an official monetary unit. In the Soviet Union in the late 1980s, cigarettes performed the function of money for a while. At that time, the value of the ruble fell to the ground when the Soviet economy fell into a bog. So, some traders preferred Marlboro, the American cigarette brand to the ruble and transacted goods and services using the Marlboro.

4

EVOLUTION OF THE MONETARY SYSTEM

In the beginning Homo sapiens used a barter system. A barter system is an economic system for trade in which one product (say, honey) is directly exchanged for another product (say, milk). The barter system dated back to more than 100,000 years ago. Consider how transactions were made under the barter system. Suppose that Tom produces milk, and Jerry produces honey. Tom wants to sell milk to buy honey. Tom must find a person (Jerry) who produces honey, and at the same time wants to buy milk. The match between any two traders was termed a double coincidence of wants by British economist William Jevons.

The double coincidence of wants made the exchanges of goods and services very complicated and inefficient. The time and effort people spent to match the double coincidence of their wants was immeasurably burdensome. People gradually began to realize the need for a medium of exchange instead of sticking to the double coincidence of wants. The inconvenience and inefficiency of the barter system led to the emergence of a new monetary system in which people used some commodities as a medium of exchange, which came to be called commodity money. Initially shells, grains such as barley or wheat, salt, and sometimes animals such as chickens, cows, and pigs were used as a medium of exchange. The monetary unit, 'shekel' that was frequently cited in the Bible was originally a unit of the weight of barley that was used as a medium of exchange at that time Considering that the term 'shekel' was used in Mesopotamia around B.C. 3000, it is presumed that commodity money appeared much earlier than B.C. 3000.

When people used animals such as cows as a medium of exchange, they realized that such items could not be easily divided according to the value of traded goods. Furthermore, such items were either not easy to store or difficult to move from place to place. Thus, commodity money that was too large or heavy was not easy to carry, and its usefulness as a medium of exchange was limited. People sought alternative commodity money items that were small, light, and easily transportable. Cigarettes were a preferred choice.

As people gradually became accustomed to using small, light, and transportable commodities as a medium of exchange, they began to turn their attention to metals that were durable, highly partitionable, and light compared with their value. Initially, precious metals were used in the form of metal chunks of various sizes. Later, coins such as copper coins, silver coins, and gold coins began to be used. Coins were first used in China around B.C. 1000 and later in Greece around B.C. 700. These coins usually had some marks inscribed on their surface. In the Roman coins that were mentioned in the Bible, the portrait and writing of Julius Caesar were engraved. The Bible tells us the details of the shape of the coin called 'denarius'. Jesus asked the Jewish to bring the coin they used for paying the tax. They brought him a denarius. Jesus asked them, "Whose portrait is this? And whose inscription?" They replied to Jesus: "They are Caesar's." Then Jesus said to them, "Give to Caesar what is Caesar's and to God what is God's." (Source: The Bible, Matthew 22:19-21)

The first paper currency began to be used in China during the Tang Dynasty (618 ~907) and gradually became widely used during the Song Dynasty (960~1279). In Europe, paper money was first used in Sweden in 1661. The original paper money was a kind of commodity currency. This is because the original paper money was issued as a certificate of ownership for a certain amount of precious metal. Then, in the United States, paper currency in which the value of the currency was backed by gold was issued in 1780, which was the beginning of the gold standard. The paper currency issued in the United States at that time was very similar to the dollar bill we use today, but it was fundamentally different from today's dollar bills in that a phrase 'Gold Certificate' was printed on the surface of the original paper currency. This was to ensure that the value of the paper currency could be exchanged for a certain amount of gold (or silver).

This gold standard system began to be used at the end of the 18th century and developed into an international gold standard by 1815. The international gold standard was maintained until 1971 when the United States officially abandoned the gold standard system. Today's currency is no longer supported by gold. In the case of the U.S. dollar bill, the phrase, 'Gold Certificate' was replaced by the phrase 'Federal Reserve Note'. This means that today's paper currency is fiat money. Paper currency does not have its own intrinsic value, but functions as money because the government requires that it be accepted as a means of payment.

Today, bank money constitutes a larger portion of money. As seen previously, money is more than currency. Banks' demand deposits are also an important form of money because they are used as a medium of exchange and as a store of value, which are important functions of money. Thus, demand deposits and other checkable deposits are an important component of money (M1 or M2). In fact, the proportion of demand deposits and other checkable deposits in M1 exceeds 50% of the entire money (M1). This means that people use these demand deposits more than currency. The sum of demand deposits and other checkable deposits is sometimes called bank money. Bank money plays an important role in the creation of money in our economy.

Lastly, we'll briefly discuss how the U.S. dollar was born and evolved. Before the American Revolution, each colony had its own currency. Interestingly, cigarettes were used as money in Maryland and Virginia. The first national currency of the United States was born by the Continental Congress shortly after the United States declared its independence in 1776. This currency was the Continental dollar. The new currency in the United States was legal tender. The Continental Congress issued huge amounts of continental dollars to support the Revolutionary War with the United Kingdom. The Continental Congress initially appealed to patriotism, fearing that people would think the dollar, a paper currency that was not guaranteed by any precious metals, was worthless. The appeal to patriotism did not last long. The result of printing paper currency recklessly was uncontrollable inflation. During the Revolutionary War, the continental dollar fell into almost worthless pieces of paper.

Appointed as the first U.S. Treasury Secretary, Alexander Hamilton, dreamed of a system in which the U.S. dollar held stable values. So, he created the dollar coin (gold coins and silver coins). The value of a dollar was set at 0.056 ounces of gold and 0.84 ounces of silver. The U.S. monetary system adopted a bimetallic (gold and silver) standard.

Until the Federal Reserve System, the central bank of the United States, was founded in 1913, the United States had operated under an economic system without a central bank. To supplement the absence of a central bank with exclusive power to issue money, the United States founded the First Bank of the United States from 1791 to 1810 and the Second Bank of the United States from 1816 to 1836. These two banks had the elements of a private bank and a central bank together, and they could be regarded as the predecessors of the Federal Reserve System. These banks issued national bank notes, which were backed by gold and silver.

Private banks also issued banknotes, and these private banks, like the two national banks, promised to exchange banknotes for coins (gold and silver coins). However, as private banks sometimes went bankrupt due to lack of funds, people avoided the banknotes issued by private banks. This dual banking system ended with the outbreak of the Civil War in the 1860s. The U.S. government issued a large amount of paper currency (= dollar bills) to procure war expenses. This paper currency was called 'Greenbacks'. It was the first green-colored dollar bill in the United States.

In 1879, the United States reintroduced the gold standard. At that time, the U.S. government set the value of one dollar equal to 0.0484 ounces of gold (or 1 ounce of gold per 20 dollars). And the main form of money was the Gold Certificate. The second attempt to adopt the gold standard developed into the international gold standard which burgeoned in the early 1800s.

5

FUNCTIONS OF MONEY

We have seen that currency is not the only money. Currency includes dollar bills such as $1 bills and $10 bills and coins such as pennies and quarters. However, money is more than currency. Could demand deposits at banks be included in the measure of money? Can we include savings deposits in the category of money? Can we include the certificates of deposits (CDs) commonly known as time deposits? Can we include government bonds such as Treasury bills and U.S. savings bonds issued by the government? Can we include commercial paper and corporate bonds issued by private firms? Can we include stocks? Can we include gold and silver? Can we include credit cards and stored-value cards? Can we include electronic money and cryptocurrencies?

Thus, it is not straightforward to define what money is in terms of the composition of money. Therefore, we need to take the 'function-first-definition-later' approach. We first stipulate the basic functions of money that money must perform and then define money as 'anything that performs the basic functions of money'. The most important function of money is that it functions as a medium of exchange or a means of payment. Money is used as a means of buying and selling goods or services and paying financial obligations. The medium of exchange function of money can be better understood by comparing it with the barter system. Under the barter system, some goods (say, milk) are directly exchanged for other goods (say, honey), but under the money system transactions are conducted through a medium of exchange, that is, money.

Let's think about how simple the transactions of goods and services are under the money system. As discussed previously, under the barter system, people had to solve the problem of the 'double coincidence of wants'. However, in a monetary economy where money is used as a medium of exchange, people who want to barter milk for honey do not have to match their specific wants with those of others who want to barter honey for milk. Suppose Tom wants to sell milk and buy honey. Then he does not have to find Jerry who wants to sell honey and buy milk. Tom can just sell milk to anyone who has money and uses the money to buy honey from anyone who wants to sell honey. Jerry is no different. She can sell honey to anyone who has money.

Money also functions as a unit of account or a common denominator. Money is used as a measure of the relative value of various goods or services. Just as we measure distance in meters and weight in kilograms, we measure the value of a good or service in terms of money. In the barter exchange, the value of a product is defined by the quantity of other goods for which it might possibly be exchanged. For example, it is like one gallon of honey is exchanged for two gallons of milk, and one gallon of milk is exchanged for three loaves of bread. Consequently, one gallon of honey is exchanged for six loaves of bread, etc. People would have to memorize all these exchange ratios. However, under the monetary economy, one gallon of honey sells for $12, one gallon of milk sells for $6, and one loaf of bread sells for $2. Thus, the money system greatly simplifies transactions by choosing one common denominator and expressing the values of all goods and services in the common denominator.

Lastly, money functions as a store of value or a store of purchasing power. Money is a convenient means of accumulating wealth. The other two functions of money—the medium of exchange and the unit of account—are unique to money, but the store of value function of money is also performed by other assets such as cash, savings, bonds, stocks, jewelry, paintings, houses, land, etc.

However, money has the advantage of being immediately usable in buying and selling goods and services and paying financial obligations compared with other types of assets. Savings deposits cannot be used directly to pay utility bills and buy groceries. You first should convert savings deposits into cash or demand deposits. This conversion is not difficult, but savings deposits cannot be used as a means of payment. Converting bonds, stocks, or precious metals into cash is more difficult and requires some time and costs. It becomes much more difficult to convert land or houses into cash. The ease with which an asset can be easily converted into cash is called liquidity, and money is the most liquid of all assets.

However, money also has disadvantages as a means of storing value. If inflation progresses, the real value of money will fall, reducing the attractiveness of money as a store of value. Thus, the holders of money will lose. Inflation works like a tax on the holdings of money. The opposite occurs when deflation occurs. In the case of deflation, the nominal value of money remains the same, but the real value of money rises. This has the same effect as receiving interest as a gift from the government.

6

MEASUREMENT OF MONEY

Modern economics reveals that money has profound effects on almost every part of the economy. When the economy is in recession or the economy is overheating, policymakers try to solve the problems by first managing the amount of money. The central bank changes the benchmark interest rate such as the federal funds rate in the United States and the bank rate in the United Kingdom by changing the supply of money in the economy. In order for policymakers to control or manage the amount of money, it is necessary to understand how the amount of money is measured in the economy.

We have discussed the three basic functions that money is supposed to perform. Based on the basic functions of money, we can define money as anything that is generally accepted in any economy as a medium of exchange, a unit of account, and a store of value. This definition is the most general definition of money that matches the basic functions of the currency.

However, this definition is not quite satisfactory as a measure of how much money a country has at some point in time. We still have to deal with some vague concepts such as 'anything' and 'generally accepted,' which need to be more specified and substantiated. In response to such needs, the central bank in each nation has developed and published indicators that further substantiate the definition of money. Although there are some degrees of variety in the measures of money across countries, there is not much difference in the basic measure of money, commonly known as M1. The Fed currently publishes two money stock measures: M1 and M2. In the past, the Fed also published M3, in addition to M1 and M2, but stopped releasing the M3 measure of the money stock. The M3 money stock is also known as broad money.

The amount of money is closely related to the operations of depository institutions. The depository institutions are financial intermediaries that accept deposits and make loans with the funds obtained from deposits. There are two types of depository institutions. Commercial banks and thrift institutions or simply thrifts. Commercial banks are traditional financial intermediaries that mainly accept transactions deposits such as checkable and savings deposits and make consumer, business, and credit card loans. On the other hand, thrift institutions include savings and loan associations (S&Ls), mutual savings banks, and credit unions that are specialized in issuing non-transactions deposits and in financing mainly home mortgages or, in the case of credit unions, consumer loans. However, during the S&L crisis that occurred from 1986 to 1995, the distinction between commercial banks and thrifts has been blurred. Commercial banks now also handle mortgage loans and accept non-transactions deposits. We first discuss how monetary aggregates are measured.

The Fed currently publishes two measures of monetary aggregates, M1 and M2. The M1 money stock is the narrowest measure of money and consists of the following items:

M1 = Currency in circulation + Demand deposits + Other liquid deposits

Currency includes Federal Reserve notes (that is, dollar bills) and coins that are in circulation. It should be noted that only currency held by the non-bank public is included in the measure of M1. Thus, currency held by the U.S. Treasury Department, Federal Reserve Banks and depository institutions are not included in the M1 money stock. Depository institutions hold some currency in their vaults to meet the reserve requirements. Currency held by depository institutions in their vaults is sometimes called vault cash, and vault cash is excluded from the measure of M1.

Demand deposits refer to the deposits that can be withdrawn on demand. Demand deposits in principle do not pay interest. There was a big change in the measurement of M1 in May 2020. Prior to May 2020, only other checkable deposits in addition to currency and demand deposits were included in M1, Other checkable deposits are deposits that can be withdrawn on demand and at the same time pay interest. These deposits include the negotiable order of withdrawal (NOW) and automatic transfer service (ATS). However, beginning May 2020, M1 also includes savings deposits. Prior to May 2020, savings deposits were included in M2. Other checkable deposits and savings deposits are collectively called other liquid deposits. Thus, part of deposits classified as components of M2 prior to May 2020 became M1. As a result of this reclassification of money, the size of M1 money abruptly increased from $4,779.8 billion in April 2020 to $16,232.9 billion in May 2020. This change has very important implications.

Other liquid deposits consist of not only other checkable deposits (NOW and ATS accounts at depository institutions, share draft accounts at credit unions, demand deposits at thrift institutions) but also savings deposits and money market deposit accounts (MMDAs). Savings deposits are a bit less liquid than demand deposits because savings deposits are not readily usable in buying and selling goods and services. The reclassification of savings deposits from M2 to M1 seems to reflect the fact that savings deposits could be easily transferred to demand deposits through Internet banking. The transaction costs involved in such transfers have been considerably reduced by Internet banking.

The M2 money stock is a little bit broader measure of money. M2 consists of small-denomination time deposits and retail money market funds (MMFs), in addition to M1.

M2 = M1 + Small-denomination time deposits + Retail money market funds

Small-denomination time deposits are those issued in amounts of less than $100,000. Retail money market funds include money market mutual fund shares (individual) and overnight repurchase agreements (RPs). Individual retirement accounts (IRA) and Keogh account balances at depository institutions are subtracted from small-denomination time deposits. Also, IRA and Keogh account balances at money market funds are subtracted from retail money market funds.

<Table 9.1> U.S. Money Stock Measures (in billions of $)

Year (December)	Currency	Demand Deposits	Other Liquid Deposits	M1	M2
1980:12	115.3	261.2		408.5	1,599.8
1990:12	246.5	276.8		824.7	3,271.8
2000:12	531.3	310.5		1,088.6	4,925.0
2010:12	918.8	516.5		1,836.7	8,801.8
2020:4	1,787.1	1,996.2		4,779.8	17,002.5
2020:5	1,819.8	2,121.2	12,291.9	16,232.9	17,835.2
2020:12	1,975.9	3,296.9	12,561.6	17,834.4	19,124.7
2022:12	2,211.5	5,135.6	12,474.8	19,821.9	21,359.2

In the past, the Fed published the M3 money stock which was a much broader measure of money. M3 included somewhat fewer liquid assets such as large time deposits, fairly long-term (2 weeks) repurchase agreements, and other assets that are somewhat harder to convert into cash.

M3 = M2 + large time deposits ($100,000 or more)
+ Money market mutual fund shares (institutional)
+ Term repurchase agreements + Term Eurodollars.

The Fed also published L (liquidity aggregates) which included much less liquid assets such as Treasury bills, U.S. savings bonds, commercial paper, etc. These items are potentially convertible into the medium of exchange items. L was equal to the sum of M3 and these forms of financial assets.

$$L = M3 + \text{Treasury bills (TBs)} + \text{U.S. savings bonds} + \text{Commercial paper (CP)} + \text{Bankers acceptances (BAs)}$$

The classification of these various monetary aggregates is mainly based on the degree of liquidity. As we expand the boundary of money from M1 to M2, M3, L, the liquidity of components of monetary aggregates decreases. The components of the previous M1 money stock (currency + demand deposits + other checkable deposits) were financial assets that could be used directly and immediately in buying and selling goods and services or making financial transactions. These items are called the medium of exchange items or spendable money. However, the new measure of M1 now includes savings deposits that are not readily usable in buying and selling goods and services. On the other hand, the components of M2 cannot be used immediately as a means of payment for transactions of goods and services or financial payments and must be converted into spendable money. However, it is still much easier to convert the components of M2 into spendable money than the components of M3 or L. As we move from M1 to L, we encounter assets that are less and less liquid.

We have seen earlier that money has significant influences on the economy. Policymakers first try to control the money supply to influence economic activity. This raises the question of which monetary aggregate, M1 or M2 should be used as a policy variable. Prior to May 2020, this debate was an important issue, because there was a big difference between M1 and M2 in terms of their composition and size. Generally speaking, M1 (narrow money) was a monetary indicator that was closer to the function of money as a medium of exchange, and M2 (broad money) was a monetary indicator that included not only medium-of-exchange items but also store-of-value items.

In a situation where the financial market is rapidly changing, new financial products are often introduced in the market, and thus the public seeks more favorable forms of financial assets that could be used as a means of payment and changes their asset portfolios from time to time. For example, in the United States, when mutual fund companies introduced new financial products called money market mutual fund shares (MMMF), many bank customers shifted from existing bank savings deposits to money market mutual funds. MMMFs are an attractive investment for investors because it is a mutual fund that invests in short-term securities that have higher liquidity and provide higher returns than bank savings deposits.

As another example, if interest rates on savings deposits go up, depositors tend to move from demand deposits that do not pay interest to savings deposits that offer higher returns. This means that M1 can fluctuate widely. The unstable movement of M1 makes the relationship between M1 and macroeconomic activity erratic and makes it inappropriate to use M1 as a policy guide. We are interested in measuring the money stock accurately to understand how closely the amount of money is related to macroeconomic activity. If the relationship is unstable, such a monetary aggregate loses its usefulness as a guide for economic policy.

In many developed countries, M1 was recognized as the most reliable indicator of monetary and financial conditions until the end of the 1970s. However, since the relationship between M1 and economic activity deteriorated since the 1980s, monetary policy based on M1 was frequently out of the mark, and the monetary authorities gradually gave up using M1 as a target variable for monetary policy and moved to M2. In many countries, M2 has been used as a target variable for monetary policy, but in recent years, M2 has also been gradually losing its importance as an indicator of monetary conditions.

However, this debate has no longer been relevant since May 2020, because most of the M2 components have become M1, and the difference between M1 and M2 has been trivial in size since 2020. Most importantly, savings deposits which were part of M2 before 2020 are now the major component of M1. More fundamentally, some economists have raised the question of whether monetary aggregates such as M1 and M2 are a useful guide for the purpose of monetary policy. The main reason is that in the rapidly changing financial environment in which new financial products continue to be introduced in the market, M2 is also showing unstable movements, and as a result, the relationship between M2 and economic activity is also difficult to predict. Therefore, countries including the United States have tended to shift the focus of monetary policy from the monetary aggregates such as M2 to interest rates such as the federal funds rate.

7

CAN BITCOIN AND OTHER CRYPTOCURRENCIES BE MONEY?

In our discussion of the measurement of monetary aggregates (M1 or M2), credit cards were not included in any measure of money. But shouldn't a credit card be included in the category of money? People sometimes call credit cards plastic money or smart money, and some stores prefer credit cards to personal checks or even cash.

However, the credit card itself is not money. Let's say you buy a flight ticket for $300 using a credit card. In this case, you pay with a credit card, but paying for the plane ticket using your credit card does not complete your transaction. It can be seen as a temporary borrowing from the card issuer. When the card issuer pays for the purchase of the flight ticket to the travel agent, the transaction is completed. Thus, when you buy the ticket using your credit card, you temporarily receive a loan from the card issuer until you pay the card issuer for the purchase of the flight ticket. In this sense, the use of a credit card only delays the payment of money. Naturally, the use of a credit card does not eliminate the use of money.

In recent years, stored-value cards (SVC) have been rapidly expanding their territory. At first glance, the stored-value card looks like a debit card or credit card, but the stored-value card is fundamentally different from debit or credit cards in that it is a prepaid card. For example, if you pay $100 for a stored-value card, you receive a prepaid card that stores the value of $100. When you purchase an item with a stored-value card, the price of the item is deducted from the balance of the prepaid card. In the case of debit cards, money is on deposit with the issuer, which is money; in the case of credit cards, the holder has a temporary loan from the card issuer.

There are various types of prepaid cards, such as phone cards issued by telephone companies, gift cards issued by department stores and shops. These stored-value cards are used for one purpose only (telephones, product purchase, etc.), but recently, credit card issuers (Visa or MasterCard) or banks issue multi-purpose prepaid cards. These multi-purpose stored-value cards have the advantage that they can be used to purchase any product and can be used anywhere. Also, as you can see from Apple Pay, money is stored on a smartphone and used like a credit card.

These multi-purpose prepaid cards can be viewed as electronic traveler's checks. The purchaser of the traveler's check pays the bank a certain amount in advance and receives it. Traveler's checks are included in M1. So, shouldn't the stored-value card be included in the M1? However, until now, such a multipurpose stored-value card has not been incorporated into M1. Since the use of these value-stored cards is expected to increase significantly in the future, it will be a matter of time before the stored-value cards are included in M1.

As the development of information technology accelerates, the monetary system is also rapidly evolving. One of such evolutions is electronic money or digital money. To date, the major e-currency issuers are Apple Pay, PayPal, a subsidiary of eBay, and Alipay, a subsidiary of Alibaba. PayPal or Alipay can be viewed as Internet banks. The mobile finance works as follows. You can open a PayPal account first and deposit money into the account via e-commerce. Money is transferred from your bank account to the PayPal account via the Internet. Or you can use your credit card to put money into your PayPal account. In order to purchase a product, you finish the transaction by transferring money from your PayPal account to an online business account. Since 2014, Apple has been offering Apple Pay services which allow consumers to make payments using iPhones that store information on their debit cards or credit cards.

As mobile banking is spreading rapidly, it is expected that banking branches that operate by dividing each region will gradually disappear. In the future, the share of electronic money will become even higher. Is electronic money included in the measure of money (M1 or M2)? It appears that people use electronic money as a means of payment. In theory, it seems to be reasonable to include electronic money in money. However, just as credit cards are not money, electronic money is not money, despite its name. After all, any transaction paid by PayPal or Apple Pay is not completed until money is taken out from bank deposits that are a component of money.

The use of cryptocurrencies such as Bitcoin is increasing, but Bitcoin has fundamentally different characteristics from electronic money. A cryptocurrency is a software object with 'tokens' that can be transferred from one owner to another, which is based on blockchain technology that is widely distributed database. Bitcoin was the first decentralized cryptocurrency that was invented in 2008 by an anonymous person or group of people who used a pseudonym, Satoshi Nakamoto. Bitcoin began to be used in 2009. Now the NYSE Bitcoin index in U.S. dollars is available. Can Bitcoin or cryptocurrencies be used as money?

As we discussed, in order for anything to be used as money, it must perform the three basic functions of money: a medium of exchange, a unit of account, and a store of value. First, people could use it to conduct transactions. Second, people could use it to measure the relative value of goods and services they transact. Third, people hold it to accumulate wealth. Does Bitcoin perform the basic functions of money? First, Bitcoin has been used to buy certain kinds of goods and services. Some vendors such as PayPal have recently supported the use of some cryptocurrencies in users' PayPal accounts. However, when users make a transaction using Bitcoin as the funding source, the transaction is not completed until the cryptocurrency is converted to fiat currency, that is, dollars, stored in their PayPal accounts. Thus, the transaction is completed only with the use of fiat money in PayPal accounts. In this regard, cryptocurrency is not a medium of exchange.

Second, prices of goods and services transacted by the use of Bitcoin are quoted in dollars, not Bitcoin. In this regard, Bitcoin does not perform the unit of account function of money. Lastly, Bitcoin can be used as a store of value. However, the prices of Bitcoin quoted in dollars have been widely gyrating, making it a very risky asset and less preferred investment. In this regard, Bitcoin is closer to stocks or bonds, rather than to money.

<Figure 9.2> Bitcoin Prices in U.S. Dollars

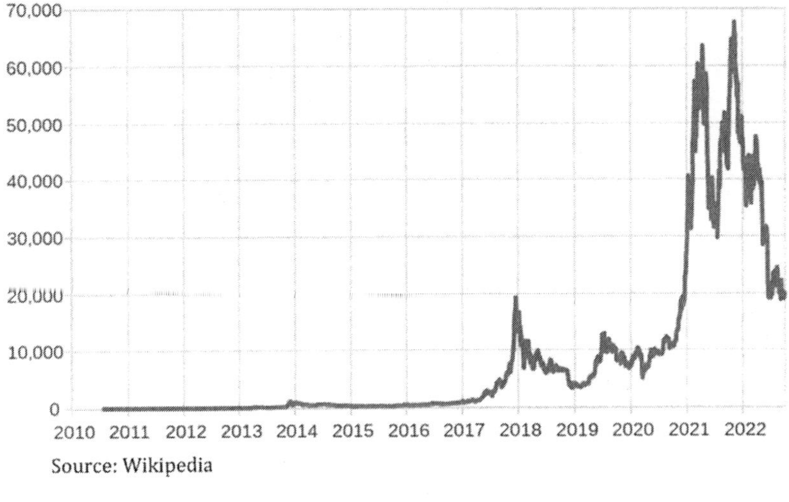

Source: Wikipedia

However, although Bitcoin does not perform the basic functions of money, it is another issue for a country to adopt Bitcoin as an official legal tender. The adoption of Bitcoin as legal currency is no different from the adoption of tobaccos as legal currency, as the State of Virginia once used tobaccos as money. The central bank of a country can decide on what can be used as a legal tender. In fact, El Salvador became the first country in the world that adopted Bitcoin as a legal tender in May 2021. In April 2022, the Central African Republic (CAR) adopted Bitcoin as its legal tender, too. These countries have adopted Bitcoin as their legal tender in the hope that they would reduce their dependency on the U.S. dollar and to promote prosperity and sustainability of their economies. Cryptocurrencies such as Bitcoin that are based on blockchain technology make it easy to trace every transaction of currency spent. Also, the use of Bitcoin has the advantage of reducing illegal transactions and money laundering and computing taxes in a more transparent and organized manner.

More countries are expected to adopt Bitcoin or other cryptocurrencies as a legal tender. However, to date, Bitcoin and cryptocurrencies do not fully perform the basic functions of money. Particularly, the prices of cryptocurrencies are highly volatile. Thus, a country that adopts a cryptocurrency will experience wide fluctuations in their stock of money, which make it difficult for the country to conduct stable and effective monetary policy. Volatile movements in a country's stock of money may also have adverse effects on international trade. Thus, the success of Bitcoin as a legal tender remains to be seen.

8

THE ECONOMICS OF GOLD: GOLD AND THE U.S. DOLLAR

The United States officially ended its gold standard in 1971 by announcing that it would no longer honor its commitment to buying or selling gold for $35 per ounce. Since then, gold prices have been freely determined in the market by demand and supply forces. At the same time, gold emerged as a competitor for the dollar as a safe asset. Now we need to understand how the price of gold is determined in the market, and how gold competes with the U.S. dollar in portfolio choices.

The human being's love for gold has a long history. Gold had been used as a form of currency since ancient times. Various kinds of gold coins were used in the Roman Empire, and the gold coin with Julius Caesar's face inscribed was mentioned in the Bible (Matthew 22:19-21).

Despite mankind's unending love for gold, it has been only 50 years since gold prices began to be freely determined in the market. The economics of gold is unique. Gold itself is a commodity and an investment target. However, gold also functioned as money under the gold standard. Although the gold standard was abolished, gold not only serves as a hedge against inflation, but also has a competitive relationship with the dollar. As inflation goes up, so does the value of gold. Also, in situations such as war fears or economic crises, the demand for gold, which is considered as a safe asset, increases, and thus the price of gold rises. Because the U.S. dollar is the safest currency, and gold is a substitute for the dollar, people try to hold either the dollar or gold during an economic crisis. Thus, the dollar and gold compete in portfolio choices. If the dollar value is expected to rise, the gold price will fall, and *vice versa*.

Gold prices are also closely related to interest rates. In general, as interest rates rise, the opportunity cost of holding gold rises by that amount. This means that if you put your money in your bank account instead of buying gold, you will earn higher interest, but you'll give up this opportunity by holding gold. Owning gold becomes more expensive, and thus people tend to convert their investments into financial assets such as bonds or deposits that pay high interest rather than gold. Gold does not pay interest or dividends, so that the price of gold moves in the opposite direction of market interest rates. If the market rate is only 1%, the opportunity cost of holding gold is only 1%. This is because, by holding gold, investors must give up 1% of the interest they can get from their investment in financial assets. However, if the market rate rises to 5%, the situation will be different. By investing in gold, you will have to sacrifice an opportunity to earn 5% interest. In order for people to invest in gold in such a situation, the rate of return on investment in gold should be at least 5% to compensate for such opportunity costs. Otherwise, people will not buy gold, and thus the demand for gold will decrease, lowering the price of gold.

However, the economic indicator most closely related to the movement of gold prices is the yield on U.S. Treasury securities. Campbell Harvey of Duke University who has investigated the movement of gold prices has found that when the yield on U.S. Treasury securities rises, the price of gold decreases, and *vice versa*. On the other hand, the relationship between gold prices and inflation is not as strong as the relationship between gold prices and bond yields. The relationship between gold prices and inflation depends on the time frame. In the short term, gold is not a good hedge against inflation. In the long run which spans decades, however, gold can be a good hedge against inflation.

Since the gold price was allowed to be freely determined in the market, gold prices have shown wide fluctuations. Market gold prices have tended to rise when the world economy was driven into an economic crisis and to fall when the world economy was in the state of tranquility. The nominal price of gold (average annual gold price) started at the price of $40.84 per troy ounce in 1971. The gold price continued to rise during the turbulent period of inflation throughout the 1970s, rising to the level of $614.73 in 1980 (except for the fall to $124.84 in 1976). Then as the spiral of inflation was mitigated, the gold price also remained relatively low and stable levels from 1981 until 2000. During the 1981~2001 period, the gold price fluctuated between $459.73 (1981) and 271.04 (2001). After the gold price bottomed out at $271.04 in 2001, the gold price began to steer toward a higher plateau, reaching $1668.88 in 2012.

As the world economy sailed smoothly after the global economy crisis, the gold price again stayed stagnant from 2013 to 2019, fluctuating between $1,160.08 and $1,392.60. However, the gold price began to soar to $1,769.10 in 2020 when the COVID-19 crisis hit the world economy and continued to go uphill to $1801.00 in 2021. On the other hand, the average monthly gold price reached the highest level so far at $2,074.88 on March 7, 2020. Since the official price of monetary gold at the price of $35.50 per ounce was abolished in 1971, it has risen more than 50 times over the past 50 years or so.

(Average annual gold prices in U.S. dollars per troy ounce: 1971: $40.84; 1972: $58.15; 1973: $97.32; 1974: $158.91; 1975: $161.02; 1976: $124.84; 1977: $147.84; 1978: $193.73; 1979: $306.68; 1980: $614.73; 1981: $459.73; 1982: $376.11; 1983: $424.02; 1984: $360.71; 1985: $317.61; 1986: $368.88;1987: $446.10; 1988: $438.94; 1989: $381.24; 1990: $383.73; 1991: $362.11; 1992: $343.82; 1993: $359.25; 1994: $384.00; 1995: $384.36; 1996: $387.73; 1997: $331.98; 1998: $294.24; 1999: $278.98; 2000: $279.11; 2001: $271.04; 2002: $310.25; 2003: $363.56; 2004: $409.72; 2005: $444.74; 2006: $603.37; 2007: $695.39; 2008: $871.96; 2009: $972.35; 2010: 1,225.53; 2011: $1,571.52; 2012: $1,668.88; 2013: $1,411.23; 2014: $1,266.39; 2015: $1,160.08; 2016: $1,251.58; 2017: $1,258.64; 2018: $1,269.50; 2019: $1,392.60; 2020: 1,769.10; 2021: 1,801.00)

9

CAN WE PREDICT THE FUTURE PRICE OF GOLD?

Gold prices are fundamentally determined by the forces of supply and demand in the market under the current international monetary system. Demand for gold is complicated by speculative demand for gold, industrial demand for gold as well as demand for gold products (jewelry) by consumers. There are two decisive factors that further complicate the determination of gold prices. One is that central banks attempt to hold a certain amount of gold as part of official reserve assets. This is a demand factor that can affect the price of gold. Another factor that can affect the price of gold is the supply-side constraint that the below-ground stock of gold reserves is limited. According to one study, there are not many remaining gold reserves that can be mined.

Goldfinger (1964), one of the 007 movie sequels deals with a plot to blow villains who attempt to take a hit on the supply of gold to disturb the international monetary system. At that time, the gold standard was still not officially abolished, and thus the attempt to destroy the supply of gold was clearly a conspiracy that could have a devastating effect on the world monetary system. The U.S. government held approximately 4,500 tons of gold in Fort Knox, Kentucky. In the movie, Goldfinger plans to drop atomic bombs on Fort Knox to contaminate the facility with radioactivity. North Korea intervenes in this plot. North Korea, which attempts to disrupt the U.S. economy by making the dollar worthless, financially supports the operation of Goldfinger. If James Bond hadn't shattered Goldfinger's conspiracy, the gold price would have risen to the ceiling, and the value of the dollar would have fallen vertically, eventually leading the U.S. economy into an uncontrollable turmoil.

Central banks hold reserves to ensure the stability of their currencies and to defend their currencies against speculation in the event of a financial crisis. The official reserves mainly consist of gold and the U.S. dollar, the major reserve currency. Also, other foreign exchanges such as the euro, the British pound, and the Japanese yen are held as reserve assets. Recently, the Chinese yuan has emerged as an important reserve asset (currently ranked 6th). The U.S. dollar accounts for more than 60% of the world's reserve assets, followed by gold. Many countries in Asia mainly hold U.S. dollars as reserve assets, and gold accounts for a small portion of total reserves, whereas in the United States and many European countries, the proportion of gold is very high in their official reserve assets. The countries in which gold reserves account for more than 50% of their total reserve assets include Portugal (68.9%), the United States (66.3%), Germany (66.0%), Italy (62.9%), France (57.8%), and the Netherlands (55.4%). Countries with the proportion of gold being less than 10% in total reserve assets include South Korea (1.3%), Singapore (2.1%), China (3.3%), Japan (3.5%), and Taiwan (4.3%).

According to the World Gold Council, all the gold ever mined, which is accounted for, totaled 190,040 metric tons as of 2019. At a price of $1,826 per ounce reached at the end of 2022, the total value of all gold ever mined would reach $12.2 trillion. The world's official gold reserves held by central banks amount to 31,812 tons, and the total private holdings of gold are estimated to be 158,000 tons. More specifically, the U.S. holding of official gold reserves was the largest at 8,133.5 tons as of the end of 2022, followed by Germany (3,359.1 tons), IMF (2,814 tons), Italy (2,451.8 tons), France (2,436.4 tons). China held 1,054.1 tons of gold reserves as of August 2014, which ranked 9th in the world, but its holding of gold reserves increased to 1,948.3 tons as of December 2022, ascending to the 6th place among 100 countries surveyed. The United Kingdom holds a relatively small amount of gold reserves. The U.K. holding of gold reserves was 10.3 tons (17th).

What will happen to the price of gold in the future? The most important demand factor that could affect gold prices in the short run is the position of the Chinese central bank. Currently, China's gold reserves constitute only 3.3% of its total reserve assets but the Chinese central bank plans to increase the holding of gold in its official reserves. If the plan is pushed forward, the amount of gold that China will buy in the future will be substantial, and the impact of the Chinese demand on gold prices cannot be ignored.

Supply-side constraints are more significant. Not long ago, *Wall Street Journal* published an analytical article on how much of the Earth's existing resources are available. The stock of gold reserves that could be mined in the future is currently estimated to be roughly 50,000 metric tons, according to the U.S. Geological Survey, although estimates vary considerably. Thus, gold reserves under the ground are expected to eventually reach the bottom in the not-too-distant future. From this point of view, gold prices will continue to fluctuate up hill and down dale in the short run, but the gold price curve will continue to rise in the long run.

Many people are interested in whether there is an appropriate level of the gold price. In this regard, Harvey's forecasting model is suggestive: when the ratio of the gold price to the consumer price index (CPI) exceeds the long-term average ratio (3.4), the gold price tends to decrease, and when this ratio is below the long-term average ratio, the gold price tends to rise. The U.S. CPI was 292.7 in 2022, and the price of gold was $1,826 at the end 2022. Therefore, the Harvey ratio is about 6.3 (=1,826/292.7). This is well above the long-term average ratio of 3.4. The Harvey model thus predicts that the appropriate level of the gold price would be about $995.2 per ounce (= 3.4 x 292.7) at the end of 2022 and that the gold price will trend downward in the future. Given the recent trend in gold prices, however, the Harvey forecasting model may be out of date.

<Table 9.2> Gold Holdings of Major Countries in the World

Rank	Country	Official Holdings of Gold (in metric ton)		% of Gold in Reserve Assets (in %)
		12/2022	9/2017	12/2022
1	U.S.	8,133.5	8,133.5	66.3%
2	Germany	3,359.1	3,374.1	66.0%
3	Italy	2,451.8	2,314.0	62.9%
4	France	2,436.4	2,435.9	57.8%
5	Russia	2,298.5	1,729.4	21.4%
6	China	1,948.3	1,842.6	3.3%
7	Switzerland	1,040.0	1,040.0	5.6%
8	Japan	846.0	765.2	3.5%
9	India	785.4	743.8	6.9%
10	Netherlands	612.5	612.5	55.4%
11	Taiwan	423.6	423.6	4.3%
17	U.K.	310.3	310.3	9.3%
27	Singapore	153.7	127.4	2.1%
36	South Korea	104.4	104.4	1.3%
World's Official Gold Reserves (3/2022)		31,812		

Source: World Gold Council

PART 10

SHORT-RUN ECONOMIC FLUCTUATIONS: THE FOUR SEASONS OF THE ECONOMY

1

THE CURSE OF SKYSCRAPERS

The Great Depression of the United States came suddenly in October 1929. Coincidentally, New York's two tycoons, Walter Chrysler of Chrysler Motors and John Jacob Rascob of General Motors were competing at the time to see who could build a taller building. The Chrysler Building was completed in 1930. The Chrysler Building (height: 366 meters) was the tallest building in the world for 11 months before the Empire State Building was built in 1931. And the Empire State Building (height: 443 meters) enjoyed the world's tallest building status for 40 years, until the Twin Towers of the World Trade Center changed the New York skyline in 1970.

Ironically, however, at the time when the tallest buildings on the earth climbed higher, the U.S. economy crashed to the lowest place. From then on, the theory that the economy would go down when the tallest building in the world went up was developed. This phenomenon is often known as the 'curse of skyscrapers'. A country that built the tallest building in the world would take pride in saying "We have done it", and the building could be used as an emblem to symbolize its national power and pride. Nevertheless, what the curse of skyscrapers suggests is that as soon as a country that built the tallest building toasted its cup, the cup turned into a poisonous grail, and the country would be cursed economically.

The Asian financial crisis of 1998 swept through the Asian region when the tallest twin towers in the world, the Petronas Towers (452 meters high) was built in Malaysia. The Petronas Towers gained the title of the tallest building in the world from 1998 to 2004. The Petronas Towers yielded its number one position to the Burj Khalifa Building (height: 828 meters) in 2010. When the world's tallest building rose through Dubai's sky in 2010, the United Arab Emirates faced the worst recession it had ever experienced.

Is the 'curse of skyscrapers' a scientifically proven theory? Andrew Lawrence (1999) devised what is called the skyscraper index. According to him, the skyscraper index generally tends to peak at the peak of the business cycle. Mark Thornton (2005) , an expert in this area, sees the curse of skyscrapers as the result of the bursting of three elements of the bubble, which are usually present during the economic expansion phase. People try to challenge the tallest building because it is easy to get a loan, the prices of land are on the rise, and people's flatulence is also heightened. In other words, his theory is that the architecture of high-rise buildings is flared by triplets that can cause bubbles. The result is a bubble collapse.

<Figure 10.1> Burj Calif Building>

Based on this theory, Thornton (2005) predicted that the world economy would once again fall into a recession in 2013. The competition to build skyscrapers was hot in 2013: (1) In February 2013, the Shard, the tallest building in Europe (height: 309 meters) climbed to show off in London, the capital of the United Kingdom; (2) In May 2013, the One World Trade Center, the tallest building in the Western Hemisphere (height: 546 meters)

appeared in the site of the World Trade Center destroyed by the 9-11 incident; (3) In August 2013, the Shanghai Tower, the tallest building in China (height: 632 meters) emerged through the clouds of the Shanghai sky. However, despite the fierce competition of skyscrapers, the world economy, especially the U.S. economy, continued to grow strongly. The curse of the skyscraper did not happen.

Jason Barr, Bruce Mizrach, and Kusum Mundra (2015) investigated the correlation between the start and completion of the world's tallest building and the peak and bottom of the U.S. economic fluctuation. They found that no statistical relationship existed between these two time series data.

This fact suggests that the curse of skyscrapers should be viewed as coincidence rather than a proven theory. In other words, there is no statistically significant relationship between the two variables. The relationship between economic variables can be divided into causality, functional relationship, correlation, sequential relationship, and coincidence according to their intensity. First, consider the functional relationship. Looking at the relationship between income and consumption, many studies have revealed that as income increases, consumption increases, and *vice versa*. In this case, we say that consumption depends on income, or consumption is a positive function of income. This relationship is called a functional relationship. Recently, several studies such as Stevens et al. (2021) have shown that drinking three or four cups of coffee a day significantly reduces heart attack. This relationship is also a functional relationship.

A stronger relationship than a functional relationship is a causal relationship. Causality can be defined in many ways, but in a nutshell, causality means that one variable is the cause of another. Granger's definition of causality has been widely used, which states that variable X (money) causes Y (inflation), if using the past history of X (money) could explain Y (inflation) better than using the past history Y (inflation) alone. The fact that prices rise when more money is supplied may indicate a functional relationship, but many studies show that the relationship between money and inflation is stronger than a functional relationship. In fact, the relationship between money and inflation is a causal relation. We observe that if there is a lot of snow, traffic accidents increase. The relationship between snow falling and traffic accidents is a causal relation.

A correlation relationship measures whether two variables (e.g. height and golf skills) move in the same direction or in the opposite direction, but it does not tell whether one variable (height) affects another variable (golf skill). If you are tall, you could play golf well, but this observation only shows that the two variables move in the same direction. In this case, we cannot say that good golf skills depend on height. Thus, there is simply a correlation between the two variables.

A lead-and-lag, or sequential, relationship means that the movement of one variable accidentally precedes the movement of another variable. The fact that when yellow leaves fall to the ground, winter is coming is a lead-and-lag relationship. Fallen leaves do not bring about winter. The observation that the economy improves about several months after the stock market turns into a bull market is also a lead-and-lag relationship. Finally, if the two variables move together but there is no statistically significant relationship between them, this is a coincidence. In the United States, stock prices sometimes flash during the summer heat wave (called 'summer rally'), but many studies indicate that there is no relationship between the summer heat wave and the rise in stock prices. The relationship between the two variables is simply a coincidence.

Economists often use probabilistic reasoning to better understand the relationship between economic variables. For example, in the process of analyzing the effect of interest rate changes on stock prices, if we find that as interest rates change 100 times, the stock price responds 90, 95, or 99 times, we can conclude that there is a very strong relationship between interest rates and stock prices. However, if the stock price responds only 40 or 50 times when interest rates change 100 times, it is difficult to draw a definitive conclusion as to whether there is a statistically significant relationship between interest rates and stock prices. In this case, we do not claim that a reliable or significant relationship between interest rates and stock prices exists.

The level of probability that economists accept as a statistically reliable level is the occurrence of at least 90 times out of 100 trials. The more commonly used probability frequency is around 95 times out of 100 trials. In this case, we say that the relationship between interest rates and stock prices is statistically significant at the 5 percent level, and we can conclude that interest rates significantly affect stock prices. A significant level of 5 percent means that there is only a 5 percent chance that the conclusion that "interest rates will affect stock prices" is wrong.

From this point of view, one can imagine that the relationship between a rise in skyscrapers and a recession will be observed much less frequently than 90% of the time. We can conclude that such a relationship is not statistically significant. Thus, economic fluctuations are unlikely to be caused by the boom and bust of skyscrapers. Like the four seasons of nature, there are four seasons of the economy. The economy also repeats the cycle of economic expansion-peak-economic contraction-trough, just like nature's cycle.

Written by Jacques Prevert and composed by Joseph Kosma, *Les Feuilles Mortes* (Dead Leaves) was made for *Le Rendez-Vous*, a ballet performance by Leland Petit that premiered in 1945. The poem is filled with the burning sun in the middle of summer, then dried leaves, and the pathetic of life. It is an inevitable phenomenon that the economy burns like red lips last summer and then goes through the process of sliding into recession as dead leaves falling to the ground on an autumn day.

Oh, I would like you so much to remember
Those happy days when we were friends, and how
Life in those times was more lovely and tender,
Even the sun shone more brightly than now.
Dead leaves are gathering as in December
You see how one never forgets…
Dead leaves are gathering as in December,
Just like the memories and the regrets.
And then the north wind comes and sweeps them
Into oblivion's icy night.
You see how I never forgot
That old song that you sang for me.
A song like us, birds of a feather,
You loving me, me loving you,
And we lived happily together,
Me loving you, you loving me.
But life tears apart gentle lovers
Who quietly obey their heart,
And the sea invades the sand and covers
The footsteps of those torn apart.

<*Les Feuilles Mortes*> (<Dead Leaves>) was later reborn as a *chanson*. In 1946 Yves Montand sang 'Dead Leaves' in the movie <*Les Portes de la Nuit*>, which showed the sublime of sweetness. Later it was translated into English, <Autumn Leaves> which was well-known for the song of Edith Piaf. It was also sung by Frank Sinatra and Nat King Cole.

The falling leaves drift by the window,
The autumn leaves of red and gold,
I see your lips the summer kisses,
The sunburned hands I used to hold,
Since you went away the days grow long…
And soon I'll hear old winter's song,
But I miss you most of all, my darling,
When autumn leaves start to fall…

2

CHARACTERISTICS OF A BUSINESS CYCLE

The economy does not stand still like the water in a lake. It is like the water flowing along a river. Sometimes the flow of water becomes rapid and sometimes becomes slow, but the river continues to flow. Similarly, the economy continues to grow in the long run, although it goes through ups and downs in the short run. As the economy grows over the long run, our living standards and economic well-being also improve.

A business cycle is a phenomenon in which real GDP and employment expand or contract over time. Economists divide the economic cycle into four phases: economic expansion, peak, economic contraction, and trough. An economic expansion refers to a phenomenon in which real GDP continues to increase, and an economic contraction refers to a phenomenon in which real GDP continues to decrease. The phase at which the economy reaches the peak of expansion is called the peak, and the phase at which the economy reaches the bottom of contraction is called the trough.

Economists also distinguish between a recession and a depression. A recession refers to a contraction phase in which real GDP continues to decline for two consecutive quarters or more. On the other hand, a depression is much more severe than a recession in the depth and duration of the contraction phase. There is no official definition of depression. An example of the depression is the Great Depression, which devastated the economies of the United States and Europe in the 1930s. This occurred in 1929 and lasted for more than 10 years. An example of the recession is the Great Recession, which hit the world economy in 2008, but it lasted only for one year and six months. Economists often distinguish between a recession and a depression by making the following joke: If your neighbor is unemployed, it's a recession. If you are unemployed, it's a depression.

The phases of economic expansion and contraction usually exhibit some characteristic patterns. One of the important features of the business cycle is that noticeable characteristic movements are detected in macroeconomic variables before the economy begins to enter an expansion phase or a contraction phase, as if any signs such as a humid and sultry weather showed up in advance before the rainy season come. When an economic variable tends to move ahead of its overall economic activity, such an economic variable is called a leading economic indicator. Therefore, by looking at the movement of leading economic indicators, we can predict the expansion and contraction phases of the business cycle to some extent.

However, there are economic variables that move simultaneously with the business cycle, and some economic variables fluctuate following the business cycle with some time lag. When an economic variable moves almost simultaneously with the business cycle, such an economic variable is called a coincident economic variable. When an economic variable moves lagging behind the business cycle, such an economic variable is called a lagging economic variable. The following variables are examples of some important leading economic variables.

- Consumers' purchases of durable goods (automobiles, home appliances, washing machines, furniture, etc.) are drastically reduced, and the inventory of these products is significantly increased. This is a typical sign of the upcoming recession. In this case, firms that produce durable goods try to cut production to reduce inventories. If the reduction in production spreads to other firms and other industries, the recession is in full swing with aggregate output falling and unemployment increasing.
- The demand for labor falls sharply. At first, working hours are reduced, and then later, layoffs increase. and eventually unemployment increases.
- Inflation slows down due to a stagnation in production activities and a decrease in consumption expenditures. Wages tend to decrease due to an increase in the unemployment rate. However, such a decrease in the price level or wages progresses more slowly than the contraction of production activity.
- Corporate profits drop significantly. As corporate profits are expected to decrease, stock prices fall. Also, the demand for funds decreases, leading to a drop in interest rates overall.

The direction as well as the timing of the movement of the leading economic indicators provide important information for understanding economic fluctuations. Some variables move in the same direction as the overall economic activity, while others move in the opposite direction. When an economic variable moves in the same direction as the overall economic trend, such an economic variable is called a 'pro-cyclical variable'. When an economic variable moves in the opposite direction to the overall economic trend, such an economic variable is called a 'counter-cyclical variable'. When an economic variable moves regardless of the overall economic trend, it is called an 'acyclical' variable.

A typical pro-cyclical variable is consumption. When the economy slows down, consumption decreases, and when the economy expands, consumption increases. A typical counter-cyclical variable is the unemployment rate. When the economy slows down, the unemployment rate rises, and when the economy expands, the unemployment rate falls. Most macroeconomic variables tend to move in the same direction as the overall economic activity, and thus can be viewed as pro-cyclical.

3

THE PATTERN OF THE BUSINESS CYCLE HAS BEEN CHANGING

The business cycle is the process in which the economy begins to enter the expansion phase followed by the peak and then enters the contraction phase followed by the trough. These four phases form one business cycle. In the past, economic theories viewed the business cycle as a repetitive pattern of the ups and downs of economic activity over a certain period of time, and much attention was paid to identifying the cause of such a pattern. According to these views, the business cycle is regarded as a wave characterized by a regular pattern. Following the names of the discoverers, the Kitchin cycle, Juglar cycle, Kuznetz cycle, and Kondratieff cycle were recognized as typical business cycle patterns. The Kitchin cycle is the shortest cycle, ranging from about three to five years from one peak to the next. The Kitchin cycle is sometimes called the inventory cycle because an increase or a decrease in inventory is considered to be the cause of the cycle.

The Juglar cycle is a medium-run business cycle with a period of 7 to 10 years from the peak to the next peak. The Kuznets cycle is a long-term wave of 15 to 25 years, and the Kondratieff cycle is known as the longest cycle, lasting about 30 to 50 years. The Kondratieff cycle is a business cycle caused by the influence of certain technological breakthroughs such as the invention of electricity, trains and aircraft, computers and the Internet, smartphones, and AI (artificial intelligence). These technological innovations are seen as a driving force for the long-term economic expansion of about 30 to 50 years.

However, in recent years, few economists believe that the economy repeats a cycle at regular intervals. If we look at the patterns of past economic fluctuations of major developed countries, it is difficult to presume that the business cycle is repeated like a wave at regular intervals. In this regard, the term 'economic fluctuations' may be more appropriate than the term 'business cycles'.

This is even more evident when looking at the pattern of economic fluctuations in the United States. The United States has been tracking business cycles developed in the United States over the past 170 years from 1854 to 2020 and has accumulated abundant statistical data on economic fluctuations. During this period, the U.S. economy experienced a total of 34 business cycles including the COVID recession in 2020. A prominent feature of recent business cycles in the United States is that the depth of economic fluctuations after World War II has become less severe than before World War II. This phenomenon is not limited to the U.S. economy but is confirmed in other countries. Looking at the U.S. economy, before the Great Depression, real output (real GDP) increased by an annual average of 5% from the long-term trend line during the economic expansion phase, while it fell by an annual average of 6% during the economic contraction phase. However, after World War II, the magnitude of fluctuations in the business cycle decreased by almost half. Real GDP increased by an annual average of 2.5% during the economic expansion period and fell by an annual average of 3% during the economic contraction period. The fluctuations in the U.S. business cycle were cut in half. (These numbers exclude the business cycles that occurred during the Great Depression and World War II because they were outliers.)

Another feature of the U.S. business cycle is that there is clear evidence that the duration of economic expansion has become longer while the duration of economic expansion has become shorter. Looking more closely at the average duration of the 33 business cycles in the United States, the contraction duration averaged 16 months, and the expansion duration averaged 42 months. The average duration of contraction from 1919 to 1945 (6 business cycles) was 18 months and the average duration of expansion was 35 months. This pattern has changed significantly since World War II. The average duration of contraction has been shortened to 11 months, and the average duration of expansion has been increased to 59 months.

<Table 10.1> Durations of U.S. Business Cycles

Business Cycles	Contraction Duration	Expansion Duration
1854 ~ 1919 (16 business cycles)	22	27
1919 ~ 1945 (6 business cycles)	18	35
1945 ~ 2014 (11 business cycles)	11	59

The phenomenon that the depth of economic fluctuations has been lessened, and the duration of economic expansion has been prolonged is almost common in many countries, although there are some differences among countries in the depth and duration of the business cycle. We can find some explanations for the phenomenon from two different perspectives. One view attributes the pattern to Keynesian economics. After the Great Depression, there was a widespread sentiment that each country's self-regulating economy could not solve economic problems, especially recession issues. Keynesian economics had profound influences on policymaking around the world, providing policymakers with a theoretical weapon to implement active government policies to prevent the next recession.

There is another view that gives some credit to the working of classical economics. From the late 1970s, neoliberalism became synonymous with deregulation and liberalization, further strengthening the self-regulating forces of the economy. Some point out that the deregulation and liberalization of the economy have contributed to reducing the extent of economic fluctuations and extending the duration of economic expansion, as Keynesian recipes did in the 1960s and 1970s. For example, the U.S. economy continued to grow smoothly after escaping from the 2008 global economic crisis until the COVID-19 crisis in 2020. Some might have a synthetic view that Keynesian prescriptions combined with the market's strengthened self-correcting function provided a foothold to recover from the global economic crisis, and since then, the U.S. economy have shown strong economic resilience compared with other countries.

4

THE INFLATIONARY GAP AND THE RECESSIONARY GAP

When the economy is in an expansion phase, a virtuous cycle occurs. Firms increase investment and production because people want to buy more goods and services. During an economic expansion period, workers' productivity tends to increase, and thus their real wages increase. As real wages increase, household income increases, and households purchase more goods and services. Business firms will hire more workers and produce more. As a result, during a period of economic expansion, a country's output (real GDP) reaches the maximum level (potential GDP) that the country can produce without stimulating inflation. However, when the economy puts the pedal to the metal further, it sometimes produces more than its potential GDP. The difference between actual GDP and potential GDP is often called the inflationary gap. When there is an inflationary gap, this is a warning sign that inflation will be forthcoming.

$$\text{Inflationary gap} = \text{Actual real GDP} - \text{Potential real GDP}$$

The reason why the gap is called an inflationary gap is that pressure on productive resources arises when the country's actual output is greater than its potential output. Firms need to hire more workers to increase production, which inevitably leads to higher wages. In addition, capital such as factories, machines and equipment must be fully utilized, which requires further investment. This will lead to an increase in inflation. Thus, if a country's economy continues to produce more than its potential output, there is an unpleasant phenomenon of higher inflation caused by the overloading of the economy. For this reason, the difference between actual GDP and potential GDP is called the inflation gap. The inflationary gap is an extraordinary phenomenon, and the inflation gap cannot last long.

<Figure 10.2> The Inflationary Gap

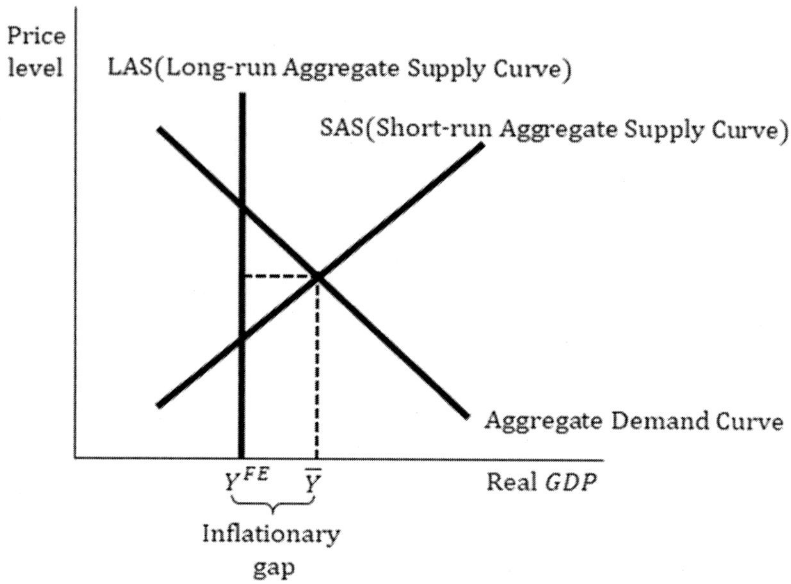

There are two reasons why firms increase their production capacity during the economic expansion phase. The first reason is that produce more goods and services beyond their production capacity to meet high demand for their products. Second, if the economy continues to expand, inflation increases, and real wages paid by firms will fall. In other words, firms can hire workers at a lower cost and thus reduce production costs. This conclusion is closer to the Keynesian view because in the classical world, nominal wages will promptly rise in response to higher inflation.

When a country's economy enters a contraction phase, the economy falls into a vicious circle as opposed to a virtuous cycle during an expansion phase. First, firms reduce production because the goods and services they produce are not selling well. In a country where the labor market is flexible, firms take steps to lay off less productive workers, because some products remain unsold. As a result, unemployment increases. An increase in unemployment inevitably reduces household real income, and consumers will reduce their consumption. When consumption decreases, firms are forced to further reduce production and lay off workers.

Thus, when the economy enters a recession, actual output will fall below the maximum level of output (potential output) that the economy can produce without inflation. The difference between potential real GDP and actual real GDP is called the recessionary gap.

$$\text{Recessionary gap} = \text{Potential real GDP} - \text{Actual real GDP}$$

When the recessionary gap deepens, prices, wages, and interest rates all fall. A recessionary gap is a warning sign that unemployment will rise.

<Figure 10.3> The Recessionary Gap

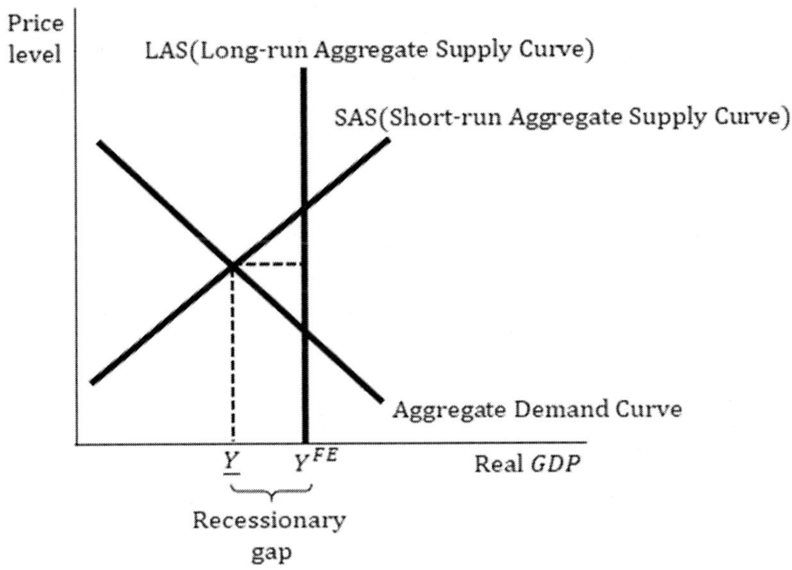

When a country experiences an inflationary gap or a recessionary gap, it means that the economy deviates from its normal trend. There is a big difference between classical theory and Keynesian theory with regards to how to solve the inflationary and recessionary gaps. Classical economists argue that it is best to let the economy take care of the inflationary or recessionary gap. The government's task is to help the market function smoothly. Classical economists support strengthening regulations that promote market competition and favor reducing regulations that hinder the

More specifically, if an inflationary gap occurs, nominal wages rise by the inflation rate if the labor market is flexible enough. As a result, real wages, which fell due to rising inflation, begin to rise again and return to the original level. Therefore, less competitive firms will leave the market. Even if firms are competitive, they will reduce production because profits will decrease due to higher production costs associated with higher real wages. Thus, the aggregate supply curve will shift to the left. This adjustment process continues until actual GDP falls to the level of potential GDP. Through the process of market adjustments, actual output falls to the level of potential output, and the inflationary gap is finally eliminated.

The opposite happens when a recessionary gap occurs. If the labor market is flexible, nominal wages will fall. Through the market adjustments, firms will hire more workers and increase production. The aggregate supply curve will shift to the right. The market's self-correcting process will continue until actual GDP rises to the level of potential GDP, and the recessionary gap is eliminated accordingly.

However, Keynesian economists are skeptical of the effectiveness of the classical prescriptions. They argue that the market is not functioning properly because wages and prices are not flexible enough to ensure the self-regulating function of the market. This is especially true when the economy deviates from its normal state. Even if the market is working properly, it takes too long for the market to eliminate the inflationary gap or the recessionary gap. Eventually, the government should intervene in the market to solve the inflationary or recessionary gap. First, if the inflationary gap occurs, the economy speeds up at full gallop, so it is necessary to cool down the economy. The economy is overheated because of strong aggregate demand, and thus policymakers should take measures to reduce aggregate demand using restrictive aggregate demand policy. Such policy includes raising interest rates and reducing government expenditures. In some cases, it might be necessary to put a break on it by raising the income tax rate or the consumption tax rate, if the inflationary gap is persistent.

The recessionary gap is caused by a lack of aggregate demand. When the recessionary gap persists, this is a signal that a recession is on the horizon, and unemployment will get worse. If wages and prices are rigid, then the market mechanism is not able to self-correct the recessionary gap. Hence, Keynesian economists suggest that the government should take steps to boost aggregate demand to eliminate the recessionary gap. Policymakers can stimulate aggregate demand by lowering interest rates or increasing government expenditures. In some cases, it might be desirable to stimulate the economy by lowering the income tax rate or the consumption tax rate.

5

WHY DOES THE ECONOMY HAVE A CYCLE? THE MULTIPLIER-ACCELERATOR MODEL

The classical school and the Keynesian school have fundamentally different positions regarding the causes of economic fluctuations. Classical economists see economic fluctuations as temporary and short-term phenomena that occur as the economy is re-equilibrated from one equilibrium position to another. When the economy temporarily overheats, the demand for labor, goods and services, and money increases, which in turn increases wages, prices, and interest rates. When wages rise, firms reduce employment; when prices rise, consumers reduce consumption, and when interest rates rise, firms reduce investment. The economy will experience a temporary contraction during this adjustment period.

Economists like Wesley Mitchell, for example, describe the business cycle as a phenomenon that comes from constraints on the production capacity and workforce. As the economy expands to the peak of a cycle, firms are almost exhausted of their production capacity and workforce and face a difficult situation to find additional labor and capital. This strong demand combined with constraints on the supply of labor and capital eventually lead to an overall increase in wages, interest rates and prices. If the rate of change of wages exceeds the rate of inflation, firms' profits decrease, and firms reduce employment and production. As a consequence, the economy enters a recession. This view indicates that the overheating of the economy fanned wage increases, leading to a recession. Today, this view is criticized for oversimplifying the causes of economic fluctuations.

Keynesian economists are more concerned with the causes of economic fluctuations than classical economists. This is because classical economists tend to emphasize the self-regulating forces of the economy, which eventually lead the economy to an equilibrium state as quickly as possible. In contrast, Keynesian economists admit that fluctuations in economic activity can be large and longer. At the same time, they support the government's active intervention to reduce the extent of economic fluctuations and to shorten the period of economic fluctuations. Keynesian theorists try to find the cause of economic fluctuations in changing aggregate demand. Variations in aggregate demand are caused by two factors. One is the rigidity of wages and prices, and the other is uncertainty about the future state of the economy. The representative model for explaining a business cycle from a Keynesian perspective is Samuelson's multiplier-accelerator model. Samuelson developed a theory on business cycles by combining Keynes' multiplier theory with the accelerator model of investment.

The multiplier effect refers to a phenomenon in which an increase in aggregate expenditure such as investment leads to an even greater increase in national income (or GDP). On the other hand, the accelerator principle refers to a phenomenon in which a change in income results in an increase in investment. By combining these two principles, one can show that there will be an explosive increase or decrease in national income triggered by a change in investment. Suppose that a firm plans to increase its production capacity. In the multiplier-accelerator model, when the demand for investment by firms increases, income increases through the multiplier effect. When income increases, the firm expects a higher demand for its products and plans to increase its target capital stock further according to the acceleration principle. In order to achieve the target capital, the firm needs to increase its investment. This increase in investment again induces a multiplier effect, which leads to an increase in income. This multiplier-acceleration interaction continues until income reaches the maximum level (potential GDP) that the economy can achieve.

If income starts to decrease after real income reaches its maximum level, the firm will reduce investment (reverse effect of the accelerator principle) because the target capital now exceeds the needed capital. The decrease in investment further reduces the national income (reverse effect of the multiplier). This reverse interaction of the multiplier and the accelerator explains why the economy repeats its expansion and contraction phases. Since the multiplier-accelerator coefficient could be large, a small downturn in investment could bring about a big decrease in GDP or a small upturn in investment could induce a large increase in GDP.

The multiplier-accelerator model also emphasizes that economic policy can be useful to avoid rapid economic fluctuations. When the economy is in recession, aggregate demand policy such as increased fiscal expenditures or reduced taxes seem to be ideal for maximizing the multiplier-accelerator interactions. If the government takes a policy to boost aggregate demand in the private sector through spending increases or tax cuts, aggregate output will start to increase through the multiplier effect. This increase in aggregate output increases investment demand through the principle of accelerator. In turn, the increased investment demand further increases income through the multiplier effect. In this way, the recovery of the economy can proceed smoothly and quickly with the aid of government intervention.

The position of the classical school on economic fluctuations is in stark contrast to that of the Keynesian model. In the classical system, an economic fluctuation is a temporary deviation from the long-run equilibrium path. Since such an adjustment toward the equilibrium path is transitory in nature, the government does not have to do anything to correct the economic fluctuation. There are two representative explanations of economic fluctuations from the classical perspective. Friedman's monetarism and Lucas' rational expectations theory. Their views fundamentally see economic fluctuations as the result of economic agents' misperception of information on prices in the market. Monetarists and rational expectations theorists view a change in the money supply as a culprit of a business cycle. A change in the money supply induces inflation, and a business cycle occurs in the process of predicting the inflation rate by economic agents because they make a systematic (monetarism) or random (rational expectations theory) error in incorporating the expected inflation into their economic behavior.

Monetarists believe monetary policy has a major impact on the economy, but do not think that it contributes to stabilizing the economy. On the contrary, they argue that capricious changes in the money supply amplify economic fluctuations. They believe that economic fluctuations are caused by discretionary and irregular changes in the amount of money. A change in the money supply has no effect on real output and employment in the long run, but in the short term it is regarded as a major source of instability of the economy, causing inflation. This happens temporarily because in the short run, economic agents make systematic errors in predicting the future price level.

However, Lucas goes further. Since Lucas' theory assumes that economic agents have rational expectations, any misperception on inflation rarely occurs. In his model, information errors are random errors and occur exceptionally. Thus, economic fluctuations occur exceptionally when policymakers implement policy in such a way that it fools economic agents. This is why his theory is sometimes called fooling theory. Lucas' new classical theory (theory of rational expectations) basically takes the same position as the monetarist's misperception theory but is more radical than that of the monetarist and more skeptical about the effectiveness of monetary policy as a tool for reducing economic fluctuations than the monetarist.

Lucas' business cycle theory seeks to find the cause of a business cycle from the fact that producers confuse a change in the general price level with a change in the relative prices of the products they produce. If producers mistake a change in the general price level (i.e., CPI) as a change in the relative price of their products, they will hire more workers and produce more to take advantage of higher prices of their products. As a result, the economy is temporarily booming. However, this kind of error occurs because of incomplete information, and hence the confusion by producers cannot last long. As more information arrives in the market, they soon realize that their perception is wrong, and the economy soon returns to the normal situation.

Thus, advocates of new classical economics predict that if economic agents form expectations rationally when making economic decisions, a business cycle will not occur, or it will be short-lived if it occurs. However, the new classical school has been criticized for being unable to explain economic fluctuations that are large and long-lasting. In other words, the new classical school cannot explain the economic fluctuations that last for months to years. The misperception of information is only a few weeks to a few months at most. For example, data on the supply of money are available in one week, and data on the price level is released every month. If so, it means that the misperception and confusion of economic agents will not exceed several weeks, and therefore, the impact of a change in the money supply on the real economy based on such misperception will not last for several weeks.

Especially in the information technology (IT) age, the misperception of information is bound to be very short run. It is no wonder that there has been some criticism that the theory of misperception cannot explain economic fluctuations that last much longer than several weeks. Another problem with the classical explanation of business cycles is that it cannot explain economic fluctuations caused by the supply shock.

Some of the explanations that came out to complement the weaknesses of the classical business cycle theory include shock propagation theory and real business cycle (RBC) theory. Propagation theory was proposed to explain how a transient (or small) impact has a relatively long-lasting (or large) impact on the economy. Classical theorists emphasize shock propagation to explain how changes in the money supply can lead to economic fluctuations that persist for months to years. Shock propagation means that a temporary (or small) shock has a relatively long-term (or large) effect on the economy.

A technological shock in the real business cycle (RBC) theory is one such example of shock propagation. RBC theory believes that in the event of a technological shock, the potential production capacity itself is affected, resulting in a short-term fluctuation in potential GDP, and accordingly actual GDP also fluctuates. Technological shocks affecting the potential production capacity include new production technologies (Ford's conveyor system, Toyota method), new inventions (computers, cell phones, the Internet and artificial intelligence), natural disasters (tsunami sweeping, COVID-19), and the discovery of new resources (shale oil and shale gas). The World Bank warned in August 2022 that "a very small shock could plumet the world economy into the spiral of recession", which seems to echo the theory of propagation.

PART 11

LONG-RUN ECONOMIC GROWTH: A DANCE MARATHON

1

Economic Growth and Living Standards: Australia Was the Richest Country 150 Years Ago

The goal of a country's economic policy is to improve the standard of living so that all members of society can enjoy an affluent life. The improvement of living standards in a country is made possible by long-term economic growth. We'll take the example of Japan and Australia to see how much economic growth makes difference in improving living standards.

According to a study by Angus Maddison (2004), in 1870 Australia's real income per capita was more than 5.5 times higher than that of Japan. In 1870, Australia was the richest country in the world, and Japan was one of the poorest countries. However, Australia's real income per capita increased by 1.1% per year over the next 110 years, and Australia's real income per capita in 1979 was 3.2 times larger compared with 1870. On the other hand, real income per capita in Japan increased by 2.7% per year from 1870 to 1979, and Japan's real income per capita in 1979 was 17.7 times bigger compared with 1870.

Japan's annual income growth rate of 2.7% does not seem to be that much different than Australia's annual growth rate of 1.1%, but after a century a small difference in the rate of economic growth made a big difference in the standard of living between the two countries. Japan's real income per capita reached the same level as Australia by 1979, and since then Japan has taken a lead over Australia in terms of income per capita. Japan, at one time, reached almost the level of U.S. income per capita and has now become one of the richest countries in the world.

The difference in the rate of economic growth is important enough to significantly change the standard of living even in the course of only one generation. The so-called Asian Tigers, South Korea, Taiwan, Singapore, and Hong Kong were among the poorest countries in the 1960s. However, there was a sea change in the standard of living in these countries over the past several decades, and by the late 1970s, they became the Newly Industrialized Countries (NICs). Countries like China, Thailand, Indonesia, Malaysia and Vietnam are now closely following the four Tigers' footsteps.

It is the magic of compound interest in economic growth that transforms a small difference in the rate of economic growth into a large difference in income per capita. The growth of a variable by compound interest means multiplicative growth, that is, geometric growth. The present value (P) of future income (F) that you'll receive n years from today is given by P = $F/(1+i)^n$, where n is the number of years, and i is the annual growth rate of income. From this PV formula, we can derive the future value (F) of income n years from today as follows: $F = P(1+i)^n$. Then income per capita 100 years from today becomes:

$$\text{Income per capita 100 years from today} \\ = (\text{Today's income per capita}) \times (1 + \text{Growth rate})^{100}$$

This kind of geometric growth occurs because last year's economic growth adds up to this year's growth rate, and this year's economic growth adds up to next year's growth rate, and so on. We can also derive the '72 rule' from the PV formula and interpret the compound interest magic using the '72 rule'. According to the '72 rule,' dividing the number 72 by the annual growth rate (percentage) gives us the number of years during which the size of a variable (say, income per capita) is doubled.

Thus, the '72 rule' gives us a different flash of comparison. Let's apply the '72 rule' to the Australian and Japanese episodes. If Australia's real income per capita continues to grow at the annual rate of 1.1%, it would take 65.5 years (72/1.1 = 65.5) for Australia's real income per capita to double. On the other hand, if Japan's real income per capita continues to grow at the annual rate of 2.7%, it would take 26.7 years (72/2.7 = 26.7) for Japan's real income per capita to double.

Before the Asian financial crisis in 1997, the South Korean economy grew at the average growth rate of about 8% a year for 30 years. If this growth trend continues, it will take approximately 72/8 = 9 years for South Korea's GDP to double its size. However, the growth rate of the South Korean economy fell almost by half (4%) beginning the mid-1990s. If the South Korean economy continues to grow at the rate of 4.0% per year, it will take about 72/4 = 18 years for its GDP to double. On the other hand, China has enjoyed an average annual growth rate of 10% over the past 30 years since it opened its economy in 1978. This means that the Chinese economy has doubled every seven years. Meanwhile, the average growth rate in the United States over the past century has been around 3.3%. If the

US economy continues to grow at the rate of 3.3% per year in the future, it will take about 22 years for the U.S. economy to double.

No one has a complete answer as to why an economy is growing, why the rate of economic growth is different across countries, and why the rate of economic growth varies over time in a country. Moreover, no one knows the recipes for high economic growth. However, economists have accumulated a considerable amount of knowledge on the sources of economic growth and the driving forces of economic growth, and thus, our understanding of long-term economic growth has now become richer.

2

ASCENSION OF THE ASIAN DRAGONS

This chapter is designed to review how Asia's Four Dragons or Tigers (South Korea, Taiwan, Singapore, and Hong Kong) ascended from the ground to the sky within a short period of time. The Four Dragons were newly independent countries after WWII. They were at the fledgling stage of development in the early 1960s when they were about to take off. They only scratched the surface of economic development at that time. We'll trace their ascension from a barren and poor land to the land of opportunity and blessing by comparing their GDP per capita. Nominal GDP refers to the value of aggregate output which is measured at the current prices of goods and services. Nominal GDP per capita is obtained by dividing the nominal GDP of a country by the number of people in that country. For the purpose of international comparison, we need to convert each country's GDP denominated in local currency into the U.S. dollar amount. Here are statistics on GDP per capita in the Four Dragons as well as in the United States and Japan. (The table for historical data on nominal GDP per capita in the Four Dragons is provided at the end this chapter.)

- In 1960, South Korea's GDP per capita was $155, making it the most lagging of the four Dragons as well as Japan. Japan was so far ahead that South Korea had to look at the success of Japan out of envy. Nominal GDP per capita in 1960 was $479 in Japan, $429 in Hong Kong and $395 in Singapore.
- South Korea, which started out as a latecomer, stepped back for a short time with the military coup that broke out in 1961. South Korea's GDP per capita declined to $92 in 1961 and stayed at $106 in 1965 when the Korea-Japan Claims Agreement ("Agreement on the Settlement of Problems concerning Properties and Claims and the Economic Cooperation") was signed. Then, in 1967, when the funds based on the Agreement began to flow in, South Korea's income per capita returned to the level of 1960 at $157, after which Korea's income per capita continued to grow steadily.

- Of the four Dragons and Japan, Japan became the first country to join the '1,000-dollar income' club. Japan ($1,059) achieved $1,000 income per capita in 1966. Subsequently, Singapore ($1,074) and Hong Kong ($1,102) reached the 1,000-dollar income level in 1971, respectively. South Korea ($1,042) reached the goal of $1,000 income per capita in 1977.
- From this point on, the race for economic growth among the four Dragons and Japan and began in earnest. These countries started to run towards the $10,000 goal. Japan ($10,218) arrived first at the '$10,000 income line' in 1981. Hong Kong ($10,667) arrived at the finish line in 1988, and Singapore ($10,711) in 1989. Taiwan ($10,573) reached the $10,000 finish line in 1992, and South Korea ($10,275) in 1994.
- In 1994, when South Korea achieved $10,000 income per capita, Japan's income per capita reached $38,759, and in the following year (1995), it climbed to the plateau of $42,516, which was even greater than U.S. income per capita in 1995 and Japan's 2021 income per capita ($39,340). (Japan's income per capita already exceeded U.S. income per capita in 1987.) It was the year when the sun rose highest over the Japanese sky, and it was also the year when the sun began to eclipse. This was the beginning of Japan's 'Lost 20 Years'. This sudden collapse of the Japanese economy was, of course, partly due to the 1995 Plaza Agreement, which brought the sharp drop in the yen's exchange rate against the U.S. dollar. A lower exchange rate of the Japanese yen means a stronger yen, which hurts the competitiveness of Japanese exports in the international marketplace. The eruptive increase in the Japanese income per capita was also partly due to the sharp drop in the yen's exchange rate.
- Singapore has outpaced Japan in per capita income since 2007. In 2007, Singapore's income per capita was $39,224, whereas Japan's income per capita was $34,038. Singapore's income per capita finally began to overtake that of the United States in 2011. In 2011, Singapore's income per capita was $52,871 while U.S. income per capita was $49,746. In 2013, Hong Kong also began to outpace Japan. Hong Kong's income per capita was $37,955 while Japan's income per capita was $37,540. Nobody in the early 1960s imagined that Singapore would catch up with the United States at the income level.
- The race between South Korea and Taiwan has been tossed about over the past several decades. South Korea was running unceasingly in the race for economic growth, finally surpassing Taiwan in income per capita in 2003. However, South Korea was surpassed

again by Taiwan in 2022 in the race. The race scores among the Four Dragons and Japan in terms of income per capita as of 2022 are as follows: (1) Singapore: $82,808; (2) Hong Kong: $49,845; (3) Japan: $33,822; (4) Taiwan: $32,643; (4) South Korea: $32,250. Singapore has been leading Japan, Taiwan, and South Korea almost by a double score, and the United States ($76,348) by a big margin in the race of economic growth.

<Table 11.1> Historical Data on Nominal GDP Per Capita in the Four Tigers (in U.S. dollars)

Year	U.S.A.	Japan	South Korea	Taiwan	Singapore	Hong Kong
1960	2,881	479	155		395	429
1965	3,665	920	106		516	678
1970	4,998	1,974	279		925	963
1975	7,517	4,514	608		2,557	2,251
1980	12,576	9,313	1,778	2,363	5,004	5,781
1985	18,232	11,464	2,542	3,271	6,782	6,557
1990	23,914	25,140	6,642	8,086	12,766	13,569
1995	28,763	42,516	12,404	12,865	24,937	23,350
2000	36,433	37,304	11,948	14,641	23,793	25,578
2005	44,218	35,781	18,658	16,023	29,870	26,554
2010	48,314	42,917	22,151	18,488	46,570	32,421
2015	56,730	35,006	28,737	22,753	55,646	42,325
2020	63,577	40,118	31,728	28,571	61,274	46,446
2021	70,160	39,883	34,998	33,186	77,710	49,845
2022	76,348	33,822	32,250	32,643	82,808	49,226

Note: The data from 1960 to 1979 are from the World Bank, and the data from 1980 to 2022 are from the IMF ("List of Countries by Past and Projected GDP (Nominal) Per Capita".)

3

TECHNOLOGICAL PROGRESS IS THE SOURCE OF LONG-TERM ECONOMIC GROWTH

The economy is characterized by undulatory fluctuations in the short run but trending growth in the long run. Improving living standards is driven by long-run economic growth. What drives economic growth? The long-term growth of an economy is largely determined by the supply side, such as increases in production resources (especially labor and capital), improvements in technology, and increases in productivity. When new production resources increase, new production and management skills are developed, or labor productivity increases, the potential production capacity (i.e., potential GDP)of the economy increases, which is identified as economic growth.

Is sustainable economic growth possible? Earlier, the Harrod-Domar growth model attempted to identify the sources of economic growth in the tradition of Keynesian economics. Savings play an important role in their model. However, the Harrod-Domar model is characterized by the 'razor's edge', which indicates that it is difficult for an economy to achieve balanced (or sustained) growth through savings. In the Harrod-Domar model, it is a coincidence that the economy maintains its equilibrium while maintaining stable growth, and that the economy can always deviate from the equilibrium path of stable growth.

A new growth model called the Solow model was proposed to improve on the weakness of the Harrod-Domar model. In the neoclassical tradition, Robert Solow developed a growth model that is constructed based on the law of diminishing marginal returns of labor and capital and the constant returns to scale. The law of diminishing marginal returns is the rule that if the amount of labor increases, while all other inputs such as capital are held constant, the productivity of one additional unit of labor will eventually decrease. The law of diminishing marginal returns also applies to capital. If the amount of capital increases under the assumption that the amount of labor is constant, the amount of output produced by one additional unit of capital will eventually decrease. Here we can easily see that the law of diminishing marginal returns is only a short-run phenomenon, for the assumption that capital is constant is valid in the short run.

What will happen in the long run? In the long run, all production factors including capital are variable. It takes some time for firms to change factories, machines, and tools, but in the long run, they can build new factories and install new machines. In this way, the law of diminishing marginal returns will not occur in the long run. Instead, we are interested in the following questions. If a firm doubles the amount of all production factors (especially labor and capital), what will happen to output in the long run? It is conceivable that output will be more than doubled or less than doubled, or just doubled. The phenomenon in which output is more than doubled is called 'increasing returns to scale' (IRTS), and the phenomenon in which output is less than doubled is called 'decreasing returns to scale' (DRTS). The phenomenon in which output is just doubled is called 'constant returns to scale' (CRTS). Thus, returns to scale are a long-run phenomenon.

In general, increasing returns to scale are more common in advanced economies or in technology-intensive industries, and decreasing returns to scale are more common in underdeveloped economies or in labor-intensive industries. Neoclassical economists presume that production technology exhibits constant returns to scale (CRTS). The assumption of CRTS maintained by neoclassical economists is related to the theory of income distribution. Neoclassical economists believe that the total amount of goods and services produced in a country must be exactly distributed among the owners of production factors involved in the production of goods and services. The exact distribution of income is possible only under the assumption of CRTS.

Solow developed a growth model on the premise of constant returns to scale. In the Solow model, the savings rate, population growth rate, and technological progress are the most important factors that influence economic growth. Particularly, it is technological progress that leads to sustained and stable economic growth.

Japan once rivaled the United States through technological progress and innovative management. Japan was once a world leader in technological progress. The products made in Japan were like specimens for new technology. Even the United States once envied Japanese production technology and management methods. However, this was the story we heard before Japan entered the 'Lost Two Decades'. Although the technological superiority of Japan seems to have shrunk now, Japan may not be squatting but crouching to jump. What has caused Japan's technological prowess to crouch? Solow's growth model may give some clue to the mysterious decline in Japan's technological powerhouse.

Japan developed countless new technologies and products that surprised the world. Among them, EKG (Electrocardiogram), endoscope camera, battery, LED (blue light emitting diode), DSLR camera, CD player, Blu-ray disc, Sony Walkman, Nintendo games console, etc. are inventions that have been loved by people all over the world. Recently, a poll was conducted on 500 Japanese people (July 2015), asking the 'invention that the Japanese are most proud of'. The results may be somewhat surprising. The rankings selected by the Japanese are as follows: (1) instant ramen (57%), (2) blue light-emitting diodes (41.4%), (3) bidets (36.8%), (4) automatic counting machine (27.2%), (5) Karaoke (25%), (6) instant curry (21.2%), (7) battery (21%), (8) rice cooker (21%), (9) endoscope camera (20%), (10) Sharp pencil (19.6%), and (11) erasable ink pen (19.6%).

The poet of the Northern *Song* Dynasty, *Ouyang Xiu* (1007~1072), praised Japanese technology 1,000 years ago in the 'Japanese Sword Song' (日本刀歌).

> The road to *Goni* is so long that it doesn't work anymore.
> Who can get a sword that cuts the jade stone whose story was passed down in the world?
> A precious sword recently came out of a country called Japan
> The merchants of Vietnam obtained it in the east of the blue sea.
> The sheath made of juniper wrapped with fish skin
> Was decorated with yellow brass and white copper.
> It was handed over at the price of the platinum by a fancier.
> If you kick it, you can defeat the weirdness and the savagery.
> According to hearsay, the country occupies a large island,
> And its soil is fertile, and its custom is good.
> They deceived people into believing that their ancestor *Shi Fu* was a *Qin*.
> When they went to the east to dig medical herbs,
> They stayed there together with young boys and girls and aged.
> Many craftsmen cultivated five kinds of grain and lived with them.
> All the things they make are still elaborate.

Shi Fu appearing in the poem was a person in *Qin* Dynasty who traveled east to get immortality herbs around 220 B.C. under the order of *Qin Shi Huang* (259~210 B.C.). Unfortunately, *Qin Shi Huang* died at the age of 51 years before he had an opportunity to get the herbs, because it was known that *Shi Fu* never returned to China. His party was known to have crossed the Korean peninsula and to have traveled to Japan. Japanese people have believed that *Shi Fu* spread the pottery culture to Japan, which was based on the record that the *Shi Fu* party brought seeds of five grain to Japan. This assertion can be confirmed in the poem by saying that "Many craftsmen cultivated five kinds of grain and lived with them". It is interesting to see that the craftwork of Japanese swords was transmitted from China.

4

SOLOW'S GROWTH ACCOUNTING EQUATION

Firms are organizations that produce goods and services using production resources. Production resources (or production factors) are often classified into four types: labor, capital, land, and entrepreneurial skills. First, labor is a physical and intellectual talent. Workers provide labor services to firms and earn wages. Second, capital includes all human-made production tools, such as factories, machines, and tools that are used for the production of goods and services. Capital also includes any equipment that can be used in the production of goods and services. Thus, capital includes cars and trucks, office buildings, and office supplies such as computers, photocopiers and telephones used in the process of production. Capital owners provide capital to firms and receive interest and dividends.

The third factor of production is land. Land includes not only the ground we usually think of, but also all the production resources that exist in the natural state. Land also includes underground minerals, oil, gas, and even water resources. Those who own land provide natural resources to firms, and in return they receive rents. This rent is similar to the concept of interest. Finally, there is entrepreneurial ability. Entrepreneurs are managers who combine labor, capital, and land to make goods and services. Entrepreneurs make decisions on production, management, finance, and market development. Their decisions involve risk. Entrepreneurs earn profits in exchange for carrying out management decisions and taking on the risk involved in their decisions.

Economists often use a production function to investigate the relationship between factor inputs (labor, capital, land, and entrepreneurship) and output (goods and services). A function is a relationship in which one variable (dependent variable) depends on another variable (independent variable). The production function represents the relationship in which output (goods and services) depends on the factors of production. The production function can be expressed as

Output = f (Labor, Capital, Land, Entrepreneurship)

Here, f denotes a functional relationship. This production function means that the amount of output depends on labor, capital, land, and entrepreneurship. When we talk about the production function for the economy as a whole, the output is aggregate output (real GDP). Since land is given to some extent, firms do not attempt to change the amount of land to increase output. In addition, entrepreneurship is an essential factor in production, but firms do not try to change the amount of entrepreneurship to increase output. Thus, firms usually change the amount of labor and/or capital to increase or decrease the production of goods or services. In this context, labor and capital are called primary factor inputs. Thus, the production function we commonly use can be expressed as follows:

Output = f (Labor, Capital)

We have seen that technological progress as well as labor and capital greatly affect the production of goods and services. Let variable A represent the level of technological progress. Solow hypothesized that technological progress affects output in the following way.

Output = A f (Labor, Capital)

This kind of technological progress is often referred to as neutral technological progress, because such technological progress affects output in a neutral way without making labor or capital more efficient. In this sense, the measure of neutral technological progress is sometimes called total factor productivity (TFP). Solow (1957) obtained the following equation from the production function with neutral technological progress, which is often referred to as Solow's growth accounting equation.

Growth rate of output = Growth rate of A
+ Share of labor x Growth rate of labor
+ Share of capital x Growth rate of capital

We can represent Solow's growth accounting equation symbolically as follows:

$$\dot{Y} = \dot{A} + S_L\dot{L} + S_K\dot{K}$$

where S_L= share of output that goes to workers, and S_K= share of output that goes to capital owners, and the dot above a variable represents the growth rate of the variable. Thus, $\dot{Y}$= growth rate of output, $\dot{L}$ = growth rate of labor, $\dot{K}$ = growth rate of capital.

The share of labor refers to the amount of GDP that goes to workers, and the share of capital refers to the amount of GDP that goes to capital owners (or capitalists). Assuming that production technology represents constant returns to scale, the sum of the share of labor and the share of capital is equal to 1. This means that GDP is exactly distributed between workers and capital owners who participate in the production of output. In the United States, about two-thirds (0.7) of GDP goes to workers, and one-third (0.3) of GDP goes to capital owners. It is known that in China, only about 40% (0.4) of China's GDP is distributed to workers and 60% (0.6) to capital owners. Capital owners in China include the owners of state-owned enterprises (SOEs). In South Korea, the share of labor accounts for about 45% of GDP, and the share of capital accounts for 55% of GDP.

Solow's growth accounting equation explains how the economic growth rate is determined. First, as the amount of labor increases, so does GDP. The rate of economic growth due to the increase in labor is given by $S_L\dot{L}$ = (share of labor) x (growth rate of labor). Next, as the amount of capital increases, so does GDP. The rate of economic growth due to the increase in capital is given by $S_K\dot{K}$= (share of capital) x (growth rate of capital).

Suppose that the share of labor (S_L) in a country is 0.7 and the share of capital (S_K) is 0.3. If the country's annual economic growth rate is 4%, the growth rate of labor is 2% per year, and the growth rate of capital is 5% per year, then the economic growth rate due to the increase in labor is (0.7) x 2% = 1.4%, and the economic growth rate due to the increase in capital is (0.3) x 5% = 1.5%. In other words, 1.4% out of the 4% economic growth is the economic growth attributable to the increase in labor, and 1.5% out of the 4% economic growth is the economic growth attributable to the increase in capital. If we sum up the economic growth rates contributed by increases in labor and capital, respectively, the sum becomes 2.9%. (= 1.4% + 1.5%). However, the country's economy grew at the rate of 4% per year. Where did the rest of the growth rate, 1.1% (= 4%−2.9%) come from? Solow's growth accounting equation explains this.

Growth rate of A = Growth rate of GDP – (Share of labor) x
(Growth rate of labor) – (Share of capital) x (Growth rate of capital)
= 4% −1.4% − 1.5% = 1.1%

Here 1.1% is the growth rate of A. Then, where did the growth rate of A, 0.5% come from? The growth rate of A measures the economic growth achieved by sources other than increases in the physical production factors, labor and capital.

The growth rate of A is known as the 'Solow residual', which is named because it is a catchall term that is not attributed to increases in labor and capital. Solow saw this as economic growth due to technological progress. For this reason, this term is also called total factor productivity (TFP) or multi-factor productivity (MFP). Economic growth associated with an increase in labor is attributed to labor productivity, and economic growth associated with an increase in capital is attributed to capital productivity, respectively, but economic growth associated with an increase in A is due to the productivity of all other factors, or the productivity of catchall factors.

At the time when Solow published his paper, the growth rate of A was called an ignorance term, because the exact nature of the residual term was not well known, but many subsequent studies have tried to uncover the nature of A. For example, a paper co-authored by Park and Yuhn (2010) reveals that total factor productivity consists of three sources: technological progress, increased production and management efficiency, and scale economies. In the case of the South Korean economy, technological progress accounts for 80% of the total factor productivity increase, production and management efficiency for 15%, and economies of scale for 5%.

After the publication of Solow's work, many studies have attempted to identify sources of growth by improving data quality and further subdividing capital and labor. Edward Denison (1974, 1985), and Dale Jorgenson (1988) contributed to the refinement of Solow's model. In particular, Denison shows that during the period from 1929 to 1982, about 30% of U.S. economic growth was driven by technological progress. Kwon and Yuhn (1990) revisited the sources of Korean economic growth from 1962 to 1981 and found that unlike the United States, the contribution of technological progress to economic growth in South Korea was only 7.6%.

5

ECONOMIC GROWTH AND LIVING STANDARDS

Solow's growth accounting equation is concerned with the sources of economic growth, more specifically, the growth of the overall economy (GDP). In another paper, Solow (1956) investigated the determinants of income per capita or living standards. In Solow's model, there are three factors that have the dominant effect on income per capita: population growth, savings, and technological progress. First of all, as the savings rate increases, the amount of funds available for investment increases. Investment is a pathway for economic growth and a basis for improving living standards. Population growth is also an important production factor, but the role of population growth in living standards is more complicated.

Population growth is the source of economic growth as Solow's growth accounting equation suggests. This is because population growth is associated with the growth of the labor force. However, higher population growth has a negative effect on the standard of living or income per capita. This is because income per person is obtained by dividing national income by the number of the population. Thus, population growth is the backbone of economic growth, but a backlash for improving living standards. When the population growth rate of a nation decreases, its per capita income and living standards increase, but its potential growth rate could decrease. Finally, technological progress is the most crucial key to improving living standards in Solow's model. This is because continuous improvements in living standards are made possible only through technological progress.

In the Solow model, the growth of population and savings acts as a limiting factor in improving living standards. In his model, if the savings rate increases by one level, the standard of living increases accordingly, but without a continuous increase in the savings rate, the standard of living also cannot improve further, other things being equal. However, there is a limit to raising the savings rate. In other words, the savings rate cannot be raised to 100% of income. People cannot save 100% of their income. In the same context, if the rate of population growth decreases by one level, the standard of living increases accordingly. However, there is a limit to lowering the population growth rate. The population growth rate cannot be dropped to 0%

(or below 0%) for an extended period. If that happens, mankind will gradually disappear on the earth. Thus, there is a limit to the policy aimed at increasing living standards by increasing the savings rate or suppressing the population growth rate.

The economic activity of the human being can be traced back to B.C. 1 million. Humanity's living standards have not changed significantly from B.C. 1 million until the Industrial Revolution (1760 ~ 1840). Harvard University's Michael Kremer (1993) and Berkeley's Bradford DeLong produced statistical data on the human being's income per capita from B.C. 1 million to A.D. 2000. Income per capita (real GDP), measured in 2000 U.S. dollar value, has remained at almost $100 levels, with slight fluctuations from B.C. 1 million to A.D. 1350. When Aristotle and Plato discussed philosophy on the streets of Athens around B.C. 500, income per capita was about $175. This golden era did not return until the advent of the Industrial Revolution around 1760. Mankind's income per capita shrunk for the next 1,000 years after the Peripatetic School of Aristotle and finally reached $120 in A.D. 400 when the Roman Empire collapsed. Even in the 1620s when the Puritans moved to the New World, income per capita did not exceed that of the Athenians around B.C. 500.

The secular stagnation of living standards in human history could be fully explained from the Solow growth accounting equation (with land and entrepreneurship added) which is given by

Growth rate of output = Growth rate of A + Share of labor x Growth rate of labor + Share of capital x Growth rate of capital + Share of land x Growth rate of land+ Share of entrepreneurship x Growth rate of entrepreneurship

Before human beings embraced the Industrial Revolution in the 18th century, they did not invent any sophisticated capital except for naïve equipment in the farming, hunting, fishing, and textile industries. Thus, the growth rate of capital was trivial. Also, there were no entrepreneurs before the arrival of the Industrial Revolution era. Thus, there was no growth rate of entrepreneurship. Before the advent of the Industrial Revolution, human beings primarily relied on the growth of labor and land to increase output and income. However, the growth rate of land was also almost fixed. Thus, the pre-Industrial Revolution production function could be represented by

Growth rate of output = Share of labor x Growth rate of labor

In this production function, the share of labor should be equal to one, because most of income consisted of labor income. Thus, the growth accounting equation becomes

Growth rate of output = Growth rate of labor

The growth rate of labor could be approximately equal to the growth rate of population.

Growth rate of output = Growth rate of population

The growth rate of output was more or less than the growth rate of population. Put simply, output (or income) increased at the same rate as the population growth rate. Therefore income per capita and living standards remained little improved from B.C. 1 million until the Industrial Revolution. The Malthusian theory of population was in line with this argument.

Then, after the Industrial Revolution, living standards (GDP per capita) began to improve exponentially. About 100 years after the Industrial Revolution, income per capita in 1850 doubled the level of 1750, and in 1950 it was more than five times the level of 1850. And in 2000, income per capita quadrupled the 1950 level. In Japan, income per capita increased by more than 17 times in 1979 compared with 1870. This quantum leap in living standards would be impossible only by increasing the savings rate or suppressing the growth rate of the population. Mankind has developed technology almost indefinitely since the Industrial Revolution. Such being the case, the only way to constantly improve the standard of living in the long run is the continual development of technology. There is no limit to technological progress. The valuable lesson we learn from Solow's growth model is that only technological progress is the most important source of steadily improving living standards, and the impact of technological progress on improving living standards will become even more important in the information technology (IT) era.

6

HOW COULD SINGAPORE CATCH UP WITH THE UNITED STATES? THE CONVERGENCE OF LIVING STANDARDS

The comparison of income per capita across major countries reveals a big disparity among them. In 1960, income per capita was $2,881 in the United States, $479 in Japan, $395 in Singapore, and $155 in South Korea. U.S. income per capita was 18.6 times larger than that of South Korea, 7.3 times larger than that of Singapore, 6 times larger than that of Japan. In 2022, however, income per capita was $79,576 in Singapore, $76,027 in the United States, $49,850 in Hong Kong, $39,243 in Japan, $36,051 in Taiwan, and $34,994 in South Korea. In 2022, U.S. income per capita was 0.96 of that of Singapore, 1.53 times larger than that of Hong Kong, 1.94 times larger than that of Japan, 2.11 times larger than that of Taiwan, and 2.17 times larger than that of South Korea. The disparity in income per capita between the United States and the four Tigers and Japan has been greatly narrowed over the past 60 years.

In fact, Japan's per capita income surpassed that of the United States for some time from 1987 to 2000 (excluding 1998). This was partly due to the fact that Japan's exchange rate was significantly lowered by the Plaza Agreement in 1985, but Japan's success also contributed to the economic achievements. However, more dramatic transformations took place in Singapore. Singapore surpassed Japan in 2007 in income per capita and began to outpace the United States in 2011. A small island nation that was filled with mulberry fields just over a half century ago was transformed into an economic paradise overtaking the United States filled with skyscrapers. What made this change possible?

In recent years, growth theorists have been paying much attention to the question of whether rich countries will get richer and poor countries will get poorer or differences in living standards between rich and poor countries will eventually be narrowed. Solow's growth model predicts that living standards among countries will ultimately converge. For convenience of discussion, we'll consider two countries. Shangri-La enjoys a high capital per worker (capital/workers) and high living standards (income per capita) while Atlantis maintains a low capital per worker and low living standards. Thus, Shangri-La is a rich country and a capital-abundant country, whereas Atlantis is a poor country and a capital-scarce country.

If Atlantis raises its savings rate and lowers its population growth rate, so that Atlantis has the same savings rate and population growth rate as Shangri-La, will Atlantis catch up with Shangri-La? These two conditions will not be sufficient for Atlantis to catch up with Shangri-La. Atlantis should have the same technological progress as Shangri-La to reach the same level of living standards as Shangri-La. Atlantis could raise its savings rate and lower its population growth rate by the appropriate use of economic and political policy. The problem lies in technological progress. It is not easy for Atlantis to raise the level of its technological progress without any help from rich countries. Fortunately, in the Solow model, technological progress is exogenously given. Metaphorically speaking, it drops from the sky like a manna. Thus, every country can get access to technology through spillovers. Thus, in the Solow model, poor countries will ultimately catch up with rich countries and enjoy the same living standards as rich countries. This proposal is called the absolute convergence hypothesis. About 60 years ago, nobody could imagine that Singapore would surpass Japan and the United States in terms of income per capita.

According to the Solow model, if the economy is open, and borrowing and lending between countries are made without constraints, growth convergence will proceed at a faster rate. In poor countries, capital per worker is significantly lower than in rich countries, and consequently the marginal rate of returns on capital in poor countries is much higher than in rich countries. Thus, investors in rich countries seek to invest in poor countries in pursuit of higher capital returns. In this way, capital flows from rich countries into poor countries, and the amount of capital per worker in poor countries gradually increases and approaches the level of rich countries. Accordingly, output per worker and living standards will also converge to the level of rich countries. However, even if income per capita rises to the level of rich countries, consumption per capita in poor countries will still be lower than that of rich countries. This is because part of the income in poor countries must be used to repay foreign debt.

William Baumol (1986) at Princeton University conducted an empirical investigation of the absolute convergence hypothesis. He used long-term time series data from 1870 to 1979 for 16 developed countries collected by Angus Madison and short-term time series data from 1950 to 1980 for 72 countries filed by Robert Summers and Alan Heston (1991). He investigated whether living standards converged among countries. To this end, he divided the sample countries into four groups: (1) 16 market economy industrialized countries, (2) planned economy countries, (3) middle-income market economy countries, and (4) low-income countries. If the standards of living among countries converge, poorer countries would grow at a faster rate, and richer countries would grow at a slower rate. Thus, there will be an inverse relationship between income per capital level and the economic growth rate.

Baumol first analyzed whether the income per capita of 16 industrialized countries converged over the past 110 years. The 16 richest market economy countries in 1870 are as follows: (1) Australia, (2) England, (3) Switzerland, (4) Belgium, (5) Netherlands, (6) Canada, (7) United States, (8) Denmark, (9) Italy, (10) Austria, (11) Germany, (12) Norway, (13) France, (14) Finland, (15) Sweden, (16) Japan. Of these 16 countries, Australia had the lowest growth rate, and Japan had the most remarkable growth rate over the period. Among the 16 countries, Baumol found that countries with a relatively high level of income per capita in 1870 grew at a slower rate, while countries with a relatively low level of income per capita in 1870 grew at a faster rate, thus significantly narrowing differences in living standards among countries.

Baumol also used short-term time series data from 72 countries and confirmed that the convergence of income per capita occurred in the middle-income market economies and planned economies, although the evidence was not as strong as in 16 developed economies. However, the convergence was not observed in low-income countries. Baumol's research on growth convergence attracted a lot of attention. However, some critics was raised, indicating that there were flaws in his research. The criticism of Bradford DeLong notes that Baumol selected the sample countries that were among the richest countries in the world as of today, which was biased to induce strong evidence in favor of convergence.

Subsequent studies of convergence have found no evidence that poorer countries have grown faster than richer countries. Instead, economists have proposed conditional convergence or relative convergence, where living standards converge in countries with similar savings, population growth, and technological progress. In addition, several studies have shown that the convergence of technology and living standards occurs in countries with similar patterns in the education level, political system, government policy, and private ownership guarantees. Thus, the conditional convergence hypothesis predicts that the convergence of living standards will occur among homogeneous countries, while the convergence of living standards will not occur among heterogeneous countries with different political systems, government policies, and education levels.

The convergence of living standards among the most homogeneous groups is the convergence of living standards in the 50 states of the United States. Because regions within a country are more homogeneous than countries, the likelihood of the interregional convergence of living standards is much higher than the possibility of the intercountry convergence of living standards. Robert Barro and Sala-i-Martin (1992, 1996) analyzed whether per capita income levels converged in 48 states in the United States from 1880 to 1988. They found that poor states grew faster, and richer states grew slower during this period. In the same vein, many studies have found strong evidence for growth convergence in Western European countries but reported weak evidence for growth convergence among OECD countries, or among Latin American and Pan-Asian countries. These countries have too many heterogeneous factors in political systems, education levels, and government policies, as well as savings and population growth.

From this point of view, it is interesting to find that South Korea's economic growth and Japan's economic growth have shown similar patterns with a time lag of 10 to 15 years. These two countries not only share values such as freedom, democracy, and market economy, but also have been in the same Confucian culture for more than 1,000 years. Furthermore, the two countries have remained homogeneity in many areas such education, human capital, institutions, law, and business practices. It is no wonder that South Korea has been closely tracing Japan over the past 60 years or so, and that the convergence of living standards showed up strongly between these two countries. One problem is that the convergence of slowing growth also occurs between the two countries.

It has also been confirmed by some economists that human capital plays an important role in the convergence of living standards. Gregory Mankiw and David Weil (1992) surveyed 121 countries to determine whether living standards in these countries converged from 1960 to 1985. First, during this period, he examined how each country's annual economic growth rate is related to income per capita in 1960. However, they did not find any inverse relationship between GDP growth and income per capita. In other words, there was no evidence of convergence of living standards. Next, they looked at the relationship between the economic growth rate and income per capita holding the savings rate and the population growth rate constant. They found that low-income countries in 1960 grew faster than high-income countries. This means that the convergence of living standards is stronger in countries with similar savings and population growth rates. The study by Mankiw and Weil supports the conditional convergence hypothesis.

Lastly, they introduced human capital into the model and made the assumption that human capital was constant across countries and analyzed the relationship between income per capita and the economic growth rate. They used the high-school-educated population as an approximation to human capital. As a result, the convergence of living standards among the sample countries was much more pronounced. Their study indicates that human capital is the most important factor in economic growth and the convergence of living standards.

Now we can find clues as to how Singapore has outpaced the United States and Japan in income per capita, and the Four Tigers have been closely chasing developed countries to close the gap in living standards. The Four Asian Tigers have been in the Confucian tradition that teaches that, “Learning and practicing scriptures are a great pleasure, too” (Confucius, The Analects) and put education as the great virtue of nation. Consequently, a great amount of human capital has accumulated in these countries. Singapore was a small island nation where mulberry fields were here and there just over a half century ago, but it has been transformed into an economic utopia. There is a Chinese proverb saying that mulberry plantations had changed into a blue sea, which mean that there has been a sea change.

The Four Tigers’ catching up advanced economies in living standards has been a great success story, but it is uncertain whether increases in human capital will continue to be a driving force behind economic growth in these countries. Almost all citizens in these countries have already achieved a sufficient level of education.

7

ECONOMIC GROWTH AND POPULATION: MALTHUS, SOLOW, AND KREMER

In Solow's growth model, population growth is a factor that has a negative effect on living standards (income per capita). However, despite the exponential increase in the world population, the living standards of humanity have improved greatly over the past 200 years or so because of the rapid advancement of technology since the Industrial Revolution. Technological progress has led income to increase more than enough to offset the decline in income per person due to population growth.

The population on earth increased at an average annual rate of 0.04% from B.C. 10000 years to the first century. This means that the world's population has only increased by 1% every 25 years. Since then, the population growth rate had not changed significantly until 1800. During 1800 years from the first century, the population increased at an average annual rate of 0.09% per year, which is a 1% increase in every 11 years. It is only in the last 200 years that the population on earth began to grow explosively after the Industrial Revolution. In the 19th century, the population growth rate rose to an average of 0.6% per year, to 0.9% in the first half of the 20th century, and to 1.8% in the second half of the 20th century. As a result, the world population exceeded 7.8 billion by 2020 and reached 8 billion in November 2022.

Malthus' theory of population explains why the population growth rate was almost fixed from B.C. 10000 to the year 1800. Initially, the smaller the population, the more resources (including land) were available per capita, and thus the standard of living improved. As living standards improved, people had more children, and the population began to increase. As the number of people increased, the standard of living began to decrease again because fewer resources and land were available per capita. Since there was not enough food to eat, the population would begin to decrease. Eventually, society was not getting better at the income level, which corresponded to a certain population growth rate, and remained stagnant at that level until the next cycle of the growth of population. This cycle was repeated until the Industrial Revolution. Thus, in the Malthusian model, the number of populations was a factor that hinders the improvement of living standards.

Ironically, when Malthus published his book titled *Essay on the Principle of Population*, Malthus' theory began to crumble. He published his book in 1788, when the world population began to show a pronounced trend to increase. Although the population began to increase, income per capita continued to increase without falling. The Industrial Revolution, which led to the advent of new production technologies, generally began in 1760 and bloomed from 1820 to 1840.

Over the past 200 years, humanity has witnessed a new phenomenon in which the population has rapidly increased, and at the same time income per capita has also increased rapidly. Malthusian theory lost its brilliance with the development of the new phenomenon. However, the failure of Malthusian theory does not mean that population growth has no effect on per capita income levels. Malthusian theory focused on the *size* of the population, but the *growth rate* of the population is still a factor influencing living standards.

The world in which Malthus lived was a world in which little capital existed, and only production resources such as labor and land determined output. But after the Industrial Revolution, capital began to emerge as an important factor of production. In the Solow model, the amount of capital held per worker is an important factor in the determination of income per capita. If the population growth rate is faster than the growth rate of capital, the amount of capital per worker will eventually decrease, and accordingly, income per capita will also decrease.

Under the influence of Malthusian theory, the suppression of population growth has been a top priority for economic policy in many countries until recently. In the tradition of the Malthusian Doomsday scenario, many countries including China and South Korea during the economic development periods followed the policy of suppressing population growth to improve their living standards under the slogan that "Let's have two babies and raise them well". Not long ago, China put the 'One Family One Child' population policy at the top of its economic policy and implemented it strictly. In many countries, however, a fundamental shift of population policy is now under way, because they have begun to realize that a decline in population growth can be a disaster for the growth of the economy. They have also been increasingly aware that in spite of the rapid increase in population growth income per capita in many countries has continued to rise because the increase in income due to technological progress has outweighed the decrease in income due to population growth.

Michael Kremer (1997) of Harvard University, in his pathbreaking paper, provides a very interesting conclusion regarding the impact of population growth on living standards. Malthus saw the *number of population* as a factor limiting income per capita, and Solow saw the *growth rate of population* as a factor limiting income per capita, but Kremer saw the *size of population* as a catalyst to promote technological advancement. Kremer, with the help of anthropologists, archaeologists, and sociologists, analyzed the determinants of the population growth rate from B.C. 1 million to 1990 and its impact on technological progress.

Kremer hypothesizes that if the population is large, technological progress is made faster because there are more scientists, inventors, and engineers in a country with more populations. He concluded that a large population is a necessary condition for technological progress. His research is divided into two parts. The first part looked at what was an important factor that determined the population growth rate from B.C. 1 million to recent years, and the second part analyzed the impact of the distribution of population across major regions on technological progress.

One million years ago, the total population on the planet was about 125,000. It surpassed 1 million people 300,000 years ago and reached 100 million people in B.C. 500. In the year (A.D. 1) when Jesus was born, 170 million people lived in the world. In A.D. 1000, 250 million people were on the earth and in 1800, shortly after the Industrial Revolution, the world population increased to 900 million people. In 1900, it increased to 1.25 billion people, and in 1990 it jumped to 5.33 billion. (The world population in November 2022 exceeded 8 billion.) He explored the relationship between the size of population and the growth rate of population. His research found that the larger the population, the higher is the population growth rate.

More convincing evidence was provided in the second part of his research. At the end of the Earth's Ice Age, the glaciers of the Arctic began to melt down around B.C. 10000, and the bridge between the continents connecting Russia and Alaska was submerged. From this time (B.C. 10000) to 1492 when Columbus discovered the new continent, the Eurasian and American continents were completely cut off for approximately 11,500 years. There were, of course, no exchanges of goods and services between the two continents, and no transfers of civilization or technology to each other.

Kremer looked at the relationship between the number of population and technological progress in five regions that were completely isolated for more than 11,500 years: (1) the Eurasian-African region called the 'Old World' (including today's Asia, Europe and Africa), (2) Americas called the

'New World' (today's North, Central, and South Americas), (3) Australia, (4) Tasmania Island to the south of Australia, and (5) Flinders Island in the middle of Australia and Tasmania. These five areas had no contact or interaction with each other for more than 10,000 years, and thus the civilization and technology they enjoyed were only theirs without external influences.

Kremer investigated the correlation between the population density and civilization in these areas. The Eurasian-Africa region had the highest population density among the five regions, with a population of 4.9 people per square kilometer. They developed a very brilliant 'Old World' civilization and technology. The next area that blossomed in the dazzling civilization was the Americas, where the population density of the region was 0.4 people per square kilometer, the second highest following the Old Continent. American people achieved the Inca and Aztec civilizations. Australia enjoyed the third highest level of civilization and technology. They engaged in hunting and developed various tools and techniques for hunting. The population density of the region was 0.03 people per square kilometer.

Tasmania was the region where little civilization was left. Residents of the region did not have the skills to make fire, nor did they make tools made of stone or bone. The population density of the region was 0.03 people per square kilometer. Flinders Island was an area far removed from civilization. The inhabitants of the island rarely enjoyed any human civilization, and their lives were no better than those of animals. Around B.C. 3000, human beings completely disappeared in the island. The population density in this island was the lowest among the five regions.

Based on these findings, Kremer arrived at the conclusion that the size of population is an essential condition for civilization and technological progress. In the Solow model, technological progress plays the most important role in improving the standard of living, but an increase in the population also works as an obstacle to technological progress. This is because, as the population grows, the amount of capital should be distributed thinly to more workers, and the amount of capital given to individual workers decreases, which hinders technological progress. However, in the Kremer model, a larger population leads to faster technological progress. It is not a coincidence that the Chinese and Indian economies have been progressing at a dazzling pace these days. In 2019, Kremer was jointly awarded the Nobel Prize in economics with Esther Duflo and Abhijit Banerjee for their experimental approach to alleviating global poverty.

8

WILL THE GROWTH OF THE FOUR TIGERS STAGNATE? 'FROM MOUNT OLYMPUS TO THE THESSALY PLAINS'

We have seen how Singapore has been catching up with Japan and the United States in living standards over a short period of time. Other Asian Tigers have also achieved quantum leaps in improving their living standards over the past 60 years or so by pursuing export-oriented growth strategies. However, beginning in the middle of the 1990s, some scholars warned that the galloping of these Asian Tigers would stop soon. The so-called stagnation theory first appeared in Krugman's 1994 article in *The Foreign Affairs*, and the paper published by Alwyn Young (1995) attracted people's attention.

First, Krugman, a Nobel laureate in economics, discovered some similarities in economic performance between the Soviet Union and the Four Asian Tigers. All these countries achieved rapid economic growth with the aid of the governments' active involvement in economic planning and the mobilization of resources (especially labor and capital). As idle resources were put into production activity, their economies grew by leaps and bounds. Buoyant with the confidence of its economic performance, the Soviet Union once had the illusion that it would soon overtake the U.S. economy in size. However, there was a limit to the mobilization of resources by the government, and the Soviet Union collapsed in the late 1980s. In the light of the Soviet experience, Krugman predicted that the growth of the Four Tigers in Asia would also slow down sharply.

Young went a step further and published a paper arguing that the miraculous economic growth in these countries is in fact just a 'tyranny of numbers'. According to him, from 1966 to 1990, the overall economy in the Four Tigers, especially GDP per capita in manufacturing, was significantly higher than that of other countries, but the high economic growth in these countries was not attributable to technological progress. A considerable portion of the growth was made by quantitative and qualitative increases in physical factor inputs (especially labor and capital). He further predicted that if the rapid expansion of production factors slowed down, growth in these countries would also slow down rapidly. Unfortunately, his predictions became reality in a few years later.

He maintained that most of the growth in these countries was driven by the participation of women in the labor force, the increase of working hours, the improvement of education, the increase of the investment rate, and the increase in production factors due to the mass inflow of idle labor into the manufacturing sector. He further argued that economic growth attributable to technological progress in these countries is insignificant. Once we take the significant increases in production factors into account, we arrive at the conclusion that the contribution of technological progress to economic growth is not much different from the historical performance of many OECD countries or Latin American countries.

Let's look more closely at his argument. Women's participation in the labor force has greatly increased in these countries since World War II due to a sharp decrease in fertility. Now that the labor force participation of women who want to work has been almost achieved in these countries, the growth resulting from the additional increase in the labor force of women will be stagnant. The inter-sectoral mobility of the labor force also played an important role. Over the past several decades, there has been a large influx of labor from the agricultural sector to other sectors, especially the manufacturing sector in the Four Tigers. Now that the influx of labor into the manufacturing sector has been almost over in these countries, the growth resulting from the inter-sectoral movement of labor will also be reduced significantly.

Rapid increases in capital in the Four Tigers also contributed sizably to their economic growth. In Singapore, the ratio of investment to GDP (investment/GDP) increased from 10% in 1960 to 39% in 1980 and again in 49% in 1984. In South Korea, this ratio was only 5% in the early 1950s, but it increased to 30% in the late 1960s and 40% in 1991. On the other hand, in Taiwan, the increase in the capital stock did not occur at an eye-catching rate, but the investment/GDP ratio, which reached 10% in the early 1950s increased to 27% in 1975 but remained around 22% by the early 1990s.

The improvement of the education level has led to the remarkable accumulation of human capital. The contribution of increases in human capital to the economic growth rate has been noticeable. The workforce with high school diplomas or higher degrees in these countries nearly tripled over the past 25 years from 1966 to 1990, especially in Singapore. The increase in human capital due to the improvement of the education level has had the effect of increasing the labor force by 1 percentage point.

In sum, the substantial part of economic growth in these countries was attributable to quantitative and qualitative increases in physical factor inputs such as increases in women's participation in the labor force, inter-sectoral transfers of workers, improvements in the education level, and increases in the capital stock. If we subtract the contribution of quantitative and qualitative increases in physical factor inputs from the total economic growth rate, we obtain the economic growth rate due to technological progress, which is called total factor productivity (TFP) growth. Young has concluded that the economic growth rate attributable to TFP growth in the Four Tigers falls from 'Mount Olympus to the Thessaly Plains', where Thessaly refers to a state in Greece. From 1966 to 1990 the average annual growth rate of total factor productivity was 1.7% in South Korea, 2.6% in Taiwan, 2.0% in Singapore, and 2.3% in Hong Kong. When comparing these numbers with the growth rate of total factor productivity in other countries, one can easily see that the growth rate in the Four Tigers is not a miracle.

Finally, Young predicted that since the quantitative and qualitative increases in the production factors (labor and capital) in these countries had almost reached a level of equilibrium, phenomenal increases in labor and capital would no longer be possible in the future. Since economic growth due to technological progress in these countries is trivial, and the rate of growth in production factors is expected to slow down, the stagnation of economic growth in the Four Tigers seems to be quite real.

It is true that the economic growth rate in the Four Tigers was almost cut in half beginning the middle of the 1990s, as predicted by Young. However, most of the Four Tigers entered an orbit of high altitude of economic growth in the 1990s. The income level of $20,000 might be the threshold level of income per capita for a country to be classified as the status of an advanced economy. Japan achieved this level of income in 1987, Hong Kong in 1993, and Singapore in 1994. Later, South Korea joined the club in 2006 and Taiwan in 2011. In a sense, the abnormally high rate of economic growth in the Four Tigers began to be normalized in the middle of the 1990s. Birds of a feather flock together. The Four Dragons under the influence of Confucius' teachings have been flying high together.

PART 12

MONETARY POLICY AND ECONOMIC STABILIZATION

1

WHAT DOES ECONOMIC POLICY AIM FOR?

Economic policy refers to any policy designed to influence economic activity. There are several different types of economic policy. Fiscal policy and monetary policy are the two pillars of economic policy. In addition, foreign exchange policy, incomes policy, and industrial policy are sometimes used by policymakers. Fiscal policy refers to changes in government expenditures, tax revenues, and transfer payments implemented by the Administration and the Parliament to influence economic activity. Fiscal policy mainly aims to promote economic growth and full employment. Monetary policy refers to changes in the money supply, interest rates, and liquidity implemented by the central bank to influence economic activity. Monetary policy primarily aims to achieve price stability. The goal of price stability pursued by the central bank often clashes with the goal of economic growth pursued by the government.

Foreign exchange policy refers to an economic policy that is designed to influence the value of a nation's currency and exchange rates with other currencies, thereby affecting imports and exports and the international balance of payments. Incomes policy is an economic policy in which the government directly regulates prices, wages, or interest rates when inflation is severe, usually seeking to establish prices and wages below market-determined equilibrium levels. Lastly, industrial policy refers to an economic policy aimed at increasing the competitiveness of a nation's industries by providing subsidies or tax benefits to firms.

The question of whether economic policy works, and whether it works as intended is the debate that has been going on since the birth of modern economics. More specifically, can economic policy solve the economic problems of unemployment and inflation or the issues of interest rate and exchange rate instability in the short run? Can economic policy promote economic growth in the long run? These questions are perennially debated, but unresolved issues. We have been discussing the effectiveness of economic policy in fragments so far. This chapter will deal with these issues comprehensively.

As we have already seen, there are roughly three different views on the effectiveness of economic policy. The first position is that economic policy influences economic activity not only in the short run but also in the long run. This position is largely maintained by people who belong to the Keynesian school. The second position is that economic policy affects economic activity only in the short term, but the effectiveness of economic policy is questionable in the long run. The third position is the view that economic policy has no effect on economic activity in the long run as well as in the short run, but rather can cause side effects such as inflation. The last two positions are largely supported by those who are in the classical tradition. Especially, people who believe in a more radical doctrine of classical economics such as the rational expectations hypothesis favor the third position, that is, policy ineffectiveness theorem.

Even those who take the position that economic policy has little effect on economic activity do not argue that economic policy should not be used. They maintain that policymakers should be cautious about using economic policy, because economic policy is more likely to do harm to the economy than to do good to the economy. Furthermore, those who believe in the self-correcting forces of the economy argue that policymakers should not use monetary policy in a discretionary manner to stabilize the economy. Discretionary monetary policy involves reducing the money supply when the economy is in a good shape and increasing the money supply when the economy is in a bad condition. Classical economists argue that this kind of discretionary monetary policy is more likely to destabilize the economy rather than to stabilize the economy. Thus, economists in the classical tradition argue that the best monetary policy is the one that is based on rules.

Those who believe in rules also support the notion of a 'small government'. If the government spends expenditures loosely, taxes will have to be raised, and government organizations will also be increased, which inevitably leads to a 'big government'. However, the allocation of resources by the government can be less efficient that the allocation of resources by the private sector, and therefore the government's activity related to economic activity should be limited to strengthening the functioning of the market.

Fiscal policy and monetary policy can be operated either in an expansionary manner or in a contractionary manner. When the economy slows down, unemployment generally increases, and inflation decreases. In such a case, policymakers (especially those taking the Keynesian stance) are tempted to boost the economy by expansionary fiscal policy or expansionary monetary policy. Expansionary fiscal policy takes the form of increasing government spending and/or cutting taxes. Expansionary monetary policy involves increasing the money supply and/or lowering interest rates. On the other hand, if the economy is booming, unemployment decreases, but inflation increases. In such a situation, policymakers are trying to cool the economy by contractionary fiscal policy or contractionary monetary policy. Contractionary fiscal policy takes the form of reducing government spending and/or increasing taxes. Contractionary monetary policy involves reducing the money supply and/or raising interest rates.

In general, monetary policy may be more effective for economic stabilization when the economy approaches its potential level of output, while fiscal policy may be more powerful for economic stimulation when the economy operates far below its potential level of output. Put it differently, monetary policy may be a more effective policy tool when the economy suffers high inflation, while fiscal policy may be a more powerful policy tool when the economy suffers high unemployment. Alternatively, monetary policy may be more effective when the economy is in a normal state, and fiscal policy may be more effective when the economy is in a recessionary phase. Also, if the economy has fewer regulations on economic activity, and prices, wages and interest rates are more flexible, monetary policy becomes more effective compared with fiscal policy. If the economy has more regulations on economic activity, and prices, wages and interest rates are more rigid, fiscal policy becomes more effective compared with monetary policy. Over the past 40 years, the world economy has become increasingly open, more flexible, and less regulated. Fiscal policy's influence on the macroeconomy is not as great as we thought before, while monetary policy's influence is growing.

Many macroeconomists now recognize that using fiscal policy as a tool for stabilizing the economy is like going out of fashion. This is especially true when the economy is in a normal state. The problem with fiscal policy is that the time lag between the occurrence of economic disturbances and the effective responses of fiscal policy to them is very long. The lag of effectiveness occurs mainly because elected policymakers are not willing to adopt a politically unpopular policy and to pursue policy that is helpful for being elected. Sometimes they try to implement fiscal policy that is not economically desirable. Furthermore, the effects of fiscal policy can be differentiated among industries, regions, and economic agents. However, fiscal policy can still be used as an important policy tool for economic stimulation because monetary policy does not work well when the economy is in serious stagnation.

It is worth noting that both fiscal policy and monetary policy are implemented mainly through supplying money to the economy. How is economic policy related to money? Fiscal policy, monetary policy, and foreign exchange policy are also very different in this respect. The most important difference between fiscal policy and monetary policy is that fiscal policy, in principle, does not involve creating new money in our economy while monetary policy entails creating new money. The government uses money collected from taxes or borrowings from investors to finance its spending programs. Thus, the government uses the existing money in the economy. When tax revenues or borrowings are not sufficient to finance its spending programs, the government borrows money from the central bank as a last resort. In such a case, fiscal policy leads to the creation of new money. In this sense, fiscal policy promotes little concern about inflation.

On the other hand, monetary policy involves supplying new money to the economy. Therefore, the central bank's supply of money means printing new money, and the total stock of money available in the economy will increase by the amount associated with monetary policy. Thus, monetary policy can always produce some upward pressure on inflation. For this reason, many developed countries take a very cautious approach to increasing the money supply.

Does the foreign exchange policy that the government uses to influence the exchange rate also affect the amount of money? Suppose that the central bank intervenes in the foreign exchange market to prevent the sharp fall in the exchange rate of the yen against the dollar (say, from ¥120 per dollar to ¥100 per dollar). The fall in the yen exchange rate or the rise in the value of the yen is due to the fact that there are too many dollars in the foreign exchange market relative to the yen. Therefore, the Bank of Japan needs to buy dollars in the foreign exchange market for the yen. In order to purchase the dollar, the Bank of Japan issues the yen through its window. Since this is the issuance of new money, the Japanese money supply increases, and some pressure on inflation may develop in Japan. This kind of foreign exchange market intervention is called unsterilized foreign exchange intervention

Lastly, both fiscal policy and monetary policy mainly affect economic activity through changes in aggregate demand. Thus, fiscal policy and monetary policy are sometimes called aggregate demand management policy. However, fiscal policy and monetary policy affect aggregate demand through different channels. Fiscal policy directly affects aggregate demand through government purchases, but monetary policy indirectly affects aggregate demand through changes in interest rates. A change in the money supply leads to a change in interest rates, which in turn, affects the components of aggregate demand such as investment, consumption, and exports.

However, it should be noted that there is some limit to what monetary policy can do. The monetary authorities can only directly control nominal interest rates and nominal exchange rates, not real interest rates and real exchange rates, which are determined by market forces. Also, the monetary authorities can only affect short-term interest rates, and long-term interest rates are determined by market forces. (However, recent quantitative easing policy is aimed at affecting long-term interest rates.)

2

The Magic of Money Creation: Tools of the Magic

The money supply itself not only affects economic activity, but also acts as a rudder for managing economic activity by changing interest rates. As a strategy of monetary policy, there are two different positions. One group of economists argue that policymakers should target the quantity of money (i.e., monetary aggregates such as M1 or M2) to influence economic activity. Another group of economists argue that policymakers should target interest rates (i.e., benchmark interest rates such as the federal funds rate) to influence economic activity. However, even if interest rates are targeted, the targeting of interest rates is achieved through controlling the money supply. Thus, it is important to understand how the money supply is determined in a country.

Today, most of money takes the form of bank money—demand deposits and short-term savings deposits in the United States. As we discussed earlier, the narrow money (M1) consists mainly of demand deposits and other liquid deposits, and the share of currency (paper currency and coins) in money is very small. The proportion of currency in M1 is only 10.6%, and the proportion of currency in M2 is 10.0% as of July 2022. Thus, it is important to understand the structure and functions of private depository institutions for the analysis of the creation of money in the economy. Commercial banks and other depository institutions receive deposits from individuals and businesses or borrow funds and lend the funds to households, businesses, and the governments. In the process of receiving and lending deposits, depository institutions create money.

Banks, like private firms aiming to maximize profits, try to make as much profit as possible by efficiently managing their assets. The operations of banks are summarized in the balance sheet of banks. The balance sheet of a bank is a table that shows how many assets and liabilities the bank has at a specific point in time. The balance sheet is simply a means of showing the balance between what one owns (assets) and what one owes (liabilities and net worth). The two sides of the balance sheet are always equal.

Assets = Liabilities + Net worth (Capital accounts)

Balance Sheet of Commercial Banks

Assets (Uses of Funds)	Liabilities (Sources of Funds)
Reserves	Checkable deposits
Cash assets (Vault cash)	Savings and time deposits
Securities	Borrowings from the central bank
Interbank loans	Interbank borrowings
Loans	Borrowings from the public
Other assets	Net worth (= Capital account)

The credit side (assets) on the balance sheet which represents the uses of funds consists of reserves, securities, loans to consumers, firms, and governments, interbank loans, and other assets. Reserves include cash held by banks in their vaults (vault cash) and reserve deposits deposited at the central bank. Cash held by banks in their vaults is not included in the stock of money and is treated as a reserve, because vault cash is not in circulation. In addition, all depository institutions must hold a certain fraction of deposits in the form of reserve deposits at the central bank. (The fraction of deposits that banks must hold is called required reserves.) Banks try to maximize profits by investing in government bonds such as Treasury bills, notes, and bonds. In the United States, banks are not allowed to hold corporate bonds and stocks, because they are too risky. Thus, the holdings of securities mainly consist of marketable Treasury securities, local government bonds (= municipal bonds or simply munis), and non-marketable U.S. savings bonds. Bank loans consist of loans to businesses, households, and the governments. Bank loans are the largest component of bank assets and the main source of revenues for banks.

The debit side (liabilities) on the balance sheet which represents the sources of funds consists of demand deposits, savings and time deposits, borrowings, and capital accounts. Demand deposits are deposits that do not pay interest, and depositors can withdraw on demand. Savings deposits are deposits that pay interest, and depositors can withdraw after a certain period in principle. Time deposits are sometimes called certificates of deposits (CDs) and have a maturity. If the depositor withdraws before the maturity date, there is a penalty for interest. Savings and time deposits are called non-transactions deposits and are the most important source of funds for banks.

Borrowings are also a major source of funds for banks. When a bank needs more money than it has, or when it falls short of required reserves, the bank has three opportunities to borrow money: it can borrow money from the central bank, other depository institutions, and corporations. First, banks can borrow money from the central bank, and banks' borrowing from the central bank is called a discount window loan. The interest rate applied to discount loans is called the discount rate. Banks can also borrow money from other banks in the federal funds market. The interest rate applied to federal funds loans is called the federal funds rate, and the federal funds rate is considered an important gauge for market interest rates.

Banks can also borrow money from corporations. Borrowing from corporations is mainly made through repurchase agreements (RPs or repos). This is a contract in which a bank sells its securities to corporations at a fixed price and agrees to buy them back at a higher price on the next business day (overnight RPs) or within a relatively short period of time (term RPs). Repurchase agreements have the same effect as borrowing money temporarily from corporations, which in nature is a temporary open market operation. The difference between the selling price of a security and the repurchase price represents the interest rate. The opposite is a 'reverse repo'. In the reverse repo, one party buys government bonds from another party for, say, \$1 million with an agreement that another party will repurchase them within a certain period for, say, \$1.02 million.

Lastly, the capital account or net worth is calculated as the difference between assets and liabilities. It includes the value of the bank's stock (face value) and the profits the bank makes as the result of its operations. As the balance sheet shows, the most typical operation of banks is to earn profits mainly by receiving deposits from depositors and lending the funds to businesses and households.

The banking system is like a living organism, creating new money as banks receive deposits and make loans with the funds. Here we have two things to keep in mind. Most importantly, one should understand that money includes not only currency, but also deposits (demand deposits and savings deposits). Secondly, it is important to note that households' deposits and banks' loans keep on rolling on. In the circular flows of deposits and loans, banks and households play an important role in creating a country's money.

There are three important players in the creation of money: the central bank, depository institutions, and depositors. Currency is issued by the central bank. Decisions on deposits are made by depositors (or the public). Finally, decisions on loans are made by depository institutions (mainly commercial banks). Thus, a country's money is created by the interactions of the central bank, banks, and depositors. More specifically, the central bank's policy variables (required reserve ratio), banks' lending capacity, and the public's preferences for currency are important variables affecting the creation of money.

Individual banks, of course, do not create money. Nevertheless, a large portion of money is created by depository institutions acting together within the fractional reserve requirement system in the process of receiving deposits and lending them. Depository institutions are required to hold a certain fraction of their deposits as reserves in the form of vault cash in their vaults and reserve deposits at the central bank. These reserves are called required reserves (RR), and the ratio of the required reserves to deposits is called the required reserve ratio.

The reserve requirements were originally designed to protect depositors. However, the reserve requirements also play an important role in the creation of money and are therefore used as an important tool of monetary policy. Depository institutions, of course, can hold reserves in excess of required reserves. These reserves are called excess reserves (ER). Total reserves (TR) are equal to the sum of required reserves (RR) and excess reserves (ER).

Total reserves (TR) = Required reserve (RR) + Excess reserves (ER)

From this definition, excess reserves are given as the difference between total reserves and required reserves.

Excess reserves (ER) = Total reserves (TR) − Required reserve (RR)

Depository institutions can use only excess reserves to make loans and invest in securities. If the required reserve ratio is 10%, and you initially deposit $1,000 in your checking account at the First National Bank (FNB), the bank must hold $100 as a required reserve. The remaining $900 is an excess reserve, and the bank can use only the excess reserve for making loans and other business operations. This is the fractional required reserve system.

3

THE MAGIC OF MONEY CREATION: PRELIMINARIES: A SIMPLE MODEL

We are now ready to discuss how money is created under the fractional required reserve system. We'll make the following assumptions to derive a simple money creation model, first.

- People deposit all the loans they receive from the bank. In other words, people don't want to hold cash.
- Banks lend all the excess reserves they hold. In other words, banks do not want to hold excess reserves.
- All deposits are demand deposits, and the required reserve ratio for demand deposits is 10%.

Now suppose an individual (Tom) deposits \$1,000 in his checking account at First National Bank (FNB). Tom's deposit at FNB has two effects. First, FNB's deposits increase by \$1,000, and accordingly, the liability item on the balance sheet increases by \$1,000. At the same time, FNB received \$1,000 in cash, which increases its total reserves by \$1,000, and thus the asset item on the balance sheet increases by \$1,000. Now that the required reserves of FNB have increased by \$100 (10% of the deposit), the total reserves of FNB (\$1,000) consists of the required reserves of \$100 and excess reserves of \$900.

Under our assumptions, FNB does not intend to hold excess reserves, and thus it will lend all the excess reserves (\$900) to other individuals (say, Jerry). Jerry will deposit the total amount of loan (\$900) she received from FNB in her checking account at Second National Bank (SNB) under our assumption that people do not want to hold cash. As a result, SNB's deposit liabilities increase by \$900. Therefore, SNB's required reserves increase by \$90 (= \$900 x 0.1), and its excess reserves increase by \$810 (= \$900 − \$90). However, SNB will not hold the excess reserves and will lend it to another individual (say, Bonnie).

Bonnie will deposit the loan she received ($810) in her checking account at Third National Bank (TNB). TNB's deposit liabilities will increase by $810. Thus, TNB's required reserves increase by $81 ($810 x 0.1) and its excess reserves increase by $729 (= $810 – $81). TNB will lend its excess reserves to another individual (say, Clyde). The process of deposit creation will not end here. How long will the process continue? As long as the bank holds excess reserves, these deposit creation processes will continue until the excess reserves created in the banking system become zero.

Thus, the total amount of deposits created in the banking system as the result of Tom's initial deposit of $1,000 at FNB is as follows. (The derivation of the equation below is presented in the appendix.)

$$\text{Total } \Delta \text{ in deposits} = \left[\frac{1}{Required\ reserve\ ratio}\right] \text{ x Initial } \Delta \text{ in deposits}$$

where Δ indicates an 'increase'.The initial increase in deposits is the same as the initial increase in total reserves (TR). Thus, the deposit creation model can be alternatively expressed as

$$\text{Total } \Delta \text{ in deposits}= \left[\frac{1}{Required\ reserve\ ratio}\right] \text{ x Initial } \Delta \text{ in TR}$$

As a numerical illustration, we can plug the numbers into the deposit creation formula (the required reserve ratio = 0.1, the initial increase in TR = $1,000):

$$\text{Total increase in deposits} = \left[\frac{1}{0.1}\right] \text{ x \$1,000m= [10] x \$1,000 = \$10,000}$$

Here we see a magical phenomenon. When an individual (Tom) initially deposited $1,000 in his bank account, total deposits of $10,000 were created in the banking system, thus creating additional deposits of $9,000 in the banking system.

When we talked about how national income was determined in the economy, we saw that some magical process known as the multiplier effect was set in motion. Here, we see that the multiplier effect also comes into play in the creation of money. In the above deposit creation formula, [1/0.1] = 10 is a money multiplier. Thus, the money multiplier is given as the inverse of the required reserve ratio (rr).

$$\text{Money multiplier} = \left[\frac{1}{Required\ reserve\ ratio}\right] = \left[\frac{1}{rr}\right]$$

The effect of the money multiplier is a phenomenon that occurs because the economy constantly moves through interactions among economic agents.

Money (M1) is given as the sum of currency and demand deposits (and other liquid deposits. Thus, when new deposits are created it means that new money is also created. How much money will be created in the money creation model? The amount of money increases by the increase of excess reserves (ER) multiplied by the money multiplier. The reason we use excess reserves instead of total reserves is that depository institutions use only excess reserves to make loans, and money is created in the process of making loans with excess reserves.

$$\text{Total } \Delta \text{ in money} = \left[\frac{1}{Required\ reserve\ ratio}\right] \text{ x Initial } \Delta \text{ in ER}$$
$$= \text{Money multiplier x Initial increase in ER}$$

If we plug the numbers into the money creation formula (the required reserve ratio = 0.1, the initial increase in ER = \$900), we obtain the following result:

$$\text{Total increase in money} = \left[\frac{1}{0.1}\right] \text{ x \$900} = [10] \text{ x \$900} = \$9{,}000$$

The increase in the amount of money is smaller than the increase in the amount of deposits, because the economy already held the currency of $1,000 before Tom deposits.

- Total money before Tom's deposit = Currency ($1,000) + Demand deposits (0) = $1,000
- Total money after Tom's deposit = Currency (0) + Demand deposits ($10,000) = $10,000
- Total increase in money = $10,000 - $1,000 = $9,000

In our simple money creation model, the amount of money created is entirely determined by the central bank. This is because the central bank sets the required reserve ratio (rr) as part of its monetary policy, and the amount of excess reserves is automatically determined once the required reserve ratio is set by the central bank. Thus, in our simple model, depositors and depository institutions have no role in the creation of money. We arrive at this conclusion because the simple model is constructed based on two simplified assumptions.

What does the money supply curve look like? As in the simple model, if the role of depositors and banks in the determination of the amount of money is ruled out, the amount of money is determined entirely by the central bank, and therefore the money supply curve is given by a vertical line. This is because the central bank determines the supply of money from the aspect of its monetary policy and is not influenced by market interest rates.

[Appendix] Derivation of the deposit and money multipliers

The total increase in deposits created by Tom who initially deposited \$1,000 in his checking account at First National Bank is given by

Total deposit increase = \$1,000 (FNB) + \$900 (SNB) + \$810 (TNB) + ...

$$= \$1{,}000 + (0.9)x\ \$1{,}000 + (0.9)^2 x\ \$1{,}000 + (0.9)^3 x\ \$1{,}000 + \cdots.$$

$$= \$1{,}000[1 + (0.9) + (0.9)^2 + (0.9)^3 + \cdots.$$

The term in parenthesis is called an infinite geometric progression. There is a convenient formula for summing the infinite geometric progression which is given by

$$S = 1 + r + r^2 + r^2 + r^2 + \cdots. = \frac{1}{1-r} \text{ and } 0 < r < 1$$

When we apply this formula to our deposit creation model, r corresponds to 0.9, and we obtain the multiplier as follows:

$$\text{Money multiplier} = \left[\frac{1}{1-0.9}\right] = \left[\frac{1}{0.1}\right] = 10$$

4

THE MAGIC OF MONEY CREATION: THE COMPLETE MODEL

The simple model of money creation we have discussed is constructed based on the assumption that depositors do not hold cash when they receive loans, and depository institutions do not hold excess reserves when they receive deposits. We made this assumption for analytical simplicity. This assumption is virtually equivalent to ignoring the roles of depositors (the public) and depository institutions (banks) in the process of creating money. The assumption that depository institutions do not hold excess reserves is not unreasonable. Because depository institutions cannot make profits if they hold all reserves as excess reserves, banks try to use as many excess reserves as possible to make loans or invest in securities. However, the assumption that depositors do not want to hold cash and want to deposit all the loans they receive is unrealistic.

In the real world, people hold some of their loans in the form of cash. Although depository institutions have very low excess reserves, in reality, they hold some excess reserves. In other words, both depositors and depository institutions play an important role in the creation of money through their decisions on their holdings of currency and excess reserves, respectively. In this chapter, we'll look at a money creation model that allows depositors to hold currency after they receive loans and allows depository institutions to hold excess reserves after they receive deposits.

To develop a model in which depositors and depository institutions as well as the central bank each play a role in the creation of money, we relax the assumptions made in the simple model above. Now depositors can hold as much currency as they want, and depository institutions can hold as many excess reserves as they want. In our complete model, the monetary base (MB) is a key variable in the creation of money. The monetary base (MB) is defined as follows.

Monetary base (MB) = Currency held by the non-bank public (C)
+ Cash held by depository institutions in their vaults
+ Reserves deposited by depository institutions at the central bank

Cash held by depository institutions in their vaults (i.e., vault cash) is not included in any measure of money (M1 or M2). The reason is that vault cash is not in circulation, and therefore it is treated as part of bank reserves. The sum of vault cash and bank reserve deposits at the central bank constitutes the bank's total reserves. Thus, the monetary base is alternatively defined as follows.

Monetary base (MB) = Currency held by the non-bank public (C)
+ Bank total reserves (TR)

The monetary base is sometimes called high-powered money or M0. Many scholars believe that the monetary base is a policy variable that the central bank can manage and control relatively accurately. The central bank can directly control currency as the issuer of currency and can have some control over the total reserves of depository institutions using the tools of monetary policy granted to the central bank. Nevertheless, the monetary base itself is not money although it is called M0, because it is not used as a means of payment for transactions.

Now we have completed the stage setup showing how a country's money is created in the complete model. In the complete model, money is created according to the following process:

Total Δ in money = Money multiplier (mm) x Initial Δ in the monetary base

The money multiplier in the complete model is of course different from the money multiplier in the simple model. The money multiplier in the complete model is given as follows.

$$\text{Money multiplier} = \frac{1 + \left(\frac{Currency}{Deposits}\right)}{Required\ reserve\ ratio + \left(\frac{Currency}{Deposits}\right) + \left(\frac{Excess\ reserves}{Deposits}\right)}$$

$$= \frac{1 + Currency\ ratio}{Required\ reserve\ ratio + Currency\ ratio + Excess\ reserve\ ratio}$$

The currency ratio (= currency/deposits) is the ratio of currency held by the non-bank public to demand deposits, and the excess reserve ratio (= excess reserves/deposits) is the ratio of excess reserves held by depository institutions to demand deposits. As already discussed, the required reserve ratio (= required reserves/demand deposits) is the ratio of required reserves to demand deposits. If the required reserve ratio is 10% (0.1), the currency ratio is 0.9, and the excess reserve ratio is 0.05, the money multiplier is as follows.

$$\text{Money multiplier} = \frac{1+0.9}{0.1 + 0.9 + 0.05} = 1.8$$

The simple money multiplier (1/required reserve ratio) is 1/0.1 = 10 in this case. Here, we can see how much the simple money multiplier is exaggerated. It follows from the money multiplier formula above that we obtain the simple money multiplier when the currency ratio and the excess reserve ratio are set equal to zero. The money multiplier (1.8) in the complete model is the magnitude of the money multiplier that is quite close to the real-world multiplier. This means that if the monetary authorities (the central bank) increase the monetary base by $1 billion, the amount of money (M1) will increase by $1.8 billion. This increase in money will affect interest rates and other financial conditions.

However, the Fed reduced the required reserve ratio on demand deposits to 0% in March 2020. Assuming that the currency ratio and the excess reserve ratio remain the same, the money multiplier under the new required reserve scheme will become:

$$\text{Money multiplier} = \frac{1+0.9}{0.9 + 0.05} = 2.0$$

The money multiplier becomes larger under the new required reserve ratio, which should be anticipated, because reserves previously classified as required reserves become free reserves, and banks' pool of funds for lending will increase by the amount of required reserves.

As our complete model shows, there are two variables that determine the amount of money in our economy: the monetary base and the money multiplier. We have seen that the central bank can control the monetary base relatively accurately. There is little disagreement that the central bank can control the monetary base in the intended direction and to the intended extent. The problem lies in the money multiplier. The difficulty associated with monetary policy is that the central bank does not have complete control over the money multiplier. Three economic agents are involved in the determination of the money multiplier. First, the central bank determines the required reserve ratio. Next, the currency ratio (currency/deposits) is mainly determined by depositors. Finally, the excess reserve ratio (excess reserves/deposits) is primarily determined by banks. The central bank cannot influence the decisions by depositors on their currency ratio and by banks on their excess reserve ratio. The Great Depression of the 1930s was prolonged and worsened because the Fed could not control the money multiplier.

We'll look at how the money multiplier is affected by the policy of the central bank and the behavior of the public and banks. First, if the central bank raises the required reserve ratio, the money multiplier will become smaller because the variable is in the denominator of the money multiplier formula. Thus, the money multiplier moves in the opposite direction to the required reserve ratio. Second, if banks hold more excess reserves, the money multiplier will also become smaller because the excess reserve ratio is in the denominator. Finally, if people want to hold more currency, the currency ratio rises. In which direction will the money multiplier move? The answer is not so simple, because the currency ratio is in both the denominator and the numerator of the money multiplier formula. However, you can easily see that even in this case, the money multiplier becomes smaller. Thus, the money multiplier moves in the opposite direction to the currency ratio. We can conclude that the money multiplier moves inversely with the required reserve ratio, the currency ratio, and the excess reserve ratio.

There is another issue that makes the money creation process more complicated. The behavior of the public and banks is also affected by market interest rates. Thus, the money multiplier is also affected by market interest rates. As interest rates rise, the opportunity costs of holding currency by the public increase. By holding currency, the public foregoes interest income. The higher the interest rate, the larger the opportunity cost of holding currency. Thus, when the interest rate rises, people want to reduce their holding of currency, and consequently the money multiplier becomes larger, *ceteris paribus*.

In addition, as interest rates rise, the opportunity costs of holding excess reserves by banks also increase. If banks use their excess reserves for making loans instead of holding them, banks can increase interest income. However, banks give up the interest income by holding excess reserves. Thus, as interest rates go up, the opportunity cost of holding excess reserves also increases. Therefore, as interest rates rise, banks try to reduce their holding of excess reserves, and accordingly, the money multiplier becomes larger, *ceteris paribus*.

To sum up, there is a positive relationship between interest rates and the money supply. When interest rates rise, the amount of money increases, *ceteris paribus*. In this way, if depositors' decision to hold currency and banks' decision to hold excess reserves are incorporated into the money creation model, the money supply is given by a curve that slopes upwardly to the right. This upwardly sloping money supply curve contrasts with the vertical money supply curve we have seen in the simple model.

We'll look at some real-world applications. When the Christmas season approaches, people go on a shopping spree. Also, when holiday seasons approach, people travel more. For shopping or traveling, people want to hold more currency, and the currency/deposit ratio will rise. Thus, during the Christmas or the holiday seasons, the money multiplier tends to decrease, and this trend will reduce the supply of money, *ceteris paribus*.

The U.S. dollar is the most preferred currency of the world. About 50% of U.S. dollar bills issued by the Fed is circulated overseas, and 80% of the 100-dollar bills are in foreigners' wallets. This is because the U.S. dollar is most preferred as a safe asset and can be used in any country in the world. Especially when a country is politically or economically unstable, the people of the country want to hold a safe and strong currency. In Russia, for example, when the value of the ruble plummeted, the Russians were eager to hold dollars. In South Korea, when the value of the Korean won plunged during the 1997 financial crisis, people struggled to obtain dollars. When foreigners' holdings of U.S. dollars increase, the currency/deposit ratio will increase, and consequently the US money multiplier will decrease. Other things being equal, the U.S. money supply will decrease.

5

THE CAUSES OF THE GREAT DEPRESSION

The Great Depression of the 1930s was a miserable event that not only disrupted the world economic order from the bottom but also drove many people to the bottom of their lives. It is still remembered as a black history to many people. The Great Depression began with the collapse of the U.S. stock market. It took more than 10 years for the U.S. economy to go through the dark tunnel of the depression. In 1933, about three years after the Great Depression, the U.S. economy was in the abyss of malaise. By 1933, one in four American families lost a job. The U.S. unemployment rose to 25% in 1933. Furthermore, 9,000 banks went bankrupt in the course of the three years.

There is still no convincing conclusion as to what caused the Great Depression, but the most persuasive explanation is that the central bank in the United States did not manage its money properly. This is the position maintained by Milton Friedman. Friedman's argument is that the Federal Reserve System failed to provide financial institutions with the right amount of money and credit. In fact, the Fed was founded in 1913, and the Great Depression occurred only 16 years later. Considering the Fed's short history, the Fed might not yet have the experience and expertise in dealing with its first major financial crisis properly.

If we look at the movement of the money multiplier and the money supply during the Great Depression, the Fed's inexperienced management of monetary policy is evident. At that time, the Fed's policymakers might not have had an accurate knowledge of how the money multiplier was determined and how it worked. As the dark clouds of the Great Depression got thicker, people began to worry about whether they could get the money they deposited in their bank. When they saw their neighbors withdrawing money from their bank, they also ran to their bank and started withdrawing money. In this way, the initial bank run (deposit withdrawal) began. This phenomenon spread across the country. After people got cash from the bank, they either kept it below the bed's mattress or put it in a coffee can and buried the coffee can in the backyard. People's holding of cash increased rapidly. As a result, the currency/deposit ratio also rose sharply. In 1931, at the early stage of the Great Depression, the currency ratio remained at the 0.09 level, but in February 1933, when the Great Depression was in full swing, it rose to almost 0.23.

Meanwhile, bank runs drove many banks into bankruptcy. Before the Great Depression, there were about 25,000 commercial banks in the United States, but 9,000 of them closed until 1933. When bank runs went out of control, President Roosevelt shut down all banks nationwide for one month in March 1933. This 'bank holiday' was intended to calm down the bank runs. Thanks to the extreme measures, bank runs began to slow down.

Meanwhile, banks also started to increase their holding of excess reserves to spearhead bank runs. This was done to reassure depositors by demonstrating that they had sufficient funds. As a consequence, the excess reserve/deposit ratio also began to rise. The excess reserve ratio was around 0.08 in 1931 but rose to near 0.12 by February 1933.

The steep increase in the currency/deposit ratio and the sharp increase in the excess reserve/deposit ratio inevitably resulted in a decline in the money multiplier. We have seen that the money multiplier is inversely related to the currency ratio and the excess reserve ratio. The Fed could have appealed to patriotism by asking depositors to reduce their holding of cash and to banks to reduce their holding of excess reserves but could not force them to do so. The money multiplier was 6.6 in March 1931 but fell to 3.6 in March 1933. It was as clear as crystal for the money supply to decrease.

The Fed also increased the monetary base by 20% during this period to quench the fire. The monetary base increased from \$6.8 billion in 1931 to \$8.2 billion by early 1933. As discussed, the creation of new money is given by the product of the money multiplier and the monetary base. The rate of increase in the monetary base (increase by 20%) was but a drop in the bucket compared with the rate of decrease in the money multiplier (decrease by 45%). The increase in the monetary base is to a mild breeze what the decrease in the money multiplier was to a strong wind. Eventually, the money supply fell from \$45 billion in 1931 to \$30 billion in March 1933. Friedman believes that this sharp decline in the money supply was the main cause of the Great Depression. Friedman's position is that in light of the seriousness of the Great Depression, a 20% increase in the monetary base could not be a bold and effective monetary response.

- 1931: Money (\$45 billion) = Money multiplier (6.6) x Monetary base (\$6.8 billion)
- 1933: Money (\$29.5 billion) = Money multiplier (3.6) x Monetary base (\$82 billion)

6

MONETARY POLICY TOOLS: OPEN MARKET OPERATIONS

A country's monetary policy is implemented by the country's central bank (and the government to a limited extent). The central bank aims to achieve goals such as price stability, high employment, and economic growth. In addition to these basic goals, the central bank also pursues the stabilization of interest rates and asset markets such as stocks, bonds, and foreign exchanges. It goes without saying that, among these goals, stabilizing prices and maintaining the value of money are the top priority of monetary policy in advanced economies.

The success of the central bank's monetary control depends on how much it can influence monetary and financial conditions including the money supply and interest rates. The central bank has three policy instruments that can influence the money supply and interest rates. These include open market operations, discount policy, and reserve requirements. These three policy instruments are traditional policy tools commonly used by central banks. However, during the global economic crisis in 2008, the central bank of the United States used quantitative easing policy, a non-traditional monetary policy tool for the first time and used again the quantitative easing policy tool during the COVID-19 pandemic crisis in 2020. Japan also began to take quantitative easing policy as Abe became the Prime Minister of Japan, and the European Central Bank followed suit.

Among the three monetary policy tools, open market operations are the most important and most frequently used monetary policy tool in advanced economies where various financial assets exist and interest rates are freely determined by market factors. On the other hand, in developing countries, open market operations have not been as effective and powerful as in developed countries since the market for financial assets (mainly government bonds) in developing countries has not been well developed and diversified for open market operations to be effectively used.

In the case of the United States, financial securities subject to open market operations are not only diverse, but the size of the market for government securities is also huge. The outstanding balance of government securities (about 10 trillion dollars) is estimated to reach about 60% of U.S. GDP. As far as Treasury securities are concerned, tens of diverse securities with different maturities are issued. Treasury securities include short-term Treasury bills with maturities ranging from one month up to one-year, medium-term Treasury notes with maturities ranging from more than one year up to 10 years, and long-term Treasury bonds with maturities ranging from more than 10 years up to 30 years. These Treasury securities are sometimes collectively called Treasurys.

U.S. Treasury securities are the most liquid and safest assets in the world. Central banks including the Fed and foreign central banks own large amounts of Treasury securities as official reserve assets. U.S. and foreign governments, and international agencies such as the United Nations, World Bank, and IMFas well as private investors from around the world also hold U.S. Treasury securities. It is known that the size of Treasury securities held by People's Bank of China's is more than $1 trillion.

Open market operations refer to monetary policy aimed at affecting the amount of money by buying or selling government securities in the open financial market. Suppose the Fed offers to buy $1 billion worth of Treasury bills for a specified price in the open financial market, and Citibank accepts the offer. In return for the securities, the Fed transfers $1 billion to the reserve bank account that Citibank holds at the Federal Reserve Bank. As the reserve deposit of Citibank increases by $1 billion, the monetary base will also increase by $1 billion, because the monetary base is equal to the sum of bank reserve deposits at the Fed and vault cash. An increase in the monetary base results in a multiple increase in the money supply. How much will the money supply (M1) increase? It depends on the size of the money multiplier. If the size of the money multiplier is 2, M1 will increase by $2 billion as the result of the central bank's purchase of government securities from Citibank.

$$\text{Increase in M1} = \text{Money multiplier x Increase in monetary base}$$
$$\Rightarrow \quad \text{Increase in M1} = [2] \text{ x } \$1 \text{ billion} = \$2 \text{ billion}$$

Thus, open market purchases increase the amount of money available in the economy and are used as a tool for expansionary monetary policy.

On the other hand, when the central bank wants to reduce the amount of money available in the economy it pursues open market sales. In the case of an open market sale, the central bank offers to sell a certain amount (say, $1 billion) of government securities for a specified price in the open financial market. Suppose that Chase Bank accepts the Fed's offer to sell government securities. Then the central bank takes \$1 billion from Chase Bank's reserve deposits at the Federal Reserve Bank. Thus, Chase Bank's total reserves decrease by \$1 billion and so does the monetary base. Then there will be a multiple decrease in the amount of money (M1). Thus, open market sales decrease the money supply and are used as a tool for contractionary monetary policy.

Decrease in M1 = Money multiplier x Decrease in monetary base
⟹ Decrease in M1 = [2] x (−\$1 billion) = − \$2 billion

The purchase or sale of government securities between the central bank and banks takes place arbitrarily because the central bank offers good prices for the securities. Banks are willing to respond to such an offer because they judge that the purchase or sale of securities at the offered prices is a good investment. When the central bank says it controls the money supply, it means a voluntary transaction between the central bank and banks, and that the central bank's control over the money supply does not entail any coercive action.

Traditional open market operations target short-term government securities, but recent quantitative easing policy targets long-term government securities and mortgage-backed securities (MBSs). The central bank does not buy or sell corporate bonds issued by private firms for open market operations because they are too risky and there could be some conflicts of interest.

Open market purchases ⇒ Increase in the monetary base
⇒ Increase in the money supply: Expansionary monetary policy

Open market sales ⇒ Decrease in the monetary base ⇒ Decrease in the money supply: Contractionary monetary policy

7

MONETARY POLICY TOOLS: DISCOUNT POLICY

Discount policy is the oldest of the Fed's monetary policy tools. Open market operations were accidentally discovered by the Fed, but discount policy was initially intended to be the primary monetary policy tool of the Fed. Discount policy refers to changes in the discount rate and discount loans. The discount rate is the interest rate applied by the central bank to banks when they borrow from the central bank. The central bank is the bank of banks. Therefore, when banks need more money, they go to their bank, the central bank, to borrow money.

Sometimes banks need more money than they have obtained from deposits. First, banks must hold a certain percentage of deposits they receive as required reserves. If the reserves held by banks are less than the required reserves, they are subject to some penalty. To maintain required reserves, banks might need to borrow money. (However, this argument is no longer relevant, because the required reserve ratio was recently reduced to 0% in the United States.) Also, banks want to borrow money when they have good investment opportunities, but they do not have enough funds to support the investment projects.

As discussed previously, banks can borrow money through three channels: borrowing from the central bank (discount window loans), borrowing from other depository institutions (federal funds loans), and borrowing from corporations (repurchase agreements or repos). Here it is important to distinguish between discount loans and federal funds loans or repurchase agreements because they have very different effects on the creation of money. When a bank borrows money from the central bank through the discount window, such borrowing brings about an increase in the money supply, but when a bank borrows money from other banks, such borrowing does not increase the money supply because it is only a transfer of existing funds between banks. By the same token, repurchase agreements also do not lead to the creation of money.

More specifically, suppose that Citibank borrows money from Chase Bank. In this case, Citibank's reserves increase as much as the amount of borrowing but at the same time Chase Bank's reserves are also reduced by the same amount, and thus there is no change in reserves for the banking system as a whole. Since there is no change in bank reserves, there is no change in the monetary base, and therefore there is no change in the amount of money. However, when a bank (say, Citibank) borrows money from the central bank, the bank's reserve deposits at the central bank increase, and consequently the monetary base increases by the amount of borrowing. Thus, the amount of change in the monetary base depends on the amount of borrowing from the central bank.

When the central bank lowers the discount rate, it has the effect of encouraging banks to borrow more money from the central bank. As banks' total reserves increase, so does the monetary base in the banking system. Such being the case, a discount loan from the central bank sets off a multiplier effect that is similar to that of open market operations, increasing the amount of money in the economy. Thus, the central bank engages in a reduction in the discount rate to pursue expansionary monetary policy. When the central bank raises the discount rate, there will be a multiple decrease in the amount of money available in the economy. The central bank engages in an increase in the discount rate to pursue contractionary monetary policy.

> Reduction in the discount rate ⇒ Increase in the monetary base⇒ Increase in the money supply: Expansionary monetary policy
>
> Increase in the discount rate ⇒ Decrease in the monetary base ⇒ Decrease in the money supply: Contractionary monetary policy

If the same goal can be achieved by open market operations, why does the central bank bother to use discount policy? Although the central bank's discount policy is less flexible than open market operations and is not as accurate as open market operations in achieving the goal of controlling the money supply, discount policy is still used as an important tool of monetary policy for several reasons. First, when the central bank changes the discount rate, it is more visible to the public than open market operations. Thus, the central bank can use discount policy as a signal to announce the direction of monetary policy in the future. This is called the announcement effect of discount policy.

Discount policy was originally introduced as a buffer to prevent financial crises. The safeguard function of discount policy is especially important in an economic system where banks can be freely established.

Financial panics could happen at any time in such an economic system. Historically, when the Federal Reserve System was founded, the main function assigned to the Fed was to act as a lender of last resort to prevent a financial panic. This is the reason why the central bank is sometimes called a bankers' bank. The discount policy is a policy instrument for the central bank to fulfill the role as a lender of last resort.

Some economists (especially monetarists) argue that the Great Depression in the 1930s worsened because the Fed failed to properly function as a lender of last resort. On the other hand, during Black Monday in October 1987 when the global stock market crashed, the Fed played an appropriate role as a lender of last resort in minimizing the impact of the financial crisis.

Although discount policy is still very useful as a tool for the central bank to act as a final lender, there are also some problems with using discount policy as a means of managing the monetary base and the money supply. First, the central bank's announcement effect can be sometimes confusing. For example, when the central bank raises the discount rate, it may be perceived as a signal of monetary tightening in the future, and banks may attempt to significantly increase borrowings from the central bank through the discount window before further increases in the discount rate. In this case, an increase in the discount rate may result in an increase in the amount of money, contrary to the intention of the central bank.

Another problem is that the central bank can change the discount rate, but the central bank cannot force banks to borrow from the central bank. Whether to borrow or not from the central bank is entirely up to the decision of the banks. This is reminiscent of the saying that "You can lead a horse to water, but you can't make the horse drink water". This is the main reason why discount policy is much less accurate in controlling the money supply than open market operations.

Finally discount loans are a privilege and not a right given to banks. Thus, discount loans could be turned down at the discount window, and banks would have to go to the federal funds market to get federal funds loans from other banks. Before January 2003, the Fed tried to keep the discount rate lower than the federal funds rate, because otherwise banks would have no incentive to borrow from the central bank, and the Fed did not want to lose this important policy tool. However, since January 2003, the discount rate has been set higher than the federal funds rate, which indicates that the Fed now wants banks to go to other banks first to borrow funds in the federal funds market rather than to borrow from the central bank.

8

MONETARY POLICY TOOLS: RESERVE REQUIREMENTS

Depository institutions are required to hold a certain fraction of deposits they receive as required reserves in the form of reserve deposits at the central bank or cash in their vaults. This is the fractional required reserve system. (However, the Fed eliminated the reserve requirements on all types of deposits in March 2020.) The ratio of required reserves to total deposits is called the required reserve ratio. The central bank's policy on reserve requirements involves changing the required reserve ratio or adjusting the amount of deposits that are subject to reserve requirements. The central bank's policy on reserve requirements is the most powerful monetary policy tool, but the least used policy tool in advanced economies because of its crude effects on the money supply and the economy. In an economic system where the financial system is not well developed, however, the policy of reserve requirements is popular because of its powerful effects on the money supply.

Originally, the required reserve system was designed to protect depositors when banks went bankrupt or were in crisis. The required reserve system is to ensure that banks always have enough funds, and that banks are ready to pay whenever depositors want to withdraw money from their bank accounts. Nowadays, many countries have been implementing measures to protect depositors such as the FDIC (Federal Deposit Insurance Corporation) in the United States. Thus, the original purpose of protecting depositors designed by reserve requirements has been dwindling.

We need to know how changes in reserve requirements affect the stock of money. The central bank's reserve requirements are fundamentally different from open market operations and discount policy in that reserve requirements affect the money supply through their effects on the money multiplier whereas open market operations and discount policy affect the money supply through their effects on the monetary base. The size of the required reserve ratio has important policy implications in relation to banks' liquidity and lending capacity. Here, we need to recall that the amount of money available in the economy is determined by the interaction of the money multiplier and the monetary base.

Money supply = Money multiplier x Monetary base

The money multiplier in the complete model of money creation is

$$\text{Money multiplier} = \frac{1+\left(\frac{Currency}{Deposits}\right)}{Required\ reserve\ ratio + \left(\frac{Currency}{Deposits}\right) + \left(\frac{Excess\ reserves}{Deposits}\right)}$$

The above formula shows that when the central bank raises the required reserve ratio, the size of the multiplier becomes smaller, *ceteris paribus*, and consequently the money supply will decrease. Thus, an increase in the required reserve ratio leads to a decrease in the money supply. When the central bank raises the required reserve ratio, part of the reserves that was previously classified as excess reserves now becomes required reserves that banks cannot use for making loans. This will reduce banks' lending capacity as much as the reduced excess reserves and reduce the amount of money through the multiplier effect.

Conversely, if the central bank lowers the required reserve ratio, the money multiplier will increase, *ceteris paribus*, and consequently the money supply will also increase. Thus, a decrease in the required reserve ratio leads to an increase in the money supply. Part of the reserves previously classified as required reserves is now converted into excess reserves, which increases the lending capacity of banks. A lower required reserve ratio will eventually increase the amount of money through the multiplier effect.

Decrease in the required reserve ratio ⇒ Increase in the money multiplier ⇒ Increase in the money supply; Expansionary monetary policy

Increase in the required reserve ratio ⇒ Decrease in the money multiplier ⇒ Decrease in the money supply: Contractionary monetary policy

On the surface, the central bank's reserve requirement policy seems to be a very powerful monetary policy tool. This nature of the policy, however, could act as a disadvantage of the tool, and the central bank's reserve requirement policy has been criticized for being a too strong and unsophisticated monetary policy tool. Since the required reserve ratio directly affects the size of the money multiplier, even a small change in the ratio could lead to a big change in the amount of money. Therefore, it is difficult to accurately figure out the effect of changing the required reserve ratio on the amount of money.

Due to the problems with the reserve requirement system, there have been increasing trends in many countries to lower the required reserve ratio or to abolish the reserve requirement system altogether. Central banks in the United Kingdom, Canada, Australia, New Zealand, Sweden, and Hong Kong have no reserve requirements. The Bank of England previously set a voluntary reserve ratio and not minimum reserve requirements. From 1971 to 1980, U.K. commercial banks agreed to a reserve ratio of 1.5%, and in 1981, this requirement was abolished. The U.S. Fed abolished reserve requirements on time deposits in December 1990 and lowered the required reserve ratio on demand deposits from 12% to 10% in April 1994. The Fed once again reduced the required reserve ratio on demand deposits to zero percent in March 2020. This action eliminated reserve requirements on all types of deposits for all depository institutions. This change in reserve requirements was made to alleviate constraints on the liquidity of depository institutions associated with the COVID-19 crisis.

Another problem is that the central bank does not pay interest on reserves deposited by banks at the central bank. (However, the central bank of the United States began to pay interest on reserves in October 2008, and this has emerged as a new monetary policy tool.) Thus, reserve requirements on deposits act like taxes to banks. Banks will ultimately transfer these costs to depositors and borrowers which causes the interest costs to increase. In the era of globalization, international competitiveness is increasingly fierce, and many central banks have lowered the required reserve ratio or abolished the system in an effort to increase the competitiveness and efficiency of banks. Thus, competitive reductions in the required reserve ratio in many countries in recent years have not been pursued as part of normal monetary policy, but rather as an attempt to increase banks' lending capacity and lower the interest rates of financial institutions by freeing funds tied to reserve requirements. A lower required reserve ratio will ultimately lower the borrowing costs of firms and stimulate investment.

Although reserve requirement policy is crude and not sophisticated as a tool for controlling the money supply and interest rates, it is quite effective as a means of providing liquidity to the banking system. Lowering the required reserve ratio increases banks' lending capacity and increases the liquidity of banks. As a result, banks can increase their business loans and consumer loans. In an economic system where the financial system is not well developed, reserve requirement policy has been widely used because it has a strong effect on the liquidity and credit conditions of banks. Another advantage of the reserve requirement policy is that it applies uniformly to all banks.

China is one of the countries that has extensively and frequently used reserve requirement policy. Especially in recent years, China has been using reserve requirements as a major tool of monetary policy, frequently raising the required reserve ratio when the economy shows signs of overheating and lowering the required reserve ratio when the economy begins to slow down. According to the CEIC website, the People's Bank of China (PBOC) has changed its required reserve ratio at least 51 times since January 1985 until May 2023. However, it has rarely used open market operations and discount policy. During the COVID-19 crisis, the PBOC lowered the reserve requirement ratio in a row, cutting the reserve requirement ratio to 8.9% in September 2021 and to 8.4% in December 2021 by 0.5% points. It continued to cut the reserve requirement ratio in April and August 2022 by 0.25% points, respectively and in March 2023 by 0.25% points to stimulate the economy. After the cuts, the weighted average reserve requirement ratio reached 7.6% and remained at that level up to May 2023. The Chinese government set the goal of 2023 economic growth at 5% after the Chinese economic growth rate slowed down to 3% in 2022, one of the weakest performances in nearly half a century. China took a different road to deal with the COVID-19 crisis from the United States: China mainly resorted to changes in the reserve requirement ratio, whereas the United States primarily relied on changes in the federal funds rate through open market operations. China's discount rate has been adjusted only once in November 2014 over the past 10 years or so.

China's approach to controlling the money supply is in sharp contrast with that of the United States and European countries including the United Kingdom. One explanation for this difference is that in China, open market operations are not well developed. Reserve requirements could be the most effective monetary policy tool in developing countries where the financial system is not sophisticated. Sometimes they need shock therapies to affect the economy but in a stable and advanced economic system, adjusting the amount of money by the use of reserve requirements is like 'sharpening a pencil with an ax'. In conclusion, reserve requirement policy is too crude to be appropriate for conducting a pinpoint management of the money supply.

9

NEW MONETARY POLICY TOOLS: QUANTITATIVE EASING (QE)

We have seen that open market operations are a very useful tool for monetary policy in advanced economies. Open market operations are designed to control the amount of money by selling or buying short-term government securities in an open financial market, which leads to changes in short-term interest rates Thus, open market operations are a major tool of traditional monetary policy.

The United States cut the short-term policy interest rate (federal funds rate) to near zero levels during the 2008 financial crisis. In such a situation, no matter how much the monetary authorities supply money, the nominal interest rate cannot go down further. This is because nominal interest rates cannot be negative. A negative nominal interest rate means that the person who lends money pays interest to the borrower. No one would do such a stupid thing unless the lender is a philanthropist.

Meanwhile, long-term nominal interest rates have a structure that is determined in the market with expected future inflation (commonly called a term premium) added to short-term interest rates. Thus, open market operations aimed at controlling short-term interest rates have little direct effect on long-term interest rates. The economic crisis in 2008 that was set off by the sub-prime mortgage problems in the United States made the housing market frozen, leading to a severe downturn in the real economy. However, the central bank could not cope with the crisis with the traditional monetary policy tool.

The stabilization of the housing market was critical to calming the economic crisis and bringing the economy back to a normal state. However, since the housing market was affected by long-term interest rates (mortgage rates) ranging over 15 to 30 years, and short-term policy rates remained near zero, traditional open market operations were not enough to revive the economy. As a result, the Fed embarked on non-traditional monetary policy by buying long-term Treasury securities and mortgage-backed securities (MBSs) from 2008 to October 2014 to stabilize the housing market. This new monetary policy has come to be known as quantitative easing policy. When we looked at the asset changes on the Fed's balance sheet, the Fed's assets were $800 billion in September 2007 before the global economic crisis, but they exploded to $2 trillion in December 2009 when the crisis ended. This happened because the Fed bought huge amounts of long-term Treasury securities and mortgage-backed securities to stabilize the economy. The Fed's quantitative easing policy is sometimes called asset purchase programs.

<Figure 12.1> The Federal Reserve Balance Sheet

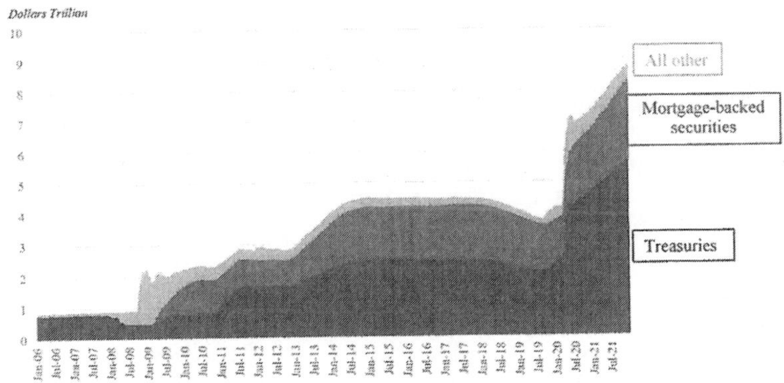

Source: Federal Reserve Bank of Saint Louis.
Note: Excludes eliminations from consolidation.

The Fed pledged to continue using quantitative easing policy until the economy reaches its potential growth rate (or full employment rate of unemployment). The Fed conducted three phases of quantitative easing (QE) from 2008 until 2014 as follows:

- ◈ QE1 (2008): Purchase of mortgage-backed securities
- ◈ QE2 (2010): Purchase of log-term government securities
- ◈ QE3 (2012): QE1 + QE2

When the U.S. unemployment rate finally fell to 5.7% in October 2014, policymakers concluded that the U.S. economy almost reached its potential output level and ended quantitative easing policy in late October 2014. As a result, the U.S. economy successfully overcame the economic crisis and regained its potential growth rate in about six years after the global economic crisis occurred. However, the United States reintroduced quantitative easing policy in 2020 to deal with the COVID-19 crisis.

When Abe was elected as Japanese Prime Minister, Japan set the escape from the 'Lost Two Decades' as the top priority of economic policy. The notorious deflation, a byproduct of the 'Lost Two Decades', crippled the Japanese economy for almost 20 years from the early 1990s. The Abe administration began to take unlimited quantitative easing policy in 2013. Unlike the United States, the Bank of Japan (BOJ) purchased private securities such as real-estate investment trusts as well as long-term government bonds and engaged in unlimited purchases of assets. It is yet premature to conclude that Japan's quantitative easing policy has succeeded as intended, because the Japanese inflation rate has not yet reached the goal of 2% per year. Although there have been some signs of success in terms of the recovery of the stock market and corporate profits and the modest rise in prices, the complete success of Japanese quantitative easing policy depends on the successful completion of the structural reforms by Abe's successor, Prime Minister Fumio Kishida, because the structural weakness of the Japanese economy is deeply bogged down in Japan.

The eurozone's economy was also struggling to recover on its own before the COVID-19 crisis. Deflation was in the offing, and differences in economic performance and conditions among member countries made it difficult for the 19 member countries to keep pace and move forward together. The European Central Bank (ECB) could not resist the temptation to implement quantitative easing and finally drew a knife in January 2015. The European Central Bank embarked on its asset purchase program in 2015 by purchasing €80 billion worth of long-term government bonds every month until the end of 2017. The ECB reduced the amount of monthly purchase of securities from €80 billion to €60 from April 2017 to December 2017 and ended the program.

The Fed has taken a new breed of monetary policy called quantitative easing, a road that has never been taken before by the Fed. It was as if Robert Lee Frost said in <The Road Not Taken> that "Two roads diverge in a yellow wood. I took the one less traveled, and that has made all the difference." As the poem sang, non-traditional quantitative easing policy changed the U.S. economy fundamentally.

Two roads diverged in a yellow wood,
And sorry I could not travel both
And be one traveler, long I stood
And looked down one as far as I could
To where it bent in the undergrowth;
Then took the other, as just as fair,
And having perhaps the better claim
Because it was grassy and wanted wear,
Through as for that the passing there
Had worn them really about the same
And both that morning equally lay
In leaves no step had trodden black
Oh, I kept the first for another day!
Yet knowing how way leads on to way
I doubted if I should ever come back.
I shall be telling this with a sigh
Somewhere ages and ages hence;
Two roads diverged in a wood, and I…
I took the one less traveled by,
And that has made all the difference.

10

HOW DOES THE CENTRAL BANK SET THE BENCHMARK INTEREST RATE (FEDERAL FUNDS RATE)?

The U.S. central bank (Fed) recently lowered the federal funds rate, a short-term benchmark interest rate in a row as an attempt to cope with inflationary expectations that have been fueled by the COVID-19 crisis. The Fed has mainly relied on changing the federal funds rate to manage the ups and downs of economic activity. The federal funds rate is the interest rate that banks charge each other for overnight loans. Thus, you may wonder how the Fed changes the interest on inter-bank loans charged by commercial banks. In fact, the federal funds rate is the short-term policy interest rate set by the central bank. Thus, when the economy slips into the phase of recession, the Fed can lower the federal funds rate, mainly by the use of open market operations. When the economy turns into the phase of inflation, the Fed can raise the federal funds rate. The following shows how the Fed has responded to the U.S. business cycles since the global economic crisis by changing the federal funds rate.

<Table 12.1> Historical Trends in the Federal Funds Rate

2008:	0 ~ 0.25% (12/16)
2015:	***0.25 ~ 0.5% (12/17)***
***2016*:**	***0.5 ~ 0.75% (12/15)***
2017:	***0.75 ~ 1.0% (3/16); 1.0 ~ 1.25% (6/15); 1.25 ~ 1.5% (12/14)***
2018:	***1.5 ~ 1.75 (3/22); 1.75 ~ 2.0% (6/14); 2.0 ~ 2.25% (9/27); 2.25 ~ 2.5% (12/20)***
2019:	2.0 ~ 2.25% (8/1); 1.75 ~ 2.0% (9/19); 1.5 ~ 1.75% (10/21)
2020:	1.0 ~ 1.25% (3/3); 0 ~ 0.25% (3/16)
2022:	***0.25 ~ 0.5% (3/17); 0.75 ~ 1.0% (5/5); 1.5 ~ 1.75% (6/16); 2.25 ~ 2.5% (7/27); 3.0 ~ 3.25% (9/21); 3.75 ~ 4.0% (11/2); 4.25 ~ 4.5% (12/14)***

where the numbers in light ink indicate federal funds rate cuts, and the italicized numbers in dark ink indicate federal funds rate hikes.

The Fed lowered the federal funds rate to a zero percent (0~0.25%) on December 16, 2008 when the global economic crisis cast a dark cloud over the U.S. economy. The zero percent federal funds rate lasted for seven more years until December 17, 2015 when the Fed raised the federal funds rate to 0.25~0.50% for the first time in seven years. The Fed judged that the U.S. economy recovered fully from the global economic crisis. Since then, the Fed continued to raise the federal funds rate eight times by a baby step (0.25% points), and the federal funds rate reached 2.0~2.25% on August 1, 2019. As the U.S. economy showed some signs of slowing down, the Fed began to shift gears toward lowering the federal funds rate again, and it lowered the federal funds rate to 2.0~2.25% on August 1, 2019, and conducted two additional baby step cuts (9/19/2019: 1.75~2.0%; 10/21/2019: 1.5~1.75%).

As the COVID-19 crisis loomed on the horizon, the Fed took a big step by lowering the federal funds rate from 1.5~1.75% to 1.0~1.25% by 0.5% points on March 3, 2020. As the COVID-19 crisis was getting worse, the Fed took a giant step in lowering the federal funds rate from 1.0~1.25% to 0~0.25% by 1.0% point on March 16, 2020. It took less than two weeks for the Fed to lower the federal funds rate twice. The federal funds rate entered the territory of zero percent. As the threat of the COVID-19 crisis began to diminish in early 2022, the Fed changed gears again toward raising the federal funds rate. This time, the specter of inflation has hung around the U.S. economy. The U.S. inflation rate recorded 40-year highs in several months in 2022, and the annual inflation rate reached 8.0% in 2022, which has been the highest level since 1981 at 8.9%. For reference, the inflation rate in the United States averaged 3.23% from 1914 until 2020, reaching an all-time high of 23.7% in June of 1920 and record low of -15.8% in June of 1921.

In order to cope with the red-hot inflation rates, the Fed raised the federal funds rate consecutively in 2022; it took a baby step (0.25% points) to raise the federal funds rate from 0~0.25% to 0.25~0.5% on March 17, 2022, and a big step (0.5% points) in raising the federal funds rate from 0.25~0.5% to 0.75%~1.0% on May 5, 2022. The Fed did not stop here and took four more giant steps (0.75% points) from 0.75~1.0% to 1.5~1.75% (6/16/2022) to 2.25~2.5% (7/27/2022) to 3.0~3.25% (9/21/2022) and to 3.75~4.00% (11/2/2022). Then, the Fed finally slowed down its step a little bit by taking a big step and raising the policy interest rate to 4.25~4.5% on December 14, 2022. Thus, the Fed continued its battle against inflation by raising its benchmark interest rate from 0~0.25% to 4.25~4.5% seven times in 2022 alone, and the federal funds rate reached its highest level in 15 years.

<Figure 12.2> Historical Trends in the Federal Funds Rate (in %)

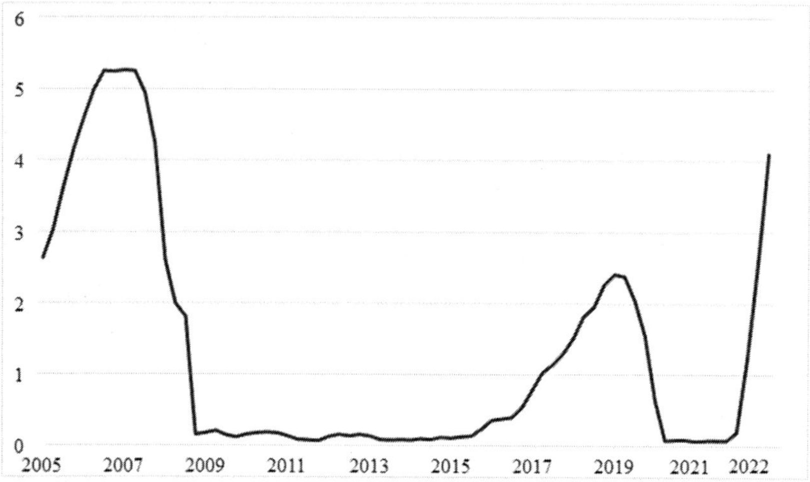

*The figure represents only the upper range of the federal funds rate after December 16, 2008.

There was a notorious episode in which the federal funds rate skyrocketed in response to rising inflation during the 1978-1982 period. At that time, the federal funds rate soared as high as 18%, and the effective federal funds rate rose close to 20%. The federal funds rate in 2022 was much lower than the federal funds rate in the late 1970s and early 1980s although the inflation rate during the COVID-19 crisis was comparable to the inflation rate during the oil crises. The following table shows a comparison of the federal funds rate between the two inflationary periods (2021 ~ 2022 and 1979 ~ 1980).

<Table 12.2> Federal Funds Rates between 1978~1982 and 2018~2022

2018 ~ 2022			1978 ~ 1982		
Year	Inflation Rate (%)	Federal Funds Rate (%)	Year	Inflation Rate (%)	Federal Funds Rate (%)
2018	1.9	2.50	1978	9.0	10.00
2019	2.3	1.75	1979	13.3	12.00
2020	1.4	0.25	1980	12.5	18.00
2021	7.0	0.25	1981	8.9	12.00
2022	8.3	4.50	1982	3.8	8.50

In order to understand why many central banks rely on changing the benchmark interest rate (federal funds rate) to influence the economy, we need to know how the federal funds rate is determined. The federal funds rate has two dimensions. First, it is a market interest rate applied to short-term loans between banks. However, it is also a policy interest rate in the sense that the central bank sets the target federal funds rate using its monetary policy. Thus, the federal funds rate is an important gauge for implementing monetary policy. The federal funds rate represents the costs of funding for banks' loans. Most interest rates determined in the market are based on the benchmark interest rate (federal funds rate) in the following manner.

Nominal market interest rate = Nominal federal funds rate
+ Market demand and supply forces + Risk factor

The interest rate on inter-bank loans is called differently across countries. As we discussed, in the United States, it is called the federal funds rate. In the United Kingdom, the interest rate is called the bank rate (or base rate), and in Japan, it is called the call rate. In South Korea, the interest rate was called the call rate until February 2008, but from March 2008, it was changed to the base rate.

Here we raise one fundamental question of how the central bank sets the benchmark interest rate at the level that it wishes to achieve. The Fed usually relies on two policy tools to change market interest rates. First, the Fed targets the federal funds rate. The Fed never forces banks to change the interest rate. Instead, the Fed attempts to lower or raise the federal funds rate by changing the quantity of money available in the banking system through open market operations.

The Federal Open Market Committee (FOMC) in the Federal Reserve System is responsible for determining whether to raise or lower the federal funds rate. The FOMC meets eight times per year. Suppose that the FOMC has decided to lower the federal funds rate. Then, the Fed supplies money to the banking system by purchasing government securities from banks in the open market. The Federal Reserve Bank of New York conducts the open market operations. The Fed offers good prices and conditions for the purchase, and banks will be willing to accept such a deal. Then the Fed credits the amount of the purchase of bonds to the reserve deposit accounts held by banks. Now that banks are given more money, they can afford to lower the federal funds rate when they lend money to other banks. Since the cost of acquiring funds is lowered, banks are now able to lower their lending rates on consumer loans, business loans, credit card loans and mortgage loans. Thus, market interest rates fall. When the Fed wants to raise the interest rate, the FOMC takes money from the banking system by selling government securities to banks. Then market interest rates will rise.

Then how can the Fed set the federal funds rate at some specific level? Suppose the Fed wants to set the federal funds rate at 3.0 percent. The Fed offers to buy any amount of government bonds at interest rates above 3.0 percent (promising unlimited open market purchases) and sell any amount at rates below 3.0 percent (promising unlimited open market sales). If the interest rate starts to move above 3.0 percent, the Fed effectively increases the money supply through open market purchases, pushing the interest rate back down to 3.0 percent. Similarly, if the interest rate starts to move below 3.0 percent, the Fed effectively decreases the money supply through open market sales, pushing the interest rate upwardly to 3.0 percent. Here we see that the Fed does not set the interest by any sort of law or coercion. The Fed's setting the federal funds rate is just like the use of open market operations on autopilot.

Another policy tool that the Fed uses (but less frequently than the federal funds rate) is to change the discount rate. The discount rate is the interest rate that the Fed charges banks when they borrow money from the Federal Reserve Bank. If the Fed lowers the discount rate, banks can borrow money from the Fed at a lower cost, which enables banks to lower their lending rates when they lend money to businesses, consumers, and home buyers. When the Fed raises the discount rate, banks will raise their lending rates when they lend money to their customers.

<Figure 12.3> Determination of the Target Federal Funds Rate

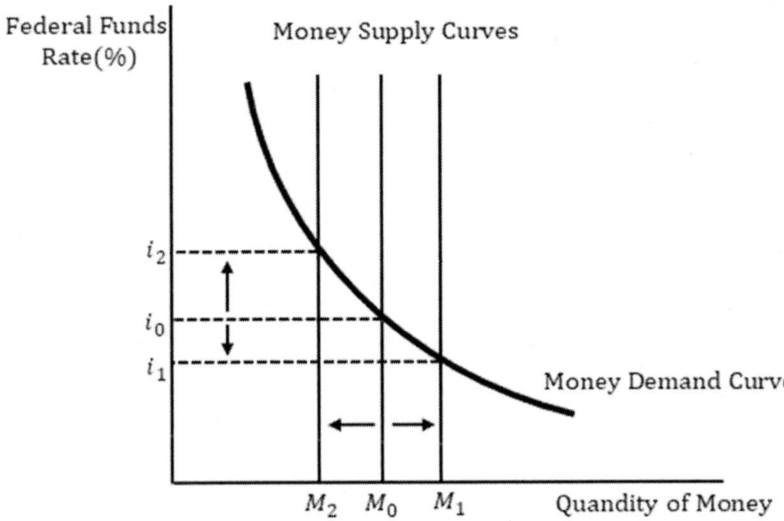

In the past, the Fed attempted to keep the discount rate lower than the federal funds rate, because the Fed did not want to lose its important monetary policy tool, discount rate policy. However, beginning January 2003, the Fed changed its position, and has maintained the discount rate to be higher than the federal funds rate. This shift reflects the Fed's intention that the Fed wants banks to go to other banks first when they need additional funds.

11

THE GOLDILOCKS ECONOMY AND THE NEUTRAL INTEREST RATE: THE TAYLOR RULE

In the economy, interest rates, inflation, and exchange rates should not be either too high or too low. There might be some medium level at which the economy can reach its optimal state. This middle point is called a 'happy medium point' in the West and *Zhongyong* in the East. *Zhongyong* is a key element of Confucian thought. Confucius regarded *Zhongyong* as the best moral rule. The core content of *Zhongyong* is that "Too much is as bad as too little".

Zhongyong is known to have been written by the grandson of Confucius. *Zhongyong* is one of the *Four Books and Three Classics*. The *Four Books* include *Analects* (*Lunyu*), *Mencius* (*Mengzi*), *Great Learning* (*Daxue*), and the *Doctrine of the Mean* (*Zhongyong*), and the Three Classics consist of the *Classic of Poetry* (*Shijing*), *Book of Documents* (*Shujing*), and *Book of Changes* (*Yijing*). The Chinese letter *Zhong* means the center that is not biased to one side, and the Chinese letter *Yong* means the normal reason. Thus, *Zhongyong* refers to the principle of maintaining the normal reasoning with being 'not too much, not too little, but just right'. We'll call *Zhongyong* the golden mean. In *Zhongyong*, human nature is innate, and therefore, human beings must follow human nature.

In fact, the doctrine of the golden mean is not a principle that applies only to human nature, but a principle that applies to the operations of the economy. This is because the economy can reach an optimal state or a normal state if economic variables are maintained at a level that is neither too high nor too low or at a level that is neither too much nor too little. Let us first consider the interest rate.

The central bank attempts to affect the equilibrium interest rate determined in the market by controlling its policy interest rate known as the benchmark interest rate (or the federal funds rate). The benchmark interest rate is the interest rate that is applied when a bank borrows money from other banks. Although the benchmark interest rate is an interest rate on short-term interbank loans, the central bank can set the target benchmark interest rate at the level that it desires to achieve through monetary policy. The central bank attempts to change the market interest rate mainly by changing the benchmark interest rate.

Suppose that the Fed raised the target federal funds rate from 1.75% to 2.50%. Since banks' cost of borrowing increases as the result of an increase in the federal funds rate, banks will raise their interest rates on consumer loans, business loans, car loans, credit card loans and mortgage loans. The central bank usually attempts to raise the benchmark interest rate when inflation is high. By raising the benchmark interest rate, the Fed can induce market interest rates to rise, and consumption and investment to be discouraged. Thus, the policy of raising the benchmark interest rate will be effective in curbing inflation, but as a side effect, unemployment will increase, and economic growth will slow down. This phenomenon is a replica of what happened in many countries after the COVID-19 crisis.

On the other hand, the central bank tries to lower the benchmark interest rate when unemployment is high. By lowering the benchmark interest rate, the Fed can induce the market interest rate to fall, and consumption and investment to be stimulated. Thus, the policy of lowering the benchmark interest rate will be effective in reducing unemployment, but as a side effect, inflationary pressure will also increase. Here, we see that if interest rates fall, economic growth speeds up, but inflation heats up. If interest rates rise, economic growth slows down, but inflation goes down.

Thus, neither too low nor too high interest rates are desirable. If the interest rate is too low, it may be good for promoting economic growth, but it can also stimulate inflation. Conversely, if the interest rate is too high, it may be good for suppressing inflation, but it can also deter economic growth. Is there any optimal level of the interest rate that neither deters economic growth nor stimulates inflation? If such an interest rate exists, that interest is an interest rate that is consistent with the state of the golden mean or *Zhongyong*. Economists have called such an interest rate the neutral interest rate and have been trying to find the neutral interest rate. The Taylor Rule is a formula for finding the neutral benchmark interest rate. The Taylor rule proposed by John Taylor (1993) is given as follows:

Target federal funds rate = Real federal funds rate + Inflation rate
+ λ [Actual inflation rate − Targetinflation rate]
+ (1- λ) [Actual economic growth rate – Potential economic growth rate]

where λ is the weight given to inflation and $(1-\lambda)$ is the weight given to economic growth. If λ is greater than 0.5, policymakers give more weight to inflation than to economic growth. If λ is smaller than 0.5, more weight is given to economic growth than to inflation. If we assume that policymakers give equal weight to both economic growth and inflation, λ is equal to 0.5. In this case, the Taylor rule becomes:

$$\text{Target federal funds rate} = \text{Real federal funds rate} + \text{Inflation rate} + 0.5\,[\text{Inflation gap} - \text{Output gap}]$$

where the inflation gap represents the difference between the actual inflation rate and the target inflation rate, and the output gap represents the difference between the actual growth rate and the potential growth rate. It is not possible to say uniformly what level of the interest rate is a neutral interest rate. This is because each country's economic situation and each country's potential economic growth rate and target inflation rate are different. In the United States, the neutral interest rate has been presumed to be 2%.

The most controversial question is whether there is a 'golden mean' or *Zhongyong* inflation rate. If inflation is too high, resource allocations are distorted. In particular, when unexpected inflation occurs, resources are allocated in a way that economic agents do not know. Also, if inflation is too high, firms can make more profits because they can sell products at a higher price, and corporate investment will be stimulated, but consumption will be adversely affected, and economic stability will be threatened. Ultimately it will lead to higher wages, higher interest rates, and higher exchange rates (or lower currency values). In the long run, high inflation also has a negative effect on economic growth.

Then if inflation is too low, will the economy be better For example, is it desirable to have zero inflation or negative inflation (deflation)? The answer is 'no'. We have already seen that deflation can have an adverse effect on the economy as much as inflation, or the adverse effect of deflation could be worse than inflation. The reason is that inflation usually comes with an economic boom, but deflation is accompanied by a severe recession. Japan's experience of the 'Lost Two Decades' tells us how serious the vicious cycle of low inflation is. When we have too low inflation, people do not want to consume today and tend to postpone their consumption, expecting prices to fall further in the future. Business profits fall, and investment decreases.

If so, what level of inflation would be most desirable? In an advanced economy, economic stability is preferred to economic growth. In general, the 2% level of inflation is deemed to be the rate of inflation that stimulates consumption and investment without sacrificing economic stability. This level of inflation rate can be viewed as a 'golden mean' inflation rate. We have already seen that economists known as 'limited inflationists' argue that some amount of inflation is needed to blow a breath of fresh air to the economy. Limited inflationists are mostly Keynesians, and they favor an annual inflation rate of 2%.

Is there any 'golden mean' or *Zhongyong* unemployment rate? The natural rate of unemployment elaborated by Friedman is close to the notion of the 'golden mean' unemployment rate. Friedman argues that a country's unemployment rate tends to approach the equilibrium rate of unemployment in the long run, and this long-run equilibrium rate of unemployment is called the natural rate of unemployment. When a country reaches its natural rate of unemployment, inflation does not accelerate and remains quite stable. For this reason, the natural unemployment rate is often referred to as the 'non-accelerating inflation rate of unemployment' (NAIRU).

The NAIRU can be viewed as a 'golden mean' unemployment rate. When the unemployment rate equals the NAIRU, output grows without inflation. When the economy reaches this state, output produced in the economy equals the level of potential output, and a country's economy can achieve its potential growth rate. Economic growth without inflation is the ultimate goal of economic policy. Can we find this 'golden mean' unemployment rate, that is, NAIRU? Unlike the golden mean inflation rate, the NAIRU varies across countries depending on their economic structure and changes over time. Thus, it is not possible to specify uniformly the NAIRU. In the United States, the NAIRU is estimated to be around 5.0~5.5%.

The exchange rate also seems to have a golden mean exchange rate. Neither a too high exchange rate (weak currency) nor a too low exchange rate (strong currency) is desirable. If a country's dollar exchange rate is too high, this means that the value of the currency of the country falls relative to the dollar. A high exchange rate is good for the country's exports and economic growth because the products of the country become cheaper in the international marketplace. However, a weak currency is not good for the country's inflation. The prices of imported goods and services (especially energy and raw materials) rise domestically, which leads to higher inflation.

If a country's dollar exchange rate is too low, this means that the value of the currency of the country rises relative to the dollar. A low exchange rate is good for the country's inflation because imported goods and services (especially energy and raw materials) become cheaper domestically, which will lead to lower inflation. However, a strong currency against the dollar is not good for the country's exports and economic growth because the products of the country become more expensive and lose their competitiveness in the international marketplace.

Thus, there seems to be a 'golden mean' *or Zhongyong* exchange rate that neither deters exports and economic growth nor promotes inflation. The exchange rate is a price variable that connects two countries. The exchange rate between any two countries is intertwined through interest rates, income, and inflation in the two countries. Theoretically, an exchange rate at which the balance of payments (BOP) reaches zero, that is, the sum of the current account balance and the capital account balance is approximately equal to zero is considered to be a golden mean exchange rate, but the golden mean exchange rate is also affected by each country's foreign exchange reserves and foreign exchange policy.

In conclusion, when an economy operates at the golden mean interest rate (i.e., neutral interest rate), it will be able to achieve its golden mean inflation rate, golden mean unemployment rate (i.e., NAIRU), and golden mean exchange rate.

The golden mean or *Zhongyong* state of the economy is sometimes likened to the Goldilocks economy. The name of the Goldilocks economy is derived from a 19th century British fairy tale titled *Goldilocks and the Three Bears* (originally titled *The Story of Three Bears*). The book featured three bears: Papa Bear (Great Big Bear), Mama Bear (Middle-sized Bear), and Baby Bear (Little Wee Bear). In the house, there are three chairs, three beds, and three bowls of porridge. They had each a chair to sit in: a little chair for Baby Bear, a middle-sized chair for Mama Bear, and a big chair for Papa Bear. They also each had a bed to sleep in: a little bed for Baby Bear, a middle-sized bed for Mama Bear, and a big bed for Papa Bear. The three bears had different tastes and preferences.

One day, they made porridge for their breakfast and poured it into their porridge bowls. While the porridge was cooling, they walked out into the wood for exercise. A little girl named Goldilocks who lived in a nearby village passed by the house owned by the three bears. She looked in the windows and peeped in through the keyhole. After she found that nobody was in the house, Goldilocks opened the door and entered the house. She saw the porridge on the table and was tempted to taste the porridge. First, she tasted the porridge of Papa Bear, and that was too hot for her. Next, she tasted the porridge of Mama bear, but that was too cold for her. And then Goldilocks finally tasted the porridge of Baby Bear, and that was neither too hot nor too cold, but just right. She liked it so much and ate it all up.

The gist of the story of the three bears lies in finding an exact middle path between two opposites. Papa Bear, Mama Bear, and Baby Bear each had different sizes of beds and chairs and different tastes and preferences of food. Goldilocks finds that one of them is always too much in one extreme (too hot food and too large bed) and one is too much in the opposite extreme (too cold food and too small bed), and one is ‘just right’. Here the Goldilocks economy has come to refer to a phenomenon in which the economy sustains moderate economic growth and low inflation, which enables policymakers to pursue a market-friendly economic policy. The Goldilocks economy is in the same vein as the *Zhongyong* (golden mean) economy.

PART 13

FISCAL POLICY AND ECONOMIC COORDINATION

1

HOW FISCAL POLICY DIFFERS FROM MONETARY POLICY

We have discussed the contents and effects of monetary policy so far. The lesson we have learned from our discussion of monetary policy is that if the monetary authorities use monetary policy to stimulate the economy rather than to manage inflation, such an attempt will not only fail, but also destabilize the economy. This conclusion is a position consistently held by monetarists. Of course, monetary policy may affect investment and output through channels other than interest rates, but such an effect is debatable.

Then, is it desirable to actively use fiscal policy, another pillar of macroeconomic policy? When Keynesian economics dominated modern economic thought, fiscal policy was often regarded as a policy with a panacea, but now few economists believe the omnipotent influence of fiscal policy. If an economy is more liberalized and self-regulated, has fewer regulations, and is closer to the normal state, fiscal policy has a limited role to play. In such an economic system, monetary policy is more flexible as a policy tool for the stabilization of the economy. However, some scholars believe that the role fiscal policy can play increases as the economic system becomes more opens. In this part, we will learn the nature, roles, and limitations of fiscal policy.

The government's functions today are not limited to national defense, diplomacy, and national security, but cover a wide range of activities, such as redressing market failures, promoting economic growth, and improving public welfare. The government spends fiscal revenues to perform these functions. Most of the revenues come from taxes, which are largely used to finance expenditures including government purchases, transfer payments, and interest payments.

All economic activities related to government revenues and expenditures are called public finance, and economic policy related to revenues and expenditures is called fiscal policy. If the government's expenditures exceed its revenues, the government has a budget deficit (or fiscal deficit), and if the government's revenues exceed its expenditures, the government has a budget surplus (or fiscal surplus). If the government's expenditures equal its revenues, the government has a balanced budget.

Tax revenues can be classified in many ways. First, taxes are comprised of federal taxes (collected by the federal government), state taxes (collected by state governments) and local taxes (collected by local governments). In 2020, taxes collected by U.S. federal, state, and local governments amounted to 25.5% of U.S. GDP, which is much lower than the OECD average of 33.5% of GDP. Taxes can be also classified according to their sources: income taxes (personal income taxes, corporate income taxes), payroll taxes (Social Security and Medicare contributions), property taxes, sales and excise taxes, estate and gift taxes, and tariffs or customs duties. Expenditures are classified into health (including Medicare) expenditures, Social Security payments, national defense, income security expenditures, and net interest payments. Expenditures can also be simply classified into defense expenditures, general government expenditures (government consumption), and fixed capital formation (government investment).

However, from the aspect of theoretical analysis, it is convenient to divide government expenditures into government purchases (G), transfer payments (TP) and interest payments (IP) and taxes into autonomous taxes and income taxes. An income tax is a tax that is dependent on income, and an autonomous or independent tax is a tax that is determined by factors other than income, regardless of the level of income. Income taxes include personal income taxes, corporate income taxes and capital gains taxes. Autonomous taxes include sales taxes, excise taxes, property taxes, and inheritance taxes.

The government can influence economic activities such as employment, growth, prices, international trade, and income distribution through fiscal policy. Government fiscal policy is implemented through changes in government purchases of goods and services (G), transfer payments (TP) and taxes (T). We have seen that government purchases of goods and services are an important component of GDP. Government purchases account for about 20% of GDP (government consumption: 15%, government investment: 5%). Government consumption includes the purchases of nondurable goods such as gasoline, cars, office supplies, and salaries for government officials and military personnel. Government investment includes the construction of highways, airports, police stations, fire stations and the purchases of weapons. In the Keynesian system, government purchases are treated as autonomous expenditures, meaning that government purchases do not depend on the level of income. The government purchases goods and services as part of fiscal policy regardless of the level of national income.

Some people receive money from the government as gifts through social programs even if they do not participate in the production of goods and services. These gifts are collectively called transfer payments or simply transfers. Transfer payments include Social Security benefits, Medicaid payments, unemployment insurance, minimum living supports, and other social security programs that individuals receive from the government. These grants are considered a redistribution of wealth and income from the well-compensated to the poorly compensated. However, transfer payments do not include subsidies paid to farmers, manufacturers, or exporters. Transfer payments are not included in GDP because these payments to individuals are not made in exchange for production activities. In developed countries including the United States, welfare benefits to the poor have reached a considerable size. Transfer payments are also treated as autonomous expenditures because transfer payments do not increase with income. Rather transfer payments are made to assist income for the low-income people. The sum of government purchases, transfer payments and interest payments is called government expenditures.

Depending on how the tax rate is determined, the tax system is divided into progressive tax, proportional tax, and regressive tax systems. The progressive tax is a tax system in which the marginal income tax rate rises with taxable income. For example, the personal income tax rate is 10% for people with annual income less than $30,000, 15% for people with annual income between $30,001 and $60,000, 20% for people with annual income between $60,001 and $100,000, and 30% for people with annual income of more than $100,000. As a country is tilted more toward a socialistic economic system or a welfare state, the progressive tax rate increases more steeply.

The proportional tax, also known as a flat tax, is a tax system in which the same marginal income tax rate applies to all taxpayers regardless of the level of income. For example, 20% of the marginal income tax rate is applied equally to people who earn $30,000 per year and people who earn more than $100,000 per year. The regressive tax is a tax system in which the tax rate decreases as the taxable income increases. For example, a tax rate of 30% applies to people with annual income less than $30,000, 25% to people with annual income between $30,001 and $60,000, 20% to people with annual income between $60,001 and $100,000 and 10% to people with annual income of more than $100,000. Sales taxes, excise taxes, and property taxes can be viewed as a regressive tax system, because lower-income individuals bear a higher relative tax burden as a percentage of their income.

We examined the effect of changes in government purchases, transfers, and taxes on national income when we discussed the multiplier effects in the Keynesian model. A policy that is aimed at increasing or decreasing government purchases, transfers, or taxes deliberately to promote or reduce aggregate demand is called discretionary fiscal policy. In the Keynesian system, the government is often tempted to engage in discretionary policy when the economy slips into a recession due to unexpected changes in consumption, investment, or net exports. The government can supplement insufficient private aggregate demand through discretionary fiscal policy. In other words, when the economy is not reaching the potential level of output due to sluggish private spending, the government can boost the economy by increasing government purchases or cutting taxes. Of course, classical economists have different views on the effectiveness of discretionary policy.

One important distinguishing feature of fiscal policy is that government expenditures, transfers, and taxes have all multiplier effects. A multiplier effect refers to a phenomenon in which a change in government expenditure, transfers, or taxes leads to an even greater change in GDP. For example, as government purchases increase by $10 billion, GDP will increase by more than $10 billion depending on the size of the multiplier. However, any increase in the money supply does not directly touch off such a multiplier effect on GDP. This is because money itself does not constitute aggregate expenditure.

Fiscal policy has unique characteristics not found in monetary policy. That is, even if the government does not purposely change transfer payments or taxes to increase or decrease aggregate demand, there is a built-in mechanism in the economic system that automatically increases or decreases transfer payments or taxes. This tendency is called an 'automatic fiscal stabilizer' or a 'built-in stabilizer', and the built-in stabilizers play an important role in stabilizing the economy.

For example, when the economy is booming, tax revenues tend to increase accordingly. Other things being equal, private consumption expenditure is suppressed as tax revenues increase. A slowdown in consumption demand will work as a brake on the booming economy through the multiplier effect and prevent the overheating of the economy. Conversely, when the economy is in deep stagnation, tax revenues tend to decrease. Other things being equal, a reduction in taxes serves as a lever to stimulate consumption and boost the economy. In this way, the income tax automatically changes even if the government does not change it deliberately and performs the function of reducing economic fluctuations.

The automatic stabilizers in the tax system can exert a greater effect when the tax system is progressive.

In addition, in a country with a well-developed social welfare system, transfer programs also play an important role as an automatic stabilizer to alleviate economic fluctuations. For example, if unemployment increases due to the sluggish economy, the number of people receiving transfer payments such as unemployment benefits increases, which stimulates consumption and boosts the economy. Conversely, when the economy is booming, many people can get jobs. As a result, the number of people who receive transfer payments decreases, and thus consumption associated with transfer programs will decrease. This eventually prevents the economy from overheating. In this way, the automatic stabilization mechanism built in transfer payments works to promote aggregate demand when the economy is in a downturn, and to decrease aggregate demand when the economy is in an upturn, alleviating economic fluctuations.

2

EQUITABLE TAXATION: PULLING THE MOST FEATHERS WITH THE LEAST SCREAMS

No one likes taxes. Whenever possible, consumers and producers alike try to avoid taxes or at least try to lower them. If consumers find a product alternative that is not taxed, but similar to a taxable product, they will be willing to buy such a substitute. If producers find products that are not taxable, but similar to taxable products, they are willing to produce such alternatives.

Arnold Harberger (1995), who published many papers on taxation, introduces an interesting anecdote that he witnessed on his trip to Indonesia. In Indonesia, a car is defined as a vehicle with four or more wheels. These cars are taxed more than two- or three-wheeled motorcycles. Interestingly, Indonesian people began to develop vehicles that are functionally the same as cars and buses but are legally classified as motorcycles. Some are classified as motorcycles with only three wheels but with benches facing each other added, which have almost the same function as buses. Harberger (1995) confesses that he was really surprised to see a motorcycle on eight people. This example shows that the market somehow is working towards minimizing tax burdens. In this way, taxpayers come up with ingenious ideas to reduce taxes as much as possible.

Jonathan Gruber (2011) introduces the following episodes:

- Uffa Fox, a British boat designer, lives in a house made of a floating bridge. When the British IRS tried to impose a property tax on the house, he pulled the house to the river and sailed up and down the river. When he finished sailing and anchored the house, the British IRS gave up trying to collect the property tax from him because his address was different from the address he left when he sailed.
- A British visitor to Cyprus in the early 1980s asked a travel guide why the houses were built with a steel frame at the top floor. The guide says that in Cyprus, taxes on buildings are imposed only on

the finished buildings, and the owner of a house with a steel frame at the top floor can claim that the house is still under construction. However, the construction of these houses will never be finished.

- The Thailand government levies taxes on business signboards. The tax rate is the lowest if the signboard advertisement is in Thai, the middle rate is applied if it is mixed with Thai and English, and the highest rate is applied if it is only in English. When you tour the city of Bangkok in Thailand, you'll see a lot of signboards that are largely displayed in English, but minimally displayed in the upper right in the Thai language. It's a mix of English and Thai, but it's really nothing different from an English signboard.

There are many heroic people who fought for equitable taxation. Lady Godiva was a legendary woman who was known to ride naked on horseback in the city of Coventry, a small English town, in the 11th century. It has been known that she did this vagary in protest of her husband, Count Leofric, who imposed excessive taxes on residents. Count Leofric founded monasteries in Coventry. Godiva's story was first introduced in the *Flores Historiarum*, published in the 13th century. Her horseback riding naked has become popular subjects of many paintings and novels. A painting drawn by John Collier in 1897 is famous.

<Figure 13.1>> Wife Godiva: John Collier (1897)

Lady Godiva was always sympathetic to the people of Coventry, who suffered from her husband's excessive taxation. Lady Godiva repeatedly protested his excessive taxation, but Count Leofric repeatedly refused her plea to cut taxes for the people. Then, her husband, who was unable to refuse Lady Godiva's request further, made the following proposal to her: "If you ride a horse naked and go around the city a round, I'll accept your request" (Source: www.wikipedia.org/Lady Godiva). Lady Godiva believed in her husband's promise and issued a decree to all the residents of Coventry to keep the window shutters pulled down and stay in the house. It was only her long hair that covered her body.

However, there was a man who didn't obey the order to close the shutter. His name was Tom, and he was a sailor. Tom made a hole in the shutter of the window and sneaked a glance at Lady Godiva on the horse through the hole. He soon became blinded by this incident and died shortly thereafter. Here, the word 'Peeping Tom' was coined. Meanwhile, her husband kept his promise and abolished the infamous tax.

The word 'Godiva' means the 'gift of God'. Modern historians question the truthfulness of the story regarding Lady Godiva. In fact, there is a surmise that she did not ride a horse without wearing any clothes but put down all the precious metals she was wearing and went around the city with a penitent attitude. (Source: www.wikipedia.org/LadyGodiva). Notwithstanding whether the story on Lady Godiva was true or not, Count Leofric's tax reform might be a godsend to taxpayers. Lady Godiva has received admiration from people in that she resisted excessive taxation in the softest way.

Today, Godiva is also famous for its chocolate brand (Godiva Chocolatier). Originally, Godiva Chocolate Company was founded in Belgium in 1926. Godiva became a multinational company by expanding its business to coffee and other drinks. It was later sold to Campbell, an American food company in 1967. Campbell sold it back to Yildiz Holding Company, a Turkish company in 2008. However, there have been some movements against the use of the name 'Godiva' on the ground that such commercialism undermines Lady Godiva's noble spirit. Pru Porretta, who led the movement, said that "Lady Godiva was a great woman who challenged her husband to stop the very harsh things happening to the people. Lady Godiva wouldn't like companies that took what was not originally theirs and used it for their own interests, not for the interests of others" (Source: www.wikipedia.org/Lady Godiva). Some people also launched a boycott of Godiva products on Facebook. However, such boycott movements may agree with the ethics of human sentiments but may be at odds with the behavior of rational economic agents who pursue their own interests.

<Figure 13.2> The Scream: Edvard Munch (1893)

The tax problem has always been a tug-of-war between tax collectors and taxpayers in human history. Historically, violent methods and bloody struggles have erupted on and off to resist excessive taxes. Excessive taxation was the background of the birth of the representative organization of the people, Congress. Thus, the issue of equitable taxation has been a political hot potato at any time in any country. The most famous principle on equitable taxation was presented earlier by Jean Baptiste Colbert (1619-

1683). He served as French Finance Minister when Louis XIV reigned France. He was known to say that "The art of taxation consists in plucking the goose as to obtain the largest number of feathers with the least possible amount of hissing" (Source: https://www.economist.com.pluck, February 20, 2014). The message of Colbert's statement is that if you handle the goose (taxpayers) too roughly to get as many feathers (taxes) as possible, then the goose will scream. Thus, you should not try to increase tax rates or taxable items too much to secure more tax revenues.

Colbert was a politician who put a lot of effort into achieving equitable taxation on various income classes. After taking office as Finance Minister, he undertook breakthrough tax reforms by the standard of the time. He tried to drastically reduce false claims for tax deduction. He also reduced direct taxes such as personal income taxes and corporate income taxes which were relatively unfair and instead raised the tax rates of indirect taxes (sales tax, excise tax, consumption tax, etc.) that could not be avoided by any privileged people. He boldly implemented mercantilism policies to increase France's wealth. He raised import tariffs to protect domestic industries and to increase tax revenues. In particular, he focused on fostering export industries such as textiles.

Some people have a misunderstanding of the truth of Colbert's 'Goose Feather' message. Some people put more emphasis on 'pulling out as many feathers as possible', but in fact, Colbert placed more emphasis on the realization of equitable taxation to minimize the goose's (taxpayers') screaming. If a tax increase is inevitable as a last resort for securing resources for welfare programs, it should be done in a way that it gives the least possible amount of suffering to taxpayers. That is, it should be done to the extent that the goose doesn't scream too much. In addition, some measures should be sought to have the least impact on the economy.

As the welfare issue has emerged as the biggest economic burden in many countries, various ways to secure welfare resources have been discussed and proposed. Depending on the type of tax, tax cuts or increases may have different effects on the economy. We are interested in the issue of which taxes get the most feathers with the least screams.

- ◈ Tax on earned income: This is a tax levied on workers' wages and salaries. These payroll taxes are the main source for various welfare programs.
- ◈ Tax on capital income: This is a tax levied on all types of income earned by individuals other than wages and salaries. Examples include taxes on interest income, rental income, dividends, and capital gains. Capital gains are income earned by selling capital

assets such as stocks and bonds, houses and other real estate, paintings, and antiques.

- Tax on corporate income: This is a tax imposed on corporate profits. Corporate taxes are sometimes controversial in relation to double taxation, but the purpose of corporate taxes is to tax the income of capital owners who have the opportunity to avoid taxation based on personal income.
- Tax on wealth: Wealth taxes are taxes on the value of the property that individuals or families own. Wealth taxes include property taxes imposed on the value of land and structures built on it and inheritance taxes imposed on the inherited property.
- Tax on consumption: The consumption tax is the oldest form of tax. The Bible tells a lot about the tax.

A consumption tax is a tax imposed on the consumption of goods or services by individuals. The consumption tax includes a sales tax that is imposed as a certain percentage of the amount of goods or services purchased, a value-added tax that is imposed on the value added at each stage of production and distribution, and an excise tax that is imposed on a certain type of products such as cigarettes, liquors, and gasoline as a certain amount of the products.

Taxes can also be divided into direct and indirect taxes. Direct taxes are taxes in which the tax payment obligor (the person who is obligated to pay the tax) and the taxpayer (the person who actually pays the tax) are the same, and the tax burden is not passed on to others. Direct taxes include income tax, corporate tax, inheritance tax, and property tax. Most direct taxes have the characteristic of the progressive tax. Indirect taxes are taxes where tax payment obligors and taxpayers are different, and the tax burden is passed on to others. Indirect taxes include value-added tax (VAT), consumption tax, sales tax, and excise tax. For example, if you pay £100 at Harrods to buy a suit, the payment (£100) includes VAT of £20. The taxpayer is the Harrods department store, but the tax is what you bear.

We have seen earlier that in order for a tax cut to have a maximum effect on the economy, it must affect marginal incentives to work, save, and invest. It is important to design a tax increase in such a way that it has the least impact on marginal incentives. Many experts agree that an increase in indirect taxes such as the consumption tax rather than an increase in direct taxes such as the income tax is the one that has the least effect on marginal incentives. A tax increase on indirect taxes is the most effective way to 'pull feathers while minimizing the screams of the goose'.

3

Is a Balanced Budget Necessary and Desirable? The Twin Deficit Problem

Should the government budget always be balanced? It is impossible for the government budget to be balanced on a monthly or quarterly basis. So, should the government budget be balanced by year? This discussion is an area that belongs to normative economics, and views on the issue are diversely divided. In the European countries and the United States, fiscal policy prior to the Great Depression aimed to maintain an annually balanced budget except the period of war. People even considered it immoral for the government to spend more than tax revenues it collected from taxpayers. This tradition was rooted in the piety of the Victorian era of England in the 19th century.

Queen Victoria's reign (1837-1901) was the time when Great Britain enjoyed economic prosperity thanks to the Industrial Revolution and the expansion of colonialism. Great Britain established the empire on which the sun never set, thus strengthening the hegemony in the world. Moral piety and utilitarian ethics dominated in many cultural and social spheres, and the entire society was overflowing with optimism. The government's spending more than tax revenues it collected was not congruous with the atmosphere of the time. This sentiment prevailed until the Great Depression.

In general, tax revenues tend to increase during the economic expansion period and tend to decrease during the economic contraction period. Therefore, in order to maintain a balanced budget for each year, it is necessary to increase government spending during the economic expansion phase and decrease government spending during the economic contraction phase. Such a policy could further amplify economic fluctuations by fanning the economic heat during economic expansion and pouring cold water into the economic downturn during economic contraction.

The cyclically balanced budget is a philosophy for balanced budgets that emerged as an alternative to the idea of yearly balanced budgets. This position does not require a strictly balanced budget each and every year. Instead, this philosophy allows the budget to exhibit a deficit during the period of recession and to achieve a surplus during the period of economic boom. However, it aims to keep the budget balanced through one business cycle.

Lastly, the functionally balanced budget is that the government's primary responsibility is to promote economic growth and achieve full employment, and thus efforts to maintain a balanced budget on a yearly basis or over a business cycle are pointless. Instead, the philosophy of the functionally balanced budget states that the government should make every effort for its GDP to reach its potential level, even if such a budget leads to a deficit. The idea that the budget deficit is good for the recovery of the economy is a Copernican revolution brought by Keynesian economics. This budget philosophy was reflected in economic policy under the name of a full-employment budget. The full-employment budget deficit is the budget deficit that an economy has when the economy is at or near full employment.

Particularly, during the time of President Kennedy in the United States, a group of young economists introduced the concept of full-employment budget deficit and actively pursued Keynesian prescriptions. They suggested that the U.S. economy was in the budget deficit in the early 1960s, but the full employment budget was still in the black, and thus there was a leeway for further tax cuts. President Kennedy accepted this proposal and implemented a series of tax cuts, which laid the foundation for the renaissance of the U.S. economy in the 1960s.

As discussed earlier, maintaining a balanced budget year by year is almost impossible and undesirable. In fact, the annual balance of the budget is just trying to adjust the budget balance to the artificial time frame of the calendar year. It would be reasonable to judge whether a country's budget is balanced on the basis of the ultimate goal of fiscal policy, that is, on the basis of full employment output. From this point of view, we are sympathetic to the 'functionally balanced budget' principle that, even if the actual budget exhibits a deficit in any year or years, there is no need to be worried about the budget deficit as long as the economy operates at the full employment level of output. In such a situation, any budget deficit will soon disappear.

In the United States, not only the federal government budget has suffered chronic deficits over the past few decades, but the trade balance has also been in persistent deficit. In the reality of the twin deficits, the U.S. economy has relied heavily on borrowing from foreign countries (especially from China, Japan, South Korea, etc.). Amid the mounting deficits and debt, however, the United States overcame the 2008 global economic crisis most successfully-among the developed economies, and as a result the U.S. stock market enjoyed the longest expansion phase until March 2020 when the

Dow Jones Industrial Index hit the highest point in U.S. history. What made the U.S. economy resilient even in the midst of the twin deficits?

The strength and resilience of the U.S. economy has something to do with the power of the U.S. dollar as a reserve currency. The United States is the only country that could afford both the budget and trade deficits for an extended period. Although the dollar standard (the Bretton Woods system) collapsed in 1973, the U.S. dollar still holds an overwhelming share in international trade and financial transactions, effectively enjoying its status as a world reserve currency. Even if the United States has the twin deficits, many investors who prefer the U.S. dollar as a safe investment are willing to lend money to the United States., that is, they are willing to buy U.S. government securities. International investors are confident that there would be no practical problem with paying back its debt. This is because the U.S. government can pay back the borrowed money by printing the dollar without limit, even though there is some domestic limit to the size of the U.S. debt. The fact that the United States can print more dollars to repay its debt is a privilege given to the U.S. dollar as a dominant key currency, which may be an envy to other countries.

4

IS THE NATIONAL DEBT EXPLOSIVE?

Many developed countries (especially the United States) have suffered significant budget deficits over the past few decades. The fiscal deficit in developed countries is largely attributable to sharp increases in spending on welfare programs. Large-scale borrowings not only impose great restrictions on the operation of domestic economic policy, but also seriously affect international transactions such as exchange rates and trade.

The fiscal deficit inevitably leads to an increase in the national debt, thus making the problem more serious. The national debt is sometimes referred to as the public debt or government debt. In general, the national debt includes a debt whose principal and interest must be repaid with taxes, and any debt that the government must pay with tax money, if it is insolvent. In the statistics published by the IMF, the government debt (also called public debt) is defined as government financial liabilities that are represented by government debt instruments. The government debt instruments include debt securities (such as government bonds and bills), loans, and government employee pension obligations. Net debt equals gross debt minus financial assets that are credit instruments. In the United States, the national debt is defined as the balance of bonds issued by federal government and federal government agencies.

In the process of coping with the global economic crisis in 2008, the U.S. government debt was snowballing as the Obama administration carried out large-scale economic stimulus packages. In 2007, before the global economic crisis broke out, the ratio of the government debt to GDP was 36.8%, but it increased to 97% in 2010 and exceeded 100% in 2011. Once again, when the COVID pandemic hit the U.S. economy, the Trump and Biden administrations pumped astronomical amounts of funds into the economy, and the debt-GDP ratio climbed to 134.2% in 2020. Although the U.S. government set a ceiling on the amount of debt that could be borrowed, the ratio has continued to rise.

<Table 13.1> U.S. Treasury Securities Outstanding (in billions of $)

Year	Marketable Securities[1)]	Nonmarketable Securities[2)]	Total
2019	16,347.3	6,372.0	22,719.4
2020	20,374.9	6,750.5	26,945.4
2021	21,878.7	6,550.2	28,428.9

1) Marketable Treasury securities include Treasury Bills, Treasury Notes, Treasury Bonds, and
Treasury Inflation-Protected Securities (TIPS).
2) Nonmarketable Treasury securities include U.S. Savings Securities.
Source: The Economic Report of the President, 2022.

When we look at the composition and ownership of U.S. debt, we find a more detailed picture of the U.S. debt situation. The amount of U.S. Treasury securities held by foreigners (general foreign investors, foreign central banks and foreign governments and institutions) amounted to $6.1 trillion, or 34% of the national debt ($17.8 trillion) in 2014, but it increased to $7.6 trillion in 2021. Foreign holdings of U.S. government securities (in billions of dollars) as of June 2021 are as follows:

Japan: $2,698; U.K.: $2.543; Cayman Island: $2,340; Canada: $1,957; China: $1,572; Iceland: $1,326; Switzerland: $1,150; Belgium: $891; Taiwan: $752; France: $662; Norway: $613; South Korea: $556; Singapore: $554; Germany: $554; Netherlands: $528; Australia: $458; Hong Kong: $450; Sweden: $356; Bermuda: $349; the rest of the world: $3,650. (Source: U.S. Treasury Department.)

It is worth noting that China has continued to reduce its holding of U.S. government securities. China has been diversifying its holdings of foreign currencies over the past several years. China was the largest holder of U.S. Treasury securities in 2014, accounting for 21% of total foreign ownership, but the size of China's holding of Treasury securities ($1.6 trillion) was slipped to the 4th place in 2021.

<Table 13.2> Ownership of U.S. Treasury Securities (in billions of $)

Ownership	2019	2020	2021
Federal Reserve & intra-governmental holdings	8,359.9	10,809.2	12,125.9
Holdings of private investors	14,841.5	16,938.6	17,491.3
Foreign & int'l institutions	6,844.2	7,070.7	7,570.9
Mutual funds	2,350.6	3,552.9	2,988.8
Depository institutions	935.1	1,264.9	1,539.6
State & local governments	793.1	1,111.9	1,397.1
U.S. savings bonds	151.3	147.1	143.6
Pension funds	1,049.5	1,218.8	1,124.7
Private	(705.3	(864.6)	(700.7)
State & local governments	(344.2	(354.2)	(424.0)
Insurance companies	368.7	398.2	417.7
Other investors	2,349.0	2,174.1	1,667.4

The debt-to-GDP ratio of the United States (134.2%, 2020) may not be too high compared with the Japanese debt-to-GDP ratio of 259% in 2020, but in terms of its content, it may be more serious than Japan. For example, in the United States, the foreign debt has increased sharply because it relied heavily on borrowing from foreigners as well as domestic investors to fill the budget deficit. This means that U.S. income and wealth has flown out to foreign countries through interest payments. On the other hand, Japan has relied mainly on borrowing from domestic residents. The amount of national wealth leaked into foreign countries is relatively small in Japan. The Japanese people have saved heavily by buying Japanese government bonds, but the frugality of Japanese people had a negative effect on Japanese consumption, which has dragged the recovery of the Japanese economy from the 'Lost Two Decades'.

In general, if the national debt of a country exceeds 100% of its GDP, this is regarded as a warning sign. Currently, among the major countries, Japan has the highest debt-to-GDP ratio (259%) followed by the Eurozone's PIGs.

Portugal: 123.0% (2012) ⇒ 135.2% (2020)
Greece: 158.5% (2012) ⇒ 211.9% (2020),
Italy: 127.0% (2012) ⇒155.3% (2020),
Ireland: 117.1% (2012) ⇒ 58.4% (2020)).

In the early 2010s, the troubled Eurozone countries were collectively called PIIGs (Portugal-Italy-Ireland-Greece). However, Ireland succeeded in reducing its national debt from 117.1% in 2012 to 58.4% in 2020, but the ratio of debt to GDP has been worsening in the PIGs (Portugal-Italy-Greece).

Other major countries, except for Germany, have witnessed an upward trend in the debt-to-GDP ratio from 2012 to 2020. For example, the ratio of debt to GDP increased from 237.9% (2012) to 259.0% (2020) in Japan, from 106.5% (2012) to 134.2% (2020) in the United States, and from 90.3%(2012) to 102.6% (2020) in the United Kingdom. The debt-to-GDP ratio also trended upwardly in Asian countries, except for Hong Kong, from 2012 to 2020. For example, the ratio increased from 22.8% (2012) to 68.1% (2020) in China, from 33.7% (2012) to 48.9% (2020) in South Korea, and from 111.0% (2012) to 152.0% (2020) in Singapore.

Given this upward trend in the debt-GDP ratio in major countries, we are concerned with whether the national debt of a country can be explosive. Eventually, this problem is related to economic growth. As long as the growth rate of real GDP is higher than the interest rate on national debt, the ratio of national debt to GDP will gradually decrease. However, if the growth rate of real GDP growth is lower than the interest rate on national debt, the debt-GDP ratio can be explosive.

<Table 13.3> Government Debt of Major Countries (% of GDP)

Country	Gross Debt		Net Debt	
	2020	2012	2020	2012
China	68.1	22.8		
Germany	68.7	82.0	46.3	57.2
Greece	211.9	158.5		155.4
Hong Kong	1.0	32.4		
Ireland	58.4	117.1	52.4	102.3
Italy	155.3	127.0	141.8	103.2
Japan	259.0	237.9	162.4	134.3
South Korea	48.9	33.7	18.4	32.2
Portugal	135.2	123.0	123.2	111.6
Russia	19.2			
Singapore	152.0	111.0		
Spain	120.0	84.1	103.0	71.9
Taiwan	32.6		30.7	
U.K.	102.6	90.3	90.2	82.8
U.S.	134.2	106.5	98.7	87.9
Venezuela	304.1			

Source: IMF

Note: The size of the debt is the total amount of the debt borne by the government, which does not include the debts of SOE (state-owned enterprises) and various pensions (national pension and government employee pensions, etc.) that must be covered by national taxes. China and South Korea have high SOE debts, so if we include them, the proportion will be much higher in these countries.

5

FISCAL DEFICITS AND RICARDIAN EQUIVALENCE: "THE BUCK STOPS HERE"

The effect of the budget deficit or fiscal deficit on the economy can be analyzed from several perspectives. First, the fiscal deficit tends to raise domestic nominal interest rates. When the government experiences a budget deficit, it must borrow funds or raise taxes. If the government borrows funds from domestic investors, some of funds that have been previously supplied to businesses and households would now be used by the government. Thus, if the government has a budget deficit, the demand for funds will increase, raising interest rates. In addition, if the government borrows funds from foreigners, foreign investors will be willing to lend money only when the government offers higher interest rates to them. Thus, when the budget deficit increases, the nominal interest rate is likely to rise.

However, it is the real interest rate, not the nominal interest rate, that affects real economic activity such as investment, savings, consumption, etc. Does the deficit raise real interest rates? We have seen that the real interest rate represents a price for giving up the current consumption of goods and services, rather than a price for using someone's money. Since the real interest rate can be viewed as the price for giving up current consumption, classical economists argue that the real interest rate is almost constant, and that the real interest rate is not affected by the demand for and supply of money. This proposition is called the Fisher hypothesis.

Suppose that the government currently maintains a balanced budget. There are two possibilities that can bring about a budget deficit. One is when government spending increases, and the other is when taxes decrease. Many economists have agreed that the fiscal deficit resulting from increased government spending raises real interest rates. However, there is much controversy over whether the fiscal deficit caused by tax cuts will raise real interest rates. Earlier, classical economist David Ricardo hypothesized that the fiscal deficit caused by tax cuts had no effect on real interest rates. This view was further refined by Harvard economist Robert Barro (1974) under the name of Ricardian Equivalence.

The proponents of Ricardian Equivalence argue that the fiscal deficit due to a tax cut does not affect the real interest rate, because consumers do not use the increased income for current consumption and instead save it, regardless of whether the tax cut is permanent or temporary. Most of all, advocates of Ricardian Equivalence see that today's tax cut will be offset by an equivalent tax increase in the future and thus today's tax cut does not increase people's permanent income or life cycle income in the long run, even though it increases their current disposable income in the short run. Permanent income or life cycle income is a stream of future income that an individual is expected to earn by working for the period of his lifetime.

According to this view, Ricardian Equivalence is an issue of whether people pay taxes now or at some point in the future. Eventually, even if the tax is cut, it is almost certain that the government will increase taxes in the future to make up the budget deficit caused by today's tax cut. Thus, the total lifetime resources that taxpayers can consume over the present and future periods remain the same. Therefore, the far-sighted consumer saves the increased income coming from the tax cut instead of using it for today's consumption. The rational consumer will use the savings when taxes are increased in the future. Thus, if a tax cut is not used for current consumption, total savings remain unchanged, and therefore the real interest rate is not affected.

Ricardian Equivalence is reminiscent of a Chinese fable. There was a farmer named *Zhogong* in the Song Dynasty who raised monkeys. There was a shortage of food for monkeys because there was a drought in the region. He came up with a trick. He offered the monkeys a deal that he would give three acorns to each of them in the morning and four acorns in the evening. However, the monkeys got mad at this offer. So *Zhogong* made a different deal and proposed that he would give four acorns in the morning and three acorns in the evening. The monkeys were very happy with the new deal. The number of acorns that the monkeys ate per day was the same, seven acorns. The monkey's perception is obviously irrational. Ricardian Equivalence demonstrates that the monkey fable does not work for rational economic agents. Rational economic agents are not fooled into thinking that the farmer's seemingly different deals are different, but they correctly perceive the two deals to be equivalent. A rational economic agent thinks that a tax cut today and an equivalent tax increase in the future are equivalent and does not easily fall into the kind of trick used by the Song Dynasty farmer.

The Ricardian Equivalence we discussed is concerned with the case in which the present generation who benefits from the tax cut will bear the burden of paying taxes later when the government raises taxes to make up the deficit. In this case, Ricardian Equivalence seems to make sense, because the present generation benefits from the tax cut and bears the burden of paying back taxes later. However, if the government imposes taxes on the descendants of the present generation, rather than the current beneficiaries, to finance the fiscal deficit, will Ricardian Equivalence still hold? In other words, will the present generation still save the increased income without spending it on today's consumption? In this case, the present generation will not pay taxes in the future in return for today's tax benefits. Thus, they don't have to increase their savings in preparation for future tax payments. It seems to be reasonable to assume that the present generation would spend the increased income for their current consumption without worrying about future tax increases.

However, Barro argues that even if the present generation benefits from tax cuts, and the future generations pay taxes later, Ricardian Equivalence remains valid. In other words, the present generation saves without consuming increased income today. Barro believes that if the present generation is concerned with the well-being of their descendants, they will not spend the increased income, and instead will save it and bequeath it to their descendants who will pay taxes later. They will not use it as a windfall income.

Ricardian Equivalence can be summarized in a figurative way: The current generation does not want to pass the buck to the future generation. The position of the present generation is that "The buck stops here in this generation".

The present generation cares for the well-being of their descendants and saves the increased income in the form of savings, gifts, and heritage for the education and health of their descendants. Eventually, the present generation's awareness that today's tax cuts will lead to tomorrow's tax increases that will be levied on their descendants in the future, and thus they will buy long-term bonds and pass them on to their descendants to ease their tax burden. Later, if the government imposes taxes on the next generations to repay the increased debt, the future generations will be able to pay taxes by selling long-term bonds they received as gifts from their parents. Again, in this case, total savings remain unchanged, and therefore the real interest rate remains unchanged.

Thus, the validity of Ricardian Equivalence ultimately depends on how much people of the present generation care about the well-being and living standards of their descendants. In order for Ricardian Equivalence to actually hold true, the present generation, who benefits from tax cuts, should not use the increased income from tax cuts for current consumption but must save it and pass the savings on to their descendants. Thus, the present generation should not pass the tax burden to their descendants. Ricardian Equivalence is, in theory, very elegant, but many economists question the validity of Ricardian Equivalence in the real world. Ricardian Equivalence may be valid in a society where the social security system is well-established and where economic agents can make far-sighted decisions, but in many countries these assumptions may not be tenable.

Moreover, although Ricardian Equivalence argues that consumers do not increase their consumption when taxes are cut, some empirical analysis shows that in reality, tax cuts are likely to increase current consumption and, consequently, reduce total savings. Thus, a budget deficit created by a tax cut will also raise the real interest rate. This is because many consumers often make near-sighted decisions rather than far-sighted ones. Many consumers are unaware that an increase in government borrowing from fiscal deficits will lead to an increase in taxes in the future, and thus they will increase their current consumption.

6

THE CROWDING-OUT EFFECT VERSUS THE CROWDING-IN EFFECT

A fiscal deficit occurs when the government spends more than it collects as taxes. In such a case, the government must borrow funds from either private investors in the capital market or the central bank to make up the deficit unless the government raises taxes. When the government borrows money from private investors, this means that some of the existing money in the economy will be transferred from the private sector to the government sector. Thus, in the event of a fiscal deficit, investment, consumption, and exports in the private sector may be reduced, as funds used for investment, consumption and exports will be used for government spending.

First, we'll see how an increase in government spending reduces consumption. Suppose the government builds a public library for $10 million and purchases 1 million books with additional funds of $10 million. We can consider three possibilities for the impact of such increases in government spending on private consumption. First, when the government spends $10 million to purchase books, private consumers reduce $10 million to purchase books. This is because consumers can borrow all the books they need from the public library or can read books in the library and they do not need to buy books. The second possibility is that consumers' book purchase expenses are halved. In both cases, consumption, i.e., the purchase of books, is reduced. The third possibility is that the purchase of books by consumers is not affected at all by the increase in government spending on books.

In the first case, we say that government spending has completely crowded out private consumption (complete crowding-out effect). In the second case, government spending has partially crowded out private consumption (partial crowding-out effect). In the third case, the government spending does not affect private consumption at all (zero crowding-out effect). Many economists acknowledge that when government spending increases, the full crowding-out (classical economists) or partial crowding-out (Keynesian economists) of private consumption could occur. Few economists argue that the crowding-out effect does not occur at all.

The crowding-out effect is most likely to occur in private investment. Suppose that the government relies on borrowing from private investors to build the library and purchase books. Then, as the government sector now competes with the private sector for a limited amount of funds available in the capital market, the market interest rate will rise, *ceteris paribus*. Since business investment moves in the opposite direction of interest rates, private business investment will certainly decrease.

Exports could also be crowded out to some extent by fiscal deficits. Exports are heavily affected by exchange rates, and exchange rates are closely related to interest rates. We have seen that interest rates could rise if the budget deficit persists. When a country's interest rate rises, the country's currency value tends to rise in the short run. This is because international funds tend to move to a country with high interest rates. A stronger currency value will make the country's goods and services more expensive in the international marketplace, resulting in a decrease in exports. Exports are reduced by an increase in government spending.

Thus, if the fiscal deficit persists, private consumption, investment and exports will be adversely affected. Such an effect is termed the 'crowding-out' effect because an increase in government spending drives out private consumption, investment, and exports. Classical economists argue that consumption, investment, and exports in the private sector are crowded out as much as an increase in fiscal spending in the government sector. An increase in government spending (G) is completely offset by an equal decrease in private spending (= consumption + investment + net exports). Thus, classical economists argue that government spending has no effect on output (GDP). They support the full or complete crowding-out effect.

On the other hand, Keynesian economists acknowledge that increasing government spending raises interest rates, which reduces investment, consumption, and exports to some extent, but the increase of interest rates is not strong enough to fully crowd out private spending. Thus, government spending still exerts a certain effect on aggregate demand, leading to an increase in output and employment. They favor the partial crowding-out effect.

Apart from the crowding-out effect, government spending sometimes has a crowding-in effect. The crowding-in effect is the opposite of the crowding-out effect. A phenomenon in which an increase in government spending leads to an increase in private expenditure, especially investment, is called the crowding-in effect. The crowding-in effect is manifested in the impact of government spending on the supply side of the economy. For example, an increase in government spending on infrastructure, or a tax cut to stimulate incentives to work, save and invest could increase a country's potential production capacity, which stimulates private investment.

The crowding-in effect contrasts with the crowding-out effect. The two effects are associated with rising interest rates due to fiscal spending. Which effect, the crowding-out effect or the crowding-in effect, is stronger? The answer depends on whether the government spending is used for government consumption or government investment for the formation of fixed capital (infrastructure). If more of the fiscal spending is used for government consumption, the crowding-out effect will be stronger than the crowding-in effect, but, if more of government spending is used for government investment, the crowding-in effect will be greater than the crowding-out effect.

7

FISCAL DEFICITS AND SEIGNIORAGE: WINDFALL GAINS TO THE GOVERNMENT?

The question of how the fiscal deficit affects inflation is a perennial debate. The issue of whether the fiscal deficit alone can lead to inflation is the focus of the debate. An increase in government spending or a reduction in taxes increase aggregate demand. However, if the increase in aggregate demand only ends up with an 'once-and-for-all increase', such an increase in aggregate demand only results in 'one-time inflation'. If the government continues to run budget deficits every year, inflation may also persist every year, but this is not a possible scenario. It is not possible in many countries for the government to increase its spending more than tax revenues continuously, maybe except for the United States. There is some limit to government spending in non-reserve currency countries.

The U.S. and Japanese budget deficits are exceptions. The United States has continued to record fiscal deficits for decades, but foreign investors (private investors, foreign central banks, foreign governments and government agencies) are eager to buy U.S. government securities or to lend money to the U.S. government, although the United State has suffered huge budget deficits year by year over the past several decades. The potential power of the U.S. economy mainly comes from the fact that the U.S. dollar functions as the *de factor* key currency in the international transactions of goods, services and financial assets and in international reserve assets. Of course, if the U.S. central bank continues to print money, dollars will be overflown in the world economy, and the value of the dollar will decrease. In such a situation, inflation originated in the United States will spread globally. This means that inflation is shared by the world citizens. Put simply, the United States exports its inflation to the rest of the world.

The case of Japan is somewhat unique. The tendency of Japanese people to save income and to invest in domestic government bonds is reputable. Thus, the Japanese government has been able to continue to finance much of its deficit through domestic capital markets enriched by domestic savings. In many countries, this kind of financing fiscal deficits is not possible.

In general, expansionary fiscal policy only leads to a 'one-time increase' in the price level, and thus an increase in government spending or a tax cut cannot be the cause of continual inflation. The only factor causing continual inflation is a continual increase in the money supply. Therefore, the answer to the question of whether the deficit causes continual inflation is the same as the question of whether the deficit brings about a steady increase in the money supply.

If the government cannot finance the budget deficit by borrowing from the private sector or by raising taxes, the government has no choice but to reach out to the central bank. This has been practiced by many developing countries and is still used as a popular means of funding the deficit in many authoritarian countries. When the government finances the budget deficit through the borrowing of money from the central bank, it is done by issuing government bonds and pressuring the central bank to buy them. This practice is known as the monetization of the budget deficit.

The monetization of the budget deficit through printing money may differ among countries. In a country such as the United States where central bank independence is guaranteed, the government cannot force the central bank to print money. Even if the government does, the central bank will not easily give in to the government's request. At best, the government asks the central bank to buy government bonds by providing appropriate prices and conditions for the securities. If the central bank voluntarily accepts such an offer, new money will be issued. However, in many developing countries and authoritarian governments, the independence of the central bank is not sufficiently ensured, and thus the government is easily tempted to pressure its central bank to print money when the budget deficit occurs.

If the government continues to borrow money from the central bank to make up the budget deficit, it almost surely increases inflation. Inflation benefits the government by reducing the real value of government borrowings. The real revenue that the government receives from inflation is called seigniorage.

To understand seigniorage, suppose that the Dystopia government issues $10 billion dollar worth of government bonds with a maturity of 10 years and forces the central bank to buy them. We further assume that the Dystopia government will use the money to build highways and power plants. New money in the amount of $10 billion has been created in the economy. There will be inflationary pressure as the result of the issuance of new money. Suppose that the country's inflation has risen by 1,000% over the period of 10 years. Then, the amount of repayment that the government will pay back to the central bank 10 years later is less than one tenth of $10 billion in real terms. The government is gaining more than $900 million in real terms due to inflation. This \$900 million becomes the government's revenue as seigniorage. For this reason, seigniorage is sometimes called the inflation tax. Of course, the size of seigniorage depends on the size of the inflation rate and the amount of money borrowed. In general, the amount of seigniorage is given as follows:

$$\text{Seigniorage} = (\text{Inflation rate}) \times (\text{Real money balance})$$

In the example above, the inflation rate is 10 (1,000%) during the period of borrowing. The real money balance is the nominal money balance divided by the price index. If the price index was 1 at the time of borrowing, the price index 10 years later becomes 11 as a result of 1,000% inflation Since the nominal money balance at the time of borrowing was \$10 billion, the amount of seigniorage becomes:

$$\text{Seigniorage} = (10) \times \left(\frac{\$1\ billion}{11}\right) = \$0.909 \text{ billion} = \$909 \text{ million}$$

The Dystopia government borrows \$1 billion and earns about \$0.9 billion. The value of \$1 billion that the government will pay back 10 years later is only about \$0.1 billion in real value. This income was collected in a secret way so that no members of society who had money noticed the inflation tax. Generally, the amount of tax is given by (tax rate) x (taxable income). In the case of the inflation tax, the inflation rate corresponds to the tax rate and the real money balance corresponds to the taxable income.

So, who pays the inflation tax collected by the government? The inflation tax is paid by the public, who holds money. Any increase in taxes can encounter resistance from the public, but the government is able to collect inflation taxes from the public invisibly and secretly through promoting inflation. It is from this context that Lenin once preached that the surest way to break down the capitalist system was to promote inflation with money.

In advanced economies such as the United States, seigniorage is negligible, because inflation is generally low. For example, the Fed estimates the amount of seigniorage in the United States to be \$11 billion to \$15 billion, which is less than 0.1% of U.S. GDP. However, in countries with severe inflation, seigniorage can be an important source of government revenues. In Israel, the proportion of seigniorage in government revenues reached more than 12% in the mid-1980s, when the average annual inflation rate in Israel reached more than 300%.

8

THE LAFFER CURVE: DO LOWER TAX RATES INCREASE TAX REVENUES?

Supply-side economists argue that lowering the marginal tax rate on wage income and corporate income not only induces more labor, more savings, and more investment, but also increases tax revenues by stimulating the economy. The rationale for this claim is that by giving people an incentive to work harder, to save more, and to invest more, the economy can produce more output (GDP), and accordingly, tax revenues also increase. Since tax revenues are equal to the tax base (taxable income) multiplied by the tax rate, the taxable income must increase sufficiently to offset the tax reduction in order for the government's tax revenues to increase.

The suggestion that tax cuts could increase tax revenues is implied in the Laffer curve, which is a diagram showing a simple relationship between tax rates and tax revenues. It is known that the Laffer curve was described by American economist Arthur Laffer (2000) on a napkin while dining with a few politicians at a restaurant in Washington D.C. When the tax rate is displayed on the horizontal axis and the tax revenue on the vertical axis, the Laffer curve takes the following shape.

The Laffer curve shows an inverted U-shaped relationship between tax rates and tax revenues. Of course, if the tax rate is 0%, the tax revenue is also zero. As another extreme case, if the tax rate were 100%, no one would try to work under this tax rate. Therefore, taxable income would be zero and tax revenues would also be zero. The real world excludes these two extreme cases. According to the Laffer curve, as the income tax rate increases, the tax revenue also increases. However, the tax revenue increases up to a specific tax rate (t^*), which can be called the optimal tax rate. When the tax rate exceeds the optimal tax rate, the tax revenue starts to decrease. The reason for the inverse U-shaped curve is that an increase in the marginal tax rate reduces the incentive for people to work more. This ultimately leads to a decrease in output and reduces taxable income. Consequently, tax revenues also decrease.

<Figure 13.3> The Laffer Curve

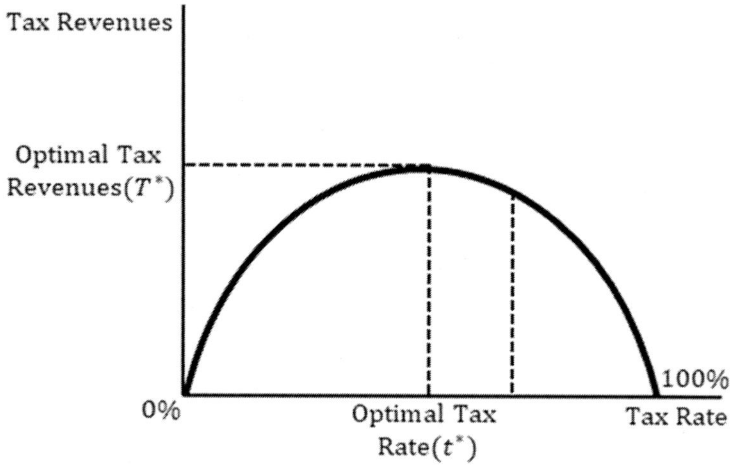

Here, the case in which a lower tax rate can lead to an increase in tax revenues corresponds to the case in which the current tax rate is higher than the optimal tax rate, that is, the current tax rate lies to the right of the optimal tax rate (t^*). If the current tax rate is lower than the optimal tax rate, a further reduction in the tax rate will only result in a decrease in tax revenues.

President Reagan of the United States drastically cut tax rates based on the supply-side prescriptions in 1981. The federal tax revenues declined by more than 6% in the period of 1981 to 1982, and the federal tax revenues during the period of 1983 to 1984 were lower than the 1981 levels. Some people argue that the significant reduction of the tax rates and the corresponding decrease in tax revenues have been largely attributable to the U.S. fiscal deficit that emerged as a serious problem in the 1980s. According to a study on the U.S. Laffer curve, the optimal tax rate that maximizes U.S. tax revenues is about 79%, more than three times higher than the current average income tax rate. The findings of this study show that the current tax rate in the United States lies on the ascending portion of the Laffer curve.

Another view, however, is that in the mid-1990s, the U.S. economy embraced a new phenomenon that was rarely experienced before. This new phenomenon was termed as a 'New Economy' where low inflation and low unemployment coexisted. Some economists argue that the New Economy is believed to be attributable to Reagan's tax cuts. In addition, a study has reported that reductions in tax rates in South Korea led to an increase in tax revenues: when the personal income tax rare that was up to 70% was lowered to 35%, and the corporate income tax rate that was up to 34% was lowered to 25%, tax revenues actually increased.

In order to get a better glimpse of some contradictory results, we need to analyze the relationship between tax revenues and tax rates as well as the tax base First, let's take a simple example:

	Tax Rate	Tax Base	Tax Revenues
Current	20%	\$100,000	\$20,000
Case 1	15%	\$120,000	\$18,000
Case 2	15%	\$140,000	\$21,000

In the above example, assuming that the current average income tax rate is 20% and the tax base is \$100,000, the tax revenue is \$20,000. Now suppose that the average income tax rate has been cut from 20% to 15%. We'll consider two possibilities that occurred as the income tax rate is lowered from 20% to 15%: (1) Taxable income is increased from \$100,000 to \$120,000; (2) Taxable income is increased from \$100,000 to \$140,000. In the first case, the tax revenue decreases to \$18,000 due to the reduction of the income tax rate, while in the second case, the tax revenue increases to \$21,000.

These results show that tax rate cuts may either increase or decrease tax revenues. It depends on whether the taxable income increases enough to offset the effect of a reduction in the tax rate. The final effects may differ depending on the economic structure and tax structure of each country and cannot be concluded uniformly. The implications of the Laffer curve are in parallel with the conclusion of supply-side economics. Supply-side economists argue that when the tax rate on personal income, corporate income, and capital gains is lowered, workers work more, savers save more, and firms invest more, resulting in higher GDP and higher taxable income, which in turn increases tax revenues (this argument corresponds to Case 2 in our example). However, the theoretical proposal of supply-side economics may show up differently among countries, and it is not clear whether the desired effects of supply-side prescriptions are supported by empirical evidence. (Refer to Romer and Romer (1998)).

Especially, a reduction in the corporate income tax is effective to the extent that it induces corporate investment. However, there is no guarantee that firms will use increased retained earnings due to the corporate tax cut for investment. When the economy is in a normal state, interest rates are an important determinant of investment. Businesses are willing to invest when the rate of return on investment is higher than the interest rate. When the economy is in a deep recession, what is more important than interest rates is expectations for the future state of the economy. When there is uncertainty about the future, firms are not willing to invest. Thus, there is no guarantee that a reduction in the marginal tax rate on corporate income will necessarily lead to investment. In 2001 and 2003, President Bush made extensive tax cuts aimed primarily at promoting investment. The tax cuts are often referred to as the Bush tax cuts. Yuhn and Bennett (2016) analyzed whether the Bush tax cuts stimulated U.S. corporate investment. Their study found that the Bush tax cuts not only failed to stimulate business investment, but in some models even reduced investment.

In conclusion, a tax cut designed to expand the supply capacity of the economy and to increase the capital stock (and investment) can achieve economic growth without inflation. This is an ideal goal of economic policy. In this case, the economy can enjoy 'stable growth without inflation', which can also increase tax revenues as a biproduct. However, the claim that a reduction in tax rates leads to an increase in tax revenues is debatable and it can vary across countries and over time.

PART 14

INTERNATIONAL TRADE AND FINANCE: SAILING BEFORE THE TRADE WINDS

1

INTERNATIONAL TRADE AND INCOME

The world is getting smaller. Even in the early 1980s, travelling to foreign countries was like a 'pie in the sky' in many countries. Foreign travel was considered a luxury item that only a limited number of people enjoyed, but now foreign travel has become a 'normal good'. Many of the goods and services that American people use and consume today are produced in foreign nations. Cell phones such as iPhones that are sold in the United States are manufactured abroad. The proportion of Chinese goods and services accounts for more than 15% of the total consumption of goods and services in the United States. There is an Amazon.com official site titled 'Shop Not Made in China', and there is a clothing brand named 'Not Made in China', which sarcastically show that people cannot live without using Chinses products in the United States.

We live in the era of great transformation in which people can easily buy and sell foreign goods, assets, and securities at any time and in any place on the Internet with just one click. The IT revolution has been squeezing the world into a global village and into a one-roof family. The rapid progress of liberalization, internationalization, and globalization has brought about great changes in domestic economic activities and the operation of domestic economic policies.

Japan and the Four Tigers (South Korea, Taiwan, Singapore, and Hong Kong) have scored a success by pursuing an export-driven growth strategy with exports being its engine of growth since the 1960s. The Four Tigers' economic growth over the past 50 years or so is regarded as a remarkable success story of export-oriented growth policy. If we look at the share of exports and imports in GDP in these countries, we can easily see how important trade has been to the Four Tigers' economic development.

<Table 14.1> Proportion (%) of Trade in GDP

Country	Exports	Imports	Total Trade	Year
Hong Kong	188.0	187.1	375.1	2017
Singapore	173.3	149.1	322.4	2017
Germany	47.5	41.9	89.4	2021
South Korea	43.1	37.7	80.8	2017
World	43.1	37.7	80.8	2016
U.K.	27.4	27.7	55.1	2020
China	18.5%	16.0	34.5	2020
Japan	12.7	12.6	25.4	2020
U.S.A.	10.2	13.3	23.5	2020

The case of South Korea is more dramatic. The ratio of exports to GDP was only 4.1% in 1960. The ratio rose to 14.9% in 1970 and to 34.6% in 1980. Since then, the share of exports in GDP has moved between 25% and 37%, and soared to 43.1% in 2017, which was the highest. The share of total trade, including imports, as a percentage of GDP reached 80.8% in 2017. In Japan and China, which have both pursued export-driven growth strategies, the proportion of total trade in GDP is much lower than that of the Four Tigers. The ratio was 34.5% (2020) in China, and 25.4% (2020) in Japan. In the United States, which has a consumption-oriented economic structure, the ratio was 23.5% in 2020, which is much lower than in the Four Tigers. The United Kingdom is in between the Asian Tigers and the United States. The ratio of total trade to GDP was 55.1% in 2020, which was relatively high.

Although the U.S. ratio of total trade to GDP is relatively low compared with other countries, the ratio has continued to rise historically over the past several decades: The U.S. ratio of trade to GDP was only 10.8% in 1970, but the ratio reached 30.8% in 2011, the highest level ever achieved in the United States. This trend manifests the increasing openness of the U.S. economy over the past 50 years or so. In the United States, the foreign sector received less attention even until the 1980s, because in the United States, domestic consumption was the most important component of GDP, which accounts for almost 70% of GDP.

1970: 10.8%; 1975: 15.5%; 1980: 20.1%; 1985: 16.6%;
1990: 19.8%; 1995: 22.5%; 2000: 25.6%; 2010: 28.2%;
(2011: 30.8%); 2015: 27.8%; 2020: 23.5%

<Figure 14.1> U.S. Trade in Goods

Source: Census Bureau.
Note: Data are seasonally adjusted.

Many countries pursue export-led growth strategies because exports have a huge impact on national income and economic growth. We have seen that a country's gross domestic product (GDP) consists of four components:

$$\text{GDP} = \text{Consumption (C)} + \text{Investment (I)} + \text{Government purchases (G)} + \text{Net exports (NX)}$$

where net exports are the difference between exports (EX) and imports (IM). From the income accounting identity, we have seen that as the items that make up GDP increase, so does GDP. However, as the Keynesian model demonstrates, if consumption increases by \$1 million, GDP does not increase simply by \$1 million. The Keynesian model shows that GDP will increase by about \$2 million. This is the multiplier effect of consumption.

It should be noted, however, that the multiplier effect occurs only when the components of aggregate expenditure such as consumption, investment, government purchases, exports and imports are autonomous. Autonomous expenditure refers to any aggregate expenditure that does not depend on income. Out of the components of aggregate expenditure, consumption and imports are induced expenditure items that vary with income. In the Keynesian model, investment, government purchases, and exports are considered as autonomous expenditure. From this point of view, the income generation effect (multiplier effect) of exports is much greater than any other aggregate expenditure item. This is especially true in countries with a large share of exports in GDP.

First, let's look at the effects of consumption and exports on income. Most of consumption depends on income, and the share of autonomous consumption is very low. Therefore, only a small portion of consumption has a multiplier effect. On the other hand, exports are all autonomous expenditure, and thus the entire amount of exports exerts a multiplier effect. In most countries, the size of exports is much larger than the size of autonomous consumption. Thus, even if consumption and exports have the same multiplier, they have different effects on GDP. Next, we'll compare the multiplier effect of exports with the multiplier effect of other autonomous expenditures such as government purchases and business investment. Since government purchases and investment are all autonomous expenditures, they also have a multiplier effect.

However, government purchases are constrained by the budget, and policymakers cannot increase them discretionally. In addition, business investment is highly affected by economic fluctuations, and thus, the multiplier effect of investment is also precarious. However, a country's exports are limited only by the conditions of the world economy, and under the WTO system pursuing free trade, each country tries to increase its exports to the maximum. From this discussion, we see that exports have a stronger income-generating effect than any other autonomous expenditures.

However, we cannot only export our goods and services to other countries. We must also import goods and services from foreign countries. Imports are a leakage of income that outflows to foreign countries in a country's circular flow of income. As imports increase, domestic income also leaks to foreign countries. Thus, the multiplier effect of net exports on income is given by the difference between an increase in income due to exports and a decrease in income due to imports. Thus, it is natural for policymakers to pay great attention to the performance of imports and exports.

Just as economic agents look at the relative prices of products when they make a decision on buying or selling products, people are concerned with the relative prices of products between two countries when they sell domestically produced products to foreigners or purchase foreign-made products from foreigners. The relative prices of products between two countries are measured by real exchange rates. The real exchange rate matters in exports and imports between the two countries. The real exchange rate is the relative price of the products of two countries and is measured as the number of units of a foreign product that can be exchanged for one unit of a home (U.S.) product. If the real exchange rate rises, one unit of a home product can buy more units of an identical foreign product, and thus a rise in the real exchange rate leads to an increase in exports, *ceteris paribus*.

Just as factors other than relative prices affect the demand for or the supply of goods and services in domestic transactions, there are factors other than the real exchange rate that affect exports and imports. These other factors include inflation, income, and interest rates in any two countries. These other factors in turn affect the real exchange rate, which affects exports and imports, and exports and imports, in turn, affect the real exchange rate. Thus, the relationship between the real exchange rate and net exports is bi-directional, which is known as a feedback effect or a cause-and-effect relation.

2

THE BALANCE OF PAYMENTS (BOP)

Cross-border transactions of goods or services necessarily involve the movements of capital across countries. The contents of international transactions are summarized in a country's balance of payments (BOP) table. The balance of payments records the receipts and payments of funds associated with the international transactions of goods, services, and assets. The statistics representing the contents of these transactions according to the double-entry bookkeeping principle are the balance of payments account. Thus, the BOP account records payment items or debits and receipt items or credits.

The flow of funds out of the country is recorded as a payment item, and the flow of funds into the country is recorded as a receipt item. The BOP traces the flows of funds that occur during a specified period (usually one year), and thus the BOP items represent flows, not stocks. The balance of payments account is largely composed of the current account, capital account, and official reserve account. Some accounts in the BOP may show surpluses, while others may show deficits. Due to the principle of double-entry bookkeeping, the surpluses and deficits cancel out each other, and thus the sum of the receipts must match the sum of the payments.

International transactions recorded in the current account include (1) transactions of goods (merchandise trade), (2) transactions of services (service trade), (3) transactions of income (investment income), and (4) transactions of transfers (unilateral transfers). The difference between receipts and payments associated with these four types of transactions is called the current account balance. The account is called the *current account* because it records the transactions of *currently* produced goods and services in the year and *currently* generated investment income and transfers in the year.

First, the merchandise trade account records the flows of funds accompanied by exports and imports of goods. Merchandise trade includes exports of, say, automobiles and semiconductors, and imports of, say, crude oil and grain. U.S. exports are listed as receipts (+) in the U.S. balance of payments, and U.S. imports are listed as payments (−). If merchandise exports exceed merchandise imports, a trade surplus occurs; if merchandise imports exceed merchandise exports, a trade deficit occurs. The United States had a trade deficit of $922.0 billion in 2020. In fact, the United States has exhibited a deficit in the merchandise trade balance over the past several decades except for a few years.

Exports and imports of services are sometimes called non-merchandise trade. Services include non-tangible items such as foreign travel, education, medical treatments, and insurance. If an American student studies at Cambridge University, the tuition and fees and all other expenses that the student spends in the United Kingdom are recorded as a payment (−) in the U.S. BOP. (Of course, the education expenses that the American student pays in the United Kingdom are recorded as a receipt (+) in the U.K. BOP.) If a British tourist travels to the United States, then all the travel expenses that the British tourist spends in the United States are recorded as a receipt (+) in the U.S. BOP. (By the same logic, all the travel expenses that the British tourist pays in the United States are recorded as a payment in the U.K. BOP.) The United States had a surplus of $245.3 billion in 2020 in the service trade balance. In contrast with the merchandise trade balance, the United States has persistently exhibited a surplus in the balance of service trade.

Investment income, the third component of the current account, refers to interest or dividend income incurred in the current year. Interest or dividends earned by American people investing in foreign assets (deposits, stocks, bonds, etc.) are recorded as a receipt item on the investment income account in the BOP (in the U.S. BOP, this balance is called the *balance on primary income*), and interest or dividends earned by foreigners investing in U.S. assets (deposits, stocks, bonds, etc.) are recorded as a payment item. The U.S. BOP shows that the United States has been losing money by buying more goods from foreign countries than selling goods to foreigners (merchandise trade balance) but has been making money from investing in foreign assets (such as deposits, stocks, bonds, etc.). In 2020, the United States had a trade deficit of $922.0 billion, but had a surplus of $188.5 billion in investment income. The United States is a net debt country with more foreigners investing in the United States than Americans investing abroad, but the income Americans earn from investing abroad is higher than the income earned by foreigners investing in the United States. This indicates that Americans have made smarter investments than foreign investors.

Finally, the transfer account records the transfer transactions that include the transfer of goods, services, and income that is made as gifts or donations. Transfer transactions include government grants to foreign countries, free donations to foreigners, pensions paid to retirees living abroad, or remittances to relatives or friends living abroad. (In the U.S. BOP, the transfer balance is called the *balance on secondary income*.) If the U.S. government, organizations, or American citizens receive such gifts or grants, the transfers are recorded as receipts in the U.S. transfer balance (or balance on secondary income); if the U.S. government, organizations, or American citizens give such gifts or grants to foreigners, the transfers are recorded as payments in the U.S. transfer balance. For example, during the Russo-Ukraine war in 2022, the U.S. government committed approximately $45 billion worth of military and humanitarian aids to Ukraine. The U.S. aids to Ukraine were recorded as a payment item in the U.S. BOP. If a U.S. organization receives relief funds from foreigners, such gifts are recorded as a receipt item in the U.S. transfer account. In the United States, the transfer balance (or balance on secondary income) had a deficit of $127.9 billion in 2020.

The current account balance is the sum of the merchandise trade balance, service trade balance, net investment income (or balance on primary income), and net transfer income (or balance on secondary income). The U.S. current account balance has been in deficit every year since 1982. The United States has exhibited surpluses in the service trade balance and investment income balance, but deficits in the merchandise trade balance and transfer balance. The surpluses in the service trade balance and investment income balance were not large enough to offset the deficits in the merchandise trade balance and transfer balance.

The capital account records the flows of funds associated with the transactions of existing financial or real assets. Capital transactions include direct investment such as the building of factories in foreign countries and acquisition of foreign firms through merges and acquisitions (M&A), portfolio investment such as the purchase of foreign stocks and bonds, and other investments such as the purchase of foreign real estate. Thus, if an American investor buys the TSMC (Taiwan Semiconductor Manufacturing Co.) stock, such a transaction is recorded as a payment in the U.S. capital account, but as a receipt in the Taiwanese capital account. But if the American investor receives dividends from the investment in the TSMC stock, such dividend income is recorded as a receipt in the U.S. current account, but as a payment in the Taiwanese current account. If TSMC invests $40 billion in Arizona to build a semiconductor factory, such investment is recorded as a receipt in the U.S. capital account, but as a payment in the Taiwanese capital account. Similarly, if a Taiwanese investor buys a 10-year-old vacation home in Miami, such investment is recorded as a receipt in the U.S. capital account, but as a payment in the Taiwanese capital account.

The fundamental difference between the capital account and the current account is that the capital account records the transactions of financial assets or real assets that already exist, while the current account records the transactions of goods or services produced in the current year or investment income and transfer income earned in the current year.

Capital transactions can take place not only at the private level but also at the government level. For example, when the government receives a loan, capital inflows occur, and when the principal is repaid, capital outflows occur. Capital transactions can also be divided into short-term capital transactions and long-term capital transactions, depending on whether the maturity of an asset (or a loan) is less than one year or more than one year. Short-term loans are riskier than long-term capital loans, and thus, short-term capital loans can show irregular movements due to the flow of speculative funds into domestic financial markets. The sum of the current account balance and the long-term capital account balance is called the basic balance, which is the primary criterion for determining the health of a country's balance of payments.

There is another important capital account item called official reserve assets. The official settlements account is part of the capital account, which represents payments or receipts of funds by central banks. However, in this book, we'll treat the official settlements account separately from the capital account for analytical convenience. Official reserve assets refer to assets held by central banks that are mainly used for international settlement or stabilizing the foreign exchange market. Official reserve assets consist of gold, major international currencies such as dollars (mainly held as U.S. Treasury securities), foreign government bonds (mainly U.S. Treasury securities), and special drawing rights (SDRs) created by the IMF. Countries with deficits in the current and capital account balances can use official reserve assets to make up the deficits. For example, if the United Kingdom has a total deficit of $10 billion in the current and capital accounts, the British government can withdraw $10 billion from the official settlements account.

An increase in official reserve assets is a payment item in a country's (say, the U.K.) BOP. The increase in official reserve assets means that the Bank of England has bought gold or foreign currencies from foreign central banks, which entails an outflow of funds form the United Kingdom to foreign countries. Thus, an increase in official reserve assets is recorded as a payment in the capital account (or the official reserve assets account). Conversely, if the Bank of England sells its official reserve assets to a foreign central bank, the transaction will result in the inflow of funds from foreign countries into the United Kingdom. Thus, a decrease in official reserve assets is recorded as a receipt in the capital account (or the official settlements account).

The current account balance and the capital account balance including the official settlements account balance must sum to zero because the BOP is constructed based on the double-entry bookkeeping principle. However, in reality, when all the balances of the BOP accounts are summed, a country's balance of payments does not always reach the theoretical value of zero. It is almost impossible to accurately record all international transactions because international transactions involve a myriad of goods and services, and thus it is almost impossible to record all the transactions accurately. There is also a possibility that people do not deliberately report some transactions to hide illegal transactions or to avoid taxes. Thus, the sum of the current account balance and the capital account balance (including the official settlements account balance) is not always equal to zero. Therefore, an adjustment item called the statistical discrepancy is needed to make the sum of the current account balance and the capital account balance (including the official settlements account balance) reach its theoretical value of zero. The residual item is sometimes marked as 'errors and omissions'.

Thus, the sum of the current account balance (CA) and the capital balance (KA) including the official settlements account balance (OA), and the 'errors and omissions' (EO) in the balance of payments should always be zero. In theory, we should have $CA + KA + OA = 0$, but in practice, we have $CA + KA + OA \neq 0$. When we add EO, we have the following relation in the BOP:

$$CA + KA + OA + EO = 0,$$

Errors and omissions sometimes become positive and sometimes negative. In the United States, the adjustment item has become significantly larger each year. Some people see the increasing errors and omissions as being associated with the increasing amount of black money flowing into the United States. It is a well-known secret that wealthy people in a country where the political situation is unstable or those who aim to avoid taxes attempt to secretly buy U.S. financial assets as a safe haven.

3

THE CURRENT ACCOUNT VERSUS THE CAPITAL ACCOUNT: *QUID PRO QUO*

We have discussed that if all the international transactions of goods, services, and assets are accurately and perfectly recorded, the sum of the current account balance (CA) and the capital account balance (KA) including the official settlements account balance (OA) in the balance of payments should always be zero. Thus, we have the following relation (here, we assume that the capital account balance includes the official settlements account balance):

$$CA + KA = 0$$

The relation can be alternatively expressed as

$$CA = -KA$$

Equivalently, we have the following relation:

$$-CA = KA$$

This relation shows that when a country has a surplus in the current account, the country must have an equivalent deficit in the capital account. Equivalently, when a country has a deficit in the current account, the country must have an equivalent surplus in the capital account.

This relationship between the current account and the capital account can be seen as *quid pro quo* in a sense. *Quid pro quo* is a Latin word that means 'something for something' or 'a favor for a favor' or 'if you do this to me, I'll do that for you'. In plain English, the term means, 'You scratch my back, and I'll scratch yours'. It is also used in the meaning of 'give and take' or 'tit for tat'.

In order to understand the relation in the simplest way, we assume that there are only two countries on the planet, Shangri-La and Atlantis. Suppose the payment currency between these two countries is dollars, and these dollars dropped from the sky like manna. Shangri-La exports $100 billion worth of goods and services to Atlantis and imports $80 billion worth of goods and services from Atlantis. Thus, Shangri-La has a trade surplus of $20 billion, while Atlantis has a trade deficit of $20 billion.

If Shangri-La does not lend $20 billion to Atlantis, international trade cannot occur between the two countries. Atlantis earns $80 billion by selling its goods and services to Shangri-La but will pay $100 billion by buying goods and services from Shangri-La. If Shangri-La does not lend $20 billion to Atlantis, Atlantis has no money to pay the difference ($20 billion), and the world trade will shrink to $80 billion. This observation shows a *quid pro quo* relationship in international trade between the two countries: "If you lend me $20 billion, I'll buy $20 billion worth of goods and services from you." The *quid pro quo* relation is reflected in the accounting principle of $CA + KA = 0$.The borrowing is reflected as a receipt in the Atlantis capital account and as a payment in the Shangri-La capital account.

Shangri-La BOP: CA (−$20 billion) + KA (+$20 billion) = 0

Atlantis BOP: CA (+$20 billion) + KA (−$20 billion) = 0

Here we make remarks about the relationship between the current account and the capital account. A trade surplus in a country represents a loan to a trade deficit country, and a trade deficit represents a borrowing from a trade surplus country. In reality, there are more than 200 countries in the world. The relation may not hold *vis-à-vis* between any two countries. Nonetheless, the relation holds true between a country and the rest of the world.

In this transaction, Shangri-La has accumulated dollar reserve assets in the amount of $20 billion. Countries accumulate foreign exchanges (mainly U.S. dollars) from selling goods and services (current account surpluses) or selling existing real and financial assets (capital account surpluses) or official reserve assets (official settlements account surpluses) to foreign countries. Countries exhaust foreign exchanges by buying goods and services (current account deficits) or buying existing real and financial assets (capital account deficits) or official reserve assets (official settlements account deficits). In the process of current and capital transactions, a country's foreign exchanges (foreign currency reserves) increase or decrease. Is there any optimal level of foreign exchange reserves, especially for emerging market countries?

If a country's holding of foreign currency reserves (mainly U.S. dollars) is too small, that situation could touch off speculative attacks on its currency. The 1997 Asian financial crisis broke out because some Asian countries such as Thailand, South Korea, Indonesia, and the Philippines were rapidly running out of their foreign currency reserves. Their currencies became the target of international speculations. On the other hand, if a country's holding of foreign currency reserves is too much, that situation increases the cost of maintaining foreign exchange reserves. For example, if the United Kingdom holds foreign currency reserves too much, some pressure on pushing the value of the pound upwardly comes into play, and the Bank of England would have to intervene in the foreign exchange market to alleviate the upward pressure on its currency. The Bank of England would have to issue its currency (pound) to buy dollars in the foreign exchange market, which will surely put an upward pressure on inflation in the United Kingdom, if it is big.

There are no established criteria for the optimal level of foreign exchange reserves. The IMF sees the appropriate size of foreign exchange reserves as the amount of a country's imports for three months. On the other hand, the Bank for International Settlements (BIS) suggests a little bit broader criterion. According to the BIS guideline, the appropriate level of foreign exchange reserves should be equal to the amount of a country's imports for three months plus one-third of the amount of international portfolio investments in stocks and bonds. In addition, the size of liquid foreign debt should be taken into account.

Here are some statistics for the holdings of foreign exchange reserves by major countries as of 2022. China holds the most foreign exchange reserves followed by Japan (2nd), Switzerland (3rd), Russia (4th), Taiwan (5th), India (6th), Saudi Arabia (7th), and South Korea (8th).

<Table 14.2> Holdings of Foreign Exchange Reserves (in billions of $)

(1) China: 3,223.8 (8/2022); (2) Japan: 1,292.1 (8/2022); (3) Switzerland: 961.4 (7/2022); (4) Russia: 549.7 (9/2022); (5) Taiwan: 545.5 (8/2022); (6) India: 537.5 (7/2022); (7) Saudi Arabia: 455.8 (8/2022); (8) South Korea: 438.6 (7/2022); (9) Hong Kong: 431.8 (8/2022);(10) Brazil: 341.0 (7/2022); (11) Singapore: 314.3 (6/2022); (12) Germany: 286.7 (6/2022);(13) U.S.: 229.1 (9/2022); (14) France: 226.3 (6/2022); (15) Thailand: 222.3 (6/2022); (16) Italy: 214.2 (6/2022); (17) U.K.: 211.7 (6/2022). (Source: IMF)

4

How Is the Exchange Rate Measured?

Just as we need money (say, pound sterling) to purchase goods or services domestically, we need foreign currency to purchase foreign goods and services, to travel abroad, or to invest in foreign assets. The market in which foreign currencies are traded is the foreign exchange market, and the equilibrium exchange rate between foreign currencies is determined in the foreign exchange market. The foreign exchange market has a long history. The Bible records two instances of Jesus cleansing the temple of money changers. He made a whip of cords and drove money changers out of the temple. The money changers in the Bible are foreign currency exchanges today. Of course, there was no official exchange rate at that time, but money changers would have determined the exchange rate according to demand and supply forces in the market. This instance shows that market forces worked even in a primitive foreign exchange market.

When a country operates in an open economy, the exchange rate affects almost all levels and dimensions of economic activity such as trade, inflation, national income, employment, interest rates and asset prices. In turn, a country's trade, inflation, national income, interest rates, and asset prices have a significant effect on exchange rates.

In order to understand the relationship between exchange rates and economic activity, we need to know exactly what the exchange rate means and how it is measured. The price of one currency (say, Japanese yen) in terms of another currency (say, U.S. dollar) is called an exchange rate. There are two ways to quote the exchange rate. One is the amount of the Japanese yen that is exchanged for one unit of the U.S. dollar. In this case, the exchange rate between two countries is expressed as '100 yen per dollar'. The other approach is to express the exchange rate as the amount of the U.S. dollar that is exchanged for one unit of local currency (say, Japanese yen) such as 0.01 dollars per yen. A common practice used in macroeconomics is to express the exchange rate (E) as the quantity of local currency that is exchanged for one unit of the U.S. dollar. The exchange rate expressed in terms of the U.S. dollar is called the dollar exchange rate. However, it is customary to express the exchange rate between the dollar and the euro or between the dollar and the British pound as the amount of the dollar exchanged for one unit of euro or pound such as \$0.98: €1 and \$1.2: £1.

In this book, we follow the dollar exchange rate except for the euro and the pound. When we follow the dollar exchange rate, we often get confused about the use of terms. For example, if the U.S. dollar exchange rate fluctuates from 100 yen per dollar to 120 yen per dollar, we say that the exchange rate has risen, which means that the value of the yen has fallen, and the value of the dollar has risen. Previously, 100 yen was needed to buy 1 U.S. dollar in the foreign exchange market, but after the exchange rate change, people need 120 yen to buy 1 U.S. dollar. Conversely, if the exchange rate falls from 100 yen per dollar to 90 yen per dollar, this indicates that the value of the yen has risen, and the value of the dollar has fallen.

Exchange rates can also be divided into nominal exchange rates and real exchange rates. We emphasized that the variables that matter in economic decision making are real variables, not nominal variables. Exchange rates are no exception. Thus, it should be noted that it is not the nominal exchange rate, but the real exchange rate that affects imports and exports. The nominal exchange rate (E) is the relative price of the currencies of two countries and is measured as the number of units of foreign currency (say, Japanese yen) that can be exchanged for one unit of the U.S. dollar. In this way, we can say that the nominal exchange rate between the U.S. dollar and the Japanese yen is 100 yen per dollar. A rise in the nominal exchange is called a nominal appreciation, which indicates that the value of the U.S. dollar relative to the value of the yen goes up or the value of the yen relative to the value of the dollar goes down. A fall in the nominal exchange is called a nominal depreciation, which indicates that the value of the U.S. dollar relative to the value of the yen goes down or the value of the yen relative to the value of the dollar goes up.

¥100: \$1 ⇒ ¥120: \$1: Nominal appreciation of the dollar
⇒ Stronger U.S. dollar (Weaker yen)

¥100: \$1 ⇒ ¥90: \$1: Nominal depreciation of the dollar
⇒ Weaker U.S. dollar (Stronger yen)

The real exchange rate is the relative price of the products of two countries and is measured as the number of units of one country's product that can be exchanged for one unit of the other country's product. (In this book, the United States is treated as a home country, and other countries such as Japan as foreign countries.) There is a close relationship between the real exchange rate and the nominal exchange rate. The real exchange rate (e) is equal to the nominal exchange rate (E) multiplied by the ratio of the price of a home product to the price of a foreign product.

$$\text{Real exchange rate} = \text{E x} \left(\frac{P}{P^F}\right)$$

where P is the average price of home (U.S.) products expressed in the U.S. dollar, and P^F is the price of foreign products expressed in foreign currency (such as the Japanese yen).

The relationship between the real exchange rate and the nominal exchange rate seems a bit complicated, but surprisingly the relationship is simple. In general, the ratio of the price of home products to the price of foreign products does not change much in the short term and is very stable. This means that the real exchange rate moves in tandem with the nominal exchange rate. When the nominal exchange rate in a country rises, the real exchange rate also tends to rise, and *vice versa*.

We have seen that the real exchange rate is the relative price of the products of two countries. That is, the real exchange rate can be expressed as

$$\text{Real exchange rate} = \left(\frac{Price\ of\ domestic\ products\ expressed\ in\ home\ currency}{Price\ of\ foreign\ products\ expressed\ in\ home\ currency}\right)$$

$$= \left(\frac{Price\ of\ domestic\ products\ expressed\ in\ foreign\ currency}{Price\ of\ foreign\ products\ expressed\ in\ foreign\ currency}\right)$$

Thus, a rise in the real exchange rate indicates that the price of home (U.S.) products rises relative to the price of foreign (Japanese) products. Conversely, a fall in the real exchange rate indicates that the price of home (U.S.) products falls relative to the price of foreign (Japanese) products. Since the real exchange rate represents the prices of products in two countries using the same currency unit, we can directly compare the prices of products between the two countries by looking at the real exchange rate.

For illustration, we'll take an example of McDonald's Big Mac hamburger. Suppose that the price of the Big Mac hamburger sold in the United States is \$3, and the price of the same Big Mac hamburger sold in Japan is 600 yen. Then the real exchange rate is calculated as follows. (We assume that the United States and Japan only produce Big Mac hamburgers.)

$$\text{Real exchange rate} = \text{Nominal exchange rate x} \left(\frac{\$3}{¥600}\right)$$

Furthermore, if the nominal exchange rate between the dollar and the yen is 100 yen per dollar (¥100/$1), the real exchange rate between the United States and Japan is given by:

$$\text{Real exchange rate} = \left(\frac{¥100}{\$1}\right) x \left(\frac{\$3}{¥600}\right) = \left(\frac{\$3}{\$1}\right) x \left(\frac{¥100}{¥600}\right) = \frac{\$3}{\$6}$$

$$= \frac{U.S. Big\ Mac\ price\ in\ \$}{Japanese\ Big\ Mac\ price\ in\ \$} = 0.5$$

Alternatively, we can express the relationship as follows:

$$\text{Real exchange rate} = \left(\frac{¥100}{¥600}\right) x \left(\frac{\$3}{¥600}\right) = \left(\frac{\$3}{\$1}\right) x \left(\frac{¥100}{¥600}\right) = \frac{¥300}{¥600}$$

$$= \frac{U.S. Big\ Mac\ price\ in\ ¥}{Japanese\ Big\ Mac\ price\ in\ ¥} = 0.5$$

Either expression is the same, showing that the real exchange rate is 0.5. What does this number mean? Since we defined the real exchange rate as the number of units of a foreign product (Japanese Big Mac) exchanged for one unit of a home product (U.S. Big Mac), the real exchange rate of 0.5 means that one U.S. Big Mac is exchanged for one half of a Japanese Big Mac. What does this real exchange rate indicate? The real exchange rate indicates that the price of the Japanese Big Mac is twice as high as that of the U.S. Big Mac. Thus, by calculating the real exchange rate, we can compare the prices of products between two countries.

A rise in the real exchange rate implies that the price of home (U.S.) products relative to that of foreign (Japanese) goods goes up, and a fall in the real exchange rate implies that the price of home products relative to that of foreign products goes down.

$3 (U.S. price)/$6 (Japanese price) = 0.5
⇒ $4 (U.S. price)/$6 (Japanese price) = 0.67:Real appreciation
⇒ Higher prices of U.S. products

$3 (U.S. price)/ $6 (Japanese price) = 0.5
⇒ $2 (U.S. price)/$6 (Japanese price) = 0.33: Real depreciation
⇒ Lower prices of U.S. products

In the above example, we computed the real exchange rate under the assumption that both the United States and Japan produce only one product, the Big Mac hamburger. However, in the real economy, both countries produce tens of thousands of goods and services, and the quantities of goods and services produced are also different. We can generalize our discussion of the real exchange rate. The real exchange rate of Country A with Country B is calculated as the weighted average of the prices of goods and services produced in Country A divided the weighted average of the prices of goods and services produced in Country B

$$\text{Real exchange rate} = \left(\frac{\textit{Weighted average of prices of home (Country A)products}}{\textit{Weighted average of prices of foreign (Country B)products}}\right)$$

The prices of home (Country A) and foreign (Country B) products are determined competitively in international markets. A rise in the prices of home products in the international market means that home products command higher prices in the international market and thus home products become more competitive. Conversely, when the prices of home products fall in the international market, it means that the international competitiveness of home products decreases. Thus, a rise in the real exchange rate indicates an increase in the international competitiveness of home products, and a fall in the real exchange rate indicates a decrease in the international competitiveness of home products.

Real exchange rate ↑ ⇒ Prices of home products ↑
⇒ International competitiveness ↑

Real exchange rate ↓ ⇒ Prices of home products ↓
⇒ International competitiveness ↓

Thus, the real exchange rate also measures the terms of trade (TOT) that are defined as the ratio of the price of exported goods to the price of imported goods in a country. The terms of trade are given by

$$TOT = \frac{\textit{Export price index}}{\textit{Import price index}}$$

Since goods and services produced in the home country are exported, and goods and services produced in a foreign country are imported, the export price index measures the average of the prices of home products, and the import price index measures the average of the prices of foreign products. Thus, the terms of trade are the same as the real exchange rate we discussed.

There are two types of foreign exchange trading. We can distinguish between spot exchange rates and forward exchange rates. A spot transaction refers to a foreign exchange transaction in which people buy or sell a certain amount of foreign currency at the current exchange rate, and the exchange rate applied to the spot transaction is the spot exchange rate. In contrast, a forward transaction refers to a foreign exchange transaction in which people buy or sell a certain amount of foreign currency at a future date at an agreed future exchange rate. The exchange rate applied to the forward transaction is the forward exchange rate.

5

THE EFFECTIVE EXCHANGE RATE AND THE U.S. DOLLAR INDEX (USDX)

The exchange rate we have discussed so far is concerned with the relative price of currencies (nominal exchange rate) or the relative prices of products (real exchange rate) in two countries. Sometimes we need a measure of the absolute value of a currency (especially the dollar). The effective exchange rate and the U.S. dollar index are intended to measure the overall value of a currency against all other currencies.

The United States engages in trading with almost every country on the planet. Thus, there are as many foreign exchange rates between the United States and the rest of the world as there are foreign currencies. The effective exchange rate of the U.S. dollar is an index number calculated as the weighted average of the values of the U.S. dollar against all currencies of its trading partners. The weight on each currency is the proportion of U.S. trade undertaken with that country. Thus, the effective exchange rate of country i is an index that shows the strength of its currency relative to the currencies of its trading partners. Suppose that country i trades with N countries, $TRADE_j$ is the amount of country i's trade with country j, and $TRADE$ is the total amount of country i's exports and imports. Then country i's effective exchange rate (EE_i) is given by

$$EE_i = E_1\left(\frac{TRADE_1}{TRADE}\right) + E_2\left(\frac{TRADE_2}{TRADE}\right) + \cdots .. + E_N\left(\frac{TRADE_N}{TRADE}\right)$$

The Bank for International Settlements (BIS) provides four sets of effective exchange rates. One pair of the measures of the effective exchange rate uses a 'narrow' set of 27 countries with data going back to 1964 for both the nominal and real effective exchange rate adjusted for inflation. The 'broad' set of the measures of the effective exchange rate uses data from 1994 for both the nominal and real series of the effective exchange rate for 61 countries.

The U.S. dollar index (USDX) should be distinguished from the effective exchange rate. We can obtain the effective exchange rate for any currency as long as the country engages in international trade. However, the U.S. dollar index is a measure of the value of the U.S. dollar relative to a basket of foreign currencies. The U.S. dollar index was established by the U.S. Federal Reserve System in 1973 after the Bretton Woods system collapsed. When the U.S. dollar index was established, the basket of foreign currencies with which the value of the U.S. dollar was compared included the Japanese yen, British pound, German mark, French franc, Italian lira, Canadian dollar, Swedish krona, Swiss franc, Dutch guilder, and Belgian franc.

The currencies included in the basket were chosen according to the size of each country's trade with the United States as of 1973. The basket was updated only once in 1999, when the euro replaced the German mark, French franc, Italian lira, Dutch guilder, and Belgian franc. Thus, the U.S. dollar index currently consists of six currencies: euro (EUR): 57.6%, Japanese yen (JPY): 13.6%, British pound (GBP): 11.9%, Canadian dollar (CAD): 9.1%, Swedish krona (SEK): 4.2%, and Swiss franc (CHF): 3.6%. The euro is by far the largest component of the U.S. dollar index. Currently, the value of the USDX is calculated according to the following scheme:

$$USDX = 50.143\ EURUSD^{-0.576} USDJPY^{0.136} GBPUSD^{-0.119} USDCAD^{0.091} USDSEK^{0.042} USDCHF^{0.036}$$

where EURUSD is the exchange rate between the euro and the dollar, USDJPY the exchange rate between the yen and the dollar, GBPUSD the exchange rate between the dollar and pound, USDCAD the exchange rate between the Canadian dollar and the U.S. dollar, USDSEK the exchange rate between the krona and the dollar, and USDCHF the exchange rate between the Swiss franc and the dollar. The number 50.143 is an indexing factor for normalization. It is worth noting that the exponents of the euro (EURUSD) and British pound (GBPUSD) are negative numbers. This is due to the way that the exchange rates of these two currencies are quoted. As we discussed, it is customary to express the exchange rate of a currency in terms of the dollar such as ¥100: $1 (dollar exchange rate), but the exchange rates of these two currencies are expressed in terms of the euro and the pound, respectively, such as $1.2: £1 and $0.98: €1.

<Figure 14.2> Nominal Broad Dollar Index

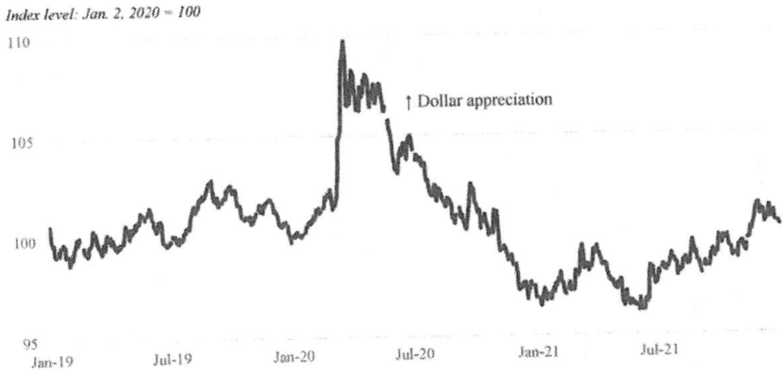

Source: Federal Reserve Board.

The USDX measures the value of the U.S. dollar from two aspects. First, the index started in 1973 with the value of the dollar in 1973 being equal to 100 (base year: 1973). Thus, if the USDX index exceeds 100, it means that the value of the dollar has risen compared with the base year (1973) value of the U.S. dollar; if it is less than 100, the value of the dollar has fallen compared with the value of the dollar in 1973. Second, if the USDX goes up, this indicates that the overall value of the U.S. dollar has risen against the value of other currencies in the basket. The USDX has fluctuated sharply in its history. It reached an all-time high in 1984 at nearly 165 and an all-time low in 2007 at almost 70. The USDX has fluctuated between 90 and 110 over the past several years.

6

EXCHANGE RATES AND ECONOMIC ACTIVITIES

Under the floating exchange rate system currently adopted by advanced economies, the exchange rate is determined by the forces of supply and demand in the foreign exchange market. Therefore, the exchange rate tends to rise or fall from minute to minute. How will fluctuations in the exchange rate affect the economy? If the exchange rate rises, will it be good for the economy or bad for the economy? We'll first look at the relationship between exchange rates and inflation. Suppose that the exchange rate between the United States and Japan has risen from 100 yen per dollar to 120 yen per dollar. This means that the value of the U.S. dollar has risen relative to the Japanese yen. Alternatively, we can say that the value of the yen has fallen relative to the U.S. dollar. The dollar has become stronger, and the yen has become weaker as the result of the exchange rate change.

A change in the exchange rate will have a significant effect on the U.S. economy as well as the Japanese economy. We'll first look at the effect of the exchange rate change on Japanese inflation. We assume that Japan imports Californian wine from the United States, and the United State imports Lexus cars from Japan. Before the exchange rate change, California wine was \$20 per bottle in the United States. Before the exchange rate change, Japanese consumers paid (\$20) (¥100) = ¥2,000 to purchase a bottle of wine. After the exchange rate change, the price of a bottle of wine in Japan will rise to (\$20) (¥120) = ¥2,400. Thus, the Japanese consumer price (CPI) will increase, and accordingly the Japanese inflation rate will go up, *ceteris paribus*. The higher the proportion of foreign goods and services in domestic consumption, the greater the effect of a change in the exchange rate on inflation. In short, because the value of the yen has fallen, Japanese consumers now will have to pay more to buy foreign goods. Thus, the Japanese inflation rate based on the CPI will increase further. However, the GDP deflator does not include the prices of imported goods or services produced in foreign countries, and thus changes in exchange rates do not directly affect the inflation rate based on the GDP deflator.

Now we'll turn our attention to the U.S. price level. To see the effect of the exchange rate change on the U.S. price level, we assume that the price of the Lexus is ¥3,000,000 in Japan. Before the exchange rate change, American consumers paid (¥3,000,000)/(¥100) = $30,000 to purchase a Lexus car. After the exchange rate change, the price of the Lexus model in the United States will fall to (¥3,000,000)/(¥120) = $25,000. Thus, the U.S. consumer price (CPI) will decrease, and the U.S. inflation rate will go down, *ceteris paribus*.

Other things being equal, an increase in the exchange rate (¥100: $1 ⇒ ¥120: $1) will have an unfavorable effect on the inflation of a currency-depreciating country (Japan) and a favorable effect on the inflation of a currency-appreciating country (U.S.).

Exchange rate ↑⇒ Value of the yen ↓ ⇒ Japanese inflation ↑

Exchange rate ↑⇒ Value of the dollar ↑ ⇒ U.S. inflation ↓

Conversely, a decrease in the exchange rate (¥100: $1 ⇒ ¥80: $1) will have the opposite effect on inflation. In such a case, the dollar has become weaker, and the yen has become stronger.

Exchange rate ↓⇒ Value of the yen ↑ ⇒ Japanese inflation ↓

Exchange rate ↓⇒ Value of the dollar ↓ ⇒ U.S. inflation ↑

A change in exchange rates also has a strong effect on trade (exports and imports). We'll continue to assume that the exchange rate has risen from 100 yen per dollar to 120 yen per dollar. Due to the rising exchange rate, the price of American wine in Japan has become relatively expensive, which will reduce the demand for American wine in Japan. The Japanese imports of American wine will decrease, and the U.S. exports of wine to Japan will decrease, *ceteris paribus*. On the other hand, Japanese goods (Lexus cars) become cheaper in the U.S. market because the U.S. dollar has more purchasing power. Thus, the Japanese exports of Lexus cars to the United States will increase and the U.S. imports of Lexus cars from Japan will increase, *ceteris paribus*.

Exchange rate ↑⇒ Value of the yen ↓ ⇒ Japanese exports ↑ and Japanese imports ↓

Exchange rate ↑⇒ Value of the dollar ↑ ⇒ U.S. exports ↓ and U.S. imports ↑

Thus, an increase in the exchange rate worsens U.S. net exports (EX – IM) or trade balances and improves Japanese net exports or trade balances. On the other hand, a decrease in the exchange rate (¥100: $1 ⟹ ¥80: $1) will have the opposite effect on trade.

> Exchange rate ↓ ⇒ Value of the dollar ↓ ⇒ U.S. exports ↑ and U.S. imports ↓

> Exchange rate ↓ ⇒ Value of the yen ↑ ⇒ Japanese exports ↓ and Japanese imports ↑

Exchange rates also have a significant impact on income (GDP) and employment. Net exports (exports - imports) are an important component of aggregate demand. In the case of an increase in the exchange rate (¥100: $1 ⟹ ¥120: $1), U.S. net exports (EX – IM) worsen or become negative, which will have a negative effect on U.S. GDP. On the other hand, Japanese net exports improve or become positive, which will have a positive effect on Japanese GDP. In the case of a decrease in the exchange rate (¥100: $1 ⟹ ¥90: $1), we have the opposite. U.S. net exports improve, and U.S. GDP will increase, whereas Japanese net exports worsen, and Japanese GDP will decrease.

As GDP increases, firms increase investment and employment. The induced effects of exports on investment and employment will be even greater in countries with a particularly large share of trade in GDP. Thus, other things being equal, an increase in the dollar exchange rate has an adverse effect on U.S. GDP and employment and a positive effect on Japanese GDP and employment.

> Exchange rate ↑⇒ Value of the yen ↓ ⇒ Japanese income and employment ↑

> Exchange rate ↑⇒ Value of the dollar) ↑ ⇒ U.S. income and employment ↓

A decrease in the dollar exchange rate (¥100: $1 ⟹ ¥90: $1) has the opposite effect.

> Exchange rate ↓⇒ Value of the yen ↑ ⇒ Japanese income and employment ↓

> Exchange rate ↓⇒ Value of the dollar ↓ ⇒ U.S. income and employment ↑

To sum up our discussion, an increase in the dollar exchange rate (¥100: $1 ⇒ ¥120: $1) has a negative effect on U.S. inflation, but a positive effect on U.S. trade, income, and employment, whereas an increase in the dollar exchange rate positively affects the inflation of U.S. trading partners (say, Japan) and negatively affects the trade, income, and employment of U.S. trading partners. Conversely a decrease in the dollar exchange rate has opposite effects on economic activity.

In this way, fluctuations in the exchange rate may either do good to the economy or do harm to the economy. Therefore, when weighing the final effect of exchange rate changes, it is necessary to carefully examine what situation the economy is currently experiencing. If the economy suffers from a recession rather than inflation, its weaker currency (or stronger dollar) will be good for the economy. Instead, if the economy worries about inflation rather than unemployment, its stronger currency (or weaker dollar) will be good for the economy.

7

THE RISE AND FALL OF THE GOLD STANDARD

The gold standard was born from the realization that the uncontrolled increase of paper currency by the monetary authorities caused inflation. Gold coins had already been used since the Greek and Roman era. However, the gold standard is different from the monetary system that uses gold coins as a medium of exchange. Under the gold standard, of course, gold coins could be used, but the gold standard has nothing to do with gold coins. The gold standard had the characteristic that the value of paper currency as a medium of exchange is backed by a certain amount of gold. For example, "one ounce of gold had a value of $20" or equivalently, "$1 is equivalent to 1/20 ounces of gold". Under the gold standard, anyone who owns $20 can exchange it for 1 ounce of gold. The ratio between a certain value of paper currency and a certain amount of gold is called the par value.

In the late 19th and early 20th centuries, the economies of many developed countries operated under the international gold standard. However, the United States had already adopted the gold standard since 1792. In 1775, a year before the United States became independent, the Continental Congress of the United States needed money to finance the War of Independence, but tax revenues were inadequate. Hence, the Continental Congress decided to print the bills to raise money. In 1775, the stock of continental currency was $6 million, but in the following year, it increased to $19 million in 1776 and $125 million in 1779.

Due to the rapid increase in the supply of continental currency, U.S. prices went sky-high. The price of gold, measured in continental currency, jumped more than 100 times in a few years. This means that the value of continental currency decreased by more than 100 times. After the sour times of inflation, when people talked about worthless things, they said that "It is not worth a continental". This experience became the background for the United States to adopt the gold standard. At the recommendation of Alexander Hamilton, who served as the first U.S. Treasury Secretary when the United States was independent in 1776, Congress adopted the gold standard in 1792 and set gold as a medium of exchange.

Thus, efforts to use gold as a medium of exchange (gold standard) originated from an attempt to curb inflation caused by the discretionary printing of paper currency. Under the gold standard, it was critically important to maintain the stability of gold prices. Since the advent of the gold standard, the gold price had shown stable movements, and inflation had also remained stable. In fact, the United States and many European countries that adopted the international gold standard from the mid-19th century to the 1930s when the gold standard virtually collapsed were more concerned about deflation than inflation. Furthermore, the fact that gold prices did not fluctuate significantly until the early 1970s when gold prices began to be determined in the market attests to the contribution of the gold standard to the stability of gold prices.

Newton, who discovered the law of universal gravity, was the former master of the Royal Mint. In 1717, he set the price of gold at 3 pounds 17 shillings and 10 pence per ounce, which remained at that level for almost 200 years until 1914. The only exception was during the war with Napoleon (1729-1821). The official gold price set by the U.S. government also changed only four times from 1792 to 1973. The official gold price determined at $19.75 per ounce in 1792, was raised to $20.67 in 1834 and $35 in 1934. It was then adjusted back to $38 per ounce in 1972 and then raised back to $42.22 in 1973. This was the last official gold price.

From 1815 to 1913, before the outbreak of World War I, the world's major economies operated under the gold standard. This is also called the classical gold standard. (As discussed, however, the United States already adopted the gold standard in 1792.) Under the classical gold standard, a nation had to meet three conditions to become a member of the system. First, each member country's money supply consisted of gold and paper currency whose value was supported by gold. Second, each member nation should define the official price of gold in terms of the units of the country's currency and be prepared to buy or sell gold at that price at any time. Third, free import and export of gold was guaranteed by member countries. Thus, the gold standard system refers to a system in which a country's currency can be converted directly into a certain amount of gold. (This gold is called specie.). For example, one dollar could be converted into 1/20 ounces of gold, and one British pound could be converted into 1/4 ounces of gold.

One important feature of the gold standard is that the amount of money in a country is constrained by the amount of gold it has. Therefore, if the amount of gold does not increase, the amount of money does not increase. If new gold mines are discovered and gold production increases, the amount of money also increases.

The gold standard had a secondary effect of stabilizing the exchange rate because there was a mechanism that established a fixed exchange rate between countries. Under the international gold standard, 1 ounce of gold was exchanged for $20 or for 4 British pounds (£4). You could buy 20 U.S. dollars or 4 U.K. pounds with 1 ounce of gold. Thus, 20 U.S. dollars are equivalent to 4 U.K. pounds. Put differently 20 U.S. dollars are on par with 4 U.K. pounds. In this way, 5 U.S. dollars could be exchanged for 1 U.K. pound, and the exchange rate between the U.S. dollar and the British pound was effectively established at 5 dollars per pound.

The classical gold standard system was in full blossom for about 30 years from 1880 to 1913. However, the importance of gold began to diminish. For example, from 1815 to 1913, the share of gold in the total money supply in the United States, the United Kingdom, and France fell from 33% to 10%. On the other hand, the share of paper currency and demand deposits in the U.S. money supply Increased to 90% in 1913.

During World War I (1914~1918), the gold standard system virtually ceased to function. After World War I, some sentiment to return to the gold standard gathered momentum. The main reason for this longing for the original gold standard was that inflation skyrocketed during the war. The United States was the first country to return to the gold standard followed by several European countries.

However, as the Great Depression broke out in the United States in 1929, the plan to return to the classical gold standard got floored. Thus, efforts to restore the original gold standard became in vain with the outbreak of the Great Depression. As the Great Depression deepened, the currency of each country also began to lose its connection with gold. In particular, when the U.S. government could not exchange one dollar for 1/20 ounces of gold due to a decrease in the value of the dollar, the government stopped redeeming dollars for gold in 1933. Other countries gradually followed suit.

The United States subsequently passed the Gold Reserve Act in 1934 that prohibited private citizens from holding monetary gold (gold bars). The law gave the government a title to all monetary gold and asked private citizens to turn in their privately held gold to the government. Furthermore, the U.S. government devalued the U.S. dollar, raising the official gold price from $20.67 per ounce to $35 per ounce. Thus, the value of the dollar fell by 41.0%.

The international gold standard system officially came to an end in 1971 when U.S. President Nixon announced that the United States would no longer honor its commitment to buying or selling gold for $35 per ounce. The U.S. government abolished the gold standard by officially announcing the demonetization of gold. Furthermore, the official price of gold ($35 per ounce) for international payments was abolished on January 1, 1975. Thus, the monetary authorities in each country would have to go to the private market to buy and sell gold at market prices. In addition, the ban on the civilian ownership of gold was completely lifted in 1975.

Under the gold standard, inflation was low and stable in each country. The stability of prices was attributable to the fact that the monetary authorities could not print money recklessly. For this reason, there are still some people who are in sympathy with returning to the gold standard to prevent inflation and stabilize the economy. However, despite some advantages of the gold standard, it is unrealistic to return to the gold standard under the complex modern economic system. In order to use gold as currency, the output of gold must increase in proportion to the amount of goods produced, which is not possible given the current underground gold reserves. The current gold reservoirs are estimated to be around 50,000 metric tons, and if gold is mined at the current rate, it is expected that the profitable gold mines would almost run out in the near future. Even now, the total amount of gold reserves is only 0.3% of the U.S. dollar-denominated monetary base. The size of gold reserves is a drop in the bucket compared with the size of transactions of goods and services produced every year.

8

THE WIZARD OF OZ

We have previously seen that unexpected inflation or deflation can lead to the redistribution of wealth and income. People who lend money generally hate inflation, and those who borrow money like inflation. Conversely, those who lend money welcome deflation, and those who borrow money abhor deflation. The effect of unexpected inflation or deflation on the redistribution of wealth and income among people has often become the cause of political strife. The most famous episode occurred in the United States in the late 1800s when deflation was serious. From 1880 to 1896, the price level in the United States fell 23%.

Deflation was blessed for bankers in the Northeastern region of the United States who lent money, but it was a nightmare for farmers in the southern and western regions who borrowed money. One solution to this problem was to replace the gold standard with a bimetallic standard that used both gold and silver as a medium of exchange. The transition to the bimetallic standard had the effect of increasing the money supply, thereby preventing deflation. Silver reserves were much bigger than gold reserves in the United States, and thus the bimetallic standard was expected to increase the U.S. money supply.

The proposal to use silver as money became the biggest issue in the 1896 U.S. presidential election. Republican presidential candidate William McKinley pledged that he would adhere to the gold standard. He was a candidate for the interests of the rich. However, Democratic presidential candidate William Jennings Bryan supported the bimetallic standard. He was a candidate for the interests of the poor. He made a famous speech in a Presidential election campaign: "You shall not crucify mankind upon a cross of gold" (Source: https://historymatters.gmu.edu/Cross of Gold) Naturally, McKinley was a candidate for the conservative powers of the Middle East, and Brian was a populist candidate for farmers in the South and West.

This debate concerning the gold standard versus the bimetallic standard once again flamed up by a novel titled *The Wizard of Oz* that was published in 1896 after the election by Frank Baum, a journalist from the Midwest.

The Wizard of Oz is better known as a movie. Year 2023 is the 80th year after the movie was released. The book and the film describe the experience of a girl named Dorothy. Dorothy landed in a strange land in a whirlwind blowing in her hometown of Kansas which was hit by a tornado. Dorothy who represents the traditional value of the United States became acquainted with three friends in the new place. They include a scarecrow (farmer), a tin woodman (industrial worker), and a lion (symbolizing Bryan).

The four of them journey along a dangerous yellow brick road (symbolizing the gold standard) in search of a 'wizard' (symbolizing McKinley) who could help Dorothy return home safely. Finally, they arrive at Oz (the symbol of Washington D.C., the capital of the United States), where people see the world through green glasses (symbols of dollars). The wizard pretends to be able to do everything for everyone, but her bragging turns out to be a scam. Dorothy's problem is solved when she realizes the mysterious power of her silver shoes (which symbolizes the silver standard).

After Republican candidate McKinley was elected president, the United States continued to maintain the gold standard, but those who advocated the silver standard were able to achieve their desired goal of rising inflation after the election. After the election, large-scale gold mines were discovered in Alaska, Australia, and South Africa. In addition, with the development of new technologies for mining gold, the amount of gold mining increased significantly. This soon led to an increase in the amount of money and inflation. U.S. prices rose 35% from 1896 to 1910. It was long before the United States experienced the blessing of rising inflation.

9

FROM THE FIXED EXCHANGE RATE SYSTEM TO THE FLOATING EXCHANGE RATE SYSTEM

The international monetary and financial order was in chaos from the Great Depression to the end of World War II because of the virtual collapse of the gold standard. With the end of World War II in 1944, the representatives of the major victorious countries gathered in Bretton Woods, a small town in New Hampshire in the United States and began to seek a new international monetary and financial system to replace the gold standard. Keynes, founder of Keynesian economics, also attended the meeting as a representative of the United Kingdom. They judged that the severe fluctuations in exchange rates in the 1930s had harmful effects on the international monetary order and agreed to adopt a fixed exchange rate system that kept exchange rates almost constant. The Bretton Woods system which became a headstone for the global monetary and financial system was born.

Under the new system, countries set the exchange value of their currencies in terms of the U.S. dollar, and the US dollar emerged as the axis of the new system, key currency, replacing gold. For example, the exchange rate was set such as 250 yen per dollar, 4 German marks per dollar, and 4 U.S. dollars per British pound. This exchange ratio is called the par value. Each country's central bank agreed to keep its par value within the plus and minus 1% ranges of the par value. For example, if the exchange rate between the yen and the dollar is set at 250 yen per dollar, the Bank of Japan was obliged to maintain the exchange rate between 247.50 yen and 252.50 yen per dollar (¥247.50 $\leq E \leq$ ¥252.50).

Under the Bretton Woods system, each country needs to hold significant amounts of dollars (mainly held in the form of U.S. Treasury securities) in order to maintain its par value. If a country's exchange rate shows signs of rising above the agreed par value (for example, 255 yen per dollar), this is a sign that there is a shortage of dollars in the foreign exchange market and that the value of the yen is too low compared with that of the U.S. dollar. There is pressure on the devaluation of the yen, an upward change in the par value of the yen. In order to avoid the devaluation of the yen and to maintain the par value (250 yen per dollar), the central bank of Japan had to intervene in the foreign exchange market by selling dollars held as official reserve assets in the market. Thus, all member nations of the IMF except for the United States had to hold a sufficient amount of dollars.

Conversely, if a country's exchange rate shows signs of falling below its agreed par value (for example, 245 yen per dollar), this means that there are too many dollars in the market, and some pressure on the revaluation of the yen, a downward change in the par value of the yen begins to come into play. Consequently, the central bank of Japan would have to engage in buying up dollars in the market to maintain the par value by printing more yen.

The Bretton Woods system granted a special privilege to the U.S. dollar, and other countries were placed in a relatively disadvantage in international transactions. If the United Kingdom excessively imported from other countries, other countries would demand the United Kingdom to pay in U.S. dollars. Then, the U.K. dollar reserves would soon run out, and it would be difficult for the United Kingdom to maintain its par value anymore. In the end, the United Kingdom would be forced to devalue its currency. For example, the United Kingdom would have to devalue the pound from $5: £1 to, say, $4.5: £1.

Under the Bretton Woods system, the United States deflected this adverse situation. If the United States imported too much, it could print dollars endlessly and pay for the imports in dollars that other countries would want. Thus, there was no need to worry about running out of its official reserves. If the U.S. government were prudent in managing its dollar, and the U.S. dollar remained stable, the special treatment given to the United States under the Bretton Woods system would be conducive to stabilizing the international monetary system. However, when the stability of the dollar was shaky, the hope that the international monetary system would remain stable on the axis of the U.S. dollar might be the same as "going up to a tree to catch fish". The saying "going up to a tree to catch fish" is a Chinese quip, indicating that people seek an implausible goal.

When the U.S. economy showed signs of overheating due to rapidly increasing expenditure for the Vietnam War in the late 1960s, two unwelcome guests, severe inflation and chronic trade deficits, annoyed the U.S. economy. The U.S. trade deficit led to the massive outflows of dollars into its trading partners (especially Germany and Japan), and these countries were faced with overflows of dollars. These countries had to continue to buy dollars in the foreign exchange market by issuing more money to maintain their fixed exchange rates with the U.S. dollar. Thus, the excessive influx of dollars continued to increase the quantity of money in these countries.

These countries were alarmed at the snowballing of their money supply and the resulting inflation. Here, speculators joined the money game. As the value of the dollar continued to decline in these countries, international speculators sold dollars and continued to buy the mark and the yen, anticipating that these countries could no longer maintain their fixed exchange rate with the dollar. The situation became worse and went uncontrollable. Finally, in March 1973, major developed countries abandoned their efforts to preserve the value of the dollar and allowed their exchange rates to be freely determined in the market. This was the end of the fixed exchange rate system and the beginning of the floating exchange rate system. Since then, major economies have adopted the floating exchange rate system.

10

DETERMINATION OF EXCHANGE RATES IN THE LONG RUN: PURCHASING POWER PARITY (PPP)

Under the floating exchange rate system, the exchange rate between any two countries is freely determined in the market-by-market forces. We have seen earlier that exchange rates have significant effects on every aspect of the economy such as trade, inflation, income, and employment. However, the exchange rate is also affected by inflation, trade, income, and interest rates. The impacts can become larger and wider when an economy becomes more open. In the economy, one variable (say, income) does not unilaterally or linearly affect the other variable (say, exchange rates). Economic variables interact with each other and move toward a general equilibrium state.

The exchange rate between any two countries is largely affected by a difference in inflation between the two countries in the long run, a difference in trade and income between the two countries in the medium run, and a difference in interest rates between the two countries in the short run. The short-term movement here refers to the movement of exchange rates over a period of days, weeks, or months. The medium-term movement refers to the movement of exchange rates over a period of 1 year to a few years, and the long-term movement refers to the movement of exchange rates over a long period such as 10 years. (However, the distinction between the short, medium, and long runs is quite arbitrary and can vary from case to case.) First, we will look at the long-term movement of exchange rates.

In order to understand how the exchange rate is determined in the long run, we need to understand the law of one price. The law states that the same product cannot be sold at different prices at the same time in different places. (This law, of course, is based on the assumption that there are no transactions costs such as transportation and information costs.) For example, the same Californian wine cannot be sold cheaper in San Francisco than in New York, or in Tokyo. If the same wine is sold at a lower price in San Francisco than in New York, people would like to buy wine in San

Francisco and sell it in New York to make a profit. As a result, more wine is supplied to New York, and the supply of wine is decreased in San Francisco, ultimately leading to a decline in wine prices in New York and a rise in wine prices in San Francisco. The price differences between San Francisco and New York will thereby be eliminated. (However, the actual wine price differs between the two areas due to differences in transportation costs, information costs, wages, rents, and taxes.) Thus, if the law of one price does not hold, there will always exist an arbitrary opportunity, which is at odds with the notion of market efficiency in a perfectly competitive market.

When we apply the law of one price to the international marketplace, we have the purchasing power parity (PPP) condition. The theory of purchasing power parity regarding the determination of exchange rates is that in the long term, the exchange rate between two currencies is determined in the way that currencies in the two countries have the same purchasing power. For example, suppose that Californian wine sells for 2,000 yen in Japan and the same wine sells for $20 in the United States. If the exchange rate between the two countries is determined at 100 yen per dollar, the purchasing power parity condition holds. First, 2,000 yen can buy a bottle of Californian wine in Japan, and 2,000 yen can also buy $20, which can buy a bottle of the same wine in the United States. Thus, 2,000 Japanese yen and 20 U.S. dollars have the same purchasing power, or equivalently, $1 has the same purchasing power as 100 yen.

According to the theory of purchasing power parity, the exchange rate between two countries is determined in the long-term at the level where the purchasing power parity condition is satisfied. In our example, the PPP exchange rate is determined at ¥100: $1. This means that in the long run, the exchange rate is determined by the relative price between the two countries. Now suppose that the price of wine in Japan rose from 2,000 yen to 2,400 yen, but the price of the same wine in the United States remains unchanged at $20. If the exchange rate is maintained at 100 yen per dollar after the price change, you can buy 24 dollars with 2,400 yen. With this money, you can buy a bottle of wine ($20) in the United States, and you have extra money of $4. There is an arbitrage opportunity. Therefore, many people will try to convert the yen into the U.S. dollar to buy wine in the United States. The demand for the dollar increases, and the supply of the yen increases. This will push the value of the dollar upwardly and the value of the yen downwardly.

How much will the dollar rise? Suppose that the value of the dollar rose from 100 yen per dollar to 110 yen per dollar. At this exchange rate, it is still advantageous to buy wine in the United States by converting the yen into the dollar. Therefore, the demand for the dollar will continue to increase, and the value of the dollar will continue to rise. This adjustment process will continue until the value of the dollar rises to 120 yen per dollar. Once the exchange rate rises to 120 yen per dollar, there is no difference between the U.S. price of wine and the Japanese price of the same wine, and the purchasing power parity condition holds. With 2,400 yen, you can buy a bottle of wine in Japan, or you can buy $20, which allows you to buy a bottle of the same wine in the United States. Thus, the arbitrage opportunity has disappeared. Now 1 U.S. dollar and 120 yen have the same purchasing power.

If the purchasing power parity condition holds true, the real exchange rate is always 1. We defined the real disease rate as the number of units of a foreign product that can be exchanged for one unit of a home (U.S.) product. Now, if the exchange rate is 120 yen per dollar, either $1 or ¥120 can buy a bottle of an identical wine. This implies that a bottle of Japanese wine is exchanged for a bottle of U.S. wine, and thus the real exchange rate becomes 1. When the real exchange rate (e) is equal to 1, the nominal exchanges rate (E) becomes:

$$E^{PPP} = \frac{P^F}{P} \text{ (Recall that } e = E\ x\ \left(\frac{P}{P^F}\right))$$

where P^F is the price of foreign products and P is the price of home (U.S.) products. According to the purchasing power parity condition, in the long run, the nominal exchange rate between the two countries moves toward the PPP exchange rate which is solely determined by the relative prices (P^F/P) in the two countries. If the Japanese price level (P^F) rises relative to the U.S. price level (P), the exchange rate between the Japanese yen and the U.S. dollar rises in the long run. The value of the yen falls, or the value of the dollar rises. If the U.S. price (P) rises relative to the Japanese. price (P^F), the opposite occurs.

The foreign price level may be represented by the foreign consumer price index (CPI), and the U.S. price level by the U.S. CPI. However, it is common to use the import price index instead of the foreign CPI and the export price index instead of the domestic CPI. We calculate the PPP exchange rate based on the export price index and the import price index as follows:

$$E^{PPP} = \frac{Import\ price\ index}{Export\ price\ index}$$

We can express this relation in terms of rate of change of the exchange rate as follows:

Rate of change of the exchange rate
= Foreign inflation rate –Home (U.S.) inflation rate

This expression restates the PPP exchange rate in terms of the rate of change. The conclusion drawn from the theory of purchasing power parity is that if the Japanese inflation rate is higher than the U.S. inflation rate, the exchange rate between the two countries will rise. The value of the Japanese yen will fall, or the value of the dollar will rise in the future. If the U.S. inflation rate is higher than the Japanese. inflation rate, the exchange rate between the two countries will fall. The value of the U.S. dollar will fall, or the value of the yen will rise in the future. For example, if the Japanese inflation rate is 4% and the U.S. inflation rate is 2%, in the long run, the exchange rate between the two countries will rise by 2%, and thus the yen will depreciate by 2%. If the Japanese inflation rate is 4%, and the U.S. inflation rate is 6%, then the exchange rate will fall by 2%, and the yen will appreciate by 2%.

11

PURCHASING POWER PARITY AND THE BIG MAC PRICE INDEX

The theory of purchasing power parity is based on the law of one price, the assumption that the same product cannot sell for different prices in different locations at the same time. According to PPP theory, the exchange rate between two currencies in the long run moves toward an exchange rate at which the law of one price holds true, that is, the purchasing power parity condition is satisfied. There is a famous index that shows how actual exchange rates accurately reflect purchasing power parity in the real world. *The Economist,* a U.K. weekly business magazine, surveys every year the prices (in local currencies) of the Big Mac hamburger sold around the world and publishes the Big Mac index. The total number of McDonald's restaurants around the world is 37,855 as of May 2019.

Every country in the world produces a myriad of products and services. Therefore, evaluating the purchasing power parity of each country's currency based on the price of the Big Mac hamburger may be too simple and has some limitations. Nonetheless, McDonald's Big Mac hamburger is almost identical everywhere in the world, and thus the Big Mac hamburger fits like a glove for comparing the PPP exchange rates among countries where the Big Mac hamburgers are sold.

	1994			2015		
Country	BigMac Price (Local Currency)	Market Exchange Rate	PPP Exchange R ate	BigMac Price (Local Currency)	Market Exchange Rate	PPP Exchange Rate
USA	$2.30	$1.00	$1.00	$4.79	$1.00	$1.00
Japan	¥391.00	¥104.00	¥170.00	¥370.00	¥117.77	¥77.24
Korea	₩2,300.00	₩810.00	₩1,000.00	₩4,100.00	₩1,083.30	₩855.95
Canada	C$2.66	C$1.39	C$1.24	C$5.70	C$1.23	C$1.19
China	9.00 Yuan	8.70 yuan	3.91 yuan	17.2 Yuan	6.21 yuan	3.59 yuan
Russia	2,900 rubles	1,775 rubles	1,261 rubles	89 rubles	65.23 rubles	18.58 rubles
Mexico	8.10 pesos	3.36 pesos	3.52 pesos	49 pesos	14.63 pesos	10.23 pesos
Germany	4.60 marks	1.71 mark	2.00 mark	€ 3.67	€ 0.86	€ 0.77
France	Franc 18.50	Franc 5.83	8.04 Franc	€ 3.90	€ 0.86	€ 0.81
Italy	4550 lira	1,641 lira	1,978 liras	€ 3.85	€ 0.86	€ 0.80

	2022 (July)		
Country	BigMac Price (Local Currency)	Market Exchange Rate	PPP Exchange Rate
USA	$5.15	$1.00	$1.00
Japan	¥390.00	¥137.87	¥75.73
Korea	₩ 4,600.00	₩ 1,313.45	₩ 893.20
Canada	C$6.75	C$1.29	C$1.31
China	24.00 Yuan	6.75 yuan	4.66 yuan
Russia	--	--	--
Mexico	70.00 pesos	20.41 pesos	13.59 pesos
Germany	€4.54	€0.98	€0.90
France	€4.54	€0.98	€0.90
Italy	€4.54	€0.98	€0.90

The table shows the Big Mac price, the market exchange rate, and the estimated PPP exchange rate in major countries that operate under the floating exchange rate system. The PPP exchange rate is obtained by dividing the local Big Mac price by the U.S. Big Mac price. For example, the Japanese PPP exchange rate is calculated as ¥390.00/$55.15 = ¥75.73/$1. We'll first look at the case of Japan. The Japanese actual exchange rate with the U.S. dollar in July 2022 was 137.87 yen per dollar, but the Japanese PPP exchange rate was 75.73 yen per dollar. If the PPP model of exchange rate determination is correct, a country's actual exchange rate should converge to the PPP exchange rate. However, there is a big divergence between the Japanese actual exchange rate and its PPP exchange rate. Can we say that the PPP theory of exchange rate determination is wrong? Not necessarily. The PPP exchange rate is a long-run exchange rate toward which a country's actual exchange rate moves. Thus, we can figure out the direction of the future movement of a country's exchange rate by looking at its PPP exchange rate. We can also use the PPP exchange rate as a basis for finding out whether the country's currency is undervalued or overvalued relative to the U.S. dollar.

If the Japanese actual exchange rate (¥137.87: $1) is higher than the PPP exchange rate (¥75.73: $1) calculated based on the price of Big Mac, the Japanese yen is currently undervalued compared with the U.S. dollar. The reason is that in the long run, one U.S. dollar could buy only 75.73 units of the yen, but currently can buy 137.87 units of the yen. Thus, the U.S. dollar is much stronger than the one predicted by the PPP exchange rate, or the Japanese yen is much weaker than the one suggested by the PPP exchange rate. When a country's actual exchange rate is higher than its PPP exchange rate, we can say that its currency is undervalued relative to the U.S. dollar, and it is reasonable to predict that the currency will appreciate, or the dollar exchange rate will fall in the future. Conversely, if a country's actual exchange rate is lower than its PPP exchange rate, then its currency is overvalued relative to the U.S. dollar, and we can predict that the currency will depreciate against the U.S. dollar, or the dollar exchange rate will rise in the future.

The major countries that are listed in the table have all higher PPP exchange rates than their actual exchange rates as of July 2022, and their currencies are thus undervalued against the U.S. dollar. Only a small number of countries has currency that is overvalued against the U.S. dollar. These countries include Canada, Sweden, Uruguay, Norway, and Switzerland.

<Table 14.4> Overvalued Currencies

Country	Actual Exchange Rate	PPP Exchange Rate	% of Overvaluation
Canada	1.29 Canadian Dollar	1.31 Canadian dollar	1.55%
Sweden	10.20 Swedish Krona	11.07 Swedish krona	8.53%
Uruguay	41.91 Uruguayan Pesos	49.51Uruguayan pesos	18.13%
Norway	9.90 Norwegian Krone	12.04 Norwegian krone	21.62%
Switzerland	0.97 Swiss franc	1.26 Swiss franc	28.90%

We have found some interesting trends in the PPP exchange rates. In 1994 before the Asian financial crisis, the currencies of most countries listed in the table were overvalued against the U.S. dollar. Looking at the Big Mac Index of 1994 reveals that currencies of all countries except for China and Russia were strong relative to the U.S. dollar. In this respect, the 1997 data on the PPP exchange rates are somewhat informative about the 1997 Asian financial crisis.

The 1997 Asian financial crisis devasted some Asian economies had something to do with the overvaluation of the currencies of the Asian countries. The experience of South Korea vividly shows this. In 1994 before the outbreak of the Asian financial crisis, the Korean actual exchange rate was 810 won per dollar, but the PPP exchange rate based on the Big Mac price was 1,000 won. The Korean currency was highly overvalued against the U.S. dollar, and the Korean currency had a lot of purchasing power to buy foreign goods and services. Thanks to the strong Korean won, Korean people enjoyed the purchasing power of their currency, spending lavishly on foreign goods and services and on foreign travel. The year 1994 was a time when the Korean economy was in its heyday, and people were excited about popping champagne. In addition, the Korean government tried to keep the exchange rate low to open the era of '$10,000 per capita income'. The Korean foreign exchange reserves ran out rapidly.

However, after 20 years, the situation was completely reversed. As of January 2015, the actual exchange rate was 1,083 won per dollar, while the PPP exchange rate was 856 won per dollar. The Korean won was greatly undervalued. The undervaluation of the Korean won means that it has less purchasing power, and thus the living standards of Korean people have been much lowered. There might be several reasons, but the undervaluation of the Korean won might reflect the weakening of South Korea's economic strength (potential growth rate) in recent years. However, the Korean *won* was not the only currency that was undervalued against the U.S. dollar.

The undervaluation of most currencies against the U.S. dollar in 2015 and 2022 might come from the fact that the U.S. economy outperformed other major countries after the 2008 global economic crisis until the outbreak of the corona pandemic crisis. In addition, policymakers in some countries intentionally maintained a low value of the currencies to promote exports. We find that in some Asian countries such as China, South Korea, and Japan, there is a considerable gap between the predicted exchange rate by PPP and the actual exchange rate. In Japan, the actual exchange rate was 138 yen per dollar as of July 2022, while the PPP exchange rate was 76 yen per dollar. Thus, the Japanese yen was also considerably undervalued. China is similar. The actual exchange rate was 6.8 yuan per dollar as of July 2022, but the PPP exchange rate was only 4.7 yuan per dollar. The yuan is also greatly undervalued. The Chinese government has been blamed for keeping the value of the yuan artificially low for decades. The undervalued currency of a country is a commonly used policy to boost exports. Coincidentally, Japan, South Korea, and China have all export-oriented growth strategies, and the currencies of all three countries have been significantly undervalued against the U.S. dollar. China and South Korea have been designated by the United States as currency-manipulating countries.

However, more importantly, the weakness of major currencies relative to the U.S. dollar seems to have reflected the strength of the U.S. dollar against other currencies. In 2015 all currencies listed in the table were undervalued against the U.S. dollar based on the PPP exchange rate. Thus, the strong U.S. dollar dominated over the past 10 years or so. This trend seems to be attributable to the outstanding performance of the U.S. economy among developed countries after the 2008 global economic crisis. However, about 30 years ago, we had a different picture. The currencies of the major countries were all overvalued against the U.S. dollar. Looking at the Big Mac Index of 1994 reveals that among the countries reviewed in the table, currencies of all countries except for China and Russia were strong relative to the U.S. dollar.

Finally, we should be aware of the limitations of the theory of purchasing power parity. The PPP exchange rate should be viewed as a wind vane for long-run movements in the exchange rate rather than as the reflection of short-run or medium-run movements in the exchange rate. Furthermore, it is difficult to use the Big Mac Index as a direct test of the theory of purchasing power parity, because a large portion of the Big Mac price is comprised of store rents, raw material prices (especially beef prices), employee wages, and taxes, which vary across countries.

12

Determination of Exchange Rates in the Medium Run: Business Cycles

The main factors that determine the medium-run movement of exchange rates are trade and business cycles. When a country's economy is booming, its income (GDP) increases, and accordingly the demand for foreign goods and services (= imports) also tends to increase. Thus, when the economy is booming, the demand for foreign exchanges (mainly dollars) increases to purchase foreign goods and services, and there will be outflows of foreign exchanges to foreign countries. As the country's dollar reserves decrease, the value of the dollar will go up, and the value of its local currency will go down. Thus, the dollar exchange rate will rise, other things being equal. When the economy enters a recession phase, the opposite occurs. The demand for foreign goods and services will decrease, and the demand for dollars will decrease as well. Hence the exchange rate will fall.

A business cycle usually lasts for a period of a few quarters to a few years. A business cycle consists of four phases. After the economy reaches a trough, the economy begins to expand (expansion phase) and climbs to a peak. After the economy reaches its peak, it begins to contract (contraction phase), and finally reaches a bottom point (trough) again. The medium-run movement of the exchange rate is closely related to the ups and downs of economic activity. Thus, the business cycle model is suitable for explaining movements of exchange rates in the medium run.

Usually, the value of a nation's currency symbolizes the political and economic power of the nation. More specifically, the value of a nation's currency reflects its economic strength and potential: when a nation is strong politically and economically, its currency tends to be strong, and when a nation is weak politically and economically, its currency tends to be weak. However, the value of a nation's currency sometimes moves in a direction that is not consistent with this prediction. When Japan was in the quagmire of the 'Lost Two Decades', the Japanese yen was strong. When the Asian countries were at the glory of economic growth, their currencies were weak. We could resolve this seeming puzzle with the help of the business cycle model.

Japan's Lost Two Decades and the 1997 Asian financial crisis illustrate how changes in exchange rates are related to a business cycle. First, Japan suffered from the severe economic contraction from the early 1990s to the early 2010s. However, we have witnessed some puzzling movements in the value of the Japanese yen. During the period of the Lost Two Decades, the value of the yen rose significantly against the U.S. dollar. The exchange rate fell as low as 76 yen per dollar on October 10, 2011 and Japan was crying out for a weak yen for many years to escape from the stagnation.

When the Japanese economy slipped into the long-lasting stagnation, Japanese people began to buy fewer foreign goods and services. Thus, the demand for dollars decreased, which would push the value of the dollar downward and the value of the yen upward. The exchange rate between the dollar and the yen went down as low as 70 yen per dollar. When a nation's economy slows down, its imports tend to decrease, and foreign currency reserves (mainly U.S. dollars) tend to increase. Thus, a contraction phase leads to a fall in the value of the dollar and a rise in the value of the yen, other things being equal.

In contrast, some Asian countries experienced economic growth at a dizzying pace in the 1990s, but ironically these countries encountered a severe financial crisis in 1997, and the value of their currencies plummeted. We can explain the 1997 Asian financial crisis using the business cycle model. Rapid economic growth and resulting excessive spending on imports were the major cause of the 1997 Asian financial crisis. Some Asian countries including South Korea, Thailand, Malaysia, and Indonesia enjoyed long-run economic expansion in the 1990s, and people in these countries went on a shopping spree to buy foreign goods and services, and to travel abroad.

Their current account worsened rapidly, and foreign reserve assets in these countries were rapidly depleted as their imports of foreign goods and services increased. Their currencies became the target of international speculators who expected the values of the local currencies to fall further. People began to sell off the local currencies in exchange for U.S. dollars, and international investors moved their dollar funds invested in these countries to safe places because they expected the local currencies to depreciate further. Consequently, the values of the currencies in these countries nosedived, and the exchange rates between their currencies and the U.S. dollar began to skyrocket.

Here we find that the exchange rate tends to rise, or the value of local currency tends to fall during the phase of expansion and the exchange rate tends to fall or the value of local currency tends to rise during the phase of economic contraction, *ceteris paribus*.

> Economic expansion ⇒ Income ↑ ⇒ Imports ↑ ⇒ Outflows of dollars ↑ ⇒ Exchange rate ↑

> Economic contraction ⇒ Income ↓ ⇒ Imports ↓ ⇒ Outflows of dollars ↓ ⇒ Exchange rate ↓

Our discussion of Japan's Lost Two Decades and the 1997 Asian financial crisis suggests that the current expansion of the economy and the expected expansion of the economy have differing effects on exchange rates. It is the expected economic expansion (or contraction) that matters in the determination of the exchange rate in the medium run. It is worth noting that self-fulfilling expectations play an important role in business cycles. If the foreign exchange market is efficient, so that information is instantaneously disseminated, the current exchange rate reflects all the information on future exchange rate movements available to market participants up to today.

If market participants expect the Japanese economy to expand in the future, they want to invest in Japanese assets such as stocks, bonds, and real estate, and therefore, the demand for the yen will increase and the supply of dollars will increase, leading to an increase in the value of the yen or a decrease in the exchange rate. Thus, the efficient market hypothesis implies that the current expansion phase of the economy will lower the value of local currency (say, Japanese yen) relative to the dollar, but the expected expansion of the economy will raise the value of local currency relative to the dollar, because self-fulfilling expectations come into play. Similarly, the current contraction phase of the economy will raise the value of local currency, but the expected contraction of the economy will lower the value of local currency.

> Expected economic expansion ⇒ Inflows of dollars ↑ ⇒ Value of local currency ↑ ⇒ Exchange rate ↓

> Expected economic contraction ⇒ Inflows of dollars ↓ ⇒ Value of local currency ↓ ⇒ Exchange rate ↑

Thus, when people expect the economy to expand in the future, its currency becomes stronger, and its dollar exchange rate will fall. This is the realization of self-fulfilling expectations. Conversely, when people expect the economy to contract in the future, its currency becomes weaker, and its dollar exchange rate will rise.

13

DETERMINATION OF EXCHANGE RATES IN THE SHORT RUN: INTEREST RATE PARITY (IRP)

Exchange rate movements in the short run such as a few days or a few weeks or a few months are mainly affected by interest rate differentials between two countries. One explanation for short-run movements in the exchange rate is the asset market approach. The asset market approach emphasizes that fluctuations in short-term exchange rates are mainly influenced by the flows of short-term funds (hot money) between countries. Since the size of the international transactions of financial assets that take place daily overwhelms the size of international transactions of goods and services (trade), the flows of financial assets between countries are the most important factor that determines short-run fluctuations in the exchange rate.

Previous explanations of the determination of exchange rates in the medium run mainly focused on the role of trade. However, technological advances in the information and communications (IT) sector and the elimination and easing of capital regulations in developed countries and emerging markets have greatly increased the volume of cross-border capital flows, and the size of cross-border capital flows significantly outstrips the size of cross-border transactions of goods and services. In 2012, the world's exports of goods and services amounted to approximately $18 trillion annually, but international currency transactions were estimated to have reached approximately $2,000 trillion annually. Capital transactions are almost 100 times larger than merchandise transactions.

Marcus Fleming (1962) and Robert Mundell (1963), a Nobel prize winner in economics observed separately in the 1960s that international capital flows were much faster and larger than merchandise and service flows. They also noted that as the world economy became more open and liberalized, international investors attempted to maximize profit opportunities by taking advantage of interest rate differentials between countries. It has become increasingly clear that when there is a difference in interest rates between two countries, large-scale movements in capital occur, which could have a significant impact on exchange rates in the short run. In contrast, they noticed that the flow of goods and services reacted very slowly to changes in economic conditions and thus did not have an immediate impact on exchange rates. Based on these observations, Mundell and Fleming separately developed their asset market models.

The exchange rate, like any other prices, is basically determined by the demand for and supply of foreign exchanges. The asset market approach states that the value of a currency (say, U.S. dollar) is determined by the interaction between the demand for and supply of dollar-denominated assets in the foreign exchange market. This approach contrasts with the explanations that the value of the dollar is largely determined by inflation differences in the long run and business cycles in the medium run. Dollar-denominated assets include deposits, bonds, stocks, and other assets issued in the U.S. dollar.

Of many factors that affect the demand for and supply of dollar-denominated assets, the most important is the expected rate of return on dollar-denominated assets relative to assets denominated in other currency such as yen-denominated assets. Other conditions being equal, the higher the expected rate of return on dollar-denominated assets, the greater is the demand for dollar-denominated assets. An increase in the demand for dollar-denominated assets leads to an increase in the value of the dollar, and consequently the exchange rate will rise (For example, ¥100: \$1 $\Rightarrow$ ¥120: \$1).

If there is no restriction on the flows of capital between countries, a difference between the expected rate of return on dollar-denominated assets and the expected rate of return on assets denominated in other currency such as the yen will induce international capital flows. There will be a continuous adjustment of the exchange rate in response to flows of funds. The exchange rate will fluctuate until the rate of return on dollar-denominated assets equals the rate of return on yen-denominated assets. The relationship between the exchange rate and the expected rate of return on assets is formally given by the interest rate parity condition.

The interest rate parity condition holds when investors make the same rate of return regardless of the currency in which assets are denominated. The interest rate parity condition states that the rate of returns on assets issued in different currencies will eventually be equalized once the expected change in exchange rates is taken into account. If the returns are not equalized in the two countries, there will be continuous flows of funds in search of a higher return, and thus the exchange rate will continue to fluctuate.

Suppose, for example, that the rate of return on one-year Japanese government bonds is 4% and the rate of return on one-year U.S. Treasury securities is 2%. We assume that the current dollar exchange rate is 100 yen per dollar. An international investor who has $100 considers two investment opportunities: Japanese government bonds that pay a fixed interest rate of 4% and U.S. Treasury securities that pay a fixed interest rate of 2% per year. As the Japanese interest rate is higher than the U.S. interest rate, the Japanese bonds seem to be an attractive investment opportunity compared with the U.S. bonds. However, the proponents of the asset market theory argue that the rate of return on both bonds will be eventually equalized if the foreign exchange market is perfectly competitive and highly efficient, and the two bonds are risk-free and have the same maturity.

We'll consider the first investment option in which the investor buys the U.S. Treasury securities that pay 2% interest annually. Then the investor will earn $2 in interest rate at the end of year. The total investment income from the U.S. bonds will be $100 (principal) + $2 (interest) = $102. Now, we'll consider the second investment option in which the investor buys Japanese bonds that pay 4% interest annually. In order to buy the Japanese bonds, the investor needs to convert $100 into the Japanese yen. Suppose that the spot exchange rate which is the exchange rate determined in the market today is 100 yen per dollar. Thus, the investor will buy 10,000 yen in exchange for $100. The investor buys ¥10,000 worth of Japanese bonds with his investment money ($100) and will earn ¥40 (= ¥10,000 x 0.04) in interest at the end of the year.

As the demand for the Japanese yen increases, the exchange rate will change in the foreign exchange market. The value of the yen rises and therefore the exchange rate will fall. How is the exchange rate adjusted? According to the interest rate parity condition, the exchange rate is adjusted in the direction that the rate of return on investment in U.S. bonds and the rate of return on investment in Japanese bonds are equalized, if the foreign exchange market is efficient.

- Interest income from investment in Japanese bonds = ¥10,000 x 0.04 = ¥400
- Total principal and interest earned from investment in Japanese bonds = ¥10,000 + ¥400 = ¥10,400

The investor wants to convert the total investment money (¥10,400) into the U.S. dollar at the maturity of the investment and bring it back to the United States. However, nobody knows what the exchange rate (the exchange rate in the future) will be one year later. We first assume that the risk of future exchange fluctuations is not covered by the contract. Here we have an 'uncovered interest rate parity' condition. When the rate of returns becomes equal between the two investments even when the risk of exchange rate fluctuations is not covered, it is said that the uncovered interest rate parity holds. We can consider three possible future exchange rates:

- Case 1: The exchange rate rises from ¥100: $1 to ¥104: $1 one year later.
- Case 2: The exchange rate falls from ¥100: $1 to ¥95: $1 one year later.
- Case 3: The exchange rate rises from ¥100: $1 to ¥101.96: $1 one year later.

We'll calculate the total investment proceeds converted into the U.S. dollar for each possibility:

- Case 1: ¥10,400/¥104 = $100
- Case 2: ¥10,400/¥95= $109.47
- Case 3: ¥10,400/¥101.96 = $102

When the first possibility occurs, the investor will lose from the investment in the Japanese bonds, because the total investment income from the U.S. investment is $102, but it is only $100 from the Japanese investment. When the second possibility occurs, the investor gains from the investment in the Japanese bonds, because the investor earns more from the Japanese investment than from the U.S. investment. Thus, in the first two cases, the interest rate parity condition is not satisfied. Only when the third possibility occurs will there be no difference between the two investments because the investor will make the same rate of return regardless of the currency in which he invests. The proponents of the IRP condition argue that the exchange rate will be adjusted toward ¥101.96: $1 one year later. However, the likelihood that the exchange rate one year later will become ¥101.96: $1 will be a coincidence. Thus, there is no guarantee that the uncovered interest rate parity condition is satisfied.

An investor's capital transaction aiming for a difference in interest rates is called arbitrage. In the above illustration, there is an arbitrage opportunity in the second case, because the investor takes advantage of the difference in the interest rate. Saying that "there is an arbitrage opportunity" is equivalent to saying that "the foreign exchange market is not efficient", or "the interest rate parity condition does not hold". Since investors are exposed to the risk of exchange rate fluctuations, they try to avoid or minimize the exchange rate risk by engaging in a forward transaction contract. Since an uncovered financial transaction is exposed to the risk of exchange rate fluctuations, investors usually make a forward transaction contract that covers foreign exchange risk. As discussed earlier, a forward contract refers to a transaction today that involves buying or selling a certain amount of foreign currency on a future date at an agreed exchange rate. When the investor uses a forward exchange rate instead of the expected future exchange rate, we have a 'covered interest parity' condition.

As an illustration, suppose that the investor enters a forward contract today to sell ¥10,400 one year later at the forward exchange rate of 101.96 yen per dollar. In this case, the investor sells the total investment proceeds (¥10,400) at the forward exchange rate of ¥101.96: $1 no matter what the actual exchange rate is on the maturity date of investment. The actual spot exchange rate one year later could be ¥104 per dollar, or ¥95 per dollar, or even ¥101.96 per dollar. Thus, under the covered interest parity, the rate of return on the Japanese bonds becomes ¥10,400/¥101.96 = $102, which is the same as the rate of return on the U.S. bonds. In this case, the covered interest rate parity condition holds. When a forward contract is made, the actual exchange rate does not matter.

The proponents of the efficient market hypothesis argue that the actual spot exchange rate one year later would converge to the one-year forward exchange rate, so that the covered interest parity condition is highly likely to hold true. Thus, they maintain that there is no difference between investing in U.S. bonds and investing in Japanese bonds in a covered interest transaction. Here we raise an important question. Is the covered interest parity condition always satisfied? In other words, will the future exchange rate converge to the forward exchange rate? This issue has been highly controversial. Many studies present little evidence in support of the covered interest rate parity hypothesis.

14

THE MARSHALL-LERNER CONDITION AND THE J-CURVE

The question of whether changes in the terms of trade (or real exchange rates) increase or decrease a country's exports or imports is a very important issue for exporting firms. As we discussed above, changes in the real exchange rate may increase or decrease a country's exports. Alfred Marshall and Abba Lerner found independently that the final effect of changes in the real exchange rate on exports and imports depends on the responsiveness of economic agents to changes in exchange rates. Since the real exchange rate and the nominal exchange rate tend to move together in the same direction in the short run, our discussion based on the nominal exchange rate will also apply to the real exchange rate.

We have so far understood that an increase in the exchange rate (or a decrease in the value of currency) increases exports and decreases imports because an increase in a country's exchange rate (say, from ¥100: $1 to ¥120: $1) or a decrease in the value of the country's currency makes its products cheaper in the international marketplace. However, the Marshall-Lerner condition shows that this simple logic is not necessarily true. Let's take the following example to understand the Marshall-Lerner condition. It is assumed that the exchange rate between Japan and the United States has risen from ¥100: $1 to ¥120: $1. This means that the prices of Japanese products have become relatively cheaper, and the prices of U.S. products have become more expensive.

For analytical simplicity, we assume that Japan exports cars to the United States and imports wine from the United States. Suppose that the average price of the *Toyota* car exported to the United States is $20,000, and the average price of wine imported from the United States is $20. Now suppose that the average unit price of *Toyota* cars exported to the United States, has dropped to $18,000 due to the rise in the exchange rate, and the average unit price of wine imported from the United States has risen to $22.

Intuitively, Japan's automobile exports will increase, and wine imports will decrease. However, this effect does not occur overnight. First,

American consumers do not change their cars to *Toyota* cars overnight. It takes some time for them to recognize that such a price change has occurred. Even if consumers recognize that the overall price has declined, consumers who have some replacement cycles of their cars will not shift to *Toyota* cars immediately. Also, for people who have preferences for American cars, it will take much time to change their consumption behavior. The situation is similar for Japanese wine consumers. It takes some time for Japanese consumers to realize that Californian wine prices have risen. And it takes a while for them to change their consumption preferences to other alternatives such as Chilean wine or Japanese *sake*.

For some time after the exchange rate has risen, Japan's automobile exports have not increased very much, but since the export price of automobiles has fallen, the amount of automobile exports may decrease initially. In addition, since the import price of wine has risen while Japan's wine imports have not decreased much, the amount of wine imports may increase. Hence, Japan's net exports or trade balance may deteriorate initially for a few months after the exchange rate has risen.

However, as time passes by, consumers in the United States and Japan begin to adapt to the relative price changes. They change consumption patterns: American consumers put *Toyota* cars on their purchase list, and Japanese consumers delete Californian wine from the shopping list. Japan's exports of cars to the United States begin to increase, and imports of Californian wine from the United States begin to shrink. If the increase in automobile exports is strong enough to offset the decline in the unit export price of cars, the amount of Japan's automobile exports will begin to increase. The responsiveness of exports to a change in the exchange rate is called the exchange rate elasticity of exports. The exchange rate elasticity of exports measures the percentage change in exports in response to a 1% increase in the exchange rate.

Similarly, if the decline in wine imports is strong enough to offset the increase in the unit import price of wine, the amount of Japan's wine imports will begin to decrease. The responsiveness of imports to a change in the exchange rate is called the exchange rate elasticity of imports. The exchange rate elasticity of imports measures the percentage change in imports in response to a 1% increase in the exchange rate.

At this stage, Japan's net exports (or trade balance) begin to improve. The final effect of a change in the exchange rate on exports and imports depends on the sign and size of the exchange rate elasticity of exports and the exchange rate elasticity of imports, respectively. What is the sign of the exchange rate elasticity of exports? A *rise* in the exchange rate (¥100: $1 $\Rightarrow$ ¥120: $1) means a *decrease* in the value of the yen, which will lead to an increase in Japanese exports and a decrease in Japanese imports. Thus, the sign of the exchange rate elasticity of exports is positive, and the sign of the exchange rate elasticity of imports is negative. (Of course, in the case of the euro and the pound, *rise* in the exchange rate ($1.2: £1 ⟹ $1.4: £1) means an *increase* in the value of the pound, which will lead to a decrease in British exports and an increase in British imports. Thus, the sign of the exchange rate elasticity of exports is negative, and the sign of the exchange rate elasticity of imports is positive.)

Thus, a rise in the exchange rate (¥100: $1 ⟹ ¥120: $1) initially decreases exports and increase imports, deteriorating the trade balance in the short run. However, over time, a rise in the exchange rate gradually increases exports and decreases imports, thus improving the trade balance in the long run. This relationship between a change in the exchange rate and net exports is known as the Marshall-Lerner condition. The shape of the Marshall-Lerner condition depends on the size of the exchange rate elasticity of exports and the exchange rate elasticity of imports, respectively.

Exchange rate elasticity of exports + Exchange rate elasticity of imports| > 1 ⇒ Trade balance (= Net exports) ↑

Exchange rate elasticity of exports + Exchange rate elasticity of imports| < 1 ⇒ Trade balance (= Net exports) ↓

Note that we take the absolute value of the exchange rate elasticity of imports, because the exchange rate elasticity of imports is negative. In the Marshall-Lerner condition, the size of the responsiveness of consumers matters. If the sum of the exchange rate elasticity of exports and the exchange rate elasticity of imports (in absolute value) is greater than 1, it means that consumers in both countries have fully adjusted their consumption behavior to changes in the exchange rate. In such a situation, a change in the exchange rate has its full effect on exports and imports. Exports increase and imports decrease, and the trade balance (= net exports) improves. Conversely, if the sum is less than 1, the trade balance deteriorates.

Why does a change in the exchange rate have a different effect on the trade balance over time? In a very short run, exports and imports do not respond to changes in the exchange rate because economic agents have little time to adjust their consumption behavior in response to changes in the exchange rate. Thus, in the short run, an increase in the exchange rate (or a decrease in the value of currency) deteriorates the trade balance. However, over time, economic agents have more time to adapt their consumption behavior to changes in relative prices between two countries, and they become more responsive to changes in the exchange rate. At this stage, an increase in the exchange rate improves the trade balance.

When we plot the effect of changes in the exchange rate on net exports (trade balance) over time, we obtain a J-shaped curve. This curve is called the J-curve. The downwardly sloping portion of the J-curve occurs when the sum of the two elasticities is less than 1, and this trend appears in the short run. The upwardly sloping portion of the J-curve occurs when the sum is greater than 1, and this pattern appears in the long run. The bottom of the J-curve corresponds to the situation in which the sum is equal to 1.

<Figure 14.3> The J-Curve

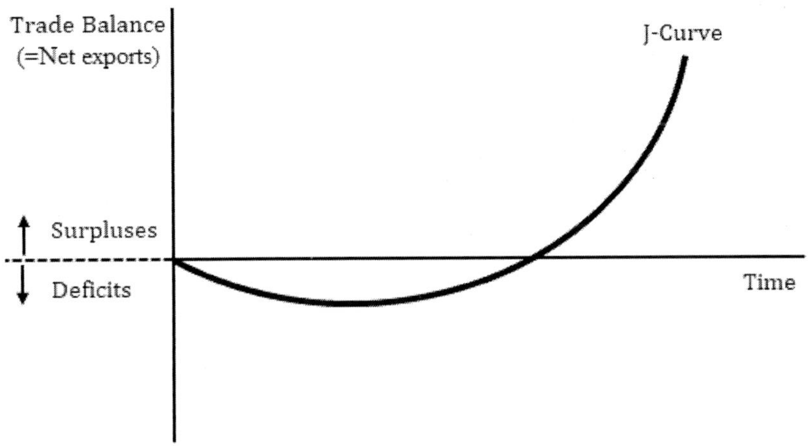

How long is the long run during which the trade balance improves? It varies from country to country and from time to time. According to one study, in the United States, Japan, Canada, and Italy, the improvement effect of a change in the exchange rate on the trade balances usually begins to show up after one year. However, in the United Kingdom, Germany and Switzerland, the improvement effect of a change in the exchange rate on the trade balance begins to show up after a longer period.

We have examined the path through which changes in the real exchange rate, or the terms of trade affect the trade balance using the Marshall-Lerner condition. It is clear that changes in the real exchange can have a profound effect on national income. The terms of trade affect net exports (NX), and net exports can influence national income through the multiplier effect of net exports. More specifically, when the sum of the exchange rate elasticity of exports and the exchange rate elasticity of imports (in absolute value) is greater than 1, an improvement of the terms of trade (or an increase in the real exchange rate) will increase national income, other things being equal. When the sum is less than 1, an improvement of the terms of trade will decrease national income.

Among the issues discussed in relation to the Marshall-Lerner condition is the exchange rate pass-through. When we talked about the Marshall-Lerner condition, we assumed that a change in the exchange rate would change the export and import prices by the same proportion. That is, if the exchange rate changes by 10%, the export price or import price has been assumed to change by 10%. However, in reality, a 10% change in the exchange rate does not cause the export price or import price to change by the same proportion. Not all of the exchange rate changes are passed to the prices of exported and imported products. The index that indicates how much a change in the exchange rate is passed to the prices of exported or imported products is called the exchange rate pass-through.

There are several reasons why exchange rate changes do not fully lead to changes in the prices of exported and imported goods. First, even if the exchange rate changes by 10%, the price of imported goods cannot be raised by 10% because importers are concerned about losing market share. By the same reasoning, the price of an export product is not reduced by 10% because exporters believe that even if they cut the price of exported goods only by half (5%), they can make more profit without losing market share. Thus, the partial pass-through is due to various factors such as corporate pricing policy, market share, and transportation costs.

For this reason, full exchange rate pass-throughs are possible, but importers and exporters are reluctant to pass all the exchange rate costs to their prices., and only partial pass-throughs usually occur. The U.S. pass-through rate for the price of imported goods is 0.42. If the U.S. exchange rate fluctuates by 10%, it means that the price of imported goods in the U.S. will fluctuate by about 4.2%. The following table shows the exchange rate pass-through in several major countries.

<Table 14.5> Exchange Rate Pass-Through (1973-2003)

OECD (average):	0.64
United States:	0.42
Eurozone:	0.81
Japan:	0.57 ~ 1.0

Source: Jose Campa and Linda Goldberg (2005), "Exchange Rate Pass-Through into Import Prices," *Review of Economics and Statistics,* pp. 984-995, Hamid Faruquee (2006), "Exchange Rate Pass-Through in the Euro Area", *IMF Staff Paper*, 63-88.

15

THE TRIFFIN PARADOX AND THE CONFIDENCE PROBLEM

Under the Bretton Woods system, the U.S. dollar was the sole key currency (or reserve currency) replacing gold. Each member nation agreed to set the value of its national currency in terms of a certain number of U.S. dollars. The U.S. dollar emerged as a key currency in international transactions of goods, services and financial assets. Thus, every nation had to hold a substantial amount of U.S. dollars to conduct international transactions and meet financial obligations. Under the floating exchange rate system, however, the U.S. dollar is no longer the official reserve currency, but still functions as a dominant reserve currency because a considerable portion of international transactions of goods, services and financial assets is still conducted in U.S. dollars.

Here we see some conflict of economic interests between the United States and the rest of the world and between long-term international objectives and short-term national goals. In order for the U.S. dollar to perform the function of a reserve currency, the United States would have to supply sufficient amounts of U.S. dollars to the rest of the world, so that they could conduct international transactions of goods, services, and financial assets. Otherwise, international transactions could not occur or shrink. The United States could supply dollars to the world through trade deficits with the rest of the world. The fact that the United States should supply dollars to the world means that the United States would have to embrace deficits in the current account and high levels of debt. Furthermore, there might be a perennial downward pressure on the U.S. dollar as long as the United States continues to supply dollars to the world. When the world is inundated with U.S. dollars, the value of the dollar would fall, and thus the United States might face the confidence problem, and this could lead the United States to lose the status of the primary reserve currency.

In an influential book, Robert Triffin (1960) saw a fundamental long-run problem of the reserve currency as the confidence problem under the gold standard and the fixed exchange rate system. Triffin realized that as international reserves held by central banks around the world grew over time, their holdings of dollars would also necessarily grow until they exceeded the U.S. stock of gold. Since the United States had promised to redeem these dollars at the price of $35 per ounce under the gold standard, the United States could no longer meet its obligations should all dollar holders simultaneously try to convert their dollars into gold. This creates the confidence problem for the U.S. dollar.

Under the current floating exchange rate system, we can still face the Triffin dilemma or Triffin paradox which states that the global reserve currency could lead to a tension between its national goals and international objectives. Put differently, a country whose currency serves as a global reserve currency faces a dilemma between short-term domestic goals (stability of the U.S. dollar) and long-term international objectives (continual supply of the U.S. dollar). Foreign nations wish to hold more dollars, and the reserve-currency nation must be willing to supply the world with an extra supply of its currency to meet the world's demand for the reserve currency.

The continuous supply of the reserve currency to the world could be done through continuous trade deficits of the United States, leading to a perennial trade deficit in the United States. Thus, the world requires an outflow of dollars out of the United States, but the United States requires an inflow of dollars to restore the confidence in the dollar, which leads to fundamental imbalances. The solution to the Triffin dilemma for the United States is to reduce the amount of dollars in circulation around the world by reducing trade deficits and raising U.S. interest rates. Such measures would attract dollars back into the United States, but both tactics would drag the world. economy into secular stagnation because there would be a shortage of dollars in the world. Naturally, the world transactions of goods and financial assets would also shrink.

16

HIGH INFLATION, HIGH INTEREST RATES AND HIGH EXCHANGE RATES: AN ECONOMIC TRIPLEDEMIC?

Many countries, especially developing countries and emerging markets frequently suffer high inflation, high interest rates and high exchange rates simultaneously. Is this phenomenon a norm or an anomaly? It is normal for inflation and nominal interest rates to go together. The relationship between the inflation rate and the interest rate is known as the Fisher equation which is given by

Nominal interest rate = Real interest rate + Expected inflation rate

Furthermore, the Fisher hypothesis states that the real interest rate is constant, and therefore there is a one-to-one relationship between the nominal interest rate and the inflation rate. The Fisher equation implies that if the inflation rate rises by one percentage point, the nominal interest rate also increases by one percentage point. Even if the Fisher hypothesis may not hold exactly, the evidence is strong that a higher inflation rate leads to a higher interest rate, and *vice versa*.

As we discussed previously, both inflation and interest rates affect the exchange rate. Then do a higher inflation rate and a higher interest rate both entail a higher exchange rate? The answer to this question is not straightforward because the inflation rate and the interest rate affect the exchange rate in a different way. Inflation affects the exchange rate in the long run, whereas interest rates affect the exchange rate in the short run. A higher inflation rate leads to a higher exchange rate (or a low currency value) in the long run. Thus, in the long run, we might have the tripledemic, or the coexistence of high inflation, high interests and high exchange rates. However, a higher interest rate tends to bring about a lower exchange rate (or a higher currency value) in the short run, *ceteris paribus*. Thus, we cannot say that the coexistence of high inflation, high interest rates and high exchange rates is a norm. Nonetheless, the economic tripledemic spread during the COVID pandemic crisis.

We should note that what matters in the determination and fluctuation of the exchange rate is not the level of the inflation rate or the level of the interest rate, but differences in the inflation rate or the interest rate between two countries. Thus, even if the interest rate is high at, say 6% in the two countries, the high interest rate will not necessarily bring a change in the exchange rate between the two countries, because in this case there is no difference in the interest rate between two countries. This implies that relative inflation rates or relative interest rates in the two countries matter in the determination and fluctuation of the exchange rate.

When higher inflation in a country brings about a higher interest rate, the exchange rate will be more strongly affected by the interest rate change rather than by the inflation rate change in the short run. Thus, when both inflation and interest rates rise higher, the exchange rate will be more likely to be affected by a higher interest rate. The mechanism through which the interest rate affects the exchange rate is that an interest rate differential between two countries induces flows of funds from a country with a low interest rate to a country with a higher interest rate.

During the inflation frenzy after the COVID-19 crisis, the United States raised the interest rate (= federal funds rate) consecutively by the use of monetary policy, widening the gap between the U.S. interest rate and the interest rates of other countries. When the United States raises the interest rate, the dollar exchange rate of its trading partners tends to rise, if other countries do not take any countermeasures, that is, do not raise their interest rates correspondingly. As long as the U.S. interest is higher than the interest rates of other countries, there will be outflows of capital into the United States. A rise in the dollar exchange rate means an increase in the value of the U.S. dollar and a decrease in the value of local currency. We'll take the Korean won as an example. Since the value of the Korean won declines relative to the dollar, the won has less purchasing power in the international marketplace, and therefore, the prices of imported products including energy and raw materials rise in South Korea. The higher prices of imported products are transmitted to the Korean price level. Thus, the consumer price index (CPI) will go up, and inflation will rise in South Korea. As a matter of fact, the United States exports its inflation to other countries by raising the U.S. interest rate.

On the other hand, if South Korea raises its interest rate to narrow the interest differential between the United States and South Korea, it might drive its economy to bay. The South Korean economy might slip into a recession. The U.S. recession, due to higher interest rates, could be transmitted to South Korea. Thus, South Korea is faced with a dilemma. If it raises its interest rates, it will have to embrace a recession. If it does not raise its interest rates, it will experience inflation as the result of the outflows of capital and the depreciation of its currency. Most countries would have no choice but to raise their interest rates because the outflows of capital could depreciate their currencies and therefore lead to higher inflation. If the stability of inflation were in jeopardy, the foundations of the economy would be shaking. This situation can be likened to 'biting the bullet.'

The governor of the Bank of Korea has been known to say that "The Bank of Korea is independent of the government, but not independent of the Fed" (Source: http://mt.co.kr/Money Today, November 16, 2022).

In the 1930s, there was some currency war between the United States and European countries including the United Kingdom. During the Great Depression, many countries suffered from high unemployment. Some countries were tempted to lower the value of their currencies to promote exports. Countries that had high unemployment were more eager to engage in such competitive currency devaluations to revitalize the economy and to reduce unemployment. A country that succeeded in lowering the value of its currency against the currency of its trading partner was able to increase its exports and to lower unemployment, while its trading partner suffered higher unemployment. Thus, lowering the value of a country's currency had the effect of exporting its unemployment to its neighboring countries. Such a policy aimed at the devaluation of currency was called 'beggar-thy-neighbor' policy. The consecutive increases of the short-term benchmark interest rate by the U.S. central bank to lower its inflation escalated by the COVID-19 crisis resembles the beggar-thy-neighbor policy of 1930s. This time, however, the United States exports its inflation to other countries that experience higher exchange rates (or lower currency values) caused by the higher U.S. interest rate.

Thus, the coexistence of high inflation, high interest rates and high exchange rates is an anomaly. A high interest rate and a high exchange rate do not necessarily go together. Rather a high interest rate leads to a low exchange rate (or a strong value of currency). A country with high interest rates sometimes experiences capital outflows because the U.S. interest rate is even higher than its interest rates.

Furthermore, what matters in international flows of capital is a differential in *real* interest rates, not *nominal* interest rates between two countries. Real variables such as real interest rates and real exchange rates matter in the international movements of goods and funds. More specifically, suppose that the U.S. interest rate rises to 6% and the Korean interest rate rises to 5% as the result of high inflation in the two countries. Then it seems that international capital will move from South Korea to the United States in pursuit of a higher U.S. interest rate. However, this conclusion is not necessarily true. We should look at real interest rates in the two countries. If the U.S. inflation rate is 5% and the Korean inflation rate is 3%, then the U.S real interest rate is 1% (6% - 5%), and the Korean real interest rate is 2% (5% - 3%). Thus, the Korean real interest rate is higher than the U.S. real interest, and international capital will flow from the United States to South Korea, although the U.S. nominal interest rate is higher than the Korean nominal interest rate. In such a situation, the inflows of capital into South Korea will push the value of the Korean won upwardly, lowering the exchange rate, say, from 1,300 won: $1 to 1,200 won: $1. In this case a higher real exchange rate leads to a higher currency (Korean won) value and a lower exchange rate.

Now suppose that the U.S. inflation rate is 3% and the Korean inflation rate 2%. Then the U.S. real interest rate is 3%, and the Korean real interest rate is 2%, and international capital will flow from South Korea to the United States, other things being equal. The outflows of capital from South Korea will drive the value of the Korean won downwardly, thus raising the exchange rate, say, from 1,300 won: $1 to 1,400 won: $1. In this case a lower real exchange rate leads to a lower currency (Korean won) value and a higher exchange rate. Thus, the economic tripledemic is not like 'having a head in the clouds', but is a variant of economic theory.

Bibliography

Akerlof, George, George Perry, and William Dickens (2000), "Near Rational Wage and Price Setting and the Long Run Phillips Curve," *Brookings Papers on Economic Activity* 1:2000, Brookings Institute

Angell, Norman (1929), *The Story of Money*, New York: Garden City Publishing

Ball, Lawrence M. (2009), *Money, Banking, and Financial Markets*, New York: Worth Publishers

Barr, Jason, Bruce Mizrach, and Kusum Mundra (2015), "Skyscraper Height and the Business Cycle: Separating Myth from Reality," *Applied Economics*, 47: 148-160

Barro, Robert J. (1974), "Are Government Bonds Net Wealth?" *Journal of Political Economy*, 82(6): 1095-1117

Barro, Robert J. and Xavier Sala-i-Martin (1992), "Convergence," *Journal of Political Economy*, 100: 223-251

Barro, Robert J. and Xavier Sala-i-Martin (1996), "Convergence across States and Regions," *Brookings Papers on Economic Activity*, 1: 107-58

Baumol, William J. (1986), "Productivity Growth, Convergence, and Welfare: What the Long-Run Data Show," *American Economic Review*, 76: 1072-85

Berger, Cynthia (2005), *Owls*, Mechanicsburg (PA): Stackpole Books

Berger, Peter (2011), *Adventures of an Accidental Sociologist*, Amherst: Prometheus Books

Bluestone, Barry and Bennett Harrison (1982), *The Deindustrialization of America*, New York: Basic Books

Boyes, William and Michael Melvin (1991), *Economics*, New York: Houghton Mifflin Co

Casiorek, Michael (2021), Broadcast: New Items, University of Sussex, January 7, 2021 (www.sussex.ac.uk)

Confucius, *The Analects of Confucius* (*The Lun Yu*), B.C. 475~221, Translated by Simon Leys (1997), New York: W. W. Norton & Co.

Cox, Jeff (2019), CNBC, May 13, 2019 (jeffcox@cnbc.com)

De Long Bradford (1988), "Productivity Growth, Convergence, and Welfare: Comment," *American Economic Review*, 78: 1138-54

Denison, Edward (1985), *Trends in American Economic Growth 1929-82*, Washington, DC: The Brookings Institute

Dickens, Charles (1850), *David Copperfield*, London: Bradbury & Evans

Easterlin, Richard (1974), "Does Economic Growth Improve the Human Lot? Some Empirical Evidence," In Paul A. David and Melvin W. Reder (eds.), *Nations and Households in Economic Growth: Essays in Honor of Moses Abramovits,* New York: Academic Press

Fayazmanesh, Susan (2006), *Money and Exchange*, London: Routledge

Fischer, Stanley (1977), "Long-Term Contracts, Rational Expectations, and the Optimal Money Supply Rule," *Journal of Political Economy*, 85: 191-206

Fleming, J. Marcus (1962), "Domestic Financial Policies under Fixed and Floating Exchange Rates," *IMF Staff Paper*, 9: 369-379

Forbes (2022), "World's Billionaires List 2022," April 5, 2022 (https://www.forbes.com/sites/forbeswealthteam/2022)

Friedman, Milton (1968a), "The Role of Monetary Policy," *American Economic Review*, 58(1): 1-17

Friedman, Milton (1968b), Presidential Address to the American Economic Association (delivered in Washington D.C. on December 29, 1967)

Friedman, Milton and Anna Schwartz (1963), *A Monetary History of the United States, 1867 ~ 1960*, Princeton: Princeton University Press

Granger, Cline (1969), "Investigating Causal Relations by Econometric Models and Cross-Spectral Methods," *Econometrica*, 37: 424-438

Gruber, Jonathan (2011), *Public Finance and Public Policy*, New York: Worth Publishers

Harberger, Arnold (1995), "Tax Lore for Budding Reformers," In Rudy Dornbusch and Sebastian Edwards, *Reform, Recovery, and Growth: Latin America and the Middle East*, Chicago: University of Chicago Press, 291-309

Hardoon, Deborah (2015), *Wealth: Having It All and Wanting More*, OXFAM Report

Harrison, Bennett and Barry Bluestone (1984), *The Industrialization of America*, New York: Basic Books

Hegel, Georg F. (1820), *Grundlinien der Philosophie des Rechts* (*Hegel's Philosophy of Right*), Translated by T.M. Knox, Oxford University Press (English Edition), 1967

Jevons, William S. (1875), *Money and the Medium of Exchange*, London: D. Appleton & Co.

Jorgenson, Dale W. (1988), "Productivity and Postwar U.S. Economic Growth," *Journal of Economic Perspectives*, 2(4): 23-41

Keynes, John M. (1936), *The General Theory of Employment, Interest, and Money*, London: Palgrave Macmillan

Kinsley, David (1989), *The Goddesses' Mirror: Visions of the Divine from East and West*, New York: SUNY Press

Kremer, Michael (1997), "Population Growth and Technological Change: One Million B.C. to 1990," *Quarterly Journal of Economics*, 108(3): 681-716

Krugman, Paul (2011), "'Eurosclerosis,' Then and Now." *New York Times*, January 22, 2011

Kwon, Jene K. and Ky-hyang Yuhn (1990), "Analysis of Factor Substitution and Productivity Growth in S. Korean Manufacturing," In Jene K. Kwon (ed.), *Korean Economic Development*, 146-166, New York: Greenwood Press

LA Times (1988), "Easy Life with Handouts Makes Monterey Pelicans 'Pier Bums'." January 24, 1988 (https://www.latimes.com)

Laffer, Arthur B., Yannis Katsell, and Yanis Varoufakis (2000), "The Laffer Curve: Past, Present, and Future," *Journal of Economic Perspectives*, 14(4):

Lawrence, Andrew (1999), "The Skyscraper Index: Faulty Towers," Property Report, Dresdner Kleinwort Waserstein Research

Maddison, Angus (2004), *The World Economy: Historical Statistics*, Development Centre, OECD

Mankiw, N. Gregory, David Romer, and David Weil (1992), "A Contribution to the Empirics of Economic Growth," *Quarterly Journal of Economics*, 107: 407-438

Modigliani, Franco (1977), "The Monetarist Controversy," *Economic Review Supplement*, Federal Reserve Bank of San Francisco

Mundell, Robert A. (1963), "Capital Mobility and Stabilization Policy under Fixed and Flexible Exchange
Rates," *Canadian Journal of Economics*, 29(4): 475-485

Nilsson, Martin (1950), *The Minoan-Mycenean Religion and Its Survival in Greek Religion*, New York: Biblo & Tannen Publisher

Nurse, Earl (2016), Marketplace Africa, May 6, 2016 (www.cnn.com)

Obama, Barack (2015), State of Union Address (delivered in the U.S. Capitol, Washington D.C. on January 20, 2015)
(https://obamawhitehouse.archives.gov)

Park, Seung R. and Ky-hyang Yuhn (2010), "Information Technology, Organizational Transformation and Productivity Growth: An Examination of the Brynjolfsson-Hitt Proposition, *Asian Economic Journal*, 24: 87-108

Pope Francis (2015): https://www.cnn.com/2015/07/07/world/pope-mass-ecuador-quito/index.html

Radford, Richard A. (1945), "The Economic Organization of a POW Camp," *Economica*, 12(48): 189-201

Romer, Christina D. and David H. Romer (1998), "Taxation and the Laffer Curve: Does Taxation Still Matter?" *American Economic Review*, 88(2)

Roosevelt, Franklin D. (1933), Inaugural Address (delivered on March 4, 1933) (https://www.fdrlibrary.org)

Samuelson, Paul (1948), *Economics*, New York: McGraw-Hill

Schneider, Friedrich and Andreas Buehn (1982), "Shadow Economies in Highly Developed Countries: What Are the Driving Forces?" Discussion Paper No. 6891, IZA, Germany

Shakespeare, William (1606), *Macbeth: New Edition*, Edited by John Seely, Richard Durant, and Frank Green (2015), London: Pearson Education Ltd.

Shapiro, Fred R. (2006), *The Yale Book of Quotations*, New Haven: Yale University Press

Sima Qian (BC 145 ~ BC 86), *Records of the Grand Historian* (*Shiji*)

Smith, Adam (1776), *The Wealth of Nations*, London: W. Strahan & T. Cadell

Solow, Robert (1956), "A Contribution to the Theory of Economic Growth," *Quarterly Journal of Economics*,70: 65-94

Solow, Robert (1957), "Technical Change and the Aggregate Production Function," *Review of Economics and Statistics*, 39: 312-320

Stevens, Laura M., Erik Linstead, Jennifer L. Hall, and David P. Kao (2021), "Association between Coffee Intake and Incident Failure Risk," *Circulation: Heart Failure*, 14(2), American Heart Association (https://doi.org/10.1161/CIRCHEARTFAILURE.119.006799)

Summers, Robert and Alan Heston (1991), "The Penn World Table (Mark 5): An Expanded Set of International Comparisons, 1950-1988," *Quarterly Journal of Economics*, 106: 327-68

Taylor, John (1993), "Discretion Versus Policy Rules in Practice," *Carnegie-Rochester Conference Series on Public Policy*, 39: 195-214

Time (1965), "We Are All Keynesians," December 31, 1965

Thornton, Mark (2005), "Skyscrapers and Business Cycles," *Quarterly Journal of Austrian Economics*, 8(1): 51-74

Thurman, Walter N. and Mark E. Fisher (1988). "Chickens, Eggs, and Causality, or What Came First," *American Journal of Agricultural Economics*, 237-238

Tolstoy, Leo (1884), *My Religion,* Chapter 8, Leo Tolstoy Archive (www.RevoltLib.com)

Triffin, Robert (1960), *Gold and the Dollar Crisis*, New Haven: Yale University Press

Twain, Mark (1876), *The Adventures of Tom Sawyer*. Toronto: Belford Brothers Publishers

Veblen, Thorstein B. (1899), *The Theory of the Leisure Class: An Economic Study of Institutions*, London: Macmillan Publishers

Viner, Jacob (1937), *Studies in the Theory of International Trade,* London: George Aleen & Unwin, Ltd.

Young, Alwyn (1995), "The Tyranny of Numbers: Confronting the Statistical Realities of the East Asian Growth Experience," *Quarterly Journal of Economics*, 110: 641-680

Yuhn, K-H., Sang B. Kim, and Joo H. Nam (2015), Bubbles and the Weibull Distribution: Was There an Explosive Bubble in U.S. Stock Prices before the Global Economic Crisis?" *Applied Economics*, 23(3): 543-552

Yuhn, K-H. and Christopher S. Bennet (2016), "A Note on the Bush Tax Cuts: Did They Succeed in Stimulating Business Investment?" *Macroeconomic Dynamics*, 20: 1623-1639